Theophrastus *On First Principles*
(known as his *Metaphysics*)

Philosophia Antiqua

A Series of Studies on Ancient Philosophy

VOLUME 119

Theophrastus of Eresus

Sources for His Life, Writings, Thought and Influence

Theophrastus *On First Principles*
(known as his *Metaphysics*)

Greek Text and Medieval Arabic Translation,
Edited and Translated with Introduction, Commentaries and Glossaries, as Well as the Medieval Latin Translation, and with an Excursus on Graeco-Arabic Editorial Technique

By
Dimitri Gutas

TUTA SUB AEGIDE PALLAS · 1683 ·

BRILL

LEIDEN • BOSTON
2010

This book is printed on acid-free paper.

Library of Congress Cataloging-in-Publication Data

Theophrastus.
[Metaphysica. Polyglot]
Theophrastus on first principles : (known as his Metaphysics) : Greek text and medieval Arabic translation, edited and translated with introduction, commentaries and glossaries, as well as the medieval Latin translation, and with an excursus on Graeco-Arabic editorial technique / by Dimitri Gutas.
p. cm. – (Philosophia antiqua, ISSN 0079-1687 ; v. 119. Theophrastus of Eresus)
English, Arabic, Greek, and Latin.
Includes bibliographical references (p.   ) and indexes.
ISBN 978-90-04-17903-5 (hardback : alk. paper)
1. Metaphysics–Early works to 1800. I. Gutas, Dimitri. II. Title. III. Series.

B626.T33M417 2010
110–dc22

2009038896

ISSN: 0079-1687
ISBN: 978 90 04 17903 5

PRINTED BY DRUKKERIJ WILCO B.V. - AMERSFOORT, THE NETHERLANDS ἰδίαις μούσαις

πρῶτον μὲν βούλομαι γενέσθαι τὰ περὶ τὸ μουσεῖον
καὶ τὰς θεὰς συντελεσθῆναι κἂν εἴ τι ἄλλο
δύναται περὶ αὐτὰς ἐπικοσμηθῆναι πρὸς τὸ κάλλιον

ἔπειτα τὴν Ἀριστοτέλους εἰκόνα τεθῆναι εἰς τὸ ἱερόν

Θεοφράστου διαθήκη (Diog. Laert. V,51)

quid? Theophrastus mediocriterne delectat,
cum tractat locos ab Aristotele ante tractatos?

Cicero, *De finibus* 1.6

CONTENTS

PART I

INTRODUCTION TO THE TEXTS

PART II

THE TEXTS AND TRANSLATIONS

PART III

COMMENTARY

PREFACE

The short essay *On First Principles* by Theophrastus, thought to have been known in the manuscript tradition as his *Metaphysics* because it was transmitted together with the books that came after Aristotle's *Physics* (τῶν μετὰ τὰ Φυσικά), occupies a distinctive position among ancient Greek philosophical writings in two ways. It survives in a rich and varied manuscript tradition that includes two early Greek manuscripts from the ninth and tenth centuries, a medieval Arabic translation from the ninth, a medieval Latin translation from the thirteenth, and a host of Renaissance manuscripts—including an Aldine edition that has been rightly regarded as a codex optimus—in which generations of hardly negligible Greek scribes and scholars tried their hands at correcting by conjecture the perceived inaccuracies or corruptions in the text. It is also in the enviable position of being arguably one of the most closely studied and scrutinized of all extant ancient Greek philosophical writings: it has enjoyed a number of pre-modern editions, three modern editions by the most respected scholars of Greek and of ancient philosophy—the latest barely fifteen years ago (Usener 1890, Ross and Fobes 1929; Laks & Most 1993)—, two shorter commentaries (Ross and Laks & Most) and two more extensive ones (van Raalte and Henrich), and a fair number of modern translations into most European languages, including Greek. In sheer numbers of pages of study and commentary in proportion to the dozen or so full pages of Greek text, the attention it has commanded is impressive, if not unique.

Under these circumstances the question is reasonably asked why there is need for yet another commented edition. To give a general answer first, I will refer to the recent discussion of the very question by Jacques Brunschwig, "Do We Need New Editions of Ancient Philosophy?"[1] For two of the three major reasons given by Brunschwig, the answer in this case is a resounding yes. The indirect tradition—the medieval Arabic and Latin translations—is rich in evidence of significance for the edition,

[1] In R.W. Sharples, ed., *Perspectives on Greek Philosophy*, Aldershot: Ashgate, 2003, 50–69.

while re-reading the known witnesses in the light of this evidence has yielded some superior ways to understand the text. The Latin translation in particular has been unjustifiably neglected (it gives us, for one, the original title of the work), while the Arabic translation, though already used to good effect by M. Crubellier in the latest edition of Laks & Most, has many more riches to offer when analyzed in detail. Specifically, and briefly put, the Arabic translation, which derives from a different transliteration of an uncial exemplar than does the rest of the tradition, gives us access to a Greek manuscript tradition that is different and older than that of our earliest extant manuscripts, the famous Viennese (J) and Parisian (E) manuscripts of Aristotle. As a result, it gives us over thirty new and superior readings (Part I, Chapter 2.2 below)—a sizeable number given the brevity of the text. In some of these cases, it corroborates suggestions and emendations made by scholars, notably those by Usener. And in view of the fact that it was made by one of the premier translators of Greek philosophical texts, Isḥāq ibn-Ḥunayn, it provides a glimpse into the way in which the text was understood by a scholar of the first classical renaissance, that in ʿAbbāsid Baghdad, who was close in both time and approach to the last phase of live Greek philosophy in late antiquity.

Re-reading the witnesses already used by my predecessors, in the context of the firmer understanding of the transmission of the text provided by the Arabic and Latin translations, gives us new confidence in the soundness of the paradosis, the text as transmitted in the Greek manuscripts, and enables us better to identify the primitive errors of the archetype (Part I, Chapter 2.5 below) and locate their place with greater precision. As a result, it has been possible to recognize as authentic and retain a number of readings previously considered corrupt and to offer corrections more consistent with the transmitted text. This edition is the most conservative of all previous ones in adhering to the text of the paradosis.

To give a more particular answer to Brunschwig's question, I should add that a related purpose of this study is to draw the attention of classical scholars to the real value of medieval Arabic translations, whenever extant, for the establishment of the Greek text. It is no exaggeration to say that there has been among scholars of Greek a certain hesitation, beyond the understandable one induced by the requirement of mastering Arabic, to engage with these translations, perhaps because of what is perceived to be "the fog and darkness of the Arabic text," in the words of Barnes 1997, 26. It is true that Barnes was talking about the text of the

Arabic translation of Ptolemy's ("al-Gharīb") life and works of Aristotle, and not of all Arabic translations, but the perception has been quite prevalent.[2] Arabic translations, like many a Greek and Latin text, may be clear or foggy and dark, depending on the case, but this has to be properly assessed and not simply stated. In the case of the libraries of both Aristotle and Theophrastus, with whose fate Barnes was concerned in that article, it is particularly inappropriate to call "foggy" Ptolemy's Arabic text, perhaps the one single document that reports something reliable and concrete about the work of Andronicus, when all the Greek evidence on the matter is darker than anything that Heraclitus himself could have produced.

On the other hand, to be fair, it must also be stated that part of the problem is that the cause of the Arabic translations has been badly served by those who studied them, generating the impression of their "fog and darkness".[3] And this applies also to the present work by Theophrastus, the value of whose Arabic translation was not properly appreciated, which led to some negative assessments.[4] It is actually a reliable translation, or, to put it more accurately, it is a useful translation to mine for the underlying Greek text. Crubellier's work in the Laks & Most edition has gone some way in establishing that, and I have followed the road to its end in the present study.

---

[2] The complaint against the disinclination by classical scholars to engage with Arabic was voiced already over half a century ago by Richard Walzer, and indeed in connection with the very Essay by Theophrastus edited in this volume: "Theophrastus' metaphysical fragment was re-edited, in Oxford, about 25 years ago, by two of the most distinguished workers in this field [Ross and Fobes]. Both of them were unaware of the fact that the Arabic text exists in the Bodleian library and had been treated by the late Laudian professor of Arabic [Margoliouth], in a paper published in 1892" ("On the Legacy of the Classics in the Islamic World," *Festschrift Bruno Snell*, München: C.H. Beck, 1956, 189–196, reprinted in his *Greek into Arabic*, Oxford: Bruno Cassirer, 1962, 35). It would be inaccurate to say that not much has changed since then, but the problem remains: the corner has not been turned yet, and classics departments are not rushing to teach Arabic as the third classical language, at least for students in Greek philosophy and science. Whence the aspirations of the present study.

[3] For example, and again in the case of the lives of Aristotle, by the work of Düring 1957, for a critique of whose statements on the Arabic evidence see my article, "The Spurious and the Authentic in the Arabic Lives of Aristotle," in *Pseudo-Aristotle in the Middle Ages. The Theology and Other Texts*, ed. by J. Kraye, W.F. Ryan, and C.B. Schmitt [Warburg Institute Surveys and Texts, 11], London, 1986, pp. 15–36; reprinted in Gutas 2000, no. VI.

[4] Like that expressed by van Raalte 113n6, that we should be warned "against putting too much faith in this source."

The main issue, or task, is that Arabic translations have to be evaluated and properly assessed and mined case by case. To that end, when it was suggested to me that I prepare critical editions of both the Greek and Arabic texts of this work by Theophrastus, I accepted mainly because I saw that the same person working on both texts would offer the opportunity to lay down some ground rules and procedures about the proper method to be followed in Graeco-Arabic editions. These procedures, as they developed in the course of my study, are presented in the Excursus at the end of Part I.

This new edition of *On First Principles* by Theophrastus thus offers, within the covers of a single volume, the Greek text—a more conservative one, with renewed faith in the soundness of the paradosis—as well as all the evidence that can be used for its establishment: a simultaneous critical edition of the medieval Arabic translation and a diplomatic edition of the medieval Latin translation. In this way a sound editorial practice that was initiated over a century ago has now reached its full implementation. My one true predecessor, the pioneer D.S. Margoliouth of Oxford, prepared critical editions of both the Greek text of the *Poetics* and its medieval Arabic translation, but he did it in separate publications and without systematically using the one for the benefit of the other.[5] In all other cases where the Arabic evidence has been used in editions of Greek works, either the Greek and the Arabic texts were edited separately by different scholars or the Greek text has not survived.[6] It is my hope that the benefits of the single-author approach adopted in this study will become sufficiently evident as to recommend it to all editors of Greek works that exist in medieval Arabic translations, most notably those of Aristotle and

---

[5] D.S. Margoliouth, *Analecta orientalia ad poeticam Aristoteleam*, London: D. Nutt, 1887, and *The Poetics of Aristotle*, London: Hodder and Stoughton, 1911.

[6] To give a brief review of the most salient publications, A. Gudeman edited again the Greek text of the *Poetics* (Berlin 1934) making full use of J. Tkatsch's earlier edition of the Arabic translation (Vienna 1928–1932), though due to the disparate approaches and understanding of proper procedures by the two scholars the result was less than satisfactory. L. Minio-Paluello's 1949 Oxford edition of the *Categories* and *De interpretatione* made use of the Syriac translations edited by Kh. Georr (Beyrouth 1948), but the extent to which the Arabic version has yet to offer new information remains to be seen. R. Walzer edited the Arabic translation of Galen's *On Medical Experience* (Oxford 1944), but the Greek text has not survived; and the same applies to the magisterial *pentapla* edition by H.J. Drossaart Lulofs and E.L.J. Poortman of Nicolaus Damascenus's *De plantis* (Amsterdam 1989). Finally, collections of fragments of ancient authors also started using the Arabic evidence—notably A. Smith's Teubner edition (1993) of Porphyry's fragments (though D. Wasserstein provided only the English translation but not the Arabic text), and FHS&G—but in these cases again the Greek text has not survived.

Galen. It is also my hope that the methodological ground rules laid down in the Excursus will be followed by future scholars and, most importantly, improved; for the Graeco-Arabist, they provide a test case of editorial procedures that will be of benefit to Arabists and classicists alike.

The Arabic translation, in addition to its value for the establishment of the Greek text, is a wonderful document also because it represents the first extant commentary on the text of Theophrastus. Here we can watch a colleague from the past—and this is particularly meaningful to those of us who have tackled the Greek text either to edit or translate it or both—grapple with the very same problems that we faced, and either admire his perspicacity when we deem him to have been right in his interpretation, especially considering the conditions under which he worked—can any modern scholar imagine working on an edition of any Greek text without LSJ, Kühner-Gerth, or, in Aristotelian studies, without Bonitz (and now, *TLG*)?—or be humbled by his mistakes in the secret hope that what now appears to us as the obviously right interpretation will not be shown by a future scholar to have been just as erroneous. After spending many (perhaps too many) hours in the company of Isḥāq trying together to solve the numerous problems presented by the text of Theophrastus, I have felt the barriers of time, place, and language that separate us dissolve and leave behind just the sheer enjoyment of shared scholarship, both philological and philosophical.

Acknowledgments

The support and help which I received in the preparation of this study by friends and colleagues in classics and ancient philosophy surpass all bounds of scholarly cooperation and generosity. The Islamic tradition, on the basis of a passage in the Qurʾān in which the Prophet is said not to have been stingy with propagating its message (*wa-mā huwa ʿalā l-ġaybi bi-ḍanīn*, Q81.24), has always considered sharing liberally one's knowledge as deserving of paradise. Leaving to Allāh the dispensation of paradise, I can only offer with genuine pleasure my sincere gratitude.

When, after the publication in 1992 of FHS&G, it was decided that the Theophrastus project would continue with an edition of his *opuscula*, Bill Fortenbaugh, our primus inter pares, suggested that I undertake the task of editing both the Greek text and the medieval Arabic translation of what has been known as Theophrastus's *Metaphysics*. Despite my reservations, I eventually agreed for the reason I state in the Preface above.

I am truly grateful to Bill (F), but also to Pamela (H) and Bob (S), for the idea, for this opportunity offered to a single person formally to work on both texts, and for the subsequent unwavering support. They should know that without their help this study could have never been completed.

In the meantime, Michel Crubellier, who had collaborated with André Laks and Glenn Most in the preparation of Laks & Most (1993) by providing information about Isḥāq's Arabic translation, and who had published a related article (1992), was himself preparing an edition of it. Crubellier decided most graciously to withdraw from his project and, with unparalleled generosity, sent me his draft edition, copies of the Arabic manuscripts, and related material. He has saved me both time and effort in this already long-winded project, and I have truly benefited from his preliminary work, to which I refer in my notes (see Part I, Chapter 3.4). There are no words to thank him, and I only hope that the result of my endeavors meets the high standards that he would have set for his own edition.

Other friends and colleagues were equally generous in sending me materials upon request and answering nagging questions. Glenn Most most kindly sent me preliminary copies of manuscripts J and P and answered questions about the apparatus criticus of Laks & Most; Marlein van Raalte obligingly sent me copies of Usener's edition of the work and related material; Enrico Berti and Pamela Huby were kind enough to share with me drafts of unpublished papers; Michel Cacouros patiently provided initial help with reading the knottier parts of manuscript P; Rüdiger Arnzen offered keen comments and sound advice on the methodological excursus; my longtime Yale colleague and friend Victor Bers provided speedy and timely responses to many an abstruse query on Greek morhology and syntax; my most recent and welcome Yale colleague Verity Harte shed much needed illumination on Heraclitean bibliography; and my student Matteo Di Giovanni obligingly cast a critical eye on Bartholomew's Latin translation and benefited me with his comments. In addition, a CNRS grant awarded through the initiative and support of Henri Hugonnard-Roche and Maroun Aouad of that venerable institution of premier research enabled me to spend a sabbatical term in Paris where I could benefit from interaction with these and other colleagues and begin working on the final stages of the project in ideal circumstances. I am deeply indebted to them all.

An earlier draft of the introduction to the Greek text (Part I, Chapter 2), the text itself with the English translation, and the commentary were read and commented upon with scholarly care and great patience by Peter Adamson, Bill Fortenbaugh, Pamela Huby, Paul Kalligas, David Reisman, Robert Sharples, Leonardo Tarán, and Marlein van Raalte. In addition, all of them were quick to respond by e-mail to queries on individual passages and problems. I greatly benefited from their learned comments, and, if I thank them collectively here instead of in many a note in the body of the work, it is only to spare the reader from my tedious repetition of gratitude which, though sparsely registered, is indeed profound. For the shortcomings that remain I alone am responsible.

My students in my Graeco-Arabic seminar at Yale, with different generations of whom I read this text by Theophrastus, not only asked penetrating questions that helped me articulate my theses and my methods better, but on occasion also provided suggestions for the proper reading of the Arabic text. Though I will introduce two of them here by name, because they appear in the apparatus—Amos Bertolacci and Alexander Treiger—all of them who participated in the seminars made invaluable contributions, for which I am truly grateful. There is no greater happiness for a teacher than to have students from whom he can learn.

On the technical side, to the libraries at Vienna (Österreichische Nationalbibliothek) and Paris (Bibliothèque Nationale), Oxford (Bodleian) and Tehran (Malik), go my thanks for the use of their invaluable manuscripts upon which this edition of Theophrastus is based. A special word of thanks is also due to the staff and the library system at Yale University, my lifelong resource, which I never took for granted. The editorial team at Brill, with Mmes Van Erp and Van der Wel, and their typesetters at TAT Zetwerk, with Messrs Geradts and Rustenburg, deserve both special thanks for their courtesy, efficiency, and professionalism, and admiration for expertly producing a very complicated text in three alphabets. I am also grateful for the excellent edition of the text in Laks & Most and its producers, a sound foundation upon which I could build, and, last but not least, for the wonder of the Internet age, the *TLG* (*Thesaurus Linguae Graecae*), without which classical and Byzantine Greek studies can now hardly be envisaged (and due to which we wonder all the more at our predecessors, who worked without it).

In closing, I wish to express my gratitude ἐκ βαθέων to my wife Ioanna, who has fashioned our life together into a welcoming space for all muses to reside, with a selfless love that surpasses understanding. This book is as much hers as it is mine.

New Haven, February 2010

ABBREVIATIONS AND REFERENCE WORKS

Allan	Notes by D.J. Allan in his copy of Ross & Fobes, as reported by Laks & Most
Blau	J. Blau, *A Grammar of Christian Arabic*, Louvain: Secrétariat du Corpus SCO, 1966
Burnikel	Burnikel 1974
CAG	*Commentaria in Aristotelem Graeca*, consilio et auctoritate Academiae Litterarum Regiae Borussicae, Berlin: Georg Reimer, 1882–1907
Crubellier	M. Crubellier, unedited draft edition of the Essay by Theophrastus
CWA	*The Complete Works of Aristotle. The Revised Oxford Translation*, edited by J. Barnes, Princeton: Princeton University Press, 1984
Denniston	Denniston, J.D., *The Greek Particles*, Oxford: Clarendon Press, 1954
DK	H. Diels and W. Kranz, *Die Fragmente der Vorsokratiker*, 3 vols, Dublin/Zürich: Weidmann, 1966^{12} (1951^{6})
Dozy	R. Dozy, *Supplément aux Dictionnaires Arabes*, Leiden: E.J. Brill, 1881; repr. Beirut: Librairie du Liban, 1968
DPhA, *-Supplement*	*Dictionnaire des Philosophes Antiques*, ed. R. Goulet, Paris: CNRS, 1989 ff.
EI^2	*Encyclopaedia of Islam*, 2nd ed., Leiden: Brill, 1960–2004
EIr	*Encyclopaedia Iranica*, Winona Lake, Indiana: Encyclopaedia Iranica Foundation, 1985 ff.
FHS&G	*Theophrastus of Eresus. Sources for His Life, Writings, Thought & Influence*, edited and translated by WilliamW. Fortenbaugh, Pamela Huby, Robert W. Sharples (Greek and Latin), and Dimitri Gutas (Arabic), 2 vols, Leiden: Brill, 1992
Fischer	W. Fischer, *A Grammar of Classical Arabic*, 3rd revised ed., transl. by J. Rodgers, New Haven: Yale University Pess, 2002
Fobes	In Ross and Fobes 1929, "that part of the Introduction which deals with the MSS" (pp. xxvi–xxxii), "the *apparatus criticus*," and "the Indexes"
GAL, *GALS*	C. Brockelmann, *Geschichte der arabischen Litteratur*, Leiden: Brill, 1943–1948^2; *Supplement* 1937–1942
GALex	G. Endress and D. Gutas, eds, *A Greek and Arabic Lexicon*, Leiden: Brill, 2002 ff.

GAS	F. Sezgin, *Geschichte des arabischen Schrifttums*, Leiden: Brill, 1967 ff.
Henrich	Henrich 2000
Humbert	J. Humbert, *Syntaxe grecque*, Paris: Klincksieck, 1972[3], 2004
Irigoin	J. Irigoin, *Règles et recommandations pour les éditions critiques*, Paris: Les Belles Lettres, 1972
K.-G.	Kühner, R., and B. Gerth, *Ausführliche Grammatik der griechischen Sprache*, 2. Teil: *Satzlehre*, 2 vols, Hannover / Leipzig: Hahn, 1898–1904
Kazimirski	A. de B. Kazimirski, *Dictionnaire Arabe-Français*, Paris: Maisonneuve, 1860; repr. Beirut: Librairie du Liban, n.d.
Kley	Kley 1936
Laks & Most	Laks and Most 1993
Lampe	G.W.H. Lampe, *A Patristic Greek Lexicon*, Oxford: The Clarendon Press, 1961
Lane	E.W. Lane, *An Arabic-English Lexicon*, London: Williams and Norgate, 1863–1893, repr. Beirut: Librairie du Liban, 1968
LSJ	*A Greek-English Lexicon*, compiled by H.G. Liddell and R. Scott, revised and augmented throughout by Sir H.S. Jones with the assistance of R. McKenzie and with the cooperation of many scholars, with a revised supplement 1996; Oxford: Oxford University Press, 1996
van Raalte	van Raalte 1993
Ross	In Ross and Fobes 1929, the Text, the English translation, the Introduction except for the part dealing with the MSS, and the Commentary
RUSCH	*Rutgers University Studies in Classical Humanities*, W.W. Fortenbaugh et al., eds, New Brunswick and London: Transaction, 1982 ff.
Schwyzer	E. Schwyzer, *Griechische Grammatik, auf der Grundlage von Karl Brugmanns Griechischer Grammatik*. 1. Band, *Allgemeiner Teil, Lautlehre, Wortbildung, Flexion*; 2. Band, *Syntax und Syntaktische Stilistik*; 3. Band, *Register* (*Handbuch der Altertumswiseschaft*, II,1.1-e), München: Beck, 1939, 1950, 1953
Smyth	H.W. Smyth, *Greek Grammar*, Cambridge, MA: Harvard University Press, 1920, 1956, 1984
SVF	J. von Arnim, ed., *Stoicorum Veterum Fragmenta*, Leipzig: Teubner, 1903–1924
Treiger	Personal communication by Alexander Treiger
Tricot	Tricot 1948
TLG	*Thesaurus Linguae Graecae*, www.tlg.uci.edu
West	M.L. West, *Textual Criticism and Editorial Technique*, Stuttgart: Teubner, 1973

WGAÜ, -S	M. Ullmann, *Wörterbuch zu den griechisch-arabischen Übersetzungen des 9. Jahrhunderts*, Wiesbaden: Harrassowitz, 2002; *Supplement* 1–2, 2006, 2007
WKAS	M. Ullmann, *Wörterbuch der klassichen arabischen Sprache*, Wiesbaden: Harrassowitz, 1970 ff.
Wright	W. Wright, *A Grammar of the Arabic Language*, 3rd ed., Cambridge: University Press, 1896–1898

Abbreviations of Works by Aristotle and Theophrastus

Aristotle

APo.	*Analytica posteriora*
APr.	*Analytica priora*
Cat.	*Categories*
DA	*De anima*
DC	*De caelo*
EE	*Eudemian Ethics*
GA	*De generatione animalium*
GC	*De generatione et corruptione*
HA	*Historia animalium*
Int.	*De interpretatione*
MA	*De motu animalium*
Met.	*Metaphysics*
Mete.	*Meteorology*
NE	*Nicomachean Ethics*
PA	*De partibus animalium*
Phys.	*Physics*
Poet.	*Poetics*
Rhet.	*Rhetoric*
SE	*Sophistici elenchi*
Top.	*Topics*

Theophrastus

CP	*De causis plantarum*
HP	*Historia plantarum*
Ign.	*De igne*
Mete.	*Meteorologica*
Vent.	*De ventis*

PART I

INTRODUCTION TO THE TEXTS

CHAPTER ONE

INTRODUCTION TO THE ESSAY[1]

1. *Date of Composition*

His deathbed complaint about the brevity of human life notwithstanding, Theophrastus lived to a ripe old age (372 / 370–288 / 286 BC).[2] In the course of the 85 years of his life, the Greek speaking world in which he grew and was intellectually, socially, and historically formed, saw tremendous changes. Before he was even fifty, the Greek city states which, as city states, constituted the only political formation he knew, lost their independence under Macedonian domination after the battle of Chaironeia (338), while the great empire of the Persian King of Kings that had dominated Greek history for some centuries was destroyed by Alexander, the former student of his teacher and colleague, Aristotle. And he lived for close to another forty years after these events to see the successor states founded by Alexander's generals take root and change forever the political and cultural scene of the Greek world and the Eastern Mediterranean. In his personal life, he went from his birthplace in the obscure village of Eresos in southwest Lesbos to become, after many turns, the scholarch of the Peripatos, a position he held for a good thirty-five years. But it was the changes in intellectual history that were the most dramatic. In his lifetime, and for the most part through his participation, philosophy developed from the early literary Socratic musings of Plato to a dominant—indeed, domineering—and established discipline of higher thought whose practice was already pursued, with different orientations and methods, in four distinct areas of Athens, the Academy, the Lyceum, the Stoa, and the Garden. As a young man he

---

[1] For the sake of brevity I will be referring to the work edited and studied in this book as the Essay.

[2] In anticipation of the commentary volume on the biographical material in FHS&G, see the critical assessment of the sources on the life of Theophrastus by Mejer 1998, complemented by Dorandi 1998. For the deathbed complaints of Theophrastus see fr. 34 FHS&G.

may have heard Plato (we are not certain),[3] but when he went (back?) to Athens with Aristotle in 335, Speusippus had already been succeeded by Xenocrates as head of the Academy, and later, when he was himself head of the Peripatos, his colleagues in the Academy were still Xenocrates and then Polemon. He was, moreover, the older contemporary of Zeno, the founder of Stoicism,[4] and of Epicurus.[5] The crucial period of the foundation of ancient philosophy—of all philosophy—which we read and study, Theophrastus lived through and helped form. Given the rapid evolution of philosophy during this lengthy period, the question of the date on which his Essay on first principles was written is of singular importance for its understanding and evaluation.

In the absence of an independent source dating the Essay, its contents and their relation to current ideas and the works of Theophrastus's contemporaries have from the very beginning constituted the means to estimate the time of its composition. The fact that in the Essay Theophrastus is prima facie seen as *criticizing* two of Aristotle's signature theories, the unmoved mover and teleology, coupled with what I interpret as an inability on the part of most scholars to entertain even the possibility that a disciple could conceivably criticize his master—and indeed the philosophical genius of all time—during the master's lifetime, led early to the view, which has survived until very recently, that the Essay was written after the death of Aristotle in 322.[6] But already in 1962, in a study of spontaneous generation, Balme suggested that the Essay may be earlier than Aristotle's *De generatione animalium* and *Historia animalium* V–VI, and

[3] For a summary of earlier views see Gaiser 1985, 24–26. Only Diogenes Laertius mentions, twice, that Theophrastus studied with Plato, at III.46 and V.36. In the former passage, in the biography of Plato, he ascribes the report to anonymous sources (ἔνιοι … φασιν), which makes it dubious, although in the latter, in the biography proper of Theophrastus, he is categorical (πρῶτον μὲν ἤκουσεν Ἀλκίππου … ἐν τῇ πατρίδι, εἶτ' ἀκούσας Πλάτωνος μετέστη πρὸς Ἀριστοτέλην). It is highly unlikely that aš-Šahrastānī (d. 1153), the only other author that states that Theophrastus was a student of Plato (fr. 241c FHS&G), had an independent source worthy of credence. Nevertheless, the evidence in Diogenes Laertius cannot be easily waived away, while the question itself is also related to the other question about the presence of Theophrastus in Assos after Plato's death; see the sensible discussions of the material by Mejer 1998, 17–19 and Dorandi 1998, 33, and cf. note 10 below.

[4] See Long 1998.

[5] See Sedley 1998.

[6] Berti 2002, 339–341 gives a very useful summary of the history of this debate, which I mostly follow. The list of the supporters of a post-Aristotelian date for the Essay include Jaeger 1923, 374; Ross p. xxv; Regenbogen 1940, 1393; Tricot p. viii; Theiler 1958,102/292; Reale 1964, 131; van Raalte 1988, 198; van Raalte 24–25; Romani 1994, 12; Dillon 2002, 176n4.

in 1971 D. Frede was able to show that Theophrastus's criticism of the unmoved mover is directed at an earlier stage of that theory. Other studies followed along these lines, to the point that today the early date of composition of the Essay has found wide acceptance.

The main argument in support of this revised view has been that Theophrastus is arguing either in favor of or against positions held by Aristotle earlier in his life, or that, had Theophrastus known the mature works by Aristotle at the end of the latter's career, he could not have written what he did, in fact, write. Briefly to review this evidence, the following arguments and passages in the Essay indicate that the Aristotelian work to which they correspond had not yet been composed and that this work was actually a *response* to Theophrastus's aporetic discussion, and thus temporally posterior.

Arguably the most telling characteristic of the Essay in this regard, as Devereux 1988 has shown, is the fact that Theophrastus knows nothing of the central and latest books of Aristotle's *Metaphysics* but concentrates all his comments on the older books and especially on book Lambda.[7] Reale 1964, 127–133, also studied the close connection between the Essay and Book Lambda but, assuming the Essay to be post-Aristotelian, wanted to argue in favor of a late date for Lambda. However, the early date of Lambda can hardly be disputed on many grounds, including the evidence from the Essay. In addition, the passage on astronomy at 5a22 in the Essay, which can be completed with the help of the Arabic translation, points unmistakably to Lambda 8, making this much discussed chapter of Book Lambda contemporary with the early date of the rest of the Book.[8]

Following the lead of Balme, Most 1988a analyzed ten biological passages, which are problematic for Aristotelian teleology, discussed at 10b7–20 and 11a10–12 in the Essay. As Most demonstrated, some of the difficulties raised by Theophrastus were subsequently resolved by Aristotle in the *De partibus animalium* and *De generatione animalium*, thus establishing the earlier date of the Essay.

In a similar vein, Devereux 1988 pointed to other features in the Essay which reflect discussions of passages in the early books of Aristotle's

[7] Theophrastus's use of Lambda was already documented by Zeller 1877, 148.

[8] Thus justifying the skepticism of Krämer 1973, 214n44 ("die Spätdatierung von Λ 8 unbewiesen und m.E. unbeweisbar ist"); see further the commentary on the first Aporia in Part III below. Frede 2000, 47–49 summarized the arguments in favor of an early and unified Book Lambda; cf. also Devereux 1988, 173 and note 33.

Metaphysics and of other early works but not the later ones, as in the case of the relation of focal meaning in analyses of knowledge (pp. 183–184). To these may be added the following from my analysis of the Essay. At 5b7–10 Theophrastus raised a problem about the motion initiated by the unmoved mover as the object of desire, a problem directed at Aristotle's *Metaphysics* Λ 7, 1072a26. Aristotle responded in the *De anima* Γ 10, 433b13–28, refining his position (see the commentary following Diaporia 8.1 in Part III below). Again, at 5b10–6a5 Theophrastus asked whether and how the influence of the first cause can penetrate into the sublunar realm and benefit the natural world; Aristotle responded in *De generatione et corruptione* B 10, 336b25–337a7 (see the commentary following Diaporia 10.1 in Part III below). In all these cases the temporal priority of the Essay is established by the fact that had the works by Aristotle in which these issues are resolved already been written and available to Theophrastus when he was writing the Essay, he could not have raised the objections or difficulties that he did.

All of the evidence listed above indicates that the Essay was written before *Metaphysics* ΓΖΗΘ, *De generatione et corruptione*, *De anima*, *De partibus animalium*, *De generatione animalium*, and *Historia animalium* V–VI. This means, essentially, that it was written before the major literary activity of Aristotle after his return to Athens in 335 BC. Specifically, it has been argued by P. Louis that *De partibus animalium* was written around 330, and by Ross that *De anima* was written after 334.[9] Accordingly the date of composition of the Essay, since it was written before both *De partibus animalium* and *De anima*, must be around 334. These dates are not precise to the year, naturally, but the bulk of the evidence makes it indisputable that the Essay must have been written at the latest at the very beginning of Aristotle's second and final stay in Athens (between 335 and 323).

This dating is fixed on the basis of the relation established by some scholars between the Essay and the works of Aristotle. Others have arrived at a similar assessment when considering the relations of Theophrastus with the Academy. Krämer 1973 in particular (as also, earlier, Krämer 1971, 12n41) documented the constant presence of "the Pythagorean-clad Platonism of the Academy" in the background—and not only—throughout the Essay, and especially the prominent place

[9] P. Louis, ed., *Aristote. Les parties des animaux*, Paris: Les Belles Lettres 1957, p. xvii; Ross 1961, 11, where the date of Aristotle's return to Athens is misprinted as 325 instead of 335.

accorded to the ideas of Speusippus, so that he could suggest (p. 214) that the Essay chronologically should be located in a period when the philosophy of Speusippus (d. 339) was still very much alive. Indeed Krämer asked a very important question (p. 213), whether the proximity to Platonic positions that are seen in the Essay (for example, the favorable presentation by Theophrastus of the unwritten Platonic doctrine of the one and indefinite dyad at 11b1 ff.; see the commentary in Part III below) is a return to Platonism or indicative of an earlier stage in Theophrastus's development, corresponding to that of the early Aristotle. Given the conclusion arrived at in the preceding paragraph about the latest date on which the Essay could have been written (ca. 334), the first alternative in Krämer's question can be safely excluded. Similar conclusions were reached by Berti (2002, preprint) when discussing the positions exhibited in the Essay about the movement of the heavens and the knowledge of the first principles. In addition to these studies, that Theophrastus in the Essay was philosophically close to Platonic positions is also shown by the fact that he seems to use the word παράδειγμα (at 7b2), meaning "paradigmatic" cause in the Platonic sense, much as it was used by Aristotle only in his esoteric works and once only in the earliest part of the *Physics* (194b26), which date from Aristotle's first residence in Athens (see the commentary on 7b2 below in Part III). All this then raises the next question, whether it is possible to date the Essay even earlier than 334 BC.

In his landmark study on the development of the natural philosophy of Theophrastus and Aristotle, Gaiser 1985, 86, dated Aristotle's *De generatione et corruptione* and *Meteorology* I–III, or at least their preliminary versions, to the period of Aristotle's residence in Assos (347–345), right after the death of Plato. Following the majority opinion (summarized on pp. 24–26), Gaiser maintained that Theophrastus also was present in Assos at the time, a thesis which his study was expressly intended further to corroborate (p. 27). Assuming that this is so,[10] and if, as mentioned

[10] There is no independent evidence for Theophrastus's sojourn in Assos other than two mutilated papyri texts, in one of which the name of Theophrastus may appear in association with Assos (Didymus, *In Demosthenem commenta*, col. 5,54 Pearson-Stephens) and in the other it may be implied (Philodemus, *PHerc.* 1021, col. V,1), both assessed positively by Gaiser 1985, 9–17 (and repeated by K. Gaiser, *Philodems Academica*, Stuttgart-Bad Cannstatt: Frommann-Holzboog, 1988, 161 and 380), but reviewed negatively by A.M. Battegazzore, "Il *Theophrast in Assos* di Konrad Gaiser," *Elenchos* 10 (1989) 217–230, at 217–220. Nevertheless, Gaiser's overall thesis can hardly

above, Aristotle's *De generatione et corruptione* responds to the Essay by Theophrastus, then there is a very real possibility that the latter was also written during the same period in Assos. Furthermore, if, as I suggest in the commentary, the word ἀτακτοτέρα at 4a4 in the Essay refers to or is an echo of Aristotle's ἀτακτοτέραν in *Meteorology* 338b20, and *Meteorology* I–III was also composed in Assos, then so was Theophrastus's Essay.

These considerations make it certainly possible, and very much probable, that the Essay may have been written in Assos, giving us 347 as the earliest date of composition. Accordingly, it can be maintained with as much certainty as is possible in such cases that Theophrastus's *On First Principles* was written in the period between 347 and 334. Beyond this we have no hard and fast evidence that will allow us to be more precise, but only personal—and considered, I might add—views. Mine is that it was written in Assos. Among considerations based on evaluation of the nature and purpose of the Essay (for a full discussion see section 3 below in this chapter), the following are of relevance.

The fourteen-year span between 347 and 334 covers a turbulent period in the lives of Aristotle and Theophrastus. After the first two or three years in Assos, which were possibly the most settled ones, they spent another two or three in Mytilene, and then the rest in Macedonia, where Aristotle was tutoring Alexander, before their eventual return to Athens in 335. The years in Assos have been seen as a continuation of the philosophical climate and milieu of the Academy: Jaeger 1948, 115, called the gathering of philosophers there "a colony of the Athenian Academy, ... the foundation of the school of Aristotle," and Gaiser 1985, 89, agreed. During this period Speusippus was head of the Academy in Athens, while Xenocrates was most probably with Aristotle and Theophrastus in Assos. And these are precisely the *dramatis personae* in the Essay: Plato and the Pythagoreans who provide the framework—with the Pythagoreans Archytas and Eurytus actually mentioned by name—Speusippus and

be discounted both on its own merits and on the basis of other circumstantial evidence, adumbrated by Dorandi 1998, 31–33. There is, finally, the added consideration that it would seem improbable that Theophrastus could have had as good an inside knowledge of, or especially a personal stake in, the discussions in the Academy, as indicated in this very Essay and as just described in the preceding paragraph, had he met Aristotle for the first time only when the latter came to Mytilene after Assos in 345, and had actually been present in an Academic environment for the first time in his life only when Aristotle returned to Athens in 335.

Xenocrates, and Aristotle, of course, and his new theories about the unmoved mover and teleology; that the pre-Socratics are but marginal at best, as Krämer 1973, 208 observed, is further indication that the Essay is not so much a systematic run-through of all opinions on the subject of first principles but a presentation of the views held by the people actually participating in the discussion, either in person or by proxy, because they set the stage for its very terms.

It is difficult to see the same kind of environment that would be conducive to the production of a work like the Essay being also present in either Mytilene or Macedonia. In particular, would the sense of proximity to Academic positions we witness in the Essay have persisted during those long years of Theophrastus's close association with only Aristotle, and after the death of Speusippus (339) and away from Xenocrates? As for the first year after the return of the two philosophers to Athens in 335, by that time they had been working together for over fourteen years, if not more, and the kind of critical discussion of Aristotle's earlier metaphysical theories that one finds in the Essay would have already taken place between them; besides, by that time Aristotle would have developed some of the later metaphysical ideas, and Theophrastus would have known about them. For in the opening of the Essay Theophrastus, very much like Aristotle in the early book Alpha of the *Metaphysics*, is still grappling with the very name of the discipline in which he is engaged, which he simply calls ἡ τῶν πρώτων θεωρία, showing no awareness that Aristotle had tried calling it, in the later books of the *Metaphysics*, in a variety of ways (see the commentary on 4a3 below in Part III). For all these considerations, as an aporetic essay historically situated at the beginning of Aristotle's new thinking about metaphysical subjects, whose function as a dialectical exercise is intended precisely to promote and abet that thinking, the Essay finds its intellectual and historical context better in Assos in 347–345 than in Athens after 335.

2. *Title and Transmission*

Two problems relating to the title of the Essay have dogged scholarship from the very beginning. One is its very name, given the glaring historical anachronism of the transmitted title, μετὰ τὰ φυσικά (if this transmitted title is taken to refer to Theophrastus's work, as it almost universally has been), since this particular title was given to Aristotle's work by that name only in the first century BC when his extant corpus was published.[11] The second is the unusual—and to some, inexplicable—syntax of the transmitted title itself, Θεοφράστου τῶν μετὰ τὰ φυσικά,[12] in which something has been thought to be missing. Furthermore, and ironically, a very helpful and learned Scholium added by some person (or persons) at the end of the Essay in some manuscripts, something which normally would have helped resolve the issue, has actually compounded the problem, due to difficulties in its interpretation. Much ink has been spilt on all these issues, but inevitably they must be revisited, for none of the proposed solutions has found universal acceptance or is, in my estimation, satisfactory.[13] First, it is necessary to provide what may be taken at this stage of scholarship to be the ascertained evidence on the basis of which a solution can be sought. There is, to begin with, the text and translation of the Scholium, separated into its three components (the capitalization of the Greek text is mine):

> [a] Θεοφράστου τῶν μετὰ τὰ Φυσικά.
>
> [b] Τοῦτο τὸ βιβλίον Ἀνδρόνικος μὲν καὶ Ἕρμιππος ἀγνοοῦσιν, οὐδὲ γὰρ μνείαν αὐτοῦ ὅλως πεποίηνται ἐν τῇ ἀναγραφῇ τῶν Θεοφράστου βιβλίων· Νικόλαος δὲ ἐν τῇ θεωρίᾳ τῶν Ἀριστοτέλους μετὰ τὰ Φυσικὰ μνημονεύει αὐτοῦ λέγων εἶναι Θεοφράστου.
>
> [c] Εἰσὶ δ' ἐν αὐτῷ οἷον προδιαπορίαι τινὲς ὀλίγαι τῆς ὅλης πραγματείας.
>
> [a] [The book] by Theophrastus of those [that come] after [Aristotle's] *Physics*.

---

[11] According to the most plausible assessment of the evidence. The occurrence of the title μεταφυσικά in the anonymous "Hesychius" catalogue of Aristotle's writings (no. 111) can be thought to be earlier than the first century BC Roman edition *only if* the text is emended to read, μετὰ ⟨τὰ⟩ φυσικά. The form μεταφυσικά as such is much later and thus can be seen in the "Hesychius" list only as an interpolation, perhaps by Hesychius himself. See the discussion of the evidence by M. Narcy in *DPhA Supplement* 226.

[12] The Paris. Gr. 1853 (P) omits τὰ in the title by haplography, but has it in the Scholium at the end.

[13] The Scholium has been studied repeatedly, and in detail, not only with reference to this Essay by Theophrastus but also in a number of other contexts; see, among the most relevant discussions for Theophrastus, Usener 1861, 259–260; Rose 1863, 183–185; Ross pp. ix–x; Jaeger 1932, 289–292; Kley 14–15; Jaeger, ed. *Metaphysics*, pp. vi–vii; Regenbogen 1940, 1366–1367, 1389; Theiler 1958, 102/292; Drossaart Lulofs 1969, 27–30; Burnikel 123–130; Berti 1982, 13–14; Vuillemin-Diem 1982, 173–198; Vuillemin-Diem 1995, 308–325; Hecquet-Devienne 2004, 171–183.

[b] Andronicus and Hermippus do not know this book, for they make no mention of it at all in the list of Theophrastus's books; Nicolaus, though, does mention it in his study of Aristotle's [books that come] after the *Physics*, saying that it is by Theophrastus.

[c] It contains some few "pre-diaporiae,"[14] so to speak, relating to the entire treatise.

(a) *The manuscript transmission of the Essay as Aristotelian together with the books of Aristotle's* Metaphysics

The Scholium itself, however it is understood, clearly puts Theophrastus's Essay in close proximity to Aristotle's *Metaphysics*, as is also obvious from the environment in which the work was transmitted in the manuscripts. In both of our oldest and most reliable independent Greek manuscripts, the Parisinus gr. 1853 (P) and the Vindobonensis phil. gr. 100 (J), the Essay is found together with the major physical, ethical, and metaphysical Aristotelian treatises. The contents of P are, in order, Aristotle's *Physics*, *De caelo*, *De generatione et corruptione*, *Meteorology*, *De anima*, *De sensu et sensibilibus*, *De memoria et reminiscentia*, *De somno et vigilia*, *De divinatione per somnium*, *De motu animalium*, *Metaphysics*, Theophrastus's Essay, the pseudo-Aristotelian *De coloribus*, Aristotle's *De partibus animalium*, *De generatione animalium*, *De incessu animalium*, *Ethica Nicomachea*, *Magna moralia*. In J the order is, *Physics*, *De caelo*, *De generatione et corruptione*, *Meteorology*, Theophrastus's Essay, Aristotle's *Metaphysics*. In P the Essay follows that of Aristotle, in J it precedes it. On the basis of her lengthy research on P and especially on the text of the *Metaphysics* in it, Hecquet-Devienne 2004 concluded in a convincing fashion that the order of these treatises in P is old and that it reflects the "state of the Lyceum library, which bears witness to ongoing research," before the death of Aristotle. Her conclusions corroborate those of Most 1988a and

[14] A "pre-diaporia", rendering the Greek προδιαπορία, is a preliminary run-through of an aporia. I have kept the Greek form because it is a technical term and, in the Greek, apparently a neologism. See the discussion on the Scholium in the commentary in Part III below. As for aporia (and its cognates, the verb ἀπορέω and the adjective ἄπορος), I keep the word, which is accepted in English. The cluster of concepts surrounding the word are crucial in the philosophies of both Aristotle and Theophrastus, and no single English word expresses them adequately. I follow Arthur Madigan, *Alexander of Aphrodisias. On Aristotle's Metaphysics 2 & 3*, Ithaca, N.Y.: Cornell University Press, 1992, 87n3, who examines the concept and refers to the discussion by J. Owens, *The Doctrine of Being in the Aristotelian Metaphysics*, Toronto: Pontifical Institute of Medieval Studies, 1963^2, 211–219. For its importance in this Essay see below in this chapter, section 3.

mine mentioned in the preceding section: Theophrastus's Essay "constitutes Theophrastus's contribution to a 'first' *Metaphysics* by Aristotle," a contribution which helped Aristotle take into account the issues raised by Theophrastus and partly respond to them. The Essay was accordingly not integrated into the works of Theophrastus and the lists of his works because it formed part of ongoing research in the Lyceum (p. 186). As Hecquet-Devienne puts it, the Paris manuscript "may be indeed the descendant of a copy of Aristotelian writings that corroborates a state of the research in the Lyceum before Aristotle achieved the revision of his works on ⟨the⟩ basis of contributions by other philosophers of the school" (p. 189). This revision seems to be clearly reflected in the programmatic opening paragraph of Aristotle's *Meteorology* (338a–339a9) where he mentions *Physics*, *De caelo*, and *De generatione et corruptione* as having been completed, *Meteorology* as the work at hand, and the animal and plant treatises as still to be written. This order corresponds quite closely to the order of the treatises in the Paris manuscript.

The presence of Theophrastus's Essay in both these manuscripts (P and J) as the only non-Aristotelian work would indicate that it was included among the writings of Aristotle and under his name from the very beginning, and almost certainly in the Roman edition of Aristotle's works in the first century BC.[15] This explains why the lists of Theophrastus's writings drawn by both Hermippus, the disciple of Callimachus the great librarian, and Andronicus (as Porphyry informs us, fr. 39 FHS&G) make no mention of the Essay, as stated in the Scholium. Both of these scholars may well have known it, but if so they knew it as Aristotelian.[16] In this regard it has been pointed out that the lists of Theophrastus's writings in Diogenes Laertius (and of Aristotle's, for that matter), which almost certainly go back to Hermippus, were thought by their author to be a complete list of all his works, based, in all probability, on autopsy of the holdings in the Alexandrian library.[17] It is thus difficult to assume that

[15] Hecquet-Devienne 2004, 189. Barnes 1997 raised enough aporiae about Andronicus of Rhodes as the author of the edition to warrant greater caution in assigning this role to him. Barnes actually gave structured argument for a position that had been implied, suggested, and stated by others before; see Lord 1986, 158, with references to Düring 1957, 415. Be that as it may, the existence of a Roman edition in that century seems beyond dispute, for Nicolaus of Damascus, about whom more later, actually used it around the turn of the eras. The actual identity of its editor is of no consequence to my argument here.

[16] For a similar assessment see Burnikel 125.

[17] Blum 1991, 60. The provenance of the lists from a library seems to be proven beyond serious doubt by the presence of the complete number of lines given by Diogenes

had the Essay been identified as Theophrastean Hermippus or Andronicus would have overlooked it.

Furthermore, with regard to the ability of these two scholars to assess the authenticity of the ascription of the Essay to Aristotle, it is important to note that modern scholarship may have criteria for such matters that are not exactly the same as those of the ancients.[18] In the case of Hermippus, Ross, p. x, believes that "it seems unlikely that Hermippus would have failed to notice the obviously unaristotelian character of the work." It is not clear why this work should have seemed so "obviously unaristotelian" to Hermippus who, if he knew anything at all about Aristotle, would have known about the aporetic character of *Metaphysics* B and N. Besides, as Moraux 1951, 221–222, depicts him, Hermippus was much more interested in a good gossipy story than in philosophical hairsplitting, while Pfeiffer says that Hermippus's biographical work was "written in a more novelistic vein ... with ... anecdotes."[19] As for Andronicus, we have his precise reasoning for declaring *De interpretatione* spurious and *De anima* authentic (as transmitted by Philoponus, *In De an.* 27.21 = Düring 1957, 418 no. 75 o), a state of affairs that should raise severe doubts, if not about his competence, then at least about his criteria. This is not to cast aspersion on Andronicus's intelligence, erudition, or service to Aristotelian studies, but merely to point out that critical judgments of this sort are always culturally determined (as are ours) and should be evaluated in that context.

All this evidence thus indicates beyond any serious doubt that the Essay was from the very beginning transmitted together with the books which were later to form Aristotle's *Metaphysics* and as part of or appendix to it, as a result of which it went unnoticed by the great Hellenistic bibliographers as one of the works of Theophrastus. And almost certainly, as already noted, it was also included as an Aristotelian work in the

---

Laertius for all the books by both Aristotle and Theophrastus (445270 and 232808 lines respectively). For this very reason it is difficult to prefer as the ultimate author of the lists Ariston of Keos over Hermippus, as argued by Moraux 1951, 221 ff. Blum's section on the libraries of Aristotle and Theophrastus, pp. 52–64, should be consulted together with the chapter by Moraux 1973, 3–31, and the recent summary of the state of affairs by Primavesi 2007, 58–59.

[18] See the discussion of this very issue, with regard to Aristotelian commentators, in Moraux 1974.

[19] R. Pfeiffer, *History of Classical Scholarship*, Oxford: Oxford University Press, 1968, 150. I wonder if today's master cataloguers could offer scholarly opinions about the authenticity of the books they are cataloguing.

Roman edition of the Aristotelian corpus; indeed, if our most ancient Aristotelian manuscripts, P and J, ultimately derive from that edition, it is difficult to see how the Essay could not have been part of it.

(b) *The identification of Theophrastus as the author of the Essay by Nicolaus of Damascus and the date and authorhip of the Scholium*

Next, we have reasonably certain evidence about Nicolaus of Damascus (born 64 BC, died after 15 AD?). The author of the Scholium credits him for restoring the work to Theophrastus in a study of Aristotle's *Metaphysics*. Drossaart Lulofs 1969, who collected most of the extant testimonia and fragments of this work by Nicolaus, very plausibly suggested (p. 23) that the reference in the Scholium must be not to an independent work by Nicolaus but to a section dealing with the *Metaphysics* in his *On the Philosophy of Aristotle*.[20] We are also relatively well informed about what Nicolaus did in that section.[21] From Averroes, who had access to an Arabic compendium of Nicolaus's work (T7.4–6 Drossaart Lulofs), we know that Nicolaus also discussed the arrangement of the subjects in Aristotle's *Metaphysics* and on occasion disagreed with it. It is reasonable to suppose that it was in the course of precisely such a discussion of the contents and the arrangement of the books of the *Metaphysics* that Nicolaus made mention of (μνημονεύει) Theophrastus's Essay, and said that it was not by Aristotle but Theophrastus (λέγων εἶναι Θεοφράστου). This implies—with little, if any, doubt—that Nicolaus found the Essay in the edition of Aristotle's works he was using and that it

[20] The Greek title of this work is Περὶ τῆς Ἀριστοτέλους φιλοσοφίας, according to Simplicius, *In De caelo* 398.36 = Test. 5.1 Drosaart Lulofs 1969. It is preserved in a highly abbreviated Syriac translation in a Cambridge University manuscript, on which Drossaart Lulofs based his edition, but also, in indirect transmission, on the citations and paraphrastic versions of this translation extant in the Syriac work of Bar-Hebraeus (1226–1286), most of which remains unedited. See Zonta 2001, who translated several passages from Bar-Hebraeus which probably derive from Nicolaus's work, and Takahashi 2005, for more details on the contents of the Syriac manuscript and the recovery of further fragments from the work.

[21] The section on Aristotle's *Metaphysics* to which the author of our Scholium refers as θεωρία τῶν Ἀριστοτέλους μετὰ τὰ Φυσικά is taken by Drossaart Lulofs 1969 (p. 11, T7) to be its very title. This, however, can hardly be right. The Greek phrase is descriptive and not literal, meaning simply "Nicolaus's study of Aristotle's books after the *Physics*." Titles descriptive of the study of something did not *themselves* contain as a rule the expression θεωρία τοῦ/τῆς/τῶν; very simply if the work was a study of something it was called Περί followed by a genitive.

was attributed there to Aristotle; for why should Nicolaus have mentioned the Essay at all in that connection unless it had been physically present in his manuscript of Aristotle's *Metaphysics* as one of the books following the *Physics*? Thus the Scholium provides further documentary support to the evidence established in the preceding section, from the study of the manuscript tradition, that Theophrastus's Essay was transmitted together with Aristotle's *Metaphysics* and as part of it.

What edition of Aristotle's works was Nicolaus using for his study? The order in which he treats Aristotle's works in it (T6 Drossaart Lulofs, and pp. 23–24) is roughly that in the Roman edition, the slight deviations from it being easily attributable to Nicolaus's quarrel with Aristotle about the arrangement of subjects in the *Metaphysics*, as mentioned above. Thus, it is most probable that it was in this edition that Nicolaus found the Essay and restored it to Theophrastus. However, what is more problematic than the actual edition used by Nicolaus is the *title* under which he found the Essay transmitted in the name of Aristotle. This is a problem to which I will come back at the end of this discussion.

Nicolaus made the correct identification of the author of the Essay in the course of the discussion, in his work Περὶ τῆς Ἀριστοτέλους φιλοσοφίας and not in a separate treatise, of the arrangements of subjects and topics in the edition of Aristotle's *Metaphysics* that he was using. The question now is, how did the scholarly world come to know about this identification, and when did this happen? The way in which the Scholium refers to the issue (μνημονεύει αὐτοῦ λέγων εἶναι Θεοφράστου) suggests that one could find out about Nicolaus's identification by reading the pertinent passage(s) in his work on Aristotle—i.e., the identification was not otherwise announced or noted in a special way. If this is so, then the question becomes, who read Nicolaus's work on Aristotle and when? The earliest references that we have to its having been read and noticed are two: one is by the scholiast, of course, who in part (b) of the Scholium refers directly to Nicolaus's restoration of the Essay to Theophrastus, and the other is by Simplicius, who also gives us the title of the work, mentioned above. Now the dates of Simplicius are known (first half of the 6th century); the question is to date the scholiast. Theoretically, it could be anybody between the first decade of the Christian era (at which time approximately Nicolaus wrote his work on Aristotle), and the time of Simplicius. But if part (c) of the Scholium, in which the work of Theophrastus is characterized as a προδιαπορία to Aristotle's *Metaphysics*, was written by the same person who wrote part (b), in which Nicolaus's work is mentioned, then this scholiast lived in late antiquity in the circle of the Neoplatonic philosophers: his technical use of the term προδιαπορία, a use which was developed only in late antiquity, attests to this (see the discussion in Part III in the commentary on 12b4).

The question whether parts (b) and (c) of the Scholium were written by the same person is contested. Hecquet-Devienne 2004, 182, basing herself on the research of Vuillemin-Diem on the Latin translation of Aristotle's *Metaphysics* by William of Moerbeke,[22] claims that they were not, principally because part (c) of the Scholium was not translated into Latin: William's "Greek model," Hecquet-Devienne concludes, "did not yet contain it." This does not really follow. The absence of that sentence in William's translation need not necessarily mean that his Greek model did not have it; William himself may have decided, for whatever reason, not to translate it.[23] However, even if William's Greek exemplar did not have it, this need not necessarily mean that part (c) of the Scholium had not yet been written by the same person who wrote part (b): William's Greek manuscript may itself have omitted it, as was the entire Scholium omitted in numerous Greek manuscripts, or it may have been omitted at some point in the Greek transmission. In any case, arguments from omissions in MSS are hardly reliable and the evidence from William of Moerbeke's Latin translation is accordingly inconclusive.

It appears much more probable that the authors of parts (b) and (c) of the Scholium were, in fact, the same person. Nicolaus's work on Aristotle—on all of Aristotle, as the Syriac and Arabic translations studied by Drossaart Lulofs indicate—was an important work, written at a time when Aristotelian scholarship began to be mainstream in Greek philosophical literature. And yet we hear nothing about this work until Simplicius. How is this to be interpreted? It was probably not by chance,

---

[22] G. Vuillemin-Diem discussed the scholium and its Latin translations extensively in her book-length article, 1982, 173–208. She later incorporated it, with slight modifications, in her book on the same subject, 1995, 308–325. In what follows I will be referring to her later, 1995, publication only.

[23] Vuillemin-Diem 1995, 317, maintains that "Wilhelm hat den übrigen Text [of the Scholium, part (b)] so sorgfältig wiedergegeben, dass er diesen aufschlussreichen Satz [part (c)] sicher nicht von sich aus weggelassen hätte." But William knew this Scholium as referring to Book A of Aristotle's *Metaphysics*, and he could hardly have agreed with the assessment in part (c) of the Scholium that Book A was merely a προδιαπορία of the entire treatise. So he may have decided to censure it.

insofar as the preponderance of evidence, though indirect, suggests otherwise. The elements of this indirect evidence are the following. Nicolaus was an outsider to the school philosophical tradition[24] and as such had no institutional context that would preserve and transmit his works. He was known because of his sheer industriousness and intelligence, and, if we can interject a contemporary cultural value into his time and immediate posterity, because he had rubbed shoulders with celebrity: Antony and Cleopatra, Herod, Augustus. He was accordingly known in a general way, and his most popular work, if one is to judge by the frequency with which it is quoted in later literature, was his multi-volume history. But in philosophy he was ignored—or if he was known to some extent, then he must have been cited by authors in works which themselves have been ignored and not survived. Thus if Nicolaus's philosophical works were not noticed in philosophical circles in his lifetime and immediately after his death, did they enter the mainstream of philosophical discussion before we first come across them in Simplicius's works? This question is crucial. By "mainstream philosophical discussion" I mean being read and studied by people who, in addition to having a philosophical education so as to appreciate Nicolaus's identification of the Essay as having been written by Theophrastus, *also had access to and were themselves responsible for manuscript production* and the further copying of philosophical texts. For it would be inane to argue that Nicolaus's works were not read by anybody between their production and Simplicius: they were available in manuscript and anybody could have read them, and there is no way we can know who. But what is important for our purposes is to know that the person who read them was someone who would be in a position to take action, commission or sponsor a new manuscript copy of the works of Aristotle, and have inserted in it the Scholium that we find in the Paris manuscript. It is in this sense that we would like to know who, if anybody, read them before Simplicius.

Drossaart Lulofs (1969, pp. 42, 131) insists that Porphyry knew the works of Nicolaus and his Περὶ τῆς Ἀριστοτέλους φιλοσοφίας, and even suggests (p. 43n17) that Simplicius might have derived his information about Nicolaus from Porphyry, but he offers no evidence whatsoever. The fact is, Simplicius is the first author who both cites the title of Nicolaus's work and offers a quotation from it (*In De caelo* 399.2 = fr. 29

[24] For his life and works, much studied in the 19th century, see Drossaart Lulofs 1969, 1–5, Moraux 1973, 445–450, Zonta 2001.

Drossaart Lulofs), while we have absolutely no evidence that Porphyry did anything of the sort. These citations by Simplicius indicate that the work of Nicolaus began to be read and appreciated by the Neoplatonic philosophers in late antiquity, and that this is the first time that it demonstrably entered the philosophical mainstream, as further indicated by its translation (among other works by Nicolaus) into both Syriac and Arabic. The philosophical tastes and predilections of authors writing in Syriac and Arabic were very much shaped by and followed the orientation of the philosophical schools in late antiquity. The fact that it is Simplicius who cites Nicolaus is also significant: given his travels in the Near East, if the manuscripts of Nicolaus of Damascus were preserved in his native city or greater Syria, it stands to reason that Simplicius may have come across them there.

Finally, two further considerations are relevant. The one is based on the fact of the complete absence of Theophrastus's Essay itself from all extant ancient philosophical literature. It is certain that it was not known until the time of Nicolaus because it was thought to be by Aristotle, as discussed above. Once Nicolaus restored it to him, however, it should have attracted some attention *if* Nicolaus's identification had become widely known—i.e., if Nicolaus's Περὶ τῆς Ἀριστοτέλους φιλοσοφίας was read in philosophical circles before the time of Simplicius. But it had not and it was not. The only comment that we have about Theophrastus's Essay is part (c) of the Scholium, which calls it a προδιαπορία on Aristotle's *Metaphysics*, a comment made by someone among, or closely affiliated with, the Neoplatonic philosophers in late antiquity (see the commentary on the Scholium in Part III below).

The second consideration relates to another scholium in the Paris manuscript (f. 231^{v}, in the margin) in which the one we are studying occurs; it concerns a comment on the word ἐκτοπωτέρως in the text of Aristotle's *Metaphysics* A 8, 989b30. This other scholium, as Vuillemin-Diem discovered (and reported by Hecquet-Devienne 2000, 147), is derived wholly from Asclepius's commentary on the *Metaphysics* (64,2–7 and 65,32–35 Hayduck). This scholiast was manifestly a Neoplatonic scholar contemporary with or younger than Asclepius (first half of 6th century). Yet a third scholium in the same manuscript remarks on the authenticity of Book A of the *Metaphysics*. These three scholia—two on Aristotle's *Metaphysics* and the one on Theophrastus's Essay—point to erudition and judiciousness in their author(s). They were all to be found in the ultimate archetype from which these sections of manuscript P were copied (by scribe E II, as termed by the specialists; see Hecquet-Devienne

2000, 147). If the authors of the three scholia were all the same person, and the indications are that they were, then he was the contemporary of or slightly younger than Asclepius.[25]

Taken together, what all this suggests is that although Theophrastus's Essay was restored to him in the work Περὶ τῆς Ἀριστοτέλους φιλοσοφίας by Nicolaus of Damascus at the turn of the Christian era, this identification was first noticed and acted upon some five centuries later by someone in the circle of the Neoplatonic philosophers who was in a position to affect manuscript production and change the ascription to the rightful author by writing or dictating the Scholium. This conclusion may be based on evidence that is, for the most part, circumstantial and from silence, but it presents the most probable course of events at this stage of our knowledge.[26] If that is the case, then parts (b) and (c) of the Scholium were either written by the same person or at any rate were roughly contemporary; they both stem from the philosophers of late antiquity.

(c) *Analysis of the syntax of the Scholiast's title,* Θεοφράστου τῶν μετὰ τὰ φυσικά

This conclusion in turn affects the question about the title of Theophrastus's Essay because it implies that this work continued to be transmitted in the manuscripts of Aristotle's works as part of or related to the latter's *Metaphysics*, carrying whatever title, or none, as the case might be.

---

[25] Hecquet-Devienne 2000, 147, who suggests as much, nevertheless does not clearly discriminate between the *author* of these scholia and the *scribe* of E II, for she seems to attribute the two scholia on Aristotle's *Metaphysics* to the scribe of manuscript P, E II. However, if that part of the manuscript was copied around the middle of the tenth century (see Hecquet-Devienne 2000, 114–115 for the documentation), it appears difficult to believe that a scholiast as learned in philosophy and its literature could have arisen at that time. The scholia are all indicative of active involvement in philosophical research and must be thought to go back to our late antique scholiast. The problem which may have disoriented Hecquet-Devienne 2000 is that the two scholia on Aristotle are written in the margin of manuscript P, while the one on Theophrastus is in the main body of the page, right after the end of the Essay. But it appears that the scribe (E II) decided to copy the Theophrastus Scholium inside the page and not in the margin as he did with the previous two because the Essay ends almost at the end of the page and he had a little writing space left which, one the one hand, was not large enough to begin copying the next treatise, *De coloribus*, and, on the other, he did not wish to leave blank. This is also indicated by the fact that at the end of the Theophrastus Scholium he still had a couple of lines space left, which he filled with an *adespoton* remark on the soul.

[26] It is true that "silence rarely proves much," as Barnes 1997, 18, aptly observed; "but this particular silence"—five centuries of complete lack of awareness of the existence of Theophrastus's Essay—"is sustained and surprising."

Philosophers until late antiquity continued to read it as Aristotle's work. Once Nicolaus's intervention was noticed by a reader who was also in a position to act on it, the manuscript of Aristotle that was next commissioned and which contained Theophrastus's Essay and the Scholium, that is, parts (b) and (c), must also have carried a title for it. What we have in the extant manuscripts is the notorious Θεοφράστου τῶν μετὰ τὰ φυσικά, which is part (a) of the Scholium. How does this relate to the rest of the Scholium and to whatever title was or was not there to begin with?

The unaffiliated genitive (τῶν) in the transmitted title has been variously interpreted. The alternatives that have been proposed are the following:

(a) Partitive genitive, indicating that the Essay is a part of a larger (actual or planned) book by Theophrastus with that title (Ross p. x; Laks & Most p. x and translation, p. 2, "Tiré de la Métaphysique de Théophraste").
(b) Genitive of origin, with the preposition ἐκ being understood, indicating that the Essay is extracted from a larger actual book by Theophrastus with that title; i.e., Θεοφράστου ⟨ἐκ⟩ τῶν μετὰ τὰ φυσικά, "From Theophrastus's *Metaphysics*" (Laks & Most p. x, note 6).
(c) Partitive genitive, indicating that the Essay is the part written by Theophrastus of *Aristotle's Metaphysics*; i.e., Θεοφράστου τῶν ⟨Ἀριστοτέλους⟩ μετὰ τὰ φυσικά (Burnikel 126: "Theophrasts Anteil an der Metaphysik des Aristoteles").
(d) Genitive of belonging, with a presumed noun, like προδιαπορίαι, to which the genitive is attached, not expressed; i.e., Θεοφράστου ⟨προδιαπορίαι⟩ τῶν ⟨Ἀριστοτέλους⟩ μετὰ τὰ φυσικά, "Diaporiae by Theophrastus on Aristotle's *Metaphysics*" (Burnikel 126n43; "Theophrasts metaphysische Diaporien," Burnikel 127n45).
(e) Partitive genitive, with a number following the title (assuming it was lost in transmission), indicating the number of the book from the *Metaphysics* which this is; i.e., Θεοφράστου τῶν μετὰ τὰ φυσικά α′ (i.e., ⟨βιβλίον⟩ πρῶτον), "The first book of Theophrastus's *Metaphysics*" (Laks & Most p. x note 6).
(f) Genitive of belonging, with a number following the title (assuming it was lost in transmission), indicating the number of books of which the work consists, even in the case of books having one book (see Moraux 1951, 198); e.g., Θεοφράστου τῶν μετὰ τὰ φυσικά α′ (i.e., ⟨βιβλίον⟩ ἕν), "Theophrastus's *Metaphysics*, one book."

(g) A title normally recorded in the nominative appears in the genitive in catalogues of titles (see Moraux 1951, 198); i.e., a presumed Θεοφράστου τὰ μετὰ τὰ φυσικά would become, Θεοφράστου τῶν μετὰ τὰ φυσικά.

Given the transmission of the work established so far, the impossible alternatives can be relatively easily eliminated. (a) and (b) rest on the assumption that whoever is responsible for the transmitted title thought that, first, the work is a fragment or part of a whole, and second that Theophrastus himself had written, or was planning to write, a work, entitled μετὰ τὰ φυσικά, from which this work was an extract. The second assumption is manifestly invalid. There is no indication anywhere that anyone until late antiquity thought that Theophrastus had written or was planning to write such a work, and in any case, even if there had been, its title could not have been μετὰ τὰ φυσικά. As Burnikel 126 duly remarks, this phrase did not express the *subject* upon which a treatise could be written but merely the *place* occupied by Aristotle's *Metaphysics* in the edition of his works, or even, if the designation μετὰ τὰ φυσικά is older than the Roman edition,[27] in the arrangement of Aristotle's works in groups. Whether the transmitted title goes back to Nicolaus or the Neoplatonic scholiast or anybody in between, μετὰ τὰ φυσικά could have meant to him only Aristotle's work so located in the edition or arrangement; Theophrastus could not have been the author of a book named μετὰ τὰ φυσικά. Accordingly, the Essay could not be a part of or extract from it.

The last three alternatives (e,f,g) have two problems. The first is what has just been mentioned, that they make μετὰ τὰ φυσικά to be a title for a book by Theophrastus, an impossibility. The second is that they represent titles as entered in a list or catalogue of books, which would imply that the person responsible for the transmitted title copied it verbatim from such a catalogue. But the problem is precisely, as the Scholium says, that there was no such title in any catalogue of *Theophrastus's* books (and this catalogue would have had to be one of Theophrastus's books because his name is mentioned in the title).

This leaves the two alternatives (c) and (d) suggested by Burnikel, which point to the right direction. The analysis of the transmitted title can again begin with what I take to be certain in the Scholium, the fact that its part (c) was written by a philosopher or scholar active in the

[27] See above, note 11.

philosophical schools in late antiquity (fifth or sixth century), as discussed above. Now first, in this part of the Scholium, the words τῆς ὅλης πραγματείας refer, without any doubt, to Aristotle's *Metaphysics*;[28] and second, in part (b) of the Scholium, the work is attributed to Theophrastus. If that is so, then as Burnikel astutely observed, the transmitted title, Θεοφράστου τῶν μετὰ τὰ φυσικά, expresses exactly the same thing as parts (b) and (c) of the Scholium.[29] But it is important to establish a temporal priority here: the title must be posterior to parts (b) and (c) because it depends on them in the sense that this title could never have been given to the Essay if the Scholium were not there. On the basis of parts (b) and (c), then, the scholiast, most likely, or some scribe after him, (re–?)named the Essay, or actually *described* it, as "*Theophrastus's* ⟨part⟩ of what comes after ⟨Aristotle's⟩ *Physics*," with the emphasis on Θεοφράστου. The insertion of the title at the *end* of the work in part (a) of the Scholium thus corroborates the analysis just given: the title is based on parts (b) and (c) and is posterior to them, semantically if not necessarily temporally, but it is necessary to add it in close proximity to the evidence that justifies it, i.e., the contents of parts (b) and (c).[30]

It appears that the difficulty we have understanding this laconic title[31] is that we are accustomed to reading the phrase μετὰ τὰ φυσικά as the *title* of the work we call *Metaphysics*; instead we should read it as a prepositional phrase, indicating a location after the Φυσικά in the edition, and see Φυσικά only as the title of *Aristotle's* work. The Neoplatonists in late antiquity, from whom this title arises, consistently understood the phrase in this fashion. Philoponus explicitly states that this is the case: θεολογικὰ μέν ἐστι τὰ μετὰ τὴν φυσικὴν πραγματείαν αὐτῷ τεταγμένα,

---

[28] The term πραγματεία, by the way, is also the one regularly used by the Neoplatonists to refer to Aristotle's *Metaphysics*: Asclepius, *In Met.* 1.6, 8, Hayduck; Syrianus, *In Met.* 1,2. The Arabic translator (Isḥāq) also understood the reference in the Scholium, some version of which he read in his Greek manuscript (Ψ), to be to Aristotle's *Metaphysics*; see next below.

[29] Burnikel 126: "Diese Worte [sc. προδιαπορίαι τῆς ὅλης πραγματείας] sagen aber ... nichts anderes aus als der Titel selbst."

[30] In subsequent copies of the Scholium the insertion of the title at the end of the work may have served another purpose, to avoid having the Scholium understood as referring to the next work copied in manuscript P, *De coloribus*. Athough τοῦτο in line 12a4 of the Scholium would normally refer to what preceded (as noted by Berti 1982, 12, and Hecquet-Devienne 2000, 148n242), the presence of the title itself in the Scholium would preclude any confusion.

[31] Laks & Most, p. x, "peu claire par elle-même;" Vuillemin-Diem 1995, 313, "das schwer verständliche τῶν;" Henrich 15, "der Genitiv τῶν nur mühsam zu konstruieren ist;" Hecquet-Devienne 2004, 176, "we do not understand its syntax."

ἅπερ οὕτω μετὰ τὰ Φυσικὰ προσηγόρευσε (*In Cat.* 5, Busse; thus to be capitalized),[32] and this understanding also appears in the titles of the commentaries on *Metaphysics*: "the book ⟨that comes⟩ after the *Physics* of Aristotle" = Σχόλια εἰς τὸ μεῖζον Α τῆς μετὰ τὰ Φυσικά Ἀριστοτέλους ⟨πραγματείας⟩ (Asclepius *In Met.* 1 Hayduck), or Περὶ τῶν ἐν τῷ Β τῆς μετὰ τὰ Φυσικά Ἀριστοτέλους πραγματείας (Syrianus, *In Met.* 1, Kroll). Thus, just as the Greek that is understood naturally from the mere title τὰ μετὰ τὰ φυσικά is, τὰ μετὰ τὰ Φυσικά ⟨Ἀριστοτέλους τεταγμένα (as in Philoponus's text) or κείμενα or ἐκδεδομένα⟩, so also if one reads μετὰ τὰ Φυσικά as it was intended by the scholiast or the person who composed the transmitted title of Theophrastus's Essay, namely, as a prepositional phrase and not as a title, the Greek that is understood from it is, Θεοφράστου τῶν μετὰ τὰ Φυσικά ⟨Ἀριστοτέλους τεταγμένων or κειμένων⟩: "Of the ⟨books that are arranged or come⟩ after ⟨Aristotle's⟩ *Physics* ⟨i.e., in the edition⟩, the one by Theophrastus."

In a sense, even Burnikel himself appears not to have fully grasped his own explanation of the title, for he translated it as (p. 126), "Theophrasts Anteil an der Metaphysik des Aristoteles," taking "Metaphysik" as the title, instead of a prepositional phrase. He thus made another suggestion, which he liked better, namely alternative (d), according to which it is assumed that some word to which the genitive τῶν would belong has dropped out. The word that he suggested is προδιαπορίαι, from part (c) of the Scholium. It is quite possible to understand the title in this fashion, especially since it appears relatively certain that the title was derived from parts (b) and (c) of the Scholium, as discussed above. The difficulty, though, is to account for the loss of the word in a title—and a crucial word for that matter—in a carefully edited manuscript from which both P and J derive.

The evidence from the Arabic translation indicates that Isḥāq may have had some of the difficulties discussed here. The colophon of the Arabic translation—it is a colophon and not a scholium—reads as follows:

"The treatise by Theophrastus, the advocate of Aristotle's arguments in metaphysics, ⟨in⟩ the translation by Isḥāq, is finished."

The phrase describing Theophrastus, "the advocate of Aristotle's arguments in metaphysics," *al-qayyim bi-huǧaǧ Arisṭūṭālis fī-mā baʿda ṭ-ṭabīʿa*, must be based on the Greek Scholium; the identification of

[32] Also more briefly in Simplicius, *In Cat.* 4, Kalbfleisch, and Olympiodorus *In Cat.* 7, Busse (where both Kalbfleisch and Busse erroneously print ἡ Μετὰ τὰ φυσικά, with a capital M instead of a capital Φ).

Aristotle's *Metaphysics* as the work to which Theophrastus's Essay relates reflects τῆς ὅλης πραγματείας in part (c) of the Scholium. The difficulty is how to understand the description of Theophrastus as the advocate, defender, custodian, curator (*al-qayyim bi-*) of Aristotle's arguments, or perhaps even one who provides and sets up arguments; theoretically, if the translator, Isḥāq, had our Scholium in front of him, this word should have reflected προδιαπορίαι. Perhaps it does, but it is difficult to argue for it. Given that the Greek word is a *hapax legomenon*, we cannot expect to find other instances of it translated into Arabic. On the other hand, as mentioned at the outset, the meaning of the Greek word is not difficult to gauge from its etymology, and the Baghdad translators of Aristotle were very good at etymological translations. Now the word ἀπορία and its derivatives in this treatise, where they occur a number of times, are normally, and properly, rendered by *šakk* and *ḥayra* and their derivatives, not by the verb *qāma bi-* and its derivatives (see the Glossary). Conversely, *qayyim bi-* in the Graeco-Arabic translation literature renders words that mean custodian and keeper, like προστάτης (*WGAÜS* s.v.), ἐπίτροπος (*WGAÜ* s.v.), and οἰκονόμος (*GA* 744b16),[33] not derivatives of ἀπορέω. Either, therefore, Isḥāq had a Greek scholium or colophon different from the one in our Greek manuscript P, or he translated according to what he thought the sense of our Scholium to be. I tend to think the latter. Isḥāq knew that Theophrastus was the faithful student of Aristotle,[34] and he could hardly envisage that προδιαπορίαι would actually mean that Theophrastus raised serious doubts about Aristotle's work. For *šakk* (doubt) in Arabic, the word for ἀπορία used in the translation, has a much stronger negative sense than (δι-)απορία does in Greek,[35] and Isḥāq accordingly used a friendly term, *qayyim bi-*, which, in this instance, would be closer in meaning to advocacy by setting up arguments. If, therefore, προδιαπορία in the Scholium means a preliminary working through of aporiae for an eventual fully articulate proof (as discussed in the following section of this chapter), then *qayyim bi-*

---

[33] In this case the Greek word is rendered by a hendiadys, *mudabbir wa-qayyim*: οἰκονόμος ἀγαθὸς ... ἡ φύσις = *aṭ-ṭibāʿ miṯla mudabbir wa-qayyim ṣāliḥ*; J. Brugman and H.J. Drossaart Lulofs, *Aristotle, Generation of Animals, The Arabic Translation*, Leiden: E.J. Brill, 1971, p. 84 (Arabic).

[34] And, according to the mistaken information in some Arabic sources, including a history of medicine by Isḥāq b. Ḥunayn himself, Aristotle's nephew; see fr. 3A FHS&G.

[35] And this is the reason why the translator of Book B of Aristotle's *Metaphysics* does not use it, which leads the unerring Commentator Averroes to appreciate it properly as an exercise in Aristotelian dialectical method.

as someone who sets up arguments for the subjects in Aristotle's *Metaphysics* is a good enough approximation. It looks highly probable that the Greek manuscript used by Isḥāq, Ψ, also contained our Scholium, except that the translator omitted the other information about Hermippus and Andronicus and Nicolaus as irrelevant for the purposes of his readers.

(d) *The Essay had an original title which* could *have been* Περὶ ἀρχῶν

If then it can be taken as established that the Essay was transmitted in the manuscript tradition, and eventually edited, along with the books that were later to form the *Metaphysics* of Aristotle and under his name, not of Theophrastus (*a*), and that the working title that was given to it, Θεοφράστου τῶν μετὰ τὰ φυσικά, was accordingly not a real title but a description by a Neoplatonic scholiast of the place of the Essay in this transmission (*b* and *c*), the question is next raised whether it had an original title and if it did what it was. A number of scholars have scoured the ancient lists of *Theophrastus's* works in order to find a title that might fit the contents of the Essay,[36] but this exercise is fruitless if, as just discussed, it was transmitted in antiquity—at the time, that is, when those lists were drawn—as a work by Aristotle; hence it is in the lists of *Aristotle's* works that it should be looked for. But this is tantamount to, and just as difficult as, asking what the original titles of the individual books that eventually comprised Aristotle's *Metaphysics* were, since for all practical purposes the Essay functioned and was transmitted as one of them.

To begin with, all evidence indicates that the Essay must have had a title originally, even if it was what we would today call a working title. This is indicated in general by the established practice, by the time of Theophrastus, of adopting as standard titles the statements in the introductory sentence(s) of a given work (White 2002, 19–20). But more specifically in the case of the Lyceum, it is also clear from the fact that Aristotle himself used such titles to give cross-references to the books of what later became his *Metaphysics* (and, of course, to his other

[36] For example, the title of Theophrastus's work Περὶ τῶν ἁπλῶν διαπορημάτων, as listed in Diogenes Laertius V,46, has found a number of supporters, for obvious reasons. It would appear that Krische was the first to make the suggestion in 1840, 343, and he was followed by Tricot (p. vii), and then by Reale 1964, 23, and Dillon 2002, 175n1; the later scholars do not necessarily credit Krische, while Dillon credits Reale. For her part, van Raalte (12n1) suggests Περὶ αἰτιῶν, Diogenes Laertius V,49.

works); thus, the title ἐν τοῖς περὶ τοῦ ποσαχῶς (*Met.* I 1, 1052a15) refers to *Metaphysics* Δ, ἐν τοῖς (δι-)ἀπορήμασιν (*Met.* M 2, 1076a39, b39) refers to *Metaphysics* B, ἐν τοῖς περὶ οὐσίας καὶ περὶ τοῦ ὄντος (*Met.* I 2, 1053b17) refers to *Metaphysics* Z and H, etc. We do not have a complete list of these working titles for all the books that were eventually included in the *Metaphysics*, but that hardly seems relevant; if some books demonstrably had titles, then they must all have, including the Essay by Theophrastus, if only for the practical purpose of referring to them during composition and discussion.[37] In any case, the practice at the time was to give titles to one's writings, and there is no good reason why Theophrastus would not have done so in this particular instance.

Secondly, it is to be noted that at least one of these working titles, the first one listed above referring to book Delta, also appears in the Hellenistic catalogue of Aristotle's writings as preserved by Diogenes Laertius and "Hesychius": Περὶ τῶν ποσαχῶς λεγομένων ἢ κατὰ πρόσθεσιν (numbers 36 and 37 respectively). Other titles of individual books by Aristotle that were eventually incorporated in the larger works, titles that were accordingly dropped from Andronicus's list as redundant and superseded, also appear in this Hellenistic catalogue.[38] It thus stands to reason that the title of Theophrastus's Essay, transmitted as it was with the books of Aristotle's *Metaphysics*, may also appear in this catalogue. On this assumption, the most likely title for the Essay would be Περὶ ἀρχῶν ("Hesychius" 21), even without any other corroborating evidence which I will next discuss: it is manifestly the most fitting title for the contents, and it is not incontrovertibly attached to any work by Aristotle. That it is fitting may well be indisputable,[39] but that it has not been assigned to any work by Aristotle requires some discussion, for it has been thought to refer to the *Physics*.

The relevant entries in the Hellenistic catalogue of Aristotle's works, most probably drawn by Hermippus (if not by Ariston of Keos, according to Moraux 1951), as preserved in Diogenes Laertius and "Hesychius," are the following:

---

[37] A complete list of Aristotle's cross-references in the *Metaphysics* to his works is provided by R. Goulet in *DPhA Supplement* 235–236.

[38] See the very useful comparative chart of the two catalogues by Diogenes Laertius and "Hesychius" in *DPhA* I,424–431 (R. Goulet), with indications of the larger works into which the books with the working titles were later incorporated.

[39] Laks & Most, who do *not* think that this is the title of the Essay, nevertheless rightly conclude, "si l'on devait le [sc. the Essay] rebaptiser, il faudrait sans doute l'intituler περὶ ἀρχῶν," p. xviii, with references to earlier scholars.

Diogenes Laertius	*"Hesychius"*
	21. Περὶ ἀρχῶν ἢ φύσεως α′
41. Περὶ ἀρχῆς α′	
90. Περὶ φύσεως γ′	81. Περὶ φύσεως α′
91. Φυσικὸν α′	82. Περὶ φυσικῶν α′

Diogenes 90–91 and "Hesychius" 81–82 are clearly the same titles, despite the slight variations, and it has been usually taken that no. 90/81 refers to books ΒΓΔ of the *Physics*, but no. 91/82 remains problematic.[40] If no. 91/82 is *Physics* A, then Diogenes 41, Περὶ ἀρχῆς, cannot be, which would leave the latter unassigned; but also conversely, if Diogenes 41, Περὶ ἀρχῆς, is *Physics* A, then the title in no. 91/82, (Περὶ) φυσικὸν/-ῶν α′, obviously referring to a physical book or books, would be unassigned. What is of greater relevance to our discussion, though, are the entries Diogenes 41 and "Hesychius" 21, which for the most part have been taken, first, to be identical, and second, to refer both to the same book, *Physics* A. But neither of these assumptions is probable, let alone certain. In the first place, the "Hesychius" 21 entry is itself problematic: it is two titles rather than a double title, for in the latter case the disjunction consists either of a proper name plus a descriptive title, or two variants of the same descriptive title,[41] whereas Περὶ ἀρχῶν ἢ ⟨Περὶ⟩ φύσεως is two titles. In addition, the ⟨Περὶ⟩ φύσεως part of this title is the doublet of "Hesychius" 81 which, according to Ross 1936 and others, refers to *Physics* B. But if, by this reckoning, Περὶ ἀρχῶν ἢ φύσεως refers to *Physics* A, we cannot have the Περὶ φύσεως part of the same title Περὶ ἀρχῶν ἢ φύσεως *also* refer to *Physics* B. As for the Diogenes 41 title, Περὶ ἀρχῆς, which is also taken to refer to *Physics* A, Moraux 1951, 83, presented arguments by which it could equally well refer to a book or parts of a book from the *Metaphysics*.

It is clear that nothing definite can be elicited from this material, and there is no point in prolonging the discussion; Ross himself was quick to admit (1936, 5) that "almost everything in the interpretation of these lists, especially those of Diogenes and Hesychius, is highly conjectural." The point I would like to make is that, given the transmission of Theophrastus's Essay among the books of Aristotle's *Metaphysics*, and the way in which the Hellenistic catalogue was compiled, the title Περὶ ἀρχῶν in

[40] Moraux 1951, 105; Ross 1936, 5–6.

[41] I.e., the title is either like Diogenes Laertius 17, Ἀλέξανδρος ἢ ὑπὲρ ἀποίκων, or, Diogenes Laertius 25, Περὶ τοῦ πάσχειν ἢ πεπονθέναι.

"Hesychius" is *as much likely* to refer to this Essay as to any book in Aristotle's *Physics* or *Metaphysics*. In other words, there is no evidence whatsoever that would contradict the assumption that the title Περὶ ἀρχῶν in "Hesychius" actually refers to Theophrastus's Essay.

The next point concerns what I have just mentioned about the way in which the Hellenistic catalogue was compiled. Thanks to recent research, most significantly by Primavesi 2007, we are in a better position to evaluate the conflicting and problematic reports about the fate of the libraries of Aristotle and Theophrastus and the transmission of their works. It now seems quite certain that there were two distinct means of transmission, one through the library bequeathed to Neleus, reportedly out of circulation for some time and eventually found again, and the other through copies extant independently in the Peripatos and acquired by the Library in Alexandria, with some works being transmitted in the one, others in the other, and the majority in both ways;[42] the disparity between the Hellenistic list of Hermippus and the post-Andronicus list of Ptolemy al-Gharīb are sufficient evidence for this. In this context, the Hellenistic catalogue of Hermippus, based on actual copies extant in the Lyceum and acquired by the Library of Alexandria, would be precisely the source to include the title of Theophrastus's Essay under the name of Aristotle, given its transmission, while the library of Theophrastus himself, bequeathed to Neleus, if it included a copy of the same Essay, would be expected to have it properly attributed to the owner of that library, Theophrastus. Accordingly, the edition of the Essay among the books constituting Aristotle's *Metaphysics*—the Roman edition, that is, that formed the basis of Nicolaus's study of that work—must have used as source a copy that came ultimately from the Lyceum but not from the library bequeathed to Neleus, and the editor, after incorporating the Essay in his edition, would have dropped its original title, just as he had dropped the original titles of the other books of Aristotle's *Metaphysics*, as mentioned just above.

The question then needs to be asked, how did Nicolaus of Damascus judge that the author of the Essay was Theophrastus? For if it is taken as established that the copy of the edition in his hands attributed it to Aristotle, but without a title, he could have studied the contents and possibly come to the *negative* conclusion that it was *not* by Aristotle,

---

[42] For a brief list of Aristotelian works demonstrably available to philosophers in Hellenistic times outside Neleus's library see Barnes 1997, 12–16, and his references there.

but what made him assert *positively* that it was by Theophrastus? Theophrastus wrote nothing on metaphysics apart from this Essay, and there was accordingly no body of doctrine by him in comparison with which one could conclude similarity of content and approach. It is therefore very unlikely that it was internal evidence that could have led Nicolaus to identify the real author, and there remains the possibility of external evidence in the form of another copy attributing the Essay to Theophrastus. If, then, Nicolaus had access to an independent manuscript by Theophrastus,[43] in all likelihood it descended from the copy in the library bequeathed to Neleus.

(e) *Positive evidence that the original title was* Περὶ ἀρχῶν

The scenario I have sketched in the preceding section (d) is only likely—it cannot be proven; on the other hand, it cannot be disproved either, and this is sufficient to render conclusive the positive evidence suggesting that the original title of the Essay was indeed Περὶ ἀρχῶν. This evidence was first used by V. Rose in 1863 in his *Aristoteles Pseudepigraphus*, p. 183, who came to this conclusion on the basis of the title of the Essay in the Latin translation by Bartholomew of Messina (see below, Chapter 2.4, and Part II,3) and a stray quotation apparently in the Greek gnomological tradition which seems to be based on it. Rose also observed that the title is attested in both Diogenes Laertius and "Hesychius" as one of the works of Aristotle. Rose did not have then the detailed knowledge about the transmission of the metaphysical books of Aristotle, but now that we do, as described above, his conclusion fits the newer findings even better.

Rose's suggestion did not find favor among classical scholars and historians of ancient philosophy.[44] The major objections were two. The

---

[43] As suggested by Drossart Lulofs 1969, 28; cf. also Mejer 1998, 23 and note 71.

[44] Most students of the Essay paid scant or no attention to it. Jaeger 1932, in his review of Ross and Fobes 1929, expressed doubts about Rose's suggestion ("das bleibt unsicher, wenn es auch prinzipiell durchaus möglich ist," p. 290), though he also pointed out the significance of Bartholomew's Latin translation in this connection (p. 294) and was instrumental in having his student, Kley, edit it. For his part, Kley 1936, 14–15, argued that the scholiast could not have said that Andronicus did not know the Essay if it was included in Andronicus's edition of the works of Aristotle. But this, first, disregards the fact that the Scholium talks about Andronicus's list, ἀναγραφή, of *Theophrastus's* books and not his edition ("Ausgabe") in which the Essay would have appeared under Aristotle's name, and second, assumes that the Roman edition of Aristotle's works was, in fact, by Andronicus, something upon which serious doubt was cast by Barnes

first was stated by Ross in his introduction (p. x) who claimed that the title Περὶ ἀρχῆς, which he ascribed to Hermippus as the probable source of Diogenes Laertius, refers to the first books of Aristotle's *Physics* and not to Theophrastus. But the invalid nature of this argument by Ross has been discussed above. The second objection, implied by Laks & Most in their edition, is that the evidence in Bartholomew's Latin translation cannot be taken as coming from an independent source because, Most claimed, Bartholomew used as exemplar the Vienna manuscript of Aristotle (J) which makes no reference to Περὶ ἀρχῶν; the title in the Latin translation, therefore, could not be but the result of a mistake. Far from using the Vienna manuscript, however, Bartholomew based his translation on a manuscript that constitutes a recension (the Messinan) distinct from that (the Constantinopolitan) of all the extant Greek manuscripts (discussed in detail below, Chapter 2.4). The independent transmission of the manuscript used by Bartholomew, therefore, makes it very likely that that manuscript (Λ) did, in fact contain a reference to the title as Ἀριστοτέλους Περὶ ἀρχῶν.

Once the independent nature of the evidence indicating the title of the Essay as Περὶ ἀρχῶν is realized, other, corroborating evidence becomes easily noticed. What appears to have been overlooked in this connection are the references that Theophrastus himself made in the Essay to his title. There is, first of all, the rather conclusive fact that in all of his extant works, and following accepted practice, as mentioned above, he referred to the title in some form in the opening sentence or paragraph; White 2002, 20–22, who documented this, even suggested the obvious (p. 22n40): "either Περὶ ἀρχῶν or Περὶ ἀρχῆς would be a reasonable title" for the Essay. But even more telling is the statement by Theophrastus at 6b21 where he said, "here, the investigation is of the first principles" (ἔνθα μὲν γὰρ τῶν ἀρχῶν ... ἡ ζήτησις). By the word ἔνθα Theophrastus meant "this here science or discipline we are engaged in," the discipline that studies the first principles *themselves* (what was later

---

1997. Kley's remaining objections are a confused jumble of elements of the transmission discussed above. Reale 1964, 26, dismissed Rose's thesis in one sentence on the grounds that no scholar has accepted it, thinking that what is stake is not the title but the authorship of the Essay; on the basis of style, he said, the Essay is, "non aristotelico." Laks & Most disregarded Bartholomew's translation for the reasons given next in this paragraph, van Raalte did not mention Rose at all, while Henrich 13 mistook Rose for Ross and attributed to Ross the suggestion that the title might be Περὶ ἀρχῶν!

to be called metaphysics),[45] and contrasted it (in the preceding ἐκείναις and the following λοιπαῖς) with the other disciplines, such as physics, in which the investigation proceeds *from* the first principles; by so doing he also identified his subject and by extension his title, Περὶ ἀρχῶν. Further down, at 7b9, he identified the first principles as the subject with which his Essay began (ἐν δὲ ταῖς ἀρχαῖς, ὅθεν δὴ καὶ ὁ πρῶτος λόγος), and thus also referred to his title.

Furthermore, if one keeps the date of composition of the Essay in mind, and that it was written at the time when Aristotle himself was grappling with the problems discussed in it and had composed book Lambda, definitely, and possibly also Alpha Meizon and Beta on the very subject, it becomes apparent how naturally Theophrastus's Essay fits in their context and continues the discussion initiated in them. The connection of the Essay with Lambda and the references to it are beyond dispute, as already discussed in section 1 of this chapter. But also in Book Alpha Meizon, 1–2, Aristotle struggled with identifying the "nature and purpose" (φύσις and σκοπός, 983a21–23) of the science that studies "the first causes and principles" (981b28–29) and with determining its name (a problem that he would revisit numerous times in the books that eventually constituted the *Metaphysics*): "the name we are looking for," he said, "refers to one and the same science," which, he continued, "must investigate the first principles and causes" (δεῖ γὰρ αὐτὴν [sc. τὴν ἐπιστήμην] τῶν πρώτων ἀρχῶν καὶ αἰτιῶν εἶναι θεωρητικήν, 982b8–9). The title of Theophrastus's Essay may easily both derive from or be reflected, if not in this very sentence, then in these and similar considerations by Aristotle. And in the very opening paragraph of the Essay, Theophrastus made reference to the question of the contents of the science sought by Aristotle in A 1–2 and how it relates to the study of nature (see further on the subject the commentary on the first Aporia, below, in Part III). Aristotle continued his search for the sought after science (ἐπιζητουμένην ἐπιστήμην, 995a24) in Book Beta and started off his first aporia on a subject which is very close to that treated by Theophrastus. Just as Aristotle asked whether the first causes are to be studied by one or more disciplines (ἔστι δ' ἀπορία πρώτη … πότερον μιᾶς ἢ πολλῶν ἐπιστημῶν θεωρῆσαι τὰς αἰτίας, 995b4–6), so also Theophrastus set the tone of his entire Essay in his opening sentence by asking what sort of objects are those which can be used to mark the boundaries of this discipline, as

[45] All translations without exception render the word as "here," "ici," etc., with the same understanding; cf. van Raalte's comment on the passage.

opposed to physics. Apart from the subject of this aporia, Theophrastus's Essay is by its very style very close to Beta, as I shall next discuss.

On the basis of all the evidence discussed in this section, it appears beyond a reasonable doubt that the title of the Essay was indeed Περὶ ἀρχῶν, and it should be restored to it, while paying homage to the perspicacity of Rose who noticed it a century and a half ago.

3. *Nature and Significance of the Work*

Long thought of as a fragment of a larger composition, Theophrastus's Essay has eventually been recognized by recent scholarship as an integral and independent work.[46] On the basis of the preceding discussion and the analysis in the commentary, it can be described as a dialectical essay of an aporetic, or rather, diaporetic nature on first principles (περὶ ἀρχῶν).[47] Its explicit purpose, stated in the opening question, is to identify and mark off the subjects which a study of first principles and of the nature of their connection to the rest of the universe must address in order to proceed to a successful resolution (εὐπορεῖν). As such it assumes and operates fully within Aristotelian (and, to the extent that Theophrastus himself contributed to their development, Theophrastean) methods of investigation. The principles of this method are well known[48] and can be summarized in some of Aristotle's familiar statements:[49]

---

[46] Hermann Usener, who first began the systematic study of the Essay in his pioneering article of 1861 entitled, "Zu Theophrasts metaphysischem Bruchstück," held the text to be fragmentary, dislocated, and lacunose. These views persisted until Ross (1929), in his Introduction, called the former charge into question (p. x) and thoroughly disproved the other two (pp. xix–xxiv). More recently Laks & Most (pp. x–xvii and 89n3) gave a sustained defense of the unity of the Essay.

[47] To avoid misunderstanding, the terms "dialectical," "aporia," and "diaporia" are to be understood in their strict Aristotelian sense as described in what immediately follows. See also above, note 14.

[48] See the collection of articles in S. Mansion 1961, and the very useful and synthetic overview of the methods of Aristotle by Berti 1989. The concept of aporia has been also much discussed; fundamental remains the article by Aubenque in Mansion 1961, while the study by Cleary 1993 provides a detailed analysis of how Aristotle actually proceeded in a diaporia, or worked through an aporia. There is a recent and exhaustive analysis of its use in Greek philosophy up to and including Aristotle in Motte and Rutten 2001.

[49] By this I do not mean to imply that these particular texts of Aristotle had necessarily been already composed at the time when Theophrastus was writing, and that he was following their letter, but that Theophrastus was operating on the basis of this

In the *Topics* Aristotle establishes the usefulness of dialectic for the study of the philosophical sciences:

> [Dialectic] is useful for the study of the philosophical sciences because if we have the ability to work initially through aporiae (διαπορῆσαι) on either side we shall more easily discern the true as well as the false in each class [of things investigated]. It has a further use in connection with the first things (πρῶτα) relating to each individual science. For, it being impossible to make any statement about them at all on the basis of the first principles proper to the particular science in hand—since these principles are prior to all things—it is by means of what is acceptable to the many or the wise (ἔνδοξα) about each that it is necessary to discuss them.[50]

Aristotle here establishes the basics of his methodology. Philosophical analyses proceeds from and on the basis of primary axiomatic truths (τὰ πρῶτα) or first principles (ἀρχαί). In the investigation of the first principles themselves, however, since there is nothing prior to them with which to investigate them, recourse must be had to the views held by the many or the wise (ἔνδοξα). The way in which these ἔνδοξα are investigated then consists of a preliminary working through the aporiae they raise, a process which Aristotle consistently calls διαπορέω.[51] This sifting, so to speak, of the aporiae results in separating the obviously false from the seemingly true, upon which then proper analysis can proceed. Aristotle discusses the process of διαπορεῖν and provides a number of examples in Book B of the *Metaphysics*:

> We must, with a view to the science which we are seeking, first recount the things about which we should first raise aporiae (ἀπορῆσαι). These include both the other opinions that some have held about them, and any points besides these that happen to have been overlooked. For those who wish to have a successful resolution of their aporiae (εὐπορῆσαι),

---

understanding he and Aristotle had about method. The statements quoted here, which may or may not have been written at the time Theophrastus was writing the Essay, reflect best this understanding.

50 *Topics* 101a34–b2; translation adapted from that by Smith 1997, 2–3. The last sentence is structured around μέν … δέ, and its two parts are integrally connected. The contrast that Aristotle is drawing through this sentence structure, and which reflects a contrast in methods, is between two prepositions, ἐκ μέν … διά δέ … : If, on the one hand, the method of analysis that starts *from* (ἐκ) the first principles in each particular science is inoperative, as in this case (because we are investigating the first principles themselves and there is nothing prior to them with which to investigate them), then on the other hand we have to have recourse to working *by means of* (διά) views accepted by the many or the wise. This structure is overlooked in the available English translations.

51 See the discussion of this and related terms in the commentary on 12b4 in Part III.

> it is advantageous first to work through them (διαπορῆσαι) well; for the subsequent successful resolution of aporiae (εὐπορία) implies the solution of those that were previously raised (ἀπορουμένων). ... Therefore one should have surveyed all the difficulties beforehand, both for the reasons we have stated and because people who inquire without first working through the aporiae (διαπορῆσαι) are like those who do not know where they have to go—besides, such a man does not know whether he has found what he was looking for or not, for to him the end is not clear, while it is clear to him who did raise aporiae at the beginning (τῷ προηπορικότι).[52]

The same approach is re-stated more forcefully and succinctly by Aristotle in a later work, *De anima* (403b20–24):

> In our enquiry concerning soul, at the same time as we proceed by working in a preliminary way through aporiae (διαποροῦντας) that need to be brought to a successful resolution (εὐπορεῖν), it is necessary also to include the views of as many predecessors as expressed themselves on the subject, in order that we may adopt (apprehend: λάβωμεν) what was stated well and, in case something was not, guard against it.

Aristotle here expands on his understanding of διαπορεῖν. It involves raising the aporiae that can be detected in an examination of what others and one's predecessors have said on a given subject and working though them in a preliminary way, and performing the same task on all other sorts of questions that may be raised. Only this ensures a successful resolution of the aporiae, what Aristotle calls εὐπορία.

The starting points of διαπορεῖν are thus what is acceptable to the many and the wise (ἔνδοξα), or what others or what predecessors have said on a subject, or any other view that may have been overlooked—in short, everything that Aristotle called the phenomena, or "appearances" (τὰ φαινόμενα).[53] In the *Nicomachean Ethics* he makes the following statement on method before entering on a discussion of incontinence:

> We must, as in all other cases, set down the phenomena (τιθέντας τὰ φαινόμενα) and, after first working out the aporiae (διαπορήσαντας), go on to prove, if possible, the truth of all that is acceptable to the many or the wise about these affections or, failing this, of the greater number and the most authoritative.[54]

---

[52] *Met.* B 1, 995a24–29, a33–b2; translation adapted from that of Ross, *CWA* 1574–1575.

[53] As analyzed in a fundamental article by Owen 1961 and further discussed in detail by Cleary 1994.

[54] *NE* VII 1, 1145b2–6; adapted from the translation by Ross/Urmson, *CWA* 1809.

The phenomena is a broad category in Aristotle and the things to which it refers depend on the science for which they are relevant and which is under investigation.[55] For the biological sciences and astronomy the reference is to empirical observations:

> It falls to experience to deliver the principles of any subject. In astronomy, for instance, it was astronomical experience that delivered the principles of astronomical science, for it was only when the phenomena (φαινόμενα) were adequately apprehended (ληφθέντων) that the astronomical demonstrations were discovered. And the same is true of any art or science whatever.[56]

The methodology encapsulated in these few citations is thus the following. For the philosophical investigation of any subject, and especially for the investigation of the principles of any subject, one starts from what Aristotle broadly calls the phenomena. Depending on the nature of the subject matter treated, these vary all the way from empirical observations to views held by the many or the wise, to the opinions of philosophers of preceding generations, and in short to any other view that commands respect. The task at hand is to identify and apprehend these phenomena (τιθέναι καὶ λαμβάνειν τὰ φαινόμενα). Before proceeding with the actual philosophical analysis of any of the subjects for which the phenomena have been collected, and in order to define the goal which one wishes to reach and winnow the true views and opinions from the false, one has to identify and raise the specific problems that are associated with the particular phenomena in each case—the aporiae—and then work through the aporiae in a preliminary way (διαπορεῖν). This lends clarity to the subject to be investigated and ensures the eventual successful resolution of the aporiae and the original problem (εὐπορία).

Theophrastus's Essay is an application, indeed a performance, of these principles or methodological guidelines. His subject being the first things (τὰ πρῶτα), it is clear that there can be no other prior principles from which to start the discussion, so recourse has to be had to the phenomena, as expressly stated by him in his *Physics* (fr. 143 FHS&G) and indicated in Diaporia 20c1 in the Essay. In this case, these consist of, first, observation of nature and the constitution of the universe (11b26), and second, the existing views and theories by the many and the wise—hence

---

[55] See Cleary's 1994 analysis of the concept of phenomena in Aristotle's methodology; cf. 90n13, "the meaning of 'phenomena' is always relative to the subject matter; e.g., physical vs. moral phenomena."

[56] *APr.* I 30, 46a17–22; translation adapted from that of Owen 1961, 84.

Theophrastus's constant reference to earlier and contemporary thinkers. These references do not constitute doxography (except accidentally) but serve the purposes of dialectic investigation.[57] The first step is to be clear about what the knowledge that is sought will consist of, or, as Theophrastus says, state precisely what the boundaries of knowing are (9a25–26). This is done by identifying and then taking hold of, or apprehending, the objective boundaries which define each thing and discriminating it from the rest; as Aristotle spoke about the necessity of apprehending the phenomena, so Theophrastus here talks of apprehending the boundaries (λαμβάνειν ὅρους) of the things investigated (9b20, 11a2, 11b25).[58] This helps setting up the aporiae which one will then work through (διαπορεῖν) as a prelude to the full investigation. Theophrastus's Essay is precisely the working through of the aporiae which he brings up, one after the other, regarding the first things. The Neoplatonist scholiast accurately perceived this nature of the Essay and called it, appropriately, προδιαπορίαι, as discussed above.[59]

---

[57] Much work has been done recently on doxographies, mainly by J. Mansfeld and H. Baltussen, which has shed precious light on their nature and function. In the case of Theophrastus, a pivotal author in the development of the genre, Baltussen points on the one hand to the significance of Aristotle's *Topics* as the starting point for Theophrastus's collection of *doxai* (Baltussen 2002, 56), and on the other to the crucial aspect of Theophrastus's philosophical production of "creating overviews on many topics ⟨which⟩ were exploited as useful reference books in later times" (Baltussen 2003, 61).

[58] These are the only three passages in the Essay in which the term ὅρος occurs. See the discussion of λαμβάνειν ὅρους used in this context by Repici 1990, 187–196. As Repici rightly points out, these boundaries are not subjective criteria to be posited by individuals, but the objective facts on the ground, the way in which reality breaks itself into well defined areas and hence enables humans to define their extent. On this understanding, it appears counterintuitive to translate the term ὅρος as "standard," as Lennox 2001, 227, does (followed by Johnson 2005, 36), and then explain that "standards" in this case is to be understood as "principles objectively based in the way the world is," because all standards—of weight, measurement, orthography, ethical behavior, literary excellence, etc.—are man-made and imply subjective epistemological categories. Theophrastus rather points to objective ontological categories in all being, very much along the lines, it seems, intended by Aristotle's use of the term ὅρος in *PA* 639a13, to which Lennox and Johnson refer. In that passage Aristotle is not talking about "standards" (Lennox, Johnson), or "canons" (Ogle in *CWA*), or "règles" (Louis), posited by humans which one adopts in the study of nature, but about different sets of objective boundaries which break reality into different categories and to which we refer in our study, as his immediately following examples make clear: boundaries established by objective or natural sets like substances (οὐσίαι, 639a16), genera (γένη a20), affections (πάθη, a22), and conditions (διαθέσεις, a22). Talking about these subjects indiscriminately, Aristotle goes on to say, is unclear (ἄδηλον) and fails to respect the proper distinctions among these sets of boundaries (ἀδιόριστον, with the term ὅρος included in the word, a22).

[59] Some scholars have tended to see this characterization as based on what the scho-

This evaluation of the nature and purpose of the Essay thus has ancient authority as well as contemporary support,[60] and I believe also corresponds most closely to its contents and structure; it also has implications for its date of composition, as discussed in section 1 above. On the other hand, given its aporetic, and hence for the most part doctrinally inconclusive impact, it has also given rise to varied interpretations, which remind one of the Indian story of the blind men and the elephant, each of whom described the animal according to the body part he felt. Thus, to give but a few examples, Reale 1964, 11, believed that the Essay expresses a crisis in the earliest Peripatos that resulted in the "liquidation of Aristotle's first philosophy"; Battegazzore 1989 felt that it promoted an empiricist approach (cf. Ross, p. xxv, "Theophrastus is first and foremost a man of science") that induced Aristotle to distance himself from Plato; Krämer 1971, 12, also with reference to the work of Weische, saw skeptical elements in it; van Raalte 1988, 189, argued that it testifies to Theophrastus's "organicistic" view of "the cosmos as an organic whole"; and Festugière 365–366 even claimed to have discerned in it the outlines of a Christian theology![61] These views are all welcome, and even though I do not believe that they constitute the main purpose of the Essay, they all point to yet further aspects of it. In a way, they attest to its richness and evocative nature, an indication of how much Theophrastus actually succeeded with his aporiae in making us think seriously about the questions he raises.

Seen from this wider perspective, Theophrastus's Essay is a window to classical Greek philosophy, offering us a rare view of it in the making. It reflects the very lively discussions in the early Academy which provide the very matrix from which it draws, and it looks forward to—and indeed

---

liast must have inferred from the last paragraph of the Essay (Theiler 1958, 102/292; Burnikel 126; Laks & Most p. xvi; van Raalte 7–8; Hecquet-Devienne 2004, 179n26). But given the accuracy of the characterization and the sophisticated understanding of Aristotelian dialectic method it betrays, together with the apposite use of the technical term (προ)διαπορία, as just described, these views can hardly be maintained.

[60] Gaiser 1985, 56, described the Essay as "ein Diskussionsbeitrag zu den ungelösten Schwierigkeiten der Prinzipientheorie des Aristoteles. Theophrast hat wohl auch hier nicht so sehr die aristotelischen Theorien nachträglich in Zweifel gezogen, sondern eher versucht, kritische Anregungen während der Ausarbeitung der aristotelischen Konzeptionen zu geben." Cf. also Laks & Most, p. xxiii, "la plus grande partie des questions posées par Théophraste ont beaucoup plus à voir avec la gestation d'un programme et d'une méthodologie de recherche qu'avec la critique d'une doctrine constituée."

[61] In addition to these, overall assessments of the Essay can be read in Usener 1861, Zeller, Theiler 1958, Krämer 1973, Botter 1999, Rudolph 2000, Dillon 2002, Berti 2002; for more details see the opening paragraphs of the Commentary in Part III.

in a real way influences—developments both in Aristotle's own later philosophy and the emerging Stoic and Epicurean thought. It is explicitly concerned with the question of first principles, thus touching upon possibly the most significant question addressed by ancient philosophy, but it is also programmatically committed to asking that question from the perspective of the contact (συναφή) and influence which these principles have with regard to the rest of the universe, especially sensible reality, thus situating itself at the very crossroads of the most basic issues raised by ancient—indeed all—philosophy: matter and form, idealism and materialism, monism and dualism. Methodologically, it is concerned not only with theoretical questions of epistemology and with brazenly asking the most fundamental question, "what is knowledge?" (9a23 ff.), but it also constantly uses in the discussion of each problem analytical and epistemological procedures and methods established in the early Academy and later in the Lyceum, procedures such as knowledge by analogy, similarity, and the like. Its non-dogmatic treatment of the issues truly brings out the crux of the matter in each instance and invites serious and sustained study, let alone commentary. Accordingly a volume could be written for virtually every paragraph, and indeed it has been extensively used in the scholarly literature in all sorts of publications.

4. *Style, Structure, and Contents of the Text*

Very much like Aristotle's *Metaphysics* Beta, as almost all modern scholars have noted since Brandis 1860, 340, Theophrastus's Essay *On First Principles* poses a number of aporiae and then works through them in a series of diaporiae, as discussed in the previous section. The aporiae themselves are related, as one follows the other in a thematic sequence with few fresh starts—essentially, the two last segments of the Essay on epistemology and teleology. The writing is continuous, with almost no natural breaks, something to be expected in so short a piece. The style, given the nature of the work just discussed and the internal audience of the philosophers (in Assos?) to which it was addressed, is elliptical, exploiting to the fullest the capacities of classical Greek for compression of meaning in elaborate periods.

The problem is accordingly how to break the text into meaningful segments for editing and presentation. Usener, who prepared the critical edition that has been normative to this day, thought that the work is a fragment, that it contains a number of lacunae, and that it is disjointed;

as a result, he divided the text into "sections"' and "chapters" which not only do not fit adequately the contents but disregard the syntax of the Greek as well. He both ran-in paragraphs that should be kept separate (at 5a5, 7b5, 9a23, etc.), and broke up individual sentences into distinct paragraphs as if they were two sentences (at 5a13, 7b9, 8b9, 11b23). All subsequent editors and translators of the Essay followed suit (at least in the second offense if not always in the first), which may have created some of the problems of interpretation. Laks & Most discarded Usener's division into nine "chapters" and introduced their own into five, based on their scrupulous analysis of the text (along "Wittgensteinian" lines, as aptly remarked by Huby 1995), but they kept Usener's division into 34 "sections." Manifestly Usener's numbering, which is arbitrary and unhelpful, cannot be maintained as the actual division of the text into paragraphs, though it has to be provided in the margins, along with his page, column, and line numbers, because all secondary literature since the first publication of his edition refers to these.

In keeping with the dialectical character of his Essay, Theophrastus is careful to identify explicitly the aporiae, and this gives the best possible clue to the building blocks of the work as well as to the natural breaks into paragraphs. He poses twenty-five aporiae in all. These he introduces in one of three ways: either he expressly identifies them as an aporia by calling it such or using a related word that clearly indicates that this is a problem that needs to be studied,[62] or he poses the aporia by asking a direct question,[63] or finally he poses the aporia in an indirect question.[64] Frequently he uses two ways simultaneously to introduce or identify the same aporia.

Following Theophrastus's lead, I have adopted as paragraphs his own breaks of the text into the several aporiae, reunited sentences that were split into two by Usener, and disregarded accordingly any artificial division into "chapters," insofar as the discussion is continuous. I assigned an integer number to each separate aporia, but in one particularly complicated case (Aporia 20), where Theophrastus re-formulates the aporia in

[62] § 13 ἀξιόω ἀποδιδόναι; §§ 11, 12, 14, 16 ἀπορέω; §§ 18, 21 ἀπορία; §§ 8, 20c1, 23 ἄπορον; § 15, 20b, 22 ἀφορισμός; §§ 9, 10, 21, 22.3 (ἐπι)ζητέω; §§ 6, 7, 15, 17 ζητεῖ (κτλ.) λόγον, σκέψιν; § 24 ληπτέον ὅρους, διστασμός.

[63] § 1 ποῖος; § 3 ἐν ποίοις; § 17 πότερον … ἤ; §§ 1, 17, 19 πῶς, §§ 3, 5, 22.1 τίς; § 22 (*passim*) τίνος ἕνεκα etc.

[64] §§ 9, 15 διὰ τί; § 15, 20c1 μέχρι πόσου; § 6, 14 ποῖος; § 20a πόσοι, ποσαχῶς; §§ 2, 4, 9, 10, 11, 14 πότερον … ἤ; § 8, 10, 14, 25 πῶς; §§ 6, 18, 20b, 20c1 τί, τίνων; § 20c2, 25 ἐν τίνι.

three successive stages, I have marked them with the letters a,b,c. Most of the aporiae are followed by a brief discussion (diaporia), which needed no special numbering; in some cases, though, the discussion extended into two or three diaporiae requiring their own paragraphs, and these have been marked with a decimal number after that of the main aporia. The "chapter" and "section" numbers of Usener are given in the right margin, the page and line numbers in the proximate left margin. My own numbering of the aporiae is inserted in bold into the text.

The aporetic character of the work has long been recognized. Ross (p. xix) called it "aporematic throughout," and Reale 1964 in particular paid special attention to this characteristic of the work (cf. Ellis 1988). He defended vigorously the originality and philosophical significance of the aporetic method, rightly insisting that raising the aporiae without resolving them is not "a mere game of hypotheses" ("un mero gioco di ipotesi," p. 17). And in his analysis of the text, he even gave a list of all the aporiae, twenty in all by his reckoning (pp. 88–90). In the main our lists coincide to a large degree, and where they differ it is primarily because Reale did not follow closely Theophrastus's separation of the aporiae. But more significantly, first, Reale did not see the aporiae as forming the structure of the Essay, at least insofar as he did not shape his translation accordingly, but followed Usener's arbitrary divisions, and second, he did not make the formulation of the aporiae specific enough to express the variations in Theophrastus's quesions.[65] Laks & Most (p. xxiv n. 24) criticized Reale's listing of the aporiae not for the shortcomings I just mentioned but rather for reducing, as they colorfully put it, "l'opuscule à une série rhapsodique d'apories." For their part, though, they went to the other extreme by introducing their own five divisions which are not indicated by Theophrastus and are by no means obvious, and they tried to claim that the Essay is well constructed beyond, it seems, what the evidence will allow. Again, as Huby 1995 put it in her review, "they at least succeed in showing that the work is less episodic than might at first appear."

[65] Thus, for example, as the final aporia of the Essay he formulates a general question about teleology ("quali sono i limiti del finalismo e della possibilità della spiegazione teleologica della realtà?"), covering the text 10a22–12a2. But in this section there are actually four aporiae mentioned by Theophrastus (22–25 according to my numbering), including the one about spontaneous causation (23) and the very significant concept for the Essay of apprehending the boundaries in nature of the extent of teleological explanation (24).

The two views of the structure of the Essay are not mutually exclusive. That it is explicitly structured in terms of the aporiae cannot be seriously doubted; its very nature, as discussed in the previous section, imposes this structure. On the other hand, it is also clear that these aporiae are not about any subject whatsoever but about first principles, whence the thematic unity characterizing the work which operates as a "leitmotif" and runs like a "red thread" through its entirety,[66] namely, understanding the connection between the intelligible and sensible worlds. Accordingly what should form the focus of attention is the aporiae themselves which follow each other in sequence, establishing the major subjects within the discussion of the first principles.

Seen from this perspective, the major subjects around which the aporiae are sequentially clustered, as one leads into the other, appear to be three. The first and main subject, occupying more than half of the Essay, is, understandably, the study, nature, and properties of the first principles (aporiae 1–17, 25). This is followed by two extensive appendices, one might say, investigating problems relating to the main subject, one on epistemology and the methods of knowing everything from the first principles down to inanimate beings—and hence, presumably, the nature of the connection between intelligibles and sensibles—(aporiae 18–21), and another on teleology, testing one view of the application of a first principle to the universe (aporiae 22–24).[67] In outline, the contents are as follows (the numbers refer to the aporiae):

A. The first principles: their study, nature, and properties

1–2, 25	Marking the boundaries of the study of first principles, as distinct from the objects of nature, to which, however, they are to be related. The concluding aporia presents the two approaches as one, the study of the universe investigating the ontological categories (intelligibles, mathematicals, sensibles) into which all beings belong and their interrelations.
3–5	The nature, number, identity, and causality of the first principles.

[66] Theiler 1958, 102–104/292–294, and Laks & Most p. xxv, respectively.

[67] Theiler 1958 ("Anhang," 102–105/292–297) identified and discussed three "leitmotifs" in the Essay, which generally correspond to the three main subjects discussed here, though he neither localized them in particular parts of the text nor related them to specific aporiae. For his part, Brandis 1860, 340, had already seen the Essay as breaking into two major sections, conflating what I present here as the two appendices into one part on epistemological principles and their application, which may be a different way of saying the same thing.

6–8 The previous aporia on the causality of the first principles brings up the question of the motion of the celestial spheres, first part.

  9–10 The previous aporia on the celestial spheres brings up the question of how they relate to the sublunar world.

11–12 After the interlude on the sublunar world, the discussion on the motion of the celestial spheres is continued, second part.

13 Review of the views of the wise (*endoxa*) on the relation of the first principles to the rest of the universe.

14–17 Properties of the first principles: whether they are indeterminate, determinate, or both (and if the latter, how to understand the division of beings into matter and form), and how to understand their property of being at rest.

B. Epistemology: knowledge and knowing all reality

18–21 The observation that all reality consists of contraries brings up the question of knowledge in general insofar as an understanding of contraries—starting from the major opposition between intelligibles and sensibles, whose connection to each other is the main subject of the Essay, to the fact that nature itself consists of differences and similarities—leads to knowledge.[68] After establishing the principle that each thing has its proper way of being known, the knowledge of the first principles is said to be through a method other than that used in natural science.

C. Teleology: Testing one view of the application of a first principle to the universe

22–24 The principle that everything has a final cause (is for the sake of something) and that nature does nothing in vain is tested by an assessment of its indiscriminate application and a brief review of alternative views.

As for the specific contents of the aporiae, each section in the commentary in Part III begins with a detailed paraphrase intended to bring out the particular issues which Theophrastus is addressing and which, given the elliptical nature of his writing, need to be spelled out for a contemporary audience. Each aporia can be accordingly judged on its own terms. Some aporiae Theophrastus simply mentions but does not discuss (e.g., §7 on the number of spheres mentioned in Aristotle's *Metaphysics* Lambda), others he discusses in detail and with syllogistic arguments (e.g. §24.1 on the one and the indefinite dyad), still others he lets his opinion about

[68] Cf. the discussion of the third leitmotif in the Essay by Theiler 1958, 104–105/296.

them indirectly be known (e.g., § 14 on the composition of the first principles, where he lets his preference for the third alternative be known by not raising any objections against it), and for yet still others he simply asserts his preference without argument (e.g., § 2 on the connection between intelligibles and sensibles), etc.[69]

The advantage of perceiving this aporetic structure of the Essay and studying each aporia on its own merit, albeit against the background of the broader theme and the "red thread" running through it, is that we can better perceive the significance of each detail for Theophrastus's immediate milieu and thus better gauge its historical moment. This is philosophy in the making, actual philosophical discussions taking place among history's premier philosophers, and the Essay gives us front row seats for that specific day. The Essay bears no explicit date, but the live issues themselves, and the determination of what argument was important for whom and when, do. As discussed in the first section of this chapter, that point in time was in all likelihood the Academic circle as reconstituted in Assos, with Speusippus in Athens as the head of the Academy.[70]

---

[69] For details on the form of argumentation in all aporiae see the commentary.

[70] The following publication appeared too late to be utilized in the present study: M. Crubellier and A. Laks, eds, *Aristotle*: Metaphysics *Beta. Symposium Aristotelicum*, Oxford: Oxford University Press, 2009.

The detailed analysis of the Aristotelian aporiae amplifies my discussion of the subject above (in section 3). Furthermore, the two editors point out (p. 19) the similar aporetic structure of Aristotle's *Metaphysics* Beta and Theophrastus's Essay, on the basis of which both they and I, independently of each other, structure our respective commentaries by the underlying aporiae. S. Menn's observation (p. 214n3) that Theophrastus uses ἀρχή and πρῶτον "equivalently" provides further evidence for my argument, following White 2002 (pp. 30–31 above), in favor of the original title of this Essay as Περὶ ἀρχῶν.

CHAPTER TWO

THE GREEK TEXT: MANUSCRIPTS, TRANSLATIONS, STEMMA CODICUM

1. *The Greek Manuscripts*

The text of Theophrastus's *On First Principles* survives in eighteen Greek manuscripts dating from the ninth to the sixteenth centuries, a medieval Arabic translation from the second half of the ninth, a medieval Latin translation from the middle of the thirteenth, two further Latin translations from the Renaissance, and an Aldine *editio princeps* from 1497 which, for the purposes of the establishment of the text, has the value of a manuscript (Burnikel 29–30). It is a rich and diverse tradition, which has engaged the attention of scholars for some time, as a result of which not only the main lines but also the details of transmission have become relatively clear. In particular after the fundamental researches of Burnikel (1974) on the manuscripts of the Essay and his establishment of a stemma codicum, and the equally fundamental edition by Laks & Most (1993) which built upon and further corroborated Burnikel's results,[1] it is now possible to proceed more expeditiously and to concentrate on all the essential evidence for the establishment of the text, eliminating what is reduntant, derivative, and misunderstood.

Briefly, the situation with the Greek manuscript tradition of the Essay is as follows. It divides into two major families, one of which is represented by the single manuscript P (Paris. gr. 1853), and the other by two sub-families: manuscripts JCL (Vindobonensis phil. gr. 100, Venet. Marcianus gr. Z 211, Florent. Laurentianus 28,45) and the manuscripts in sub-family Σ (as called by Burnikel, pp. XXXVIII–XXXIX), which includes fourteen manuscripts and the Aldine edition of 1497. These manuscripts are described and discussed extensively by Fobes (pp. xxvi–xxxiii), Burnikel, and Laks & Most (pp. xl–lxxx) in a way that renders

[1] The approach and conclusions of Burnikel in this study were also favorably reviewed by N.G. Wilson in *Gnomon* 51 (1979) 59–60.

repetition nugatory; the interested reader is referred to these works. Here only the manuscripts and translations immediately relevant to the establishment of the text of the Essay in this edition will be discussed.

P Paris. gr. 1853

One of the two most ancient (tenth century) and reliable manuscripts containing the works of Aristotle (manuscript E of the Aristotelian treatises), the Parisinus has been repeatedly studied and analyzed in the literature, most recently by Hecquet-Devienne 2000 and 2004. It "is the result of a strong 'editorial' project ... carried out by three scribes capable of correcting transliteration errors and other types of copying errors. It is the result of a collation of models [i.e., exemplars], which were themselves carefully executed" (Hecquet-Devienne 2004, 172). It contains both the *Metaphysics* of Aristotle and the Essay by Theophrastus, in that order, and at the end of the Essay it has the Scholium about its authorship and nature (12a3–12b5) discussed above in Chapter 1.2. The fact that other scholia of this nature in the same manuscript transmit information also from the commentary on Aristotle's *Metaphysics* by Asclepius, the student of Ammonius (fl. early sixth century), and that these scholia must have been present in at least one of the exemplars from which P was copied and with which it was collated, constitutes another indication among others that will be discussed later, that the text of Theophrastus's Essay in this manuscript ultimately goes back to a Neoplatonic archetype from the period of Asclepius. This information accords well with the findings resulting from a study of the readings in P of the Essay: P has by far the largest number of correct readings in common with Ψ, the Greek exemplar of the Arabic translation, which itself also ultimately derives from the same Neoplatonic archetype but from a line independent from that of P (see the list of these readings below in this chapter, section 3). This indicates the reliability of the text in P vis à vis that in the other extant Greek manuscripts. However, P was copied from (a) minuscule manuscript(s) (e.g., at 11b5 ἄνευ, corrected as such by the scribe, was written originally ἂν ἐν) ultimately deriving from the same transliteration from uncials to minuscule writing as manuscript J.[2]

[2] For a discussion and the evidence see Irigoin 1997, 183–187.

Sub-family JCL

J Vindob. phil. gr 100, the famous Viennese Aristotle, also contains Theophrastus's Essay together with Aristotle's *Metaphysics*, but in this manuscript the Essay precedes the *Metaphysics* and does not contain the Scholium at the end. It is our earliest witness to the text in the Greek tradition, and is completely independent from P, having no common errors with it. Burnikel 119 records only two such, a spelling error of ἐνμόρφους at 7a6, which has little evidentiary value, and ἔχουσαι at 10b22, which is almost certainly not an error but the correct text (see the commentary on that passage). J itself was copied from a minuscule manuscript, as it appears from its error at

6b12 δόξειεν ἂν P Ψ CL A : δόξει ἐρᾶν J

as noted by Fobes (p. xxvi). This variant also indicates that

C and L, which have the correct reading, were not copied from J but from a common ancestor, independently of each other. C (Venet. Marcianus gr. Z 211) and L (Florent. Laurentianus 28,45) exhibit numerous errors of transcription due mostly to misread abbreviations, of omission, and of commission in editorial attempts. In particular the Florentine manuscript (L) contains an inordinate number of errors which would indicate a lengthy tradition of copying from the common ancestor it has with C (Burnikel 113).

Although CL do derive ultimately from a common ancestor with J, they nevertheless have been so corrrupted in the process of transmission that they no longer carry any correct readings, independently of J, which are not due to conjectural emendations. This can be shown in the following table of all readings in CL that are not present in either of the two independent manuscripts, P and J, and their correctors. To complete the documentation, the table also contains the readings of the other two independent manuscripts, Ψ and Λ, as they become evident from the Arabic and Latin translations respectively (for which see sections 2 and 4 below). The readings adopted in the text as correct are always listed first.

4a6 ταὐτὰ Λ (*eadem*) C^{2} Tiph. Steph. : ταυτα P, ταῦτα J CL : τὰ αὐτὰ A : Ψ om. in lac.] The correct reading in C (ταὐτὰ) does not come from an independent source but is a correction by a second hand. But the evidence of C here is not needed as the correct reading is found in Λ. The Arabic translation is missing the first page of the text where this passage occurs.

5b8 κρεῖττον PJ Ψ : κρείττων Λ L A, κρεῖττων C] Here the PJ and Ψ reading is the correct one, even if only for stemmatic reasons (see the stemma codicum in section 6 below), though Burnikel 121 suggests that L A should be preferred (see the commentary); but even if that were so, κρείττων in L A would still not be more that an "obvious" conjectural emendation.

10a4 ἢ μερῶν CL et Spengel, sed corruptelam susp. ego : ἠμερῶν PJ, ἡμέρων A : ⟨τῶν εἰρ⟩ημένων ut vid. Ar. (*allatī qulnā*), an etiam Ψ? : Lat. om. in lac.] It is almost certain the reading ἢ μερῶν is corrupt; the wrong breathing in PJ and the nonsensical reading in A of the Σ sub-family ("tame"?) suggest a deeper problem than the one for which the too obvious scribal correction in CL would provide a solution. It is not impossible that some form of εἰρημένων, the reading in the Arabic translation, may underlie the corrupt form. In any case, CL do not offer an independent reading but a conjectural correction of the reading in the paradosis as represented by PJ.

10a12 κινεῖται CL B : κινῆται PJ Ψ A [Λ]] This is an instance of a correction necessary for the sentence to become complete; a verb in the indicative is needed to provide an apodosis, which otherwise would be lacking, in the temporal clause. It is not evidence of an independent source of CL (and B, which belongs to the Σ sub-family).

10b22 ἔχουσαι PJ Ψ Λ : ἔχουσι CL A] ἔχουσαι is almost certainly the correct reading; see the commentary. The presence of ἔχουσι cannot be explained other than as a conjecture intended to restore the broken syntax of the sentence.

This evidence indicates that all that CL contribute to the text is the conjecture emending to the indicative at 10a12; the dubious separation of the two words at 10a4 is an attempt to correct the probably corrupt passage. One may safely conclude that CL do not have any independent and original readings beyond what is to be found in PJ and Ψ and Λ. As a result, they contribute no independent readings for the establishment of the text and hence their evidence need not be taken in the main apparatus except, for the purposes of full documentation, in problematic passages. Their readings are, however, fully registered in the supplementary apparatus.

Sub-family Σ

According to Burnikel's researches (66), further corroborated by Laks and Most, this large sub-family of manuscripts derives from a single late thirteenth century manuscript,

A Vaticanus gr. 1302. It belongs to the same family as JCL, but since it and those that directly derive from it cannot be subsumed under any of the three, JCL, they form their own sub-family (Burnikel 121).

For a listing of the other manuscripts in this sub-family see the Sigla, and for a description see Burnikel and Laks & Most. Manuscript A is distinctive through a number of unique characteristics. It is the oldest extant manuscript that contains the Essay by Theophrastus together with eight other of his opuscula and independently of Aristotle's other works and especially the *Metaphysics*. It also contains the Scholium (12a3–12b5) about the history of the text. Its quality as witness to the text, however, is marred by numerous peculiar mistakes. These alterations to the text are due both to errors and to a substantial revision of the text at some point in the forebears of A (Burnikel 121). In addition, the corrections that have been effected on the manuscript itself by at least two hands appear to be all based on conjecture rather than on readings from other manuscripts, and hence there is no question of contamination (Burnikel 69). Because of these shortcomings, both Ross and Fobes as well as Jaeger 1932 in his review of Ross & Fobes showed little appreciation for the manuscript. Their verdict is basically correct. As Burnikel summarizes it (123), A has no original and independent readings against the consensus of P and J. In the entire text, manuscript A and any of the other manuscripts in sub-family Σ have a reading that is not carried by P and J and their correctors only in the following passages (as in the preceding table, the readings of Ψ and Λ are also included, and in the entries the reading adopted as correct in the text is listed first):

4a23 αὑτῶν Ψ Λ O : αυτῶν P : αὐτῶν JCL A] αὑτῶν is a correction by the learned scribe of manuscript O (Ottobonianus gr. 153) of the sub-family Σ, Theodore of Gaza. His conjecture, however, is not needed for the establishment of the text since the original reading is independently provided in Ψ and Λ.

4b9 ἐχούσας PJ Ψ Λ C : ἔχουσαν L A] ἐχούσας is the lectio difficilior and is to be retained (though Burnikel 121 argues for the singular form); see the commentary. The unnecessary "correction" to the singular was independently made both by A and L and, in modern times, by Usener.

4b18 πιστικωτέρως PJ Ψ Λ CL A : πειστικωτέρως D] The difference here is a matter of spelling: there is no doubt that the paradosis had the spelling with iota only, and that the epsilon iota was added conjecturally by the knowledgeable scribe of manuscript D (Ambrosianus P 80 sup.), for D was ultimately copied from A which has πιστικωτέρως. I believe that the form with the iota only is correct for the reasons I discuss in the commentary.

5b8 κρεῖττον PJ Ψ : κρείττων Λ L A, κρεῖττων C] The neuter form in PJ Ψ is correct. This was discussed above, under the sub-family JCL.

6a26 τὰ ἄλλα P : τ' ἄλλα JCL: τἆλλα A [Ψ] [Λ]] Whether there is crasis or elision here, and if the former, whether a coronis is to be used to write it, are all matters of orthography and editorial preferences, whose conventions changed over the centuries; this has no bearing on the question of independent readings in Σ. I prefer to adhere to the oldest recoverable paradosis, τὰ ἄλλα.

7b13 ἀντιμεταλλακτέον D : τι μεταλλακτέον PJ C^1L A [Ψ] : τὴν μεταλλακτέον C : μεταλλακτέοι ut vid. Λ] Here the scribe of manuscript D corrected the primitive error by haplography in the entire paradosis as it appeared in his source, manuscript A (ἐνέργειαν ⟨αν⟩τι μεταλλακτέον).

8a11 ὂν pr. Ψ B^2O : ἓν PJ Λ CL A] This variant indicates that manuscripts Ψ and P J derive from different transliterations from uncials (see below, section 2). The common source of P and J had thus ἓν, which was corrected by Theodore of Gaza (the scribe of O) and the corrector of B into ὂν.

8b4 μέλανα PJ CL [Λ] : τὰ μέλανα A et ut interpr. Ar.] Burnikel 121 may be right in arguing that the article is needed to avoid making the expression a hendiadys and thus misrepresenting the meaning, but given the context, there is little danger of misunderstanding. The reading in A would again be a correction and not independent, while the Arabic translation represents the correct understanding of the passage whether or not the article was present in Ψ.

8b20 γένη ... εἴδη Ψ Λ A Tiph. : γένη ... εἴδει L : γένει ... εἴδει PJ CL^1.] The correct reading, divined by A by writing the plural nominative, is present independently in manuscripts Ψ and Λ as reflected in the Arabic and Latin translations respectively.

9a23 ὁρατόν PJ Ψ Λ CL : ἀόρατον A] Here actually ὁρατόν is the correct reading, and A is an attempt at emendation; see the Appendix.

10a12 κινεῖται CL B : κινῆται PJ Ψ A [Λ]] A reads the erroneous subjunctive. This variant was discussed above, under the sub-family JCL.

10b22 ἔχουσαι PJ Ψ Λ : ἔχουσι CL A] A reads the erroneous ἔχουσι. This was discussed above, under the sub-family JCL.

11a8 αὐτὸ Λ : αὐτὰ J^{II} CL [Ψ] : αύτος P : αὔτως A] The correct reading is apparently uniquely carried by Λ, though αὐτὰ in J^{II}, if it reflects the reading in the now lost original J, may be equally correct; see the commentary. A's "correction" to αὔτως creates an intolerable redundancy with ὁμοίως later on in the sentence and is to be rejected.

11b5 τ' PJ^{II} CL [Ψ] [Λ] : τε A] As with all cases of elision in Greek manuscripts, not much can be elicited from this variant.

11b14 τὰς Ψ OV^{a2} : τε P CL [Λ] : τε τὴν J^{II} : om. A] The correct reading is carried independently by Ψ and then, by emendation, by two representatives of the Σ sub-family of manuscripts; the correction, which is obvious, was apparently made by the discerning Theodore of Gaza in manuscript O and then copied by a reader of V^{a2}. The

Arabic translation has the correct form reflecting τὰς μεταβολάς (*at-taġāyīr*), but even if Ψ read τε for τὰς the translator would have made the obvious correction in his version.

This evidence indicates that A and the manuscripts of sub-family Σ contribute no independent readings but only two conjectures, at 7b13 and 10a12. Three other correct readings, the nominatives at 8b20, the rough breathing for the reflexive form at 4a23, and the accusative feminine plural article at 11b14 are found as original readings in Ψ and/or Λ but must be seen as conjectures in A and sub-family Σ and hence do not constitue independent evidence. In the remaining cases the reading of the oldest two Greek manuscripts, P and J, is indeed the correct one and not that of the manuscripts in sub-family Σ (as thought by some earlier editors). As in the case of CL, the manuscripts in sub-family Σ and especially A have no independent readings to contribute and accordingly can be ignored in the establishment of the text except in these few instances where they provide ancillary help. Burnikel 73 calls sub-family Σ "nahezu Bedeutungslos" for this purpose, and he is right. Only his admiration for the editorial and scribal work of Theodore of Gaza (manuscript O) makes him advise (122) that "der Apparat einer Neuausgabe der Mt [Metaphysik] müsste die konjekturale Tätigkeit des Gazes gebührend berücksichtigen." The advice is well taken, though hardly necessary, for the exemplar of the Arabic translation (which Burnikel did not know) actually provides a number of those readings.

2. *Manuscript Ψ, Exemplar of the Arabic Translation by Isḥāq Ibn-Ḥunayn*

Ψ The only information that we have about the Greek manuscript on which the Arabic translation was based (Ψ) is what we can gather from the translation itself; there is no external evidence. The translation was made by Isḥāq ibn-Ḥunayn, and because we know that Isḥāq did translate a number of books of Aristotle's *Metaphysics* (but not A; see now Bertolacci 2005, 270), we could guess that the manuscript also included the Aristotelian work, as do both of our earliest Greek manuscripts, J and P. It may also be possible to speculate that Aristotle's work followed that of Theophrastus, as in the Greek manuscript J, and that since Ψ most likely contained the Scholium at the end of Theophrastus's Essay (see Chapter 1.2), this may have caused the misunderstanding that Book A of

Aristotle's *Metaphysics* was actually by Theophrastus and hence led to its not being translated into Arabic[3]—but there is no evidence for any of this with regard to manuscript Ψ. As a matter of fact, Book Alpha eventually was translated as part of Aristotle's *Metaphysics* by Naẓīf in the second half of the tenth century; but we know the reason neither of what led to the translation of Alpha in the tenth century nor of its neglect over a century earlier at the time of al-Kindī.

With regard to Ψ itself, there is some evidence in the translation that it was a manuscript in a minuscule hand; in at least two passages there is a mistaking of omicron iota for alpha, a mistake which is more likely to have happened in minuscule:

> 4b10 πρώτοις **α** Λ : πρώτας Ψ ut vid.
> 6a4 ὅμοια **α** Λ : ἅμα ἃ Ψ

If this is so, the question arises whether Ψ derives from the same transliteration from an uncial ancestor as J and P. The evidence is provided by the variant at

> 8a11 ὂν Ψ B²O : ἓν **α**

where the erroneous reading ἓν came about through a confusion of the round capital letters O and E in an uncial exemplar.[4] This indicates that Ψ derives from a transliteration from an uncial manuscript that is different from that of J and P. This is also suggested by the fact that whenever Ψ P and J do not all have the same reading, Ψ agrees almost as many times with J as it does with P,[5] something which would not have been the case had Ψ been related with either through the same transliteration. Ψ therefore, through the Arabic translation, represents a tradition of the text that has no immediate relation to that of J and P and is therefore a primary carrier of a number of independent readings. As a matter of fact, Ψ carries the correct reading over J and P, and thus helps establish the text, in no less than 31 passages; in some of these, the correct reading had already been divined either by knowledgeable scribes or emenders in

---

[3] This is an old hypothesis that goes back to Albert the Great; for some recent discussions see Martini 2002, 81–84.

[4] Cf. the same mistake, also deriving from two different transliterations, in Aristotle's *Met.* 1025b8, listed by Irigoin 1997, 186.

[5] Counting variants due to accents and breathings, Ψ agrees with J against P 17 times, and Ψ agrees with P against J 23 times; see below, section 3.

some late Greek manuscripts[6] or by modern scholars, whose conjectures have been thus dramatically corroborated. Some others are also to be found in the exemplar of the Latin translation (Λ), also registered below, which indicates the independence of that branch of the tradition, as will be discussed later (in section 4 below). In his introduction to the edition of Laks & Most and then in his article, Crubellier (p. LXXVI in Laks & Most, and p. 39n56 in Crubellier 1992) signalled some of the correct readings independently carried by Ψ as they can be recovered from the Arabic translation; I give here a complete list, together with the names of scribes and scholars who corrected them in the Greek text.

4a23 αὑτῶν Ψ Λ, corr. O
4b2 οἷά τε Ψ, prop. Hoffmann apud Us.[1]
5a4 ⸢καὶ⸣ κατ' ἐκεῖνο Ψ, suppl. Gutas
5a22 ⸢οἰκεῖος⸣ Ψ, suppl. Gutas
5b3 ψυχῇ Ψ, corr. Us.[1,2]
5b6 ὅμως ⸢ὡς⸣ ἐμψύχοι⸢ς⸣ Ψ, coni. Us.[1]
5b18 ἀσύνδετον Ψ, prop. Us.[2]
6b3 χρόνος θ' ἅμα καὶ οὐρανὸς [θ' pro δ' coni. Us.[1]] Ψ, corr. Gutas
6b7 πως Ψ Λ, corr. recc.
7a2 ⸢πλὴν ὀλίγαις⸣ Ψ, suppl. Gutas
7a7–8 [τὰς τ' ἐμμόρφους καὶ τὰς τῆς ὕλης] om. Ψ, secl. Gutas
7a15 ⸢ὡς⸣ Ψ, coni. Hommel et Marcovich 1978, 2001
7a15 ὁ ante κόσμος om. Ψ, secl. Wim.[1,2] et Ross, del. Us.[1,2]
7a20 αὖ τὸ Ψ, prop. Zeller
7b3 ἐτησίους Ψ, coni. Us.[2]
8a11 ὂν pr. Ψ, corr. O
8a13 ᾗ Ψ, coni. Us.[1]
8a22 περιεργία τὸ ζητεῖν Ψ Λ, prop. Dirlmeier
8b20 γένη ... εἴδη Ψ Λ, corr. A
8b25 κοινῇ Ψ Λ, corr. edd.
9a14 ⸢τὰ⸣ Ψ, add. Wim.[1,2]
9b20 τε ⸢τὰς⸣ Ψ, suppl. Gutas
10a4 ᾗ μερῶν CL et Spengel, sed corruptelam susp. ego : ἡμερῶν P J, ἡμέρων A : ⟨τῶν εἰρ⟩ημένων Ar. (*allatī qulnā*), an etiam Ψ?
10a16 ἆρ' Ψ Λ, corr. O
10b2 ⸢καὶ ἀναχωρήσεις⸣ Ψ, add. Us.[2]
10b19 του Ψ, coni. Us.[1,2]
10b20 ταὐτὰ Ψ, coni. Brandis
10b25 δὴ ut vid. Ψ, corr. Gutas

---

[6] Burnikel 60 (also 121–122) again praises the editorial acuity and accuracy of the manuscript edition of six of Theophrastus's opuscula copied by Theodore of Gaza in the third quarter of the fifteenth century (Ottobonianus gr. 153), "ein Werk, das der Aldina ebenbürtig ist;" see above, section 1.

10b26 ᾗ Ψ, coni. Oporinus
11b12 ἐν Ψ Λ, add. L[1]
11b14 τὰς Ψ, corr. O

3. *Relation of Ψ to J and P*

The relation of J to P has been investigated and established by Burnikel and then by Laks & Most, as briefly mentioned above. In addition, because J and P are two of the most important manuscripts for a number of Aristotelian works and in particular his *Metaphysics*, their relationship has been independently studied and verified, as already mentioned, and needs no further discussion.[7] The question now is to determine how our third independent source for the Greek text of Theophrastus's Essay, manuscript Ψ, is related to the other two, so that it can be placed in the stemma accordingly. The agreement of Ψ with either one against the other provides the answer.

Ψ agrees with P against J in the following 23 passages; when the agreement is in error, it is marked with an asterisk. The (correct) reading adopted in the text is given first, while for later reference the readings of the fourth independent source for the Greek text, the exemplar of the Latin translation (Λ), are also given.

4a16 τῶν φθαρτῶν PJ[II] Ψ Λ[8] : τῶν ἀφθάρτων J
4a23 περιτιθέντων P Ψ Λ : -τεθ- J
4a23 αὑτῶν Ψ Λ, αυτῶν P : αὐτῶν J
6a1 δὴ P Ψ Λ : δεῖ J
6a13 εἰ J[II] Ψ Λ, εἱ P : η J
6a27 ὅσον P Ψ Λ : ὅσων J
6b12 δόξειεν ἂν P Ψ : δόξει ἐρᾶν J : Lat. om. in lac.
7a19 τὰς δ' P Ψ Λ : τὰς J
7b18 λογῶδες P Ψ : λογωιδες J : λογωειδες J[1] : λογοειδὲς Λ
*7b19 καὶ J Λ : om. P Ar. (an etiam Ψ?)
8a16 κατ' αὐτήν P, Ψ ut vid. : καθ' αὐτήν J, καθ' αὑτήν Λ

[7] See in particular, Harlfinger 1979 and his stemma codicum on p. 27.

[8] The Latin has *corruptibilibus*, which prima facie would seem to indicate τοῖς φθαρτοῖς, and hence in agreement with neither P nor J, but it appears that Bartholomew used the ablative, as with the preceding *principiis*, because he understood the word φθαρτῶν to be governed by the preposition *sub* (for ὑπὸ), despite the accusative in ὑπὸ τὰς ἀρχάς. Alternatively, Burnikel 129 thinks that the confusion may arise from an incorrect reading by Bartholomew of an abbreviation for the suffix in φθαρτ-ῶν. In either case, what determines the reading in Λ and its affiliation with P and Ψ and not with J is that the word in Latin reflects φθαρτός and not ἄφθαρτος, as in J.

κατ' αὐτὴν P Ψ : καθ' αὐτὴν J [Λ]
8b12 ὑποβάλλει P Ψ : ὑπερβάλλει J Λ
8b15 τῷ P Ψ Λ : τὸ J
8b21 ἤ P Ψ Λ : εἴ J
8b27 τέλεος δ' ἤ P Ψ : τέλος δὲ J Λ
9b7–8 τις ἀρχή P Ψ Λ : της αρχηι J
9b27 κατάλοιπον P Ψ : κατὰλοιπόν J [Λ][9]
10a1 τά τε P Ψ : τὰ δὲ J Λ
10a5 εἰ P Ψ : ἤ J Λ
10b16 μέγιστον P Ψ Λ : μάλιστα J
11a17 ἐμψύχων P Ψ Λ : ἀψ- J^{II}
11b14 μεταβολὰς P Ψ Λ : -λὴν J^{II}
11b23–24 πέρι σκεπτέον P Ψ : περισκεπτέον J^{II} Λ

For its part, Ψ agrees with J against P in the following 17 passages, agreement in error being marked again with an asterisk. The correct reading adopted in the text is listed first and the readings of the Latin exemplar, Λ, are also given.

4a12 δέ πως J Ψ Λ : δεπῶς P
4a21 τοῦ παντὸς J Ψ, Λ ut vid. : παντός P
5a26 ὁμοίως J Ψ Λ : om. P
* 5a28 εἰ δ' ἤ PJ^{II} : εἰ δὴ J Ψ Λ
* 5b17 ἐρύσαιμ' P : ἐρυσαίμ' J et Ψ ut vid. [Λ]
6a11 τοιαῦτ' ἄττα J Ψ Λ : τοιαυτ' αττι P
6b5 δ' οὐδ' J Ψ Λ : δ' P
6b14 ἀρχὰς J Ψ : ἀργὰς P : Lat. om. in lac.
* 7b12 τις P : τῆς J Ψ Λ
8a20 εἴ J Ψ Λ : ἤ P
9a4 ταὐτὸ J Ψ Λ : ταυτωι P
10a3 θέσις J Ψ : θέσεις P : Lat. om. in lac.
* 10a17 μηδ' ἐν P : μηδὲν J Ψ Λ
* 10a18 οὐδ' ἐν P Λ : οὐδὲν J Ψ
10b3 πρὸς J Ψ Λ : πρὸ P
* 11a19 τι P Λ : τε J^{II} Ψ
11b5 δ' J^{II} Ψ Λ : P om.

If then Ψ agrees with P against J 23 times and with J against P 17 times, Ψ agrees with J one fourth fewer times than it does with P. This 4:3 (23:17) ratio is statistically consistent (in a relatively small sample that is the short text of Theophrastus's Essay) with an assumption that there is no direct stemmatic affiliation of Ψ with either J or P after the translitera-

[9] The Latin has *hec reliquerunt* for τούτοις κατάλοιπον in the Greek, which would stand for ταῦτα κατέλιπον, as Kley 26 suggests. However, it appears that Bartholomew did not understand the Greek, which may have been corrupted in his exemplar.

tion of their respective uncial parents into minuscule. Accordingly, the agreement of Ψ with either one of them carries the correct reading while the odd man out represents an individual error by that manuscript or its immediate source. This is what happens with great preponderance in the two lists of agreements just given. Problems for the accuracy of this stemmatic relationship among the manuscripts concerned arise when Ψ agrees with either J or P in error, which implies that either an identical error or an identical correct conjecture was made by two scribes independently of each other. These problematic passages, marked with an asterisk in the two lists, need to be discussed.

The agreement of Ψ with P is almost perfect: in 22 of the 23 instances of congruence they do indeed carry the correct reading and, correspondingly, J or its immediate source is in error. Only in one passage (7b19) do they agree in error, omitting the conjunction καί. Crubellier (in Laks & Most p. LXXVI note 151) makes a good case that we cannot be certain that Ψ did not carry καί, for the translator may have seen it in his source (Ψ) but decided not to translate it; in which case the omission would be unique to P. However, the variant itself (the presence or absence of καί) is of such great currency that other alternative explanations may be just as valid. To begin with, the original reading in the parent manuscript may have been without the conjunction (the passage makes just as good sense without it) and its addition would be a deliberate insertion by J or its immediate source; or two scribes may have indeed omitted it independently of each other. In short, not much can be made of this particular variant.

The situation with the agreement of Ψ with J is at first sight more problematic, insofar as six of the seventeen instances of agreement between them are in error (i.e., the cases marked in the list above with an asterisk), but upon closer inspection there are only two contestable passages. To begin with, 5b17 is a matter of accents and not a common error properly speaking, given the practices of scribes, while 5a28, 10a17 and 10a18 concern word breaks which were not at all or not evenly observed in either uncial or early minuscule manuscripts.

This leaves only two problematic passages which present a stemmatic incongruity: 7b12 (τις P : τῆς J Ψ Λ) and 11a19 (τι P Λ : τε J^{II} Ψ). If Ψ and J, and indeed, also Λ, agree on a reading, then according to the stemma (below, section 6) it must be correct; they cannot agree in error unless one assumes independently made identical errors or conjectural corrections. In the first of these two passages, it is unlikely that all three independent sources (J Ψ and Λ) would have committed the same error (τῆς) for a reading transmitted correctly only by P (τις); the correct reading in P has accordingly to be seen as a correction made by P or its immediate source of the primitive error in the Neoplatonic archetype (the source of all our manuscripts together).[10] In the second passage, the correct reading is carried by both P and the exemplar of the Latin translation (Λ); the identical erroneous readings in Ψ and J^{II} can only be seen as having occurred independently of each other.

In short, the agreement of Ψ with J also favors the view of the independence of Ψ from both J and P, suggesting the stemma given below. The two passages (7b12 and 11a19) which seem to contradict this view do not, in the end, present difficulties substantive enough to counterbalance the overwhelming evidence supporting it.

4. *Manuscript Λ, Exemplar of the Latin Translation by Bartholomew of Messina*

The Latin translation by Bartholomew of Messina commands attention by its very date: it was commissioned by King Manfred of Sicily (reigned 1258–1266). It survives in a unique manuscript in Padua, Antoniana XVII 370 (ff. 62^r–64^r), dating from the early 14th century.[11] An annotated transcription of the text, without editorial intrusions (a diplomatic edition), was prepared by Kley 1936, which was reviewed extensively by Dirlmeier 1938 and briefly by A. Mansion 1938 and Ross 1938. The accuracy of the transcription was further confirmed by Most 1988c, who also added a few corrections (p. 170n6).

Bartholomew based his translation on a lost Greek manuscript to which I give the siglum Λ. Most 1988c argued at length that Λ is, in fact, the manuscript of the Viennese Aristotle, J, or a manuscript directly deriving from it. Accordingly, the edition of Laks & Most disregarded Bartholomew's Latin translation as evidence for the Greek text. Most based his argument both on a comparison between the readings in Λ and the Greek manuscripts, and on external circumstances. In the latter case, William of Moerbeke, who himself used J for his translation of Aristotle's *Metaphysics*, took the manuscript with him from Constantinople to Italy between 1260 and 1267. Since this is precisely the period during which

[10] According to Hecquet-Devienne's analyses (2000; 2004, 172) of the copying of P, this would be due to corrections made to P in the process of its constitution.

[11] See the detailed description by Franceschini 1935.

Bartholomew prepared the translation of Theophrastus's Essay, it is not unlikely, Most 1988c, 181, argued, that Bartholomew had access to J or to a copy deriving from it. This circumstantial evidence, however, cannot be decisive, as Vuillemin-Diem 1995, 311, remarked, for it cannot be proven that Bartholomew and William actually met. More importantly, the evidence from the comparative readings in Λ and the Greek manuscripts that Most collects fails to establish a close connection between the Latin translation and J (or the identity of Λ and J). Of the four passages listed by Most to this end,[12] only one is a unique error in J which is repeated in the Latin translation, an omission of καί; but this is hardly decisive, for as Most himself notes (180), the Latin text in the Padua manuscript "elsewhere occasionally omits καί." The other three readings occur in other Greek manuscripts as well and thus cannot show a unique relationship between J and the Latin translation. Furthermore, and more significantly, the Latin translation has the correct reading when J is in error in twenty-five (25) places, as listed by Most 1988c, 181–183. This lack of agreement in error is fatal to Most's argument, even though Most explains it away by claiming (183) that none of the correct readings in the Latin translation "was beyond the capacity of the *divinatio* of Bartholomaeus." But, first, Bartholomew was not the kind of translator who would correct his exemplar in the course of his work; his extant translation of two Hippocratic treatises from a Greek manuscript which we actually possess, Vaticanus gr. 276, shows that he was a literal and slavish translator, reproducing all the unique readings and errors of his exemplar. And second, twenty-five is too large a number of correct readings in such a short text to qualify as *divinatio* by such a translator, especially when they are attested in the other manuscripts of the tradition. Besides, if Bartholomew was ingenious and sophisticated enough to correct all those errors in J, the question remains why he failed to correct some others that were more obvious, like, e.g., ἦ at 8a6 (correct: ᾗ), or τῆς at 7b12 (correct: τις). It appears certain that neither J nor a copy of it were the source of Bartholomew's Latin translation.[13]

[12] Most 1988c, 179; the fifth passage, 11a4, occurs in the last section of J, J^{II}, which was copied after Bartholomew's translation, and thus we do not know what J originally had.

[13] Vuillemin-Diem 1995, 311, makes all these points convincingly. In note 121 on p. LXIV in Laks & Most, Most claims that Vuillemin-Diem reported to him privately that the possibility could not be excluded that the Latin translation was based not on J but on a closely related ("très proche") manuscript. In her 1995 book on the Latin

Already in 1974, Burnikel, who made a complete collation of the Latin translation with the Greek, found that it is not possible to associate its Greek exemplar, Λ, with a specific family of Greek manuscripts because the errors that Λ has in common with them are distributed fairly evenly among them ("ziemlich gleichmässig," p. 128). This indicated to Burnikel (129–130) that Λ was a representative of a separate family in the manuscript transmission, and Vuillemin-Diem 1995, 311, fully concurred.

If this is so, the question then is from which point in the transmission of the text Λ and its source branch off. A first test would be to examine whether it shares the primitive errors found in the Greek manuscripts PJ and in Ψ in order to establish whether or not it descends from the same archetype. From the table of these primitive errors given in section 5 below, it becomes clear that Λ shared them with the rest of the extant witnesses for the text and thus it does not derive from an archetype different from that represented by the Greek manuscripts and Ψ.

Next, Λ shares the key common mistake with all the main Greek manuscripts (PJ CL A = **α**) against Ψ at

> 8a11 pr. ὂν Ψ : ἓν **α** Λ (*unum*).

This indicates that Λ derives from the same transliteration from uncials as the extant Greek manuscripts but not from that of the source of Ψ. If then Λ is related to the two families of the Greek manuscripts (the one represented by P and the other by the two sub-families JCL and Σ), but it does not belong to either one of them but has its own family, as stated above, it must be placed in the stemma close to but separate from the common ancestor of the two families, i.e., from the "Constantinopolitan recension," as identified by Burnikel (127).

These stemmatic relations, as indicated by the researches of Burnikel and Vuillemin-Diem on the basis of common errors in manuscripts, are further corroborated by an analysis of the correct readings which Λ shares with Ψ and the two Greek families of manuscripts. In the first place, Λ shares some correct readings with Ψ against the Constantinopolitan recension (P and J CL A = **α**), something that would have been impossible had it been dependent on the latter. Of the correct readings

---

Metaphysics (p. 310n67), she wrote that note 121 in Laks & Most appears to be based on a misunderstanding ("der Anmerkung n. 121 scheint allerdings ein Missverständnis zugrunde zu liegen").

that are particular to Ψ and absent from all extant Greek manuscripts that were listed above in section 2, the following are also found in Λ:[14]

4a23 αὑτῶν Ψ Λ (*se ipsa*) : αυτῶν P, αὐτῶν JCL A
6b7 πως Ψ Λ[15] : πῶς PJ
8a22 περιεργία τὸ ζητεῖν Ψ Λ (*otiositas inquirere*) : περιεργίαν τοῦ ζητεῖν **α**
8b20 γένη ... εἴδη Ψ Λ (*genera ... species*) A[16] : γένει ... εἴδει P J CL[1]
8b25 κοινῇ Ψ Λ (*comuni*) : κοινὴ P J
10a16 ἆρ' Ψ Λ (*utrum*) O[17] : ἀρ' P, ἄρ' JCL A[18]
11b12 ἐν Ψ Λ (*in*) : om. **α**

To these may be added two further correct readings which are unique to Λ:

4a6 ταὐτά Λ (*eadem*) : ταυτα P, ταῦτα J : Ar. om. in lac.
11a8 αὐτὸ Λ (*hoc*) : αὐτὰ J[II] CL [Ψ] : αὑτος P, αὕτως A

Second, in the preceding section (3), the agreement in readings among P, J, Ψ, and Λ were listed in two lists, one of the agreement of Ψ with P against J, and the other the agreement of Ψ with J against P. Of the forty variants that were discussed in the two lists combined, the reading in Λ agreed 20 times with J against P and 15 times with P against J; in the remaining five instances either the Latin text was missing or its evidence was inconclusive.[19] This almost equal distribution of agreement of Λ with P and J in correct readings also shows the independence of Λ from either one of them. Furthermore, in these forty instances, Λ never agrees in error with P, though it agrees with J in error in ten of them. However, the nature of the errors in these instances is such that it is stemmatically inconsequential. One of them (7b12) is a primitive

[14] Some of these were first pointed out as uniquely correct readings in Λ by Dirlmeier 1938, 136, and Ross 1938, neither of whom, however, knew of the Arabic translation. Thus although not all of their suggestions in this regard can be accepted on the basis of our knowledge now of Ψ (see the commentary for a discussion of the passages in question), they deserve credit for taking the text represented by the Latin translation seriously, Dirlmeier more so than Ross.

[15] The Latin has *omnimode* for ἅπαντά πως, which Bartholomew took as a single semantic unit (whether it was written as one word or two), similar to ἁπανταχοῦ or πανταχῶς. Ἅπαντά πως is clearly the reading in Λ and not, as Kley 21 suggests, a different wording such as πάντως, etc.

[16] The correct reading in A is conjectural.

[17] The correct reading in manuscript O is a conjecture by the redoubtable Theodore of Gaza.

[18] Cf. Kley 26 and Ross 1938, 16.

[19] These uncertain passages are, 5b17, 6b12, 6b14, 9b27, and 10a3.

error of the Neoplatonic archetype (see the next section) that is carried by all witnesses except P, which indicates that the correction is due to the editors of P (see above, section 1). Three others are erroneous word divisions (5a28, 10a17, 11b24), one is the result of an ētacism (10a5), another is a matter of spelling (7b18), and yet another a matter of breathings, with the rough breathing occasioning a scribal correction of κατ' to καθ' (8a16). The wrong variant (8b12) ὑπερβάλλει may have been an original error during the transcription from uncials (possibly occasioned by the preceding ὑπερβατός at 8b9), and thus carried by both Λ and J but corrected by the editors of P, while the correct ὑποβάλλει in Ψ would be the original reading from the archetype; and similar would appear to be the cases with the two remaining common errors at 8b27 and 10a1. None of these errors is such as to point incontrovertibly to a stemmatic dependence of Λ from the source of J; to the contrary, as already mentioned at the beginning of this section, twenty-five errors in J are not reproduced in Λ.

Genetically, therefore, Λ represents a witness to the Greek text that is indepedent of the Constantinopolitan recension, or the extant two families of Greek manuscripts. The independent derivation of Λ is also evident in, and supported by, two other peculiarities: the environment in which it is transmitted, and the title it gives to the Essay. The Padua manuscript of Bartholomew's Latin translation of the Essay includes the following treatises:[20] *Problemata, De principiis* (i.e., Theophrastus's present Essay), *Mirabilium auscultationes, De eupragia, Physiognomica, De signis, De inundatione Nili, De mundo, De animalibus, De differentia spiritu et animae, De motu animalium*. These are all mostly pseudo-Aristotelian treatises. Since as a rule it is the availability of source texts that determines what texts are to be translated, it is reasonable to assume that the Greek exemplar (Λ) from which Barholomew worked also contained some or most of these treatises.[21] Hence Theophrastus's Essay was transmitted in this manuscript together with other pseudo-Aristotelian works, not the canonical corpus, as is the case with the oldest extant Greek manuscripts, J and P (see above, Chapter 1.2). This would indicate that the Theophrastean Essay, after its transliteration from uncials, was transmitted initially in its traditional environment—the mature Aristotelian treatises and especially the *Metaphysics*—as represented by

[20] See the contents of the manuscript given by Franceschini 1935.

[21] See Harlfinger 1971a, 62–63, about the transmission of these pseudo-Aristotelian works: "Die Entscheidung darüber, was übersetzt wird, ist also offensichtlich eng mit der Frage des Zugangs zu bestimmten Texten verbunden."

the manuscripts P and the sub-family JCL. After a while, however, it was detached from this environment and on the one hand was joined to the other extant opuscula in the ancestor of manuscript A of the Σ sub-family, and on the other was associated with several Aristotelian pseudepigrapha in the tradition from which derives the recension of the ancestor of manuscript Λ.

Secondly, the title of the Essay is given in Bartholomew's Latin as *Liber Aristotelis De principiis*, or, in Greek, Ἀριστοτέλους Περὶ ἀρχῶν. Valentin Rose 183–185, who first looked into these matters in some detail, took this evidence seriously and concluded that this is the original and ancient title of Theophrastus's Essay. Usener almost completely disregarded the issue, while subsequent scholars paid litle attention or importance to the evidence of the Latin translation and Rose's suggestion. The demonstrable independent derivation of Λ, however, as just indicated, requires that the question be revisited (see Chapter 1.2). These peculiarities of Λ indicate that although it is derived from the same transcription from uncials as both families of the Greek manuscripts, it represents a separate recension, one possibly prepared for or in Messina, which accordingly was named "recensio Messanensis" by Burnikel 127. There is a good analogue to this situation in the two recensions, Constantinopolitan and Messinan, of the *Eudemian Ethics*, as discussed by Harlfinger 1971b, 6–9. The Messinan recension of Theophrastus's Essay, and the ultimate parent for Λ, branch off from the transcription into minuscule before the formation of the Constantinopolitan recension.[22]

The readings of Λ, as they can be reconstructed from Bartholomew's Latin translation, are accordingly consulted and recorded. The value of Λ as a fourth independent witness to the text, in addition to preserving the original title of Theophrastus's Essay and the two unique correct readings listed above, also lies in corroborating the state of the text as transmitted, after one transliteration into minuscule, in the two oldest representatives of the two families of Greek manuscripts, J and P, and, after another transliteration, in the Arabic translation reflecting manuscript Ψ (whence its agreement with Ψ against P and J in the seven passages listed above). The value of this attestation provided by Λ lies in the greater confidence that it imparts in the transmitted readings (unless they manifestly belong to the primitive errors of the Neoplatonic archetype, for which see the next section). For this reason the readings of the paradosis

[22] Burnikel 130: "B ist also ... Zeuge eines Zustandes vor der byzantinischen Edition."

deserve careful scrutiny before they are emended. It has been possible in this edition to rehabilitate and preserve the largest possible number of the transmitted readings, eliminating some of the hasty conjectures of earlier editors.

On the other hand, it is also clear from the state of the Latin translation that it contains numerous unique errors due to the transmission both within Greek between the transliteration and manuscript Λ, Bartholomew's exemplar, and within Latin after the translation by Bartholomew.[23] The evidence from either of these stages of corruption is of no interest for the establishment of the Greek text and accordingly it is not registered in the apparatus.

5. *The Neoplatonic Archetype of the Extant Manuscript Tradition*

The two uncial manuscripts, from which derive the minuscule transliterations that were the sources of Ψ on the one hand and PJ and Λ on the other, go back to a common ancestor, for there are certain errors in the text—I call them primitive errors—that are common to the representatives of all families of manuscripts: the exemplar of the Arabic translation, Ψ; the exemplar of the Latin translation, Λ, representing the Messinan recension, and the two independent Greek manuscripts, J and P, representing the Constantinopolitan recension. These primitive errors indicate the most ancient stage of corruption from which all our extant manuscripts and translations derive.

In the following list of these primitive errors, the first variant in each entry is that of the erroneous reading as contained in all four independent sources for the text—the Greek manuscripts PJ and the exemplars of the Arabic and Latin translations, Ψ and Λ respectively—followed after the colon by the emendation and its first author. In the case of manuscript sigla, the reference is to the manuscript whose scribe or source made the emendation. The details about the readings in each case can be found in the corresponding entries in the apparatus criticus. This list of the errors of the archetype revises the one first given by Fobes, pp. xxvii–xxviii. Some of the errors on that list have been shown not to have been those of the archetype, insofar as Ψ, which was not known to Fobes, had the correct reading, and some others turned out not to have been errors at all. The readings in each case are discussed in detail in the commentary.

---

[23] Many of these errors are discussed by Kley in his notes.

5b2 διαφορὰν : μεταφορὰν J[II]
6b19 ἐκείνοις : ἐκείναις Camotius[24]
7b8 εἰ : ἢ J[II]
7b12 τῆς : τις P
7b13 τι μεταλλακτέον : ἀντιμεταλλακτέον D
7b15 ἐν : secl. Us.[2]
7b16 κινοῦν : κινούμενον Ross
7b20 δεῖ : δεῖν Laks & Most
8a2 εἰ : τί Us.[2]
8a2 οὖσιν ἀκολουθεῖ : οὐ συνακολουθεῖ Ross
8a6 ἡ vel ἢ : ᾗ Us.[1,2]
8b27–9a1 ἔστιν δ᾽ ἔνια τῶν μὲν : εἰσὶ δ᾽ ἔνιαι μὲν ὧν Gutas
9b24 πέφυκεν ⟨* * *⟩ ὅσοι : lac. ind. Us.[1,2]
10a4 ἡμερῶν vel ἢ μερῶν corruptelam susp. Gutas
10a11 καὶ ἡ : καὶ ⟨εἰ⟩ ἡ Gutas (εἰ ἡ Wimmer)
10a12 κινῆται : κινεῖται CL B
10a17 τε : γε Sylburg
10a23 θ᾽ add. Us.[1,2]
10b4 ἢ : ᾗ Bignone
10b20 δ᾽ ἐν : δ᾽ ⟨αἱ⟩ ἐν Gutas
11a18 καὶ : κἂν homo italicus quidam
11a19 πλῆθος : πλήθει Laks & Most
11a20 †οὐκ εἰ† locus corruptus necdum sanatus
11a22 †ει locus corruptus necdum sanatus
11b1 γ᾽ : τ᾽ Gutas, δ᾽ Ross
11b18 τε : γε Ross

We have no direct evidence for the identity and provenance of the manuscript that contained these errors and ultimately became the archetype from which all our knowledge of the text of the Essay derives. But we know that it contained the Scholium at the end of the Essay and that this Scholium, as I hope to have demonstrated (above, Chapter 1.2), derives from the Neoplatonic school in late antiquity. We also know that some of the other scholia in manuscript P on the *Metaphysics*, scholia which necessarily derive from this archetype, are by Asclepius, the Neoplatonic philosopher. Both these indications clearly point to the sixth Christian century as the *terminus a quo* for the archetype, assuming that the scribes and editors of P took both their text of the *Metaphysics* with Theophrastus's Essay and the accompanying scholia from the same archetype and not from two different manuscripts. Since

[24] It is not clear that this is a primitive error in the uncial Neoplatonic archetype; it could also have arisen in the transmission in minuscule, as represented in all the extant Greek manuscripts. See the commentary.

the latter alternative seems rather unlikely, it appears relatively certain that the archetype dates from the sixth century.

With the identification and correction of the primitive errors in this archetype listed above, our reconstruction of the text can aspire to go beyond the sixth century. The hope is that the text as established in the present edition might represent its state in the Roman edition of the first century BC, or even earlier; but we have no way of knowing.

6. *Stemma Codicum*

(Dates in parentheses are conjectural and are intended merely as suggestions to provide some plausible time frame.)

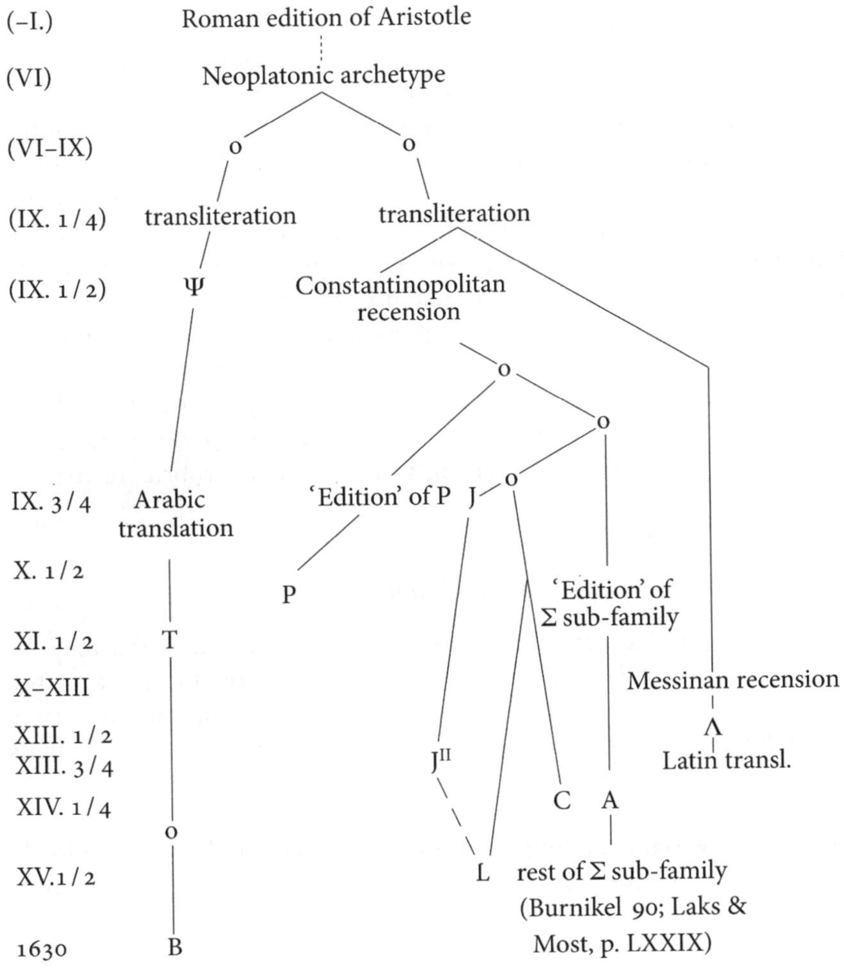

7. *Sources and Principles of the Greek Edition*

a. *Sources of the text*

As discussed in the preceding analysis, represented in the stemma codicum, there are four independent witnesses for the text of Περὶ ἀρχῶν by Theophrastus: the Greek manuscripts J and P, the Arabic translation by Isḥāq ibn-Ḥunayn based on the lost Greek manuscript Ψ, and the Latin translation by Bartholomew of Messina based on the lost Greek manuscript Λ. In preparation for the edition, I accordingly (1) collated anew manuscripts J and P from high quality photographs, (2) prepared a critical edition of the Arabic translation (below, Part II,2) in order to elicit with accuracy the readings of Ψ, and (3) examined in detail, for the same purpose, the Latin translation in the diplomatic edition by Kley (presented below, Part II,3). The edition is based on these primary sources and on the corrections of their primitive errors (above, section 5) that have been offered over the centuries by scribes and scholars.

According to the analysis in section 1 above, manuscripts CL of the sub-family JCL, and manuscript A of the sub-family Σ do not contribute any independent and correct readings, apart from four conjectural emendations by scribes, and in addition have many mistakes of their own. In particular L and A are error ridden. Accordingly I did not examine any manuscripts in sub-family Σ and manuscripts CL in sub-family JCL but reproduced instead the evidence as presented in the apparatus of the edition by Laks & Most. Insofar as whatever acceptable readings they have are the result of scribal emendations, their readings can be treated like the emendations of modern scholars and have been reported in the main apparatus sporadically, with their sigla listed under the rubric "raro citantur."

b. *The apparatus criticus: main and supplementary*

The main apparatus includes all the readings of P and J, the relevant readings of Ψ and Λ as they are reconstructed on the basis of the Arabic and Latin translations respectively, and the appropriate scribal and scholarly emendations. In particular, the main apparatus contains the following information:

(1) All the variant readings of P and J, except for those of a merely orthographic nature (such as movable final ν) and those which show

differences of breathing and accents, when in both cases they do not represent real alternatives. Variants which are due to the slip of the pen and produce nonsense (what we would call today "typos", as, e.g., τινσος in P at 6b10 for τινός, and ὀεγεσθαι in J at 6a10 for ὀρέγεσθαι) have been recorded in the supplementary apparatus.

(2) All the relevant variant readings of Ψ as they are reconstructed from the Arabic translation, according to the rules established in the Excursus following Part I below. By "relevant" is meant those readings that bear upon the establishment of the Greek text. In essence, what is recorded is all instances of departure by the Arabic translation from the transmitted Greek text which are not clearly due to corruption strictly within the Arabic tradition—i.e., corruption of a text which, though correctly translated and reflecting the Greek text we have, was manifestly due to the vicissitudes of transmission from one Arabic manuscript to the other; such variants which are of no relevance to the establishment of the Greek text are listed in the apparatus criticus of the edition of the Arabic translation (Part II,2). The decision to include in the apparatus, irrelevant mistakes apart, all the evidence provided by the Arabic translation is justified by an analysis of the possible ways of corruption of the Arabic text, as discussed in the Excursus. In more general terms, it is justified by the fact that the Arabic translator, Isḥāq ibn-Ḥunayn, is the very first commentator on our text, and much closer than we are to both the ancient Greek manuscipt tradition and the tradition of Aristotelian scholarship and understanding of late antiquity. In this regard his opinion about and understanding of Theophrastus's text is to be respected and documented—in any case, it certainly is not any less respectable than those of the Renaissance humanists and modern scholars; the fact is, the Graeco-Arabic translators of the early ʿAbbāsid era are our first humanist scholars after continuous Greek scholarship came to an end in late antiquity, and for the reasons just listed their opinions ought to be recorded.

Readings in Ψ are not recorded when it is impossible to tell from the Arabic what the Greek had, either because in general terms the syntax and word order of the Arabic do not reveal the details of the Greek or because, more particularly, certain characteristics of Greek, like most particles and variations of accents that do not affect the meaning of the word, cannot be adequately represented in Arabic. In all such cases where the Arabic translation does not yield the reading in Ψ, this is indicated in the apparatus entry with square brackets placed around the siglum, [Ψ].

The Arabic evidence which explains and justifies my derivation of the readings of Ψ, as recorded in the apparatus, is discussed in every instance in the notes to the translation of the Arabic text, except when such explanation or justification becomes obvious from my translation. I have added in the apparatus the Arabic word(s) behind the reconstructed Greek, in transliteration, only when the reconstructed reading does not agree with an extant Greek reading; that is, in cases where the Arabic fills a lacuna, corroborates an emendation, or presents an alternative reading. In such cases I did not translate the Arabic into Latin, as Irigoin 25 recommends, for I considered it superfluous: readers who do not read Arabic will understand what it says from the conjectural Greek reading included in the apparatus.

(3) All the variant readings of Λ, as they are reconstructed from the Latin translation, that bear upon the establishment of the Greek text. The Latin translation, as opposed to the Arabic, is painfully literal and follows the Greek word order, conspicuously reflecting the underlying Greek text. Accordingly, variants that are due to unique errors in the Greek forebears of Λ and in the subsequent Latin tradition, and are of no relevance to the establishment of the Greek text, are not recorded at all.

(4) Selected readings from later manuscripts (recentiores) when they contain scribal emendations that are adopted in the text, or are useful in providing full documentation for the readings adopted or rejected.

(5) Selected emendations by modern scholars. As already mentioned, this Essay by Theophrastus has enjoyed inordinate attention from scholars, and indeed from among the most competent and influential in both classical scholarship and ancient philosophy. This has proven overall extremely beneficial, for many primitive errors in the common Neoplatonic archetype of all our main manuscripts have been restored to reasonable soundness (see the list of primitive errors above, section 5). However, each age has its own approach to scholarship, and the alacrity with which classical philologists in the nineteenth and the first half of the twentieth centuries fell to "correcting" any Greek text they encountered resulted in numerous unnecessary emendations.[25] Our age tends to be

[25] This is not intended to cast doubts on the practice of offering emendations, or deny some of our great predecessors their insight—and the credit due to them—when their emendations are corroborated by the Arabic translation or other evidence.

more conservative in this regard (I consider myself a staunch supporter of this attitude); already the most recent edition by Laks & Most restored many of the readings of the manuscripts. The apparatus, however, should not continue to be burdened with some of the less felicitous suggestions of our great forebears, so that some weeding is necessary.[26] Accordingly, the main apparatus contains selected conjectures by previous scholars only when they have been confirmed by Ψ (in order to acknowledge their merit) and when they suggest a fruitful line of approach to the passage. These conjectures or corrections are registered only in the name of the scholar who first made them, not those of subsequent editors who also adopted them.

However, the information that has been withheld from the main apparatus for the reasons just given is not completely superfluous. An apparatus containing it may be consulted for fuller documentation of the readings in the manuscript tradition, the character of individual manuscripts and their scribes, and the fruits of all past scholarship on the text. To this end I have included a supplementary critical apparatus in Part II at the end of the Greek text and the facing English translation.[27] It contains all the readings of manuscripts CL and those in sub-family Σ (that are not included in my main apparatus) as recorded by Laks & Most, other incidental or mistaken readings of the main manuscripts, as well as the suggestions for emendations and comments offered by modern scholars. In the latter case I collated anew all the editions beginning with that by Brandis (1823); for the earlier editions, including the Aldine (for references to which see Ross and Laks & Most), I presented their readings again as recorded by Laks & Most.

The apparatus is essentially mixed, positive when the variants presented are real alternatives, negative when they are aberrations. In the presentation of the material in the apparatus, I bunch together the readings that represent one alternative, separated by commas, and I use the colon, more than once if necessary, to separate alternative readings.[28] Thus shortened and sharpened, the apparatus will be more accesible, I

[26] I consider Irigoin's well-phrased statement of the purpose of the apparatus sufficient justification for this weeding (p. 23): "L'apparat critique a pour but de fournir au lecteur non pas toute l'histoire de la tradition ni celle des éditions imprimées."

[27] A practice actually recommended by West 86n12.

[28] I have found helpful the guidelines offered by West, especially pp. 86 ff. In general I have found them more flexible and more expressive than those suggested for the Budé series by Irigoin.

hope, to readers, more responsive to the needs of researchers, and more conducive to a better understanding of this fascinating text and its transmission.

c. *The apparatus of parallel passages (Loci Paralleli)*

Given the highly referential character of the Essay, I have thought it useful to add to the text an upper apparatus of parallel passages as a study aid. Two things need to be emphasized about it. First, it is an apparatus of loci paralleli and *not* an apparatus fontium. Its aim is to cite not only passages in the works of other philosophers to which Theophrastus was responding or referring, but also those passages in Aristotle, mainly, to which Theophrastus's aporiae may have given rise; also passages which reflect the oral discussions between Aristotle and Theophrastus, which may have found their way formulated in one of Aristotle's subsequent treatises. Second, it is selective; its aim is to include the passages that earlier scholars and I have found to be most immediately relevant to the subjects discussed by Theophrastus, but both the extent and immediacy of the choice can claim neither comprehensiveness nor infallibility.

d. *Punctuation*

I have revised throughout the punctuation of the Greek text to accord with the flow of the argument as indicated by the syntax and choice of particles, and restore the cohesion and sequence of meanings intended by Theophrastus. In a number of instances in previous editions not only a period but even a paragraph and chapter break were placed between two parts of the same sentence, as, e.g., at 7b5–11 and 8b8–12, both cases of clear μέν ... δέ sentences. Such practices, usually established by an earlier and respected editor and followed dutifully by subsequent ones, hinder the understanding of the internal cohesion of the work and on occasion lead to unusual interpretations.

Traditional punctuation of classical Greek texts tends to use the Greek colon (a point above the line) to excess; none of the several languages I know uses naturally so many major breaks within the same sentence, and certainly not classical Greek. To a certain extent, this may reflect manuscript usage, but this is the convention of writing Greek from the ninth to the fifteenth centuries, not that of the time of Theophrastus, and in any case we do not write in perfect imitation of the Greek manuscripts. I see no reason to follow these conventions rather than one that is closer to our custom of reading texts. I have thus introduced (like others before me) two additional punctuation marks to the traditional Greek four. I have employed the dash rather more frequently than has been customary (though H.H. Joachim's edition of Aristotle's *De generatione et corruptione* uses it to great benefit, as does Ross's edition of the *Metaphysics*), and I have also used, though sparingly, the English colon (:) according to our usage, for in some instances it is clearly preferable to the Greek colon or comma (e.g. at 5b13).

e. *Layout of the editions*

Hermann Usener's critical edition of 1890, like that of Bekker for Aristotle, has set the standard form of reference to this work by Theophrastus. It covers pages 4 to 12 in his edition, in two columns, which are accordingly referred to as a and b, exactly as in the case of Bekker's Aristotle. Usener had a different conception of the structure of the Essay, judged by almost all subsequent students of it as inappropriate, and thus his division into sections and chapters cannot be easily adhered to. However, because of the established convention—now a hundred and twenty years old—of referring in secondary literature to the text by his page, column, and line numbers, these must necessarily be followed to the extent feasible. For this edition, I have followed the paragraph breaks indicated by the series of aporiae discussed by Theophrastus (see above, Chapter 1.4) and thus have introduced many more paragraph breaks than those used by Usener. This has necessitated a variation in the contents of some lines, but to the extent possible I have kept precisely to the line lengths and numbers in Usener's original edition.[29] I have, however, added into the text new paragraph numbers, in bold, to correspond to the number of aporiae discussed, but also printed in the right margin Usener's "chapter" numbers in Roman numerals and section numbers in Arabic numerals in brackets. Words divided between two lines are always referred to, in the commentary, the glossaries, and elsewhere, by the line in which they begin (e.g., the word πολυ-χουστέρα would be referred to as occurring at 4a3, not 4a3–4).

[29] An inevitable shift in this regard has also occurred in the editions of Ross and Laks & Most. In this edition, the only lines that do not match Usener's exactly are the following: 5a13–22, 8b9–14, and 11b23–12a1.

The line numbers being the one invariable standard, I have also added them in raised numerals into the Arabic and Latin translations. This only minimally disturbs the reading of the text but it facilitates and simplifies reference and obviates the need to introduce yet another set of numbers for references to the translations. In their case, Greek words divided between two lines are also counted as belonging to the line in which they begin, and thus the translation of the Greek word that follows the divided word is counted as starting the next line. For the layout of the Arabic text in particular see also below, Chapter 3.5.

f. *The translation and annotation of the Greek text*

Given the aporetic nature of Theophrastus's Essay and the context of live discussion which it betrays and to which it aims to contribute, his style of writing is challenging to the translator. He is brief, elliptic, referential, allusive; and if at times he seems ambiguous, the ambiguity is rather to be imputed to our ignorance of the full context and the references and allusions, than to his style; for he is also grammatical and intelligible. "Fidelity is the only virtue which a translator need cultivate," avers Jonathan Barnes (1994, xxiii), further specifying, "fidelity in the matter of sense." Yes, but the question is, which sense? or, whose understanding of the sense? Even if the answer to the first be, "the sense intended by the philosopher," in reality it is reducible to the answer to the second, "the translator's"—the translator's understanding of the sense or the translator's understanding of the sense intended by the philosopher. Fidelity therefore in this context requires that the translator inform the reader where the author's sense ends and the translator's understanding of it begins. I have done so by adding in square brackets those words and phrases which are not in the Greek but are required either by English syntax or the Greek sense, as I understood it; the only exception is that I have not bracketed the unexpressed verb εἰμί (to be) when used as copula. In cases where an adequate English version could present the same ambiguity as that perceived by me in the Greek, I explained the situation in a footnote. I have also used the footnotes to present problems relating to key terminology as well as to identification of personalities mentioned and subjects discussed.

In my understanding of the sense and sweep of each argument in the Essay I found it useful to pay special attention to the particles. This is hardly a novel observation but I believe in this instance it bears repeating in order to explain my vigorous translation of them, using whatever phrases in idiomatic (but not slangy) English are commonly added to our language to indicate emphasis, tone, and color to what we say. Written English does not use these particles as freely, but the style and meaning of Theophrastus are enhanced by their use so that an English translation that highlights them benefits the rendering of the corresponding sense. In this effort van Raalte's commentary has proven invaluable, and if I sometimes disagree with her it is only because she has quickened our attention to the particles. In the commentary I discuss as a rule the particles and my choice of translation.

My translation tries to steer a middle course between an interpretive version and a slavishly literal one that offends English usage by means of the compromise of discriminating, through the use of bracketed words and phrases, between what the Greek definitely says and what (I argue) it implies, and of explaining the latter in the notes and commentary.[30] This may rob it of some elegance but makes it more objective and a better tool for study, which is the aim of this publication. My task was lightened considerably by the existing fine translations of my predecessors: whenever I agreed with their interpretations of the Greek and the style of their translated sentences or phrases, I did not hesitate to borrow freely the wording of the English versions of Ross and van Raalte, or, in Anglicized form, the versions in languages other than English. It is my pleasure to acknowledge my debt and gratitude to these scholars as I restate my belief in the principle that there is no point in reinventing the wheel just to be "different" or "original."

g. *The commentary*

The transmission of the text of the Essay is complicated, as described. The choice of variants in each case needs to be explained and justified, especially when the evidence is in Arabic or Latin. The commentary accordingly discusses all such cases of editorial decisions, as well as of choices in the translation, with the aim to help the reader understand the philosophy of the Essay by establishing a text that is as sound as

---

30 There are numerous disquisitions on the appropriate method of translating Greek philosophical texts into modern languages, the most useful of which I have found to be those by Jonathan Barnes in the first and second edition of his translation of Aristotle's *Posterior Analytics* as well as his comments in the *CWA*, p. xi, and by Henrich, in a more theoretical vein, in his introduction. But being aware of the difficulties and challenges presented by the enterprise and consciously trying to solve them while translating are more important than talking about them.

philologically possible. Given the aporetic nature of the work, also as described, the meaning and purpose of Theophrastus in the Essay will continue to be debated for a long time; but it should be possible to agree for the time being on those aspects of it which can be settled philologically.[31]

Thus conceived primarily as a study aid, the commentary is divided into the aporiae which constitute the building blocks of the work, and it opens with a paraphrase, in italics, of the argument of Theophrastus, together with whatever discussion is necessary to give a basic understanding of it. As a rule, I have engaged in a discussion of the philosophical content of the aporiae only to the extent necessary to establish the text; for strictly philosophical analyses, the reader is referred to the commentaries of Ross, Laks & Most, van Raalte, and especially Henrich, and to the many publications in the secondary literature cited.

[31] To borrow the elegant phrasing of F.M. Cornford 1937[1], p. v, the Essay by Theophrastus *On First Principles*, "is a subject on which agreement may never be reached; but there is some hope of persuading scholars that a Greek sentence means one thing rather than another."

CHAPTER THREE

THE ARABIC TEXT: MANUSCRIPTS, TRANSMISSION, EDITIONS

1. *The Arabic Manuscripts*

The Arabic translation of the Essay by Theophrastus *On First Principles* survives in two known manuscripts, one in the Malik library in Tehran and the other in the Bodleian at Oxford. The first,

T Tehran Malik 5925, pp. 2–28, according to the numbering of the pages by Crubellier 2013, is written in an airy and slightly angular scholar's *nasḫ*, almost completely devoid of diacritical points. The title page and the first page are missing; the text of the Essay thus begins at 4a12 (see the apparatus of the Greek text). It is dated 461 Hijra / 1069 AD in its colophon, which reads,

> The treatise by Theophrastus, the advocate of Aristotle's arguments in metaphysics, ⟨in⟩ the translation by Isḥāq, is finished.
>
> I, Yaḥyā ibn-Jarīr, the physician from Tikrīt, transcribed it from a corrupt copy, in Mayyāfāriqīn in the year 461. Praise be to God.
>
> It was collated with its exemplar, which was very corrupt.

The scribe is the Jacobite Christian medical scholar and theologian, Abū-Naṣr Yaḥyā ibn-Jarīr at-Tikrītī, student of Ibn-Zurʿa, the Baghdad Aristotelian philosopher from the school of Yaḥyā ibn-ʿAdī. According to Ibn-Abī-Uṣaybiʿa, who has a brief notice on him (I,243), he was still alive eleven years after he copied this manuscript, in 472 / 1079–1080. His medical works mentioned by Ibn-Abī-Uṣaybiʿa concern sexual hygiene (Graf 1947, 260, refers to possible extant copies), but he also wrote an astrological piece which is extant, though its authorship is contested (*GAS* VII,19; *GALS* I,862, Graf 1947, 260). His major theological work is *Kitāb al-Muršid*, *The Guide*, in which he mentions that he visited Constantinople in 450 / 1058 (Graf 1947, 260–262). Like most of the scholars of his time he was a man of many talents and of apparent interest who deserves to be studied beyond the few essays that have been devoted to his theological views.[1]

The manuscript was copied in Mayyāfāriqīn, just west of lake Van in eastern Anatolia, at the sources of the Tigris. It contains, following Theophrastus's Essay, al-Fārābī's *Principles of the Opinions of the People of the Perfect State* (*Mabādiʾ ārāʾ ahl al-madīna al-fāḍila*), and it was used by R. Walzer 1985 for his edition of that text (cf. pp. 22–25). The manuscript has marginal notes and corrections by the same scribe, one of which, in both Syriac and Arabic in the part on al-Fārābī, refers to "Gregory of Nyssa or some other Gregory" (Walzer p. 24). The manuscript is defective both at the beginning and end; it is missing at least two pages at the beginning—a title page and the first page of Theophrastus's text—and a few pages at the end of al-Fārābī's text. This is unfortunate, because we are deprived of the title which Theophrastus's Essay carried in this manuscript; the colophon gives a description of its contents, which in all likelihood reflects the Scholium in some Greek manuscripts (see above, Chapter 1.2), but not the title.

The probable provenance of this manuscript bears some discussion, given that it is the chief witness for one independent branch of the transmision of the text of Theophrastus's Essay. It was copied, as just mentioned, in Mayyāfāriqīn in 1069–1070. Mayyāfāriqīn at that time was the seat of the court of the Marwānid dynasty which ruled the region of Diyārbakr (380/990–478/1085).[2] The city had come to prominence as political and cultural center already during the time of Sayf-ad-Dawla and the previous dynasty of the Ḥamdānids, who were overthrown by the Marwānids in 380/990–991, and it enjoyed a further period of cultural efflorescence under the long and illustrious reign of the Marwānid Naṣr-ad-Dawla (401/1011–483/1061). Yaḥyā's brother, al-Faḍl ibn-Jarīr, served as the physician of Naṣr-ad-Dawla (Ibn-Abī-Uṣaybiʿa I,243), and in all likelihood Yaḥyā moved to Mayyāfāriqīn together with his brother, where he stayed and worked also through the reign of Naṣr-ad-Dawla's successor, his son Niẓām-ad-Dīn (453/1061–472/1079). It was during the rule of Niẓām-ad-Dīn that Yaḥyā copied our manuscript, and it is interesting to note that Ibn-Abī-Uṣaybiʿa gives this ruler's date of death as the year through which Yaḥyā was known

[1] For this, his major surviving work, see Mouawad 1997, with further references.

[2] For the Marwānids see, most conveniently, the article by C. Hillenbrand in *EI*², VI,626–627.

to have lived. We do not know whether this coincidence is significant for the date of Yaḥyā's own death and his relation with Niẓām-ad-Dīn.

The fact that the manuscript contains also al-Fārābī's *Principles* (*Mabādi'*), a work that was completed in Damascus towards the end of his life in 943, points to its probable provenance. At that time al-Fārābī had left Baghdad and lived in Syria, where he died, as his biographers say, in 339/950–951 "under the protection" of Sayf-ad-Dawla, the Ḥamdānid ruler at Aleppo. Since the Marwānids were, in essence, the successors of the Ḥamdānids in the area and particularly in Mayyāfāriqīn, and adherents (and inheritors?) of their cultural policies, it stands to reason that manuscripts both by al-Fārābī himself and in his possession would be available and accessible, after his death, not only in Damascus and Aleppo but also in Mayyāfāriqīn. It is accordingly most probable that the Essay by Theophrastus, just like al-Fārābī's *Principles* (*Mabādi'*), came ultimately from the library of al-Fārābī himself. It is known that al-Fārābī started his *Principles* in Baghdad but finished it in Damascus;[3] which means that when he moved from Baghdad to Damascus after the end of 330/September 942, he carried with him his library, or at least some portion of it. Theophrastus's Essay, as translated in Baghdad by Isḥāq ibn-Ḥunayn, was among these books.

Yaḥyā ibn-Jarīr twice tells us in his colophon that the exemplar from which he copied Theophrastus's Essay was corrupt, "very" corrupt. It is not entirely clear whether "corrupt," *saqīm*, literally "diseased," refers to the physical state of the manuscript—i.e., torn or worm-ridden—or to the state of the text in it, error-ridden. The former seems more probable, given that some of the omissions in the text are in all probability due to a physically defective exemplar. There are certainly numerous places in the text where the mistake is clearly due to defects in the Arabic writing, and obvious corrections can be made on the basis of the Greek (see the apparatus of the Arabic edition). In some cases, however, these mistakes occur in clusters, where it would appear that there may have been some sort of physical damage to the exemplar in those places; e.g., section 9b20–21, where there are three important omissions (see below, section 2). If that is the case, then it is almost certain that the exemplar of T, a manuscript affiliated with al-Fārābī, was an old copy from Baghdad, transcribed in the circle of the Baghdad Aristotelians to whom al-Fārābī belonged. It was thus very close to Isḥāq's autograph, its

[3] For the details of al-Fārābī's life at the end of his life and his literary activities see my article on his biography in *EIr*. IX,210a.

direct provenance from which can hardly be disputed. That the exemplar of T was in al-Fārābī's possession means that he had read it, and it remains to be investigated whether an echo of it can be found in his writings. The same applies to the scholar scribe, Yaḥyā ibn-Jarīr, despite the fact that he does not indicate in his colophon that he had copied it for himself (*li-nafsihī*).

The second manuscript,

B Oxford, Bodleian, Ouseley 95, ff. 92ᵛ–95ᵛ, is part of a larger miscellany (*majmūʿa*) of philosophical treatises, written in a beautiful Persian *taʿlīq*, almost fully provided with diacritical points. It is not dated, but it is written in Ṣafavid times and can be dated ca. 1630 AD.[4] It is unfortunate that it has been destroyed apparently by book worms, so that all the pages are torn obliquely with very few lines surviving intact; as a result, about half of the text is missing (cf. Margoliouth 1892, 192). The loss, however, hardly matters, for it is quite certain that this manuscript (B) was copied, through an intermediary, from the Tehran manuscript (T), for the following reasons.

First, that B derives from T, whether directly or at some remove, is indicated by the following:

(1) B also omits the first paragraph and a half of the text and begins in the middle of a sentence with exactly the same words as T, *minhā munfaṣilun*. If B was copied from an exemplar that derived from a manuscript other than T, then it will have to be assumed against all odds that T and that other manuscript finished the first page of the text at exactly the same place independetly of each other, and that the opening page of that manuscripts was also lost.

(2) At 8a26, the name of Euripides is spelled with exactly the same skeletal text (*rasm*) in both manuscripts: اورسوسس. Not only are all the ridges after the *rāʾ* and after the second *wāw* the same, despite the lack of diacritics—something difficult to achieve even in direct copying—but the two transcriptions also share the same mistake, writing a second *wāw* towards the end of the name instead of the original *dāl* or *ḏāl*.

[4] See the description of the manuscript in E. Sachau and H. Ethé, *Catalogue of the Persian, Turkish, Hindûstânî, and Pushtû Manuscripts in the Bodleian Library*, Oxford: The Clarendon Press, 1889, 865 and 871, no. 1422.

(3) At 11a23, T has السربف for الشريف, but writes the *sīn* (*šīn*) in a peculiar way, doubtless due to the scribe's momentary carelessness: the first of the three ridges of the *sīn* is written much taller than the other two, thus giving the impression that the first ridge constitutes a different letter from the following two. B reproduces this as التشريف, interpreting the first ridge, justifiably, as a *tā'*, but failing to see (or disregarding) that the following ridges are two, not three, and do not constitute a *sīn* or *šīn*.

(4) At 11b15 T has هذه, but the initial هـ is written in a way that the first downward stroke of the letter goes straight down rather than at a slant and it is not later met at the top of the letter by the upward stroke to close the circle, so that that first downward stroke can look like a بـ, while the loop on the left side of the letter looks accordingly as a separate letter, in fact like ـعـ or ـفـ. Thus the reading in B for هذه comes out as بعده, a misreading that could have occurred only in a copy made from this particular manuscript (T).

(5) Finally, at 11b6 T writes كانها but the initial *kāf* is written without the top bar and with the loop of the *kāf* more closed than open so that it is possible to misread it as a *fā'* or *qāf*, which is how B read it for he writes, فانها. In all of these cases the mistranscription is due to the peculiarities of the particular manuscript T, and not to normal copying errors in Arabic manuscripts.

Second, B does not seem to derive directly from T but through at least one intermediary.

(1) At 11b8 T writes بصمون for يضيفون. Although the loop of the *fā'* is written slightly above the line and the line connecting it with the previous letter is slightly longer than normal, the letter is still recognisable as a *rasm* of *fā'*/*qāf*. But B writes بصعمون, misreading the letter as an *'ayn*. Though one can understand why the misreading has occurred, it still cannot be justified on the basis of T, so it seems plausible that there was an intermediary that caused the error.

(2) More significantly, at 6b10, T writes, ان سن without diacritics for ان يبين. B misreads this as ان من, which is unwarranted on the basis of T, for the three ridges in سن cannot be misread as a *mīm*. There accordingly must have been at least one intermediary where the three ridges were transcribed in a way that could evoke a *mīm*.

(3) Finally, B, or the intermediary, was copying the text of T only, without the marginal material. The few explanatory additions in the margins of T are not included in B, and neither is the marginal correction of the text at 4b11b.

It is thus established that the Bodleian manuscript (B) derives from the Tehran manuscript (T) through at least one intermediary. This makes it impossible for B to carry any independent readings, but the fact that the Arabic skeletal text is pointed throughout is useful in determining the readings in T and the extent to which the scribe understood what he was copying.

By the same token, the Bodleian manuscript cannot inform us about the title of the Essay; not only does it derive from T, and hence has no independent information to offer, but is itself mutilated and the colophon, if there was one, is missing. The scribe of B just added at the beginning of the text as title, *Maqāla li-Ṯāwufrasṭus*, *Essay by Theophrastus*, which indicates that he took the name of the author from the colophon in T and its copy.

2. *The Arabic Translation*

The Arabic translation is of high quality, indicative of the translator's competence and familiarity with the subject matter. The relatively frequent inaccuracies in the translation are partly due to mistakes in the Greek exemplar upon which it is based, and partly to the difficulty of the text. All in all, the translation is accurate and quite faithful, and it helps establish the Greek text in a number of places, as discussed above in Chapter 2.2.

At the same time, the Arabic translation differs from the Greek text as we have it in certain ways which have to be properly described and assessed. In the first place, as mentioned in Chapter 2.2 above, the Arabic translation is based on a Greek manuscript (Ψ) that derives from a different transliteration from uncials than that which formed the exemplar of the extant Greek manuscripts. The textual differences between the Greek text and the Arabic translation that derive from this fact were analyzed above; this feature makes the Arabic translation an indispensable witness for the establishment of the Greek text.

Second, other discrepancies between the Greek text as we have it and the Arabic translation have different sources: some are additions and others omissions. Minor additions of a few words (there are no major insertions of extraneous material in this brief Essay) are as a rule glosses and explanatory remarks with reference to a particular word or sentence in the text. The origin of these glosses is not insignificant. The Essay was translated in Baghdad, by a scholar who was close to the Aristotelian school, on the basis of a lost Greek manuscript about whose origins we have no information. It is likely that this Greek manuscript itself may have carried some marginal glosses, or that some of the scholars in Baghdad who first studied this treatise added their own comments, or finally that even the scribe himself, Yaḥyā ibn-Jarīr, who was educated in the same tradition, may have been responsible for some of them. These glosses occur in the following passages: 4b6, 5a13, 5b27, 8a10, 11b5, 11b6. The first two are marginal, the last four have been inserted into the text; they are all translated in the notes to these passages.

Third, minor omissions of a word or two may be either accidental, having occurred either in the Greek or the Arabic tradition, or deliberate, on the part of the translator; their precise nature has to be assessed because of their potential interest to the establishment of the Greek text. The guidelines and principles on the basis of which these minor discrepancies are to be registered in the Greek and Arabic apparatuses are described in detail in the methodological Excursus at the end of Part I.

Finally, there are a few omissions of some length in the Arabic translation. The origins of such omissions are notoriously difficult to assess. They (1) may have already been present in the Greek exemplar of the Arabic translation; (2) the translator himself may have been responsible for them either (a) by accidentally skipping a line or a phrase as he was translating, or (b) by deliberately not translating a sentence or phrase, for a variety of reasons; and finally, (3) even if the text was translated faithfully, some sentences or phrases may have fallen out accidentally in the course of the transmission within the Arabic tradition. Assessing in which category an omission belongs is significant for the way in which and where it will be recorded. Case (1) is of significance for the establishment of the Greek text in one way and of the Arabic text in another. A verifiable omission in a Greek manuscript that is no longer extant—as is the case with all Greek texts translated into Arabic—may be significant evidence that the phrase or sentence in question was itself an addition in the Greek tradition and not part of the author's original text; it is therefore imperative that it be recorded in the Greek apparatus. By the same token, such an omission in the Greek exemplar of a translation signifies that the Arabic text itself from the very beginning lacked that passage and hence was integral without it; that is, in trying to edit the translation and reconstruct the text as it left the pen of the translator, that particular passage plays no role and hence cannot be considered as a lacuna *in the Arabic text*; if at all, it will be recorded in an Arabic apparatus only for the purposes of comparison of the two texts and not of the establishment of the Arabic text. Cases (2) and (3), by contrast, do not concern the establishment of the Greek text, though in different ways, relatively and absolutely. Case (3) does not absolutely, for obvious reasons: the fact that some Arabic scribe neglected to copy a phrase or two of a text that was an accurate and complete translation of the Greek original is of no interest to the Greek editor. In case (2a), however—in cases, that is, of accidental omissions—there is almost never any certainty that the line or phrase accidentally omitted by the translator was also not missing from the Greek exemplar (for very much the same reasons of haplography, homoeoteleuton, etc.). This uncertainty makes it necessary, for the sake of completeness, to record that omission in the Greek apparatus so that it may be compared with similar omissions, if they exist, in the extant Greek manuscripts of the work. Case (2b), on the other hand, is of no interest to the Greek editor—for it does not say anything about the Greek text, which was fully present in the translator's exemplar, but only about his decision not to, or inability to, translate the pasage in question—except for comparative purposes. Also for comparative and not textual purposes are of interest to the Arabic editor both cases (2a) and (2b); for regardless whether the omissions occurred by accident or design, the fact is that the Arabic text that was produced by the translator did not have those passages, and hence its reconstitution in the edition need not take them into consideration. Case (3), by contrast, though of no use to the Greek editor, as mentioned, is central to the Arabic apparatus and should be dutifully recorded.

In this treatise there are eight cases of such omissions, briefly listed below; the details of their occurrence are discussed fully in the commentary.

1) 6b25–26, the words ὥσπερ ὅσοι πῦρ καὶ γῆν ἢ μεμορφωμένας are not translated at all, the omission being manifestly due to a homoeoarcton: somebody skipped in the Greek text from ὥσπερ in line 6b25 to ὡς in line 6b26. This was either the scribe of the Greek manuscript from which the translation was made (Ψ, or possibly one of his predecessors), or the translator himself as he was reading the manuscript. The omission is an example of case (1) or (2a) above.

2) 8b27, the words ἢ ἐξ ἀμφοῖν εἰσὶ δ' were omitted either in the Greek exemplar Ψ, or by the translator as he was reading it, by haplography: someone skipped from δ' before ἢ ἐξ to δ' before ἔνιαι. This is also an example of an omission in case (1) or (2a) above.

3) 9a16–17, the Arabic words corresponding to ἔχει δὲ καὶ … τὰ μαθήματα were omitted by a scribe in the Arabic tradition, who skipped from the word *at-taʿālīm* to *at-taʿālīm* in *fī t-taʿālīm ⟨ayḍan fa-inna li-t-taʿālīm⟩ anfusihā ḫtilāfan*. A proper lacuna in the Arabic text, it represents case (3) above.

4) 9b20–21, the words καὶ περὶ τὰς ἔτι προτέρας were translated but dropped out in subsequent Arabic tradition because of an omission by homoeoteleuton; they are easily restored: *ʿilmu umūri ṭ-ṭabīʿati ⟨wa-ʿilmu mā qabla ṭ-ṭabīʿati⟩*. This is another example of a proper lacuna in the Arabic text, as in case (3) above.

5) 10a10–12, the translation of the words τοῦ οὐρανοῦ … καθ' ἕκαστον was omitted in the Arabic tradition; see the discussion of the details of this omission in the commentary. This is also a proper lacuna in the Arabic text, and another example of case (3) above.

6) 10b8–9, the words καὶ τοῖς θήλεσιν ἡ πρόεσις εἴπερ μὴ συμβάλλεται, on female emission, were not translated. There is no break in the Arabic syntax, which would suggest that the omission was deliberate, either because of the difficulty of the passage or, though less likely, because of the sensitivity of the subject. This is an example of case (2b) above.

7) 10b13–16, the longish passage, καὶ ὡς ἔνια δὴ … λάβοι τις ἂν τοιαῦτα, consists of a few more examples of apparent purposelessness in animal life. There is again no break in the Arabic syntax, and the omission appears to be deliberate, most likely on account of the difficulty of the technical terms involved, in addition to the fact that the philosophical point about teleology had already been made. This is yet another example of case (2b) above.

8) 11a11–12, the words καὶ ἐν τῇ μέσῃ κοιλίᾳ τῆς καρδίας τὴν κρᾶσιν ἀρίστην ὅτι τὸ μέσον τιμιώτατον are missing in Arabic. This is a difficult case to call, for theoretically the omission could have occurred both in

the Greek and Arabic tradition. For reasons discussed in the note to the translation, it appears more likely that it was deliberate on the part of the translator, and thus an example of case (2b).

The results of this analysis of the differences between the Greek text and the Arabic translation have been entered accordingly in the critical apparatuses of the two texts.

3. *The Translator, Isḥāq Ibn-Ḥunayn*

Concerning the identity of the translator, the ascriptions are not unanimous. The scribe of the Tehran manuscript, Yaḥyā ibn-Jarīr, explicitly ascribes it in the colophon to Isḥāq ibn-Ḥunayn (d. 910–911; see *EI*[2] IV,110), as cited above. In his *Index*, however, which was completed in 987, Ibn-an-Nadīm says (*Fihrist* 252.9, fr. 3A FHS&G) that the translation was made by Yaḥyā ibn-ʿAdī (d. 974; see *EI*[2] XI,245), the Aristotelian scholarch in Baghdad, a statement to which the great Syriac scholar Bar-Hebraeus (d. 1286) later added that the translation was done from Syriac into Arabic (fr. 3B FHS&G). Now the evidence in the colophon of the manuscript should be decisive, especially in the case of this manuscript which, as discussed above, descends from an exemplar in all probability copied some time in the tenth century in Baghdad in the Aristotelian circles frequented by al-Fārābī. On the other hand, Ibn-an-Nadīm received his information about philosophical manuscripts and translations from Yaḥyā ibn-ʿAdī himself, and his authority cannot be easily impugned. The two ascriptions need not necessarily be in conflict, though, insofar as Isḥāq could have translated it in the first place and Ibn-an-Nadīm's report could mean either that Yaḥyā ibn-ʿAdī revised Isḥāq's translation or that he, Ibn-an-Nadīm, heard of or possessed a copy of Theophrastus's Essay from the library of Yaḥyā ibn-ʿAdī. In this case, however, the evidence provided by Bar-Hebraeus, that Yaḥyā's translation was done from the Syriac, cannot stand, for that would mean that Isḥāq translated the Greek text into Syriac and Yaḥyā the Syriac text into Arabic, whereas in the colophon the scribe ascribes to Isḥāq the *Arabic* translation which he has just finished copying. Since the evidence provided by the scribe, Yaḥyā ibn-Jarīr, must trump all others, it is most likely that the translation was transmitted as just described: Isḥāq ibn-Ḥunayn made the translation into Arabic from the Greek, and this translation became current in the circles of the Baghdad Aristotelians where al-Fārābī found it and acquired a copy. Yaḥyā ibn-ʿAdī, the scholarch of the Aristotelians after al-Fārābī's departure from Baghdad in mid-tenth century, either corrected or most likely "edited" or "published" the text, and Ibn-an-Nadīm learned about it on the authority of Yaḥyā ibn-ʿAdī and inaccurately reported it as having been translated by Yaḥyā. As both Isḥāq and Yaḥyā ibn-ʿAdī are known to have translated books of Aristotle's *Metaphysics*,[5] they doubtless found the Greek text in the Greek manuscript(s) of the Aristotelian work which would have included, as discussed in Chapter 1.2, also the Essay by Theophrastus.

The stylistic pecularities of the translation provide additional corroboration that it came from the pen of Isḥāq ibn-Ḥunayn. It is true that, in general, we are far from the stage where we can distinguish with absolute certainty, on this basis, between the styles of Isḥāq and Yaḥyā ibn-ʿAdī. It is also true that very few translations by Yaḥyā are extant; however, in this particular case the following indications appear to be conclusive.

Isḥāq ibn-Ḥunayn was arguably the most accomplished translator of Greek philosophical texts, and Yaḥyā was active at a time when the translation movement was winding down and coming to an end; accordingly the translations had reached a high level of accuracy, sophistication, and consistency in technical terminology. Under these circumstances, it becomes difficult to argue conclusively about identities of translators on the basis of words chosen to translate technical terms. The assumption must be, and given the ubiquitous practice of later scholars of revising or "touching up" earlier translations, that such terminology would be similar enough and flexible enough as to make definite pronouncements about the identity of the translator inadvisable. What remains is to analyze the way in which some very common, functional, words are translated and seek to identify turns of Arabic phrase that may be unique to a translator. That said, we can have a look at Aristotle's *Sophistics*, almost the one work which we know for certain to have been translated by Yaḥyā ibn-ʿAdī, and the *Physics*, a work translated beyond the shadow of a doubt by Isḥāq.

The word ἴσως (perhaps) occurs eight times in the *Sophistics*. In four of these Yaḥyā consistently translates it with *ʿasā* (175b23, 180a14, 181b32, 33), once with *laʿalla* (179b26), once literally, *ʿalā l-musāwāt* (170b21), and twice he does not translate it at all (170a22, 180a16). In the Arabic translation of the *Physics*, Isḥāq translates the word in a number of ways, depending on the context, but most frequently by *ḫalīqun an* (185b11,

[5] See the detailed discussion in Bertolacci 2005, 270, and *passim*.

200b4, 202b33, 212b18, 224b15, 228a15, 231a16, 241b15, 253a15, 261b12) and *aḫlaqu bi-* (217a8, 252b31). By contrast, he uses *ʿasā* only once (256b12) and *laʿalla* only twice (202a22, 229a29), *rubba-mā* once (223b7) and, characteristically, also *fī-mā aḥsibu* (238b9, 253a13). In the Essay by Theophrastus, ἴσως occurs four times, in one of which (6a6) it is not translated at all, and in the other three it is translated by *aḫlaqu bi-* (4b13), *ḫalīqun an* (8a3), and *fī-mā aḥsibu* (6a12). The close correspondence between the idiom of Isḥāq in the *Physics* and the translator of the Essay is obvious. Particularly noteworthy is the use of the expression *fī-mā aḥsibu* ("as I reckon") to render ἴσως. It is a brilliant rendering, and also uncommon, in that it gives not the strict lexical meaning of the word but its sense in the particular context. I am not sure whether this rendering of ἴσως is unique to Isḥāq, but in this case it points to the identicalness of the translator of both the *Physics* and Theophrastus's Essay.

A similar conclusion is obtained from a consideration of the translation of the word μάλιστα. Yaḥyā ibn-ʿAdī translates it essentially in two ways in the *Sophistics*. The first is the painfully literal, but in the Arabic context rather barbaric expression, *akṯara*, "more" or "most" (165b18, 176b27,[6] 182b32 and 33, 182b38 twice; *kaṯīran* 169a33); the second is the generic *ḫāṣṣatan* (169a35, 172b13, 174b9,[7] 176a26, 176b21). In only one case does Yaḥyā use a more elegant construction to express the sense of the word, translating μάλιστα δριμύς with the elative only, *aḥaddu* (183a3). The procedure adopted by Yaḥyā in translating μάλιστα in this way is understandable. Since he was translating from a Syriac translation of *Sophistici Elenchi* and not from the Greek,[8] he was bound by the choices that had been made by the Syriac translator, and hence he translated mechanically the Syriac term with the same Arabic word in each occurrence; in other words, he did not have the possibility to express the nuances of the use of the word that a Greek context would have given him. But this is precisely what we see in Isḥāq's translation of the *Physics*, where he renders the word μάλιστα in a variety of ways, always sensitive to its meaning in context. First, Isḥāq never uses plain *akṯara* to translate it, but in the few places where he does use this elative form, he uses it either in the expression *akṯaru mā* (197b32, 199b30, 203b22), or *akṯara*

---

6 With the word *ḫāṣṣatan* added here above the line in the Paris manuscript which has preserved the Arabic translations of the *Sophistics*.

7 It is interesting to note that in these three passages just referred to, somebody wrote *akṯara* above the word *ḫāṣṣatan* in the Paris manuscript.

8 The Syriac translation was made, we are told by Ibn-an-Nadīm (*Fihrist* 249.27), by Theophilus of Edessa (d. 785), the court astrologer of the caliph al-Mahdī (775–785).

followed by the *maf'ūl muṭlaq* of the word modified by μάλιστα (199a20, 262a12). Second, other than these uses of *akṯar*, Isḥāq does not use only *ḫāṣṣatan* (198a11, 204a1, etc.), like Yaḥyā, but numerous other ways to translate μάλιστα. In both these aspects the translator of Theophrastus's Essay does the same: he never uses *akṯara* and he always translates according to sense. The following instances show the identical procedures in the translation of the *Physics* and in the Essay. In a few places, Isḥāq translates μάλιστα in the *Physics* with *awlā bi-* (265a5, 267b4) and *aḥaqqu bi-* (247b2); the translator of the Essay also uses *awlā bi-* (5b9, 11b17), and in one place even *aḥaqqu wa-awlā bi-* in hendiadys (6b26). Second, noteworthy is the extremely innovative but accurate rendering of the difficult expression ὅτι μάλιστα in the two translations: With *Physics* 205b6 ὅτι μάλιστα μὴ κινεῖται τὸ ὅλον = *ab'ad al-mawāḍi' min an tataḥarraka ilayhi jumlatun* (p. 244 Badawī), and *Physics* 210b13 ὥστ' εἰ ὅτι μάλιστα ἐν ἀλλήλοις εἶεν = *fa-in kāna qad yajūzu bi-wajhin mina l-wujūhi an yakūna kullu wāḥidin minhumā fī ṣāḥibihī* (p. 295 Badawī), compare the Essay 8a4, ὅτι μάλιστα σύμφωνον ἑαυτῷ = ⟨*fī*⟩ *ġāyati mā yumkinu an takūna 'alayhi mina l-ittifāqi*. Similarly note the similarity in rendering the superlatives with *aḥaqqu bi-* in *Physics* 223b19, (ἡ κυκλοφορία ἡ ὁμαλὴς) μέτρον μάλιστα = *fa-aḥaqqu l-ḥarakāti bi-an takūna al-muqaddirata* (*l-ḥarakatu 'alā l-istidārati l-mustawiyati*) (p. 479 Badawī), and in the Essay 6a1 τὸ θειότατον = *aḥaqqu l-ašyā'i bi-annahū llāhu*.

From this comparison there clearly results that the translators of the *Sophistics* on the one hand and of the *Physics* and Theophrastus's Essay on the other were two different people, and if Yaḥyā ibn-'Adī was the translator of the *Sophistics*, then he could not have been the translator of the other two. There also results that if Isḥāq was the translator of the *Physics* then it is highly probable that he was also responsible for the translation of Theophrastus's Essay. This probability comes close to being certainty in such cases when it is noted that some other peculiarities of expression, or mannerisms, in the *Physics* translation are also present in the translation of the Essay. The first is the habit of Isḥāq on occasion to introduce a direct or, mostly, indirect question with the Arabic expression, *layta ši'rī*, "I wish I knew." From the relative frequency and casualness of its use in the *Physics* translation—casual in the sense that the Greek text has no word or structure indicating urgency in the question that is being asked—it would seem that the expression had lost its strict literal meaning and was used as a question marker in the Arabic of Isḥāq's Baghdad. Thus, for example, Isḥāq uses it in *Physics* 185b12 and 203b32 to translate questions introduced by πότερον ... ἤ and ποτέρως (pp. 13 and 214 respectively), and in 185a22 and 215a6 to translate questions introduced by πῶς (pp. 10 and 362 Badawī, respectively). The same use of *layta šiʿrī* is also seen in the translation of the Essay by Theophrastus, marking questions introduced by ἀξιώσειεν ἄν (6a16), ἆρα (10a16), and πόθεν (10a24).[9]

Another mannerism is Isḥāq's habit of adding the word *aʿnī*, "I mean," when he introduces subordinate clauses, explanatory or parenthetical phrases, or attributive phrases following a noun in the Greek, when they run the risk of being misunderstood if rendered paratactically in Arabic. For example, *Physics* 252a19–21, διόπερ βέλτιον ὡς Ἐμπεδοκλῆς ... ἐν μέρει τὸ πᾶν ἠρεμεῖν καὶ κινεῖσθαι πάλιν = *fa-inna qawla Anbāduqlis ... ajwadu, aʿnī anna l-kulla yaskunu marratan ṯumma yataḥarraku* (p. 814 Badawī); and *Physics* 234a19–20, ἀνάγκη τὸ αὐτὸ εἶναι τὸ ἐν ἑκατέρῳ νῦν = *fa-wājibun an yakūna l-āna wāḥidan bi-ʿaynihī, aʿnī l-āna llaḏī fī kulli wāḥidin minhumā* (p. 640 Badawī); etc. This use of *aʿnī* is also quite frequent in the translation of the Essay by Theophrastus (7a16, 7a21, 7b20, 8a8, 8a22, 8b12, 9b14, 10b24, 11a5). This particular mannerism may not be unique to Isḥāq, for it is also encountered in the earlier translator of *De caelo*, Yaḥyā ibn-al-Biṭrīq (see *GALex* I, p. 17*), but it appears not to have been common among translators of Isḥāq's generation and later.

Finally another rendering that is common to the translations of both the *Physics* and Theophrastus's Essay is the term ἄλογον, translated as *ġayr munqās*, "unreasonable." This is an unusual rendering, and indeed one that Isḥāq uses only once in the *Physics* (255a10) although the Greek term itself occurs frequently enough, but it also occurs in the Essay at 7a10 and later, in the form *laysa bi-munqās*, to translate μὴ ἔχειν λόγον at 10b25. Apart from the startling occurrence of this unusual term in the two translations, its derivation also bespeaks an advanced stage in the development of technical terminology. Since λόγος was usually translated also with the word *qiyās*, Isḥāq—if it was Isḥāq who first thought of using *munqās* in this connection—thought that he would use a word in Arabic etymologically deriving from the same root as *qiyās*, just

---

[9] Ullmann in *WGAÜ* 552 registers two more uses of *layta šiʿrī* in the translation of Themistius's paraphrase of the *De anima*; this is as it should be, for all indications are that this work also was translated by Isḥāq. However, the evidence collected here indicates that *layta šiʿrī* does not properly translate enclitic ποτε, as Ullmann has it, but simply introduces the questions that follow in the text.

as ἄλογον derives from λόγος in Greek. He thus used *munqās* ("logos-ed," i.e., reason-ed, reasonable), the participle of the passive verbal form *infaʿala*, together with a negative.

The whole question of the identity of the translators of individual Greek works during the Graeco-Arabic translation movement remains a thorny and difficult field, not yet fully researched, though significant advances have recently been made.[10] Under these circumstances, the evidence collected here indicating that the translator of Theophrastus's Essay was indeed Isḥāq ibn-Ḥunayn makes the identification as certain as can be achieved at present.

4. *Editions of the Arabic Text*

1) Margoliouth. The article by Margoliouth 1892 was the first to study the Arabic translation, only about half of which was available to him in the damaged Bodleian manuscript; the Tehran manuscript was not discovered until much later. Margoliouth's purpose in this article was to introduce, edit, and translate a Persian version of the *Book of the Apple* (*Kitāb at-tuffāḥa*) from the Bodleian manuscript, which also contains the Essay by Theophrastus, so his interest in the latter was only incidental. In the introduction he devoted a few pages (192–201) to the work, in which he presented a transcription of a whole passage (11a1–11b1) and numerous other sentences for the purpose, primarily, of assessing the value of the Arabic translation for the establishment of the Greek text. In a few places his readings and suggestions for the text are accurate and have been adopted (indicated in the apparatus), while his critical comments have been referred to in the commentary. But in several other places his transcription is inaccurate or wrong, given the deficient manuscript from which he was working. These need not clutter the Arabic apparatus, for they contribute nothing to the establishment of the text, but are listed in a separate apparatus in Part II at the end of the Arabic text and facing English translation.

2) Alon. The first complete edition of the Arabic translation, based on both extant manuscripts, was offered by Alon 1985 in an article that

[10] Cf. *GALex* I, p. 9*, and the reviews of *WGAÜ* by P. Pormann in the *Journal of the Royal Asiatic Society* 13 (2003) 105–107, and by O. Overwien in *Bulletin Critique des Annales Islamologiques* 20 (2004) 130–132.

drew upon his doctoral dissertation. Alon's edition is very uneven. At times he offers valuable readings and suggestions for corrections, though almost always without indicating that he is altering the manuscript readings; and at other times his text contains numerous serious mistakes in transcription,[11] omissions, and inaccurate information about manuscript readings. These also need not clutter the main Arabic apparatus and have been listed in the separate apparatus at the end of the Arabic text and English translation.

Whenever I accepted one of Alon's corrections of a faulty reading in the Arabic manuscripts because it was consonant with the translator's practice and the Greek text, I took the liberty, following my practice, of indicating in parenthesis next to the corrected reading in the apparatus the reading of the Greek text on whose basis this correction is warranted, even if Alon himself did not make such an explicit justification for the correction. Thus at 10a10 Alon reads *ḫāṣṣatan* (p. 200, translated as "especially," p. 214) instead of the manuscript reading *ḫāṣṣiyya*. Alon's reading is correct because it translates καὶ μάλιστα, as it does on an earlier occasion at 9b19. I note this in the apparatus in parentheses next to his correction, although Alon has no note about it but only a vague reference to the following lacuna without even specifying its extent or exact location in the text.

3) Crubellier. The publication of the 1992 article by Crubellier marked an advance in the study of the contribution the Arabic translation could make to the establishment of the Greek text. In this study, undertaken in conjunction with the preparation of a new edition of the Greek text by Laks & Most, Crubellier offered a close translation of the Arabic text with copious notes explaining the Arabic translation and offering corrections and emendations. Many of these contributions to the history of the Greek text found their way in the apparatus criticus of Laks & Most under the siglum "Isḥāq"[12] or, when "Isḥāq" agreed with all the Greek manuscripts, under the siglum of **ω**. I refer to Crubellier's article with the siglum Crub.[1]

[11] Such mistakes were not without consequences. For example, Alon's mistranscription *munqasiman* for the reading *munfasiḫan* attested in the manuscript at 5a4b led Pines (in Alon 1985, 186n24) to conjecture unnecessarily a reading of λέγοιτο for the actual λύοιτο in the Greek text.

[12] For the inadequacy of this siglum, because it covers a number of discrete phenomena, see section III in the Excursus and note 11.

At the same time Crubellier had prepared the draft of a new edition of the Arabic translation, which he most generously placed at my disposal (see the Preface). I have gratefully benefited from this draft edition, to which I refer with the siglum Crub.[2]

5. *The Present Edition and Translation of the Arabic Text*

The Arabic edition aims to reproduce, to the extent possible, the state of the text as established by the translator in order to derive maximum benefit in divining the readings of its Greek exemplar, Ψ. The procedure that has been followed is described in the Excursus on Graeco-Arabic editorial technique at the end of Part One.

In the edition of the Arabic text, the enumeration of the lines with small raised numbers follows that of the Greek text. Since Greek and Arabic syntax are different and do not follow the same word order, the following guidelines have been adopted in order to reduce arbitrariness in assigning the line numbers. Normally, the line number is placed before the Arabic word translating the first complete Greek word in that line (divided words in the Greek are included in the line in which they start). If, because of the requirements of Arabic syntax, that word is integrated in the sentence of the preceding or following line, then the line number is placed before the second full word of the line. In cases where this happens with more than two or three words, then the line numbering is split into two segments (in exceptional cases three) identified with a and b (and c in the exceptional case) after the number of the line. This is a general rule of thumb which it may not have been possible to apply absolutely consistently. But on balance, and despite the somewhat distracting presence of the numbers inside the text, this procedure appeared less cumbersome and infinitely less confusing than introducing yet another set of numbers to refer to the lines of the Arabic translation. As it is, the reader can identify on the spot the precise passage that corresponds to the Greek text because it bears precisely the same number.

The critical apparatus accompanying the Arabic text is positive. With only one, essentially, manuscript at our disposal for the establishment of the text, it has been possible to give full documentation of all the evidence in the apparatus without unduly cluttering it. In practice, and with regard to diacritical points, which are almost entirely absent in T, this means that in all instances in which even a slight doubt existed about the reading of a word lacking its diacritics, the skeletal form of that word, as well as the reading offered in B, have been fully recorded. In the case of the personal prefixes of verbs in the imperfect, variants between the two manuscripts and among editors due to the pointing of the third person masculine and feminine, and first person plural, have been mentioned only when absolutely crucial for the meaning. Meritorious suggestions and readings offered by earlier editors have also been recorded, while the obvious errors in the transcripts of Margoliouth and Alon are listed in the supplementary apparatus at the end of the Arabic edition and English translation.

Given the nature of the mistakes in a manuscript that are due to the peculiarities of Arabic writing, it is important to discriminate among them and register them differently in the apparatus. These are, to list them by their Arabic name, (a) *taḥrīf*, mistakes due to a miswritten skeleton (*rasm*), whose correction is indicated in the apparatus by writing "corr(ected by)," or "corr(ection in)"; (b) *taṣḥīf*, mistakes due to different pointing of the same skeleton, indicated in the apparatus by writing "read(ing by or in)"; and (c) *taḥrīk*, variants due to different vowel signs placed on the same skeleton with the identical pointing, indicated in the apparatus by "voc(alization by or in)".

On occasion it has been possible to correct the Arabic text on the basis of the Greek. In such cases, it is clear that the suggested emendation or reading, which constituted a translation of the text as it appeared in the Greek exemplar, Ψ, existed in the translator's autograph but that it was corrupted in the process of the Arabic transmission. These emendations are registered with an asterisk (*) following the name of the scholar who made them, itself followed in parentheses by the Greek word(s) justifying the emendation.

The English translation of the Arabic text tries to be literal without sacrificing intelligibility. In places where the Greek and Arabic say exactly the same thing, an attempt has been made to render the Arabic text with the same words as the Greek, to make meaningful the comparison of the two translations. The translation is also heavily annotated. This semed preferable to both adding a second commentary for the Arabic text alone and to incorporating the Arabic notes into the Greek commentary. The notes discuss every deviation of the Arabic from the Greek as well as any other peculiarity of the translation in order to explain the choices that I made for the readings of Ψ that I registered in the Greek apparatus criticus.

EXCURSUS

PRINCIPLES OF GRAECO-ARABIC TEXTUAL CRITICISM AND EDITORIAL TECHNIQUE

Establishing the Arabic Edition and the Greek Apparatus

The edition of the Arabic translation of Theophrastus's *On First Principles* (or the Arabic translation of any classical Greek text) contains the following parts: (**a**) a critical edition of the Arabic translation; (**b**) apparatus criticus for the Arabic text; (**c**) apparatus criticus for the Greek text, containing information for the Greek text that is gained from the Arabic edition; (**d**) English translation of the Arabic translation; (**e**) philological commentary on the details of the Graeco-Arabic translation; (**f**) Greek-Arabic and Arabic-Greek glossaries. The purpose of each part and what it ought to contain are briefly described below.

1. *Stages in the Transmission of Texts*

The Arabic translation of *On First Principles* (or of any classical Greek text) represents three different stages in the transmission of the text which have to be kept separate if the Arabic edition can be of use to the establishment of the Greek text. Starting with the known and proceeding to the unknown, we have:

(1) *Extant manuscripts*. The Arabic text of the translation as found in the extant manuscripts (in this case, manuscripts T and B). These all derive ultimately from the translator's autograph, or final clean copy. They contain, however, numerous variations from that autograph or clean copy which are due to mistakes, misreadings, miscopyings, omissions, inclusions, interpolations, etc., that occurred in the process of the transmission of the text *within* the Arabic tradition. The purpose of the Arabic apparatus (**b**) is to register the appropriate information which these manuscripts contain.

(2) *The translator's autograph or clean copy*. This is not physically extant, but since all the extant manuscripts derive from it, it is possible to reconstruct it to the extent allowable by the evidence provided in the manuscripts and the Greek text. The purpose of the Arabic edition of the text (**a**) is to reproduce, to the extent possible, the text as it stood in the translator's autograph or clean copy.

(3) *The Greek exemplar used by the translator*, also not extant. This is the manuscript on the basis of which the translation was made (in this case, Ψ); the translation, therefore, as it stood in the translator's autograph, reflects the readings of this manuscript. The readings of this Greek exemplar, to the extent that they can be recovered with certainty from the Arabic translation as established in the critical edition (**a**), will be recorded either in the edition of the Greek text or, in case they are not accepted by the editor in the edition, in the Greek apparatus criticus (**c**). When they cannot be established at all because the Arabic translation is not precise enough or specific enough to express the underlying Greek word (as in the case of particles, for example), this fact is registered in the Greek apparatus with square brackets placed around the siglum of the Greek exemplar, [Ψ] (see above, Chapter 2.7b, § 2).

2. *Relation between Stages 1 and 2*

Establishing the translator's autograph or clean copy (Stage 2) from the extant manuscripts (Stage 1) is done as in any edition of an Arabic text with regard to selecting variants and identifying and correcting errors. The variants that have not been selected for inclusion in the text and the various erroneous readings are registered in the Arabic apparatus and marked by the siglum which represents the manuscript where they occur. However, in establishing the critical edition of the Arabic translation of a Greek text we have an additional source of information which tells us what the autograph should have said: the Greek original. If we can ascertain that the translator translated a particular passage or word accurately but that the correct original translation was subsequently corrupted in the transmission within the Arabic tradition, it is possible to correct such mistakes and misreadings on the basis of the Greek text. These corrections are registered in the Arabic apparatus (**b**) in a special manner, with an asterisk next to the name of the person making the correction, followed by the Greek word in parentheses (see the Sigla for the Arabic apparatus below).[1] When this correction is also used to corroborate the reading in the Greek text, then it is registered in the Greek apparatus (c) with an asterisk following the siglum representing the Greek exemplar of the Arabic translation (Ψ*).[2]

3. *Relation between Stages 2 and 3*

Determining how the Arabic translation relates to the Greek exemplar from which it was made involves comparing the received Greek text with the Arabic edition, as established in section II above. If there is disparity between the Greek and the Arabic at any specific point, its cause is either determinable or indeterminable, each of which must be registered *differently* in the Greek apparatus (c).

(1) A disparity whose cause is determinable is when it can can be ascertained that the Greek manuscript used by the translator (Ψ) had a different reading from that of the Greek received text. If that variant also appears in other Greek manuscripts of the work, the siglum Ψ will be added to those representing the variant in the Greek apparatus. If that variant does not appear in any known manuscript, then it will have to be reconstructed in Greek and registered in the Greek apparatus (c) under the siglum Ψ (see the Sigla for the Greek apparatus), followed in parentheses with the transliterated Arabic word(s) which led to the reconstruction.

(2) Frequently, however, the cause of the disparity is indeterminable. This means that it is not possible to determine at which of the three stages in the transmission of the text (as described in section I above) the disparity occurred. This occurs most frequently with omissions in the Arabic translation: (i) they may be due to the scribe(s) of the extant

[1] For this and all following examples, see the entries in the Greek and Arabic apparatus to which reference is made. For an example of the use of the Greek text to emend an erroneous Arabic word, see Crubellier's correction of the mistaken *mawǧūd* to *madḫūl* for ἐπεισοδιῶδες at 4a14, a mistake based on the misreading of a similar skeleton in Arabic for the two words. In the footnote to the translation, references are given from the translation literature further to substantiate this correction.

[2] For example, at 4b11 the transmitted *iḏ* (ἐπεί) is corrected to *in* (εἰ) because *iḏ* does not fit the sense of the sentence, and the correction is registered also in the Greek apparatus because there is some variation in the Greek evidence.

manuscript(s) or to their immediate source from which they derive—the possibility that such an omission may have taken place is very large when only one or two manuscripts of the work survive, as in the present case; (ii) they may be due to the translator himself, who either neglected to translate or skipped over a word or words; (iii) and they may also be due to the Greek exemplar used for the Arabic translation (Ψ), even if such omission may not be attested in any extant Greek manuscript.[3]

Other kinds of disparity, however, are just as difficult to determine. An addition of a word in the Arabic translation may indicate an extra word in the Greek original, but then it may be a semantic elaboration on the part of the translator. A disparity may also occur from a misreading by the translator of the Greek exemplar or from a correct reading of a slightly different Greek original than the received text, the precise nature of which may not be readily identifiable. All such information from the Arabic translation, despite its indeterminacy, could possibly relate to the Greek exemplar and is thus of interest to the Greek editor. It should therefore be registered in the Greek apparatus in a distinct way and attributed to the Arabic tradition in general, using the abbreviation "Ar." (see the Sigla). This indicates what the Arabic text has in its extant form and informs the reader that it cannot be specified to which of the three stages of the transmission of the text this reading is to be attributed.[4]

However, when a disparity between the Greek and Arabic texts can be explained within the context of the Arabic tradition itself and corrected accordingly, then this variant in the Arabic tradition will not be registered in the Greek apparatus with "Ar." Example: in 9a16–17 the Greek has, ὥσπερ καὶ ἐν τοῖς μαθηματικοῖς· ἔχει δὲ καὶ αὐτὰ τὰ μαθήματα διαφοράν. The Arabic manuscripts read, *ka-mā fī t-taʿālīm anfusihā ḫtilāfan*, which is clearly defective: some Greek words are not translated (καὶ … ἔχει δὲ καὶ … τὰ μαθήματα), and the accusative of *iḫtilāfan* has no governing word. The latter provides the clue that something has been omitted within the Arabic manuscript transmission and is not due to something omit-

[3] The Greek manuscripts used by the translators were either old uncial manuscripts of the sixth or early seventh centuries or the newly minted minuscule manuscripts of the ninth (no Greek secular manuscripts were copied between about the mid-seventh to the early ninth century). In either case, the Greek manuscript used by the translator could well represent a branch in the transmission that left no descendants, as with the present work.

[4] Examples: 4a19, 6a6 (omission); 5a3 (addition); 6a4 ὅμοια—ἅμα ἅ (misreading due to minuscule exemplar).

ted in the Greek manuscript or misread by the translator. The omitted words can be easily reconstructed and the omission itself attributed to haplography: one thus adds to the Arabic text, *ka-mā fī t-taʿālīm* ⟨*ayḍan fa-inna li-t-taʿālīm*⟩ *anfusihā ḫtilāfan*, where one scribe skipped from the first *taʿālīm* to the second and omitted the intervening words. In such cases, the omission and its correction are registered in the apparatus of the Arabic text but not in that of the Greek text.[5]

There are three cases of disparity, however, in which it is possible to be more precise about its cause and thus further specify the general designation "Ar." in the apparatus:

(2.1) The translator may have had the same text as the received text but interpreted it either according to his own understanding of the subject of the treatise (which may be different from our own) or according to the purposes for which he was making the translation.[6] In either case, his interpretation is of interest for the establishment of a difficult text, to say nothing of its significance for the history of ideas. It should therefore be registered in the Greek apparatus with the specification, "ut interpr(etatus est) Ar." ("as interpreted in the Arabic;" see the Sigla).[7]

(2.2) The translator may have had the same text as the received text but misunderstood it either because he did not understand the vocabulary involved or did not parse or punctuate the sentence correctly. However,

---

[5] A slight problem in this correction is generated by the fact that the Greek has two different words in this text, τοῖς μαθηματικοῖς and μαθήματα, both of which are translated by *taʿālīm*. Μαθήματα occurs only once in this work, but there is no doubt that its translation is properly and correctly *at-taʿālīm*, since that is what the word means in both Greek and Arabic, the science of mathematics. Τοῖς μαθηματικοῖς, however, refers to mathematical *objects*, not to the discipline, and its translation by *at-taʿālīm*, if the addition proposed in the emendation of the text is to be correct, would be inaccurate. It seems, however, that the translator did in fact mistake τοῖς μαθηματικοῖς as referring to the discipline rather than to its objects, and thus *our* addition of *at-taʿālīm*, representing the translator's mistake, is correct. In the two other passages in this work where τὰ μαθηματικὰ (with the article) occurs (4a18, 11b20), referring to the objects of mathematics, the translator renders the word also with *at-taʿālīm* and not with *al-ašyāʾ* (or *al-umūr*) *at-taʿālīmiyya*, as he does in 6b9, where the Greek word is found without the article and thus clearly refers to mathematical "things" and not to the discipline itself.

[6] See Gutas 1998, 141–150.

[7] Examples: 4a15, 5b8–9, and see the corresponding notes in the translation of the Arabic text.

the possibility that he might have had a slightly different text than the received text, or a corrupt text, can never be entirely ruled out. How the translator misunderstood the sentence is of potential interest to the Greek editor of the text and should therefore be registered in the Greek apparatus with the specification, "ut intell(exit) Ar." ("as understood in the Arabic;" see the Sigla).[8]

(2.3) In some cases of omission, i.e. when the Arabic does not translate a word in the Greek, it is posible to attribute the omission not to any of the three reasons given above but to the translator's deliberate decision not to translate the text. This may occur for two reasons:

(a) The translator may have decided not to translate a word because he felt that the Arabic sentence as constructed somehow included the sense of the word left untranslated. This occurs most frequently with the translation of Greek particles: In their case, there is first the question of the extent to which the Graeco-Arabic translators understood their precise force and implication; the subject of how well scholars of Greek in ninth and tenth century Byzantium and their colleagues in the Islamic world knew the classical Greek particles has, to my knowledge, not been investigated. But in addition to particles, the same observation applies to related words—adverbs, conjunctions, pronouns—which lend nuance and emphasis to the sentence rather than a concrete concept. In all such matters of nuance, the translator, even if he understood the full force of the particles or related words, may have felt either that Arabic could not express it adequately or that the way in which he had translated the Greek sentence by and large covered the said nuance without the need for a specific and additional Arabic word or phrase. Thus the absence of a specific Arabic word or phrase translating any of these Greek words would not indicate that that Greek word was absent at any one of the three levels indicated above, but that it is due to the translator's decision not to translate it. In these cases the Greek word not translated will be indicated by the notation "non vert(it) Ar." However, in the case of particles, it would be otiose to record the relatively frequent absence of their translation with this notation every time it occurs; in this regard the editor will have to exercise his judg-

---

[8] Examples: 4b15 (example of auditory mistake), 7b19, and see the corresponding notes in the translation of the Arabic.

ment and record only those instances in which the particle in question contributes decisively to the signification of the sentence. Apart from this, all the other similar words not translated for this reason will be noted by "non vert. Ar." ("not translated in the Arabic"); see the list of Abbreviations.[9]

(b) The translator may have decided not to translate a word, sentence, or passage in the Greek text because mainly he did not understand it or somehow felt that the text, as he found it in his exemplar, did not contribute anything to the subject of the treatise being translated. This kind of deliberate omission during the work of translation is explained by no less an authority than Isḥāq's father, Ḥunayn himself, when he mentioned that while translating Galen, he would omit some poetic passages (Aristophanes) because he neither understood them nor found them germane to Galen's treatise.[10] In Theophrastus's *On First Principles*, examples of such passages which were not translated are the sentences with biological content at 10b8–9 and 10b13–16, apparently because Isḥāq did not properly understand them. In these cases, the notation "non vert. Ar." in the Greek apparatus is used to indicate that there was no omission or lacuna in the Greek exemplar (or, a fortiori, in the Arabic manuscript tradition), something that the notation "om. Ar." is intended to convey. This is the difference between "om. Ar." and "non vert. Ar."

[9] Examples: 10a14 κἄν; 10b4 αὐτῇ. With regard to the latter, it is to be noted that the translator is selective in his translation of emphatic αὐτός: in some cases he translates it properly with *nafs* (e.g., 7b22, 9b14), but in others he does not. With regard to this intensive pronoun, an interesting case illustrating how the way in which a sentence was translated into Arabic may adequately cover the nuance of such words in Greek is the Homeric citation in 5b17, where emphatic αὐτῇ occurs twice. Isḥāq translates, *jabarahum ḥawla l-arḍi maʿa l-baḥri kullihī*, where the word *kullihī* at the end clearly intends to cover the signification of the second αὐτῇ. In this context, if Isḥāq had attempted to translate also the first αὐτῇ and said something like either *ḥawla l-arḍi kullihā* or *ḥawla l-arḍi nafsihā*, the Arabic style of the resulting sentence would have been rather unsatisfactory. Thus it seems that Isḥāq decided not to translate the first αὐτῇ and was content to allow the word *kullihī* at the end somehow to convey the force of both intensive Greek pronouns. Yet another example of Isḥāq's decision not to translate something because he thought it redundant is provided by the passage at 10b1 where ἤ τίνος is not translated. The notation "non vert. Ar." in the apparatus draws attention to this fact, for it can hardly be thought that he did not actually have ἤ τίνος in his exemplar (Ψ); whereas a notation "om. Ar." could have implied that it would be permissible to suppose that Ψ actually had omitted these words.

[10] See the discussion in Gutas 1998, 140.

Finally, a word of caution. The apparatus of the Greek text should not be cluttered with information that belongs strictly to the apparatus of the Arabic text. A discrimination has to be made between variant readings that are due solely to the tranmission within the Arabic tradition and those that are due to the transmission within the Greek tradition as represented by the Greek manuscript used by the translator.[11]

4. *Accessories*

(1) The *English translation* of the Arabic translation is of benefit to the Greek scholar. It conveys in detail what the translator read in his exemplar, how he punctuated each sentence, and how he understood the sweep of the argument. It is also of benefit to the Arabic scholar interested in the history of the translated texts and their doctrines, and in their diffusion and acceptance in Arabic philosophy.

(2) A philological *commentary* always accompanies the English translation (in this case as running notes to the text). Its purpose is to analyze every discrepancy between the Greek text and the Arabic translation and explain in detail the precise way in which each Greek word and sentence in the exemplar of the translation (Ψ) was either (mis)read and (mis)understood by the translator or represents the correct text that has been corrupted in the extant Greek manuscripts. This in turn will give the reader to understand the editorial decisions that went into the making of the Arabic and the Greek apparatus.

[11] For example, in the apparatus at 8a10, Laks & Most register two omissions by "Isḥāq". This entry, however, does not belong here but in the Arabic apparatus. The text of the original translation as written by Isḥāq was not the one transmitted in the existing Arabic manuscript T because the latter makes no sense and it has to be assumed that Isḥāq wrote intelligible Arabic. The text of this sentence was therefore corrupted within the Arabic tradition—and not because of any mistake in Isḥāq's exemplar—and has to be corrected in order for it to make sense grammatically (see my correction of the Arabic text). But this mistake then and its correction have no bearing on Ψ, the Greek exemplar of the translation, since it contained the correct Greek text. Accordingly the references in the apparatus of Laks & Most to the omission of these words are inappropriate because they say nothing about the transmission of the work in Greek (which is the purpose of the Greek apparatus); they should be transferred to the Arabic apparatus. For another example see 4b9 and 10 (ὀλίγοις—περιττοῖς) and the corresponding note in the translation of the Arabic text.

(3) The need for and benefits of the *Greek-Arabic and Arabic-Greek glossaries* are obvious as indices of words used. They also contribute to Greek and Arabic lexicography in general and most particularly to the continuing efforts to compile lexica of the translated literature.[12]

[12] For the benefits of the Graeco-Arabic translated literature for Arabic lexicography see *WKAS* II,2, pp. IX–XI. For Graeco-Arabic lexicography see, in general, *GALex*, and especially the recent glossaries compiled by M. Ullmann, *WGAÜ* and *WGAÜS*.

PART II

THE TEXTS AND TRANSLATIONS

1. THE GREEK TEXT WITH ENGLISH TRANSLATION

SIGLA

Semper citantur

J	Vindobonensis phil. gr. 100; ca. 850 AD
J^{II}	manus recentior (saec. XIV) librarii qui f. 137^{r-v} supplevit[1]
P	Parisinus gr. 1853; saec. X
Ψ	archetypus graecus translationis Isaaci arabicae deperditus; saec. IX
Ψ*	lectio cod. Ψ a nobis correcta[2]
[Ψ]	quid interpres legerit ignoramus[3]
Ar.	lectio in transl. Arab. incertae originis, aut e cod. Ψ sumpta aut interpretis coniectura vel errore orta[4]
Λ	archetypus graecus translationis Bartholomaei latinae deperditus; saec. XIII (?) (= recensio Messanensis)
[Λ]	quid interpres legerit ignoramus
Lat.	lectio in transl. Lat. incertae originis, aut e cod. Λ sumpta aut interpretis coniectura vel errore orta
ω	codicum JP Ψ Λ consensus (4a1–11a1), J^{II}P Ψ Λ consensus (11a1–12a2)

Raro citantur

C	Marcianus gr. 211; saec. XIII exeuntis vel XIV ineuntis
L	Laurentianus 28,45; AD 1445
A	Vaticanus gr. 1302; saec. XIII exeuntis vel XIV ineuntis
α	codicum JP CLA consensus (4a1–11a1), J^{II}P CLA consensus (11a1–12a2) (= recensio Constantinopolitana)

Occasione oblata citantur

B	Bernensis 402; saec. $XV^{4/4}$
D	Ambrosianus P 80 sup. (gr. 630); saec. XV
H	Leidensis Vossianus gr. Q. 25; ca. 1487 AD
N	Neapolitanus III D 1; 20/i/1497 AD
O	Vaticanus Ottobonianus gr. 153; saec. $XV^{3/4}$

---

1 See Burnikel 116n11.
2 See the Excursus § II.
3 See the Excursus § I.3.
4 See the Excursus § III.2.

R	Palatinus Vaticanus gr 162; 1442–1457 AD
S	Londinensis BL Add. 5113; 1480–1487 AD
V	Vaticanus gr. 1305; saec. $XV^{2/2}$
V^a	Vaticanus Urbinas gr. 108; saec. $XV^{1/2}$
z	Parisinus gr 2277; ca. 1479 AD
Ald.	editio princeps: Venetiis apud Aldum Manutium, 1/vi/1497 AD
Steph.	translatio Latina a Henrico Stephano confecta, ed. Parisiis 1515 AD
Tiph.	translatio Latina a Georgio Tiphernate confecta, Vat. Urbinas lat. 208; saec. XV

Cam.	Camotius 1551
$Jaeger^1$	Jaeger 1923 / 1948^2
$Jaeger^2$	Jaeger 1932
$Us.^1$	Usener 1861
$Us.^2$	Usener 1890
$Wim.^1$	Wimmer 1862
$Wim.^2$	Wimmer 1866
Zeller	Zeller 1879

⟨ ⟩	nostra vel aliorum coniectura suppleta
⌜ ⌝	lectio in Ψ et Λ quae in codd. deest graecis
[ ]	nostra vel aliorum coniectura seclusa
* * *	lacuna coniectura nostra indicata
X^1	librarius X se ipsum corrigens
X^2	secunda manus

Contractiones[5]

add.	addidit
adn.	adnotatio (= Part III, Commentary)
alt.	alterum
app. crit. alt.	apparatus criticus alter (= Part I, Chapter 2.7b)
codd.	codices
coni.	coniecit
corr.	correxit
del.	delevit
dist.	distinxit
dubit.	dubitanter
edd.	editores, editiones
fort.	fortasse
inc.	incipit
ind.	indicavit
iter.	iteravit

[5] For the abbreviations of the names of scholars and the references to their publications see the list of Abbreviations and the Bibliography.

l.	linea
lac.	lacuna
litt.	litterae
om.	omisit
pr.	prius
prop.	proposuit
ras.	(in) rasura
recc.	recentiores
sc.	scilicet
secl.	seclusit
s.l.	supra lineam
susp.	suspicatus est/sum
transp.	transposuit
ut intell.	ut intellegit[6]
ut interpr.	ut interpretatus est[7]
ut vid.	ut videtur
v.	vide
vert.	vertit[8]

[6] See the Excursus § III.2.2.
[7] See the Excursus § III,2.1.
[8] See the Excursus § III.2.3.

ΘΕΟΦΡΑΣΤΟΥ ⸢ΠΕΡΙ ΑΡΧΩΝ⸣

[τῶν μετὰ τὰ Φυσικά]

(1) Πῶς ἀφορίσαι δεῖ καὶ ποίοις τὴν ὑπὲρ τῶν Usener I [1]
πρώτων θεωρίαν; Ἡ γὰρ δὴ τῆς φύσεως πολυχουστέρα καί, ὥς γε δή τινές φασιν, ἀτακτοτέρα, μεταβολὰς ἔχουσα παντοίας· ἡ δὲ τῶν πρώτων ὡρισμένη καὶ ἀεὶ κατὰ ταὐτά, διὸ δὴ καὶ ἐν νοητοῖς οὐκ αἰσθητοῖς αὐτὴν τιθέασιν, ὡς ἀκινήτοις καὶ ἀμεταβλήτοις, καὶ τὸ ὅλον δὲ σεμνοτέραν καὶ μείζω νομίζουσιν αὐτήν.

(2) Ἀρχὴ δέ, πότερα συν- [2]
αφή τις καὶ οἷον κοινωνία πρὸς ἄλληλα τοῖς τε νοητοῖς καὶ τοῖς τῆς φύσεως ἢ οὐδεμία, ἀλλ' ὥσπερ ἑκάτερα κεχωρισμένα, συνεργοῦντα δέ πως εἰς

4a2–3 τὴν ὑπὲρ τῶν πρώτων θεωρίαν] Arist. *Met.* A 1, 981b28–29 τὴν ὀνομαζομένην σοφίαν περὶ τὰ πρῶτα αἴτια καὶ τὰς ἀρχὰς. A 2, 982b8–9 ἐπὶ τὴν αὐτὴν ἐπιστήμην πίπτει τὸ ζητούμενον ὄνομα· δεῖ γὰρ αὐτὴν τῶν πρώτων ἀρχῶν καὶ αἰτιῶν εἶναι θεωρητικήν. Xenocrates fr. 6 Heinze τὴν σοφίαν ἐπιστήμην τῶν πρώτων αἰτιῶν καὶ τῆς νοητῆς οὐσίας. **4a4** ἀτακτοτέρα] Arist. *Mete.* 338b20–21 λοιπὸν δ' ἐστὶ μέρος τῆς μεθόδου ταύτης ἔτι θεωρητέον ... ταῦτα δ' ἐστὶν ὅσα συμβαίνει κατὰ φύσιν μέν, ἀτακτοτέραν μέντοι τῆς τοῦ πρώτου στοιχείου τῶν σωμάτων. **4a6–7** ἐν νοητοῖς οὐκ αἰσθητοῖς αὐτὴν (*sc.* τὴν τῶν πρώτων θεωρίαν) τιθέασιν] Theophr. fr. 319 FHS&G ἡ ἐπιστήμη ἡ θεωρητικὴ ταὐτὸ τοῖς πράγμασιν ... τῷ νῷ τὰ μὲν νοητὰ ἀεὶ ὑπάρχει, τὰ δὲ ἔνυλα ὅταν νοηθῇ καὶ αὐτὰ τῷ νῷ ὑπάρξει. Arist. *DA* 402a3–4, 430a4–5 τὴν τῆς ψυχῆς ἱστορίαν εὐλόγως ἂν ἐν πρώτοις τιθείημεν. ... ἡ γὰρ ἐπιστήμη ἡ θεωρητικὴ καὶ τὸ οὕτως ἐπιστητὸν τὸ αὐτό ἐστιν. **4a7–8** αἰσθητοῖς ... ἀκινήτοις καὶ ἀμεταβλήτοις] Arist. *Met.* Λ 1, 1069a30–31, 33; 1069b3 οὐσίαι δὲ τρεῖς, μία μὲν αἰσθητή, ἧς ἡ μὲν ἀΐδιος ἡ δὲ φθαρτή, ... ἄλλη δὲ ἀκίνητος, ... ἡ δ' αἰσθητὴ οὐσία μεταβλητή. **4a8–9** σεμνοτέραν καὶ μείζω] Arist. *Met.* A 2, 983a4–5 οὔτε τῆς τοιαύτης [sc. ἐπιστήμης] ἄλλην χρὴ νομίζειν τιμιωτέραν· ἡ γὰρ θειοτάτη καὶ τιμιωτάτη.

4a1 Θεοφράστου **α** Ψ : Ἀριστοτέλους Λ | Περὶ ἀρχῶν Λ (*de principiis*), Περὶ ἀρχῶν vel Περὶ ἀρχῆς prop. Rose, Laks & Most : deest **α** Ψ **1a** τῶν μετὰ τὰ φυσικά [τῶν om. CL, τὰ om. P] **α**, Ar. in coloph. (*maqālat Ṯāwufrasṭus fī mā baʿda ṭ-ṭabīʿa*) : deest Λ, secl. Laks & Most (v. part. I, cap. 1.2) **2–12** πῶς—ἀλλ' ὥσπερ lac. in codd. Ar. **6** ταὐτά Λ (*eadem*) : ταυτα P, ταῦτα J **9** πότερα P Λ, ποτερα J : πότερόν ἐστιν J^{II} | πότερα δ' ἀρχὴ ut interpr. Lat. **12** ab ἑκάτερα inc. codd. Ar. | δέ πως J Ψ Λ : δεπῶς P

THEOPHRASTUS 4a1

⌜*ON FIRST PRINCIPLES*⌝

[transmitted as]

[(The book) by Theophrastus of Those (that Come) after (Aristotle's) *Physics*][1]

(**1**) How and with what sort of [things] should one mark the boundaries of the study of the first [things]? For surely the [study] of nature is more multifarious and, at least as some actually say, more lacking in order,[2] involving as it does all sorts of changes; but the [study] of the first [things] is bounded and always the same, for which reason, indeed, they[3] even place it among[4] the intelligibles but not the sensibles, on the ground that the [intelligibles] are unmovable and unchangeable, and on the whole consider it more venerable and more important.

(**2**) The starting point is, whether [there is] some connection and something like a mutual association between intelligibles and the [things] of nature or [there is] none, but the two are, as it were, separated, though

---

[1] The original title, *On First Principles*, is preserved only by the Latin translation, which, however, ascribes the work to Aristotle. The Essay was transmitted together with the books that make up what was later called Aristotle's *Metaphysics* under this title, which was assigned to it by scribes and which was descriptive of the place it occupied in the edition of Aristotle's works. See Chapter 1.2.

[2] Theophrastus echoes here an understanding of the issue that was common both to Aristotelian conceptions, as reflected in the opening paragraph of Aristotle's *Meteorology*, and to members of the Academy. See the commentary.

[3] Apparently the same people as the "some" in the preceding sentence, though it is not certain; see the commentary.

[4] I.e., as operative among them; see the commentary.

τὴν πᾶσαν οὐσίαν. Εὐλογώτερον δ᾽ οὖν εἶναί τινα συναφὴν καὶ μὴ ἐπεισοδιῶδες τὸ πᾶν, ἀλλ᾽ οἷον τὰ μὲν πρότερα τὰ δ᾽ ὕστερα, καὶ ἀρχὰς τὰ δ᾽ ὑπὸ τὰς ἀρχάς, ὥσπερ καὶ τὰ ἀΐδια τῶν φθαρτῶν.

(3) Εἰ δ᾽ οὖν οὕτω, τίς ἡ φύσις αὐτῶν καὶ ἐν ποίοις; Εἰ μὲν γὰρ ἐν τοῖς μαθηματικοῖς μόνον [3] τὰ νοητά, καθάπερ τινές φασιν, οὔτ᾽ ἄγαν εὔσημος ἡ συναφὴ τοῖς αἰσθητοῖς οὔθ᾽ ὅλως ἀξιόχρεα φαίνεται τοῦ παντός. Οἷον γὰρ μεμηχανημένα δοκεῖ δι᾽ ἡμῶν εἶναι σχήματά τε καὶ μορφὰς καὶ λόγους περιτιθέντων, αὐτὰ δὲ δι᾽ αὑτῶν οὐδεμίαν ἔχει φύσιν· εἰ δὲ μή, οὐχ οἷά τε συνάπτειν τοῖς τῆς φύσεως ὥστ᾽ ἐμποιῆσαι καθάπερ ζωὴν καὶ κίνησιν αὐτοῖς, οὐδὲ γὰρ αὐτὸς ὁ ἀριθμός, ὅνπερ δὴ πρῶτον καὶ κυριώτατόν τινες τιθέασιν.

4a14 μὴ ἐπεισοδιῶδες τὸ πᾶν] Arist. *Met.* Λ 10, 1076a1 οἱ δὲ λέγοντες τὸν ἀριθμὸν πρῶτον τὸν μαθηματικὸν ... ἐπεισοδιώδη τὴν τοῦ παντὸς οὐσίαν ποιοῦσιν. N 3, 1090b19–20 οὐκ ἔοικε δ᾽ ἡ φύσις ἐπεισοδιώδης οὖσα ἐκ τῶν φαινομένων, ὥσπερ μοχθηρὰ τραγῳδία. *Poet.* 9, 1451b34–35 λέγω δ᾽ ἐπεισοδιώδη μῦθον ἐν ᾧ τὰ ἐπεισόδια μετ᾽ ἄλληλα οὔτ᾽ εἰκὸς οὔτ᾽ ἀνάγκη εἶναι. **4a16** πρότερα ... ὥσπερ καὶ τὰ ἀΐδια τῶν φθαρτῶν] Arist. *Met.* Θ 8, 1050b6–7 τὰ μὲν γὰρ ἀΐδια πρότερα τῇ οὐσίᾳ τῶν φθαρτῶν. **4a18–21** εἰ μὲν γὰρ ... τοῦ παντός] Arist. *Met.* N 3, 1090b14–21 περὶ μὲν τοῦ ἀριθμοῦ παντὸς καὶ τῶν μαθηματικῶν τὸ μηθὲν συμβάλλεσθαι ἀλλήλοις τὰ πρότερα τοῖς ὕστερον, ... τοῖς δὲ τὰς ἰδέας τιθεμένοις τοῦτο μὲν ἐκφεύγει ... **4a21–4b2** μεμηχανημένα ... οὐδεμίαν ἔχει φύσιν] Speusippus fr. 28,10–13 Tarán φυσικωτάτην αὐτὴν [sc. τὴν δεκάδα Σπεύσιππος] ἀποφαίνων καὶ τελεστικωτάτην τῶν ὄντων, οἷον εἶδός τι τοῖς κοσμικοῖς ἀποτελέσμασι τεχνικόν, ἐφ᾽ ἑαυτῆς ἀλλ᾽ οὐχ ἡμῶν νομισάντων ἢ ὡς ἔτυχε θεμένων ὑπάρχουσαν. **4b2–4** εἰ δὲ μή ... ἀριθμός] Arist. *Met.* Λ 10, 1075b27–28 εἴ δ᾽ ἔσται τὰ εἴδη ἢ ⟨οἱ⟩ ἀριθμοί, οὐδενὸς αἴτια· εἰ δὲ μή, οὔτι κινήσεώς γε. **4b5** πρῶτον] v. ad 4a14

13 πᾶσαν om. Ar. | τινα non vert. Ar. **14** post ἐπεισοδιῶδες add. εἶναι J[II] **15** καὶ PJ Λ : καὶ τὰ μὲν J[II], ut interpr. Ar., dubit. Us.[1] **16** τῶν φθαρτῶν PJ[II] Ψ CL, τοῖς φθαρτοῖς Λ (sed v. cap. 2.3, notam 8) A : τῶν ἀφθάρτων J **19** ἄγαν om. Ar. **20** ἀξιόχρεα P, ἀξιοχρέα J [Ψ] [Λ] **21** τοῦ παντός J Ψ, Λ ut vid. : παντός P : πάντως prop. Jaeger[2] **23** περιτιθέντων P Ψ Λ : περιτεθέντων J | αὑτῶν Ψ Λ, αυτῶν P : αὐτῶν J **4b2** ἔχει **ω** : ἔχειν B[2], coni. Wim.[1,2] | οὐχ οἷά τε Ψ, prop. Hoffmann apud Us.[1] : οὐχ οἷόν τε A[2] : οὐχ ὥστε **α** Λ : οὐχ οὕτως γε coni. Us.[2] : οὐδ᾽ ὥς prop. Us.[1]

somehow both contributing to [bring about] all of existence.[5] At any rate, it is more reasonable that there is some connection and that the universe is not episodic,[6] but rather that the former are, as it were, prior and the latter posterior—and first principles, too, and the latter subordinate to the first principles—just as eternal [things] too are to the perishable.[7]

(**3**) If so, then, what is their[8] nature and among what sort of [things are they]? For if, on the one hand, [it is] among the mathematicals only that the intelligibles are, as some say,[9] neither is [their] connection with the sensibles very conspicuous nor do they appear to be at all serviceable with regard to the universe. For they seem, as it were, to have been devised by us as figures, shapes, and proportions that we ascribe [to things], while they in themselves have no nature at all; or, if not,[10] they are not able to have a connection with the [things] of nature that would produce in them something like life and motion—no, not even number itself,[11] the very one which some people[12] rank as first and most dominant.

---

[5] Existence (*ousía*) here is used in the sense of all that exists. See the commentary on the various uses of the word in this Essay.

[6] I.e., it does not consist of a series of disconnected and unrelated episodes, "like a wretched tragedy," as Aristotle says, using the literary term (*Poet.* 1451b33–34) in a metaphysical context (*Met.* 1090b19, 1076a1) to criticize Speusippus to whom Theophrastus too is alluding; see the commentary on Diaporia 2.

[7] I.e., "are [prior] to the perishable," as also in the Arabic translation.

[8] I.e., the intelligibles. The plural pronoun could refer either to the first things or to the intelligibles. But the preceding paragraph, on the basis of which ("if so") Theophrastus now asks the main question, has in essence made "the intelligibles" coextensive with "the first things" (cf. van Raalte 100n6), and the following sentence speaks of "the intelligibles" as the subject under discussion, so there can be little doubt about the referent of the pronoun.

[9] Theophrastus is referring to both Speusippus and Xenocrates here, though views differ. See Henrich 81–83 for a discussion of the alternatives.

[10] I.e., if they have not been devised by us.

[11] I.e., is able to do this.

[12] The Pythagoreans and their followers in the Academy, Speusippus and Xenocrates.

(4) Εἰ δ' ἑτέρα τις οὐσία προτέρα καὶ κρείττων ἐστίν, ταύτην πειρατέον λέγειν πότερον μία τις κατ' ἀριθμὸν ἢ κατ' εἶδος ἢ κατὰ γένος. Εὐλογώτερον δ' οὖν ἀρχῆς φύσιν ἐχούσας ἐν ὀλίγοις εἶναι καὶ περιττοῖς, εἰ μὴ ἄρα καὶ πρώτοις καὶ ἐν τῷ πρώτῳ. [4]

(5) Τίς δ' οὖν αὕτη καὶ τίνες, εἰ πλείους, πειρατέον ἐμφαίνειν ἁμῶς γέ πως εἴτε κατ' ἀναλογίαν εἴτε κατ' ἄλλην ὁμοίωσιν. Ἀνάγκη δ' ἴσως δυνάμει τινὶ καὶ ὑπεροχῇ τῶν ἄλλων λαμβάνειν, ὥσπερ ἂν εἰ τὸν θεόν· θεία γὰρ ἡ πάντων ἀρχή, δι' ἧς ἅπαντα καὶ ἔστιν καὶ διαμένει. Τάχα μὲν οὖν ῥᾴδιον τὸ οὕτως ἀποδοῦναι, χαλεπὸν δὲ σαφεστέρως ἢ πιστικωτέρως.

(5.1) Τοιαύτης δ' οὔσης τῆς ἀρχῆς, ἐπείπερ συνάπτει τοῖς αἰσθητοῖς, ἡ δὲ φύσις ὡς ἁπλῶς εἰπεῖν ἐν κινήσει καὶ τοῦτ' αὐτῆς τὸ ἴδιον, δῆλον ὡς αἰτίαν θετέον ταύτην τῆς κινήσεως. Ἐπεὶ δ' ἀκίνητος καθ' αὐτήν, φανερὸν ὡς οὐκ ἂν εἴη τῷ κινεῖσθαι τοῖς τῆς φύ- [5]

4b6 εἰ ... ἐστίν] Arist. *Met.* A 6, 987b14–18 Πλάτων ... παρὰ τὰ αἰσθητὰ καὶ τὰ εἴδη, τὰ μαθηματικὰ τῶν πραγμάτων εἶναί φησι μεταξύ, διαφέροντα τῶν ... εἰδῶν τῷ τὰ μὲν πολλ' ἄττα ὅμοια εἶναι τὸ δὲ εἶδος αὐτὸ ἓν ἕκαστον μόνον. **4b7–8** πότερον ... γένος] Arist. *Met.* Z 1, 1028b4–6 τίς ἡ οὐσία· τοῦτο γὰρ οἱ μὲν ἓν εἶναί φασιν οἱ δὲ πλείω ἢ ἕν, καὶ οἱ μὲν πεπερασμένα οἱ δὲ ἄπειρα. Δ 6, 1016b31–32 τὰ μὲν κατ' ἀριθμόν ἐστιν ἕν, τὰ δὲ κατ' εἶδος, τὰ δὲ κατὰ γένος, τὰ δὲ κατ' ἀναλογίαν. **4b8–11** εὐλογώτερον ... πρώτῳ] Arist. *PA* 665b14–15 ὅπου γὰρ ἐνδέχεται, μίαν (sc. ἀρχὴν εἶναι) βέλτιον ἢ πολλάς. **4b11** τίς ... πλείους] Arist. *Met.* Λ 8, 1073a14–15 πότερον δὲ μίαν θετέον τὴν τοιαύτην οὐσίαν ἢ πλείους, καὶ πόσας, δεῖ μὴ λανθάνειν. **4b15** θεία γὰρ ἡ πάντων ἀρχή] Arist. *Met.* A 2, 983a8–9 ὅ τε γὰρ θεὸς δοκεῖ τῶν αἰτίων πᾶσιν εἶναι καὶ ἀρχή τις. K 7, 1064a34-b1 εἴπερ ὑπάρχει τις οὐσία τοιαύτη, λέγω δὲ χωριστὴ καὶ ἀκίνητος ... ἐνταῦθ' ἂν εἴη που καὶ τὸ θεῖον, καὶ αὕτη ἂν εἴη ⟨ἡ⟩ πρώτη καὶ κυριωτάτη ἀρχή. **4b16** δι' ἧς ... διαμένει] Arist. *DC* 279a18–30 τἀκεῖ [sc. οὐράνια σώματα] ... ἀναλλοίωτα καὶ ἀπαθῆ ... διατελεῖ τὸν ἅπαντα αἰῶνα ... ὅθεν ... ἐξήρτηται ... τὸ εἶναί τε καὶ ζῆν.

9 ⟨οὐσίαν⟩ ἀρχῆς add. Us.[1,2] | ὀλίγοις **ω**, v. adn. **10** περιττοῖς **ω**, v. adn. : πρώτοις prop. Zeller | καὶ alt. om. Lat. : καὶ ἐν O | πρώτοις καὶ **α** Λ : πρώτοις, καὶ dist. Allan (privatim), Laks & Most : πρώτας (sc. οὐσίας) ut vid. Ψ (prop. Treiger) : del. Zeller | ἐν om. Lat. **11** εἰ J Ψ* Λ : εἰ P **15** fort. ὥσπερ Ψ | εἰ PJ : εἴ⟨η⟩ vel ᾖ ut intell. Ar. : om. Lat. **17** οὖν PJ Λ : οὐ ut intell. Ar. (cf. χαλεπόν) **18** πιστικωτέρως **ω**, v. adn. : πειστικωτέρως D **23** τῷ PJ Λ : τοῦ ut intell. Ar.

(**4**) But if, on the other hand,[13] some other substance is prior and more powerful, one ought to try to say whether it is one such in number, or in species, or in genus. At any rate, it is more reasonable that, having the nature of a first principle, they[14] are among few and extraordinary [things]—if not, indeed, even among the first [things] as well as in[15] the first.

(**5**) What, at any rate, this[16] is, or what they are, if they are more, one ought to try to reveal somehow or other, whether by analogy or by some other [procedure through] similarity. Perhaps it is necessary to apprehend [it or them] by means of some power and superiority over others, as if [we were apprehending] god, for divine is the first principle of all, through which all [things] both are and abide. And yes, maybe it is easy to provide an explanation in this manner—but more explicitly or more convincingly, difficult.

(**5.1**) Such being the first principle,[17] then, since it is connected with sensibles, and nature[18] is, to put it simply, in motion (which is the property unique to it),[19] it is evident that it should be posited as the cause of movement. But since it is in itself motionless, it is obvious that it could

[13] This responds to the first "if" introducing the second sentence in § 3.

[14] I.e., substances like the one that was just assumed—a substance prior and more powerful than the mathematicals. See the commentary.

[15] I.e., in the set of things that contains only one item, the first thing. See the commentary here and on 4a17–18.

[16] The feminine pronoun refers ultimately to the first principle, as is evident from the answer to this question given at the beginning of the next paragraph, "Such being the first principle."

[17] I.e., divine. See the commentary.

[18] Nature, that is, in the sense of "the things of nature," as in what follows. See the commentary.

[19] "Unique property," which I borrow from Robin Smith 1997, 62, catches best the meaning of the term *ídion*.

σεως αἰτία, ἀλλὰ λοιπὸν ἄλλῃ τινὶ δυνάμει κρείττονι καὶ προτέρᾳ· τοιαύτη δ’ ἡ τοῦ ὀρεκτοῦ φύσις, ἀφ’ ἧς ἡ κυκλικὴ ἡ συνεχὴς καὶ ἄπαυστος. Ὥστε ⸢καὶ⸣ κατ’ ἐκεῖνο λύοιτο ἂν τὸ μὴ εἶναι κινήσεως ἀρχὴν ἢ εἰ κινούμενον κινήσει.

(6) Μέχρι [6] μὲν δὴ τούτων οἷον ἄρτιος ὁ λόγος, ἀρχήν τε ποιῶν μίαν πάντων καὶ τὴν ἐνέργειαν καὶ τὴν οὐσίαν ἀποδιδούς, ἔτι δὲ μὴ διαιρετὸν μηδὲ ποσόν τι λέγων ἀλλ’ ἁπλῶς ἐξαίρων εἰς κρείττω τινὰ μερίδα καὶ θειοτέραν (οὕτω γὰρ μᾶλλον ἀποδοτέον ἢ τὸ διαιρετὸν καὶ μεριστὸν ἀφαιρετέον· ἅμα γὰρ ἐν ὑψηλοτέρῳ τε καὶ ἀληθινωτέρῳ λόγῳ τοῖς λέγουσιν ἡ ἀπόφασις), τὸ δὲ μετὰ ταῦτ’ II [7] ἤδη λόγου δεῖται πλείονος περὶ τῆς ἐφέσεως, ποία καὶ τίνων, ἐπειδὴ πλείω τὰ κυκλικὰ καὶ αἱ φοραὶ τρόπον τινὰ ὑπεναντίαι καὶ τὸ ἀνήνυτον καὶ οὗ χάριν ἀφανές. Εἴτε γὰρ ἓν τὸ κινοῦν, ἄτοπον τὸ μὴ πάντα τὴν αὐτήν· εἴτε καθ’ ἕκαστον ἕτερον αἵ τ’ ἀρχαὶ πλείους—ὥστε τὸ σύμφωνον αὐτῶν εἰς

5a1–2 ἄλλῃ … προτέρᾳ] Arist. *Met.* Δ 11, 1018b22–23 πρότερα καὶ ὕστερα λέγεται … τὰ δὲ κατὰ δύναμιν· τὸ γὰρ ὑπερέχον τῇ δυνάμει πρότερον καὶ τὸ δυνατώτερον. **5a2** ἡ τοῦ ὀρεκτοῦ φύσις] Arist. *Met.* Λ 7, 1072a25–26 ἔστι τι ὃ οὐ κινούμενον κινεῖ, ἀΐδιον καὶ οὐσία καὶ ἐνέργεια οὖσα· κινεῖ δὲ ὧδε τὸ ὀρεκτὸν καὶ τὸ νοητόν. **5a3** ἡ κυκλικὴ ἡ συνεχὴς] Arist. *Met.* Λ 6, 1071b10–11 κίνησις δ’ οὐκ ἔστι συνεχὴς ἀλλ’ ἢ ἡ κατὰ τόπον, καὶ ταύτης ἡ κύκλῳ. Λ 7, 1072a21–22 καὶ ἔστι τι ἀεὶ κινούμενον κίνησιν ἄπαυστον, αὕτη δ’ ἡ κύκλῳ. **5a4** ἄπαυστος] Arist *DC* 279b1–3 καὶ ἄπαυστον δὴ κίνησιν κινεῖται (sc. τὸ θεῖον) εὐλόγως· πάντα γὰρ παύεται κινούμενα ὅταν ἔλθῃ εἰς τὸν οἰκεῖον τόπον, τοῦ δὲ κύκλῳ σώματος ὁ αὐτὸς τόπος ὅθεν ἤρξατο καὶ εἰς ὃν τελευτᾷ. **5a4–5** τὸ μὴ εἶναι … κινήσει] Plato *Phaedr.* 245d6–7 οὕτω δὴ κινήσεως μὲν ἀρχὴ τὸ αὐτὸ αὑτὸ κινοῦν. Arist. *DA* 404a7–8 καὶ κινεῖν τὰ λοιπά, κινούμενα καὶ αὐτά (sc. τὰ ἄτομα, Δημόκριτος καὶ Λεύκιππος) **5a7–8** τὴν ἐνέργειαν καὶ τὴν οὐσίαν] Theophr. fr. 152.3–5 FHS&G τὴν γὰρ ἑκάστου οὐσίαν καὶ τὸ οἰκεῖον εἶδος ἐνέργειαν εἶναι ἑκάστου, μὴ οὖσαν ταύτην κίνησιν. **5a8–11** μὴ διαιρετὸν … ἀφαιρετέον] Arist. *Phys.* Θ 10, 267b24–26 τὸ δέ γε πρῶτον κινοῦν … ἀδιαίρετόν ἐστι καὶ ἀμερὲς καὶ οὐδὲν ἔχον μέγεθος. *Met.* Λ 7, 1073a5–7 μέγεθος οὐδὲν ἔχειν ἐνδέχεται ταύτην τὴν οὐσίαν, ἀλλ’ ἀμερὴς καὶ ἀδιαίρετός ἐστιν.

5a2 φύσις ut ex nota marginali λύσις correctum susp. Gercke apud Us.[2] **3** post κυκλικὴ add. κίνησις Ar., Us.[1,2] **4** ἄπαυστος J : άπαυτος P [Ψ] [Λ] | καὶ (*ayḍan*) κατ’ ἐκεῖνο Ψ : κατ’ ἐκεῖνο **α** Λ : κἀκεῖνο coni. Cam., καὶ ἐκεῖνο coni. Us.[1,2] **5** εἰ del. J[II] **12** ἅμα non vert. Ar. **15** ποία Ψ Λ : ποια J : ποῖα P J[II] **16** post ἀνήνυτον dist. van Raalte not be a cause to the [things] of nature by being in motion but, as the remaining [alternative], by some other, superior and prior, power; and such is the nature of the desirable, from which [there springs] the circular, continuous and unceasing [motion]. And so on this [basis] ⌜also⌝ [the difficulty] could be resolved that there can be no beginning of motion unless something in motion initiate it.[20]

(**6**) Now up to these [arguments], the account has all its parts in place, so to speak: it both posits a single first principle for all [things] and provides [its] actualized state[21] and essence,[22] and it further says that it is neither something divisible nor quantifiable, but exalts it in an absolute sense to some better and more divine rank (for it is better that one should provide such an account rather than that one should remove [from it] divisibility and partitionability, because those who make the negative statement [above make it] in an argument that is at the same time loftier and closer to truth);[23] but what [comes] immediately after these [arguments] needs further discussion about the impulsion[24]—of what kind and towards which [things] it is—because the rotating [bodies] are more than one and the[ir] motions are somehow opposed, while [their] interminableness and "[that] for the sake of which"[25] are not apparent. For if the mover is one, it makes no sense that all not with the same [motion];[26] and if it is different for each and the first principles are more than one, [the consequence is such] that the concord of [the rotating

[20] I.e., establishing the desirable as a first principle accomplishes two objectives: it (a) accounts for movement in nature (b) and ensures that it is initiated by an unmoved mover; it "also" resolves, that is, the difficulty generated by the Platonic (and Pythagorean and atomist) position that only something in motion itself can initiate motion in others.

[21] *Enérgeia*, in this special sense used by Aristotle and Theophrastus. See the commentary.

[22] Essence here and elsewhere translates one of the meanings of *ousía*; see the commentary at 4a13.

[23] I.e., slightly to paraphrase the explanation by Ross 43, it is better to say that the first principle belongs a priori (because it is divine?) to a class of things which could not be divisible into parts than it is to put it into a class, like that of material things, which would naturally be divisible, and then deny divisibility of it.

[24] I.e., towards the unmoved mover. Theophrastus uses here a different word (*éphesis*) for desire than the one he uses elsewhere (*órexis*, at 5a20, etc.). See the commentary for the apparent nuance differences.

[25] I.e., the final cause of the motions.

[26] I.e., either "that all the rotating bodies do not move with the same motion," or "that the mover does not move all the rotating bodies with the same motion." See the commentary.

ὄρεξιν ἰόντων τὴν ἀρίστην οὐθαμῶς φανερόν. (7) Τὸ δὲ κατὰ τὸ πλῆθος τῶν σφαιρῶν τῆς αἰτίας μείζονα ζητεῖ λόγον· οὐ γὰρ ⌜οἰκεῖος⌝ ὅ γε τῶν ἀστρολόγων. [8]

(8) Ἄπορον δὲ καὶ πῶς ποτε φυσικὴν ὄρεξιν ἐχόντων οὐ τὴν ἠρεμίαν διώκουσιν ἀλλὰ τὴν κίνησιν. Τί οὖν ἅμα τῇ μιμήσει φασὶν ἐκεῖνο ὁμοίως ὅσοι τε τὸ ἓν καὶ ὅσοι τοὺς ἀριθμοὺς λέγουσιν; καὶ γὰρ αὐτοὶ τοὺς ἀριθμούς φασιν τὸ ἕν.

(8.1) Εἰ δ' ἡ ἔφεσις, ἄλλως τε καὶ τοῦ ἀρίστου, μετὰ ψυχῆς, εἰ μή τις λέγοι καθ' ὁμοιότητα καὶ μεταφοράν, ἔμψυχ' ἂν εἴη τὰ κινούμενα. Ψυχῇ δ' ἅμα δοκεῖ καὶ κίνησις ὑπάρχειν (ζωὴ γὰρ τοῖς ἔχουσιν, ἀφ' ἧς καὶ αἱ ὀρέξεις πρὸς ἕκαστον, ὥσπερ καὶ τοῖς ζῴοις, ἐπεὶ καὶ αἱ αἰσθήσεις

5a20–22 τὸ δὲ κατὰ τὸ πλῆθος τῶν σφαιρῶν ... οὐ γὰρ ⌜οἰκεῖος⌝ ὅ γε τῶν ἀστρολόγων] Arist. *Met.* Λ 8, 1073b3–5, 1074a14–17 τὸ δὲ πλῆθος ἤδη τῶν φορῶν ἐκ τῆς οἰκειοτάτης φιλοσοφίᾳ τῶν μαθηματικῶν ἐπιστημῶν δεῖ σκοπεῖν, ἐκ τῆς ἀστρολογίας. ... τὸ μὲν οὖν πλῆθος τῶν σφαιρῶν ἔστω τοσοῦτον, ὥστε καὶ τὰς οὐσίας καὶ τὰς ἀρχὰς τὰς ἀκινήτους ... τοσαύτας εὔλογον ὑπολαβεῖν· τὸ γὰρ ἀναγκαῖον ἀφείσθω τοῖς ἰσχυροτέροις λέγειν. **5a24–25** οὐ τὴν ἠρεμίαν ... κίνησιν] Arist. *Phys.* Θ 9, 265b1–8 κινεῖταί τε καὶ ἠρεμεῖ πως ἡ σφαῖρα· τὸν αὐτὸν γὰρ κατέχει τόπον. ... διὰ δὲ τὸ τοῦτο μένειν ἀεί τε ἠρεμεῖ πως τὸ ὅλον καὶ κινεῖται συνεχῶς. **5a26–27** ὅσοι τοὺς ἀριθμούς] Arist. *Met.* A 6, 987b11–13 οἱ μὲν γὰρ Πυθαγόρειοι μιμήσει τὰ ὄντα φασὶν εἶναι τῶν ἀριθμῶν, Πλάτων δὲ μεθέξει, τοὔνομα μεταβαλών. **5a27–28** τοὺς ἀριθμούς φασιν τὸ ἕν] Xenocrates fr. 16 Heinze, 214 Isnardi Parente (= Favonius Eulogius, *Disputatio de Somnio Scipionis* V,6–7, 6.17–23 Scarpa) Estque numerus, ut Xenocrates censuit, animus ac deus; non enim aliud est quam quod ei subest. ... Quantam enim velis colligas quantitatem, ducetur ab uno texetur ab uno desinetque in unum. Ac pereuntibus aliis, quae id recipere possunt, immutabile perseverat. Arist. *Met.* M 8, 1083a23–25 εἰσὶ δὲ οὗτοι ὅσοι ... οἴονται ... τὰ ... μαθηματικὰ εἶναι καὶ τοὺς ἀριθμοὺς πρώτους τῶν ὄντων, καὶ ἀρχὴν αὐτῶν εἶναι αὐτὸ τὸ ἕν. ... τὸ ἓν μὲν εἶναί τι πρῶτον τῶν ἑνῶν, ὥσπερ ἐκεῖνοί φασι. **5a28–5b1** ἡ ἔφεσις ... μετὰ ψυχῆς] Arist. *DA* 433a31–32 ἡ τοιαύτη δύναμις κινεῖ τῆς ψυχῆς ἡ καλουμένη ὄρεξις **5b3–7** ζωὴ ... γίνονται] Arist. *DA* 413b1–2 τὸ μὲν οὖν ζῆν διὰ τὴν ἀρχὴν ταύτην (sc. τὴν ψυχήν) ὑπάρχει τοῖς ζῶσι, τὸ δὲ ζῷον διὰ τὴν αἴσθησιν πρώτως. **5b4** ἀφ' ἧς] Arist. *DA* 408b14–16 τὸν ἄνθρωπον τῇ ψυχῇ (sc. ἐλεεῖν ἢ μανθάνειν ἢ διανοεῖσθαι βέλτιον λέγειν)· τοῦτο δὲ μὴ ὡς ἐν ἐκείνῃ τῆς κινήσεως οὔσης, ἀλλ' ὁτὲ μὲν μέχρι ἐκείνης, ὁτὲ δ' ἀπ' ἐκείνης.

22 οἰκεῖος Ψ (*ānas*) : om. **α** Λ | post ἀστρολόγων add. ἱκανός J^{II} et alii alia, v. app. crit. alt. **26** ὁμοίως om. P **28** εἰ δ' ἡ PJ^{II} : εἰ δὴ J Ψ Λ **5b1** ἀρίστου PJ^{II} Ψ Λ : ἀορίστου J | ὅτι post λέγοι ut intell. Ar., add. Us.^{1} **2** μεταφοράν J^{II} A^{2} Tiph., Hampke apud Us.^{1,2} : διαφοράν **α** Ψ* Λ | post μεταφορὰν non dist. Ar. | ἔμψυχ' P : ἔμψυχα J **3** ψυχῇ Ψ, corr. Us.^{1,2} : ψυχὴ J Λ, ψυχη P bodies], as they proceed in fulfillment of the best desire,[27] is by no means obvious. (**7**) As for the [matter] of the great number of spheres, it calls for a fuller account of the reason [for it]; for the one [given] by the astronomers, at any rate, is not ⌜pertinent⌝.[28]

(**8**) Also a matter of aporia[29] is how on earth it is that they,[30] though possessed of a natural desire, pursue not rest but motion. Why, then, is it at the same time with imitation that this[31] is maintained, alike by those who uphold the one and by those who uphold the numbers?[32]—for the latter, too, maintain that the numbers are the one.[33]

(**8.1**) And if impulsion, especially towards the best, entails soul, then unless one speak by simile and metaphor, the [things] in motion will be ensouled. But movement also seems at the same time to pertain to soul[34] (for [soul] is life to those who have it—and from it also [start] the desires for each [thing]—just as [it is] to animals, too, for even sense-

[27] I.e., the concord of the motion of the spheres as they proceed in fulfillment of their desire for the best, the unmoved mover. See the commentary.

[28] I.e., the account given by the astronomers Eudoxus and Calippus in Aristotle's *Metaphysics* Lambda 8 to which Theophrastus is directly referring. See the commentary.

[29] On the use of the word aporia see Chapter 1.2, note 14, and for its importance in this Essay, Chapter 1.3.

[30] I.e., the rotating bodies.

[31] I.e., the statement that they pursue not rest but motion. See the commentary.

[32] These are, variously or even jointly, the Pythagoreans and Plato, together with his followers Xenocrates and Speusippus.

[33] I.e., the numbers are unmoved like the one because they are ultimately derived from it and reducible to it, as Xenocrates reportedly maintained. For the point of this rhetorical question and the passage in general see the commentary.

[34] I.e., at the same time as desire or impulsion. See the commentary.

καίπερ ἐν τῷ πάσχειν οὖσαι δι' ἑτέρων, ὅμως ⌜ὡς⌝ ἐμψύχοι⌜ς⌝ γίνονται). Εἰ δ' οὖν τῆς κυκλικῆς αἴτιον τὸ [9] πρῶτον, οὐ τῆς ἀρίστης ἂν εἴη· κρεῖττον γὰρ ἡ τῆς ψυχῆς, καὶ πρώτη δὴ καὶ μάλιστα ἡ τῆς δια-
5b10 νοίας, ἀφ' ἧς καὶ ἡ ὄρεξις.

(9) Τάχα δὲ καὶ τοῦτ' ἂν τις ἐπιζητήσειεν, διὰ τί τὰ κυκλικὰ μόνον ἐφετικά, τῶν δὲ περὶ τὸ μέσον οὐθὲν καίπερ κινητῶν ὄντων: πότερον ὡς ἀδύνατα ἢ ὡς οὐ διικνουμένου τοῦ πρώτου; Ἀλλὰ τοῦτό γ' ἄτοπον, εἰ δι' ἀσθένειαν· ἰσχυρότερον γὰρ ἄν τις ἀξιώσειεν τοῦ Ὁμήρου Διός, ὅς φησιν,

αὐτῇ κεν γαίῃ ἐρύσαιμ' αὐτῇ τε θαλάσσῃ.

Ἀλλὰ λοιπὸν ὥσπερ ἄδεκτόν τι καὶ ἀσύνδετον εἶναι.

5b7–9 τῆς κυκλικῆς ... τῆς ψυχῆς] Arist. *DA* 407b5–12 ἄδηλος δὲ καὶ τοῦ κύκλῳ φέρεσθαι τὸν οὐρανὸν ἡ αἰτία· οὔτε γὰρ τῆς ψυχῆς ἡ οὐσία αἰτία τοῦ κύκλῳ φέρεσθαι, ἀλλὰ κατὰ συμβεβηκὸς οὕτω κινεῖται, οὔτε τὸ σῶμα αἴτιον, ἀλλ' ἡ ψυχὴ μᾶλλον ἐκείνῳ. ἀλλὰ μὴν οὐδ' ὅτι βέλτιον λέγεται· καίτοι γ' ἐχρῆν διὰ τοῦτο τὸν θεὸν κύκλῳ ποιεῖν φέρεσθαι τὴν ψυχήν, ὅτι βέλτιον αὐτῇ τὸ κινεῖσθαι τοῦ μένειν, κινεῖσθαι δ' οὕτως ἢ ἄλλως. **5b8–10** κρεῖττον γὰρ ἡ (sc. κίνησις) τῆς ψυχῆς, καὶ ... ἡ τῆς διανοίας] Arist. *DA* 410b12–14 τῆς δὲ ψυχῆς εἶναί τι κρεῖττον καὶ ἄρχον ἀδύνατον· ἀδυνατώτερον δ' ἔτι τοῦ νοῦ. Theophr. fr. 159,27–29 FHS&G Θεόφραστος εἰκότως ἀρχὴν κινήσεως τὴν ψυχὴν εἰπὼν οὐδὲν ἄλλο πρὸ αὐτῆς ὑποθέμενος, ἀρχῆς οὐκ οἴεται δεῖν ἀρχὴν ἐπιζητεῖν. **5b8–10** ἡ (sc. κίνησις) τῆς ψυχῆς ... ἡ ὄρεξις] Arist. *DA* 433a17–20, b11–12 δύο ταῦτα φαίνεται τὰ κινοῦντα, ὄρεξις καὶ διάνοια πρακτική· τὸ ὀρεκτὸν γὰρ κινεῖ, καὶ διὰ τοῦτο ἡ διάνοια κινεῖ, ὅτι ἀρχὴ αὐτῆς ἐστι τὸ ὀρεκτόν. ... τὸ ὀρεκτὸν ... κινεῖ οὐ κινούμενον τῷ νοηθῆναι ἢ φαντασθῆναι. **5b12** τῶν περὶ τὸ μέσον] Arist. *GC* 335a24–25 ἐπεὶ δ' ἐστὶν ἔνια γενητὰ καὶ φθαρτά, καὶ ἡ γένεσις τυγχάνει οὖσα ἐν τῷ περὶ τὸ μέσον τόπῳ ... **5b13–14** οὐ διικνουμένου τοῦ πρώτου] Arist. *GC* 336b28–31 τὸ εἶναι ... ἐν ἅπασιν ἀδύνατον ὑπάρχειν διὰ τὸ πόρρω τῆς ἀρχῆς ἀφίστασθαι.

6 ὅμως ὡς Ψ (*illā annahā ʿalā ḥālin*), coni. Us.[1] : ὅμως PJ Λ | ἐμψύχοις Ψ (*tunsabu ilā anna lahā anfusan*), coni. Us.[1,2] : ἔμψυχοι **α** Λ : ἐν ψυχῇ coni. Ross **8** τῆς ἀρίστης PJ Λ : τοῦ ἀρίστου ut interpr. Ar. | κρεῖττον PJ Ψ : κρείττων Λ **8 et 9** ἡ sc. αἰτία ut interpr. Ar. **17** αὐτῇ pr. non vert. Ar. | ἐρύσαιμ' P : ἐρυσαίμ' J, ἐρυσαίμ⟨ην⟩ ut intell. Ar., v. adn. : [Λ] (*librabit*; fort. *liberavi*?) **18** ἀσύνδετον Ψ (*lā muḥtamil li-l-irtibāṭ*), prop. Us.[2] : ἀσύνθετον PJ Λ : ἀσύνετον coni. Us.[1,2]

perceptions, though they consist in being affected by others,[35] yet take place in [animals] ⌜as⌝ ensouled [beings]). If, then, the first [mover] is the cause of the circular [movement], it will not be [the cause] of the best [movement]; for the [movement] of the soul is a more effective [thing], and first indeed and foremost is the [movement] of thought, from which the desire also [starts].[36]

(**9**) Perhaps one might incidentally ask this, too, why the rotating [bodies] alone are actuated by impulsion, but none of those about the center,[37] although they are mobile: is it because they are incapable, or because the first does not get through? But certainly the latter would make no sense, if because of weakness—for one would expect [the first] to be stronger than Homer's Zeus, who says,

With the earth would I hale [you] up, and therewithal the sea.[38]

So then what remains is to be like something unreceptive and unconnected.[39]

---

[35] And not, that is, by the soul.

[36] The movement of the soul—i.e., movement whose *source* is the soul (as the parallel formulation by Theophrastus in his fr. 159,28 FHS&G has it), and especially thought—is more effective than the unmoved prime mover in causing movement because it is itself the source of desire in the moved object. For a different understanding of the referent in the phrase "that [i.e., movement] of the soul" in the Arabic translation see the corresponding note.

[37] I.e., the sublunar world, considered to be the center of the universe. It is the realm of generation and corruption (Aristotle, *GC* 335a25), or, as Theophrastus says in the beginning of his *Physics* (fr. 143 FHS&G), the world of motion and of alteration and being affected.

[38] *Iliad* VIII,24. The translation is by Arthur S. Way, *The Iliad of Homer done into English verse*, London: Sampson Low, etc., 1886, vol. I, p. 184, whose Victorian version, in addition to being surprisingly literal, perhaps conveys the same distance existing between it and modern English as there existed between Homer's Greek and Greek in the time of Theophrastus.

[39] The Greek does not specify whether what is like something unreceptive and unconnected is the center itself (singular subject, so interpreted by Ross, Tricot, and Reale 1964) or "those about the center" (plural subject, so interpreted by Laks & Most, van Raalte, and Henrich). The singular neuter adjectives "unreceptive" and "unconnected" would tend to favor the former.

[10] **(10)** Τάχα δὲ πρότερον ζητήσειεν ἄν τις πῶς ἔχει, πότερα μέρη ταῦτα ἢ οὐ μέρη τοῦ οὐρανοῦ, καὶ εἰ μέρη, πῶς μέρη· νῦν γὰρ οἷον ἀπεωσμένα τῶν ἐντιμοτάτων οὐ μόνον κατὰ τὰς χώρας ἀλλὰ καὶ κατὰ τὴν ἐνέργειαν, εἴπερ ἡ κυκλικὴ τοιαύτη· συμβαίνει γὰρ οἷον κατὰ συμβεβηκὸς ὑπὸ τῆς κυκλικῆς περιφορᾶς καὶ εἰς τοὺς τόπους καὶ εἰς ἄλληλα τὰς μεταβολάς.

(10.1) Εἰ δὲ καὶ τὸ ἄριστον ἀπὸ τοῦ ἀρίστου, κάλλιον ἄν τι παρὰ τοῦ πρώτου δέοι τῆς κυκλοφορίας—εἰ μὴ ἄρ᾽ ἐκωλύετο τῷ μὴ δύνασθαι δέχεσθαι—τὸ γὰρ δὴ πρῶτον καὶ θειότατον πάντα τὰ ἄριστα βουλόμενον. Τάχα δὲ τοῦτο μὲν οἷον ὑπερβατόν τι καὶ ἀζήτητον—ἀξιοῖ γὰρ ὁ τοῦτο λέγων ἅπανθ᾽ ὅμοια καὶ ἐν τοῖς ἀρίστοις εἶναι, μικράν τιν᾽ ἢ μηδεμίαν ἔχοντα διαφοράν— **(11)** τόδε δ᾽ [11] ἄν τις ἴσως ἀπορήσειεν πρὸς αὐτὸν τὸν πρῶτον

5b20 μέρη τοῦ οὐρανοῦ] Arist. *DC* 278b11–21 ἕνα μὲν οὖν τρόπον οὐρανὸν λέγομεν τὴν οὐσίαν τὴν τῆς ἐσχάτης τοῦ παντὸς περιφορᾶς. … ἄλλον δ᾽ αὖ τρόπον τὸ συνεχὲς σῶμα τῇ ἐσχάτῃ περιφορᾷ τοῦ παντός. … ἔτι δ᾽ ἄλλως λέγομεν οὐρανὸν τὸ περιεχόμενον σῶμα ὑπὸ τῆς ἐσχάτης περιφορᾶς. **5b21–26** οἷον ἀπεωσμένα (sc. τὰ περὶ τὸ μέσον) … τὰς μεταβολάς] Arist. *GC* 337a2–7 τἆλλα ὅσα μεταβάλλει εἰς ἄλληλα κατὰ τὰ πάθη καὶ τὰς δυνάμεις, οἷον τὰ ἁπλᾶ σώματα, μιμεῖται τὴν κύκλῳ φοράν· … κύκλῳ φαμὲν περιεληλυθέναι τὴν γένεσιν διὰ τὸ πάλιν ἀνακάμπτειν· ὥστε καὶ ἡ εὐθεῖα φορὰ μιμουμένη τὴν κύκλῳ συνεχής ἐστιν. **5b25–26** εἰς ἄλληλα τὰς μεταβολὰς] Theophr. *Ign.* 1.1–2 ἀὴρ μὲν γὰρ καὶ ὕδωρ καὶ γῆ τὰς εἰς ἄλληλα μόνον ποιοῦνται μεταβολὰς φυσικάς. **5b26–27** ἄριστον ἀπὸ τοῦ ἀρίστου] Arist. *Met.* A 4, 985a9–10 εἴπερ τὸ τῶν ἀγαθῶν ἁπάντων αἴτιον αὐτὸ τἀγαθόν ἐστι. **5b26–6a2** Εἰ δὲ … βουλόμενον] Arist. *GC* 336b25–337a1 ἀεὶ δ᾽ … συνεχὴς ἔσται ἡ γένεσις καὶ ἡ φθορά …, τοῦτο δ᾽ εὐλόγως συμβέβηκεν. ἐπεὶ γὰρ ἐν ἅπασιν ἀεὶ τοῦ βελτίονος ὀρέγεσθαί φαμεν τὴν φύσιν, βέλτιον δὲ τὸ εἶναι ἢ τὸ μὴ εἶναι …, τοῦτο δ᾽ ἐν ἅπασιν ἀδύνατον ὑπάρχειν διὰ τὸ πόρρω τῆς ἀρχῆς ἀφίστασθαι, τῷ λειπομένῳ τρόπῳ συνεπλήρωσε τὸ ὅλον ὁ θεός, ἐνδελεχῆ ποιήσας τὴν γένεσιν—οὕτω γὰρ ἂν μάλιστα συνείροιτο τὸ εἶναι διὰ τὸ ἐγγύτατα εἶναι τῆς οὐσίας τὸ γίνεσθαι ἀεὶ καὶ τὴν γένεσιν. τούτου δ᾽ αἴτιον … ἡ κύκλῳ φορά· μόνη γὰρ συνεχής. **6a1–2** τὸ γὰρ δὴ πρῶτον … βουλόμενον, **3–4** ὁ τοῦτο λέγων] Plato *Tim.* 30a2, 6–7 βουληθεὶς γὰρ ὁ θεὸς ἀγαθὰ μὲν πάντα … θέμις δ᾽ οὔτ᾽ ἦν οὔτ᾽ ἔστιν τῷ ἀρίστῳ δρᾶν ἄλλο πλὴν τὸ κάλλιστον. Arist. *Met.* Λ 10, 1075a11–19 ποτέρως ἔχει ἡ τοῦ ὅλου φύσις τὸ ἀγαθὸν καὶ τὸ ἄριστον. … οὐ γὰρ οὗτος (sc. ὁ στρατηγὸς) διὰ τὴν τάξιν ἀλλ᾽ ἐκείνη διὰ τοῦτόν ἐστιν. … πρὸς μὲν γὰρ ἓν ἅπαντα συντέτακται.

22 καὶ PJ[1] Ψ : om. J Λ **23** συμβαίνει **ω** (sc. γίνεσθαι; v. adn.) : λαμβάνει coni. Us.[1,2] **24** οἷον PJ Ψ : om. Lat. : εἶναι prop. Zeller **6a1** δὴ P Ψ Λ : δεῖ J | post θειότατον dist. Ar. **2** post βουλόμενον add. ἦν J[II] **4** ὅμοια **α** Λ : ἅμα ἃ Ψ vel Ar. | post εἶναι dist. Ar., Us.[1], add. τὰ χείριστα J[II] **6** πρῶτον om. Ar.

(**10**) But perhaps one might ask beforehand what the situation is: whether these[40] are or are not parts of the heavens, and if parts, how so;[41] for as it is,[42] they have been pushed, so to speak, away from the [things] held in highest honor not only as regards the[ir] locations but also as regards the[ir] activity—if indeed the circular [movement] is such:[43] for it happens as it were by accident that the[ir] changes, both into the[ir several] places and into each other, [take place] by means of the circular rotation.

(**10.1**) And if, too, the best [comes] from the best, something better than rotation will be needed [to issue] from the first—unless of course they were prevented[44] by being unable to receive—for surely the first and most divine is that which wills everything that is best. But while this [claim] is perhaps like something inordinate and unexamined—for he who maintains this demands that everything should be alike and among the best, having little or no differentiation[45]—(**11**) the following aporia might fairly be raised with reference to the first heaven itself: whether

---

[40] I.e., "those about the center."

[41] Aristotle (*De caelo* 278b10–21) identified three senses for "the heavens" (*ouranós*), one of which is the entire universe, whence Theophrastus's question.

[42] "As it is" (the temporal adverb *nun*) could refer either (a) to Theophrastus's account of the Aristotelian cosmos given in the preceding paragraphs, or (b) to the way things actually are.

[43] I.e., one of the things held in highest honor; for the sublunar elements do not move naturally in a circle.

[44] The subject of this verb is not stated explicitly by Theophrastus and opinion has been divided about it. Some have claimed that it is the heavenly spheres ("the rotating bodies"), while others think that it continues to be "those about the center," i.e., the sublunary elements and bodies which, it is suggested, not only lack rotation, but even had they had it it would not have been the best possible outcome of the influence by the first. I tend to favor the second alternative (which is also supported by an apparently authoritative gloss in the Arabic translation); see the discussion in the commentary at Diaporia 10.1.

[45] Cf. 8a27–8b1 and 11b7–10 where Theophrastus refers again to this objectionable theory, apparently of Plato (cf. Dillon 2002, 179; Berti 2002, 350); see the Loci Paralleli.

οὐρανὸν ἀναφέρων, πότερον ἡ περιφορὰ τῆς οὐσίας ἐστὶν αὐτοῦ καὶ ἅμα τῷ πεπαῦσθαι φθείροιτ' ἄν, ἤ, εἴπερ ἐφέσει τινὶ καὶ ὀρέξει, κατὰ συμβεβηκός· εἰ μὴ ἄρα σύμφυτον αὐτῷ τὸ ὀρέγεσθαι καὶ οὐθὲν κωλύει τοιαῦτ' ἄττα τῶν ὄντων ὑπάρχειν. **(12)** Ἴσως δ' ἂν εἴη καὶ ἀφελόντα τὴν ὄρεξιν ὑπὲρ αὐτῆς τῆς κινήσεως ἀπορεῖν, εἰ ἀφαιρεθεῖσα φθείροι ἂν τὸν οὐρανόν.

(13) Καὶ τοῦτο μὲν ὥσπερ ἑτέρων λόγων, ἀπὸ δ' οὖν ταύτης ἢ τούτων τῶν ἀρχῶν ἀξιώσειεν ἄν τις (τάχα δὲ καὶ ἀπὸ τῶν III ἄλλων ἄρ', ἄν τις τίθηται) τὰ ἐφεξῆς εὐθὺς ἀποδιδόναι καὶ μὴ μέχρι του προελθόντα παύεσθαι. Τοῦτο γὰρ τελέου καὶ φρονοῦντος ὅπερ Ἀρχύτας ποτ' ἔφη ποιεῖν Εὔρυτον διατιθέντα τινὰς ψήφους· λέγειν γὰρ ὡς ὅδε μὲν ἀνθρώπου ὁ ἀριθμός, ὅδε δὲ ἵππου, ὅδε δ' ἄλλου τινὸς τυγχάνει. Νῦν δ' οἵ γε πολλοὶ μέχρι τινὸς ἐλθόντες καταπαύονται, καθάπερ καὶ οἱ τὸ ἓν καὶ τὴν ἀόριστον [12] δυάδα ποιοῦντες· τοὺς γὰρ ἀριθμοὺς γεννήσαντες καὶ τὰ ἐπίπεδα καὶ τὰ σώματα σχεδὸν τὰ ἄλλα παραλείπουσιν πλὴν ὅσον ἐφαπτόμενοι καὶ το-

---

6a7–10 πότερον ... συμβεβηκός] Arist. *DA* 407b5–9 ἄδηλος δὲ καὶ τοῦ κύκλῳ φέρεσθαι τὸν οὐρανὸν ἡ αἰτία· οὔτε γὰρ τῆς ψυχῆς ἡ οὐσία αἰτία τοῦ κύκλῳ φέρεσθαι, ἀλλὰ κατὰ συμβεβηκὸς οὕτω κινεῖται, οὔτε τὸ σῶμα αἴτιον, ἀλλ' ἡ ψυχὴ μᾶλλον ἐκείνῳ. **6a13–14** ὑπὲρ αὐτῆς ... τὸν οὐρανόν] Plato *Theaet.* 153d1–5 καὶ δηλοῖ ὅτι ἕως μὲν ἂν ἡ περιφορὰ ᾖ κινουμένη καὶ ὁ ἥλιος, πάντα ἔστι καὶ σῴζεται τὰ ἐν θεοῖς τε καὶ ἀνθρώποις, εἰ δὲ σταίη τοῦτο ὥσπερ δεθέν, πάντα χρήματ' ἂν διαφθαρείη. **6a17** τὰ ἐφεξῆς] Arist. *Phys.* E 3, 226b34–227a1, 227a17–24 ἐφεξῆς δὲ οὗ μετὰ τὴν ἀρχὴν ὄντος ἢ θέσει ἢ εἴδει ἢ ἄλλῳ τινὶ οὕτως ἀφορισθέντος μηδὲν μεταξύ ἐστι τῶν ἐν ταὐτῷ γένει καὶ οὗ ἐφεξῆς ἐστιν ... φανερὸν δὲ καὶ ὅτι πρῶτον τὸ ἐφεξῆς ἐστι, κτλ. ... ὥστε ἡ σύμφυσις ὑστάτη κατὰ τὴν γένεσιν. **6a20–22** Εὔρυτον] Arist. *Met.* N 5, 1092b10–13 καὶ ὡς Εὔρυτος ἔταττε τίς ἀριθμὸς τίνος, οἷον ὁδὶ μὲν ἀνθρώπου ὁδὶ δὲ ἵππου ... οὕτως ἀφομοιῶν ταῖς ψήφοις τὰς μορφὰς τῶν φυτῶν. **6a24–26** οἱ τὸ ἓν ... καὶ τὰ σώματα] Sextus Empiricus, *Adv. Math.* X,282 ἐκεῖνοι (*sc.* οἱ Πυθαγόρειοι) μὲν γὰρ ἐκ δυεῖν ἀρχῶν, τῆς τε μονάδος καὶ τῆς ἀορίστου δυάδος, ἐποίουν τοὺς ἀριθμούς, εἶτ' ἐκ τῶν ἀριθμῶν τὰ σημεῖα καὶ τὰς γραμμὰς τά τε ἐπίπεδα σχήματα καὶ τὰ στερεά.

9 ἐφέσει ... ὀρέξει transp. Ar. **11** τοιαῦτ' ἄττα J Ψ Λ : τοιαυτ' αττι P **13** εἰ J[II] Ψ Λ, εἱ P : η J **14** φθείροι PJ Λ : φθείροιτ' A et fort. Ψ **17** ἄρ' ἄν PJ A, 'ἄρ' ἄν C, ἆρ' ἄν Λ : ἃς ἄν J[II], ὅς ἄν L : ἀρ(χῶν) ἂν coni. Wim.[1,2] : ἅμα ut intell. Ar. | ἄν τις ἄρα transp. Us.[1] **18** του P Ψ J[II] : τοῦ J Λ **21** γὰρ om. J **26** καὶ alt. del. J[II] | τὰ ἄλλα P : τ' ἄλλα JCL : τἆλλα A [Ψ] [Λ] **27** ὅσον P Ψ Λ : ὅσων J the rotation is of its essence and with cessation it would perish, or, if indeed [the rotation occurs] through some impulsion and desire, [it is] accidental—unless, of course, desiring is innate to it and nothing prevents some beings from being such.[46] (**12**) But perhaps one might, even while setting desire aside,[47] raise an aporia about the motion itself, whether its removal would destroy the heavens.[48]

(**13**) Now this may well be [more appropriately] discussed elsewhere,[49] but for the present it is from this or these first principles[50] (and perhaps also from the others, I suppose, were one to assume [them]) that one could demand that [they] provide right away an account of the [things that come] next and not, having proceeded up to a [point], stop. For this is what a sensible adult [would do], which is exactly what Archytas once said Eurytus did as he arranged certain pebbles: for Eurytus said [according to Archytas], that this happens to be the number of man, this of horse, and this of something else.[51] At present, however, having arrived at a certain [point], many, certainly, stop completely, as do too those who posit the one and the indefinite dyad;[52] for having generated numbers and planes and solids, they leave out almost everything else except to the extent

[46] I.e., innately desiring, or acting upon their innate desire. See the commentary.

[47] I.e., removing it from consideration in the discussion in the second part of this apparent thought experiment; the first is stated in the preceding sentence.

[48] "The heavens" here may be taken in any one of its three significations (see above, note 41), but the net outcome would be the same; Theophrastus is clearly referring here to the very existence of everything.

[49] Theophrastus touches upon the related question whether the motion of the heavens is essential to them later in this Essay (10a9–19), but it is not clear whether he actually discussed the subject (and the thought experiment?) elsewhere. See the commentary.

[50] The reference is to the preceding discussion of first principles at 4b11–5a5, before it was interrupted for a critical review of the theory of desire.

[51] The Pythagoreans Archytas and Eurytus, both of Tarentum, were roughly contemporaries of Plato; Archytas had special relations with him. See *DPhA* I, § A322, and III, § E150 (both by Centrone).

[52] The Pythagoreans and Plato, to whom Theophrastus explicitly ascribes this doctrine below (at 11a27–11b5), and perhaps also Plato's "orthodox" followers in the Academy other than Speusippus and Xenocrates who are mentioned separately later in the paragraph (as Ross 54 observes; cf. also Happ 1971, 244n833).

σοῦτο μόνον δηλοῦντες, ὅτι τὰ μὲν ἀπὸ τῆς ἀορί-
6b1 στου δυάδος, οἷον τόπος καὶ κενὸν καὶ ἄπειρον, τὰ δ' ἀπὸ τῶν ἀριθμῶν καὶ τοῦ ἑνός, οἷον ψυχὴ καὶ ἄλλ' ἄττα: χρόνος θ' ἅμα καὶ οὐρανὸς καὶ ἕτερα δὴ πλείω· τοῦ δ' οὐρανοῦ πέρι καὶ τῶν λοιπῶν οὐδεμίαν ἔτι ποιοῦνται μνείαν. Ὡσαύτως δ' οὐδ' οἱ περὶ Σπεύσιππον, οὐδὲ τῶν ἄλλων οὐθεὶς πλὴν Ξενοκράτης· οὗτος γὰρ ἅπαντά πως περιτίθησιν περὶ τὸν κόσμον, ὁμοίως αἰσθητὰ καὶ νοητὰ καὶ μαθηματικὰ καὶ ἔτι δὴ τὰ θεῖα. Πειρᾶται δὲ καὶ [13]
Ἑστιαῖος μέχρι τινός, οὐχ ὥσπερ εἴρηται περὶ τῶν πρώτων μόνον. Πλάτων μὲν οὖν ἐν τῷ ἀνάγειν εἰς τὰς ἀρχὰς δόξειεν ἂν ἅπτεσθαι τῶν ἄλλων εἰς τὰς ἰδέας ἀνάπτων, ταύτας δ' εἰς τοὺς

6b2 τὰ δ' ἀπὸ τῶν ἀριθμῶν καὶ τοῦ ἑνός, οἷον ψυχὴ] Xenocrates fr. 68, 14–21 Heinze γενέσθαι τὸν ἀριθμὸν τοῦ ἑνὸς ὁρίζοντος τὸ πλῆθος καὶ τῇ ἀπειρίᾳ πέρας ἐντιθέντος ... τοῦτον δὲ μήπω ψυχὴν τὸν ἀριθμὸν εἶναι ... τοῦ δὲ ταὐτοῦ καὶ τοῦ ἑτέρου συμμιγέντων ... ψυχὴν γεγονέναι. Arist. *DA* 404b19–21 Πλάτων ἐν τῷ Τιμαίῳ (35a–36d) ... αὐτὸ μὲν τὸ ζῷον ἐξ' αὐτῆς τῆς τοῦ ἑνὸς ἰδέας καὶ τοῦ πρώτου μήκους καὶ πλάτους καὶ βάθους. **6b2–3** ψυχὴ καὶ ἄλλ' ἄττα: χρόνος θ' ἅμα καὶ οὐρανὸς] Plato *Tim.* 36d8-e1, e5–6, 38b6–7 ἐπεὶ δὲ ... πᾶσα ἡ τῆς ψυχῆς σύστασις ἐγεγένητο, μετὰ τοῦτο πᾶν τὸ σωματοειδὲς ἐντὸς αὐτῆς ἐτεκταίνετο ... καὶ τὸ μὲν δὴ σῶμα ὁρατὸν οὐρανοῦ γέγονεν ... χρόνος δ' οὖν μετ' οὐρανοῦ γέγονεν, ἵνα ἅμα γεννηθέντες ἅμα καὶ λυθῶσιν. Arist. *Met.* Λ 6, 1072a2–3 ὕστερον γάρ (sc. τῆς κινήσεως), καὶ ἅμα τῷ οὐρανῷ, ἡ ψυχή, ὡς φησίν (sc. ὁ Πλάτων). **6b7–9** Ξενοκράτης ... θεῖα] Arist. *Met.* Z 2, 1028b24–27 ἔνιοι δὲ τὰ μὲν εἴδη καὶ τοὺς ἀριθμοὺς τὴν αὐτὴν ἔχειν φασὶ φύσιν, τὰ δὲ ἄλλα ἐχόμενα, γραμμὰς καὶ ἐπίπεδα, μέχρι πρὸς τὴν τοῦ οὐρανοῦ οὐσίαν καὶ τὰ αἰσθητά. **6b11–15** Πλάτων ... εἰρημένων] Arist. *EN* I 4, 1095a30-b1 διαφέρουσιν οἱ ἀπὸ τῶν ἀρχῶν λόγοι καὶ οἱ ἐπὶ τὰς ἀρχάς· εὖ γὰρ καὶ ὁ Πλάτων ἠπόρει τοῦτο καὶ ἐζήτει, πότερον ἀπὸ τῶν ἀρχῶν ἢ ἐπὶ τὰς ἀρχάς ἐστιν ἡ ὁδός. **6b13–14** τὰς ἰδέας ἀνάπτων ... εἰς τοὺς ἀριθμούς] Sextus Empiricus *Adv. Math.* x,258 κατὰ τὸν Πλάτωνα ... ἑκάστη ἰδέα κατ' ἰδίαν μὲν λαμβανομένη ἓν εἶναι λέγεται, κατὰ σύλληψιν δὲ ἑτέρας ἢ ἄλλων δύο καὶ τρεῖς καὶ τέσσαρες, ὥστε εἶναί τι ἐπαναβεβηκὸς αὐτῶν τῆς ὑποστάσεως τὸν ἀριθμόν, οὗ κατὰ μετοχὴν τὸ ἓν ἢ τὰ δύο ἢ τὰ τρία ἢ τὰ τούτων ἔτι πλείονα ἐπικατηγορεῖται αὐτῶν.

6b2 ψυχὴ P Ψ Λ, ψυχη J, ψυχῆι J[1] **3** χρόνος θ' ἅμα καὶ οὐρανός [θ' coni. Us.[1]] Ψ (*miṯla ... az-zamāni ma'a s-samā'i*) : χρόνον δ' ἅμα καὶ οὐρανὸν **α** Λ **3–4** post πλείω (non post ἄττα) dist. Ar. | χρόνος—πλείω del. J[II], om. L, secl. Us.[1,2] **5** δ' οὐδ' J Ψ Λ : δ' P **7** post γὰρ del. ἂν J[1] | πως Ψ (*'alā waǧhin min al-wuǧūh*) Λ (*(omni)mode*) v. cap. 2.4 notam 15 : πῶς P J | περιτίθησιν PJ Λ [Ψ] : διατίθησιν prop. Us.[2], coni. van Raalte **8** post ὁμοίως dist. Ar. **10** ἑστιαῖος J : ἐστι αἶος P, ἔστι ὡς vel ὃς (?) Λ (*est quod*) [Ψ] **12** post ἀρχὰς add. τὰ ὑπὸ τὰς ἀρχὰς J[II] | δόξειεν ἂν Ψ P : δόξει ἐρᾶν J : Lat. om. in lac. **12–14** δόξειεν—ἀρχάς Λ vel interpres om. e homoeoteleuton (ἀρχὰς—ἀρχάς)

of apprehending and declaring only this much, that some things are [generated] from the indefinite dyad—such as place, the void, and the 6b1
infinite—and others from the numbers and the one—such as soul and some others: time together with the heavens, and quite a few more[53]—but of the heavens and the rest they make no *further* mention whatsoever. And likewise neither do those around Speusippus[54] nor anyone of the others except Xenocrates;[55] for he does somehow provide everything about the universe, alike sensibles, intelligibles, mathematicals, and, what is more, the divine [things]. Hestiaeus,[56] too, tries, up to a [point], and not, as mentioned, only with regard to the first [things]. And yes, in reducing [things] to the first principles, Plato[57] would seem to be treating of the others[58] by relating [them] to the ideas, these to the numbers, and

[53] Given the high degree of congruence between the ideas presented here and the Platonic cosmogony in the *Timaeus*, it is clear that Theophrastus is referring to discussions in the Academy. See the commentary on 6b3–4.

[54] Fragment 59 Tarán 1981, 87 Isnardi Parente 1980.

[55] Fragment 26 Heinze 1892, 100 Isnardi Parente 1982.

[56] Of Perinthus, an otherwise little known disciple of Plato. For a review of all the extant information on him see *DPhA* III, § 111 (Dorandi).

[57] Test. Plat. 30 Gaiser 1968, App. 3,8 Krämer 1990.

[58] I.e., of the things other than the first things.

ἀριθμούς, ἐκ δὲ τούτων εἰς τὰς ἀρχάς, εἶτα κατὰ τὴν γένεσιν μέχρι τῶν εἰρημένων· οἱ δὲ τῶν ἀρχῶν μόνον—ἔνιοι δὲ καὶ τὴν ἀλήθειαν ἐν τούτοις· τὰ γὰρ ὄντα μόνον περὶ τὰς ἀρχάς. Συμβαίνει δὲ τοὐναντίον ἢ ἐν ταῖς ἄλλαις μεθόδοις· ἐν ἐκείναις γὰρ τὰ μετὰ τὰς ἀρχὰς ἰσχυρότερα καὶ οἷον τελεώτερα τῶν ἐπιστημῶν· τάχα δὲ καὶ εὐλόγως· ἔνθα μὲν γὰρ τῶν ἀρχῶν, ἐν δὲ ταῖς λοιπαῖς ἀπὸ τῶν ἀρχῶν ἡ ζήτησις.

(14) Πῶς δέ ποτε χρὴ καὶ ποίας τὰς ἀρχὰς ὑποθέσθαι, τάχ' ἂν ἀπορήσειέν τις, πότερον ἀμόρφους καὶ οἷον δυναμικάς, ὥσπερ ὅσοι πῦρ καὶ γῆν, ἢ μεμορφωμένας, ὡς μάλιστα δέον ταύτας ὡρίσθαι, καθάπερ ἐν τῷ Τιμαίῳ φησίν· τοῖς γὰρ τιμιωτάτοις οἰκειότατον ἡ τάξις καὶ τὸ ὡρίσθαι. IV [14]
(Φαίνεται δὲ καὶ ἐν ταῖς λοιπαῖς σχεδὸν ἔχειν οὕτω ⌜πλὴν ὀλίγαις,⌝ καθάπερ ἡ γραμματικὴ καὶ μουσικὴ, καὶ ταῖς μαθηματικαῖς, συνακολουθεῖ δὲ καὶ τὰ μετὰ

6b14–15 κατὰ τὴν γένεσιν] *v. ad* 6a17. **6b16–17** ἔνιοι δὲ καὶ τὴν ἀλήθειαν ... τὰς ἀρχάς] Arist. *Met.* α 1, 993b19–31 ὀρθῶς δ' ἔχει καὶ τὸ καλεῖσθαι τὴν φιλοσοφίαν ἐπιστήμην τῆς ἀληθείας. ... οὐκ ἴσμεν δὲ τὸ ἀληθὲς ἄνευ τῆς αἰτίας· ... ὥστε καὶ ἀληθέστερον ⟨ἀεὶ⟩ τὸ τοῖς ὑστέροις αἴτιον τοῦ ἀληθέσιν εἶναι· διὸ τὰς τῶν ἀεὶ ὄντων ἀρχὰς ἀναγκαῖον [ἀεὶ] εἶναι ἀληθεστάτας ... ὥσθ' ἕκαστον ὡς ἔχει τοῦ εἶναι οὕτω καὶ τῆς ἀληθείας. **6b25–26** ὅσοι πῦρ καὶ γῆν] Theophr., Περὶ τῶν φυσικῶν, fr. 227C,8–9 FHS&G Παρμενίδης ... δύο ποιῶν τὰς ἀρχάς, πῦρ καὶ γῆν, τὸ μὲν ὡς ὕλην τὸ δ' ὡς αἴτιον καὶ ποιοῦν. **6b27** ἐν τῷ Τιμαίῳ] Plato, *Tim.* 30a2–6 βουληθεὶς γὰρ ὁ θεὸς ἀγαθὰ μὲν πάντα ... πᾶν ὅσον ἦν ὁρατὸν παραλαβὼν οὐχ ἡσυχίαν ἄγον ἀλλὰ κινούμενον πλημμελῶς καὶ ἀτάκτως, εἰς τάξιν αὐτὸ ἤγαγεν ἐκ τῆς ἀταξίας, ἡγησάμενος ἐκεῖνο τούτου πάντως ἄμεινον. **6b28–7a3** ἡ τάξις καὶ τὸ ὡρίσθαι ... ταῖς μαθηματικαῖς] Arist. *Met.* M 3, 1078a36-b2 τοῦ δὲ καλοῦ μέγιστα εἴδη τάξις καὶ συμμετρία καὶ τὸ ὡρισμένον, ἃ μάλιστα δεικνύουσιν αἱ μαθηματικαὶ ἐπιστῆμαι.

14 ἀρχάς J Ψ : ἀργὰς P : Lat om. in lac. **19** ἐκείναις Cam. : ἐκείνοις **α** [Ψ] [Λ] **20** post ἐπιστημῶν add. ἐνταῦθα δὲ τὸ κράτιστον ἡ ἀρχή J^{II} **21** ἔνθα **ω** : ἐνταῦθα J^{II} **25–26** ὥσπερ—μεμορφωμένας Ψ vel interpres om. e homoeoarcton (ὥσπερ—ὡς) **27** post καθάπερ add. Πλάτων Us.^{1} **7a2** πλὴν ὀλίγαις (*mā ḫalā š-šāḏḏi minhā*) Ψ, v. adn. : om. **α** Λ | καθάπερ ἡ γραμματικὴ καὶ μουσική, καὶ (post μουσική dist.) Ψ : καθάπερ ἡ γραμματικὴ καὶ μουσικὴ καὶ PJ Λ : καθάπερ ἐν γραμματικῇ καὶ μουσικῇ καὶ J^{II} et edd. a Us.^{2}, et alii alia, v. app. crit. alt. **3** συνακολουθεῖ [-ουσθεῖ P] **ω** : -ουθεῖν coni. Us.^{2}

from these to the principles,[59] and then, in order of generation, all the way [down] to the [things] mentioned;[60] but the others [treat] of the principles only—and some, even, [say] that reality itself consists of these,[61] for the [things] that exist pertain exclusively to the first principles. This is the opposite of what happens in the other disciplines: for in those, the [parts] of knowledge [that come] after the principles are firmer and, as it were, more complete; but maybe reasonably so: for here[62] the search is for the first principles whereas in the rest it is from the first principles.

(**14**)[63] Perhaps one might raise the aporia, how and of what sort one should at all suppose the first principles to be: whether shapeless and, as it were, potent (as [do] those who [posit] fire and earth),[64] or already shaped, on the ground that it is necessary most of all for these to be determined, as he says in the *Timaeus*;[65] for order and being determined are most appropriate to the [things] of greatest value. (This, incidentally, seems to be so also in almost all the rest [of the disciplines,] ⌜except for a few⌝ like grammar and music, as well as in the mathematical ones, while the [things] after the first principles, too, follow suit; and further,

---

[59] The anacoluthon is in the original. Theophrastus here changes the construction of the sentence, which was based on the verb "relating [them] to" (*anáptōn*); from here on and for the next phrase an intransitive verb of motion, like "proceeding," is apparently to be understood (cf. van Raalte 274).

[60] I.e., the things that "come next" in the sensible world mentioned earlier, at 6a17, as examples of which Theophrastus cited the theories of Eurytus about men and horses; see the commentary. Also to be noted is the reservation implied in Theophrastus's circumspect expression and the fact that he mentions Plato *after* Xenocrates and Hestiaeus; see the commentary.

[61] The neuter pronoun refers to all the various first principles mentioned previously—the one, the indefinite dyad, etc. See the commentary.

[62] I.e., in the study of the first principles, what was later to be called metaphysics; this appears to be a direct reference to the title of the Essay, "On First Principles".

[63] The argumentation in this aporia and the following diaporiae is too convoluted to include the precise numbering of the different sections in the text and translation; see the discussion in the commentary.

[64] It would seem that the reference here is to Parmenides, who viewed earth and fire as the material and efficient principles, or possibly even to a Pythagorean like Philolaus. See the commentary.

[65] This is not an exact quotation but a general reference to views expressed in Plato's dialogue at 30a.

τὰς ἀρχάς· ἔτι δὲ καὶ κατὰ τὰς τέχνας ὁμοίως, αἵπερ τὴν φύσιν μιμοῦνται: καὶ τὰ ὄργανα καὶ τὰ ἄλλα κατὰ τὰς ἀρχάς.) Οἱ μὲν οὖν ἐμμόρφους πάσας, οἱ δὲ μόνον τὰς ὑλικάς, οἱ δ᾽ ἄμφω [τὰς τ᾽ ἐμμόρφους καὶ τὰς τῆς ὕλης,] ὡς ἐν ἀμφοῖν τὸ τέλεον, οἷον γὰρ ἐξ ἀντικειμένων τὴν [15] ἅπασαν οὐσίαν.

(14.1) Ἄλογον δὲ κἀκείνοις δόξειεν ἄν, εἰ ὁ μὲν ὅλος οὐρανὸς καὶ ἕκαστα τῶν μερῶν ἅπαντ᾽ ἐν τάξει καὶ λόγῳ, καὶ μορφαῖς καὶ δυνάμεσιν καὶ περιόδοις, ἐν δὲ ταῖς ἀρχαῖς μηθὲν τοιοῦτον ἀλλ᾽ ὥσπερ «σάρξ, εἰκῇ κεχυμένων ὁ κάλλιστος», ⌜ὥς⌝ φησιν Ἡράκλειτος, «κόσμος». Καὶ κατὰ τοὐλάχιστον δ᾽ ὡς εἰπεῖν λαμβάνουσιν ὁμοίως ἐν ἀψύχοις καὶ ἐμψύχοις· ὡρισμέναι γὰρ ἑκάστων αἱ φύσεις ὡς εἰπεῖν καίπερ αὐτομάτως γινομένων, τὰς δ᾽ ἀρχὰς ἀορίστους εἶναι.

(14.2) Χαλεπὸν δὲ πάλιν αὖ τὸ τοὺς λόγους ἑκάστοις περιθεῖναι

7a4–6 κατὰ τὰς τέχνας ... κατὰ τὰς ἀρχάς] Arist. *Phys.* B 8, 199a15–20 ὅλως δὲ ἡ τέχνη τὰ μὲν ἐπιτελεῖ ἃ ἡ φύσις ἀδυνατεῖ ἀπεργάσασθαι, τὰ δὲ μιμεῖται. εἰ οὖν τὰ κατὰ τέχνην ἕνεκά του, δῆλον ὅτι καὶ τὰ κατὰ φύσιν· ὁμοίως γὰρ ἔχει πρὸς ἄλληλα ἐν τοῖς κατὰ τέχνην καὶ ἐν τοῖς κατὰ φύσιν τὰ ὕστερα πρὸς τὰ πρότερα. **7a7** οἱ δὲ μόνον τὰς ὑλικάς] Arist. *Met.* A 3, 983b6–8 τῶν δὴ πρώτων φιλοσοφησάντων οἱ πλεῖστοι τὰς ἐν ὕλης εἴδει μόνας ᾠήθησαν ἀρχὰς εἶναι πάντων. **7a10** ἄλογον δὲ κἀκείνοις δόξειεν ἄν] Arist. *Met.* K 5, 1062a31–35 ταχέως δ᾽ ἄν τις καὶ αὐτὸν τὸν Ἡράκλειτον ... ἠνάγκασεν ὁμολογεῖν μηδέποτε τὰς ἀντικειμένας φάσεις δυνατὸν εἶναι κατὰ τῶν αὐτῶν ἀληθεύεσθαι· νῦν δ᾽ οὐ συνιεὶς ἑαυτοῦ τί ποτε λέγει, ταύτην ἔλαβε τὴν δόξαν.

5 αἵπερ τὴν φύσιν PJ Λ : ἅσπερ (sc. τὰς ἀρχάς) τὴν φύσιν (accus. e synecdoche = τῇ φύσει) ut interpr. Ar. | post μιμοῦνται non dist. Ar. | καὶ pr. non vert. ut vid. Ar. **6** ἐμμόρφους J[II], ἐνμόρφους PJ, [Ψ] [Λ] **7** post πάσας add. τίθενται J[II] | post μόνον add. ἀμόρφους J[II] **7–8** ἄμφω, τάς τ᾽ PJ Λ : ἄμφω Ψ : ἀμφοτέρας coni. Wim.[1,2] | τὰς τ᾽— ὕλης PJ Λ : om. Ψ, seclusi ut glossema **12** λόγῳ PJ Λ : λόγοις ut intell. Ar. | post λόγῳ dist. Us.[2] **14** σὰρξ **ω** CL A : σάρον Bernays apud Schuster, Us.[2] : σάρμα Diels et alii alia, v. app. crit. alt. | post σάρξ dist. Gomperz, Viano (v. adn.) | κεχυμένων **α** Λ : κεχυμένη ut interpr. Ar., Tiph. (*caro fusa*) Bergk : κεχυμένον Us.[2] : κεχυμέν⟨η ἀνθρώπ⟩ων Friedländer : κεκυ(η)μένων Mouraviev | ὁ secl. Gomperz, del. Bergk **15** ὥς Ψ (*ʿalā mā*), coni. Hommel apud Marcovich 1978, et Marcovich 2001 : om. PJ Λ | ὁ ante κόσμος **α** [Λ] : om. Ψ, secl. Wim.[1,2] et Ross ut addendum scriptoris cuiusdam, del. Us.[1,2] **16** τοὐλάχιστον J, τοὐλάχιστου P [Ψ] [Λ] **17** ἀψύχοις καὶ ἐμψύχοις transp. Ar. **19** τὰς δ᾽ P Ψ Λ : τὰς J : οἷον τὰς J[II] **20** αὖ τὸ Ψ (*ayḍan an naǧmaʿa*), prop. Zeller : αὐτὸ PJ Λ : αὐτὸ ⟨τὸ⟩ Wim.[1]

[this is] similarly [so] also in accordance with the crafts, which, in fact, imitate nature: both the instruments and the rest [are] in accordance with the first principles.[66]) So, then, some [suppose that there is] nothing but enshaped[67] [first principles], others only material ones, and still others both, on the ground that whatever is complete consists of both since all of existence[68] is [constituted], as it were, from opposites.

(**14.1**) It would, however, seem unreasonable[69] even to these [people] if, on the one hand, the entire heavens and each of the parts were all orderly and formally principled in respect of shapes and of powers and of periods [of time], while on the other hand there were nothing of the kind in the principles, but [it were] like "flesh,[70] of [things] poured out at random, the most beautiful," ⌜as⌝ Heraclitus says, "arrangement."[71] And they even take it [to be so] as a rule down to the smallest [thing], alike in inanimate and animate [things]; for the natures of each [set] of them are, as a rule, determinate—even when they come into being spontaneously—but the principles [they say,] are indeterminate.

(**14.2**) Again, it is difficult[72] to ascribe to each [set of things] its [*own*] formal principles by a collective referral to "for-the-sake-of-which"[73] in

[66] The exceptive phrase in this parenthetical statement, preserved only in the Arabic translation, provides some discrimination, with regard to the order and determinacy of their respective first principles, between grammar and music on the one hand and mathematics on the other. See the commentary.

[67] I.e., endued with shape and form; cf. "ensouled". The Greek word, *émmorphos*, appears to be a neologism, most likely coined by Theophrastus himself, for this is its first occurrence in extant Greek literature, and was used very sparingly after him—interestingly, mostly by Christian authors.

[68] Existence (*ousía*) in the sense of all that exists. See the commentary at 4a13.

[69] This first set of objections to the "materialists," introduced by "unreasonable," is followed in the next paragraph (14.2) by objections to the "formalists."

[70] I.e., the fleshly contour of the human body; see the commentary.

[71] Fragment 124 DK, 107 Marcovich 2001, T 209 Mouraviev 1999.

[72] This second set of objections to the "formalists" follows upon the first directed at the "materialists" in the preceding paragraph.

[73] I.e., a final cause.

πρὸς τὸ ἕνεκά του συνάγοντας ἐν ἅπασιν—καὶ ἐν ζῴοις καὶ φυτοῖς καὶ ἐν αὐτῇ πομφόλυγι—πλὴν εἰ συμβαίνει τῇ ἑτέρων τάξει καὶ μεταβολῇ μορ-
7b1 φάς τε παντοίας καὶ ποικιλίας γίνεσθαι τῶν περὶ τὸν ἀέρα καὶ τὴν γῆν· ὧν δὴ μέγιστόν τινες παράδειγμα ποιοῦνται τὰ περὶ τὰς ὥρας τὰς ἐτησίους ἐν αἷς καὶ ζῴων καὶ φυτῶν καὶ καρπῶν γενέσεις, οἷον γεννῶντος τοῦ ἡλίου.

(15) Καὶ ταῦτα μὲν ἐνταῦθά που ζητεῖ τὴν σκέψιν, ἀφορισμὸν ἀπαιτοῦντα μέχρι πόσου τὸ τεταγμένον καὶ διὰ τί τὸ πλέον ἀδύνατον ἢ εἰς τὸ χεῖρον ἡ μετάβασις,
(16) ἐν δὲ ταῖς ἀρχαῖς, ὅθεν δὴ καὶ ὁ πρῶτος λό- V [16]
γος, εἰκότως ἄν τις καὶ τὸ περὶ τῆς ἠρεμίας ἀπορήσειεν. Εἰ μὲν γὰρ ὡς βέλτιον, ἀνάψειεν ἂν ταῖς ἀρχαῖς· εἰ δ᾽ ὡς ἀργία καὶ στέρησίς τις κινήσεως, οὐκ ἀνάψει, ἀλλ᾽ εἴπερ, τὴν ἐνέργειαν ἀντιμεταλλακτέον ὡς προτέραν καὶ τιμιωτέραν, τὴν δὲ κίνησιν [ἐν] τοῖς αἰσθητοῖς. Ἐπεὶ τό γε διὰ τοῦτ᾽

7a22 πομφόλυγι] Arist. *GA* 762a21–22 γίνονται δ᾽ ἐν γῇ καὶ ἐν ὑγρῷ τὰ ζῷα ... ἐμπεριλαμβάνεται δὲ καὶ γίνεται θερμαινόμενον τῶν σωματικῶν ὑγρῶν οἷον ἀφρώδης πομφόλυξ. **7a23** τῇ ἑτέρων τάξει καὶ μεταβολῇ] Arist. *GA* 777b28–30 γενέσεις ... φθοράς· τούτων δ᾽ ἔχουσι τὸ πέρας καὶ τῆς ἀρχῆς καὶ τῆς τελευτῆς αἱ τούτων κινήσεις τῶν ἄστρων. similia ap. Theophr., v. van Raalte 317–322. **7b2–3** παράδειγμα] Arist. *Met.* Δ 2, 1013a26–27 = *Phys.* B 3, 194b26–27 ἄλλον δὲ (sc. τρόπον αἴτιον λέγεται) τὸ εἶδος καὶ τὸ παράδειγμα, τοῦτο δ᾽ ἐστὶν ὁ λόγος τοῦ τί ἦν εἶναι. **7b3–5** παράδειγμα ... ἡλίου] Arist. *Met.* Λ 5, 1071a13–16 ὥσπερ ἀνθρώπου αἴτιον τά τε στοιχεῖα ... καὶ ἔτι τι ἄλλο ἔξω οἷον ὁ πατήρ, καὶ παρὰ ταῦτα ὁ ἥλιος καὶ ὁ λοξὸς κύκλος (cf. *Phys.* B 2, 194b13). **7b12** ἠρεμία ... στέρησίς τις κινήσεως] Arist. *Phys.* Θ 8, 264a27 ἡ γὰρ ἠρεμία στέρησις κινήσεως. **7b13–14** ἐνέργειαν ... τιμιωτέραν] v. supra ad 5a7–8

21 ἕνεκά του PJ Λ : ἓν ἕκαστον ut intell. Ar. | καὶ om. Ar. ut vid. **23** ἑτέρων **ω** : ἀστέρων coni. Us.[1,2] **7b1** ποικιλίας PJ Λ : ποικίλας Ψ J[II] **3** ἐτησίους Ψ (*as-sana*), coni. Us.[2], ἐστησιους P : αἰτίους J CL, αἰτίας ut intell. Lat., ἐτείους A **6** που P : ποῦ J Λ : non vert. Ar. **7–8** post ἀδύνατον dist. Laks & Most, post τεταγμένον dist. Ar. et edd. **8** ἢ J[II] (J?) : εἰ Ψ Λ, εἱ P **9** ἀρχαῖς P[1] J Λ : ἀρχᾶς P [Ψ] **12** ἀρχαῖς J Λ : ἀρχᾶς P [Ψ] | τις P : τῆς J Ψ Λ **13** ἀντιμεταλλακτέον D : τι μεταλλακτέον PJ C[1]L A [Ψ] : μεταλλακτέοι ut vid. Λ (*transmutandi*) : τὴν μεταλλακτέον C : ἀντικαταλλακτέον coni. Us.[1,2] **15** ἐν **ω** : secl. Us.[2], del. Us.[1] | διὰ τοῦτ᾽ om. Ar. **15–16** τοῦτ᾽ ἠρεμεῖν [ἡρεμεῖν J] PJ : τοῦθ᾽ ἠρεμεῖν J[II] [Ψ] [Λ]

all [cases]—both in animals and in plants and even in the very bubble[74]—unless it happens that, by reason of the order and change of *others*, there come about all manner of shapes and varieties of atmospheric 7b1
and terrestrial [things]; of which in particular some make the greatest paradigmatic [cause] to be the [things] relating to the seasons of the year, in which [seasons] there are generated alike animals and plants and fruits, with the sun being, as it were, the begetter.[75]

(**15**) Now while these call for investigation somewhere here,[76] demanding that one mark the boundaries of how far what is endowed with order [extends] and [answer] why more [of it] is impossible lest the change be for the worse, (**16**) yet regarding the first principles—from which, it is to be noted, the very discussion first [began][77]—one might reasonably raise an aporia also about their rest. For if [rest is taken] as [something] better, one would ascribe [it] to the first principles; but if as cessation and a certain privation of motion, one will not [so] ascribe [it]—but no, if anything, an actualized state[78] should be substituted in [its] stead, on the ground that it is prior and more valuable, while motion [should be ascribed] to the sensibles. For to be at rest on account of this—[viz.,] that it is impossible

[74] In all likelihood Theophrastus is referring here to a minimal form of organic life, or to the moment of transition from inorganic to organic life in spontaneous generation. According to Aristotle (*GA* 762a21–25, p. 1180 *CWA*), "living things form quickly whenever this air and vital heat are enclosed," and "the corporeal liquids being heated, there arises as it were a frothy bubble."

[75] The reference is apparently to Peripatetic circles; cf. van Raalte 319 and Laks & Most 53n24.

[76] I.e., in this Essay. Theophrastus returns in §§ 22–24 below to the issue of the determinacy of the principles and to answering the two questions he asks in this paragraph, viz., how far what is ordered extends and why more of it would be for the worse.

[77] Theophrastus restates here the main subject of his essay and obliquely also refers to his title.

[78] *Enérgeia*, for which see the commentary at 5a7.

ἠρεμεῖν—ὡς ἀδύνατον ἀεὶ κινούμενον εἶναι τὸ κινοῦν,
οὐ γὰρ ἂν εἴη πρῶτον—κίνδυνος μὴ
λογῶδες καὶ ἄλλως οὐκ ἀξιόπιστον, ἀλλὰ μείζω
7b19 τινὰ αἰτίαν ζητεῖ.

19 **(16.1)** Δοκεῖ δὲ καὶ ἡ αἴσθησις τρόπον
20 τινὰ συναυδᾶν ὡς ἐνδεχόμενον μὴ δεῖν τὸ κι-
νοῦν ἕτερον εἶναι καὶ ὃ κινεῖ διὰ τὸ ποιεῖν
καὶ πάσχειν· ἔτι δ' ἐάν τις ἐπ' αὐτὸν ἄγῃ τὸν
23 νοῦν καὶ τὸν θεόν.

23 **(16.2)** Ἄτοπον δὲ καὶ τὸ ἕτερον λε-
8a1 χθέν, ὡς οὐ μιμοῦνται τὰ ὀρεγόμενα τοῦ ἠρεμοῦν-
τος· τί γὰρ αὐτοῖς οὐ συνακολουθεῖ ἡ τῶν ἄλλων;
Πλὴν ἴσως οὐχ ὁμοίως ληπτέον ὡς εἰς τὸ ἀμερὲς
ἄγοντας, ἀλλ' ὅπως ὅ τι μάλιστα σύμφωνον ἑαυ-
5 τῷ καὶ ἀπηρτισμένον ὡς ἂν πόλις ἢ ζῷον ἢ ἄλλο

7b16–17 ἀδύνατον ... πρῶτον] Arist. *Met.* Λ 7, 1072a24–25 ἐπεὶ δὲ τὸ κινούμενον καὶ κινοῦν [καὶ] μέσον ... ἔστι τι ὃ οὐ κινούμενον κινεῖ. *MA* 698a7–10 ὅτι μὲν οὖν ἀρχὴ τῶν ἄλλων κινήσεων τὸ αὐτὸ ἑαυτὸ κινοῦν, τούτου δὲ τὸ ἀκίνητον, καὶ ὅτι τὸ πρῶτον κινοῦν ἀναγκαῖον ἀκίνητον εἶναι, διώρισται πρότερον. **7b19–21** ἡ αἴσθησις ... ὃ κινεῖ] Arist. *Phys.* Θ 6, 259b1–3 ὁρῶμεν δὲ καὶ φανερῶς ὄντα τοιαῦτα ἃ κινεῖ αὐτὰ ἑαυτά, οἷον τὸ τῶν ἐμψύχων καὶ τὸ τῶν ζῴων γένος. **7b20–21** μὴ δεῖν ... ὃ κινεῖ] Theophr., Περὶ κινήσεως, fr. 271,3–6 FHS&G αἱ μὲν ὀρέξεις καὶ ἐπιθυμίαι καὶ ὀργαὶ σωματικαὶ κινήσεις εἰσὶ καὶ ἀπὸ τούτου τὴν ἀρχὴν ἔχουσιν, ὅσαι δὲ κρίσεις καὶ θεωρίαι, ταύτας οὐκ ἔστιν εἰς ἕτερον ἀναγαγεῖν, ἀλλ' ἐν αὐτῇ τῇ ψυχῇ καὶ ἡ ἀρχὴ καὶ ἡ ἐνέργεια καὶ τὸ τέλος. Arist. *MA* 698b18–21 ἀνάγκη δὲ τοῦτο (sc. ἀκίνητόν τι) ἕτερον εἶναι τοῦ κινουμένου ... εἰ δὲ μή, οὐ κινηθήσεται. **7b23** νοῦν] Theophr. fr. 307A,13–14, 26–27 FHS&G τῷ δὲ ἀρχὴν πάντων εἶναι (sc. τὸν νοῦν) καὶ ἐπ' αὐτῷ τὸ νοεῖν ... ἀπ' αὐτοῦ (sc. ἡ ἀρχή ἐστιν). ... τὸ παθητικὸν ἐπ' αὐτοῦ οὐχ ὡς τὸ κινητὸν ληπτέον, ἀτελὴς γὰρ ἡ κίνησις, ἀλλ' ὡς ἐνέργειαν. **8a3** τὸ ἀμερές] Arist. *Met.* Λ 7, 1073a5–7 μέγεθος οὐδὲν ἔχειν ἐνδέχεται ταύτην τὴν οὐσίαν (sc. τὸ πρῶτον κινοῦν) ἀλλ' ἀμερὴς καὶ ἀδιαίρετός ἐστιν. **8a5** πόλις ἢ ζῷον] Arist. *MA* 703a29-b2 ὑποληπτέον δὲ συνεστάναι τὸ ζῷον ὥσπερ πόλιν εὐνομουμένην κτλ.

16 post ἠρεμεῖν add. δεῖ J[II] | κινούμενον corr. Ross : κινοῦν **ω** CL A | κινοῦν **α** Ψ : om. Lat. : κινούμενον coni. Us.[1,2] | post κινοῦν add. ἄτοπον J[II] **16–17** εἶναι τὸ κινοῦν οὐ γὰρ in spatio vel ras. 9 litt. J[1] **17** πρῶτον κίνδυνος PJ Λ : κίνδυνος τὸ πρῶτον ut intell. Ar. | post πρῶτον add. καὶ J[II] **18** λογῶδες Ψ P : λογωειδες [-ωιδ- J] J[1], λογοειδὲς Λ CL A **19** καὶ J Λ : om. P, non vert. Ar. **20** δεῖν Laks & Most : δεῖ **ω** : ἀεὶ coni. Wim.[1,2] : πᾶν Kley (falso; v. infra text. Lat.) **21** κινεῖ **ω** : κινεῖται coni. Us.[1,2] [*mouetur* Tiph. Steph.] | ποιεῖν **ω** : ποιοῦν coni. Us.[1,2], τὸ ποιοῦν prop. Fobes **22** δ' ἐάν P : δὲ ἂν J [Ψ] [Λ] | ἄγῃ [ἄγει JC] **α** Λ : ἀνάγῃ prop. Us.[2], ἄγῃ vel ἀνάγῃ Ψ (*yarudda*) **8a1** μιμοῦνται **ω** : κινοῦνται coni. Us.[2] [*moueri* Steph.] | τοῦ ἠρεμοῦντος PJ Λ : τὰ ἠρεμοῦντα J[II], ut intell. Ar. **2** τί Us.[2] : εἰ **ω** C A : ἢ J[II]L, ᾗ Bignone | οὐ συνακολουθεῖ ἡ corr. Ross : οὖσιν ἀκολουθεῖ ἡ P Ψ, οὖσιν ἀκολουθείη J Λ CL A : οὖσιν ἀκολουθοίη prop. Sylburg for what causes movement to be [itself] in every instant moved, because then it would not be first[79]—runs the risk of being [an argument] of [mere] words and otherwise not worthy of belief, and rather calls for some better reason [to be given for it].

(**16.1**) And even sense-perception seems in some manner to concur in that it is possible for what causes movement not to have to be different from what it moves on the ground that [it] both acts and is acted upon[80]—and beyond this, [the same holds true] if one were to apply [it] to intellect itself and to god.[81]

(**16.2**) Neither does the other thing that has been said make any sense,[82] that the [things] that desire what is at rest do not imitate;[83] for why 8a1
aren't they accompanied by that of the others?[84] Except that, perhaps, one should not conceive [of these things] in the same way as if he were reducing to something without parts, but rather in such a way that the entire heavens[85] too—which, famously, they maintain to be most perfect—shall be as much as possible in harmony with themselves and

[79] I.e., because it would require something else to set it in motion, and so on in an infinite regress.

[80] For the interpretation of this phrase see the commentary. Theophrastus here appeals to the observable fact of self-movement in living beings (cf. Ross 63), something granted also by Aristotle (*Phys.* 259b1 ff.), but without accepting Aristotle's further and ultimate refutation of self-movement.

[81] That is, the same argument of the identity of mover and moved—of the possibility of self-movement—also applies, and much more cogently, to objects that the senses cannot perceive, intellect and god.

[82] I.e., at 5a23–25 above.

[83] The Greek has no object for "imitate;" it has been understood that the reference is to "what is at rest," or "it."

[84] The text of this elliptical sentence is uncertain. As reconstructed, it may mean, "why in the case of the heavenly bodies is desire not accompanied by imitation, as in all other cases?" See the commentary.

[85] The heavens are used here in the sense of the entire universe; see above, note 41.

τι τῶν μεριστῶν ᾖ καὶ ὁ ὅλος οὐρανός, ὃν δή φασιν εἶναι τελεώτατον.

(17) Ἐπιποθεῖ δέ τινα καὶ τὰ τοιάδε λόγον: πῶς ποτε τῶν ὄντων ὁ μερισμὸς εἰς ὕλην καὶ μορφήν; πότερον ὡς τὸ μὲν ὄν, τὸ δὲ μὴ ὄν, δυνάμει δ᾽ ὂν καὶ ἀγόμενον εἰς ἐνέργειαν; ἢ ὂν μέν, ἀόριστον δέ, καθάπερ ἐν ταῖς τέχναις, ἡ δὲ γένεσις ἢ οὐσία γ᾽ αὐτῶν τῷ μορφοῦσθαι κατὰ τοὺς λόγους; Ἀλλ᾽ οὕτω γ᾽ εἰς μὲν τὸ βέλτιον τάχ᾽ ἂν ἡ μετάβασις εἴη, τὸ δ᾽ εἶναι οὐθὲν ἂν ἧττον ἀληθὲς ὑπάρχοι κατ᾽ αὐτήν (οὐ γὰρ ἂν οὐδὲ γίνοιτο μὴ ὑπαρχούσης), ἀλλὰ τὸ μήτε τόδε μήτε ποιὸν μήτε ποσόν, ὡς ἀόριστον τοῖς εἴδεσιν, δύναμιν δέ τιν᾽ ἔχον. Ὅλως δὲ κατ᾽ ἀναλογίαν ληπτέον ἐπὶ τὰς τέχνας καὶ εἴ τις ὁμοιότης ἄλλη. VI [17]

(18) Δόξειεν δ᾽ ἂν καὶ τοῦτ᾽ ἔχειν ἀπορίαν, εἰ μὴ ἄρα περιεργία τὸ ζητεῖν, τί δή ποτε ἡ φύσις καὶ ἡ ὅλη δ᾽ οὐσία τοῦ παντὸς ἐν ἐναντίοις ἐστίν, καὶ σχεδὸν ἰσομοιρεῖ τὸ χεῖρον τῷ βελτίονι, μᾶλλον δὲ καὶ πολλῷ πλέον ἐστίν, ὥστε δοκεῖν καὶ Εὐριπίδην καθόλου λέγειν ὡς VII [18]

8a17–18 τὸ μήτε τόδε μήτε ποιὸν μήτε ποσόν] Arist. *Met.* Z 3, 1029a20–21 λέγω δ᾽ ὕλην ἣ καθ᾽ αὑτὴν μήτε τὶ μήτε ποσὸν μήτε ἄλλο μηδὲν λέγεται οἷς ὥρισται τὸ ὄν. **8a19–20** κατ᾽ ἀναλογίαν ληπτέον ἐπὶ τὰς τέχνας] Arist. *Phys.* A 7, 191a7–12 ἡ δὲ ὑποκειμένη φύσις ἐπιστητὴ κατ᾽ ἀναλογίαν· ὡς γὰρ πρὸς ἀνδριάντα χαλκὸς … τὸ ἄμορφον ἔχει πρὶν λαβεῖν τὴν μορφήν, οὕτως αὕτη πρὸς οὐσίαν ἔχει καὶ τὸ τόδε τι καὶ τὸ ὄν. **8a23** ἡ ὅλη δ᾽ οὐσία τοῦ παντὸς ἐν ἐναντίοις ἐστίν] Arist. *Met.* A 5, 986b3 οἱ Πυθαγόρειοι … ὅτι τἀναντία ἀρχαὶ τῶν ὄντων. Γ 2, 1005a3–5 πάντα γὰρ ἢ ἐναντία ἢ ἐξ ἐναντίων, ἀρχαὶ δὲ τῶν ἐναντίων τὸ ἓν καὶ πλῆθος. **8a24–25** ἰσομοιρεῖ τὸ χεῖρον … πλέον ἐστίν] Plato *Theaet.* 176a5–6 οὔτ᾽ ἀπολέσθαι τὰ κακὰ δυνατόν, … ὑπεναντίον γάρ τι τῷ ἀγαθῷ ἀεὶ εἶναι ἀνάγκη. Arist. *Met.* A 4, 984b32–985a2 τἀναντία τοῖς ἀγαθοῖς ἐνόντα ἐφαίνετο ἐν τῇ φύσει, καὶ οὐ μόνον τάξις καὶ τὸ καλὸν ἀλλὰ καὶ ἀταξία καὶ τὸ αἰσχρόν, καὶ πλείω τὰ κακὰ τῶν ἀγαθῶν καὶ τὰ φαῦλα τῶν καλῶν, κτλ.

6 ᾖ corr. Us.[1,2] : ἡ P J, ἢ Ψ Λ CL A **11** ὂν pr. Ψ B²O, prop. Zeller : ἓν **α** Λ **12** ἡ δὲ **ω** CL A : ᾗ δὲ coni. Ross : εἰ δὲ coni. Us.[1,2] : ἡ prop. Fobes, coni. Laks & Most **13** ἢ Ψ (*aw*), coni. Us.[1] : ἡ PJ Λ CL : ἣ A | γ᾽ PJ C, γε L A [Ψ] : δ᾽ Λ, prop. Fobes | τῷ P Ψ Λ J¹ : τῶν J **16** κατ᾽ αὐτήν P et Ψ ut vid. (*fī l-uḫrā*, v. adn.) : καθ᾽ αὐτήν J, καθ᾽ αὑτήν Λ (*secundum se ipsum*) **20** εἴ J Ψ Λ : ἤ P **22** περιεργία τὸ ζητεῖν Ψ (*al-baḥṯu huwa mina l-fuḍūli*) Λ (*otiositas inquirere*), prop. Dirlmeier : περιεργίαν τοῦ ζητεῖν [τοῦ ζητεῖν iter. P, περιέργειαν J] **α** : περιεργίαν, τοῦ ζητεῖν dist. Laks & Most : περιεργίαν, τὸ ζητεῖν Jaeger² **23** δ᾽ **α** : om. Λ [Ψ] : γ᾽ prop. Ross 1938 **26** καθόλου **α** Λ : ὀρθῶς (*ṣawāb*) vel similia ut intell. Ar.

integrated, as if they were a city or an animal or something else with parts.[86]

(**17**) In addition, also the following require some discussion. However is the division of beings into matter and shape [to be taken]?[87] Whether the one as being and the other as not-being, but as being potentially and driven[88] towards actuality? Or, as being, but indeterminate, as in the crafts, while generation, or at any rate their[89] substance,[90] [would come about] through being shaped in accordance with formal principles? But of course, in this [latter] way on the one hand the change would be likely for the better, and on the other, being would be no less truly predicated [of things] with respect to [their matter] (for they would not even come into being at all if [matter][91] did not exist), though [it would be being], as something indeterminate with regard to forms, that is neither this nor such nor so much but having a certain potentiality. In general, our understanding must be based on analogy with reference to the crafts and, if [there is] any other similarity, [on that one].

(**18**) It would seem that the following, too, involves an aporia—unless it is pedantry [even] to inquire—why in the world it is that nature, and indeed the entire substance[92] of the universe, consists of contraries, with the worse almost equaling the better—or rather being greater by far—so that even Euripides would seem to be making a universal statement when

---

[86] Theophrastus here is apparently arguing that the imitation in question should be of the harmony and orderliness of the first principle and not of its rest.

[87] Or, according to Laks & Most, "how is the division into matter and form at all [to be related] to beings?"

[88] The Greek participle, *agómenon*, is ambiguous: it could be either middle voice, "in progress towards," or passive, "being led towards" (cf. van Raalte 364–365). "Driven" is intended to reproduce this ambiguity: either driven inwardly or by an external agent.

[89] The pronoun must refer to the "beings" mentioned in the initial question in 8a9; see the commentary.

[90] *Ousía*, as used in this sense in the corresponding Aristotelian passage (*Phys.* 191a11); see the Loci Paralleli and the commentary at 4a13.

[91] Both here and in the preceding line the feminine pronoun and participle refer unequivocally to matter (*hýlē*).

[92] *Ousía* here in the sense of formal constitution; cf. 10a3 and 11b26 and see the commentary at 4a13.

8b26|27 οὐκ ἂν γένοιτο | χωρὶς ἐσθλά.
27 Ὁ δὲ τοιοῦτος λόγος ἐγγὺς τοῦ
8b1 ζητεῖν ὅ τι οὐ πάντ᾽ ἀγαθὰ οὐδὲ πάντα ὅμοια,
καὶ ὅ τι κατὰ πάντων μὲν τὸ εἶναι λέγομεν, οὐ-
θὲν δὲ ὅμοιον ἀλλήλοις, καθάπερ τὰ λευκὰ καὶ
4 μέλανα ἐν αὐτοῖς.

4 **(18.1)** Ἔτι δὲ τὸ δοκοῦν παραδοξότε-
5 ρον, ὡς οὐχ οἷόν τε τὸ ὂν ἄνευ τῶν ἐναντίων.

(18.2) Οἵ δ᾽ ἔτι πλέονι τῷ παραδόξῳ χρώμενοι καὶ τὸ
μὴ ὂν μηδὲ γεγονὸς μηδὲ μέλλον προσκαταριθμοῦ-
σιν εἰς τὴν τοῦ παντὸς φύσιν. Ἀλλ᾽ ἥδε μὲν οἷον
ὑπερβατός τις σοφία, τὸ δὲ ὂν ὅτι πολλαχῶς, VIII [19]
10 φανερόν. Ἡ γὰρ αἴσθησις καὶ τὰς διαφορὰς
θεωρεῖ καὶ τὰς αἰτίας ζητεῖ· τάχα δ᾽ ἀληθέσ-
τερον εἰπεῖν ὡς ὑποβάλλει τῇ διανοίᾳ τὰ μὲν
ἁπλῶς ζητοῦσα, τὰ δ᾽ ἀπορίαν ἐνεργαζομένη,
δι᾽ ἧς, κἂν μὴ δύνηται προβαίνειν, ὅμως ἐμ-
15 φαίνεταί τι φῶς ἐν τῷ μὴ φωτὶ ζητούντων
ἐπὶ πλέον. Τὸ ἐπίστασθαι ἄρα οὐκ ἄνευ δια-
φορᾶς τινος. Εἴ τε γὰρ ἕτερα ἀλλήλων διαφορά
τις, ἔν τε τοῖς καθόλου πλειόνων ὄντων τῶν ὑπὸ
τὰ καθόλου διαφέρειν ἀνάγκη καὶ ταῦτα, ἐάν τε
20 γένη τὰ καθόλου ἐάν τ᾽ εἴδη.

8b3–4 καθάπερ τὰ λευκὰ καὶ μέλανα ἐν αὐτοῖς] Arist. *Cat.* 14a20–22 λευκὸν μὲν γὰρ καὶ μέλαν ἐν τῷ αὐτῷ γένει· χρῶμα γὰρ αὐτῶν τὸ γένος. **8b6–8** τὸ μὴ ὂν ... φύσιν] Theophr. *Phys. Opin.* fr. 8 (Diels 483–484) ἔτι δὲ οὐδὲν μᾶλλον τὸ ὂν ἢ τὸ μὴ ὂν ὑπάρχειν, καὶ αἴτια ὁμοίως εἶναι τοῖς γινομένοις ἄμφω. ... τῷ κενῷ ... ὅπερ μὴ ὂν ἐκάλει καὶ οὐκ ἔλαττον τοῦ ὄντος εἶναί φησι. **8b9** τὸ δὲ ὂν ὅτι πολλαχῶς] Arist. *Met.* Γ 2, 1003b5–10 τὸ ὂν λέγεται πολλαχῶς ... μὴ ὄν φαμεν. **8b10–12** ἡ γὰρ αἴσθησις ... ὑποβάλλει τῇ διανοίᾳ] Theophr. fr. 301B FHS&G Θεόφραστος δὲ τὴν αἴσθησιν ἀρχὴν εἶναι πίστεώς φησιν· ἀπὸ γὰρ ταύτης αἱ ἀρχαὶ πρὸς τὸν λόγον τὸν ἐν ἡμῖν καὶ τὴν διάνοιαν ἐκτείνονται. **8b10–11** διαφορὰς, αἰτίας] Arist. *HA* 491a9–12 ἵνα πρῶτον τὰς ὑπαρχούσας διαφορὰς καὶ τὰ συμβεβηκότα πᾶσι λάβωμεν, μετὰ δὲ τοῦτο τὰς αἰτίας τούτων πειρατέον εὑρεῖν.

26 οὐκ P[1]J Ψ Λ : οὐδ᾽ P **8b4** τὰ μέλανα A, ut interpr. Ar. [Λ] | post μέλανα dist. Ross, van Raalte | ἔτι non vert. Ar. **12** ὑποβάλλει P Ψ : ὑπερ- J Λ **13** ἐνεργαζομένη P : ἐνεργαζομένηι J : ἐργαζομένη CL A et fort. Λ : ἐνεργαζόμενα ut intell. Ar. **15** τῷ P Ψ Λ : τὸ J | post ζητούντων add. ἡμῶν A[2] Ar. **17** εἴ **ω** : ᾖ coni. Us.[2] **20** γένη ... εἴδη Ψ Λ A Tiph. : γένει ... εἴδει PJ CL[1] : γένη ... εἴδει L he says,

"Good things cannot come to pass alone."[93]

But such a way ofspeaking[94] comes near to wanting to know why [things] 8b1
are not all of them good or all of them alike, and why, though we predicate being of all [things], there is nothing [through which they are] similar to one another as [there is between] white and black [things] among them.[95]

(**18.1**) Further, what appears more paradoxical: that being cannot be without contraries.

(**18.2**) And again, those who indulge in even greater paradox add to the nature of the universe also that which is not and has not been and will not be. Now this in particular may well be a sort of "wisdom" that has gone too far, but that "that which is" is manifold, is evident. For sense perception both observes the differences and seeks the causes;[96] though perhaps it is closer to the truth to say that it prompts the faculty of thought partly by simply searching and partly by producing an aporia through whose consideration, even if it is not able[97] to advance, some light still makes its appearance in the non-light as [we] search further. Knowing, then, [does] not [occur] without some difference.[98] For both, if [things] are other than each other, there is some difference, and, in the case of universals where the [things that fall] under the universals are more than one, these too differ of necessity, be the universals genera or species.

---

[93] *Aeolus*, fr. 21 Nauck. The sense of "even" here in "even Euripides" (*kai Euripídēn*), "Euripides, too," would seem to be that even a literary person and not a philosopher could be making universal statements with philosophical import. Cf. van Raalte 384.

[94] I.e., asking why nature consists of contraries.

[95] I.e., the genus color shared by black things and white things.

[96] I.e., the differences distinguishing one being from another and their causes. Cf. the Arabic translation.

[97] The subject of this verb is taken universally by commentators to be the faculty of thought.

[98] I.e., without the presence of some difference.

8b20 **(18.3)** Σχεδὸν δὲ καὶ ἐπι- [20]
στήμη πᾶσα τῶν ἰδίων· ἥ τε γὰρ οὐσία καὶ τὸ
τί ἦν εἶναι καθ᾽ ἕκαστον ἴδιον, τά τε θεωρούμενα
καθ᾽ ἑαυτὰ καὶ οὐ κατὰ συμβεβηκὸς ἦν ἄν τι κατὰ
24 τινός.

24 **(18.4)** Ὅλως δὲ τὸ ἐν πλείοσιν τὸ αὐτὸ συνι-
25 δεῖν ἐπιστήμης, ἤτοι κοινῇ καὶ καθόλου λεγόμενον
ἢ ἰδίᾳ πως καθ᾽ ἕκαστον, οἷον ἀριθμοῖς γραμμαῖς,
ζῴοις φυτοῖς· τέλεος δ᾽ ἡ ἐξ ἀμφοῖν. Εἰσὶ δ᾽
9a1 ἔνιαι μὲν ὧν καθόλου τέλος (ἐν τούτῳ γὰρ τὸ
αἴτιον), τῶν δὲ τὸ ἐν μέρει, καθ᾽ ὅσα διαίρεσις
εἰς τὰ ἄτομα, καθάπερ ἐν τοῖς πρακτοῖς καὶ ποιη-
τοῖς· οὕτως γὰρ αὐτῶν ἡ ἐνέργεια. Ταὐτὸ δ᾽ ἐπι- [21]
5 στάμεθα καὶ οὐσίᾳ καὶ ἀριθμῷ καὶ εἴδει καὶ γένει
καὶ ἀναλογίᾳ καί, εἰ ἄρα, παρὰ ταῦτα διαιρέσει,
διὰ πλείστου δὲ τὸ κατ᾽ ἀναλογίαν, ὡς ἂν ἀπέ-
χοντες πλεῖστον, τὰ μὲν δι᾽ ἡμᾶς αὐτούς, τὰ δὲ
διὰ τὸ ὑποκείμενον, τὰ δὲ διὰ τἄμφω.

10 **(19)** Πλεοναχῶς δ᾽ ὄντος τοῦ ἐπίστασθαι, πῶς ἕκα- [22]
στα μεταδιωκτέον; Ἀρχὴ καὶ μέγιστον ὁ οἰκεῖος
τρόπος, οἷον τὰ πρῶτα καὶ νοητά, καὶ τὰ κινητὰ
καὶ ὑπὸ τὴν φύσιν, αὐτῶν τε τούτων τὰ ἐν ἀρχῇ

8b20–22 ἐπιστήμη ... ἴδιον] Arist. *Top.* Α 4, 101b19–23 τοῦ ἰδίου τὸ μὲν τὸ τί ἦν εἶναι σημαίνει ... καὶ καλείσθω ... ὅρος, τὸ δὲ λοιπὸν κατὰ τὴν κοινὴν ... ὀνομασίαν προσαγορευέσθω ἴδιον. **9a4–6** ταὐτὸ ... διαιρέσει] Arist. *Met.* Δ 9, 1018a5–7 τὰ δὲ (sc. λέγεται ταὐτὰ) καθ᾽ αὑτὰ ὁσαχῶσπερ καὶ τὸ ἕν· καὶ γὰρ ὧν ἡ ὕλη μία ἢ εἴδει ἢ ἀριθμῷ ταὐτὰ λέγεται καὶ ὧν ἡ οὐσία μία. Δ 6, 1016b31–2 τὰ μὲν κατ᾽ ἀριθμόν ἐστιν ἕν, τὰ δὲ κατ᾽ εἶδος, τὰ δὲ κατὰ γένος, τὰ δὲ κατ᾽ ἀναλογίαν. *Top.* Δ 1, 120b36 εἰ μὴ ἐν τῇ αὐτῇ διαιρέσει τὸ γένος καὶ τὸ εἶδος, ἀλλὰ τὸ μὲν οὐσία τὸ δὲ ποιόν, κτλ.

21 ἥ P Ψ Λ : εἴ J **23** ἄν τι κατὰ τινός Ross : ἄν τι κατά [κατα J] τινος PJ : ἄν τι κατὰ τινός Us.[2] **24** ὅλως **ω** : ὁμοίως coni. Us.[1,2] : ὅμως prop. Fobes **25** κοινῇ Ψ (*ʿāmmiyyan*) Λ (*comuni*) : κοινὴ PJ | καὶ om. J **26** πως non vert. Ar. | post γραμμαῖς dist. Ar. **27** τέλεος δ᾽ ἡ [ἡ om. Ar., v. infra] Ψ (*wa-l-maʿrifa al-kāmila*), τελεος δ᾽ ἡ P : τέλος δὲ J Λ CL A : τέλος δ᾽ ἡ Brandis | ἡ ἐξ ἀμφοῖν εἰσὶ δ᾽ om. Ψ vel interpres e homoeoteleuton (δ᾽—δ᾽) | εἰσὶ ego, v. adn. : ἔστιν **α** Λ : om. Ar. in lac. **9a1** ἔνιαι μὲν ὧν ego, v. adn. : ἔνια τῶν μὲν PJ[1] (μὲν om. J, add. s.l. J[1]) Ψ Λ CL A : ἔνια ὧν μὲν coni. Laks & Most, ἔνια, ὧν coni. van Raalte : ἐνίων μὲν τὸ coni. Wim.[1,2] : ἐνίων μὲν coni. Ross : ἔνθα τῶν μὲν coni. Us.[2] **2** δὲ τὸ **ω** : δ᾽ Us.[1] **3** πρακτοῖς PJ Ψ A : πρακτικοῖς Λ CL **4** ταὐτὸ J Ψ Λ : ταυτωι P **6** post εἰ ἄρα, distinxi **7** τὸ **ω** : τῷ coni. Us.[1,2] | ἀπέχοντες **α** Ψ : ἀπέχοντα Λ (*distantia*), prop. Dirlmeier : ἀπέχοντος coni. Ross

(**18.3**) In addition, almost all knowledge is of unique properties, for both, on the one hand, the essence and "the what-it-is-to-be" for each are unique properties, and, on the other, what [things] are observed essentially and not accidentally would be in each case something *of* something.[99]

(**18.4**) In general, though, to perceive simultaneously the identical in many is [the task] of knowledge, whether, in fact, it is said [of them] in common and universally or in some unique way with regard to each, as, for example, in numbers and lines, and animals and plants; complete is the one [consisting] of both. There are, however, some [knowledges] whose end is the universal (for therein is their cause), while of others it is the particular, those in respect of which division[100] [can proceed] down to the individuals,[101] as in the case of [things] done and [things] made: for this is how their actualized state is.[102] Well, the identical we come to know with respect to essence, to number, to species, to genus, to analogy, and with respect to a division besides these, if there is one at all; across the greatest [distance], though, [we come to know] that [which is identical] with respect to analogy, insofar as we are, as it were, the farthest removed, partly owing to ourselves, partly to the subject matter, and partly to both.

(**19**) Since, then, knowing [occurs] in very many ways, how is each [class of things] to be pursued? The starting point and the most important is the appropriate manner [of pursuing each class], such as the first and intelligible [things], the [things] that are movable and [fall] under

---

[99] I.e., an essential attribute belonging to some concrete thing. The least interpretive reading of this clause would be, "what are observed [to be] essential and not accidental [attributes] would be in each case a certain thing [belonging] to some other [particular] thing." See the commentary.

[100] Division here and in what immediately follows refers specifically to the systematic classification of things into categories as practiced in the Academy (cf. Laks & Most 66n24).

[101] In the original, etymological sense of individual, in Greek (*átomon*) as in English, indivisible entity.

[102] *Enérgeia*; see the commentary at 5a7.

καὶ ⸢τὰ⸣ ἑπόμενα μέχρι ζῴων καί φυτῶν καὶ ἐσχάτων τῶν ἀψύχων. Ἔστιν γάρ τι καθ' ἕκαστον γένος ἴδιον, ὥσπερ καὶ ἐν τοῖς μαθηματικοῖς· ἔχει [23] δὲ καὶ αὐτὰ τὰ μαθήματα διαφορὰν καίπερ ὁμογενῆ πως ὄντα· διῄρηται δ' ἱκανῶς. Εἰ δὲ καὶ ἔνια γνωστὰ τῷ ἄγνωστα εἶναι, καθάπερ τινές φασιν, ἴδιος ἂν ὁ τρόπος εἴη, διαιρέσεως δέ τινος δεῖται· τάχα δ' ἐφ' ὧν ἐνδέχεται, κατ' ἀναλογίαν οἰκειότερον λέγειν ἢ αὐτῷ τῷ ἀγνώστῳ, καθάπερ εἴ τις τῷ ἀοράτῳ τὸ ὁρατόν.

(20a) Πόσοι δ' οὖν τρόποι καὶ ποσαχῶς τὸ εἰδέναι, πειρατέον διελεῖν. **(20b)** Ἡ [24] δ' ἀρχὴ πρὸς αὐτὰ ταῦτα καὶ πρῶτον τὸ ἀφορίσαι τί τὸ ἐπίστασθαι. Χαλεπώτερον δ' ἂν δόξειεν· οὐ γὰρ οἷόν τε καθόλου καὶ κοινόν τι λαβεῖν ἐν τοῖς πλεοναχῶς λεγομένοις. **(20c1)** Ἢ καὶ τοῦτ' ἄπορον ἢ οὐ ῥᾴδιόν γε εἰπεῖν μέχρι πόσου καὶ τίνων ζητητέον αἰτίας ὁμοίως ἔν τε τοῖς αἰσθητοῖς καὶ νοητοῖς· ἡ γὰρ εἰς τὸ ἄπειρον ὁδὸς ἐν ἀμφοῖν ἀλλοτρία καὶ ἀναιροῦσα τὸ φρονεῖν. Ἀρχαὶ δὲ τρόπον τινὰ ἄμφω· τάχα δ' ἡ μὲν ἡμῖν ἡ δ' ἁπλῶς, ἢ τὸ μὲν τέλος ἡ δ' ἡμετέρα τις

9a16–18 ἔχει … ἱκανῶς] Arist. *Met.* E 1, 1026a25–27 οὐ γὰρ ὁ αὐτὸς τρόπος οὐδ' ἐν ταῖς μαθηματικαῖς (sc. ἐπιστήμαις), ἀλλ' ἡ μὲν γεωμετρία καὶ ἀστρολογία περί τινα φύσιν εἰσίν, ἡ δὲ καθόλου πασῶν κοινή. **9b2** ἄπορον ἢ οὐ ῥᾴδιόν γε εἰπεῖν] Arist. *Met.* M 9, 1085a29 εἰ μὴ ῥᾴδιον δεῖ λέγειν τὸ ἀδύνατον. **9b4–5** ἡ γὰρ εἰς τὸ ἄπειρον ὁδὸς … φρονεῖν] Theophr. fr. 159.2–5 FHS&G εἰ γὰρ καὶ τῶν πρώτων τὰ αἴτια ζητήσομεν καὶ τῶν αὐθυποστάτων γενέσεις ἐπινοήσομεν, εἰς ἄπειρον προϊόντες λησόμεθα καὶ τέλος οὐδὲν ἔχον τῆς θεωρίας. Arist. *Met.* α 2, 994b20 οἱ τὸ ἄπειρον ποιοῦντες … τὸ ἐπίστασθαι ἀναιροῦσιν οἱ οὕτως λέγοντες, κτλ. Γ 4, 1006a6–9 ἔστι γὰρ ἀπαιδευσία τὸ μὴ γιγνώσκειν τίνων δεῖ ζητεῖν ἀπόδειξιν καὶ τίνων οὐ δεῖ· ὅλως μὲν γὰρ ἁπάντων ἀδύνατον ἀπόδειξιν εἶναι· εἰς ἄπειρον γὰρ ἂν βαδίζοι, ὥστε μηδ' οὕτως εἶναι ἀπόδειξιν. **9b6–7** ἀρχαὶ … ἁπλῶς] Arist. *APo.* 72a1–3 πρὸς ἡμᾶς μὲν πρότερα καὶ γνωριμώτερα τὰ ἐγγύτερον τῆς αἰσθήσεως, ἁπλῶς δὲ πρότερα καὶ γνωριμώτερα τὰ πορρώτερον.

14 τὰ Ψ (*mā minhā*), add. Wim.[1,2] : om. **α** [Λ] **19** γνωστὰ J : γνωτὰ P [Ψ] [Λ] **22** ἢ Ψ Λ CL A : ἡ P, η J : ᾗ J[1] ut vid. **23** ὁρατόν **ω** CL : ἀόρατον A, edd. a Ross (praeter van Raalte) **23–26** πόσοι—ἐπίστασθαι om. Lat. **23** δ' οὖν P Ψ : δὲ J : om. Lat. **26** τί PJ[1] Ψ : om. J Lat. **9b1** ἢ **ω** : ᾗ coni. Ross **3** αἰτίας PJ Λ : ἀρχὰς ut interpr. Ar. **6** ἀρχαὶ P[1]J[1] Ψ, ἀρχὰ J : ἀρχας P : ἀρχῆς CL, ἀρχὴ Λ A **7–8** τις ἀρχὴ P Ψ Λ : της αρχηι J nature, and of these latter, those at the head[103] and ⸢those⸣ that follow, right down to animals, plants, and lastly to inanimate [things]. For there is something unique[104] relating to each genus [of things], as also in mathematicals; furthermore, even mathematics itself is differentiated despite being somehow homogeneous—but the distinction has been made sufficiently.[105] And if, in addition, some [things] are known by being unknown, as some maintain, this manner would be unique [to them] but needs some sort of division;[106] though perhaps, for those [cases] in which it is possible, it is more appropriate to call [this manner of knowing knowing] by analogy than by the very [attribute of being] unknown, as if one [were to call seeing] what is seen by means of [its being] unseen.[107]

(**20a**) One should try to distinguish, then, how many manners [of investigation there are], and in how many ways knowing [occurs]. (**20b**) The starting point with reference to these [things] themselves and the first [step] is to mark the boundaries of what knowing is. But this would seem more difficult,[108] for it is not possible to apprehend something universal and common in the case of [things] said in very many ways. (**20c1**) Or actually *this* is a matter of aporia, or at least not easy to say, how far and up to which [things] search for causes should extend, alike in the case of sensibles and of intelligibles, for the route to infinity is in both cases inappropriate and destructive of understanding. (Both are, in some manner, starting points: perhaps the one for us and the other absolutely, or the one is an end and the other some starting point of

---

[103] I.e., the celestial bodies.

[104] I.e., in the manner of being investigated.

[105] Presumably, as Ross 67 observes, in the Peripatetic School.

[106] I.e., some sort of list arrived at by division as practiced in the Academy (for which see Ross 1951, 144–145, and Laks & Most 66n24), and especially by Speusippus (if this passage refers to him; see the Appendix); cf. the divisions list mentioned in the preceding paragraph at 9a5–6.

[107] For the analysis that led to the translation presented here see the Appendix. It is not known precisely to what and to whom Theophrastus is referring in this passage, though it is more than likely that he has Speusippus in mind (as elsewhere in this Essay) who held that a thing is defined (and thus known) through the complex of its relations to all other things.

[108] I.e., marking the boundaries of knowledge, or determining with precision what its objects are, is more difficult than distinguishing the different ways of knowing; see the structure of this whole argument given in the commentary at 9b1.

ἀρχή. Μέχρι μὲν οὖν τινὸς δυνάμεθα δι᾽ αἰτίου [25] θεωρεῖν, ἀρχὰς ἀπὸ τῶν αἰσθήσεων λαμβάνοντες· ὅταν δὲ ἐπ᾽ αὐτὰ τὰ ἄκρα καὶ πρῶτα μεταβαίνωμεν, οὐκέτι δυνάμεθα, εἴτε διὰ τὸ μὴ ἔχειν αἰτίαν εἴτε διὰ τὴν ἡμετέραν ἀσθένειαν ὥσπερ πρὸς τὰ φωτεινότατα βλέπειν. Τάχα δ᾽ ἐκεῖνο ἀληθέστερον ὡς αὐτῷ τῷ νῷ τῶν τοιούτων ἡ θεωρία θιγόντι καὶ οἷον ἁψαμένῳ, διὸ καὶ οὐκ ἔστιν ἀπάτη περὶ αὐτά. **(20c2)** Χαλεπὴ δὲ καὶ εἰς αὐτὸ [26] τοῦθ᾽ ἡ σύνεσις καὶ ἡ πίστις—ἐπεὶ καὶ ἄλλως μέγα καὶ πρὸς τὰς καθ᾽ ἕκαστα πραγματείας ἀναγκαῖον καὶ μάλιστα τὰς μεγίστας—ἐν τίνι ποιητέον τὸν ὅρον, οἷον περί τε ⌜τὰς⌝ τῆς φύσεως καὶ περὶ τὰς ἔτι προτέρας. Οἱ γὰρ ἁπάντων ζητοῦντες λόγον ἀναιροῦσιν λόγον, ἅμα δὲ καὶ τὸ εἰδέναι· μᾶλλον δ᾽

9b8–12 μέχρι … μὴ ἔχειν αἰτίαν] Arist. *APo.* 87b37–88a8 αἰσθάνεσθαι μὲν γὰρ ἀνάγκη καθ᾽ ἕκαστον, ἡ δ᾽ ἐπιστήμη τὸ τὸ καθόλου γνωρίζειν ἐστίν. … ἐκ τοῦ θεωρεῖν τοῦτο πολλάκις συμβαῖνον τὸ καθόλου ἂν θηρεύσαντες ἀπόδειξιν εἴχομεν. … τὸ δὲ καθόλου … δηλοῖ τὸ αἴτιον· ὥστε περὶ τῶν τοιούτων ἡ καθόλου τιμιωτέρα τῶν αἰσθήσεων καὶ τῆς νοήσεως, ὅσων ἕτερον τὸ αἴτιον· περὶ δὲ τῶν πρώτων ἄλλος λόγος. **9b10** αὐτὰ τὰ ἄκρα καὶ πρῶτα] Plat. *Epist.* VII 344d5 ἔγραψέν τι τῶν περὶ φύσεως ἄκρων καὶ πρώτων. Cf. *Phaedo* 78d1–4, *Resp.* 493e3, etc. αὐτὸ τὸ καλόν, *Resp.* 534c4 αὐτὸ τὸ ἀγαθόν, Arist. *Protrept.* fr. 48,3 αὐτῶν τῶν πρώτων. **9b12–13** εἴτε διὰ τὴν ἡμετέραν ἀσθένειαν … βλέπειν] Arist. *Met.* α 1, 993b8–11 οὐκ ἐν τοῖς πράγμασιν ἀλλ᾽ ἐν ἡμῖν τὸ αἴτιον αὐτῆς (sc. τῆς τῆς περὶ τῆς ἀληθείας θεωρίας κατὰ δεύτερον τρόπον χαλεπότητος)· ὥσπερ γὰρ τὰ τῶν νυκτερίδων ὄμματα πρὸς τὸ φέγγος ἔχει τὸ μεθ᾽ ἡμέραν, οὕτω καὶ τῆς ἡμετέρας ψυχῆς ὁ νοῦς πρὸς τὰ τῇ φύσει φανερώτατα πάντων. **9b14–16** αὐτῷ τῷ νῷ … ἀπάτη περὶ αὐτά] Arist. *Met.* Θ 10, 1051b17–32 περὶ δὲ δὴ τὰ ἀσύνθετα … τὸ μὲν θιγεῖν καὶ φάναι ἀληθές … τὸ δ᾽ ἀγνοεῖν μὴ θιγγάνειν … ὅσα δή ἐστιν ὅπερ εἶναί τι καὶ ἐνεργείᾳ, περὶ ταῦτα οὐκ ἔστιν ἀπατηθῆναι ἀλλ᾽ ἢ νοεῖν ἢ μή. **9b21–22** οἱ γὰρ ἁπάντων ζητοῦντες λόγον … τὸ εἰδέναι] Arist. *APo.* 72b5–7 ἐνίοις μὲν οὖν διὰ τὸ δεῖν τὰ πρῶτα ἐπίστασθαι οὐ δοκεῖ ἐπιστήμη εἶναι, τοῖς δ᾽ εἶναι μέν, πάντων μέντοι ἀπόδειξις εἶναι· ὧν οὐδέτερον οὔτ᾽ ἀληθὲς οὔτ᾽ ἀναγκαῖον. *Met.* Κ 6, 1063b10–11 μηθὲν γὰρ τιθέντες (sc. οὐ μηκέτι λόγον ἀπαιτοῦσιν) ἀναιροῦσι τὸ διαλέγεσθαι καὶ ὅλως λόγον. Theophr. fr. 159.5–8 FHS&G ὥσπερ γὰρ ὁ πάντα ἀποδεικτὰ νενομικὼς αὐτὴν μάλιστα τὴν ἀπόδειξιν ἀναιρεῖ, τοῦτον τὸν τρόπον καὶ ὁ πάντων αἰτίας ἐπιζητῶν ἄρδην ἀνατρέπει τὰ ὄντα πάντα καὶ τὴν τάξιν αὐτῶν τὴν ἀπό τινος ὡρισμένης ἀρχῆς προϊοῦσαν.

8 τινὸς Ψ Λ : τίνος P : τινος J | δι᾽ αἰτίου **α** : αἰτίας ut interpr. Ar., δι᾽ αἰτίας ut interpr. Lat. **13** βλέπειν PJ Λ : βλέποντες ut intell. Ar., coni. Us.[1,2] **15** θιγόντι corr. Wim.[1] : θίγοντι **α** [Ψ] [Λ] **17** σύνεσις **α** Λ : ζήτησις Ψ (*baḥt*; cf. 6b22) **19** ἐν τίνι P Ψ : ἕν τινι J Λ **20** τε τὰς Ψ (*ʿilm*) v. adn. : τε **α** Λ : τὰς coni. Us.[2], τὴν Us.[1], τὰ prop. van Raalte ours.[109] Up to a point, then, we are able to conduct studies by means of a cause[110] by taking starting points from sense-perceptions; but when we move on to "the first and highest" [things] themselves, we are no longer able to, either because they have no cause or because of our own lack of strength, as it were, to look in the direction of the brightest [things]. But perhaps *that* is closer to the truth, that the contemplation of such [things] is by means of the intellect itself as it makes contact with and touches [them], as it were, which is also why there can be no deception about them.) **(20c2)** So, reaching understanding and conviction, seeing that it is otherwise important and necessary in studies of each particular [thing] and especially [in] the most important ones, is difficult with regard to this very [issue] here: at which [point] to set the boundary—[the boundary], that is, both regarding ˹the˺ [studies] of nature and regarding those even prior.[111] For[112] those who seek proof of everything do away with proof, and at the same time with

[109] The chiasmus in this construction has been noted by the commentators. The sensibles constitute the starting point for us (who proceed from down up) while the intelligibles are starting points absolutely (i.e., containing, as they do, the explanation of the universe from top down); but if so, as absolute starting points in this sense, they also constitute the end toward which we tend when we start from some sensibles.

[110] I.e., we are able "to acquire knowledge of them by identifying their cause" (van Raalte 454), which is in keeping with Theophrastus's statement about the search for causes. Studies by means of a cause, however, cannot go on indefinitely because "the route to infinity"–infinite regress—must be avoided.

[111] I.e., studies on subjects that are prior to the objects of nature, viz., mathematics and metaphysics. For the concept of boundaries existing in reality and which should be observed in the search for knowledge see Part I, Chapter 1.3 and note 58.

[112] The function of "for" (*gar*) here is to give the reason why setting a boundary in the various disciplines of inquiry is difficult: if no boundary is set, one would go on seeking proof for everything ad infinitum. See the commentary at 9b24 for a statement of the argument.

ἀληθέστερον εἰπεῖν ὅτι ζητοῦσιν ὧν οὐκ ἔστιν οὐδὲ πέφυκεν ⟨ * * * ⟩ ὅσοι τὸν οὐρανὸν ἀΐδιον ὑπο-
9b25 λαμβάνουσιν, ἔτι δὲ τὰ κατὰ τὰς φορὰς καὶ τὰ [27] μεγέθη καὶ τὰ σχήματα καὶ τὰς ἀποστάσεις καὶ ὅσα ἄλλα ἀστρολογία δείκνυσιν, τούτοις κατάλοι-
10a1 πον τά τε πρῶτα κινοῦντα καὶ τὸ τίνος ἕνεκα λέγειν καὶ τίς ἡ φύσις ἑκάστου καὶ ἡ πρὸς ἄλληλα θέσις καὶ ἡ τοῦ σύμπαντος οὐσία, καὶ ὑποβαίνοντι δὴ πρὸς τὰ ἄλλα καθ' ἕκαστον τῶν εἰδῶν ἢ μερῶν ἄχρι ζῴων καὶ φυτῶν.

(21) Εἰ οὖν ἀστρολογία συνεργεῖ μέν, οὐκ ἐν τοῖς πρώτοις δέ, τῆς φύσεως ἕτερα τὰ κυριώτατ' ἂν εἴη καὶ πρότερα· καὶ γὰρ δὴ καὶ ὁ τρόπος, ὥς οἴονταί τινες, οὐ φυσικὸς ἢ οὐ πᾶς. Καίτοι τό γε κινεῖσθαι καὶ ἁπλῶς τῆς φύσεως οἰκεῖον καὶ μάλιστα τοῦ οὐρανοῦ. Διὸ καὶ ⟨εἰ⟩ ἡ ἐνέργεια τῆς οὐσίας ἑκάστου καὶ τὸ καθ' ἕκαστον ὅταν ἐνεργῇ καὶ κινεῖται, καθάπερ ἐν τοῖς ζῴοις καὶ φυτοῖς (εἰ δὲ μή, ὁμώνυμα), δῆλον ὅτι κἂν ὁ οὐρανὸς ἐν τῇ περιφορᾷ κατὰ τὴν οὐσίαν εἴη, χωριζόμενος δὲ καὶ ἠρεμῶν ὁμώνυμος· οἷον γὰρ ζωή τις ἡ περιφορὰ τοῦ παντός. ᾿Αρ' οὖν εἴ [28] γε μηδ' ἐν τοῖς ζῴοις τὴν ζωὴν ἢ ὡδὶ ζητητέον,

---

9b23–24 ζητοῦσιν (sc. λόγον) ὧν οὐκ ἔστιν οὐδὲ πέφυκεν] Arist. *Met.* Γ 6, 1011a12–13 λόγον γὰρ ζητοῦσιν ὧν οὐκ ἔστι λόγος· ἀποδείξεως γὰρ ἀρχὴ οὐκ ἀπόδειξίς ἐστιν. **10a12–16** κινεῖται ... παντός] Arist. *DA* 413a22–24 πλεοναχῶς δὲ τοῦ ζῆν λεγομένου, ... ζῆν αὐτό φαμεν, οἷον νοῦς, αἴσθησις, κίνησις, κτλ.

24 lac. ind. Us.[1,2], v. adn. | ὅσοι ⟨δὲ⟩ prop. Zeller : τοῖς οὖν prop. Us.[2] **27** ἀστρολογία δείκνυσιν [post ἀστρολογία add. δὲ J] **ω** : ἀστρολογικὰ δεικνῦσιν coni. Us.[1,2] | τούτοις κατάλοιπον P Ψ : τούτοις κατὰλοιπόν· J : ταῦτα κατέλιπον ut interpr. Lat. **10a1** τά τε P Ψ : τὰ δὲ J Λ **3** θέσις J Ψ : θέσεις P : om. Lat. in lac. **4** τῶν om. J | ἢ μερῶν CL et Spengel, sed corruptelam susp. ego : ἡμερῶν PJ, ἡμέρων A : ⟨τῶν εἰρ⟩ημένων Ar. (*allatī qulnā*), an etiam Ψ? : om. Lat. in lac. **5** post φυτῶν add. καὶ ἀψύχων Steinmetz 1964 | εἰ P Ψ : ἡ J : ἡ μὲν Λ **6** post δὲ dist. Laks & Most : post φύσεως dist. JP Ar. edd. [Λ] **7** κυριώτατ' P : κυριώτατα J [Ψ] [Λ] **10–11** τοῦ οὐρανοῦ—καθ' ἕκαστον om. Ar. | καὶ ⟨εἰ⟩ ἡ addidi : καὶ ἡ PJ [Λ], om. Ar. in lac. : εἰ ἡ coni. Wim.[1,2] : καὶ εἰ coni. Us.[2] **12** κινεῖται CL B : κινῆται PJ Ψ A [Λ] **13** μὴ ὁμώνυμα non dist. Ar. **14** κἂν PJ Λ C A : οὐκ ἂν L : non vert. Ar. **16** ἆρ' Ψ (*layta šiʿrī*) Λ (*utrum*) O : ἀρ P : ἄρ' J CL A **17** γε Sylburg : τε **α** Λ [Ψ] | μηδ' ἐν P : μηδὲν J Ψ Λ | ἢ ὡδὶ edd., η ωδὶ sic P : η ωδει J : ἢ τόδε ut intell. Ar. : δὴ ut intell. Lat.

knowing, too;[113] or rather, it is closer to the truth to say that they seek [proof] of [things of] which there neither is nor by their very nature can be any. ⟨* * *⟩ those who assume the heavens to be eternal[114] and, further, what has to do with the movements and the sizes and the figures and the distances and whatever else astronomy shows—for these [people] it remains to state both the first movers and "that for the sake of which," as well as what the nature of each is, the position of the one relative to the other, and the substance[115] of the universe; and then, for someone progressing downwards to the rest [of the things, there remains to state the same] for each species or part[116] individually down to animals and plants.

(**21**) If, then, astronomy helps, but not with regard to the first [things], the principal [things] will be other than and prior to nature;[117] and certainly also the method, as some think, is not that of nature,[118] or not entirely. In fact, being in motion, at least, is proper both to nature in general and to the heavens in particular. Hence, ⟨if⟩ the actualized state[119] of each [thing] is of its *essence*, and each individual [thing] is also in motion when in an actualized state, as in the case of animals and plants (otherwise [they would be animals and plants] in name [only]), then it is obvious that the heavens, too, in [their] rotation, would be in accordance with their essence, but when divorced [from movement] and at rest, [they would be the heavens] in name [only]—for the rotation of the universe is, as it were, a kind of life. So I wonder, if even in the case of animals life is not to be investigated except in this way,[120] isn't then also movement, in the case

---

[113] Proclus, who cites a similar passage by Theophrastus (*In Tim.* 35A = fr. 159 FHS&G), says that this is directed against Plato's inquiry into the origins of the soul in the *Timaeus*.

[114] It is necessary to assume a lacuna at this point. See the discussion in the commentary. The missing sentence would have read something like, "⟨Though finding such a boundary is difficult, one should on the other hand beware of stopping too short in the quest of causes, as is done by⟩ those who assume the heavens to be eternal ... ."

[115] Substance (*ousía*) here in the sense of formal constitution; cf. at 8a23 and 11b26 and see the commentary at 4a13.

[116] In all likelihood "or part" is a corruption and should be substituted by "mentioned above," i.e., "for each species mentioned above," as in the Arabic translation. See Chapter 2.1, section on "Sub-family JCL."

[117] I.e., either mathematicals or the intelligibles studied in metaphysics.

[118] I.e., that used in the study of nature, or physics.

[119] *Enérgeia*, see the commentary at 5a7.

[120] I.e., an explanation of life, or movement, is to be investigated in a metaphysical inquiry on first principles by considering it as belonging to the essence of animals.

οὐδ’ ἐν τῷ οὐρανῷ καὶ τοῖς οὐρανίοις τὴν φορὰν ἢ τρόπον τινὰ ἀφωρισμένον; Συνάπτει δέ πως ἡ νῦν ἀπορία καὶ πρὸς τὴν ὑπὸ τοῦ ἀκινήτου κίνησιν.

(22) Ὑπὲρ δὲ τοῦ πάνθ’ ἕνεκά του καὶ μηδὲν μάτην, ἄλλως ⟨θ’⟩ ὁ ἀφορισμὸς οὐ ῥᾴδιος, καθάπερ πλεονάκις λέγεται (πόθεν δ’ ἄρξασθαι χρὴ καὶ εἰς ποῖα τελευτᾶν;), καὶ δὴ ἔνια τῷ μὴ δοκεῖν ἔχειν οὕτως ἀλλὰ τὰ μὲν συμπτωματικῶς τὰ δ’ ἀνάγκῃ τινί, καθάπερ ἔν τε τοῖς οὐρανίοις καὶ ἐν τοῖς περὶ τὴν γῆν πλείοσιν. IX

(22.1) Τίνος γὰρ ἕνεκα αἱ ἔφοδοι καὶ ἀνάρροιαι θαλάττης, ἢ τίνος αἱ προχωρήσεις ⌜καὶ ἀναχωρήσεις⌝ ἢ ἀναξηράνσεις καὶ ὑγρότητες, καὶ ὅλως πρὸς ἄλλοτ’ ἄλλο μεταβολαὶ καὶ φθοραὶ καὶ γενέσεις, ᾗ αἱ μὲν ἐν αὐτῇ τῇ γῇ ἀλλοιώσεις καὶ μεταβολαὶ γίνονται πρὸς ἄλλοτ’ ἄλλο μεθισταμένων καὶ ἕτερα δ’ οὐκ ὀλίγα παρόμοια τούτοις; [29]

10a18 ἐν τῷ οὐρανῷ καὶ τοῖς οὐρανίοις τὴν φορὰν] Theophr. fr. 159,27–30 ὁ μὲν Θεόφραστος εἰκότως ἀρχὴν κινήσεως τὴν ψυχὴν εἰπών … ἔμψυχον … εἶναι δίδωσι τὸν οὐρανόν καὶ διὰ τοῦτο θεῖον. **10a22** ὑπὲρ δὲ τοῦ πάνθ’ ἕνεκά του καὶ μηδὲν μάτην] Arist. *Met.* A 2, 982b10 τἀγαθὸν καὶ τὸ οὗ ἕνεκα ἓν τῶν αἰτίων ἐστίν. A 3, 983a31 τετάρτην δὲ … αἰτίαν … τὸ οὗ ἕνεκα καὶ τἀγαθόν. **10a28-b4** τίνος … γενέσεις] Arist. *Mete.* 353a22–24 τῆς δὲ θαλάττης τὰ μὲν ἀπολειπούσης τὰ δ’ ἐπιούσης ἀεὶ φανερὸν ὅτι τῆς πάσης γῆς οὐκ ἀεὶ τὰ αὐτὰ τὰ μέν ἐστιν θάλαττα τὰ δ’ ἤπειρος, ἀλλὰ μεταβάλλει τῷ χρόνῳ πάντα.

18 οὐδ’ ἐν P Λ : οὐδεν J, οὐδὲν Ψ **22** μάτην secl. Zeller **23** ἄλλως [αλλως P] PJ Ψ L : ἀλλ’ ὥς Λ C A | post ἄλλως dist. Ar. Zeller | θ’ add. Us.[1,2] **24** λέγεται PJ Λ : λέξεται Ψ (*sa-naqūlu*) | δ’ **ω** : τ’ prop. Zeller : secl. van Raalte **25** ἔνια τῷ P Λ CL A : ἔνια τῶν J [Ψ] : τῷ ἔνια Us.[1] : ἐνίων τῷ prop. Us.[2] **10b1** ἢ τίνος non vert. Ar. | ἢ—προχωρήσεις secl. Ross **2** καὶ ἀναχωρήσεις Ψ (*wa-ǧazruhū*), add. Us.[2] : om. PJ Λ **3** πρὸς J Ψ Λ : προ P **4** ᾗ Bignone : ἢ **ω** CL A | αὐτῇ non vert. Ar. | τῇ PJ[1] : om. J [Ψ] [Λ] **6** δ’ om. A Lat.

of the heavens and the heavenly [bodies, not to be investigated] except in some manner whose boundaries have been marked?[121] The present aporia[122] is in a way also connected with the movement [caused] by the unmoved.

(**22**) With regard to "all [things] are for the sake of something" and "nothing is in vain," marking the boundaries is in any case not easy, as is frequently stated—from which point is it necessary to begin and at what sort [of things] to end?[123]—and in particular some [things are not easily marked within boundaries] by not seeming to be thus,[124] but rather [by] some of them [seeming to occur] by coincidence and others by some necessity, as in the case of both celestial and the majority of terrestrial [things].

(**22.1**) To wit: for the sake of what [thing do] incursions and refluxes of the sea [occur], or of what [thing] advances ⌜and regressions⌝, or drynesses and humidities, and, in general, changes now in this direction and now in that, and passings-away and comings-to-be[125] through which there occur the alterations and changes in the earth itself as [things] shift now towards this and now towards that place, and not a few other [things] besides, similar to these?

[121] I.e., in a manner proper to metaphysics ("not that of nature," at 10a8 above), whose objects of study are well marked off, as the opening sentence of this Essay wishes to investigate.

[122] I.e., the question that was asked in the preceding sentence, where Theophrastus hints that the metaphysical investigation into the movement of the heavens—that is, that it is essential to the heavens and thus not to be sought beyond this—bears directly upon, and obviates, Aristotle's theory of the unmoved mover. For a different interpretation see van Raalte 484.

[123] Theophrastus returns here to Aporia 15 which he mentioned earlier at 7b5–8. "Marking the boundaries" refers to the question he posed there, "mark the boundaries of how far what is endowed with order extends," and where disorder begins, as he repeats here.

[124] I.e., they do not seem to be manifestly for the sake of something and not in vain.

[125] Theophrastus is apparently referring here to the entire set of issues eventually discussed in Aristotle's *On Coming-to-be and Passing-away* (whose title is here adumbrated), viewed as problematic when considered from the point of view of their final cause.

10b7 **(22.2)** Ἔτι δ᾽ ἐν αὐτοῖς τοῖς ζῴοις τὰ μὲν ὥσπερ μάταια, καθάπερ τοῖς ἄρρεσιν οἱ μαστοὶ καὶ τοῖς θήλεσιν ἡ πρόεσις, εἴπερ μὴ συμβάλλεται, καὶ πώγωνος δ᾽ ἐνίοις ἢ ὅλως τριχῶν ἔκφυσις ἔν τισιν τόποις· ἔτι δὲ κεράτων μεγέθη καθάπερ τῶν ἐλάφων τοῖσδε καὶ λελωβημένων κινήσει τε καὶ παραιωρήσει καὶ ἐπιπροσθήσει τῶν ὀμμάτων· καὶ ὡς ἔνια δὴ βίᾳ ἢ παρὰ φύσιν, ὥσπερ ὁ ἐρῳδιὸς ὀχεύει καὶ τὸ ἡμερόβιον ζῇ· καὶ ἕτερα οὐκ ὀλίγα λάβοι τις ἂν τοιαῦτα. Καὶ τὸ μέγιστον δὴ καὶ μάλιστα [30] δοκοῦν περὶ τὰς τροφὰς καὶ γενέσεις τῶν ζῴων· οὐθενὸς γὰρ ταῦθ᾽ ἕνεκα, ἀλλὰ συμπτώματα καὶ δι᾽ ἑτέρας ἀνάγκας. Ἔδει γάρ, εἴπερ ⌜του⌝ χάριν, ἀεὶ κατὰ ταὐτὰ καὶ ὡσαύτως.

10b8 τοῖς ἄρρεσιν οἱ μαστοὶ] Arist. *PA* 688a17–22 τὰ μὲν τετράποδα τῶν ζῴων οὐκ ἔχει μαστούς … τοῖς δ᾽ ἀνθρώποις διὰ τὴν εὐρυχωρίαν καὶ τὸ σκεπάζεσθαι δεῖν τὰ περὶ τὴν καρδίαν … τοῖς μὲν ἄρρεσι διὰ τὴν εἰρημένην αἰτίαν. **10b9** τοῖς θήλεσιν … μὴ συμβάλλεται] Arist. *GA* 739a20–21 ἡ γιγνομένη ὑγρότης μετὰ τῆς ἡδονῆς τοῖς θήλεσιν οὐδὲν συμβάλλεται εἰς τὸ κύημα. **10b10** πώγωνος δ᾽ ἐνίοις] Arist. *APo.* 96a10–11 οὐ πᾶς ἄνθρωπος ἄρρην τὸ γένειον τριχοῦται, ἀλλ᾽ ὡς ἐπὶ τὸ πολύ. **10b10** τριχῶν ἔκφυσις ἔν τισιν τόποις] Arist. *PA* 658a18–24 σκέπης γὰρ χάριν αἱ τρίχες … τοῖς δ᾽ ἀνθρώποις ἐπεὶ ἐξ ἴσου διὰ τὴν ὀρθότητα τὰ πρόσθια τοῖς ὀπισθίοις, τοῖς τιμιωτέροις ὑπέγραψεν ἡ φύσις τὴν βοήθειαν. **10b11** κεράτων μεγέθη] Arist. *PA* 663a10 τὸ γὰρ μέγεθος αὐτῶν (sc. τῶν κεράτων) … μᾶλλον βλάπτει ἢ ὠφελεῖ (sc. τὰς ἐλάφους). **10b14–15** ὥσπερ ὁ ἐρῳδιὸς ὀχεύει] Arist. *HA* 609b24–25 κράζει τε γὰρ καὶ αἷμα, ὥς φασιν, ἀφίησιν ἐκ τῶν ὀφθαλμῶν ὀχεύων. **10b15** τὸ ἡμερόβιον ζῇ] Arist. *HA* 552b21–23 ζῇ δὲ καὶ πέτεται μέχρι δείλης, καταφερομένου δὲ τοῦ ἡλίου ἀπομαραίνεται καὶ ἅμα δυομένου ἀποθνήσκει βιῶσαν ἡμέραν μίαν, διὸ καὶ καλεῖται ἐφήμερον. **10b17** τροφὰς καὶ γενέσεις] Arist. *GA* 778a10–11 περὶ μὲν οὖν τῆς ἔσωθεν τροφῆς τῶν ζῴων καὶ τῆς θύραζε γενέσεως εἴρηται, cf. *GA* IV,10. **10b18–19** συμπτώματα … ἀνάγκας] Arist. GA 777b29–30, 778a3–4 τούτων (sc. τῶν γενέσεων καὶ φθορῶν τῶν ζῴων) δ᾽ ἔχουσι τὸ πέρας καὶ τῆς ἀρχῆς καὶ τῆς τελευτῆς αἱ τούτων κινήσεις τῶν ἄστρων. … τῆς δὲ τῶν ἄστρων τούτων περιφορᾶς τάχ᾽ ἂν ἕτεραί τινες εἶεν ἀρχαί.

7 τοῖς om. P **8–9** καὶ—συμβάλλεται non vert. Ar. **12** τοῖσδε Us.[1,2], τοῖσδὲ J, τοισδε P : τοῖς δὲ Ψ CL A : om. Lat. : τοῖς ⟨οὐκ ὠφελουμένοις, τοῖς⟩ δὲ add. Ross | κινήσει **α** Ψ, non vert. Lat. : κνήσει coni. edd. a Us.[1,2], v. adn. **12–15** τοῖσδε—ὀχεύει non vert. Lat. **13–16** καὶ ὡς—τοιαῦτα non vert. Ar. **14** δὴ P : δεῖ J **16** μέγιστον P Ψ Λ : μάλιστα J **17** τροφὰς καὶ γενέσεις transp. Ar. **19** καὶ non vert. Ar. | του Ψ (*šay'*), *alicuius* Tiph. Steph., coni. Us.[1,2] : τούτων **α** Λ **20** ταὐτὰ Ψ (*'alā ḥālin wāḥidatin*), *eadem* Tiph., *idem* Steph., coni. Brandis : ταυτα P : ταῦτα J Λ CL A

(**22.2**) Furthermore, even in the case of animals[126] some [things] are, as it were, purposeless, like the breasts in males and the emission in females (if indeed it makes no contribution), and the growth of beard in some or of hair altogether in certain places; and further, the large size of horns, like those of deer, by which they are even harmed as the [horns] sway, dangle, and block [their] line of vision; and then again, the way in which some [things] are with violence or unnatural, like the copulation of the heron[127] and the life of the day-fly—one could cite quite a few other [things] of this kind. And finally, the most important and most generally accepted [thing] has to do with the [different kinds of] food and generation of animals; for these are not for the sake of anything, but are rather coincidences and due to other necessities. For if indeed they were for the sake ⌜of something,⌝ they would have to be ever uniform and invariable.[128]

---

126 "Even (*autoís*) in the case of animals" because animals seem to illustrate best Aristotle's teleology.

127 Aristotle says that (*HA* 609b23–25) the ash-colored heron "screams during the union, and it is said drips blood from its eyes" (p. 950 *CWA*).

128 The structure of this paragraph about animals is in ascending order of difficulty for maintaining teleology: first are mentioned parts of animals which seem to have no purpose, then parts which actually hamper their living, and then behavior which does violence to them or is against nature. These three sets represent individual difficulties that apply to some animals and not to others. The paragraph ends by mentioning the most difficult problem with teleology of all, one that applies to all animals, insofar as it affects their nourishment and generation: the bewildering variety of forms of nourishment and generation cannot all be for the sake of the same end; for if they were, they would all have to be uniform and invariable. Theophrastus uses the same argument against the theory of the prime mover causing movement by being desired: if this were so, and the prime mover is one and invariable, then all celestial bodies would move with the same motion (above, 5a17–18).

(22.3) Ἔτι δ' ⟨αἱ⟩ ἐν τοῖς φυτοῖς καὶ μᾶλλον τοῖς ἀψύχοις ὡρισμένην τιν' ἔχουσαι φύσιν, ὥσπερ δοκοῦσιν, καὶ μορφαῖς καὶ εἴδεσιν καὶ δυνάμεσιν, τίνος ἕνεκα ταῦτα ζητήσειεν ἄν τις. **(23)** Αὐτὸ γὰρ τοῦτο ἄπορον, τὸ μὴ ἔχειν λόγον καὶ ταῦτ' ἐν ἑτέροις δὴ ποιοῦσιν προτέροις καὶ τιμιωτέροις· ᾗ καὶ ἔοικεν ὁ λόγος ἔχειν τι πιστόν, ὡς ἄρα τῷ αὐτομάτῳ ταῦτα καὶ τῇ τοῦ ὅλου περιφορᾷ λαμβάνει τινὰς ἰδέας ἢ πρὸς ἄλληλα διαφοράς.

(24) Εἰ δὲ μὴ τοῦθ' ἕνεκά του καὶ [31] εἰς τὸ ἄριστον, ληπτέον τινὰς ὅρους καὶ οὐκ ἐπὶ πάντων ἁπλῶς θετέον, ἐπεὶ καὶ τὰ τοιάδε ἔχει τινὰ διστασμὸν καὶ ἁπλῶς λεγόμενα καὶ καθ' ἕκαστον. Ἁπλῶς μὲν ὅτι τὴν φύσιν ἐν ἅπασιν ὀρέγεσθαι τοῦ ἀρίστου καὶ ἐφ' ὧν ἐνδέχεται μεταδιδόναι τοῦ ἀεὶ καὶ τοῦ τεταγμένου, ὡς δ' αὐτὸ καὶ ἐπὶ τῶν ζῴων ὁμοίως: ὅπου γὰρ οἷόν τε τὸ βέλτιον, ἐνταῦθα οὐδαμοῦ παραλείπειν, οἷον τὸ ἔμπροσθεν τὴν φάρυγγα τοῦ οἰσοφάγου—τιμιώ-

---

10b28 τῇ τοῦ ὅλου περιφορᾷ] Arist. *GC* 336a31–b4 οὐχ ἡ πρώτη φορὰ αἰτία ἐστὶ γενέσεως καὶ φθορᾶς ἀλλ' ἡ κατὰ τὸν λοξὸν κύκλον. ... τῆς μὲν οὖν συνεχείας ἡ τοῦ ὅλου φορὰ αἰτία, τοῦ δὲ προσιέναι καὶ ἀπιέναι ἡ ἔγκλισις. **11a5–7** τὴν φύσιν ... τοῦ ἀεὶ] Arist. *PA* 687a16–17 ἡ δὲ φύσις ἐκ τῶν ἐνδεχομένων ποιεῖ τὸ βέλτιστον. *GA* 788b20–21 τὴν φύσιν ὑποτιθέμεθα ... οὔτ' ἐλλείπουσαν οὔτε μάταιον οὐθὲν ποιοῦσαν τῶν ἐνδεχομένων περὶ ἕκαστον. *DA* 415a26–28 φυσικώτατον γὰρ τῶν ἔργων τοῖς ζῶσιν ... τὸ ποιῆσαι ἕτερον οἷον αὐτό ... ἵνα τοῦ ἀεὶ καὶ τοῦ θείου μετέχωσιν ᾗ δύνανται. **11a10–11** τὸ ἔμπροσθεν ... τιμιώτερον γάρ] Arist. *PA* 665a22–25 ἀεὶ τὸ βέλτιον καὶ τιμιώτερον ... τοῦ ... ἔμπροσθεν καὶ ὄπισθεν ἐν τοῖς ἔμπροσθεν.

20 αἵ (sc. γενέσεις vel μεταβολαὶ) addidi, v. adn. **21** τιν' non vert. Ar. **22** ἔχουσαι **ω** : ἔχουσι CL A **25** post λόγον dist. Ross | καὶ non vert. et τοῦτ' (*ḏālika*) pro ταῦτ' legisse vid. et post τοῦτ' dist. Ar. | δὴ ut vid. Ψ (*ṯumma*) : μὴ **α** Λ **26** ᾗ Ψ (*fa-*, ut statuit Treiger), *quatenus* Steph., coni. Oporinus : ᾗ Ald. : ἡ P, ἢ J, ἢ Λ CL A | ἔχειν **α** Λ : ἔχων ut intell. Ar. **27** καὶ non vert. Ar. **28** ἰδέας **ω** : ἰδίας J[II] | ἢ om. J **11a1** διαφοράς PJ Λ : διάφορας ut intell. Ar. | μὴ τοῦθ' **ω** CL A : μή, τοῦ θ' edd. a Us.[1,2] : μὴ ταῦθ' prop. Zeller : μή, τοῦ γ' coni. van Raalte | post τοῦθ' desinit J ante corr. | του om. J[II] **2** post ἄριστον dist. Ar. **4** καὶ alt. om. J[II] **7** τοῦ ἀεὶ καὶ τοῦ τεταγμένου transp. Ar. **8** αὐτὸ Λ (*hoc*) : αὐτὰ J[II] CL [Ψ] : αὐτος P, αὕτως A | ὁμοίως non vert. Ar. **9** παραλείπειν ego, prop. Fobes : παραλείπει **α** Λ [Ψ]

(**22.3**) And yet again, ⟨those⟩ [generations and changes],[129] in the case of plants and still more of inanimate [things], which have, as they seem, a fully determinate nature pretty much in terms of shapes and forms and powers, one might investigate for whose sake these [things] are. (**23**) For this very thing is a matter of aporia, that these [things] too have no cause in *other* agents [that are] prior and nobler—for which reason there seems to be some credibility in the account that, allegedly, these acquire certain forms or differences in relation to one another spontaneously and through the rotation of the universe.

(**24**) But if this is not "for the sake of something" and "with a view to the best," one should apprehend some boundaries[130] and not posit [these two principles] for everything without qualification, for in fact the likes of the following are somewhat ambiguous when said both without qualification and with reference to each [species]. Without qualification, when [it is said] that nature in all [things] desires the best and, wherever possible, gives a share in the eternal and orderly;[131] and [with reference to each species] when something like this [is said] similarly about animals: for where the better is possible, there it is never lacking, like the windpipe being in front of the oesophagus—for it is nobler—and the mixture [of

[129] For the assumption of these words in the structure of this sentence see the commentary.

[130] I.e., as exhibited in things themselves or in objective reality; see Part I, Chapter 1.3 and note 58, and cf. Repici 1990, 187–193.

[131] Literally, gives a share in the "always" and the "orderly arranged."

τερον γάρ—καὶ ἐν τῇ μέσῃ κοιλίᾳ τῆς καρδίας τὴν κρᾶσιν ἀρίστην—ὅτι τὸ μέσον τιμιώτατον—· ὡσαύτως δὲ καὶ ὅσα κόσμου χάριν. Εἰ γὰρ καὶ [32] ἡ ὄρεξις οὕτως, ἀλλ' ἐκεῖνό γ' ἐμφαίνει διότι πολὺ τὸ οὐχ ὑπακοῦον οὐδὲ δεχόμενον τὸ εὖ, μᾶλλον δὲ πολλῷ πλεῖον· ὀλίγον γάρ τι τὸ ἔμψυχον, ἄπειρον δὲ τὸ ἄψυχον· καὶ αὐτῶν τῶν ἐμψύχων ἀκαριαῖον, κἂν βέλτιον, τὸ εἶναι. Τὸ δ' ὅλον σπάνιόν τι καὶ ἐν ὀλίγοις τὸ ἀγαθόν, πολὺ δὲ πλήθει τὸ κακόν †οὐκ εἰ† ἀοριστία δὲ μόνον καὶ οἷον ὕλης εἴδη, καθάπερ τὰ τῆς φύσεως ἀμαθεστάτου †ει καὶ γὰρ οἱ περὶ τῆς ὅλης οὐσίας λέγοντες, ὥσπερ Σπεύσιππος σπάνιόν τι τὸ τίμιον

11a11–12 ἐν τῇ μέσῃ ... τιμιώτατον] Arist. *PA* 665b18–21 ἔχει δὲ καὶ ἡ θέσις αὐτῆς (sc. τῆς καρδίας) ἀρχικὴν χώραν· περὶ μέσον γάρ. ... ἐν τοῖς γὰρ τιμιωτέροις τὸ τιμιώτερον καθίδρυκεν ἡ φύσις. **11a20–21** ἀοριστία ... φύσεως ἀμαθεστάτου] Arist. *GA* 778a4–7 βούλεται μὲν οὖν ἡ φύσις ... τὰς γενέσεις καὶ τὰς τελευτάς, οὐκ ἀκριβοῖ δὲ διά τε τὴν τῆς ὕλης ἀοριστίαν καὶ διὰ τὸ γίγνεσθαι πολλὰς ἀρχάς, αἳ τὰς γενέσεις τὰς κατὰ φύσιν καὶ τὰς φθορὰς ἐμποδίζουσαι πολλάκις αἴτιαι τῶν παρὰ φύσιν συμπιπτόντων εἰσίν. **11a23–25** Σπεύσιππος ... ἑκατέρωθεν] Arist. *EN* 1109a 20–30 ἐστὶν ἡ ἀρετὴ ἡ ἠθικὴ μεσότης ... δύο κακιῶν, τῆς μὲν καθ' ὑπερβολὴν τῆς δὲ κατ' ἔλλειψιν ... διὰ τὸ στοχαστικὴ τοῦ μέσου εἶναι. ... ἐν ἑκάστῳ γὰρ τὸ μέσον λαβεῖν ἔργον ... διόπερ τὸ εὖ καὶ σπάνιον καὶ ἐπαινετὸν καὶ καλόν. *Met.* Λ 7, 1072b31–34 Σπεύσιππος τὸ κάλλιστον καὶ ἄριστον μὴ ἐν ἀρχῇ εἶναι· ... τὰς ἀρχὰς αἴτια μὲν εἶναι, τὸ δὲ καλὸν καὶ τέλειον ἐν τοῖς ἐκ τούτων.

11–12 καὶ—τιμιώτατον om. Ar. in lac. **13** post χάριν non dist. Ar. | γὰρ PJ Λ, non vert. Ar. : δὲ coni. Tricot | post γὰρ dist. Brandis, Us.[2] | καὶ alt. non vert. Ar. **14** γ' P, γε J^{II}CL A : δὲ Λ **16** πολλῷ om. J^{II} | τι non vert. Ar. **17** ἐμψύχων P Ψ Λ : ἀψύχων J^{II} **18** ἀκαριαῖον, κἂν βέλτιον, τὸ homo Italicus quidam : ἀκαριαῖον καὶ βέλτιον τὸ **ω** : ἀκαριαῖον, κεἰ βέλτιον, τὸ prop. Fobes, alii alia v. app. crit. alt. **19** τι P Λ : τε Ψ J^{II} CL A | πλήθει corr. Laks & Most (v. adn.) : πλῆθος · ἡ P, πλῆθος ἢ Λ (*multitudo est*) J^{II} CL A : πλῆθος εἶ D, πλῆθος εἰ coni. Us.[2] : πλῆθος εἶναι Ald. : πλῆθος ut intell. Ar. (*kaṯīr al-ʿadad*), L^{1}, coni. Wim.[1,2], prop. Zeller **20** τὸ κακόν **ω** CL A : τοῦ κακοῦ coni. Us.[2] | οὐκ' ει sic P, locus corruptus necdum sanatus | οὐκ **α** Λ : οὗ ut intell. Ar. : del. Us.[2] : δοκεῖ prop. dubit. Us.[1] | ει P, εἰ CL A : ἡ J^{II}, ut intell. Ar. : δὲ ut interpr. Lat. : ἐν coni. edd. a Zeller | ἀοριστία **ω** CL A : ἀοριστίᾳ coni. edd. a Zeller **20–21** καὶ οἷον ὕλης εἴδη non vert. Ar. **21** εἴδη P A : εἴδει Λ J^{II} CL : *speciebus* Tiph. **22** ει· καὶ γὰρ sic P A^{2} Tiph., locus corruptus necdum sanatus : εἰ καὶ γὰρ A : καὶ γὰρ J^{II}, ut intell. Ar. : εἰ γὰρ καὶ C, ut interpr. Lat. : καὶ L : ἐστί· καὶ γὰρ Us.[1] : εἰκῇ γὰρ edd. a Sylburg **23** post Σπεύσιππος dist. Ar.

the blood] being the best in the central ventricle of the heart—because the center is the noblest—; and similarly with whatever [is said to be] for the sake of order. For[132] if it is true that desire [functions] in this manner,[133] this here, nevertheless, clearly reveals that there is much that neither obeys nor receives the good—or rather, it is much more by far:[134] for the animate is something little, while the inanimate is infinite; and the existence of the animate [things] themselves, though better, is momentary. In general, the good is something rare and in few [things], whereas evil is much in number,[135] †not if† indeterminacy only and, as it were, the forms of matter, just like those of the nature of a most ignorant one; †if for in fact, those who speak about all of existence,[136] just as Speusippus makes the noble, which is about the place of the center,

[132] "For" here explains the ambiguity mentioned in the preceding sentence, before the listing of examples.

[133] I.e., for the best, a reference to 11a6.

[134] I.e., than what obeys and receives the good; cf. the Arabic translation.

[135] The text is irremediably corrupt in the next three lines, in the places marked with a dagger. Ross presents a text, approved by Tarán 1981, 444, that is a hodgepodge of scribal and scholarly emendations, which he translates as follows: "But to say that *in general* the good is something rare and found only in few things, while the evil is a great multitude, and does not consist solely in indefiniteness and exist by way of matter, as *is* the case with the things of nature, is the act of a most ignorant person. For quite random is the talk of those who speak of the whole of reality as Speusippus does when he makes the valuable element to be something scanty, namely, what is found in the region of the centre of the universe, the rest forming the extremes and being to each side of the centre. Rather, reality in fact is and always has been good."

[136] *Ousía* in the sense of all that exists. See the commentary at 4a13.

ποιεῖ τὸ περὶ τὴν τοῦ μέσου χώραν, τὰ δ' ἄκρα
11a25 καὶ ἑκατέρωθεν. Τὰ μὲν οὖν ὄντα καλῶς ἔτυχεν ὄντα,

(24.1) Πλάτων δὲ καὶ οἱ Πυθαγόρειοι μακρὰν τὴν [33]
11b1 ἀπόστασιν, ἐπιμιμεῖσθαι τ' ἐθέλειν ἅπαντα· καίτοι καθάπερ ἀντίθεσίν τινα ποιοῦσιν τῆς ἀορίστου δυάδος καὶ τοῦ ἑνός, ἐν ᾗ καὶ τὸ ἄπειρον καὶ τὸ ἄτακτον καὶ πᾶσα ὡς εἰπεῖν ἀμορφία καθ' αὑτήν, ὅλως δ' οὐχ οἷόν τ' ἄνευ ταύτης τὴν τοῦ ὅλου φύσιν, ἀλλ' οἷον ἰσομοιρεῖν ἢ καὶ ὑπερέχειν τῆς ἑτέρας, ᾗ καὶ τὰς ἀρχὰς ἐναντίας. Διὸ καὶ οὐδὲ τὸν θεόν, ὅσοι τῷ θεῷ τὴν αἰτίαν ἀνάπτουσιν, δύνασθαι πάντ' εἰς τὸ ἄριστον ἄγειν, ἀλλ' εἴπερ, ἐφ' ὅσον ἐνδέχεται· τάχα δ' οὐδ' ἂν προέλοιτ', εἴπερ ἀναιρεῖσθαι συμβήσεται τὴν ὅλην οὐσίαν ἐξ ἐναντίων γε καὶ ⌜ἐν⌝ ἐναντίοις οὖσαν.

(24.2) Φαίνεται δὲ [34]
καὶ ἐν τοῖς πρώτοις ἐπιθεωρούμενα πολλὰ καὶ ὡς ἔτυχεν, οἷον τὰ περὶ τὰς τῆς γῆς λεχθέντα μετα-

---

11a25–26 Τὰ μὲν οὖν ὄντα καλῶς ἔτυχεν ὄντα] Arist. *Met.* Λ 10, 1076a3–4 τὰ δὲ ὄντα οὐ βούλεται πολιτεύεσθαι κακῶς. **11b7–9** οὐδὲ τὸν θεόν … δύνασθαι πάντ' εἰς τὸ ἄριστον ἄγειν] Theophr. *Mete.* 14,14–17, Daiber 1992, 242–243 وليس من الله تكون الصواعق ولا شئ ممّا [*sic leg.*] ذُكر وذلك أنّه ليس ينبغي أن نجعل [*sic leg.*] الله سببَ تشويس العالم بل سبب تعديله وترتيبه وذلك لأنّا نضيف تعديله وترتيبه إلى الله [عز وجل] وتشويش العالم إلى طبيعة العالم (Neither thunder nor anything of what has been mentioned is from god. The reason is that we should not posit god [to be] the cause of the disorder of the world but the cause of its harmonious order; this is because we ascribe its harmonious order to god and the disorder of the world to the nature of the world.) **11b8–10** τὸν θεόν … δύνασθαι πάντ' εἰς τὸ ἄριστον ἄγειν … ἐφ' ὅσον ἐνδέχεται] Plato *Timaeus* 29e1–3, 30a6–7 ἀγαθὸς ἦν (sc. ὁ θεός) … πάντα ὅτι μάλιστα ἐβουλήθη γενέσθαι παραπλήσια ἑαυτῷ. … θέμις δ' οὔτ' ἦν οὔτ' ἔστιν τῷ ἀρίστῳ δρᾶν ἄλλο πλὴν τὸ κάλλιστον.

24 ποιεῖ **α** Λ : ποιοῦσι ut intell. Ar. | δ' **ω** : τ' prop. Zeller **25** καὶ del. Zeller | post καὶ add. τὰ dubit. Us.[1] | post ἑκατέρωθεν add. μὴ τοιαῦτα J[II], non dist. Ar. | τὰ μὲν οὖν non vert. Ar. **11b1** ἐπιμιμεῖσθαι **ω** CL A : ἐπεὶ μιμεῖσθαι coni. Laks & Most (et iam Allan) | τ' ἐθέλειν ego : γ' ἐθέλειν P, γε θέλειν J[II] Ψ Λ, γ' ἐθέλειν Us.[2]: δ' ἐθέλειν coni. Ross **2** σύνθεσιν ut vid. Λ (*compositionem*; cf. Kley 27) **4–5** καθ' αὑτὴν non vert. Ar. **5** ὅλως δ' Ψ Λ J[II] CL A : ὅλως P : ὡς δ' coni. Us.[2] | ἄνἐ[υ] cum litura ex -ἐν corr. P[1] **7** ᾗ corr. Ross : ἡ P, ἢ Ψ Λ J[II] **12** ἐν Ψ (*fī*) Λ (*in*) L[1] B[2], Tiph. Steph., coni. Sylburg : om. **α** **14** τὰς Ψ OV[a2] : τε P CL [Λ] : τε τὴν J[II] : om. A | μεταβολάς P Ψ Λ : μεταβολὴν J[II]

something rare, and the rest, extremes and on either side.[137] The things 11a25
that are happen to be good;[138]

(**24.1**) Plato and the Pythagoreans [make] the distance[139] a great one and 11b1
[make] all [things] wish to imitate fully; and yet, they make a certain opposition, as it were, between the indefinite dyad and the one, in which [dyad reside] the infinite and the disordered and, in general, all shapelessness as such, and [they make] the nature of the universe altogether impossible [to be] without [the dyad], but rather [make the dyad] almost balance, or even predominate over the other [first principle]; on which account, [they make] also the first principles contrary [to one another].[140] For this reason, those who ascribe the cause to god [claim] that not even god is able to lead all [things] towards the best, but, if [at all, only] so far as is possible; though perhaps he wouldn't even choose to, if indeed it would result in the destruction of all existence,[141] given that it [is constituted] from contraries and consists of contraries.

(**24.2**) Even in the case of the first [things] there appear upon closer inspection many [things which are] also at random, such as what has

---

137 The sentence, as we have it in the corrupt text, has no finite verb.

138 Theophrastus here seems to be echoing Aristotle's final words in *Metaphysics* Lambda 10, 1076a3–4: "The things that are do not want to be badly governed;" though because of the corruption in the preceding sentence, the precise force of the statement and its connection to the rest of the sentence about Plato remain ambiguous.

139 I.e., the distance separating the first principle(s) and everything else, apparently in contrast to Speusippus; see the references in van Raalte 565–566.

140 An implied syllogism in this sentence is rejected for another. The implied syllogism, "All things wish to imitate the first principles, the first principles are the best, therefore all things imitate the best," is rejected and is substituted by, "All things wish to imitate the first principles, the first principles are contary and include both order and disorder, therefore all things imitate and include order and disorder." The words "and yet" signal the beginning of the argument that leads to the major premise, "the first principles are contrary," which is substituted for the implied one; see the commentary.

141 *Ousía* in the sense of all that exists. See the commentary at 4a13.

βολάς· οὔτε γὰρ τὸ βέλτιον οὔτε τὸ τινὸς χάριν, ἀλλ' εἴπερ, ἀνάγκῃ τινὶ κατακολουθεῖν· πολλὰ δὲ καὶ ἐν τῷ ἀέρι τοιαῦτα καὶ ἐν ἄλλοις. Μάλιστα δ' ἂν δόξειεν ἔχειν τήν γε τάξιν τῶν μὲν αἰσθητῶν τὰ οὐράνια, τῶν δ' ἄλλων, εἰ μὴ ἄρα καὶ πρότερα τούτων, τὰ μαθηματικά: εἰ γὰρ καὶ μὴ πᾶν, ἀλλ' ἐν τούτοις πλέον τὸ τεταγμένον (πλὴν εἴ τις τοιαύτας λαμβάνοι τὰς μορφὰς οἵας Δημόκριτος ὑποτίθεται τῶν ἀτόμων)· ἀλλὰ δὴ τούτων μὲν πέρι σκεπτέον, ὃ δ' ἐξ ἀρχῆς ἐλέχθη, πειρατέον τινὰ λαμβάνειν ὅρον, καὶ ἐν τῇ φύσει καὶ ἐν τῇ τοῦ σύμπαντος οὐσίᾳ, καὶ τοῦ ἕνεκά του καὶ τῆς εἰς τὸ βέλτιον ὁρμῆς. **(25)** Αὕτη γὰρ ἀρχὴ τῆς τοῦ σύμπαντος θεωρίας, ἐν τίσιν τὰ ὄντα καὶ πῶς ἔχει πρὸς ἄλληλα.

[Θεοφράστου τῶν μετὰ τὰ Φυσικά.
Τοῦτο τὸ βιβλίον Ἀνδρόνικος μὲν καὶ Ἕρμιππος ἀγνοοῦσιν, οὐδὲ γὰρ μνείαν αὐτοῦ ὅλως πεποίηνται ἐν τῇ ἀναγραφῇ τῶν Θεοφράστου βιβλίων· Νικόλαος δὲ ἐν τῇ θεωρίᾳ τῶν Ἀριστοτέλους μετὰ τὰ Φυσικὰ μνημονεύει αὐτοῦ λέγων εἶναι Θεοφράστου. Εἰσὶ δ' ἐν αὐτῷ οἷον προδιαπορίαι τινὲς ὀλίγαι τῆς ὅλης πραγματείας.]

11b17–19 μάλιστα … τὰ οὐράνια] Arist. *PA* 641b18–19 τὸ γοῦν τεταγμένον καὶ τὸ ὡρισμένον πολὺ μᾶλλον φαίνεται ἐν τοῖς οὐρανίοις ἢ περὶ ἡμᾶς. **11b22** Δημόκριτος] Theophr. *CP* VI,17.11 τά γε σχήματα Δημοκρίτου, καθάπερ ἐλέχθη, τεταγμένας ἔχοντα τὰς μορφάς. Cf. Arist. *GA* 789b3–4 Δημόκριτος δὲ τὸ οὗ ἕνεκεν ἀφεὶς λέγειν πάντα ἀνάγει εἰς ἀνάγκην οἷς χρῆται ἡ φύσις.

15 τὸ βέλτιον οὔτε τὸ **ω** CL A : τῷ βελτίονι οὔτε τῷ prop. Us.[2] : τῷ βέλτιον οὔτε τῷ prop. Jaeger[2] **18** γε Ross : τε P J^{II} [Ψ] [Λ] **22** λαμβάνοι P : λαμβάνει J^{II} [Ψ] [Λ] **23–24** πέρι σκεπτέον P Ψ : περισκεπτέον Λ J^{II} **25** λαμβάνειν P Λ [Ψ] : λαβεῖν J^{II} **12a3** Θεοφράστου—φυσικά P A : om. J^{II} CL Ar. | post φυσικὰ add. α⁀ A **12a4-b5** τοῦτο—πραγματείας P A : om. J^{II} CL : in Ar. paraphrasis scholii legitur, v. part. I, cap. 1.2 **4** τὸ A : om. P **12b4** δ' P : δὲ A | οἷον P : om. A | προδιαπορίαι P : προδιαπορήσεις A been said about the changes of the earth,[142] for [they are] neither "the better" nor "that for the sake of which" but, if anything, [appear] to comply with some sort of necessity; there are many things of this sort both in the air and elsewhere. And it would seem that among sensibles, the celestial [things] above all would possess at least order, and, among other [things],[143] the mathematicals (if, that is, there are no [things] even prior to these): for if it is true that the ordered is not everything, it is nevertheless the greater part in these (unless one were to take the shapes of atoms to be such as those Democritus assumes[144]); but while these [are all things] one should certainly look into, the main [point] that has been made[145] [is that] one should try to apprehend some boundary, both in nature and in the substance[146] of the universe, and both for "that for the sake of which" and for the impulse towards "the better." (**25**) For *this* is the starting point of the study of the universe, among what [things] beings are[147] and how they relate to one another.

[The book] by Theophrastus of Those [that Come] after [Aristotle's] *Physics*. Andronicus and Hermippus do not know this book, for they make no mention of it at all in the list of Theophrastus's books; Nicolaus, though, does mention it in his study of Aristotle's [books that come] after the *Physics*, saying that it is by Theophrastus. It contains some few "pre-diaporiae,"[148] so to speak, relating to the entire treatise.[149]

---

142 Above, at 10a25–10b7.

143 I.e., the intelligibles.

144 I.e., ordered, as Theophrastus himself mentions on another occasion (see the Loci Paralleli), and thus ontologically prior to both the heavenly bodies and mathematicals.

145 I.e., at the beginning of this Aporia (24), at 11a1–3, which is here repeated.

146 Substance (*ousía*) in the sense of formal constitution; cf. 8a23 and 10a3, and see the commentary at 4a13. For the concept of boundary referred to here see Part I, Chapter 1.3 and note 58.

147 I.e., as in the opening aporiae, the determination whether beings are among intelligibles, mathematicals, or sensibles (on the use of the preposition *en* see the commentary on 4a17–18).

148 I.e., preliminary reviews, or runnings through, of aporiae, apparently a neologism. See the commentary.

149 I.e., Aristotle's *Metaphysics*. For a discussion of this crucial Scholium see Part I, Chapter 1.2.

1A. SUPPLEMENTARY CRITICAL APPARATUS TO THE GREEK TEXT

4a1a tit. Περὶ τῶν ἁπλῶν διαπορημάτων prop. Krische, Reale : Περὶ αἰτιῶν αʹ (apud Diog. Laert. V.49) prop. van Raalte **2** πῶς PJ Λ CL A^2 Tiph. : ὡς A **3** πολυχουστέρα PJ Λ C (ut vid.) L : -χεστέρα A, -χιδεστέρα C^2 **4** καὶ PJ Λ CL : ἢ A **5** μεταβολὰς PJ Λ L A : -βολὴν C | παντοίας **α** Λ : παντοίαν C^2 **6** ταὐτὰ C^2 Tiph. Steph., Brandis : ταῦτα CL : τὰ αὐτὰ A **9** πότερα O Tiph., ποτερα A^2, ποτέρα A : προτέρα C : πρότερον ἔστι L **10** κοινωνία πρὸς ἄλληλα PJ Λ A : πρὸς ἄλληλα κοινωνία CL **12** ἑκάτερα post κεχωρισμένα transp. $Us.^1$ **13** δ' om. A **14** post μὴ add. εἶναι L | ἐπισωδιῶδες J **15** δ' pr. P JCL : δὲ A **16** καὶ **α** Ψ Λ : αἴτια $Us.^1$ **18** μόνον **ω** C : μόνοις L A **20** ἀξιόχρεα CL, ἀξιοχρέα A **21** τοῦ παντός CL : παντός A : περᾶναί τι $Us.^1$: αἰτιά τινος prop. $Us.^2$ | μεμηχανημένα **ω** A, -νημνʹ C : -νημένη L **22** δι' **ω** CL : δ' A **23** περιτιθέντων L O^1 : περιτεθέντων C A | αὑτῶν O : αὐτῶν CL A.

4b2 ἔχει CL A **3** ἐμποιῆσαι [εμποιησαι P] PJ Ψ A [Λ] : ἓν ποιῆσαι L, ἓν ποιῆ C **3–4** ζωὴν καὶ κίνησιν PJ Ψ A : ζωὴ καὶ κίνησις Λ CL **6** εἰ **ω** CL A^2O Tiph. : ἡ A **9** ἐχούσας **ω** C : ἔχουσαν L A | ὀλίγοις CL A **10** εἶναι καὶ **ω** CL : εἰ ἦν A : εἰ ἦν ἐν A^2 | περιττοῖς CL A **11** εἰ CL Tiph. : οἱ A **12** εἴτε κατ' ἀναλογίαν iter. A **17** οὖν CL A **18** πιστικωτέρως CL A **19** τῆς om. CL | ἐπείπερ **ω** CL A : εἴπερ prop. $Jaeger^2$ **21** ταύτην **ω** A : ταύτης CL.

5a4 ἄπαυστος CL A **5** κινούμενον PJ Ψ* Λ C^1L A : κινοῦμεν C **8** μὴ ... μηδὲ **α** [Ψ] [Λ] : μήτε ... μήτε coni. Cam. **10** θειοτέρα J **12** ἅμαι P **13** ταῦτ' PJ A : ταῦτα CL [Ψ] [Λ] **15** ποία CL A **16** ανήνυτον **ω** CL A : ἀκίνητον A^2 Tiph. : ἄριστον prop. Zeller **19** ἔτ' ἀρχαὶ J **20** ἰόντων **ω** A : ὄντων CL | οὐθαμῶς PJ CL : οὐδαμῶς A [Ψ] [Λ] **21** τῆς αἰτίας **ω** C A : τὰς αἰτίας εἶναι L : περὶ τῆς αἰτίας $Us.^1$ **22** post γὰρ prop. ⟨ἀρκεῖ⟩ $Us.^{1,2}$, ⟨ἀξιόπιστος⟩ van Raalte | ὅ **ω** CL : οἵ A | post ἀστρολόγων prop. ⟨λόγος ἱκανός ἐστιν⟩ $Jaeger^1$, ⟨ἀξιόλογον⟩ dubit. Fobes **24** ὄρεξιν **ω** CL : ἕξιν A **25** μιμήσει CL A | post μιμήσει add. κι A^2 (*imitando moueri* Tiph.) **26** ἐκεῖνο **ω** C A : ἐκεῖνοι B^2, ἐκίνει L **27** αὐτοὶ ⟨οἱ⟩ prop. van Ophuijsen apud van Raalte 188 **28** εἰ δὴ CL A^2 : ἐδὴ A.

5b1 ἀρίστου CL A | λέγοι PJ CL : λέγει A [Ψ] [Λ] **2** ἔμψυχ' C A : ἔμψυχα L | ἂν εἴη **α** Λ [Ψ] : εἶναι coni. $Wim.^{1,2}$ **3** ψυχὴ L A : ψυχὴν C | ἅμαι P | καὶ κίνησις PJ L A : καὶ κίνησιν C, κατὰ κίνησιν Λ **4** αἱ om. A **5** ὥσπερ καὶ τοῖς (τοῖς P^1, τοῦ P) **ω** CL A : ἀνθρώποις τε καὶ $Us.^1$ | αἱ om. A **6** ἑτέρων PJ CL : ἑτέροις A [Ψ] [Λ] | ὅμως CL A : μόνοις prop. $Us.^2$ **8** κρείττων L A, κρεῖττων C | ἡ om. L **9** ψυχῆς J Ψ Λ CL A : ψῆς P | alt. καὶ om. L O **10–26** τάχα—μεταβολάς secl. $Us.^1$ **11** μόνον PJ Λ C A : μόνα L [Ψ] **12** τὸ μέσον **ω** CL^1 A : τῶν μέσων L | οὐθὲν PJ A : οὐδὲν CL [Ψ] [Λ] **13** ἀδύνατα **α** Λ [Ψ] : ἀδυνάτων prop. $Us.^2$ | οὐ **ω** L^1 A : om. CL **17** κεν PJ CL : κ' ἐν A : μὲν ut vid. Λ [Ψ] **18** ἀσύνθετον CL A **20** οὐρανοῦ **ω** CL : ἀνθρώπου A : ὅλου A^2 Tiph. **22** καὶ CL A **23** συμβαίνει CL A **24** οἷον CL A **25** περιφορᾶς **ω** CL : περιφορᾶ A **26** post μεταβολὰς add. ἔχειν Cam. | τὸ ἄριστον ἀπὸ τοῦ **ω** CL H^2 : om. A in lac. : ἐφετικὴ A^2 Tiph. **27** παρὰ **ω** L A : περὶ C | δέοι **ω** C A : δέχοιτο L.

6a1 δὴ CL A **2** post βουλόμενον add. ἦν L **3** τι **ω** CL A^2 Tiph. : τε A : γε O **4** post ὅμοια add. εἶναι L **4–5** εἶναι μικράν **ω** CL : transp. A **5** τόδε **ω** C A : τό τε L **6** ἀπορήσειεν ἴσως CL **10** ὀεγεσθαι sic J, ὀρέ- corr. J[1] **11** οὐθὲν PJ, οὐδὲν CL A [Ψ] [Λ] | τοιαῦτ' ἄττα A : τοιαῦτάτα C : τοιαῦτα L **12** ἴσως **ω** L A : ἴ C **13** εἰ C[1]L A : οἱ C **14** φθείροι CL O Tiph. Steph. | ἂν secl. Wim.[1,2] **15** λόγων PJ Λ C A [Ψ] : λόγος L | ἀπὸ **ω** CL : αὐτὸ A **17** τίθηται τὰ PJ CL : τιθῆται τὰς A [Ψ] [Λ] **18** τοῦ προελθόντος C A : τοῦ -θόντας L : του -θὼν Us.[1] **19** ὅπερ **ω** CL Tiph. : ὅπως A **21** λέγειν PJ Λ A [Ψ] : λέγει CL **22** ὅδε pr. **ω** L A : ὃ C | δὲ ἵππου ὅδε om. A **24** ante τὴν add. οἱ L **26** καὶ alt. om. L **27** ὅσον CL A | τοσοῦτο PJC A, τοσοῦτον L [Ψ] [Λ].

6b2 ψυχὴ CL A **3** ἀλλ' ἄττα **ω** L A : τἄλλάτα C **4** οὐρανοῦ **ω** CL A : ἀνθρώπου prop. Laks & Most **5** οὐδεμίαν P Ψ B[2] : οὐδὲμίαν J, οὐδὲ μίαν Λ CL : οὐδεμένων A | ποιοῦνται **ω** CL : ποιοῦντα A | δ' οὐδὲ L : δ' οὐδυ' C : δ' A **6** σπεύσιππον PJ Ψ A[2]B[2]Nz[1] Tiph., σπεύσιπτον ABz : πέσσιππον C Λ, πέσσιπον L **7** οὗτος **ω** A : οὕτως CL | περιτίθησιν CL A **10** τινσος sic P **11** μόνον **ω** CL O Tiph. Ald. : μόνων A **12** post ἀρχὰς add. τὰ ὑπὸ τὰς ἀρχὰς L | δόξειεν ἂν CL A **14** ἀρχάς CL A | κατὰ **ω** CL A : κατάγων coni. Us.[2] **15** τὴν om. L **21** ἔνθα CL A **23** καὶ ποίας **ω** CL : καὶ ὁποίας B[2], ὁποίας A **24** ἀπορήσειέν P CL : ἀπορήσειέ J A [Ψ] [Λ] **27–28** καθάπερ—ὡρίσθαι om. C **28** οἰκειώτατον J.

7a2 καθάπερ ἡ γραμματικὴ καὶ μουσικὴ καὶ [γραμ-, μουσ- transp. CL] CL A : καθάπερ τῇ γραμματικῇ καὶ μουσικῇ καὶ coni. Wim.[1,2] : καθ' ἅσπερ ἡ γραμματικὴ καὶ ἡ μουσική, κἂν coni. Us.[1] **3** συνακολουθεῖ CL A **4** τὰς alt. om. A **5** αἵπερ τὴν φύσιν CL A **6** ἐμμόρφους CL : εὐμόρφους A : ἀμόρφους Wim.[1,2] **7** post πάσας add. τίθενται L | post μόνον add. ἀμόρφους L **7–8** ἄμφω, τάς τ' CL A | τάς τ' ἐμμόρφους καὶ τὰς τῆς ὕλης [τ' ἐμμόρφους CL Tiph. : τε ἀμόρφους A] CL A **9** τέλεον PJ CL : τέλειον A [Ψ] [Λ] | post τέλεον add. ὄν Us.[2] **10** κἀκείνοις **ω** CL A : κἀκεῖνο Bergk **12** ἅπαντ' PJ C [Ψ] [Λ], ἅπαντα L : ἅπαντά τ' A | λόγῳ CL A **14** σὰρξ CL A : σωρὸς prop. Us.[1,2] Wim.[1,2], σωρῶν coni. Laks & Most : στράγξ sive ἐξ ἀστρίων sive ἀστραγάλων Bergk | εἰκῆ J, εἰκη P **15** ὡς om. CL A **15–19** καὶ—εἶναι secl. Us.[2] **16** τοῦ λάχιστον C : τοῦτο ἐλάχ- L : τοῦ ἐλάχ- A **18** γεινομένων P **19** τὰς δ' C A : εἰς τὰς L | post εἶναι add. λέγουσι L | χαλεπὸν **ω** A : λεπὸν C : λεκτέον L **20** αὐτὸ CL A **21** ἕνεκά του CL A | συνάγοντας **ω** CL A[2]B[2] Tiph. : συναγόνας AB | ἅπασι J Us.[2] **22** ante φυτοῖς add. ἐν CL | πομφόλυγι P A : παμφόλυγι J : παμφόλυγγι CL [Ψ] [Λ] **23** ἑτέρων CL A.

7b1 τε **ω** CL : τὰς A | ποικιλίας A : ποικίλας CL **3** ποιοῦνται **ω** CL B[2] : ποιοῦντες AB **5** post οἷον add. ἡ C **6** ποῦ (sic) post ζητεῖ transp. A : om. CL | ζητεῖ PJ Λ L A : ζητεῖν C [Ψ] **7** πόσου **ω** L A : ποσοῦ C **8** τὸ pr. om. A | ἢ L B[2] : εἰ C AB | ἡ om. A **9** ἀρχαῖς CL A **12** ἀρχαῖς CL A | post ἀρχαῖς iter. ὅθεν—ἀπορήσει C e lin. 9–11 | τις Tiph. : τῆς CL A **15** ἐν CL A **15–16** τοῦτ' ἠρεμεῖν A : τοῦθ' ἠρεμεῖν CL **16** post ὡς add. εἰ L | post κινοῦν add. ἄτοπον L **17** πρῶτον καὶ [καὶ om. C] κίνδυνος CL : κίνδυνος πρῶτον A **19** post τινὰ del. τι L[1] | καὶ CL A **20** μὴ **ω** C A : καὶ ὡς L | δεῖ L : δὴ C A **21** κινεῖ CL A | ποιεῖν CL A **22** δὲ ἂν CL A.

8a1 μιμοῦνται CL A | τοῦ ἠρεμοῦντος CL A **2** αὐτοῖς **ω** CL A : ἂν τοῖς coni. Us.[2] **3** post ληπτέον add. δὲ L **5** post ἢ alt. add. καὶ A **6** καὶ καὶ J | ὁ om. A **11** δ'] δὲ Wim.[2], μὲν coni. Wim.[1] **12** δὲ pr. **ω** CL : δέον A **13** ἢ—τῷ **ω** CL A : τῆς οὐσίας ἕνεκα τὸ coni. Wim.[1,2] | τῷ L : τῶν C : τὸ A **14** βέλτιον PJ Λ C A [Ψ] : βέλτιστον L **15** τάχ' PJ CL, τάχα A [Ψ] [Λ] | οὐθὲν **ω** CL R[1]B[2] : ἀθὲν A **16** post ὑπάρχοι [ὑπάρχει CL] add. καὶ L | κατ' αὐτήν B[2] : καθ' αὑτήν C[1]L AB : καθ' αὐτήν C **17** οὐδὲ **ω** C A : οὐδὲν L **18** post μήτε pr. add. τὸ CL **19** τιν' **ω** C A : τινες L | ἀναλογίαν PJ CL : ἀνολογίαν A [Ψ] [Λ] **20** ληπτέον **ω** CL A : ἀντιτέον prop. Us.[1] | ἐπὶ **ω** CL A : ἐστὶ coni. Us.[2] | εἴ CL A **23** ἐν **ω** Tiph. : om. C A : ἢ L **26** εὐριπίδην PJ CL : εὐριπίδης A [Ψ] [Λ] | οὐκ CL A

8b1 post οὐ add. ποτε L **3** post ἀλλήλοις add. ἀλλὰ Us.[1] **4** μέλανα PJ Ψ C A : μέλαινα

L [Λ] | αὐτοῖς **α** Ψ : αὐτοῖς Λ, prop. Ross 1938 : ἐναντίοις Us.[1] | post δὲ add. καὶ A **7** ὃν J, ὸν P[1] : ων P **12** ὑπερβάλλει CL A **14** προβαίνειν **ω** CL : παρα- A **15** τῷ CL A **16** ante τὸ add. καὶ L | ἄρα **ω** A : ἔστιν CL **17** εἴ CL A **18** post ὄντων add. καὶ L **19** διαφέρειν **ω** C A : διαφέρει γὰρ L **20** τὰ καθόλου om. L | τ' PJ CL, τε A [Ψ] [Λ] **21** ἤ CL A **23** ἑαυτὰ PJ A : αὑτὰ CL [Ψ], lac. in Lat. **23–24** ἦν—τινός susp. Wim. **24** ὅλως CL A **25** λεγόμενον **ω** CL : λέγομεν A **26** ιδία πῶς PJ | post οἷον add. ἐν Us.[1]

9a2 δὲ τὸ CL A **4** ταὐτὸ CL A | δ' PJ A : δὲ CL [Ψ] [Λ] **6** εἰ ἄρα PJ Λ A [Ψ] : εἰ ἔστι C : ἔτι L | παρὰ PJ Ψ L A : περὶ Λ C | διαιρέσει **ω** L : διαιρέσεις A : διαίρεσις CVSO **7** τὸ CL A **10** ἕκαστα PJ Λ CL [Ψ] : ἕκαστον A **13** post καὶ add. τὰ L **15** γένος iter. L **16–18** ἔχει—ἱκανῶς secl. Us.[1] **17** ὁμογενῆ **ω** CL : ὁμοιογενῆ A **19** γνωστὰ CL A **23** δ' οὖν CL A **26** τί CL : om. A.

9b1 πλεοναχῶς P J A : πολλαχῶς CL [Ψ] [Λ] | ἢ καὶ CL A : ἐπεὶ καὶ coni. Wim.[1,2] : ante ἔστι δὲ (pro ἢ) καὶ lac. ind. Us.[1] : post η et ante καὶ lac. ind. et ἡ⟨γούμεθα οὖν ἐπίστασθαι.⟩ καὶ prop. Us.[2] **2** γε PJ : τε CL A [Ψ] [Λ] **7–8** τις ἀρχή CL A **8** τινὸς L A : τίνος C **9** λαμβάνοντες **ω** CL B[2]O Tiph. : -ται A : -τας Ald. **10** πρῶτα **ω** L A : πρῶτον C **13** φωτεινότατα [φωτιν- J] **ω** CL B[2] : ποθειν- A | βλέπειν CL A **14** τῶν τοιούτων PJ Ψ : om. CL A Lat. **15** καὶ pr. om. CL **17** alt. ἡ om. CL **19** ἔν τινι CL : ἔν τι A **21** οἱ **ω** CL A[2]B[2]O Tiph. : εἰ A **22** καὶ om. A **27** post ἄλλα add. τοῦ [ἀπὸ τοῦ C] C[1] | ἀστρολογία δείκνυσιν CL A | καταλοιπὸν CL A[2] : κατὰ λοιπὸν A.

10a1 τὰ δὲ CL : ταῦτα δὲ τὰ A | λέγειν **ω** A : λέγει CL **3** θέσις CL A **5** εἰ A : ἡ CL | ἀστρολογία **ω** CL : ἀστρολόγος A **7** post ἕτερα add. γὰρ L | κυριώτατα CL A **8** φυσικὸς **ω** C[1]L A : φυσικῶς C **10–11** καὶ ἡ CL A **17** μηδ' ἐν L A : μηδὲν C | η ωδει C : ἢ ὧ δεῖ A : ἢ ὧδε A[2] Tiph. : om. L | ζητητέον J Ψ CL A : ζητέον P **18** οὐδ' ἐν CL A **23** ῥάδιος **ω** C[1]L A : ῥάδιον C **24** λέγεται CL A | δ' CL : δὲ A | χρὴ **ω** CL : χρὴν A **28** ἕνεκα post ἔφοδοι transp. A.

10b2 καὶ ἀναχωρήσεις om. CL A | καὶ ὑγρότητες [post καὶ add. αἱ L[1]] **ω** CL A : τῆς ὑγρότητος coni. Wim.[1,2] **3** post ὅλως add. αἱ L | πρὸς CL A **4** τῇ CL A **4–6** ἢ—μεθισταμένων secl. Us.[2] **8** μαστοὶ PJ CL B : μασθαὶ A [Ψ] [Λ] **10** ἐνίοις **ω** C A : ἔνιοι L **12** λελωβημένων PJ CL [Ψ] : λελωβημένοις A : om. Lat. **14** δὴ CL A **16** μέγιστον CL A **18** οὐθενὸς PJ L : οὐδενὸς C A [Ψ] [Λ] **21** τιν' L A : τινες C **23** εἴδεσιν **ω** CL : εἴδει A | post τίνος add. γ' A | ταῦτα post ζητήσειεν ἄν τις transp. L **25** ποιοῦσιν **ω** CL A : πεφυκότα οὖσι vel dubit. ποιούσης Us.[1] : προσοῦσαν coni. Us.[2] **26** καὶ τιμιωτέροις om. CL **27** ἄρα **ω** C A : ἔστι L **28** ἰδέας CL A.

11a1 διαφοράς A : -ρά C, -ράν L | του om. CL **2** καὶ om. A **3** τὰ PJ[II] Ψ L A [Λ] : κατὰ C **4** διστασμὸν P C[1]L : δισταγμὸν C ut vid. et A, δυσταγμὸν J[II] [Ψ] [Λ] | λεγόμενα **ω** L O : λέγομεν ἃ C A | ἕκαστον PJ[II] Λ CL [Ψ] : ἑκάστου A **5** post ἁπλῶς iter. θετέον—ἔχει e l. 3 del. A[1] | post φύσιν add. εἰκὸς Us.[2] | post ἅπασιν add. ἀνάγκη Us.[1] **8** ὅπου **ω** CL : ὅποι A **10** φάρυγγα PJ[II] A : -γγαν CL[1], -γκαν L [Ψ] [Λ] | οἰστοφάγου P **13** post χάριν lac. ind. Wim.[1,2] | γὰρ CL A **14** ἡ om. L | γε CL A | ἐμφαίνει διότι **ω** CL A : ἐμφαίνεται ὅτι prop. Fobes | πολὺ **ω** C[1]L A : πολλὰ C **17** ἐμψύχων CL A **18** ἀκαριαῖον καὶ βέλτιον τὸ CL A : *momentaneum et infirmum* Tiph. : ἀκαριαῖον τὸ βέλτιον καὶ τὸ prop. Zeller : ἀκαριαῖον καὶ βέλτιον τῷ coni. Us.[1,2] : ἀκαριαίου καὶ βέλτιον τὸ coni. Ross **21** καθάπερ τὰ **ω** CL A : καθάπτεσθαι Us.[1] : καθαιρεῖν τὰ coni. Us.[2] | post φύσεως add. ὡς L, lac. ind. Zeller **23** σπεύσιππος P Ψ Λ A, σπεύσιπος CL : πεύσιπος J[II] **24** δ' CL A | ἄκρα **ω** CL A : ἀθρόα Us.[1] **25** ἑκατέρωθεν **ω** CL : ἑκατέρω A

11b1 ἐπιμιμεῖσθαι] ἀποστάντα μιμεῖσθαι Us.[1] : ἐπι⟨νοοῦντες τῶν τῇδε ἀποφαίνονται τὸ ἓν⟩ μιμεῖσθαι prop. Us.[2] : ἐπι⟨νοήσαντες τῶν ἀρχῶν οἴονται τὸ ἓν⟩ μιμεῖσθαι Diels (DK) | γε θέλειν CL A : om. Tiph. : τὸ θεῖον Us.[1] **5** τ' PJ[II] CL : τε A [Ψ] [Λ] **7** ἢ CL A **9**

ἄριστον **ω** CL : ἀόριστον A **11** οὐσίαν **ω** CL A^2 Tiph. : ἁγίαν A **12** γε **α** [Ψ] : τε V Us.[1] : δὲ (? *autem*) Λ **14** τὰ **ω** CL V^aB : τὸ A | μεταβολάς A : μεταβολὴν CL **15** τινὸς PJ^{II} Ψ C A [Λ] : τίνος L **18** τε CL : om. A | post τάξιν lac. ind. et ⟨καὶ τὸ ὡρισμένον⟩ dubit. prop. Us.[2] **20** μαθηματικά PJ^{II} Ψ C A : μαθητικά L, μαθηματικῶν Λ **22** λαμβάνοι A : λαμβάνει CL **23–24** πέρι σκεπτέον L A : περισκεπτέον C **25** λαμβάνειν CL A **26** σύμπαντος PJ^{II} Λ L A [Ψ] : παντὸς C.

2. THE ARABIC TEXT WITH ENGLISH TRANSLATION

SIGLA

T	Tehran, Malik 5925, pp. 2–28, dated 461 Hijra / 1069 A.D.
T^1	additions or corrections by the original scribe
T^2	additions or corrections by a second hand
B	Oxford, Bodleian, Ouseley 95, ff. 92^v–95^v, dated ca. 1630 A.D.
B^1	additions or corrections by the original scribe
{B}	text missing because of physical damage in the manuscript
Alon	edition of the Arabic text in Alon 1985
Bertolacci	private communication by Amos Bertolacci
Crub.^{1}	readings suggested by Crubellier 1992
Crub.^{2}	unedited draft edition of the Arabic text
Gutas	contributions to this edition
Marg.	readings suggested by Margoliouth 1892
Treiger	private communication by Alexander Treiger
⟨ ⟩	editorial additions to the transmitted text
[ ]	editorial deletions from the transmitted text
* * *	editorial conjecture of a lacuna in the transmitted text
*	An asterisk after the name of an editor indicates that the Arabic reading or emendation suggested by him is based on the Greek text (provided immediately following in parentheses; see the Excursus § II).

Abbreviations

add.	added by, addition in
app.	critical apparatus
appar.	apparently (*ut videtur*)
codd.	codices, when all the manuscripts agree on a reading
conj.	conjectural reading of a word or words admitted in the text, in lieu of what is transmitted in the extant manuscripts
corr.	corrected by, correction in, in cases of changes to the skeleton of a word (*taḥrīf*; see Chapter 3.5)
del.	deleted by, deletion in
ind.	indicated by or in
indeterm.	indeterminable
interpr.	interpreted by, interpretation in
lac.	lacuna in
mrg.	margin
om.	omitted by, omission in
prop.	proposed reading suggested by, in an apparatus or commentary

read.	reading by, of unpointed or wrongly pointed skeleton (*taṣḥīf*; see Chapter 3.5)
secl.	secluded by
voc.	vocalized by or in (*taḥrīk*; see Chapter 3.5)
w.p.	without points; completely unpointed skeleton (*rasm*) of a word

[مقالة لثاوفرسطس]

4a **(2)** * * * [12]⟨كلّ واحد⟩ منهما منفصل عن الآخر ⟨إ⟩لّا ⟨أ⟩نّهما يتعاونان على وجه من الوجوه على [13]الجوهر والأولى فى [اتّصال] القياس أن يكون بينهما [14]اتّصال وألّا يكون الكلّ مدخولاً لكن كأنّ [15]بعضَها متقدّمةٌ ومبادئُ وبعضَها متأخِّرةٌ [16]وتحت تلك المبادئ كتقدّم الأشياء الأزليّة للأشياء القابلة للفساد

(3) [17]فإنْ كان الأمر كذلك فما طبيعتها وفى [18]أىّ الأشياء وجودها فإنّه إن كانت الأشياء المعقولة إنّما هى فى التعاليم فقط [19]على ما يقول بعض الناس فليس [20]اتّصالها بالأشياء المحسوسة بيّناً ولا هى بالجملة ممّا [21a]يُحتاج إليه

Title added by the scribe of B on the basis of the colophon; see Part I, Chapter 3.1 **4a12** كل واحد prop. Crub.[1], add. Gutas* (ἑκάτερα) | إلّا أنهما prop. Alon, add. Gutas* (δέ); cf. *GALex* I,266 § 3.1, and below at 6a23 : لانهما T {B} | يتعاونان read. Alon : ىعاوىان T {B} **13** اتصال secl. Gutas **14** perhaps ⟨ما⟩ اتصال is to be added* (τινα συναφήν); cf. 4b6 etc. | والا T, B : ولا Crub.[2] | مدخولا corr. Gutas : مدخول corr. Crub.[1,2]* (ἐπεισοδιῶδες) : موحود T, موجود B : موجودا Alon | كأنّ read. Gutas* (οἷον) : كان T B

[1] The Arabic manuscripts, lacking the first page of the text, are missing the original title. This title is given to the treatise by the scribe of B, on the basis of the mention of Theophrastus's name and metaphysics in the colophon. See above, Part I, Chapter 3.1.

[2] The manuscript has *li-annahumā*, for which there is no basis in the Greek tradition of the text. The correction to *illā annahumā* is warranted. For *illā anna* translating δέ (in συνεργοῦντα δέ πως) without a preceding μέν see *GALex* I,266, *illā anna* 3.1.

[3] Isḥāq chose the meaning of "substance," *jawhar*, for οὐσία. The omission of πᾶσαν could be attributed to any stage in the transmission.

[4] Isḥāq used here the etymological translation *al-awlā fī l-qiyās*, "more according to analogical reasoning," for εὐλογώτερον; elsewhere (4b8) he will translate it simply by *al-awlā*, "it is more reasonable." The manuscript reads, *al-awlā fī ttiṣāl al-qiyās*, but the word *ittiṣāl* manifestly has been mistakenly introduced into this place from the following line and is to be deleted.

[ESSAY BY THEOPHRASTUS][1]

(2) * * * ⟨each one⟩ of the two is separate from the other, except that[2] 4a12
they cooperate somehow with regard to substance.[3] It is more reasonable[4] that there *is* a[5] connection between the two and that the universe is[6] not uncoordinated,[7] but that some [parts] of it, as it were, are prior and principles, and some [others] are posterior and subordinate to those principles,[8] just as eternal things are prior to the perishable.

(3) If this is so, then what is their nature and in which[9] things do they exist? For if intelligible things are just in mathematicals alone, as some people say, then their connection with sensible things is not obvious,[10] nor are they, in general, among[11] what is needed and of use[12] with regard

---

[5] The Arabic does not have here the indefinite particle *mā*, "some," that would correspond to Greek τινα; Isḥāq apparently felt that the indefinite *ittiṣālun* covered sufficiently the concept.

[6] The Arabic does use here the verb to be, *yakūna*, but this need not reflect a Greek εἶναι either after μή, as in L, or after ἐπεισοδιῶδες, as in J^II, apparently two scribal "corrections" in the Greek manuscripts; the addition of *yakūna* is required by the Arabic syntax.

[7] For the correction of the transmitted *mawjūd* to *madḫūl* here see Crubellier 1992 27n13. Ἐπεισοδιώδης is glossed as *madḫūl* in the Arabic translation of the *Poetics* 1451b33–34, ed. Tkatsch I,240.20 and note 33 = ed. Badawī 105.3–4 and note 1. In Arabic *madḫūl* essentially means "unsound," "defective" (see Lane, s.v., and cf. J. Ragep, "Freeing Astronomy from Philosophy," *Osiris* 16, 2001, p. 66); in this context, where the defect can be cured by having prior and posterior elements, and principles which provide coherence and subordinate elements that follow them, it would have been possible for the Arabic reader to elicit the sense of "uncoordinated" from the word.

[8] Isḥāq understood, if not actually read in his exemplar, two sets of τὰ μέν … τὰ δέ clauses, viz., τὰ μὲν πρότερα τὰ δ᾽ ὕστερα, καὶ τὰ μὲν ἀρχὰς τὰ δ᾽ ὑπὸ τὰς ἀρχάς (as the Greek text is actually corrected in J^II), and combined the two μέν phrases and the two δέ phrases.

[9] Isḥāq definitely read ποίοις, but translated it in its Middle Greek meaning of "which" rather than in the classical "what kind of".

[10] The stage at which ἄγαν was omitted here is unspecifiable.

[11] Isḥāq undertranslated φαίνεται, "appear," through the use of an indefinite expression, "they are among."

[12] Isḥāq translated ἀξιόχρεα with a hendiadys, in which he used both senses of the constitutive χρεία in ἀξιόχρεα, need and use.

ويُنتفع به فى الكلّ وذلك أنّ [22]الأشكال والأشباه والنسَب قد يُرى فيها [21b]إنّما
هى بمنزلة ما نخترعه نحن [23]فنضعه وصفاً وأمّا هى فى أنفسها فليست [2]لها 4b
طبيعة قائمة وإن لم تكن لها طبيعة قائمة فليس يمكن أن تتّصل [3]بالأشياء
الطبيعيّة حتّى تُحدث فيها حياةً [4a]وحركةً مثلاً وذلك أنّ العدد نفسه فضلاً
عن غيره —— [5]وهو الذى يعتقد فيه بعضُ الناس أنّه أوّل هذه وأعظمها خطراً
—— [4b]ليس له طبيعة قائمة

(4) [6]وإن كان هاهنا جوهرٌ مّا آخر أشدّ تقدّماً وفضلاً [7]فقد ينبغى أن نروم
القول فيه هل هو واحد فى [8]العدد أو واحد فى النوع أو واحد فى الجنس

21a وينتفع read. Marg. : T (w.p.), وبنفع B **21b** نخترعه read. Marg. : نخترعه B : نحرعه T : نخبر عنه Alon **23** فنضعه read. Marg. : فنصعه B : T (w.p.; a smudge on top of the ع could either be accidental or an attempt to change the reading to فنصفه in view of the following *maf'ūl muṭlaq*) | وصفا T : وضعا B **4b2** وان لم تكن لها طبعه قائمه B, add. mrg. T[1] **3** تحدث B, T (w.p.) **4b** after قائمة break (.:.) ind. T **6** جوهر ما آخر أشدّ تقدّماً] يريد طبيعة الأشياء المعقولة add. mrg. T[1]

[13] Arabic *al-kull*, with the article, means the universe, thus translating τοῦ παντός, also with the article. Margoliouth 1892, 195 (followed by Alon 1985, 206), had suggested reading πάντως, but there is no evidence for this; apart from the fact that, as discussed in the commentary on the Greek text, πάντως is not a viable alternative in this passage, in two translations which are almost certainly the work of Isḥāq, the *NE* and *Phys.*, πάντως is translated, not by *fī l-kull*, the text we have here, but by *lā maḥālata* (*NE* 1124b9 = 263.16 ed. Badawī, 1128a5 = 281.5; *Phys.* 251b2 = 807.2 ed. Badawī), *'alā l-wujūhi kullihā* (*Phys.* 198b5 = 140.16), and *'alā kulli ḥālin* (*Phys.* 217b22 = 401.2). The sense of the Arabic passage here is very close to van Raalte's (105) interpretation of the Greek: mathematicals are not of use with regard to (explaining) the universe because "they are not real enough or not powerful enough to account for the universe as we know it."

[14] Isḥāq misread the syntax of this sentence and wrongly took "figures, etc." as the object of both participles (μεμηχανημένα = *naḫtari'uhū*, and περιτιθέντων = *naḍa'uhū waṣfan*). The latter translates etymologically the Greek participle: *waḍa'a* translates τίθημι and *waṣf* renders the concept of enveloping something with a description, included in the preposition περι-. In the other two instances in the treatise where the same verb occurs (6b7 and 7a20) Isḥāq used different words according to sense.

to the universe.[13] The reason is that figures, images, and proportions may be thought to be like something which we devise only ourselves and posit as descriptions[14]—but as for them in themselves, they have no self-standing nature.[15] And if they do not have a self-standing nature,[16] 4b
then it is not possible[17] for them to connect with the things of nature so as to produce in them life and movement, for example; the reason is that number itself—let alone anything else[18]—about which some people believe that it is the first of these and the most significant, has no self-standing nature.[19]

(4) But if there is another substance prior and superior,[20] we ought to[21] seek to say about it whether it is one in number, or one in species, or one in genus. What is more reasonable, given that their[22] nature is the nature

---

[15] The Arabic *qāʾima*, "self-standing," is a semantic elaboration added by Isḥāq intended to temper the absolute sense of the Greek οὐδεμίαν. The implication, even in the Greek, is not that intelligibles, if they consist only of mathematicals, have absolutely no nature—they would be ineffable otherwise—but that they would have, in this understanding, no constitutive nature in things, a nature that could be described as self-standing or having independent subsistence.

[16] Isḥāq took εἰ δὲ μή not as negating δοκεῖ μεμηχανημένα εἶναι, but as a specific negative affecting only the immediately preceding verb, ἔχει (φύσιν).

[17] The Arabic *laysa yumkinu* almost certainly translates here an original οὐχ οἷόν τε or οὐχ οἷά τε; *yumkinu* invariably translates οἷόν τε whenever it occurs in this work: 8b5, 9a27, 11a8, 11b5. On the basis of the Arabic it is not possible to decide between the two Greek alternatives, though the structure of the Greek sentence would suggest the second; see the commentary.

[18] This phrase is not a gloss but renders the force of αὐτός as amplified by the negative οὐδέ in οὐδὲ γὰρ αὐτὸς ὁ ἀριθμός.

[19] "Self-standing nature" is added by Isḥāq to complete the elliptical sentence—as is done by modern translators also—though he understands it differently; see the commentary.

[20] A marginal gloss added by the scribe, Yaḥyā ibn-Jarīr, explains, "He means the nature of intelligible things."

[21] In the construction *qad yanbaġī* for πειρατέον *yanbaġī* renders the suffix -τέον while the particle *qad* followed by the imperfect lends emphasis. This use of the particle with the imperfect, which can be either emphatic, as here, or factual, though not noted in formal grammars (neither Wright's nor Fischer's grammar has it), is frequent not only in this text and in other Graeco-Arabic translations but also in standard medieval Arabic generally. For the emphatic use see H. Reckendorf, *Die syntaktischen Verhältnisse des Arabischen*, Leiden: E.J. Brill, 1895–1898, 300, and for the factual G. Graf, *Der Sprachgebrauch der ältesten christlich-arabischen Literatur*, Leipzig: Harrassowitz, 1905, 34.

[22] The Arabic translation scrupulously preserves the plural in ἐχούσας, with the general reference to substances being understood. See the commentary.

والأولى [9]إذا كانت طبيعتها طبيعةَ مبدأ أن يكون وجودها فى أشياء كثيرة 4b
[10]زائدة اللهمّ إلّا أن تكون أوائلُ وجودُهًا فى [11a]الأوّل

(5) [12a]فقد ينبغى أن نلتمس أن نوضح على وجه من الوجوه [11b]أىّ جوهر هو هذا الجوهر إن كان واحداً أو أىّ الجواهر هى إن كانت ⟨كثيـ⟩ـرة [12b]إمّا بياناً عن ذلك بطريق المقايسة [13]أو بطريق من التشبيه آخر وأخلق بنا أن نكون فى ذلك مضطرّين إلى [14b]إدراك [15a]الله [تعالى] على ما هو عليه [14a]بقوّة ما وفضل على سائر الأشياء [15b]وذلك أنّ مبدأ جميع الأشياء كلّها إلهىٌّ [16]وبه وجود جميع الأشياء وبقاؤها وأخلق [17]بالوفاء بذلك على هذا الوجه ألّا يكون سهلاً وأيضاً فإنّ سلوك سبيل أخرى [18]هى أوضح من هذه أو أقرب إلى التصديق ربّما صعب

(5.1) فإذ كان [19]المبدأ يجرى هذا المجرى من قِبَل أنّه يتّصل بالأشياء المحسوسة [20]والطبيعة على الإطلاق من القول هى فى الحركة وهذا الأمر [21]هو الأمر الذى يخصّها فمن البيِّن أنّه ينبغى أن نجعل هذا سبباً [22]للحركة لكن

---

10 زائدة read. Marg. : زايده B : رايده T : ذاتية Alon | تكون read. Marg. : يكون T B | أوائلُ وجودُها voc. Treiger **11b** first أىّ corr. Alon* (τίς) : فهى T and appar. B (partly damaged) | second إن corr. Gutas* (εἰ) : اذ B : اد T | ره كانت … add. in mrg. T[1] with صح notation, om. B : ⟨كثيـ⟩رة add. Alon* (πλείους) omitting the marginal كانت **12b** إما corr. Alon* (εἴτε) : اما T : انا B | بياناً corr. Gutas : سنا T : بينا B : بينّا *sic* Alon **13** آخر read. Alon : احر T : ⟨ا⟩حرى B **15a** تعالى secl. Gutas **15b** جميع T (w.p.) {B} : om. Alon **16** وبقاؤها read. Alon : T (w.p.) {B} **17** الا T : الا ان B | سبيل read. Crub.[2] : T (w.p.) B (w.p.) : سبل Alon **18** فاذ read. Crub.[2] : T (w.p.) {B} : فان Alon **19** من corr. Gutas : فمن T {B} | يتصل read. Alon : T (w.p.) : نفصل B | after المحسوسة break (∴) ind. T

[23] The mistranslation here is due to Isḥāq's wrong choice of meaning for περιττοῖς, which he understood in its primary sense, "beyond the regular number, excessive," rather than what Theophrastus apparently intended here, "extraordinary." If this is so, then

of a principle, is that they exist in many and excessive things[23]—unless, 4b9
of course, there are first [things][24] whose existence is in the first.

(5) We accordingly ought to try and make clear somehow what substance this substance is, if it is one, or what substances they are, if they are many, in an exposition about this either[25] by way of comparison or by some other way of similarity. It is likely that in this regard we need to apprehend god as he is in himself,[26] through some power and superiority [he has] over the rest of things. The reason is that the first principle of all things, all of them, is divine, and through it all things exist and abide. It is likely that carrying this out in this manner is not[27] easy; furthermore, following another way which would be clearer than this or more credible may be[28] difficult.

(5.1) Since the first principle is such due to[29] the fact that it is connected with sensible things, and nature, absolutely speaking, is in motion—something which is its unique property—it is evident that we ought to posit this as cause of motion. But insofar as it is motionless in itself,

---

clearly ὀλίγοις could not stand, in his view, and ὀλίγοις was either rendered by Isḥāq himself as "many", *kaṯīra*, or, if not, what Isḥāq might have originally written for it, *qalīla*, was "emended" to *kaṯīra* by a later scribe or reader to fit the meaning, as Crubellier 1992, 28n14 suggests. In any case, the Arabic evidence here concerns only the transmission within the Arabic tradition and is of no interest for the Greek text.

24 Isḥāq read πρώτας for πρώτοις, and possibly either missed or disregarded the following καί which might have stood in Ψ; he thus read, εἰ μὴ ἄρα καὶ πρώτας [καὶ] ἐν τῷ πρώτῳ, *sc.* εἶναι.

25 Alon's correction of the transmitted *anā* here to *immā* is warranted by the Greek text. For *immā ... aw* translating εἴτε ... εἴτε see *GALex* I,356.

26 "As he is in himself," *'alā mā huwa 'alayhi* translates ὥσπερ ἂν ᾖ or εἴη, which is what Isḥāq most likely understood, rather than read, for ὥσπερ ἂν εἰ in the Greek text. It is also likely, though perhaps less so, that he read ὅσπερ for ὥσπερ; ὅσπερ, as a matter of fact, would be perfectly rendered in Arabic by *'alā mā huwa 'alayhi*, "as he is in himself": cf. LSJ s.v. § 5b. For the ὥσπερ/ὅσπερ confusion in Greek manuscript readings see Daiber 1980, 333. Isḥāq thus read and punctuated the main sentence as, ἀνάγκη δ' ἴσως λαμβάνειν ὥσπερ (or ὅσπερ) ἂν ᾖ (or εἴη) τὸν θεόν, δυνάμει τινὶ καὶ ὑπεροχῇ τῶν ἄλλων, where τὸν θεόν is taken as the object of λαμβάνειν.

27 Isḥāq read the negation οὐ here for οὖν in the Greek text.

28 Isḥāq understood the δέ after χαλεπόν to introduce a second alternative for τάχα, as if the structure were τάχα μὲν οὐ ῥᾴδιον ... τάχα δὲ χαλεπόν.

29 The manuscript reading (T only; B has a lacuna) has *fa-min qibali*, but the *fa-* clearly needs to be secluded. It is in all likelihood a scribal addition intended to make the *min qibali* clause the apodosis after the initial *in kāna*. The proper apodosis, however, following the Greek, comes in line 4b21 with *fa-min al-bayyin*.

من قبل أنّه هو فى نفسه غير متحرِّك فمن [23]البيِّن أنّه ليس هو سببَ الحركة
للأشياء [1]الطبيعيّة لكن الذى بقى أن يكون يحرِّكها بقوّة ما أخرى أفضل 5a
[2]وأقدم وهذه هى طبيعة المتشوَّق إليه [3]وعنها تكون الحركة الدوريّة المتّصلة
التى [4a]لا تفترّ فيجب من ذلك أن يكون القولُ بأنّه ليس هو [5]مبدأَ الحركة أو
إن كان يحرِّك فهو بتحرُّكه يكون ⟨محرِّكاً⟩ [4b]منفسخاً أيضاً

(6) فأمّا إلى [6]هذا الموضع فكأنّ القول كامل إذ جعل المبدأ [7]لجميع الأشياء
واحداً ووصف فعْلَه [8]وجوهرَه وذكر فيه أنّه ليس بشىء متجزِّئ ولا ذى
مقدار [9]بل رفع على الإطلاق إلى مرتبة هى أفضل من ذلك [10]وأشبه بالله فإنّ
وصْفَه على هذا النحو أولى [11]من أن يُرفَع التقسيمُ والتجزّؤُ عنه [12a]وذلك
أنّ [13a]السلب لمن قال به فيه [12b]فى مرتبة أعلى وأصدق [13b]وأمّا ما بعد ذلك
[14]فيُحتاج فيه إلى قول أبلغ من هذا القول فى التشوُّق [15]أىّ شىء هو وأىّ

5a2 المتشوق corr. Alon. : التشوق corr. Marg.* (ὀρεκτοῦ) : المسوب T B **4a** تفتر corr. Crub.[1,2]* (ἄπαυστος) : سعر T {B} : تتغير Alon **5** بتحركه corr. Gutas* (κινούμενον) : سحرىكه T {B} : بتحريكه read. Alon | محركا add. Gutas **4b** منفسخاً read. Crub.[1,2] : T (w.p.) {B} : منقسما Alon | after ايضا break ind. (∴) T **6** فكأن read. Alon* (οἷον) : T (w.p.), B (w.p.) | إذ corr. Gutas* (ποιῶν *participium coniunctum*; cf. *GALex* I,150) : ان T {B} **8** متجزئ read. Crub.[1,2], T (w.p.) {B} : متحرك Alon **11** يرفع corr. Gutas* (ἀφαιρετέον) : بوقع T {B} : يوقع read. Alon | والتجزّؤ read. Gutas : والىحرى T {B} : والتجزئ read. Crub.[1,2] : والتحرك Alon | عنه corr. Gutas : فيه T {B} **13a** under السلب gloss in bottom mrg. (truncated in the photographs) . . . يريد أن . . . بالـ . . . بالله T[1] : . . . ⟨ا⟩لمعر⟨فة⟩ باللـ⟨ـه⟩ . . . mrg. gloss B[1] (truncated in the photograph); cf. 5b27 below

[30] Isḥāq apparently read or understood the genitive τοῦ for the dative τῷ (at 4b23) in his exemplar, and this caused the misinterpretation of the sentence.

[31] The use of the word "movement" (*ḥaraka*) here in the Arabic need not necessarily imply that the word κίνησις was present in the manuscript, as Usener conjectured. The Arabic translation, just like the modern language translations, could not be as elliptical as the Greek original.

it is evident that it is not the cause of[30] motion for natural things, but what remains is that it moves them by some other, superior and prior, power, and this is the nature of the desirable, from which there comes into being the continuous circular movement[31] that does not abate. From this it becomes necessary that the view[32]—which maintains that *it* is not the source of motion, or[33] that if it *does* initiate motion it does ⟨so⟩[34] by being [itself] in motion—be invalidated also.[35] 5a

(6) Up to this point, then, it is as if the account is complete, since it makes the first principle of all things [to be] one, describes its activity and substance, and mentions about it that it is not something divisible or quantitative but raises [it] absolutely unto a rank that is better than that[36] and more like god. For that it should be described in such a manner is more appropriate than that division and partition be removed from it. The reason is that the negative statement,[37] by those who maintain it in this connection, is on a level[38] that is loftier and[39] closer to truth. As for what [comes] after that, it is in need of a more extensive account than

[32] "The view," *al-qawl bi-* (a doctrine which one holds), renders the implication of τό in τὸ μὴ εἶναι.

[33] Isḥāq failed to understand the use here of the discjunctive ἤ in the sense of πλήν.

[34] The addition of *muḥarrikan* here to complete the thought seems to be necessary. The transmitted sentence in Arabic can be read two ways. (a) *In kāna yuḥarraku, fa-huwa bi-taḥrīkihī yakūnu*, assuming Isḥāq did not understand the sentence and translated literally and blindly, because this corresponds one to one to the Greek, εἰ κινούμενον (sc. ἐστί) = *in kāna yuḥarraku*, κινήσει (sc. κινούμενον ἔσται) = *bi-taḥrīkihī*. The final *yakūnu* can be taken to be either elliptical, i.e., *yakūnu yuḥarraku*, translating the presumed κινούμενον ἔσται, or a repeated *yakūnu* harking back to *yajibu min ḏālika an yakūna l-qawlu … yakūnu munfasiḥan*. (b) Assuming Isḥāq did understand the sentence, then by changing the *taḥrīk* to *taḥarruk* for κινούμενον and adding *muḥarrikan* to complete the thought, a perfect match to the Greek sense can be obtained, since it is clear that Isḥāq had exactly the same Greek text that we do.

[35] The Arabic reads *ayḍan*, which indicates that Ψ read καὶ κατ' ἐκεῖνο. Usener's conjecture (and Camotius's) was thus partly correct, in that καί does not substitute for κατ' but is to be added to it.

[36] The words "better than that" (*afḍal min ḏālika*) would seem to render the force of the indefinite τινά, which is not otherwise translated: "some better rank" is a "rank that is better than that," i.e., other ranks.

[37] Under "negative" there is a marginal gloss by the scribe, Yaḥyā ibn-Jarīr, that is partly legible: "He means that the knowledge of God …". Cf. below at 5b27.

[38] What is to be understood is clearly, "is ⟨an argument (λόγῳ) that is⟩ on a level," where Isḥāq did not explicitly translate λόγῳ, since it is adequately covered by *as-salb*, "negative statement," and added the implied "level," or "rank," *martaba*.

[39] Isḥāq translated the very common locution ἅμα τε καί with a simple "and" (*wa-*).

الأشياء يتشوّق إليه المتشوِّقُ من قبل أنّ الأشياء الدوريّة ليست بواحدة بل 5a
أكثر من واحد [16a]وحركاتها متضادّة على وجه من الوجوه [17a]وممّا يخفى أيضاً
من أمرها [16b]أنّها لا تفترُ [17b]والسببُ [فى] الذى له صار ذلك كذلك فإنّ
المحرِّك إن كان واحداً فشنعٌ [18]ألّا تكون كلّها إنّما تتحرّك حركةً واحدةً بعينها
وإن كان لكلّ واحد منها محرِّكٌ غير المحرِّك للآخر [19]والمبادئ أكثر من واحد
فيكون اتّفاقها حتّى [20]صارت إلى هذه الشهوة التى هى أفضل الشهوات ليس
هو بيِّناً بوجه من الوجوه (7) [21a]فأمّا كثرة الأكر فإنّ السبب فيها [22a]يقتضى
كلاماً [21b]أجلّ من ذلك [22b]فإنّى لم آنَسْ إلى كلام المنجّمين فى ذلك

(8) [23]وممّا يُتحيّر فيه أيضاً السبب الذى له [24a]صارت هذه الأكر لمّا كانت فيها شهوة طبيعيّة [25a]إنّما تطلب الحركة [24b]ولا تطلب السكون فى وقت من الأوقات [25b]فلمَ صار [26b]القائلون بالواحد والقائلون بالأعداد يقولون [25c]مع

---

15 واحد T {B} : واحدة Alon **16b** تفتر corr. Gutas* (ἀνήνυτον) : تعر T {B} : تغير read. Crub.[2] : تتغير Alon **17b** فى secl. Gutas; cf. 5a23 below | فشنع corr. Treiger* (ἄτοπον; cf. 5b14 below) : فبديع T {B} : مدبع read. Crub.[2] : om. Alon **18** للآخر read. Crub.[2], T (w.p.) {B} : للآخرة Alon **19** والمبادئ corr. Gutas* (τ') : فالمبادى T {B} **20** after الوجوه break (∴) ind. T **22b** آنس read. Gutas : انس T {B} : انسب Alon **23** يتحير read. Alon* (ἄπορον) : T (w.p.) {B}

[40] Isḥāq took the phrase οὗ χάριν, "for whose sake," i.e., the "reason," to mean the "reason for the interminableness" of the movements of the celestial spheres. This seems to be due to the fact that this phrase (οὗ χάριν) does not have the article τό prefixed to it, which would have made it unambiguously refer to the final cause. Without the article, Isḥāq took the phrase to refer to the reason for which the interminableness (τὸ ἀνήνυτον) exists, and so what his Arabic sentence means is, "What is also unknown about the movements of the rotating things is, first, that they do not abate, and second, the

this account on desire: what [kind of] thing it is and what things the one 5a14
who desires desires, insofar as the rotating things are not one but more than one and their movements are somehow opposed to one another. What is also unknown about [the movements] is that they do not abate and the reason why that is so.[40] For if the mover is one, it is unseemly[41] that not all of them move with the identical one motion only; and if each one of them has a mover different from the mover of the other, and[42] the first principles are more than one, then their concord, with a view to[43] arriving at this desire which is the best of desires,[44] is by no means evident. (7) As for the multiplicity of spheres, the reason for it requires a discussion more weighty than this, for I did not find congenial[45] the discussion on the subject by the astronomers.

(8) Also perplexing is the reason why these spheres, having a natural desire, have come to seek only motion and not rest at any time.[46] Why, then, have the adherents of the one and the adherents of numbers come

---

reason for which they do not abate." Modern interpretations tend to view the οὗ χάριν phrase to refer to the final cause of their movement, not the (proximate) cause of their interminable movement.

[41] For the Arabic translation of ἄτοπον here and at 5b14 and 7b23 see the commentary.

[42] The manuscripts have *fa-* here, which would make this point the beginning of the apodosis of the second conditional εἴτε sentence, but it is difficult to see how Isḥāq could have made this error. Since the apodosis begins properly with *fa-yakūnu* in the next clause, the *fa-* in *fa-l-mabādiʾ* is in all probability a mistake within the Arabic transmission, in which case the original *wa-* of Isḥāq is to be restored.

[43] Isḥāq took ὥστε not as introducing the apodosis (correctly; see the commentary), but with the participle (apparently against normal usage), ὥστε εἰς ὄρεξιν ἰόντων, *ḥattā ṣārat ilā hāḏihi š-šahwa*.

[44] Isḥāq took "the best of desires" literally, rather than as "desire for the best;" see the note to the translation of the Greek and the commentary.

[45] The verb used here, *lam ānas*, is first person singular jussive of *anisa*, the *maṣdar* of which, *anasatun*, is used in the Arabic translation of Aristotle's *Rhetoric* to render οἰκειότης; in all likelihood it stands for οἰκεῖος in this passage (see *GALex* I,523). It would seem that Isḥāq took οἰκεῖος as meaning "congenial or familiar" to "me", i.e., Theophrastus, rather than the intended "proper to the subject under discussion," and thus added the first person singular, *fa-innī lam ānas*. It seems more probable to assume this than the other alternative, namely that Ψ read μοι οἰκεῖος, which would make less sense in the Greek context, because it would then mean, "an account that is proper or belonging to me, Theophrastus," rather than the subject under discussion.

[46] Isḥāq misread ποτε as a temporal enclitic instead of intensive or exclamatory.

قولهم بالتقيُّل [26a]هذا القولَ على مثال واحد [27a]فإنّ القائلين أيضاً بالأعداد [28a]يقولون إنّ الواحد [27b]فى الأعداد

(8.1) [28b]فإنْ كان هاهنا تشوُّق ″ وكان مع ذلك تشوُّق ″ إلى [1]أفضل الأمور 5b
فذلك مع نفس إلّا أن يقول قائل إنّ بالشَبَه [2]والاختلاف تكون الأشياء المتحرِّكة ذوات أنفس [3a]وقد يُرى أنّ مع وجود النفس الحركةَ وذلك أنّ [4a]ما له نفس [3b]فله حياة، [4b]عنها تكون الشهوات الداعية إلى كلّ واحد ممّا يُشتهى [5]كما نجد ذلك فى الحيوان فإنّ الحواسّ [6]وإن كان وجودها إنّما هو فى الانفعال بغيرها إلّا أنّها على حال تُنسَب إلى أنّ لها [7]أنفساً فإنْ كان الأوّل إنّما هو سبب

25c بالتقيل read. Alon* (μιμήσει) : T (w.p.) {B} : بالتقبل read. Crub.[2] **27b** فى T {B} : هو prop. Gutas **5b1** إنّ *sic* T (w.p.) instead of إنه, {B} | بالشبه read. Crub.[2], T (w.p.) {B} : بالتشبه Alon **2** والاختلاف corr. Alon* (διαφοράν) : والاحلاط T {B} : والاختلاط read. Crub.[1,2] **3a** يرى read. Crub.[2], T (w.p.) {B} : ترى read. Alon **6** الانفعال corr. Alon* (πάσχειν) : الافعال T {B} | تنسب read. Alon : ننسب T {B} : نسبت Crub.[2] **7** انفسا corr. Gutas : انفس T {B}

[47] This elliptical sentence baffled Isḥāq as much as modern interpreters. To begin with, Isḥāq took τὸ ἕν to be the subject of the sentence in indirect speech, not τοὺς ἀριθμούς, as modern translators do. For the rest, we have two alternatives: either Isḥāq interpreted the Greek to mean "the one is *among* (*fī*) the numbers" in order to avoid translating literally the Greek sentence and ending up with what he may have felt was relatively meaningless, "the one is the numbers," or, there is a slight textual corruption with the preposition *fī*, "in," which does not exist in the Greek, and which can accordingly be corrected to *huwa* for *fī*, thus reading, *yaqūlūna inna l-wāḥida huwa l-aʿdādu*, "they say that the one is the numbers," rendering precisely the Greek with τὸ ἕν as the subject, as mentioned earlier. Either of these alternatives seems more plausible than assuming that Isḥāq had a variant Greek text in Ψ, something like ἐν τοῖς ἀριθμοῖς or τῶν ἀριθμῶν for τοὺς ἀριθμούς, as suggested by Crubellier 1992, 30n22.

[48] Isḥāq read in Ψ εἰ δή, the reading also in J, and not εἰ δ' ἤ. See the second following note.

[49] Isḥāq read here διαφοράν, *iḫtilāf*, along with all the Greek manuscripts, reproducing the primitive error in the Neoplatonic archetype.

to maintain, at the same time that they adhere to imitation, this statement in the same way? For the adherents also of numbers maintain that the one is among the numbers.[47]

(8.1) And if there is[48] desire, and there is along with it desire towards the best of things, then this involves soul, unless one were to maintain that 5b
it is through resemblance and variance[49] that things that are in motion come to possess souls.[50] As a matter of fact, it seems[51] that with the existence of the soul there is motion,[52] the reason being that whatever has soul also has life, from which there come the desires propelling toward each individual object of appetite, as we find that [to be the case] with[53] animals. For although the existence of the senses consists only in being affected by others, they are nevertheless such due to the fact that they have souls.[54] So if the first is the cause of just the circular motion, then it

[50] Isḥāq understood as follows the syntax of the original: εἰ δὴ ἔφεσις (*sc.* ἔστιν), ἄλλως τε καὶ τοῦ ἀρίστου (*sc.* ἔστιν ἔφεσις), μετὰ ψυχῆς (*sc.* ἄρα)· εἰ μή τις λέγοι, ⟨ὅτι⟩ καθ' ὁμοιότητα καὶ διαφορὰν ἔμψυχ' ἂν εἴη τὰ κινούμενα. I would think that it was his misreading of the syntax that led him to assume ὅτι after λέγοι (and thus everything after λέγοι as part of the reported speech) rather than that ὅτι actually was present in his manuscript Ψ, as Usener[1] conjectured. It is to be noted that in 5b1 *inna* (that) is used without a following accusative, a characteristic of Middle Arabic; see Blau § 402.2 (p. 512).

[51] *Wa-qad yurā*, factual use of *qad* with the imperfect; see above, note 21.

[52] The presence of the word *wujūd* indicates that Isḥāq took the Greek ὑπάρχειν to mean existence (and not, to belong to, with the dative), which led him to the following analysis of the sentence (leaving δοκεῖ aside): ἅμα τῇ ψυχῇ καὶ κίνησις ὑπάρχει = ἅμα τῇ ὑπάρξει τῆς ψυχῆς καὶ κίνησις ὑπάρχει, transferring the concept of ὑπάρχειν also to ψυχή, which is implied in the Greek anyway. Then in order to avoid redundance, he translated only once the concept expressed by ὑπάρχειν, thus: ἅμα τῇ ὑπάρξει τῆς ψυχῆς καὶ κίνησις = *maʿa wujūdi n-nafsi l-ḥaraka*. It is clear that Isḥāq read ψυχῇ in the dative, corroborating Usener's conjecture, though in his case he understood ἅμα as a preposition governing the dative and not as an adverb (see the commentary). The Arabic follows closely the Greek word order (*wa-qad yurā anna maʿa wujūdi n-nafsi l-ḥarakata*). The nominal sentence used here would normally have the subject come first because it is definite (*al-ḥaraka*), and it would read, *inna l-ḥarakata maʿa wujūdi n-nafsi*. The inversion does have the desired effect of emphasis, though it seems a bit forced.

[53] Isḥāq misunderstood the syntax of τοῖς ζῴοις; he did not realize that it is parallel to τοῖς ἔχουσιν and translated it as "with regard to," *fī*.

[54] The Arabic indicates that the Greek in Ψ read ὅμως ὡς ἐμψύχοις, with *illā annahā* rendering ὅμως, *ʿalā ḥālin* ὡς, and *tunsabu ilā anna lahā anfusan* ἐμψύχοις; *tunsabu ilā* in particular renders the dative in ἐμψύχοις. Usener's conjecture is spectacularly corroborated.

5b الحركة الدوريّة [8]فليس هو سبب أفضل الأمور وذلك أنّ سبب [9]النفس أفضل منه وأقدم منه وأولى بأن يكون سبب الفهم [10]الذى عنه تكون الشهوة

(9) وفيها أنا قائله أيضاً [11]موضع طلب وبحث أعنى لِمَ صارت الأجسام الدوريّة دون غيرها ذوات تشوُّق [12]فأمّا سائر الأجسام التى تلى الوسط فليس فيها ولا واحدٌ له تشوُّقٌ — هذا على أنّها متحرِّكة —[13]هل ذلك من قِبل ضعفها وعجزها أو من قِبل أنّ [14]الأوّل لا يبلغ إليها إلّا أنّه إن كان إنّما لا يبلغ إليها للضعف والكلال فذلك شَنِعٌ [15]وذلك أنّه على كلّ حال أقوى من [16]زاوس الذى قال فيه اميروس إنّه

[17]جَبَرَهم حول الأرض مع البحر كلّه

---

10 after الشهوة break (∴) ind. T **11** وبحث read. Alon, T (w.p.), B (w.p.) **14** للضعف والكلال corr. Gutas* (δι' ἀσθένειαν) : الضعف والكلال T {B} : ضعف وكلال corr. mrg. T[1] | شنع read. Gutas : بشع appar. T {B} : شنيع Alon Crub.[2] **16** زاوس read. Alon, T (w.p.) {B} | اميروس read. Crub.[2], T (w.p.) {B} : اوميروس Alon **17** جَبَرَهم read. Gutas* (reading ἐρυσαίμ⟨ην⟩ for ἐρύσαιμ' in the transmitted text) : حبرهم T {B} : يجرهم Alon : جرهم Crub.[2] : حيّرهم prop. Treiger

[55] The neuter form κρεῖττον confused Isḥāq—as it did later Greek scribes who "corrected" it to the feminine form, κρείττων, to go with ἡ κίνησις (see the commentary). But having too much respect for his text to attempt facile emendations, Isḥāq, unlike the Greek scribes, tried to understand it in context. If κρεῖττον is neuter, Isḥāq thought, the only noun it could refer to in the sentence would be τὸ αἴτιον of the preceding line. He thus translated, "the cause is better," apparently interpreting the femine article in ἡ τῆς ψυχῆς as ἡ ⟨αἰτία⟩, allowing Theophrastus the licence to alternate between the neuter and feminine forms of the word. For consistency, Isḥāq continued with the same referent, cause, also in the next sentence, and translated ἡ τῆς διανοίας not as "the motion of comprehension" but as "the cause of comprehension." The neuter in κρεῖττον would also seem to have influenced Isḥāq's understanding of τῆς ἀρίστης, which he translated also in the neuter as if it were τοῦ ἀρίστου: "the best of things" instead of "the best movement." The resulting mistranslation inadvertently shifts the discussion from a comparison of motions—the one initiated by the first versus the one by the soul—to a comparison of causes: the first cannot be just the cause of circular motion, because then the cause of

will not be the cause of the best of things; the reason is that the cause of 5b8
the soul is better than it, prior to it, and more fitting that it be the cause of comprehension, from which springs desire.[55]

(9) There is a point to be investigated and researched also in what I will now say, namely, why the rotating bodies alone have come to posses desire. As for the rest of the bodies that are adjacent to the center, there is among them not even one that has desire, despite [the fact] that they are mobile. Is that due to their weakness and impotence or due to the [fact] that the first does not reach them? Except that if it does not reach them on account of [its] own[56] weakness and fatigue, that would be unseemly.[57] The reason is that [the first] is throughout[58] stronger than Zeus, about whom Homer[59] says that

> he restored them[60] around the earth,[61] together with all the sea.

---

soul would be better than it, and this is unacceptable for the first. This view would not be alien to the neoplatonized Aristotelianism of the Baghdad Aristotelians who were both patrons and consumers of translations of philosophical texts like this.

[56] This emphasis would appear to be the force of *innamā* here: "if the first does not reach them on account of precisely the weakness *it* has ...", i.e., on account of its *own* weakness. For the emphatic use of *innamā* see *GALex* I,501, § 11.

[57] For the Arabic translation of ἄτοπον see the commentary at 5a17.

[58] "Throughout," *ʿalā kulli ḥālin* (literally, "in every case"), stands in the translation in the place of ἄν τις ἀξιώσειεν, hardly an appropriate rendition. There can be no question that Isḥāq knew the meaning of the word, for in the other two passages where it occurs it is translated in acceptable fashion (6a3 *awjaba*, 6a16 *layta šiʿrī*). ἀξιόω itself is normally rendered with some form of the root *ʾhl* in the translation literature (*GALex* I,572–576), but this also is far from being the case here. Manifestly something went wrong in Ψ at this point. On the basis of the Arabic, *ʿalā kulli ḥālin* ("in every case") for ἄν τις ἀξιώσειεν, it would appear that Isḥāq read something like ἅπασι ὡς εἶεν ("as they might be for all"), though the corruption is difficult to guess.

[59] The spelling of the name of Homer here, *ʾmīrūs*, is relatively unusual.

[60] The Arabic has a skeleton (حرهم) which can be pointed to read *jabarahum*, the only feasible reading given the skeleton. *Jabarahum* means "he rescued, restored them," translating ἐρυσαίμ⟨ην⟩ instead of ἐρύσαιμ' in the transmitted text, an accenting of the word that is also found in Greek manuscript J. The former is aorist optative middle, 1st person, for ἐρύομαι (ῥύομαι), "to rescue, deliver," while the original (ἐρύσαιμ') is aorist optative active for ἐρύω, "to draw, drag." Isḥāq manifestly chose the "rescue" meaning, taking the verb to be in the middle voice. Crubellier suggested reading *jarrahum* (draw), which would be a precise rendering of the correct ἐρύσαιμ'; but this reading would also require to correct the transmitted skeleton of the Arabic word given above.

[61] The first intensive αὐτῇ is not translated because apparently Isḥāq felt that it is well represented in *kullihī* after *al-baḥr*.

[18]فقد بقى أن يكون ذلك من طريق أنّ هذا شئٌ غير قابل ولا محتمل للارتباط

(10) [19]وأخلق بباحث أن يبحث قبل ذلك عمّا أنا قائله كيف الحال فيه هل
[20]هذه الأجسام أجزاء للسماء أو ليست أجزاءً لها وإنْ كانت [21]أجزاءً لها فكيف
صارت أجزاءً لها وذلك أنّا نجدها كأنّها قد قذَفت بها عنها وأقْصَتْها الأجسامُ
[22]التى هى فى غاية الشرف فى أماكنها و[23]فى فعلها إن كانت الحركة الدوريّة
كذلك فإنّا نجد [26a]انتقالها [25b]من موضع إلى موضع وبعضِها إلى بعض [24]كأنّه
عرضٌ لزمها عن [25a]الحركة الدوريّة

(10.1) [26b]وإن كان ما هو فى غاية الفضيلة إنّما يكون ممّا هو فى [27]غاية الفضيلة
فقد يُحتاج من الأوّل إلى شىء هو أفضل من [28]الحركة الدوريّة إلّا أن يكون
إنّما امتنع ذلك منها من قِبل عجزها عن [1]قبوله فإنّ الأوّل إنّما كان أحقّ 6a
الأشياء أيضاً بأنّه الله [2]لأنّه لا يشاء من الأمور كلّها إلّا أفضلها فأمّا هذا
المعنى فأخلق به أنّه يكون كأنّه [3]موضعٌ تُخُطِّى وممّا لا يقع فيه بحثٌ [عن

18 شئ corr. Gutas* (τι) : الشئ T (w.p.), B | للارتباط read. Crub.[1,2], T (w.p.) : الارتباط B : للاوساط Alon 21 قذفت read. Alon : فدفت T {B} | وأقصتها read. Gutas, T (w.p.) {B} : واقصيها read. Crub.[2] : وامضتها Alon 26b انما corr. Gutas : فانما T B 27 after الاول gloss يريد الأجسام التى تلى الوسط add. T B (cf. 5a13a above) : om. Crub.[1] : secl. Crub.[2] 28 امتنع read. Alon, T (w.p.), B (w.p.) 6a2 انه T {B} : ان Alon 3 تُخُطِّى read. voc. Gutas : T (w.p.), ⟨بحـ⟩طى B : يخطى Alon Crub.[2] | يقع read. Bertolacci : نمع T : ⟨بقـ⟨ـع B : نفع read. Alon | بحث read. Gutas* (ἀζήτητον) : بحث B : بحب T with the dot under ب appar. crossed out : يجب read. Alon | عن corr. Gutas : من T B | عن هذا المعنى secl. Bertolacci

[62] Isḥāq mistook the genitive of separation in τῶν ἐντιμοτάτων as referring to the subject.

There remains that it should come about because this is something that is not receptive or admitting of connection.

(10) One might likely investigate beforehand what I am about to say—how the situation is: Are these bodies parts of heaven or are they not parts of it, and if they are parts of it how have they come to be parts of it? The reason is that we find them as if they have been thrust and driven away by[62] the bodies which are the most noble with respect to their localities and[63] activity, if the circular motion is such. For we find that their change from place to place and of the one into the other is as if it were an accident that accompanies them as a result of the circular motion.

(10.1) And if what is best comes only from what is best, something that is better than circular motion may be required from the first,[64] unless this is unattainable for them[65] on account of their inability to receive it. For 6a
the first is also the most deserving of things to be god,[66] because it wishes only the best of all things.[67] As for this concept, it is likely that it is, as it were, something that is passed over[68] and what is not investigated;[69] for he

[63] Isḥāq here does not follow the Greek structure of the sentence, οὐ μόνον … ἀλλὰ καί, but joins the two parts with a simple "and", *wa-*. Cf. M. Ullmann in *Der Islam* 60 (1983) 3–36.

[64] After "the first" there is added in the text in T a gloss by the scribe, Yaḥyā ibn-Jarīr, also copied in B, "He means the bodies which are adjacent to the center." Cf. the gloss at 5a13a above.

[65] The gloss in both Arabic manuscripts astutely identifies the referent here as "the things about the center." See the note to the translation of the Greek and the commentary on Diaporia 10.1.

[66] "Most deserving … god" translates the superlative θειότατον, most divine.

[67] Isḥāq read this sentence with the implied verb "to be" (ἐστί) understood as coming after θειότατον rather than the final βουλόμενον, thus making θειότατον the predicate of πρῶτον and the conjunction καί to mean "also". This in turn caused βουλόμενον to be understood as a circumstantial participle (*li-annahū*, "because").

[68] Vocalizing the Arabic skeleton as *tuḫuṭṭiya*, which literally translates ὑπερ-βαίνω, pass over; for the usage cf. al-Kindī's *Rasāʾil* in the edition of M. Abū Rīda, Cairo 1950, I,293.7, and see Abū Rīda's note 4.

[69] After *baḥṯ*, investigation, there is added in the manuscript the prepositional phrase *ʿan hāḏā l-maʿnā*, "on this subject." This is a doublet from the preceding clause (*hāḏā l-maʿnā*) and clearly redundant, perhaps added as a gloss; it is to be deleted.

هذا المعنى] فإنّ القائل بذلك يوجب [فى] [4]جميعَ الأشياء معاً وهى التى قد 6a توجد أيضاً فى أفاضل الأمور [5]إلّا أن يكون بينها من الاختلاف يسيرٌ أو لا يكون بينها اختلافٌ أصلاً (11) فأمّا ما أنا قائله فهو [6]موضع تشكّكٍ إذا جعل الناظر نظره فى أمر [7]السماء فبحث عن حركتها هل هى لجوهرها [8]ومع سكونها يكون بطلان السماء [9]أو هى بشهوة وتشوّق فتكون بطريق العرض [10]اللهم إلّا أن يكون التشوّق غريزيّاً فيها [11]وليس يمنع مانع أن يكون بعض الأشياء الموجودة كذلك (12) [12]وللباحث أيضاً فيها أحسب أن يحذف الشوق [13]ويجعل بحثه فى أمر الحركة نفسها هل إذا زالت كان بزوالها [14]بطلان السماء

(13) وأخلق بقائل أن يقول إنّ الكلام فى هذا المعنى [15a]ليس هذا موضعه [16b]لكن ليت شعرى للإنسان أن يعتقد ⟨أنّه⟩ [15b]من هذا المبدأ أو من هذه [16a]المبادئ أو من [17]سائر المبادئ معها يكون دفعةً سائرُ الأشياء التى تتّصل بها [18]وليس إنّما تبلغ إلى مدّة ما ثمّ تنقطع وتنحلّ [19]فإنّ هذا فعل الكامل

3 فى secl. Gutas **5** after اصلا break (∴) ind. T **6** تشكك read. Gutas, T (w.p.) {B} : بشكك read. Alon : يشكك read. Crub.[2] **7** فبحث T (w.p.) : فسحث B : فيجد Alon **8** after بطلان add. حركها and crossed out T **10** غريزيّاً read. Gutas, عربربا B : عربراً T : غزيرا Alon : غريزا Crub.[2] **11** after كذلك break (∴) ind. T **12** يحذف read. Alon, T (w.p.), B (w.p.) **16b** انه add. Gutas **18** تنحل read. Alon : تنحل B : سحل T, appar. corrected to سحل T[2]

[70] "Together, which are those," stands for *maʿan wa-hiya llatī*, which translates ἅμα, ἅ, a misreading of ὅμοια in the transmitted text. So either Ψ actually read, or Isḥāq misread, ἅπανθ' ἅμα, ἃ καὶ ἐν τοῖς ἀρίστοις.

[71] *Illā an* here would seem to translate the concession expressed by the circumstantial participle in the Greek ἔχοντα; cf. *GALex* I,259, *illā an* 9.

[72] The Arabic omits πρῶτον, "first" heaven. The stage at which this omission occurred is indeterminable.

[73] Reading *ġarīziyyan*, as in B instead of *ġarīzan* [?] the reading suggested by the skeleton in T. The reading in B may be a correction of that in T, as *ġarīz* appears to be unattested in this signification (for σύμφυτος) and unlikely that it would be coined as a passive form expressing it.

who maintains this requires all things [to be] together, which are those[70] that may be found also among the best things, unless[71] there is between 6a4 them slight or no difference at all. (11) As for what I am about to say, it is a place to raise doubts when one looks into the question of heaven[72] and investigates whether its motion is of its substance and with its cessation there would come about the annihilation of heaven, or whether it is by means of desire and craving and thus it comes about accidentally—unless, indeed, desire is innate[73] in it and nothing prevents some existing things from being like this. (12) As I estimate, an investigator also might take away desire and make his inquiry on the question of motion itself: whether, once it is removed, there would come about with its removal the annihilation[74] of heaven.

(13) One might more appropriately[75] say that this is not the place[76] to discuss this subject, though one would wish to believe ⟨that⟩, from this principle or from these principles, or from the rest of the principles together, there come about at once the rest of the things[77] that are connected with them, and that it is not the case that they go up to a certain moment only and then break off and dissipate. For this is the act of a perfect and intelligent man, which is what Archytas once said,

---

[74] The reflexive expression in the Arabic, *kāna buṭlānu s-samāʾi*, would indicate a Greek original middle voice in the original, φθείροιτ', as in A, rather than φθείροι in the rest of the manuscripts, though active/middle or passive transformations in the Graeco-Arabic translation process are relatively common: cf. *GALex* I,B46.

[75] *Aḫlaqu bi-* here, in addition to its regular usage translating τάχα and ἴσως, renders ὥσπερ, which is quite appropriate for the meaning of ὥσπερ in this context, "it would seem as if" in the sense of "may well be," "perhaps."

[76] The Arabic rendition here is paraphrastic but it does mean, "this needs to be discussed elsewhere," which is also what the Greek says. There seems to be no reason to assume any variants in the Greek exemplar of the Arabic.

[77] Isḥāq slightly misunderstood this complicated sentence; the underlying Greek text in all probability was the one transmitted in the Greek manuscripts. The only discrepancy is that Isḥāq seems to have understood ἅμα for ἄρ' α[ν] = *maʿahā*, and omitted the following τις or left it untranslated. Otherwise, he understood the syntax as follows: ἀξιώσειεν ἄν (*layta šiʿrī*) τις (*li-l-insāni*) ἀποδιδόναι (*an yaʿtaqida*) ἀπὸ δ' οὖν ταύτης ἢ τούτων τῶν ἀρχῶν (*lākin min hāḏā l-mabdaʾi aw min hāḏihi l-mabādiʾi*) τάχα δὲ καὶ ἀπὸ τῶν ἄλλων ἅμα (*aw min sāʾiri l-mabādiʾi maʿahā*) [τις] τίθεσθαι τὰ ἐφεξῆς εὐθύς (*yakūnu dufʿatan sāʾiru l-ašyāʾi llatī tattaṣilu bihā*), where τίθεσθαι seems to have been understood for τίθηται or τιθῆται in the transmitted text.

العاقل وهو ما قاله مرّة أرخوطس [20]أن يجعل ما يجعله سَلِسَ الجَرْى بعد
أن يصير له حصص ما [21]فإنّه يقول إنّ هذا العدد المشار إليه من شأنه أن
يكون للإنسان [22]وهذا العدد للفرس وهذا العدد لشىء آخر غيرهما [23]إلّا أنّا
نجد الكثير من الناس إنّما يبلغون بهذه إلى موضع من المواضع ثمّ يعطّلونها
[24]بمنزلة القوم الذين يقولون بالواحد [25]وبالاثنوة غير المحدودة فإنّ هؤلاء
لمّا ولدوا من هذين الأعداد [26]والسطوح والأجسام كادوا أن [27]يمسكوا عن
سائر ما سوى ذلك إلّا أنّهم بقدر ما يدركون ذلك [28]ويدلّون عليه فقط قالوا
إنّ بعض الأشياء كان من [1]الاثنوة غير المحدودة مثل المكان والخلاء وما لا 6b
تناهى [2]وبعضها كان من الأعداد ومن الواحد مثل النفس [3]وغيرها والزمان
مع السماء [4]وأشياء أخر كثيرة فأمّا النظر فى أمر السماء وفى سائر الأشياء [5]فلم
يذكروه أصلاً فضلاً عن أن يشرعوا فيه ولم يذكر ذلك ولا [6]شيعة سبوسبس
ولا أحد غيره ما خلا [7]كسانوقراطيس فإنّ هذا يجعل على وجه من الوجوه
جميعَ الأشياء [8]فى العالم على مثال واحد المحسوسة منها والمعقولة [9]والتعاليميّة
ومع ذلك الإلهيّة ويروم [10]أن يبيِّن أنّه يتداول إلى مدّة ما ولا يقف عند

19 ارخوطس read. Alon : ارحوطس T B **20** الجرى read. Alon, T (w.p.) {B} | حصص T {B} : حصى Alon* (ψήφους), but see comm. **25** بالاثنوة read. Alon, T (w.p.), B (w.p.) **6b1** الاثنوة read. Alon, الاثنوه B, T (w.p.) **5** يشرعوا read. Alon, T (w.p.), B (w.p.) : يسرعوا Crub.[2] **6** سبوسبس corr. Alon* (Σπεύσιππον) : سوسلس T B **7** كسانوقراطيس read. Alon : كسانوقراطس T, {B} **10** أن يبين read. Alon : ان سن T : ان مں (with three dots over them) B : ازتيس conj. Crub.[1,2] | يتداول B, T (w.p.) : متداول Alon

[78] Isḥāq mistook the proper name here for an adjective, which he translated etymologically, deriving it from εὖ and ῥέω (εὖ + ῥυτός); he thus read the main clause as, τοῦτο γὰρ τελέου καὶ φρονοῦντος: ποιεῖν εὔρυτον, i.e., "for this is [the act] of a perfect and intelligent man: to make [the thing he makes] easy to flow." Isḥāq's etymological analysis is quite accurate and not "inexacte" (pace Crubellier 1992, 32n28). It is only to be noted

to make the thing he makes easy to flow,[78] after there having accrued to him some allotted parts.[79] For he says that this particular number by its nature belongs to man, and this number to horse, and this number to something else other than the two. Except that we find many people take these[80] as far as a certain point only and then stop using them, like those who hold the doctrine of the one and the indefinite dyad: for once these [latter people] have generated from these two [principles] numbers and planes and solids, they disregard almost everything else except that, to the extent that they grasp that and point to it only, they say that some things come from the indefinite dyad, like place, void, and the infinite, 6b
and some [others] come from the numbers and the one, like soul and other things—time together with heaven and many other things. But as for investigating the question of heaven and the remaining things, they did not mention it at all let alone broach it.[81] This was mentioned not even by the followers of Speusippus, nor by anyone else except Xenocrates, for this [man] somehow assigns all things in the universe equally[82]—the sensible things, the intelligible, the mathematical, and, additionally, the divine. He wishes to make clear that he is deliberating[83] up to a certain

that Isḥāq added the verbal noun *fiʿl* and the indefinite verbal complement *mā yajʿaluhū* to flesh out his translation of ποιεῖν, *an yajʿala*, thus using three words to translate one. This is parallel to the translation of Laks & Most, who also use three words to flesh out ποιεῖν: "Car c'est le *fait* d'un homme ... de *procéder* comme Archytas jadis affirmait qu' Eurytos le *faisait* ...".

79 "Allotted parts" translates *ḥiṣaṣ* (ψήφους), as in the manuscript, rather than Alon's emendation of the manuscript reading into *ḥaṣan* to make it mean "pebbles," an emendation also approved by Crubellier 1992, 32n29. Isḥāq translated the Greek word ψήφους in the metaphorical meaning, "lots, votes", rather than the literal one of "pebbles."

80 Isḥāq added a plural pronoun here. Its proximate antecedent would be *ḥiṣaṣ*, the allotted parts just mentioned; in context, however, it appears that the antecedent is the "principles" of the preceding sentence, to which the final "them" in this sentence also refers.

81 The addition of the phrase "let alone ..." here would appear to render the emphasis in the original indicated by ἔτι at 6b5.

82 Isḥāq placed the comma after ὁμοίως (6b8), not before, as do the modern editions.

83 It seems clear that Isḥāq misunderstood another proper name, that of Hestiaeus, and translated what he understood of it. Crubellier's 1992, 32n30, attempt to read the name of Hestiaeus in the skeleton of the words in the manuscript, *an yubayyina* is not very successful. In all likelihood *yarūmu an yubayyina* stands for πειρᾶται only, whereas καὶ Ἑστιαῖος is somehow understood to mean *annahū yatadāwalu*, "he is deliberating." The subject is clearly Xenocrates, continuing with the previous sentence to which Isḥāq's understanding of the meaning comes as an acceptable sequel.

[11]الأوائل فقط على ما وصفنا فأمّا افلاطن فإنّه عند ردّه [12]إلى المبادئ قد يُظَنّ أنّه قد شرع فى سائر الأشياء [13]بأنّه ردّ الأشياء إلى الصور وردّ الصور إلى [14]الأعداد وترقّى من الأعداد إلى المبادئ فلمّا أخذ فى الكلام فى [15]التولّد بلغ إلى الصور وبعض الناس إنّما ذكر [16]المبادئ فقط وبعض قال إنّ الحقّ أيضاً إنّما هو فى [17]هذه فإنّ الموجودات إنّما هى فى المبادئ فقط وقد عرض [18]أنّ المأخذ فى هذه السبيل والمأخذ فى سائر السبل ⟨متضادّان⟩ [19]وذلك أنّ ⟨في⟩ سائر السبل ما خلا هذه السبيل ما بعد المبادئ ⟨من⟩ العلوم أقوى [20]وكأنّه أكمل، وأخلق بذلك أن يكون [21]واجباً من قبل أنّ البحث فى هذه السبيل إنّما هو عن المبادئ أنفسها والبحث فى [22]سائر السبل يأخذ من المبادئ

(14) [24]وأخلق بالإنسان أن يتشكّك [23]فى أمر المبادئ كيف ينبغى أن توضع وأىّ الأشياء هى هل هى غير مشكّلة [25]وكأنّها أشبه بالقوى [26]من قبل أنّ المبادئ أحقّ وأولى [27]بالتحديد كما قيل فى الكتاب المنسوب إلى طيماوس فإنّ [28]الترتيب والتحديد هو بأشرف الأمور أولى وأحقّ [1]وقد نجد ذلك كذلك 7a

11 after وصفنا break (.:.) ind. T   12 شرع B (though there is a dot or smudge over the ع): T (w.p.), Crub.[1,2] (w.p.)   13 second رد appar. om. B (though it may be missing because of the damage in the MS), om. Marg.   18 و before the second المأخذ appar. missing in T, though a smudge before it may be the letter و add. later in T : و om. B | متضادان add. Gutas* (τοὐναντίον: cf. 11b7–12) : ⟨مخالفان⟩ Alon   19 فى add. Crub.[2]* (ἐν) | من add. Alon : ⟨فى⟩ prop. Crub.[1], add. Crub.[2]

moment and that he does not stop at the first principles only, as we described. As for Plato, in referring [things] to the first principles, he may be thought to have gone into the remaining things by referring the things to the forms and the forms to the numbers, and by progressing from the numbers to the first principles; and once he began the discussion on[84] generation, he arrived at the forms.[85] Some people mentioned the first principles only, and some [others] said that reality also is only in these, for the things that exist are [found] only in the principles. But it happens that the procedure in this method and the procedure in the other methods[86] ⟨are opposite⟩; the reason is that in the other methods except ⟨in⟩ this one, the sciences that [come] after the principles[87] are more powerful and, as it were, more complete. It is likely that this is unavoidable, insofar as the investigation in this method is of the very principles themselves, while the investigation in the other methods begins from the principles.

(14) One might likely raise doubts concerning the first principles: how they ought to be posited and what [kinds of] things they are—are they shapeless and, as it were, more like powers,[88] insofar as first principles are more deserving of and better suited to being defined, as it is said in the book of Timaeus? For being ordered and being defined are better suited to and more deserving of the most noble things. Now we find this to be 7a

---

[84] Κατά is misunderstood here to mean "about".

[85] Isḥāq understood "the forms," *aṣ-ṣuwar*, to be what τῶν εἰρημένων, "the things discussed," refers to.

[86] Isḥāq understood the regular meaning of "method" from the Greek μεθόδοις rather than the sense of "discipline" intended here.

[87] Isḥāq took the genitive of τῶν ἐπιστημῶν with μετὰ τὰς ἀρχάς; cf. the commentary.

[88] The Arabic omits here the words, ὥσπερ ὅσοι πῦρ καὶ γῆν, ἢ μεμορφωμένας. The omission is due either to a homoeoarcton in Ψ, where the scribe (or one of his predecessors) jumped from ὥσπερ in the omitted phrase to ὡς in the next phrase, or to Isḥāq who himself skipped those words as he was reading his manuscript. The Arabic sentence is grammatically correct, thus nothing seems to be missing here, though the resulting contradiction in the principles' being described both as "unshaped," *ġayr mušakkala*, and "better suited to being defined," *awlā bi-t-taḥdīd*, should have bothered the readers.

7a فى سائر العلوم، [2]ما خلا الشاذّ منها مثل الكتابة والموسيقى، وكذلك يجرى
الأمر [3]فى التعاليم ويتبع ذلك ويلزمه ما بعد [4]المبادئ وعلى هذا المثال تجرى
الأمور أيضاً فى الصناعات [5b]فإنّ آلاتها [6a]وسائر ما فيها [5a]تتقيّل فى طبعها
[6b]المبادئ وتجرى بحسبها فبعضٌ قال إنّ المبادئ كلّها مشكّلة [7]وبعضٌ قال
إنّ المشكّلة منها إنّما هى المبادئ المشاركة للمادّة فقط وبعضٌ قال إنّ الصنفين
جميعاً كذلك [8]إذ كان الكمال إنّما هو فيهما جميعاً [9a]وذلك أنّ [10a]الجوهر كلّه
[9b]كأنّه عن المتضادّات

(14.1) [10b]ولأولائك أن يقولوا إنّ هذا غير منقاس [11]أن تكون السماءُ
بأسرها وكلّ واحد من جميع أجزائها [12]تجرى على نظام ونسَب وأشكال وقوى
[13]وأدوار ولا يكون فى المبادئ شىء [14a]من ذلك لكن [15a]أجلّ الأمور [14b]بمنزلة

7a2 الشاذ read. Alon : الساد T {B} **3** يتبع read. Alon : سع T : سعى B **3–4** التعاليم ... ايضا فى repeated and then crossed out in T {B} **5a** تتقيل read. Gutas, T (w.p.) {B} : يتقيّل read. Alon : يتقبل read. Crub.[2] **6b** وتجرى read. Gutas, T (w.p.) {B} : ويجرى read. Alon **13** وادوار read. Alon* (περιόδοις) : وادواز appar. T {B}

[89] "Except for a few," *mā ḫalā š-šāḏḏ minhā*, after *sā'ir*, may stand for one of two things: (a) it may render Greek σχεδόν (Crubellier 1992, 33n34), which Isḥāq took to modify ἐν ταῖς λοιπαῖς rather than οὕτω. Σχεδόν is translated in exactly the same way in Aristotle's *Categories* 10a29, σχεδὸν ἐπὶ πάντων, *fī jamīʿihā illā š-šāḏḏi minhā* (Badawī *Manṭiq* I,59.5). *Aš-šāḏḏ* here has the meaning of "a few," as is evident also from the use of *yasīr* in the paraphrastic translation of σχεδόν in *Top.* 154b18, σχεδὸν δὲ καὶ τὰ λοιπὰ πάντα, *wa-jamīʿu l-ašyā'i l-bāqiyati … illā l-yasīru* (Badawī *Manṭiq* II,686.-2, ed. 1952). The only difference between this phrase in these examples and in the Arabic translation of Theophrastus is that in the latter the exceptive particle is *mā ḫalā* rather than *illā*. However, (b) the expression *mā ḫalā š-šāḏḏ minhā* may render an additional

so in the rest of the sciences except for a few,[89] like writing and music, 7a1
and the situation is the same with the mathematical [sciences]. This is followed and attended by what comes after the first principles. Similar also is the case with the crafts, for their instruments and everything else in them imitate by nature[90] the first principles and act in accordance with them. Some people say that all the first principles are endowed with shape, others say that those endowed with shape among them are the first principles which partake of matter only, and still others say that both classes together are such, since completeness consists precisely in both of them together, the reason being that substance, in its entirety, consists, as it were, of opposites.

(14.1) It is up to them to say that this is unreasonable:[91] that heaven in its entirety and each one of all its parts would involve order and proportions[92] and shapes and powers and periods, while in the first principles [themselves] there would be none of that but the most sublime thing would be like flesh scattered to no purpose, as Heraclitus said.[93] Indeed

---

Greek phrase not extant in the Greek manuscripts, because *aš-šāḏḏ* also translates in the translation literature words such as ἔνιοι and παῦροι: *Categories* 10a32, ὡσαύτως δὲ καὶ ἐπὶ τῶν ἄλλων. ἐπ' ἐνίων δέ …, *wa-ka-ḏālika fī sā'irihā wa-ammā fī š-šāḏḏi minhā* … (Badawī *Manṭiq* I,59.7), and οἱ παῦροι in the Ps.-Pythagorean *Golden Verses*, *aš-šāḏḏa mina n-nāsi* (F. Rosenthal, "Some Pythagorean Documents Transmitted in Arabic," *Orientalia* 10, 1941, 113). Since *mā ḫalā* in the Arabic translation of Theophrastus renders πλήν (6b6), the expression *mā ḫalā š-šāḏḏ minhā* may actually stand for Greek ⟨πλὴν παύροις or ὀλίγοις⟩ or a similar phrase. The second alternative seems more plausible; see the discussion in the commentary.

90 Τὴν φύσιν was understood as an accusative of specification (synecdoche) by Isḥāq, as if it were a dative of respect, so the translation *fī ṭabʿihā* is accurate from this point of view. The question is why—and how—Isḥāq took "principles" as the object of the verb to "imitate": most likely he read—or understood—ἅσπερ for αἵπερ. Then the subject of μιμοῦνται became necessarily τὰ ὄργανα καὶ τὰ ἄλλα, but this would also necessitate the omission of the first καί in line 7a5, unless Isḥāq took καί to mean "both … and," which he did not explicitly render in his translation.

91 For "unreasonable" = *ġayr munqās* see above, Part I, Chapter 3.3 at the end.

92 Isḥāq apparently understood the plural λόγοις for λόγῳ here.

93 Isḥāq read this sentence as follows: ἀλλ' ὥσπερ σὰρξ εἰκῇ κεχυμένη ὁ κάλλιστος, ὥς φησιν Ἡράκλειτος, κόσμος. See the commentary.

لحم منثور باطلاً [15b]على ما قال إراقليطس وقد [16]يستعملون أيضاً النظر فى أصغر الأمور مثلاً على هذا المثال أعنى [17]فى ذوات الأنفس والعديمة للنفس فإنّ طبائع كلّ واحد من هذه محدودة [18]مثلاً وإن كانت تحدث من ذاتها [19]فأمّا مبادئها فغير محدودة

(14.2) وقد يصعب [20]أيضاً أن نجمع حدودها حتّى نردّ كلّ ما فيها [21]إلى الواحد فى جميع الأشياء أعنى [22]الحيوان والنبات وفيما هو أيضاً بين الحيوان والنبات إلّا [23]أن يكون قد يلزَم نظامَ أشياء وتغيّرَها [1]حدوثُ صور أُخَرَ 7b
غيرها كثيرة مختلفة ممّا فى [2]الهواء وفى الأرض وقد يجعل بعض الناس أعظمَ دليل على ذلك [3]أمر أوقات السنة [4]فإنّه يتولّد فيها أصنافُ الحيوان والنبات والثمار [5]كأنّ الشمس تولّدها

(15) فأمّا هذا المعنى [6]فقد يَحتاج فى هذا الموضع إلى بحث [7]يقتضى أن نحدّ إلى أين يبلغ المنظومُ ولِمَ [8]صار الأكثرُ عاجزاً إن كانت النقلة إلى ما هو أخسّ **(16)** [9]وأمّا المبادئ وهى التى منها ابتدأ⟨نا⟩ بالكلام [10]فبالواجب قد يتحيّر الإنسان من أمرها فى أمر السكون [11]فإنّه إن قال إنّ ذلك لها على طريق الأمر الأفضل فقد شاب [12]المبادئَ وإن قال ⟨إنّه⟩ يدلّ على طريق التعطيل وعدم الحركة [13]فلم يَشْبُهْا لكن قد ينبغى أن يتغيّر الفعل [14]إذ كان أشدّ تقدّماً وفضلاً

15b اراقليطس read. Alon, T (w.p.) {B} **7b5** after تولدها break (∴) ind. T **7** نحدّ read. Gutas* (ἀφορισμόν), T (w.p.) {B} : نجد Alon Crub.[2] | أين corr. Alon* (πόσου) : ان T {B} **8** إن T (εἰ) {B} : او conj. Alon (ἤ) **9** ابتدأ⟨نا⟩ add. Gutas : اىدا T {B} : ابتدئ Alon **10** يتحير read. Alon, T (w.p.) {B} **11** شاب read. Gutas : شاب T, {B} : سآت Alon : شآت Crub.[1,2] **12** إنه add. Gutas **13** يشبها read. Gutas : ىسها T {B} : ينسبها Alon : يشئها *sic* Crub.[1] | يتغير corr. Alon* (-μεταλλακτέον) : ىصر T {B} they engage also in theoretical inquiry, for example, into the smallest of things in this manner—I mean into the animate and the inanimate; for the natures of each one of those are definite, for example, even though they come about by themselves; but as for their first principles, they are indefinite.

(**14.2**) But again, it is difficult for us to collect their definitions[94] in order to reduce each of its contents to the one[95] in all things—I mean [in] animals and plants and in what is also between animals and plants[96]—unless the order and transformation of things should be accompanied by the origination of many and various other forms of what is in the air and 7b
on the earth. As a matter of fact,[97] some people make the seasons of the year the greatest evidential proof for that, for [different] sorts of animals, plants, and fruits are generated in them as if the sun were generating them.

(**15**) As for this subject, it may need here an investigation that requires us to delimit how far the ordered extends, and why what is most has come to be incapable,[98] if[99] the transition is to what is baser; (**16**) but as for the first principles, which are those from which we started the discussion, one might be duly perplexed about them with regard to the issue of [their] rest. For if he says that they possess this [rest] by way of what is the best, then he has tarnished[100] the first principles; and if he says that it indicates the manner of suspension [of activity] and the privation of[101] motion,

---

94 Here ἑκάστοις, taken as a dative of attribution, is translated as if it were ἑκάστων, *ḥudūdahā*, the attached pronoun *-hā* rendering ἑκάστοις. The Arabic would also seem to corroborate Zeller's emendation of the transmitted reading αὐτό to αὖ τό.

95 Isḥāq read, or understood, ἓν ἕκαστον instead of ἕνεκά του in the extant Greek manuscripts.

96 Apparently Isḥāq did not understand the word πομφόλυξ, if he had it in his text, and wrote something generic in its stead (as Crubellier 1992, 34n38 notes), perhaps taking as model a similar statement at 7a8–9.

97 Noteworthy is again the factual use of *qad* with the imperfect, translating the Greek particle δή in 7b2.

98 Isḥāq translated τὸ πλέον ἀδύνατον literally, choosing to render the second word as "incapable" rather than as "impossible." It is doubtful that he understood the precise import of this phrase.

99 Ψ read εἰ for ἤ here together with some of the other independent witnesses.

100 Isḥāq did not perceive that the intended object of ἀνάψειεν is ἡ ἠρεμία and thus took the verb to mean "to attach to" the principles something bad, i.e., to tarnish or adulterate them.

101 Ψ read the genitive article τῆς for the indefinite τις here.

والحركة [15]فى الأشياء المحسوسة وذلك أنّ [16]السكون لا يكون إلّا من قِبل عجز المحرِّك عن أن يكون محرِّكاً دائماً [17]فإنّه ليس يخاف أن يكون الأوّل غير [18]ذى نطق ولا ذلك أيضاً ممّا يستحقّ أن يصدَّق به لكن الأمر [19]يقتضى سبباً هو أعظم من ذلك

(16.1) وقد يُظنّ بأنّ الحسّ [20]يشهد على وجه من الوجوه بأنّ ذلك ممكن أعنى أنّه ليس يجب أن يكون المحرِّك [21]غير الشىء الذى يحرِّكه من قِبل الفعل [22]والانفعال وللإنسان أيضاً أن يردّ هذا القول إلى [23]العقل نفسه وإلى الله

(16.2) ومن القبيح أيضاً القول الآخر الذى قيل فيه [1]إنّ 〈الأشياء〉 المتشوِّقة 8a
ليس تقتدى بالساكن [2]فإنّه وإن كان يتبع وجودَها وجودُ سائر الأشياء [3]فإنّه

16 محركا T {B} : متحركا conj. Alon **17** فانه ... غير] فانه يخاف الا يكون (الـمحرك) الاول وهذا غير prop. Alon **8a1** الأشياء add. Gutas | المتشوقة corr. Alon* (τὰ ὀρεγόμενα) : المسوبه T {B} | تقتدى read. Crub.[2] : نقدى T {B} : تعتدى Alon

[102] For τι μεταλλακτέον in the Greek manuscripts, the Arabic manuscript T has what appears to be *yunṣara*, "to be defended, supported," which is rather unwarranted in the context. Alon's correction of the Arabic skeleton to *yataġayyara* is plausible, though what Isḥāq understood by it is unclear.

[103] The Greek exemplar of the Arabic translation, Ψ, together with all extant Greek manuscripts, read κινοῦν here; κινούμενον is Ross's emendation.

[104] The Arabic translation reads as if the Greek text had, κίνδυνος τὸ πρῶτον. It appears, however, that this is how Isḥāq understood this difficult passage rather than that he had a text different from that in J and P.

[105] It is to be noted that the use of *qad* with the imperfect is also connective continuative, adding a new point ("furthermore," "also"), like that of *qad* with the perfect.

[106] Isḥāq did not translate καί before ἡ αἴσθησις; it is not clear whether this was because the word was missing in Ψ, as in P, or because Isḥāq felt that the notion of "also" was already covered by the *qad yuẓannu* formulation he just used (see the preceding note).

then he does not tarnish them, but it becomes necessary for activity to undergo change[102] since it is prior and of higher merit, while motion is [present] in the objects of sense. The reason is that being at rest does not come about except on account of the inability of the mover always to be producing motion,[103] for there is no fear that the first[104] would be without speech, nor is this again something that deserves credence, but the matter requires a cause that is greater than this.

(16.1) It is also[105] thought that sense-perception[106] somehow attests that this is possible, namely, that it is not necessary[107] for what imparts movement to be different from the thing which it moves on account of acting and being-acted-upon. One may also refer this argument to intellect itself and to god.

(16.2) Bad,[108] too, is the other statement that has been made about it,[109] that the ⟨things⟩[110] that desire do not imitate what is at rest;[111] for even if 8a

[107] Isḥāq clearly read some form of δεῖ in Ψ; the question is whether he read δεῖ or the infinitive δεῖν as required by the syntax and corrected by Laks & Most. Judging from the fact that Isḥāq breaks the continuity of the Arabic sentence with the inclusion of the word *aʿnī*, "I mean," "namely," i.e., he makes two sentences out of the (theoretically correct) one Greek sentence ἐνδεχόμενον μὴ δεῖν ..., it would appear that he read δεῖ and, properly taking it not to belong to the same syntactical structure as ἐνδεχόμενον but as anacolouthon, he read the sentences as if there were a colon after ἐνδεχόμενον, as follows: ὡς ἐνδεχόμενον: μὴ/οὐ δεῖ τὸ κινοῦν .... He thus translated δεῖ as if it were a finite verb in an independent sentence (pace Crubellier 1992, 35n42). It seems that δεῖ is one of the primitive errors of the Neoplatonic archetype; see Part I, Chapter 2.5.

[108] For the Arabic translation of ἄτοπον see the commentary at 5a17.

[109] That is, on this subject.

[110] The addition of ⟨*al-ašyāʾ*⟩ *al-mutašawwiqa* for τὰ ὀρεγόμενα is necessary here; *al-mutašawwiqa* by itself, as in the transmitted text, would mean "the group of people who desire," i.e. as if it were translating οἱ ὀρεγόμενοι, which is not a variant attested in the tradition. Furthermore, in the next sentence, *al-mutašawwiqa* is referred to by the pronoun *-hā*, which indicates that the referent is a thing and not a personified entity (in which case the pronoun would have been *-hum*).

[111] Isḥāq appears to have read, or understood, τὰ ἠρεμοῦντα for τοῦ ἠρεμοῦντος (cf. the similar correction in J^{II}), which he took as object of μιμοῦνται, not of τὰ ὀρεγόμενα as in the Greek. However, given that the Greek μιμοῦνται, which takes its object in the accusative, has no object in the sentence, it is also likely that Isḥāq may have understood even the genitive τοῦ ἠρεμοῦντος as the object of μιμοῦνται. Hence it is not certain that Ψ had τὰ ἠρεμοῦντα, and thus the reading of the translation is listed in the apparatus as "ut intell. Ar."

خليق أن يكون ليس ينبغى أن تؤخذ على مثال واحد حتّى تُردُّ إلى ما لا جزء 8a
له [4]لكن على أنّها ⟨فى⟩ غاية ما يمكن أن تكون عليه من الاتّفاق [5]والنظام
بمنزلة مدينة أو حيوان أو شىء آخر [6]من الأشياء الجزئية أو بمنزلة السماء
بأسرها وهى التى [7]يقولون فيها إنّها ⟨في⟩ غاية الكمال

(17) [8]وقد تقتضى هذه الأشياءُ أيضاً التى أنا ذاكرها الكلام فيها [و]أعنى كيف [9]صارت قسمة الأشياء الموجودة هى إلى المادّة والصورة [10]⟨أ⟩ذلك على ⟨أنّ⟩ إحداهما ⟨موجودةٌ⟩ والأخرى غير موجودة إلّا أنّها بالقوّة [11]موجودة وقد تُخرَج إلى الفعل أو على أنّها موجودة [12]إلّا أنها غير محدودة بمنزلة ما فى الصناعات لكن حدوثها [13]أو وجودها إنّما هو بقبول الصورة على حسب [14a]نسبها إلّا أنّ الأمرَ إن كان ⟨كـ⟩ذلك [15a]فأخلق بالنُقلة أن تكون [14b]إلى الأمر الأفضل [15b]إلّا أنّ القول بأنّها موجودة ليس [16]يكون من الصحّة على دون ما

---

4 على corr. Gutas* (ὅπως) : عُلم T {B} | فى add. Gutas (cf. 5b22, 26) **7** فى add. Gutas **8** و secl. Gutas, cf. 5b11 **10** أ . . . أن . . . موجودة add. Alon | إحداهما corr. Gutas : احدبهما T, {B} : احديهما Alon : احد بهما Crub[2] | after احداهما add. نعنى الماده T, {B}, om. Crub.[1], secl. Crub.[2] **12** محدودة corr. Alon : موحوده T, {B} **14a** after انّ add. اى T B (by dittography) : del. Gutas | الا ان اى الامر ان كان ذلك om. Crub.[1], secl. Crub.[2] | ⟨كـ⟩ذلك add. Gutas* (οὕτω; cf. 4a17)

[112] Manuscript Ψ had the same reading here as all the Greek manuscripts, εἰ … οὖσιν, and Isḥāq understood the participle in its existential sense, "being, existing." Under the influence of this understanding he then took the pronoun ἡ in ἡ τῶν ἄλλων as referring to a supposed subject ἡ οὐσία. He thus read the passage as follows, εἰ γὰρ αὐτοῖς, οὖσιν, ἀκολουθεῖ ἡ ⟨οὐσία⟩ τῶν ἄλλων: "for (even) if they, while existing, are followed by the existence of the others," and took the clause beginning with πλὴν ἴσως as the apodosis of the conditional sentence beginning with εἰ.

[113] According to the structure of the Arabic here, the subject of the verb *tu'ḫaḏa* (ληπτέον) can be either "the things that desire" or "the rest of the things," most likely the latter. If the verb were to be read in the masculine, *yu'ḫaḏa*, then the referent would be *wujūd*, existence, which makes little sense in the context.

their existence is followed by the existence of the rest of the things,[112] it is 8a2
nevertheless likely that they[113] ought not to be taken in the same manner as being reduced[114] to what has no parts; but [they should be taken] as being ⟨at⟩ the highest [level] of congruity and orderliness that is possible for them, like a city or an animal or something else with parts, or like the entire heaven, about which they say that it is ⟨at⟩ the highest [level] of perfection.

(17) Also these things which I am about to mention require discussion, namely, how has the division of existing things into matter and form come to be? ⟨Was it⟩ as one of them[115] ⟨existing⟩ and the other not existing but potentially existing and sometimes brought out to actuality? Or, as existing, but unlimited, like what [obtains] in the crafts, whereas[116] their origination, or their existence, comes about through their reception of a form precisely in accordance with their proportions?[117] If this is so, however, the transferral is likely to be towards the best thing, except that the statement professing its existence is no less sound than the statement about the other.[118] The reason is that they are not such

---

[114] Reading *turaddu* (not in the subjunctive) in the passive, referring to the things, rather than in the active, *naruddu*, as the Greek would require (ἄγοντας), because in that case the Arabic would have to supply an object (*narudduhā*), as in the preceding sentence, where it provides the missing object in the Greek, ἄγῃ τις, which is rendered as, *li-l-insāni an yarudda hāḏā l-qawla* (with the addition of *hāḏā l-qawla*).

[115] A marginal note in Arabic, which has actually entered into the text here, explains, "He means 'matter'." But as Crubellier 1992, 35n45 notes, this marginal note was inserted after the wrong word, for it explains the term "the other" that follows immediately.

[116] "Whereas," *lākin*, translating δέ, as in all the Greek manuscripts.

[117] "Proportions," *nisab*, translates λόγους, indicating that Isḥāq opted for a mathematical interpretation of the word.

[118] Isḥāq took the pronoun αὐτήν in κατ' αὐτήν to refer to *ṣūra* (μορφή), form, so he understood the prepositional phrase to mean "than the statement about the other" (*al-qawlu fī l-uḫrā*), i.e., about form, in order to complete the comparison implied in the Greek "less" (ἧττον). He says, in effect, "The statement professing the real existence of matter is no less sound than the statement about the real existence of form" (= the "other" item in the two subjects which this paragraph discusses).

عليه القول فى الأخرى وذلك أنّها [17]لم تكن لتحدث لو لم تكن موجودة ⟨إلّا⟩ ألّا تكون هذا الشئَ المشارَ إليه [18]ولا كيف ولا كم كأنّه للصور خروج عن الحدّ [19]إلّا أنّه قوّة ما لها وبالجملة فقد ينبغى أن نفهم الأمر فى ذلك على قياس ما [20]هو فى الصناعات وإن كان هاهنا مشاكلة فى شىء من غير الصناعات

(18) [21]وقد يظنّ أنّ فى هذا أيضاً موضعَ تشكّكٍ ـــ إن لم يكن [22]البحث عن مثل هذا هو من الفضول ـــ أعنى لِمَ صارت الطبيعة [23]وجوهر الكلّ بأسره إنّما وجودهما فى المتضادّات [24]ويكاد أن يكون الأخسّ من الأمور معادلاً للأفضل منها بل [25]هو أكثر منه كثيراً حتّى قد يُظنّ أنّ [26]قول اوريبيديس قول صواب وهو أنّه قال إنّه ليس توجد الخيرات [27]على الانفراد وهذا القول قريب
من أن نكون [1]نبحث فيه لِمَ لا كانت الأشياء كلّها خيراً ولِمَ لا كانت كلّها 8b
متشابهةً [2]ولِمَ صرنا نقول فى الأشياء كلّها إنّها موجودة وليس [3]هى متشابهة بعضها لبعض بمنزلة الأشياء البيض [4]والأشياء السود فيها

(18.1) وما يُظنّ به أنّه أبدع من هذا [5]أنّه ليس يمكن أن يكون الموجود خلِواً من المتضادّات

---

17 إلا add. Gutas* (ἀλλά); cf. *GALex* I,255 § 4.2 **19** نفهم read. Crub.[2], T (w.p.) : نفهم or نفهم B : يفهم Alon **21** تشكك read. Gutas, T (w.p.) : شكك B : لشكك Alon Crub.[2] **26** اوريبيديس corr. Crub. : اورسوس T B : اويبيدس Alon **27 – 8b1** نكون نبحث read. Gutas, T (w.p.) : يكون يبحث read. B **8b1** خيرا B : حر T

[119] The absence of a clear subject for γίνοιτο is reflected in this verb, apparently to be read as *li-taḥduṯa*, where the feminine pronoun could stand for an unidentified "it" or an understood plural "things" (*al-ašyāʾ*). But if the singular "it" is understood, it could

as[119] to come into being had it not existed, ⟨except⟩ that they do not become this particular thing or quality or quantity, as if the forms had indeterminacy,[120] but they have some potentiality. In general, we ought to understand this issue by analogy with what is in the crafts and if there is a similarity in anything other than the crafts.

(18) It may be thought that doubts can be raised about this point also—if investigating the likes of this were not superfluous—namely, why is it that the existence of nature and of the entire substance of the universe is[121] just in the contraries? And the meanest thing is almost equivalent to the most excellent (no, rather it is more than it by far), to the point that it may be thought that Euripides' statement is true?[122] He said, namely, that the good things are not found by themselves. This statement comes close to our inquiring about it why all things are not good and why they 8b
all are not alike, and why we come to affirm of all things that they exist and yet they are not alike, one to another, like the white things and the black things among them.

(18.1) That [opinion] which is thought to be more uncommon[123] than this is that it is impossible for what exists to be devoid of contraries.

only refer to matter, the subject under discussion (the immediately preceding *nuqla* is also feminine, but sense requires that it not be considered), in which case the resulting sentence—"it (matter) is not such as to come into being had it (matter) not existed"—would make little sense, and so the attentive reader would guess that the feminine pronoun should refer to the plural "things" mentioned at the outset. The Arabic uses here the expression *mā kāna li-* with the subjunctive (= not to be such that; see *WKAS* I,458b) to translate the negative optative in ἂν οὐδὲ γίνοιτο, a masterful rendering.

120 Isḥāq misunderstood the dative of respect in τοῖς εἴδεσιν for a dative of possession, and, failing in addition to pay proper attention to the absence of the article before ἀόριστον, he read as if the text said, ὡς τοῖς εἴδεσιν τὸ ἀόριστον, "as if the forms had indeterminacy."

121 Isḥāq translated Greek ἐν with amplification, *wujūduhumā fī*, "their existence [is] in," which appears to be the correct rendering in this case. Cf. the note by Ross 65 for the meaning of the preposition.

122 Isḥāq wrote *ṣawāb* to translate καθόλου in the sense, perhaps, that it means "in a general way" = generally true. Crubellier 1992, 36n49, suggests that Isḥāq must have had difficulties with the universal implications of the Greek word and substituted a more "banal" term (though it is difficult to see how "correct" can be more banal than "universal").

123 Isḥāq did not explicitly translate ἔτι. If he took it to complement παραδοξότερον, then in all likelihood its meaning would be included in the comparative force of the elative, *abdaʿ min hāḏā*.

(18.2) [6]وقد استعمل قوم من الشناعة ما هو أبدع من هذا [7]فأدخلوا ما ليس 8b
بموجود ولا كان موجوداً ولا يكون موجوداً فى عداد [8]ما يدخل فى طبيعة الكلّ لكن هذا الأمر كأنّه [9]حكمة تتجاوز كلّ حدّ وأمّا الموجود فمن البيّن أنّه على أنحاء شتى [10]وذلك أنّ الحسّ يقف على فصوله [11]ويبحث عن أسبابها وأخلق بهذا القول أن يكون أصحّ [12]أعنى أنّه يُوقِع للفكر أشياء [13]يبحث عنها على الإطلاق وأشياء تُحدِث له الشكّ والحيرة [14]فهو وإن لم يتهيّأ له بالفكر أن ينجح فيها إلّا أنّه على حال قد يظهر له [15]شىء من الضوء فى الموضع الذى لا ضوء فيه إذا نحن أمعنّا فى البحث والتفتيش، [16]والمعرفة إذن ليس تكون بغير اختلاف [17]ما وذلك أنّ الأشياء إن كان بعضها غير بعض فقد وقع الاختلاف [18]والأشياء الكلّيّة إذ كان ما تحتها كثيرة [19]فقد يجب ضرورة أن تختلف هذه أيضاً كانت [20]الكلّيّات أجناساً أو كانت أنواعاً

(18.3) وأخلق [21]بكلّ معرفة أن تكون إنّما هى معرفة بالأشياء الخاصّيّة وذلك أنّ الجوهر [22]وما هو الشىء خاصٌّ فى كلّ واحد من الأشياء والأشياء التى تُعلم [23]بذاتها لا على طريق العرض إنّما هى شىء فى [24a]شىء

---

6 من الشناعة prop. to seclude as a gloss Crub.[1] **9** after حد break (∴) ind. T, blank space of three letters B **10** الحس corr. Alon* (αἴσθησις) : الحسى T : الجنس B | على (يقف) corr. Gutas* (θεωρεῖ); cf. 8b24, 9a4, 11a2 : عند T B **13** تحدث read. Alon : نحدث T : يحدث B, perhaps read ⟨بها⟩ يُحدث له? **14** ينجح read. Gutas* (προβαίνειν) : ىنحح B, T (w.p.) : يتحجّ *sic* Alon : يتحج Crub.[2] **16** والمعرفة B : فالمعرفه T **18** كثيرة sic T B : كثيراً is to be read **20** الكليات read. Alon* (τὰ καθόλου) : الكلات B : الكلمات appar. T **21** انما repeated in T

[124] "Others which produce in it" = *ašyāʾa tuḥdiṯu lahū š-šakka wa-l-ḥayrata*, is supposed to render τὰ δ' ἀπορίαν ἐνεργαζομένη, though the Arabic text as it stands now would be translating ἐνεργαζόμενα, the subject being τὰ δ'. The feminine participle in Greek refers to sense-perception, which is the subject that produces the aporia. In Arabic, if the text as transmitted is kept, the subject of the verb in this relative clause would have to be the "things", *ašyāʾa tuḥdiṯu*. The translation would be more accurate if we read *ašyāʾa*

(18.2) And some people employed unreason that is more uncommon than this and introduced what does not exist, did not exist, and will not exist among what is included in the nature of the universe—but this is, so to speak, a wisdom that has exceeded all bounds. As for the existent, it is evident that it comes in various modes. The reason is that sense-perception perceives its differences and investigates their causes; but it is more likely that this statement is truer, namely that [sense-perception] submits to [the faculty of] thought some things which it simply investigates and some others which produce in it[124] doubt and perplexity. So [sense-perception], even if it is not able to succeed through [the faculty of] thought[125] with regard to these [things], it nevertheless is such that[126] some light does appear to it in the place where there is no light when we are assiduous in inquiry and investigation. Knowing, therefore, does not occur without some difference. The reason is that if things are unlike each other, then difference occurs; and since what [falls] under the universal things is many, these too must differ of necessity, whether the universals are genera or species. 8b6

(18.3) It is more likely[127] for every knowledge to be knowledge only of things that are [unique] properties; the reason is that substance and what a thing is[128] are proper to every single thing, and the things that are known essentially and not accidentally are something precisely in something.[129]

---

yuḥdiṯu lahū ⟨*bihā*⟩ *š-šakka wa-l-ḥayrata* "and others, ⟨by means of which,⟩ it (= sense-perception) produces in it (thought) doubt and perplexity," where the ⟨*bihā*⟩, though it does not appear in Greek, is required by the Arabic syntax.

125 Isḥāq took the feminine pronoun in δι' ἧς to refer to διάνοια and not to ἀπορία, most likely because he understood the subject of δύνηται to be αἴσθησις and not διάνοια.

126 "Such that" translates *ʿalā ḥālin*, which does not appear in the Greek. Normally this expression renders Greek ὥς, as in 5b6, where we have the same Arabic, *illā annahū ʿalā ḥālin* rendering Greek ὅμως ⸢ὥς⸣. Here it does not seem that there was an identical Greek text, with ὥς again being lost in transmission. In all likelihood *ʿalā ḥālin* was added by Isḥāq to complete the sense as he understood it.

127 Isḥāq translates here σχεδόν with the term normally used to translate τάχα, *aḫlaqu bi-*, whereas in the three other occurrences of the word in this work it is rendered either with the more usual term *kāda* (6a26, 8a24) or with *qad* and the imperfect (7a1). It would appear that Isḥāq interpreted the force of σχεδόν as applying to the whole phrase and not only to one word, like Laks & Most ("au sens d'une affirmation atténuée," p. 64).

128 It is interesting to note that the technical phrase τὸ τί ἦν εἶναι is rendered here literally by *mā huwa š-šayʾ* and not by the more usual term *māhiyya*.

129 Isḥāq also took the technical term τὶ κατὰ τινός in its ontological and not predicative sense; see the commentary.

(18.4) وبالجملة [25a]فإنّ حقَّ المعرفة الوقوفُ على [24b]الشىء بعينه الذى يقال فى أشياء كثيرة [25b]إمّا عامّيّاً كلّيّاً [26]وإمّا خاصّيّاً فى كلّ واحد بمنزلة ما يقال فى الأعداد وفى الخطوط [27]وفى أصناف الحيوان والنبات والمعرفة الكاملة هى [1]من الأمور الكلّيّة كالغاية المقصود إليها فإنّ السبب إنّما وجوده فى هذه [2]وهى 9a
من الأمور الجزئيّة بقدر القسمة [3]إلى الأشخاص بمنزلة ما يوجد فى الأشياء التى تُفعل وتُعمل [4]فإنّ فعلها يجرى هذا المجرى وقد نقف على أنّ الشىء واحد بعينه [5]بالجوهر وبالعدد وبالصورة وبالجنس [6]والمقايسة ومع ذلك أيضاً بالقسمة إن كانت القسمة خارجة عن هذه [7]إلّا أنّ أكثر ما نقف به على ذلك بالمقايسة إذ كنّا نبعد بها بعداً [8]كثيراً فى بعض الأمور من قِبلنا أنفسنا وفى بعضها [9]من قِبل الشىء الموضوع وفى بعضها من قِبلهما جميعاً

---

27 after والنبات break (∴) ind. T **9a1** المقصود corr. Gutas : والمقصود T B | اليها T B : اليه prop. Marg. **4** نقف read. Marg., نقف B, T (w.p.) : يقف read. Alon **7** بها corr. Gutas : بهما T B : om. Alon **9** الموضوع corr. Gutas* (ὑποκείμενον) : الموصع T : الموضع B | قبلهما B : فبلهما T

[130] One would have expected *yuqālu ʿalā*, "is predicated of," rather than *yuqālu fī* here.

[131] Isḥāq read a defective Greek text here due to homoeoteleuton: either the Greek text in Ψ or Isḥāq himself in reading it jumped from δ' to δ' in line 8b27, skipping over the words ἢ ἐξ ἀμφοῖν ἔστιν δ' (and thus missing not only ἔνια as indicated by Crubellier 1992, 37n52). Isḥāq accordingly read, τέλεος δ' (*sc.* ἐπιστήμη ἐστὶ) ἔνια τῶν μὲν καθόλου ⟨ὡς⟩ τέλος … τῶν δέ …, with ὡς apparently understood by Isḥāq himself in order to make τέλος fit the syntax of the mutilated sentence. That Isḥāq skipped the words indicated above is clear from the fact that he omitted translating ἀμφοῖν, a word which he diligently translated in the other five instances in which it occurs in this small work: in 7a7, 7a8, 9a9, and 9b6 ἄμφω is translated by the dual of the noun or pronoun concerned with the addition of *jamīʿan*, and in 9b5 with the dual only; it is only in this passage that

(18.4) In general, the task of knowledge is to perceive the same thing which is said with regard to[130] many things, either in common and universally or in a particular way with regard to each—like what is said with regard to numbers and lines and to the [different] kinds of animals and plants. Perfect knowledge consists of [some of] the universal 9a
matters as the goal aimed at,[131] (for the existence of the cause [resides] in this alone), and of [some] of particular matters commensurate with the division into individuals, like what is found with regard to things which are done and made, for their actuality is of this kind. Now we recognize that something is the same[132] through substance, number, form,[133] genus, and analogy, and, additionally, also through division, if indeed division is not among these.[134] However, for the most part we recognize [the same] by means of analogy,[135] since by means of it we are at a very great distance—in some things on account of us ourselves, in others on account of the subject matter, and in yet others on account of them both.

---

it is not translated at all, which indicates that Isḥāq did not see it or did not have it in Ψ. As for ἔνια, it appears to be reflected in the preposition *min* in the Arabic version (and not to be missing as indicated by Crubellier 1992, 37n52), *wa-l-maʿrifa al-kāmila hiya min al-umūr al-kulliyya*, "perfect knowledge consists of some of the universal things." This stands for, as just discussed, τέλεος δ' (*sc.* ἐπιστήμη ἐστὶ) ἔνια τῶν μὲν καθόλου. Although when ἔνια is used in this work to refer to things and not people (ἔνιοι, when it is translated by *baʿḍ*) it is translated by the indefinite noun *ašyāʾ*, "things" (as at 9a18, 10a25), here the preposition is sufficient to indicate ἔνια. For if Isḥāq had missed ἔνια in his exemplar and thus read the sentence as, τέλεος δ' (sc. ἐπιστήμη ἐστὶ) τῶν μὲν καθόλου, he would have translated, "perfect knowledge consists of the universal things." Thus the preposition *min* indicates that Isḥāq read ἔνια τῶν, which is also the reading of all the extant Greek manuscripts.

[132] Isḥāq understood ταὐτὸ ἐπιστάμεθα in its current sense of "we recognize the same thing," instead of the technical use of ταὐτό as "the identical," "we recognize the [quality] 'same'."

[133] Isḥāq chose this meaning of εἶδος instead of "species."

[134] This is one of two ways in which the elliptical sentence in the Greek can be read, but not the correct one. See the commentary.

[135] Isḥāq misunderstood διὰ πλείστου to refer to the degree of recognition ("for the most part we recognize"), rather than to the distance through which recognition takes place. Cf. the note to the Greek text for modern interpretations of this passage which caused difficulties to most translators.

(19) [10]فلمّا كانت المعرفة قد تكون على وجوه كثيرة كان الوقوف على الطريق 9a الذى به [11]ينبغى أن نبحث عن كلّ واحد من الأشياء على الوجه الملائم هو مبدأ الأمر ومَلاَكه [12]ومثال ذلك البحث عن الأوائل المعقولة وعن الأشياء المتحرِّكة [13]الداخلة تحت الطبيعة وما من هذه فى المبادئ [14]وما منها لواحق إلى أن نبلغ إلى الحيوانات والنباتات وننتهى بأخرة إلى [15]التى لا نفس لها وذلك أنّ فى كلّ واحد من هذه جنساً [16]خاصّاً كما فى التعاليم ⟨أيضاً [17]فإنّ للتعاليم⟩ أنفسها اختلافاً على أنّها [18]كأنّها من جنس واحد وقد لُخّص ذلك تلخيصاً بالغاً وإن كان هاهنا أشياء [19]تُعلم من طريق أنّها غير معلومة على ما يقول بعض الناس [20]فجهة البحث عن هذه خاصّيّة وتحتاج إلى قسمة ما [21]وأخلق بالقول بالمقايسة — فيما يمكن فيه أن يقال بالمقايسة — أن يكون [22]أليق من القول به يُعلم من طريق أنّه غير معلوم كما [23]لو قال قائل فى شئ من الأشياء إنّه مبصَر من طريق أنّه غير مبصَر

(20a) [24]فقد بقى أن نلتمس تمييز الجهات التى تقع بها المعرفة وعلى كم يقال فى الشىء إنّه يُعلم **(20b)** [25]والمبدأ فى ذلك وأوّله أن نلخِّص [26]المعنى فى قول القائل إنّ الشىء يُعلم ما هو وقد يُظنّ بهذا الأمر أنّه أصعب من ذاك [27]وذلك

10 كان corr. Gutas : فاذا B, T (w.p.) **11** الملائم read. Alon : الملايم B : الملام *sic* T **14** بأَخرَةٍ read. Gutas (cf. *GALex* I,94), T (w.p.) : باخره B : بآخره Alon : باخره Crub.[2] **15–16** جنساً خاصاً corr. Gutas : جنس خاص T (w.p.), B **16–17** add. Gutas* (ἔχει δὲ καὶ … τὰ μαθήματα); see the Excursus, § III **20** خاصية وتحتاج corr. Gutas : خاصى ويحتاج T (w.p.), B : خاصّ ويحتاج Alon **22** أليق read. Gutas* (οἰκειότερον) : الق T {B} : البق Crub.[2] : التى Alon **24** تمييز read. Crub.[2] : نمسز T {B} : بخير Alon

(19) Since knowledge comes about in many ways, recognizing[136] the 9a10 method by means of which we ought to investigate everything in an appropriate manner is the starting point and basic prerequisite. An example of that is the investigation of the intelligible first [things], of the movable things that fall under nature, and of the latter, those that are among the principles and those of them that are concomitants, until we reach animals and plants and finish in the end with the inanimate. The reason is that each one of these has a uniquely proper genus, just as in mathematics ⟨also, for mathematics⟩[137] itself has a differentiation although it is, as it were, a single genus; this has been set down with sufficient precision. And if there are things which are known by way of being unknown, as some people say, the way to investigate them is uniquely proper [to them] and in need of some sort of division; it is more likely that arguing by analogy, with regard to those [things] for which it is possible to argue by analogy, is more fitting than an argument through which knowledge is gained by way of being unknown,[138] just as if one were to say about something, that it is seen by way of being unseen.

(20a) There remains to try and distinguish the ways in which knowledge occurs and in how many [ways] it is said about something that it is known. **(20b)** The starting point and first [thing] in this respect is for us to state with precision what is meant when one says that something is known. It may be thought about this matter that it is more difficult

---

[136] The transmitted text *fa-iḏan* is almost certainly a corruption of *kāna*; *fa-iḏan* is hardly correct in context, and there is no justification for it in the Greek. Although Isḥāq recast the initial two sentences in the Greek (the interrogative and the nominal one following it) into one affirmative sentence, he did, in the end, say the same thing as the Greek; *fa-iḏan*, "therefore," as a semantic addition to the text is not indicated, and the inferential implication it adds in Arabic is already covered by the initial *lammā*, just as in the Greek it is expressed by the genitive absolute.

[137] These words were omitted in the Arabic manuscript tradition through extended haplography by jumping from *at-taʿālīm* to *at-taʿālīm*, as suggested by Crubellier 1992, 38n53. The accusative in *iḫtilāfan*, which otherwise would be unexplained, is the fossil that indicates this. It needs a word that governs the accusative, and this is *fa-inna* in the missing words, *ayḍan fa-inna li-t-taʿālīm*. Isḥāq mistook the first "mathematicals" as referring to the discipline of mathematics and not to its objects.

[138] Isḥāq quite properly understood, and accordingly translated, this sentence by supplying the implied words: τάχα δέ, ἐφ' ὧν ἐνδέχεται ⟨κατ' ἀναλογίαν λέγειν⟩, κατ' ἀναλογίαν οἰκειότερόν ⟨ἐστιν⟩ λέγειν ἢ ⟨λέγειν⟩ αὐτῷ τῷ ἀγνώστῳ ⟨γνωστόν⟩. It appears that he understood αὐτῷ as a personal rather than an intensive pronoun.

9b أنّه ليس يمكن أن يؤخذ شيءٌ كلّيٌّ عامّيٌّ فى [1]الأشياء التى تقال من جهات شتى (20c1) ولعلّ هذا ممّا [2]يُرتبك فيه أو ليس بالسهل أن يقال إلى أىّ موضع ينبغى أن ينتهى الطلب فى الأشياء التى [3]ينبغى أن نبحث عن مبادئها وأىّ الأشياء هى فى الأشياء المحسوسة [4]والأشياء المعقولة على مثال واحد فإنّ سلوك طريق ما لا نهاية له [5]فيهما مجتنب غير مألوف وخارج عن المعقول [6]وهما جميعاً مبادئ على وجه من الوجوه إلّا أنّى أقول إنّ الأخلق بتلك أن تكون مبادئ لنا [7]وهذه مبادئ على الإطلاق أو تكون تلك غاية يُقصد لها وهذه مبادئ لنا [8]فأمّا إلى موضع من المواضع فقد يمكنّا أن ندرك أسباباً [9]بأن نأخذ لتلك أوائلَ من الحواسّ [10]فأمّا إذا ترقّينا إلى الأطراف الأُوَل أنفسها [11]⟨ف⟩لم نقدر حينئذ على ذلك إمّا من قِبل أنّه لا سبب لها [12]وإمّا من قِبل عجزنا نحن أنفسنا بمنزلة [13]ما يعرض لنا عند التماس النظر إلى الأشياء التى فى غاية الضياء وأخلق بهذا القول الآخر أن يكون [14]أصحّ أعنى أنّ النظر فى أشباه هذه من الأمور كان ⟨بـ⟩العقل نفسه [فيها] [15]بمساس الأمر المطلوب وكأنّه يماسّه ولذلك صار لا [16]يقع فيها الزلل (20c2) والبحث أيضاً عن هذا نفسه صعب

9b2 يرتبك read. Gutas : برسك T {B} : يشك Alon Crub.[2] **3** وأى corr. Alon : والى T B **5** مجتنب read. Gutas : محسب T {B} : مختلف Alon Crub.[2] **6** من repeated, the first crossed out T, {B} **7** second مبادئ read. Alon : مادٍ T, مباد B **9** after الحواس break (∴) ind. T **10** ترقينا corr. Gutas* (μεταβαίνωμεν) : بوفسا T {B} : توفينا read. Alon **11** add. Gutas **13** after الضياء break (∴) ind. T **14** كان T {B} : كأن read. Alon | بـ add. Gutas* (τῷ νῷ) | فيها secl. Gutas **15** بمساس corr. Crub.[1,2*] (θιγόντι) : بماس T {B} : بقياس read. Alon **16** after الزلل break (∴) ind. T

139 In order to complete the comparative χαλεπώτερον, Isḥāq adds "than that," which is to be understood, in context, as referring to the precise determination of what knowledge is; in other words, he seems to have understood the sentence as saying that the problem of the different ways and aspects of knowledge is more difficult than the mere determination of what the meaning of knowledge precisely is.

than that;[139] the reason is that it is not possible to receive a universal and common thing in the case of things which are said in various ways. (**20c1**) 9b
Perhaps[140] this is something which is intractable, or it is not easy to say up to which point should extend the search for things whose principles[141] we ought to investigate, and which things these are, alike among the sensible things and intelligible things; for following the path to infinity in both cases is to be avoided and not accosted, and it is unreasonable. These two together are starting points in some manner, except that I would say that[142] it is more likely for the former to be starting points for us and the latter starting points absolutely, or for the former to be an end aimed at and the latter[143] starting points for us. Up to a certain point, then, it is indeed[144] possible for us to perceive causes[145] by taking starting points from the senses for those [things]; but when we advance to the first extremes themselves, we are not able then to do that, either because they have no cause or on account of *our* impotence, like what happens to us when we attempt to look at things that are extremely bright.[146] It is likely that this other statement is more correct, namely, that the theoretical investigation into the likes of these things is ⟨by means of⟩ the intellect itself[147] through contact with, and as if it touches, the object sought; and for this reason no error can occur about them. (**20c2**) Also,

---

140 Isḥāq read in Ψ ἤ, "or," as in all other Greek manuscripts.

141 Isḥāq rendered αἰτίας ("causes") as "principles" (*mabādi'*), in clear divergence from his usual practice of translating the word in all its other occurrences in the work as *asbāb* (except for 11b8 where it is translated with the related word *'illa*. See the glossary). It does not seem likely that he read ἀρχάς for αἰτίας in Ψ, though interpretive marginal glosses to that effect cannot be excluded.

142 The Arabic adds these words to complete the sense of the sentence, just like modern translators do; cf. Ross 27: "Perhaps we may say that …".

143 Isḥāq apparently missed the chiasmus of the construction, if the pronouns *tilka* and *hāḏihī* that he uses are interpreted in their customary sense; thus, in the second alternative, the sensibles would be the end and the intelligibles our starting point.

144 Note again the emphatic use of *qad* with imperfect.

145 Isḥāq understood or interpreted δι' αἰτίου θεωρεῖν as if it were αἰτίας θεωρεῖν; it does not seem as if he had a different text: "looking into things by means of a cause" is close in meaning to "perceiving a cause."

146 Isḥāq read the ὥσπερ πρὸς τὰ φωτεινότατα phrase as a clause, interpreting (rather than reading?) the infinitive βλέπειν as βλέποντες. A thousand years later Usener suggested the same correction.

147 The Arabic of this sentence as transmitted is ungrammatical. The preposition *bi-* before *'aql* must have dropped out and subsequently *fīhā* must have been added after *nafsihī* to compensate for it by providing, through the pronoun in *fīhā*, which refers to the preceding *ašyā'*, some connection with the opening nominal clause *an-naẓar … al-umūr*.

[17]وكذلك التصديق به وذلك أنّ هذا الأمر عظيم الغَناء [18]ويُحتاج إليه مع ذلك حاجةً ضرورةً فى كلّ واحد من العلوم [19]وخاصّةً فى أجلّها أعنى فى أىّ شىء ينبغى أن نجعل [20]⟨حدَّ⟩ ذلك ومثالُه علمُ أمور الطبيعة ⟨وعلم ما [21]قبل الطبيعة⟩ فإنّ الذين طلبوا الحجّة فى العلوم ⟨كلّها⟩ قد يبطلون [22]الحجّة ويبطلون مع ذلك المعرفة بل [23a]أصحّ القولين قول [24b]الذين يعتقدون فى السماء أنّها أزليّة [23b]يلتمسون حجّة فيما لا حجّة فيه [24a]ولا من شأنه أن تكون فيه حجّة [25]وأيضاً فإنّ الذين يذكرون أمر حركاتها [26]ومقاديرها وأشكالها وأبعادها
[27]وسائر ما يُبيَّن بصناعة النجوم فقد يبقى عليهم أن يذكروا [1]الأوائلَ المحرِّكة 10a
والسببَ الذى ⟨له⟩ صار ذلك كذلك [2]وما طبيعة كلّ واحد منها ووضعُها بعضها مع بعض [3]وجوهرُ الكلّ بأسره وإذا انحطّوا [4]إلى سائر الأشياء ذكروا مثل ذلك فى الأنواع التى قلنا [5]إلى أن بلغوا إلى الحيوان والنبات

---

17 الغناء read. Gutas: العا T {B}: العناء Alon **20** حد add. Gutas* (ὅρον) | ذلك T {B} : الحد Alon **20–21** add. Gutas* (καὶ περὶ τὰς ἔτι προτέρας); see above, Part I, Chapter 3.2 **21** add. Alon* (ἁπάντων) **22–25** بل اصحّ ان يقال انهم يلتمسون حجة فيما لا حجة [بل اصح . . . وايضا فيه ولا من شأن ان تكون فيه حجة وقول الذين يعتقدون فى السماء انها ازلية وايضا conj. Alon **23a** قول T {B} : ⟨بأنّ⟩ قول conj. Crub.[2] **24b** يعتقدون read. Alon, T (w.p.) {B} **24a** after حجة break (∴) ind. T **27** يُبيَّن voc. Gutas* (δείκνυσιν), T (w.p.) {B} : يبين read. Crub.[2] : تبين read. Alon | يبقى read. Gutas : سمى T {B} : بقى Alon : نبغى conj. Crub.[2] **10a1** add. Gutas* (τίνος; cf. 10a28, 10b23)

[148] The Arabic text here (9b17) has *baḥṯ*, which corresponds to ζήτησις, as in 6b22. It has to be assumed that Ψ had actually ζήτησις rather than the transmitted σύνεσις, for it is difficult to see how this well known word (σύνεσις) could have been misunderstood by Isḥāq.

[149] Isḥāq translated πίστις in its later, Christian, meaning of "belief."

[150] Isḥāq appears not to have grasped the implication of ἄλλως, unless it is assumed that he understood something like ὅλως from it.

the investigation[148] of this [question] itself is difficult, and so is believing it.[149] The reason is that this matter is of great moment[150] and there is, in addition, necessarily need for it in every one of the sciences, and especially in the grandest of them—namely, at which thing we should set ⟨the boundary⟩[151] of that, such as the science of the objects of nature ⟨and the science of what is prior to nature⟩.[152] For those who seek proof in ⟨all⟩[153] the sciences actually destroy proof and destroy knowledge as well; rather, the more correct of the two statements is the statement of those who believe that heaven is eternal: they attempt [to find] proof in connection with what neither admits of proof nor is in its nature to admit of proof.[154] Also, for those who mention [heaven's] movements, sizes, figures, distances, and everything else that is explained by astronomy,
there remains to mention the first movers, the reason ⟨on account of⟩[155] 10a
which this came to be so, what the nature of each one of them is, their position relative to one another, and the substance of the entire universe; and when they[156] descend to the rest of the things they mention the like of this concerning the species we talked about[157] until they reach animals and plants.

---

[151] The word, which dropped from the text in the Arabic transmission, clearly needs to be restituted.

[152] The phrase *wa-ʿilmu mā qabla ṭ-ṭabīʿa* dropped from the text through homoeoteleuton.

[153] Alon's (1985, 199) addition of *kullihā* here to reproduce ἁπάντων (9b21) is necessary for the sentence to make sense.

[154] Due to the lacuna in line 9b24 in Ψ, as in all Greek manuscripts, Isḥāq read this sentence (9b23–25) as follows: Μᾶλλον δ' ἀληθέστερον εἰπεῖν ὅτι ζητοῦσιν ⟨λόγον⟩ ὧν οὐκ ἔστιν οὐδὲ πέφυκεν ὅσοι τὸν οὐρανὸν ἀΐδιον ὑπολαμβάνουσιν, making ὅσοι the subject of ζητοῦσιν in the ὅτι clause (as suggested by Crubellier 1992, 39n58). Alon's (1985, 200n104) rearrangement of the Arabic to fit the Greek is unnecessary.

[155] *Lahū* is to be added here: *wa-s-sabab allaḏī ⟨lahū⟩ ṣāra ḏālika*, translating καὶ τὸ τίνος ἕνεκα; cf. τίνος γὰρ ἕνεκα αἱ ἔφοδοι … (10a28), translated as, *as-sabab allaḏī lahū ṣāra l-amr yajrī* … .

[156] In line 10a3 ὑποβαίνοντι, singular in Greek, was understood by Isḥāq as referring to the plural τούτοις at 9b27 and translated as plural, *inḥaṭṭū*. Laks & Most 17n55 also understood it this way, a misinterpretation based on improper appreciation of the particle δή in line 10a4; see the commentary at 10a4.

[157] In 10a4 after καθ' ἕκαστον τῶν εἰδῶν Isḥāq apparently read τῶν εἰρημένων, i.e., "those we mentioned" one by one, *allatī qulnā*. It is not unlikely that Ψ may indeed have had this reading instead of the rather pointless ἢ μερῶν (if that is how the manuscript readings are to be understood).

(21) فإذا كانت صناعة النجوم [6]قد تعين بعض المعونة إلّا أنّها لا تنظر فى 10a
أوائل الطبيعة [7]فالأمور التى هى أجلّ قدراً وأشدّ بعداً هى غير هذه فإنّ [8]هذا
الفنّ على ما يظنّ بعض الناس ليس هو طبيعيّاً أو [9]ليس هو بأسره طبيعيّاً، هذا
على أنّ الحركة على الإطلاق [10]أمر ملائم للطبيعة وخاصٌّ بها وخاصةً * * *
[12]إنّما يكون إذا فعل وتحرّك بمنزلة ما عليه الأمر فى [13]الحيوان والنبات فإن
لم يكونا سَمِيَّيْن فمن البيِّن أنّ [14]السماء على حال حركتها تكون على جوهرها
[15]حتّى إذا فارقت الحركة وسكنت كانت سميّة [16]وذلك أنّ حركة الكلّ هى
بمنزلة حياة ما فَيَا ليت شعرى هل [17]الحياة ليست هى شيئاً للحيوان أو قد

6 تعين read. Alon, T (w.p.) {B} **7** بعداً T B : بدائياً prop. Crub.[1] **10** وخاص corr. Gutas : وحاصا T {B} | وخاصة corr. Alon* (καὶ μάλιστα; cf. 9b19) : وحاصه T {B} : وخاصية read. Crub.[1,2] **10–12** lac. (τοῦ οὐρανοῦ … καθ' ἕκαστον) ind. Crub.[1]; see above, Part I, Chapter 3.2 **12** وتحرك read. Crub.[2]* (κινεῖται), T (w.p.) {B} : يحرّك (om. و) Alon **13** يكونا T (w.p.) {B} : فيكونا Alon | سميين corr. Gutas* (ὁμώνυμα; cf. 10a15) : سماين T {B} : سمائين Alon **17** ليست corr. Alon : ليس T {B}

[158] Isḥāq also read, like most modern scholars, τοῖς πρώτοις δὲ τῆς φύσεως, without a comma after δέ.

[159] "Farthest away," i.e., in time; *ašaddu buʿdan* translates πρότερα, apparently intended to be taken in a temporal sense.

[160] A line is missing here from the translation, apparently a copyist's omission within the Arabic tradition. Crubellier 1992, 40n60, had already correctly identified the extent of the Greek text to which this omission corresponds (τοῦ οὐρανοῦ … καθ' ἕκαστον, from 10a10 to 12), placing the lacuna in the Arabic text correctly after what the manuscript (T) has as *ḫāṣṣiyya*. He ascribed the omission to a homoeoteleuton in the Arabic transmission, thinking that the word *ḫāṣṣiyya*, as we actually have it in the manuscript, formed a homoeoteleuton with the same word in a presumed expression *al-ašyāʾ al-ḫāṣṣiyya* which, he claimed, stood for τὸ καθ' ἕκαστον at 10a11–12 at the other end of the lacuna. However, in this translation, *ḫāṣṣiyya*, whether with *al-ašyāʾ* or without it, never stands for καθ' ἕκαστον, for which almost uniformly Isḥāq uses *kull wāḥid* (e.g. at 5a19, 8b22, 8b26, 9a15, 9b18, etc., and see the Glossary), but it uniformly translates ἴδιον and its derivatives; as a matter of fact, at 8b21, *al-ašyāʾ al-ḫāṣṣiyya* translates τὰ ἴδια. The word *ḫāṣṣiyya* in this passage, which should actually be read *ḫāṣṣatan*, stands for Greek μάλιστα at 10a10, as it does at 9b19, where the exactly identical expression, καὶ μάλιστα, is translated as

(21) So if astronomy does help somewhat but does not investigate the first [things] of nature,[158] the things which are of the highest moment and farthest away[159] are other than these. For this discipline, as some people think, is not about nature, or it is not entirely about nature, despite [the fact] that motion in an absolute sense is something suited to nature and proper to it, and especially * * *[160] comes about only when it acts and is in motion, as is the case with animals and plants. If they are not homonymous[161] then it is clear that heaven, when in a state of motion, is in accordance with its substance, such that when it is separated from the motion and is at rest, it is homonymous—the reason is that the motion of the universe is like some sort of life. I thus wish I knew whether[162] life is 10a5

wa-ḫāṣṣatan. (The previous phrase in the Arabic text, *wa-ḫāṣṣun bihā*, does not stand for μάλιστα but is actually a hendiadys for οἰκεῖον in the expression *mulā'im bi-ṭ-ṭabīʿa wa-ḫāṣṣ bihā*, where the pronoun in *bihā* naturally refers back to *ṭabīʿa*. Had the word *ḫāṣṣ* been used to translate μάλιστα here with reference to οὐρανοῦ, Isḥāq would have said, *wa-ḫāṣṣ bi-s-samā'*, and not used the pronoun in *bihā*.) Thus although the lacuna may indeed be due to a homoeoteleuton, the specific one was not between *ḫāṣṣiyya* ⟨* * * *al-ašyā' al-ḫāṣṣiyya*⟩ *innamā yakūnu*.

As for the lacuna itself, it could be thought that it occurred already in the Greek text on account of the possible homoeoteleuton in two successive lines which end in μάλιστα and καθ' ἕκαστον respectively. However, the Arabic syntax in the translation of this sentence precludes this because it indicates that Isḥāq did have the full text in front of him and that it was the same as that transmitted in the oldest Greek manuscripts, J and P: διὸ καὶ ἡ ἐνέργεια τῆς οὐσίας ἑκάστου καὶ τὸ καθ' ἕκαστον ὅταν ἐνεργῇ καὶ κινῆται. Since he read ἡ instead of εἰ (or actually, εἰ ἡ) and κινῆται instead of κινεῖται (see the commentary), he was missing a main verb in the sentence, and he assumed it to be something like ἐστί (e.g., understanding something like, καὶ τὸ καθ' ἕκαστόν ἐστι), for he must have translated, "⟨Hence, the actuality of the substance of each thing and each thing itself⟩ comes about only when it acts and is in motion." The text I place in angular brackets is what has been lost, but the second half of the sentence, what is extant, presupposes it because of the existence of "comes about only" (*innamā yakūnu*) in the Arabic text and the masculine verbs *faʿala* and *taḥarraka*. Had the omission occurred in the Greek tradition and Isḥāq read, jumping from μάλιστα to ὅταν, τό γε κινεῖσθαι καὶ ἁπλῶς τῆς φύσεως οἰκεῖον καὶ μάλιστα ὅταν ἐνεργῇ καὶ κινῆται, he would have translated, "Motion in an absolute sense is something suited to nature and proper to it, and especially when it [fem., for nature] acts and is in motion," or in Arabic ... *amrun mulā'imun li-ṭ-ṭabīʿati wa-ḫāṣṣun bihā wa-ḫāṣṣatan iḏā faʿalat wa-taḥarrakat*. Thus the *innamā yakūnu* as we have it in the text as well as the masculine verbs cannot be explained. The omission therefore occurred in the Arabic tradition and there is accordingly a lacuna in that text. By the same token, it is also clear that Ψ had the same (erroneous) Greek text as J and P, constituting some of the primitive errors of the Neoplatonic archetype (see Part I, Chapter 2.5).

161 Isḥāq read μὴ ὁμώνυμα without a comma between the two words.

162 Isḥāq read, together with all the Greek manuscripts, εἴτε, not having the benefit of the correction by Sylburg into εἴ γε.

ينبغى أن نبحث عن هذا أيضاً [18]إنّ الحركة ليست شيئاً للسماء وللأجرام السماويّة [19]أو ذلك على جهة ما محدودة إلّا أنّ هذا الشكّ كأنّه مقرون [20]بالشكّ فى الحركة عن غير متحرِّك

(22) [23b]فأمّا تلخيص هذا الأمر [22]حتّى يُعلم أنّ الأشياء كلّها إنّما تكون من أجل شىء وأنّه ليس شىء باطل [23a]لا معنى له فليس هو بسهل على ما [24]سنقول فى مواضع كثيرة فمن أىّ الأمور ليت شعرى ينبغى أن نبدأ وإلى [25]أيّها ينبغى أن ننتهى فإنّا قد نجد أشياء قد يُظنّ بها أنّها ليس تجرى [26]هذا المجرى لكن بعضها يجرى على طريق الاتّفاق والعَرَض وبعضها يجرى بضرورة تدعو إليه [27]كما نجد ذلك فى كثير من الأمور السماويّة والأمور [28]الأرضيّة

(22.1) فإنّ للسائل أن يسأل عن السبب الذى له صار الأمر يجرى على
ما يجرى عليه مذاهب [1]ماء البحر ومجترفاته وتشعّبه، وجَزْرُهُ عن مواضع 10b

18 وللاجرام corr. Alon : وللاجرم T {B} **20** after متحرك break (.·.) ind. T **24** نبدأ read. Gutas, T (w.p.), B (w.p.) : تبدأ read. Alon **25** ليس T {B}: ليست corr. Alon **28** عن add. above the line T[1] **10b1** ومجترفاته read. Crub.[2] : T (w.p.), B (w.p.) : ومجيراته *sic* read. Alon | وتشعبه read. Crub.[2] : وشعبه T B : وتشيعه Alon

[163] Having read εἴτε in the preceding phrase, Isḥāq naturally took the ἤ as disjunctive. See the commentary.

[164] Isḥāq apparently understood (or read?) ἢ τόδε for what editors have corrected to ἢ ὡδί. The Greek manuscripts have a variety of forms; see the Greek apparatus.

[165] Isḥāq clearly could not understand this difficult sentence, though to his credit, he translated literally, which makes little sense. It is particularly nonsensical in the preceding sentence, which puts in the mouth of Theophrastus the outlandish claim that "motion is

not something belonging to animals, or[163] we ought to investigate this[164] also: motion is not something that belongs to heaven and the heavenly bodies, or that[165] is in some manner limited, except that this doubt is, as it were, connected with the doubt concerning motion [caused] by the unmoved.

(22) As for the precise delimitation of this matter with a view to knowing that all things come to be on account of something and that there is nothing that is in vain, meaningless, it is not easy,[166] as we shall state[167] in many places. From which things, I wish I knew, ought we to begin? And at which of them ought we to stop? For we do find things of which it is thought[168] that they do not follow this course, but some of them occur by way of coincidence and accidentally, while others occur by a necessity that brings them about, as we find this [to be the case] in connection with many celestial things and terrestrial things.

(22.1) For one may ask about the reason why things are as they are: [why there are] incursions[169] of sea water sweeping [things] away and 10b
spreading out,[170] [why there is] its ebbing from places which dries them

---

not something that belongs to heaven and the heavenly bodies," even if this is taken as a hypothetical question. Consequently, "that" in the following sentence, *ḏālika*, has no proper referent; it cannot refer to motion because *ḥaraka* is feminine, except perhaps in a general way. It is regrettable that this work was not studied in the Arabic tradition; it would have been interesting to see what a philosophically minded reader would have made of this passage.

166 Isḥāq read here in Ψ, as in all the Greek manuscripts, μηδὲν μάτην ἄλλως, ὁ ἀφορισμὸς οὐ ῥᾴδιος, which he translated as, *laysa šay'un bāṭilun lā maʿnā lahū fa-laysa huwa* (sc. *talḫīṣ hāḏā l-amr*) *bi-sahlin*, where *bāṭil* translates μάτην and *lā maʿnā lahū* translates ἄλλως in its sense of precisely "purposeles, meaningless." Without any particle following ἄλλως, he read μάτην ἄλλως as a hendiadys.

167 Isḥāq used the future tense, indicating that he read in the Greek text λέξεται for λέγεται, or at least so understood the text.

168 Isḥāq understood, καὶ δὴ ἔνιά ⟨ἐστι⟩ τῶν/τῷ μὴ δοκεῖν, "there are some things of/by which it is thought [of them] that they do not ...," which gave rise to the translation, "for we do find things of which it is thought that they do not ..." As for the contested reading τῶν/τῷ, it appears that the Arabic translation most readily would derive from a reading of τῶν in Ψ, though it is also possible that a reading of τῷ could have occasioned a similar translation; the Arabic is not specific enough to allow a definite decision.

169 "Incursions" stands for *maḏāhib*, translating ἔφοδοι.

170 *Mujtarifāt wa-tašaʿʿub*, hendiadys for misunderstood ἀνάρροιαι.

[2]وجفافُه عنها، ومدُّه إلى مواضع وبَلّـُه إيّاها [3]وبالجملة عن التغايير التى 10b
تعرض فيه إلى شىء بعد شىء [4]وأصناف الكون والفساد وكذلك يسأل عمّا
يعرض فى الأرض من [5]الاستحالات والتغايير والتنقّل من شىء إلى شىء
[6]وعن أشياء أُخر ليست باليسيرة نظائر [7]لهذه

(22.2) وقد يكون فى الحيوان أيضاً أشياء كأنّها [8]باطلة بمنزلة الثديين فى
الذكورة [10]واللحية فى بعضها وبالجملة نبات الشَعر فى [11]مواضع من البدن وممّا
يجرى أيضاً هذا المجرى القرون العظيمة التى توجد لبعضها بمنزلة [12]الأيائل
حتّى أنّ بعضها قد يتأذّى فى الحركة [13]والاستقلال وستر العينين [16]وأعظم ما
[17]يدخل الشكّ فيه من ذلك وأخصّه به أمر تولّـُد الحيوان وأغذيته [18]فإنّ هذه
ليست من قِبل شىء بل إنّما هى أعراض لزمت [19]من قِبل أشياء أخر ضرورية
وذلك أنّها لو كانت من أجل شىء [20]لقد كان يجب أن تكون دائماً على حال
واحدة وعلى مثال واحد

---

2 ومده T (w.p.) {B} : ومدة read. Alon **4** يسأل read. Alon : سل T B : نسأل read. Marg. **6** نظائر read. Alon, T (w.p.), B (w.p.) **8** باطلة corr. Gutas : باطل T (w.p.) {B} | الثديين read. Alon : T (w.p.) {B} **13** والاستقلال read. Marg. : T (w.p.) : والاسقلال B : والاستعلاق Alon **17** امر B, appar. T (which has امو with a haček on the و intended to correct it to read ر) : امور Crub.[2] **19** ضرورية (اشياء) corr. Gutas* (ἀνάγκας) : ضرورة B, T (w.p.) **20** كان corr. Gutas : كانت T (w.p.), appar. B (only the ـب is visible: ⟨كانـ⟩ـب)

[171] The Greek-Arabic correspondences here are the following: *jazr* = ἀναχωρήσεις, *jafāf* = ἀναξηράνσεις, *madd* = προχωρήσεις, and *ball* = ὑγρότητες. Isḥāq took ἀναχωρήσεις with ἀναξηράνσεις and προχωρήσεις with ὑγρότητες. "For why is there the ebbing of the sea from places and its drying them up, and the flowing into places and its moistening them?" Thus Isḥāq had what would, strictly speaking, correspond to, ἢ τίνος αἱ ἀναχωρήσεις καὶ ἀναξηράνσεις, ἢ αἱ προχωρήσεις καὶ ὑγρότητες; But it seems clear that Isḥāq himself joined ἀναχωρήσεις with ἀναξηράνσεις and προχωρήσεις with ὑγρότητες for the sake of meaning, and that the text in front of him had what is established here. Alternatively, the Arabic may suggest that the Greek text was, ἢ τίνος αἱ

up, and its flowing into places and drenching them,[171] and, in general, 10b2
[what the reason is] for the changes into one thing after another which take place in this connection, and for the various sorts of coming to be and passing away. One may similarly ask about the alterations and changes and the shifting from one thing into another that occur in the earth, and about other things, which are not few, similar to these.

(22.2) In animals, too, there do occur[172] things which are purposeless, as it were, like breasts in males[173] and beards in some, and in general the growth of hair in some parts of the body. What is also analogous to this is the enormous horns which are found in some of them, such as deer, to the point that some of them actually suffer harm[174] as [the horns] move, rise high [above the deer's head],[175] and cover their eyes.[176] The most important [thing] of all this about which there is doubt and the one to which [doubt] most properly belongs[177] is the matter of the generation and nourishment[178] of animals, for these are not for the sake of anything, but rather are accidents that are concomitant only on account of other, necessary things. The reason is that, had they been for the sake of something, they would have been necessarily always in the same state and in the same way.

⟨ἀναχωρήσεις καὶ⟩ προχωρήσεις ἢ ἀναξηράνσεις καὶ ὑγρότητες, putting the terms that go together first and second in each phrase respectively, but the chiasmus in the text as suggested by Usener works just as well if not better.

172 The emphatic *qad* with imperfect here render the emphasis in αὐτοῖς τοῖς ζῴοις.

173 "And the emission in females, if indeed it makes no contribution" (10b8–9, καὶ τοῖς θήλεσιν … συμβάλλεται) was not translated by Isḥāq. Since there is no break in the syntax the omission would appear to be deliberate. See Part I, Chapter 3.2.

174 It is not possible to decide whether Ψ had λελωβημένων or -μενοις. Isḥāq clearly took τοῖς δέ and λελωβ- to refer to the deer (*baʿḍahā*), but if he had -μένοις in front of him he would still have understood it from the context to refer to τοῖς.

175 This seems to be the intended meaning of *istiqlāl*, which renders παραιωρήσει. See Kazimirski s.v. The suggested emendation by Alon 1985, 201, and Crubellier 1992, 41n62, *istiʿlāq*, is not attested in the dictionaries.

176 The next few lines in the Greek text, 10b13–16 (καὶ ὥς ἔνια … τοιαῦτα), are left untranslated. It may be that Isḥāq could not decipher either the elliptical syntax or the rare vocabulary, or possibly both. See Part I, Chapter 3.2.

177 Isḥāq correctly took the noun implied by τὸ μέγιστον δὴ καὶ μάλιστα δοκοῦν to be ἀπορία. He perceived the rhetorical crescendo in the paragraph and ended with the intended phrase, "and the greatest aporia of all is …"

178 Isḥāq transposed the two words, apparently in order to list them in chronological sequence, taking τροφάς to refer to actual feeding.

(22.3) [24a]وللإنسان أيضاً أن يبحث [21]من أمر النبات بل من أمر الأنفس [23b]عن السبب الذى له [22]صار لها طبيعة محدودة، على ما يرون، [23a]بالصور والأنواع والقوى **(23)** [24b]فإنّ هذا نفسه موضع حيرة أعنى أنّه ليس [25]بمنقاس أن يكونَ ذلك ثمّ يُجعلَ فى غيرها ممّا هو أقدم [26]وأشرف منها فأخلق بالقول الذى فيه [27a]شىء ممّا يجب أن يُوثَقَ به هو أنّ هذه خليق أن تكون إنّما [28b]تقبل الصور [1a]والأصناف المختلفة [27b]من ذاتها [28a]من حركة الكلّ

(24) [1b]فإنْ لم تكن هذه من قِبل شىء [2]قُصد به الأمر الأفضل فقد ينبغى أن 11a
نقف على حدود ما ولا [3]نضعَ هذا القول على جميع الأشياء مطلقاً وذلك أنّ هذه الأشياء كأنّ القول فيها يميل إلى [4]الجهتين إذا قيلت على الإطلاق وإذا قيلت على واحد واحد [5]أعنى بالقول على الإطلاق أنّ الطبيعة فى كلّ شىء [6]تتشوّق إلى الأفضل وأنّها فيما يحتمل ذلك [7]تفيده النظام والدوام [8]وكذلك يجرى الأمر فى الحيوان وذلك أنّها حيث يمكن [9]الأمرُ الأفضلُ فليس يقصُر فى موضع من المواضع ومثال ذلك [10]أنّ الحنجرة جُعلت من مقدّم المرىء

---

21 الانفس *sic* T (w.p.), الانفس B : اللا نفس conj. Alon, but this negative formation is not usual with this translator; perhaps ⟨مـ⟩ـا لا نفس ⟨له⟩ is to be read for the Greek τοῖς ἀψύχοις: cf. 11a17, 9a15; but see the comm. **24b** اعنى انه T : اعنى ان نكون انه B, with signs ind. the deletion of the words ان نكون **25** بمنقاس read. Alon : نمماس T : نمماس B : بمقياس Crub.[2] | لا يجعل conj. Alon **27a** يوثق read. Treiger* (πιστόν) : نونق T : بوثف B : يوفق Alon : نوفق Crub.[2] **11a2** نقف read. Marg., يقف B, T (w.p.) | حدود ما corr. Crub.[1,2]* (τινάς; cf. 4b6, 4b14, etc.) : حدودها T B **3** كأنّ read. Marg. : كل appar. T, كان or كانه T[1] (the final *nūn* is slightly smudged) : كانه B **7** تفيده read. Marg. : نعده appar. T B : تعيده read. Crub.[2] **8** الحيوان T {B} : الحيوانات Marg. **9** يقصر read. Alon, T (w.p.) : نقصر B : تقصر read. Marg.

[179] The Greek has "inanimate things," and it is tempting to correct the Arabic *al-anfus* to read ⟨*m*⟩*ā lā nafsa* ⟨*lahū*⟩, but it does not seem that this was what Isḥāq wrote. See the commentary.

(22.3) One also ought to investigate, with regard to plants—or still more, with regard to souls[179]—the reason why they have a nature that is delimited, as they believe, by forms, species,[180] and powers; (23) for this very [thing] is perplexing, namely, that it is not reasonable[181] for this to be [so] and then to be applied[182] to something else which is prior and nobler than they.[183] So the argument that is more likely to contain something that should be relied upon is that these are apt to be receiving forms and different sorts[184] just spontaneously from[185] the movement of the universe.

(24)[186] If, then, these do not come about on account of something 11a
through which the best is aimed at,[187] we ought to recognize certain boundaries and not posit this statement for all things without qualification. The reason is that it is as if[188] a statement about these things tends toward two directions, when it is said without qualification and when it is said for each individual. By "statement without qualification" I mean that nature in everything desires the best and that it bestows order and perpetuity upon whatever can admit them. The same applies in the case of animals. The reason is that wherever the best is possible, it does not fail in any place. For example, the windpipe is placed in front of the

---

180 Isḥāq selected the inappropriate of the two meanings of εἶδος, form and species, apparently because he already translated μορφαῖς as "forms."

181 For Arabic *munqās* rendering ἔχειν λόγον see above, Part I, Chapter 3.3 at the end. The form of the word as it is used here is beyond dispute (cf. above at 7a10), for the skeleton of the word in the Tehran manuscript is clearly that of *munqās*. The Bodleian manuscript, through a metathesis of the second and third letters in the word *bmnq's*, reads *bmqy's* (*bi-miqyās*), which is almost tolerable (and accepted by Crubellier) except that *miqyās* is a noun meaning a measuring instrument.

182 Isḥāq took ποιοῦσιν not as a participle but as a verb, "they do/apply," which he then translated in the passive, "to be applied."

183 Isḥāq apparently read the following Greek text in Ψ and punctuated it thus: αὐτὸ γὰρ τοῦτο ἄπορον, τὸ μὴ ἔχειν λόγον [καὶ] τοῦτ', ἐν ἑτέροις δὴ ποιοῦσιν προτέροις καὶ τιμιωτέροις, apparently disregarding καί.

184 It is not clear how *al-aṣnāf al-muḫtalifa* is supposed to be translating πρὸς ἄλληλα; a textual corruption may be involved.

185 Unless one is to emend the Arabic text and add ⟨*wa-*⟩*min*, Isḥāq appears not to have translated καί in 10b27, understanding the following phrase as complementing and explaining the preceding.

186 Aporia 24 was translated by Margoliouth 1892, 194.

187 Isḥāq read in his manuscript the transmitted μὴ τοῦθ' and punctuated after ἄριστον: εἰ δὲ μὴ τοῦθ' ἕνεκά του καὶ εἰς τὸ ἄριστον, ληπτέον ....

188 Margoliouth's suggestion to read *ka-anna* here (instead of *kāna*) is well taken: it expresses the indefiniteness of τινά in ἔχει τινὰ διστασμόν.

[11]لأنّها أشرف منه [13]وكذلك جُعل كلّ ما تتهيّأ به الزينة إذا كانت [14]الشهوة 11a
تجرى هذا المجرى إلّا أنّه قد يظهر أنّ [15]ما لا يؤاتيها ولا يقبل الأمر الأفضل
كثير بل هو [16]أكثر كثيراً ممّا يقبله وذلك أنّ ذا النفس قليل [17a]وما لا نفس له
فلا يحصى كثرةً [18a]وأسرع تكوُّناً [17b]ممّا له نفس [18b]وأجود وجوداً وبالجملة فإنّ
[19]الجيّد يسير وفى أشياء يسيرة والردىء كثير العدد [20]وخروج هذا عن الحدّ
فقط هو [21]بمنزلة ما يكون فى طبيعة غاية الجهل [22]فإنّ الذين تكلّموا فى الجوهر

13 جعل Marg., appar. B (partly damaged) : فعل T : فعل read. Alon : يجعل Crub.[2] | كل ما read. Gutas : كلما T {B} | تتهيأ read. Alon : T (w.p.) {B} | الزينة read. Crub.[2], Alon in app. crit. : الرسه T {B} : الريئة Alon **15** يؤاتيها read. Marg., T (w.p.), B (w.p.) **17a** فلا read. Alon, ملا T : ولا B **22** الجوهر T : الجواهر B

[189] The words καὶ ἐν τῇ μέσῃ κοιλίᾳ τῆς καρδίας τὴν κρᾶσιν ἀρίστην ὅτι τὸ μέσον τιμιώτατον are missing in Arabic. It is difficult to decide what caused this omission. On the face of it, there is no reason why Isḥāq should not have translated this passage on the excellence of blood mixture in the middle ventricle of the heart. However, in view of the fact that (1) Theophrastus has just said that body parts occypying a front position are nobler, this statement about the center being "the noblest" may seem contradictory; as a matter of fact, there may indeed be a doctrinal problem with this passage, as discussed by Laks & Most 83n38. So it is doubtful that an omission even in the Greek tradition can be ruled out. Secondly, (2) the presence of the words τιμιώτερον and τιμιώτατον at the end of two sentences may have given rise to a textual corruption in the Greek through homoeoteleuton (even if not exact; i.e., τιμιώτερον γάρ at 11a10–11 and τιμιώτατον at 11a12). On the other hand, the same two considerations may have been operative, and perhaps more plausibly so, in the Arabic tradition. Isḥāq, who was certainly knowledgeable and sensitive to cultural and philosophical issues, (3) may not have translated the sentence for the same doctrinal reason—the center could not be the noblest—while (4) it is more likely that the same Arabic word for both the comparative τιμιώτερον and the superlative τιμιώτατον, *ašraf*, could have given rise to a homoeoteleuton omission within the Arabic tradition. I decide in favor of option (3) because there are two additional considerations. First, the Arabic syntax before and after the missing sentence is immaculate, and thus an accidental omission in the Arabic tradition is rendered more improbable; second, and more important, are considerations of context. Isḥāq understood the word κόσμος in the following sentence to mean "ornament" (see the following note, and cf. Laks & Most 83n39) and missed or

oesophagus because it is nobler than it,[189] and whatever is conducive to ornament,[190] if[191] desire functions in this manner, is similarly placed; except that it does appear that what neither complies with it[192] nor receives the best is much—no, rather, it is much more by far than what does receive it. The reason is that the animate is scarce[193] while the inanimate is immeasurably plentiful, and faster of generation than the animate and better of being.[194] In general, the good is little and in few things, while the bad is great of number, and the departure of this from the limit only is like what happens in the nature of extreme igno- 11a10

disregarded the particle γάϱ right after it. In the ensuing sentence, as read by Isḥāq (i.e., ὡσαύτως δὲ καὶ ὅσα κόσμου χάϱιν εἰ καὶ ἡ ὄϱεξις οὕτως), it makes semantically little sense to say that the noblest body parts are in the center rather than in front because, as the Arabic translation has it, "whatever is conducive to ornament (literally, "everything by means of which ornamentation presents itself or is formed") when desire follows this course" must refer to physical beauty in animate beings, and this is not in their center. It thus appears that there is more justification for considering the omission deliberate on the part of Isḥāq than for any of the other alternatives, and I so note it in the edition.

190 Interestingly, Isḥāq, just like Ross in modern times, chose this meaning of κόσμος as most appropriate in this context. See the commentary.

191 For *iḏā* translating εἰ see *GALex* I,161–163, §§ 2.1–2.3. It is interesting to note that Isḥāq did not translate γάϱ in 11a13, and so took the words ὡσαύτως ... οὕτως as one sentence. It is impossible to know whether he had a defective text or had problems with γάϱ similar to those faced by modern readers and decided not to translate the word; see the commentary.

192 The feminine singular pronoun here would be taken to refer, because of the context and the following *al-amr al-afḍal*, "the best," to *zīna*, "ornament," rather than to the immediately preceding *šahwa*, "desire."

193 Greek τι is not translated in the Arabic.

194 Isḥāq took ἄψυχον also as the subject of the following clause, and the final τὸ εἶναι as an accusative of respect (unless he read the dative τῷ εἶναι in Ψ which would amount to the same thing). He thus read the genitive in τῶν ἐμψύχων as the genitive after the comparative βέλτιον and the positive ἀκαϱιαῖον, which he interpreted as a comparative (more momentary = faster): ἄπειϱον δὲ τὸ ἄψυχον καὶ αὐτῶν τῶν ἐμψύχων ἀκαϱιαῖον καὶ βέλτιον τὸ/τῷ εἶναι. It is interesting to see that in order to make his rendering fit what he interpreted as two comparatives in the Greek text, he translated τὸ εἶναι twice, in two different meanings of the word, generation and being. Isḥāq must have thought that "faster of generation," i.e., faster to be generated, refers to the fact that inanimate things do not need a long gestation period to be generated. (The discussion of this passage by Merlan 1968, 140, is based on an inaccurate understanding of the Arabic.)

بأسره [23]مثل سبوسبس جعلوا الشريف [24]فى الموضع الوسط قليلاً عزيزاً فأمّا النهايات [25]وما عن جنبتى الوسط فهى عندهم على ما ينبغى

(24.1) [27]فأمّا أفلاطن وشيعة فوثاغورس فإنّهم باعدوا الأمر [1]بعداً كثيراً بما 11b
رأوه من الأشياء كلّها يتقيّله هذا [2]على أنّهم وضعوا سببها بالتضادّ [3]للاثنوة غير المحدودة وللواحد يدخل فيها الخروج عن التناهي [4]وعن النظام وبالجملة الخروج عن صورة، [5]وبالجملة فإنّه ليس يمكن أن تكون طبيعة الكلّ خلواً من تلك [6]لكنّها كأنّها مضاهية للأخرى أو تفضل [7]عليها أو تكون المبادئ أيضاً متضادّة ومن قِبل ذلك [8]صار الذين يضيفون العلّة إلى الله لا يقولون ولا فيه إنّه يقدر [9]أن يقود الأشياء كلّها إلى الأمر الأفضل لكن إذ [10]كان به

---

23 سبوسبس read. Alon, T (w.p.), B (w.p.) : سوسيس read. Marg. | الشريف read. Marg. : السريف T : التشريف B **24** عزيزاً read. Marg. : عربرا T B : غزيرا Alon | فاما T (w.p.) : واما B **25** جنبتى B : حسى T : جنبى Alon | after ينبغى break (∴) ind. T **27** فوثاغورس corr. Marg. : فوباعورسن T : فوباعوريين B | after باعدوا break (∴) ind. T **11b1** كثيرا read. Alon, T (w.p.), B (w.p.) | راوه T : رواه B | يتقيله read. Gutas, T (w.p.) : بقيله B : يتقبله read. Marg. : متقيّلة Alon **3** غير T B : الغير Marg. | فيها corr. Gutas* (ἐν ᾗ); cf. the fem. pronouns in تلك لكنها in ll. 5–6 below : فيه T (w.p.), B (w.p.) **5** after تلك add. يعنى الرداه T, يعنى الرداءة B : gloss ind. Marg. : om. Crub.[1], secl. Crub.[2] **6** كأنّها read. Alon : كانها T : فانها B | للاخرى T : الاخرى B | after للاخرى add. يعنى الحروره T B : gloss ind. Marg. : om. Crub.[1], secl. Crub.[2] **8** يضيفون read. Crub.[2] : نصمون T : نصعون B : يصبقون *sic* Alon **9** اذ T (w.p.), B (w.p.) : اذا Alon

[195] Given the corrupt nature of the text, Isḥāq had problems with its interpretation just like modern scholars. The text that he read in Ψ in all likelihood looked like this, with curly brackets placed around words he did not translate: Τὸ δ᾽ ὅλον, σπάνιόν τε καὶ ἐν ὀλίγοις τὸ ἀγαθόν, πολὺ δὲ πλῆθος {η} τὸ κακὸν οὐ{κ} εἰ/ἡ ἀοριστία {δὲ} μόνον {καὶ οἷον ὕλης εἴδη} καθάπερ τὰ τῆς φύσεως ἀμαθεστάτου. First, it is clear that he read οὗ ἡ for οὐκ εἰ, either because that is what he had in his text or, more probably, because that is how he interpreted it; see the commentary. Second, since the bad is presented in the text as being numerous, he interpreted ἀοριστία—literally translated as "departure from the limit"—as referring to the boundless instances of the bad itself, not to the indefiniteness and unformed nature of prime matter (as modern scholars do). And third, in the final phrase, he understood ἀμαθεστάτου as being the genitive of τὸ ἀμαθέστατον (the state

rance.[195] For those who spoke about substance in its entirety, like Speusippus, placed[196] the noble in the center place, as something scarce and rare.[197] As for the extremes and what is on either side of the center, they are, in their opinion, as they should be.[198]

(24.1) As for Plato and the followers of Pythagoras, they put the matter at a very great distance[199] because they thought that all things imitate[200] 11b
this, though they posited their[201] cause in opposition to the indefinite dyad and to the one, which [dyad][202] includes a departure from finitude and from order, and, in general, from form. In general, it is impossible for the nature of the universe to be free of that,[203] but it corresponds, as it were, to the other[204] or is superior to it, or[205] the principles are also contrary to each other. On account of this, those who attribute the cause to god have come to say that not even he is able to guide all things to the

---

of extreme ignorance) not ὁ ἀμαθέστατος (the most ignorant person) and thus, reading τῆς φύσεως ἀμαθεστάτου together, made sense of the καθάπερ phrase as meaning, "like what [happens] in the nature of extreme ignorance." In this way he could make some sense of the whole sentence by seeing in it a comparison (καθάπερ, *bi-manzilat*) between bad beyond limits on the one hand and a state of extreme ignorance on the other. Given this understanding of the sentence, the phrase καὶ οἷον ὕλης εἴδη, "and, as it were, the forms of matter," makes no sense: the phrase is clearly parallel to ἀοριστία but it cannot refer to the bad as ἀοριστία does; what would "the forms of matter of the bad" mean? So apparently Isḥāq just decided not to translate the phrase. (Previous discussions of the Arabic, presented by Tarán 1981, 444–445, are based on inaccurate analysis of the text.)

196 Isḥāq punctuated after Σπεύσιππος and read, or interpreted, ποιεῖ as if it were ποιοῦσιν, thus compensating for the absence of a finite verb in the sentence. See the commentary.

197 This is a hendiadys for σπάνιον, with *qalīl* emphasizing the numerical rarity of the thing and *ʿazīz* its preciousness.

198 Isḥāq read τὰ δ' … ἔτυχεν ὄντα as one sentence, and was forced to disregard the words τὰ μὲν οὖν; it does not appear as if he had a defective text.

199 It is not clear what Isḥāq, or especially his readers, understood by this phrase.

200 *Taqayyala*, "to imitate," not broadly attested in medieval dictionaries, would appear from this passage to have been more common. Cf. Dozy s.v.

201 I.e., of all things.

202 The manuscript has the masculine pronoun, *fīhi*, which, however, cannot be what Isḥāq wrote because further down, ll. 5–6, the same entity, the dyad, is referred to with feminine pronouns, *tilka lakinnahā*.

203 After "that" (*tilka*) the manuscripts add what is obviously a later marginal gloss, *yaʿnī ar-radaʾata*, "i.e., badness," which cannot be attributed to Isḥāq.

204 After "the other" (ἑτέρας = *uḫrā*), the manuscripts add another marginal gloss, *yaʿnī al-ḫayrūrata*, "i.e., goodness," also not to be attributed to Isḥāq.

205 Isḥāq read in Ψ ἤ as in all the other manuscripts; ᾖ is Ross's emendation.

أيضاً ألّا يكون يشآء ذلك أصلاً إذ [11]كان قد يعرض أن يرتفع جوهرها بأسره من قِبل أنّه من أشياء متضادّة [12]وفى أشياء متضادّة

(24.2) وقد نجد [13]أيضاً فى الأوائل أشياء كثيرة لحقت على طريق [14]الاتّفاق مثل ما ذكرنا من التغايير التى تعرض فى الأرض [15]فإنّ هذه لم يُقصد بها الأمرُ الأفضل ولا جُعلت من أجل شىء [16]لكنّها لزمت وتبعت إماماً ضروريّاً وقد نجد [17]فى الهواء مثل ذلك وفى أشياء أُخَر غيره إلّا أنّ أوْلى الأشياء بأن [18]يُظنّ بها أنّ فيها نظاماً إمّا من الأشياء المحسوسة [19]فالأجرام السماويّة وإمّا من سائر الأشياء — إلّا أن تكون هذه متقدّمة [20]لتلك — فالتعاليم فإنّ هذه وإن لم تكن كلّها [21]على نظام فأكثرها كذلك إلّا أن يعتقد معتقد [22]ما كان يعتقده ديموقريطس فى صور [23]الأجزاء التى لا تتجزّأ إلّا أنّ هذا أمر [24]ينبغى أن نبحث عنه فأمّا ما قلناه منذ أوّل الأمر فقد ينبغى أن نلتمس [25]حدّاً ما فى الطبيعة وفى [26]جوهر الكلّ ولِمَا هو من أجل شىء [27]وللحركة إلى الأمر الأفضل **(25)** فإنّ هذا مبدأ [1]النظر فى الكلّ وننظر أيضاً فى أىّ الأشياء وجود 12a
الموجودات وكيف [2]حالها بعضها عند بعض

---

12 نجد read. Crub.[2] : نحد T : بجد B : تجد read. Alon **14** ذكرنا T : ذكرناه B **15** هذه read. Marg. : هده T : بعده *sic* B : هذا Alon | لم T : om. B **16** تبعت read. Alon, T (w.p.) : يبعث B **18** يظن read. Crub.[2], T (w.p.) {B} : نظن read. Alon **20** فالتعاليم corr. Gutas* (τὰ μαθηματικά; cf. 4a18, 9a16) : بالعلم T {B} : فالتعليم Crub.[2] : بالتعلم Alon **22** ديموقريطس read. Alon, T (w.p.) : دموفريطس B **23** تتجزأ read. Alon : سحرا T : سحرى B best, but since he *is* in a position [to do so as well,[206] they say] that he would not wish that at all since their entire substance would come to be eliminated as a result, given that it is from contrary things and in contrary things.

(24.2) We also find among the first [things] many things attached [to them] by way of chance, like the changes[207] we mentioned that happen in the earth, for neither the best was intended by these nor were they effected for the sake of anything, but rather they concomitantly follow some leading necessity.[208] We find in the air their likes and others in other things. However, the thing that is most deserving to be thought of as having order is either the heavenly bodies among sensible things, or[209] the mathematicals[210] among the rest of the things—unless these are prior to the former. For even if not all of these possess order, yet most of them do—unless one believes what Democritus used to believe about the forms of atoms—though this is something on which we ought to do research.[211] As for what we said from the very beginning, we ought to search for some boundary in[212] nature and in the substance of the universe, and for what is for the sake of something and for the movement toward the best, (25) for this is the starting point of the theoretical investigation into 12a
the universe; and we also [ought to] investigate in which things beings exist and how they relate to one another.

---

206 The Arabic has, *lākin iḏ kāna bihī ayḍan*; see *WKAS* I,452 for *kāna bihī*.

207 "The changes," *at-taġāyīr*, most likely translates Greek τὰς μεταβολάς so that it can be assumed that the text in Ψ read, τὰ περὶ τὰς τῆς γῆς λεχθέντα μεταβολάς. See the discussion of this passage in Part I, Chapter 2.1, in the section on "Sub-family Σ".

208 Literally, "some necessary leader," though it is clear from the context that "leader" (*imām*) is not to be taken anthropomorphically.

209 The translation of a simple μέν … δέ construction with only two items in the series by *immā … wa-immā* is not widely attested; see *GALex* I,354, § 5.2.

210 Isḥāq clearly understood the structure and meaning of the sentence; accordingly, the manuscript reading of *bi-t-taʿallum* (though unpointed in manuscript T, بالعلم; B is lacunose at this point) needs to be corrected. Crubellier effected the first correction, changing the initial particle from *bi-* to *fa-*, to coordinate it with *fa-l-ajrām* in the preceding clause, and *taʿallum* to *taʿlīm* to designate mathematics. However, in other passages in this work (see the Glossary) Isḥāq uses properly the plural form, *taʿālīm*, to denote mathematics, so this correction is also necessary.

211 Isḥāq properly took this last sentence as completing the previous paragraph; see the commentary.

212 "In," *fī*, here means, as it normally does, "in" in the sense of "with respect to," which is quite unambiguous, *pace* Repici 1900, 191n22.

[تمّت مقالة ثاوفرسطس القيّم بحجج ارسطوطالس فى ما بعد الطبيعة ⟨بـ⟩ترجمة إسحاق

وكتبتها أنا يحيى بن جرير المتطبّب التكريتى من نسخة سقيمة بميفرقين سنة ٤٦١ ولله الحمد

قوبل بها من أصلها وكان سقيماً جدّاً]

Colophon ⟨بـ⟩ترجمة add. Gutas

[Colophon]

The treatise by Theophrastus, the advocate of Aristotle's arguments in metaphysics, ⟨in⟩ the translation by Isḥāq, is finished.

I, Yaḥyā ibn-Jarīr, the physician from Tikrīt, transcribed it from a corrupt copy, in Mayyāfāriqīn in the year 461. Praise be to God.

It was collated with its exemplar, which was very corrupt.

2A. SUPPLEMENTARY CRITICAL APPARATUS TO THE ARABIC TEXT

The following apparatus contains readings in the texts edited by Margoliouth and Alon that are not included in the main critical apparatus; see Part I, Chapter 3.4. The sigla and signs used are the same as those in the main apparatus.

4a20 بالجملة T B : فى الجملة Marg. **21b** نحن T B : om. Marg.

4b8 والاولى T : واولى Alon **13** فى T {B} : مع Alon **22** هو T B : om. Alon

5a2 اليه T B : التى Marg. **3** وعنها T B : وعنه Alon : عنها Marg. | الحركة الدورية T B : حركة الدور Marg. **5** يكون T {B} : om. Alon | after ايضا add. باطلا Alon **24a** الاكرّ read. Alon **25a** first تطلب T {B} : تطالب Alon

5b2 تكون T {B} : فتكون Alon **6** انها T {B} : انه Alon **9** واقدم T (w.p.) {B} : وامدح Alon **18**[1] **24** كانه T B : كانها Marg.

6a1 ايضا T B : om. Alon | لانه T B : om. Alon **5** ان T {B} : om. Alon | يسير او T (w.p.) : سير ان الكلام فى هذا الكلام فى : T B ان الكلام فى هذا المعنى Marg. | لقائل : T B بقائل **14** Alon يسيرا او : B او هذا المعنى Alon **17** دفعة B, T (w.p.) : وقعة Marg. **22** غيرهما T B : غيرها Alon

6b1 لا تناهى T B : هى Alon[2] **4** فاما T {B} : واما Alon **6** and **19** خلاء Alon instead of خلا **20** بذلك T B : فذلك Alon

7a2 خلاء Alon instead of خلا **16** اصغر T {B} : احقر Alon | مثلا T {B} : ومثلا Alon **17** للنفس T {B} : النفس Alon **20** نرد T {B} : نؤد Alon

7b9 وهى T {B} : om. Alon **20** يشهد T (w.p.) {B} : شهد Alon **22** يرد T (w.p.) {B} : يؤد Alon **23** نفسه T {B} : om. Alon

8a3 ترد T (w.p.) {B} : يؤد Alon | حر له (i.e., جزء له) T {B} : حركة Alon **4** ان تكون T {B} : om. Alon | اتفاق T (w.p.) {B} : اتقان Alon **6** او T {B} : و Alon **7** الكمال T (τελεώτατον) {B} : الجمال Alon **14a** الامر T B : الامور Alon **18** عن T {B} : على Alon **26** وهو T B : om. Alon

---

[1] Frequently Alon is given to blaming the translator (Isḥāq) for his own misreadings or misunderstandings. In this case, he misreads *li-l-irtibāṭ* as *li-l-awsāṭ*, and says, "The Arabic *lil-awsāṭ* is Isḥāq's addition, which hardly makes this sentence any clearer" p. 189, note 41.

[2] Though the translation is correct: "the infinite."

8b4 السود T B : الاسود Marg. **9** واما T B : فاما Alon **11** ويبحث T (w.p.) : وسحث B : ويفحص Alon **14** وان T B : ان Alon

9a3 الاشخاص T B : اشخاص Marg. **21** second بالمقايسة T {B} : المقايسة Alon

9b10 الاطراف T B : الاطراق Alon **13** في T {B} : هي في Alon **25** يذكرون T {B} : يذكروا Alon

10a20 متحرك T (w.p.) {B} : محرك Alon **22** انها T {B} : om. Alon **25** ايها T (w.p.), B : اين Alon | فانا T (w.p.), B : فاما Alon

10b2 عنها T {B} : منها Alon **12** ان T {B} : أن إن Alon **17** به T B : له Marg.

11a3 يميل T (w.p.), B : يجعل Alon **19** يسيرة T (w.p.), B : يسير Alon **20** وخروج T B : وحرف Alon **25** وما T B : و om. Marg.

11b4 first عن T B : om. Marg. **8** العلة T B : om. Alon[3] | يقولون T (w.p.), B : يقبلون Alon **12** وقد T B : فقد Alon **15** ولا T : B unclear : وان Marg.

12a2 عند T {B} : مع Alon

colophon تمت T {B} : om. Alon | بميفرقين T (w.p.) {B} : om. Alon

---

[3] Alon even adds a note (135) saying that "the Arabic text omits to translate the Greek *aitia* (cause)"!

3. THE LATIN TRANSLATION BY BARTHOLOMEW OF MESSINA

INTRODUCTION

Bartholomew's Latin translation of the Essay, which survives in a single manuscript in Padua, Antoniana XVII 370, ff. 62^r–64^r, was published in a diplomatic edition by Kley 1936, 3–13, with a slight philological commentary (14–28). Because of its significance for the establishment of the Greek text (see above, Part I, Chapter 2.4), and in order to provide in one volume all the evidence regarding it, I am copying it here. As a diplomatic edition, Kley's text reproduced exactly the wording, spelling, capitalization, and punctuation in the manuscript. Not having seen the manuscript myself, but also because of the nature of the slavishly literal translation, I have thought it best to print the text here as published by Kley except for the following features which are intended to enhance the usefulness of the Latin translation for the student of the Greek text of Theophrastus.

I have eliminated all periods from the text which, according to Kley, are to be found in the manuscript, because they are randomly and erroneously placed and hamper the reading of the text. I have, however, not introduced any punctuation or capitalization, but rather divided the text into my numbered aporiae of the original Greek and introduced Usener's line numbers for easy reference. Finally, Most 1988c, who collated the manuscript against Kley's edition, found a few mistaken transcriptions (p. 170n6), and I have accordingly incorporated his corrections into the text. None of this changes the text from being an exact copy of that in the manuscript.

The Latin text presented as such here is adequate for the purpose of providing evidence for the establishment of the Greek text. The Latin translation, however, may also deserve treatment in its own right and a proper edition, but for this it would be necessary to consult the Padua manuscript, something that could not have been undertaken in the present work. For the same reason, it would have been incautious to have added a Latin and Greek glossary without having first ascertained the readings in the manuscript and their status in the transmission of the text. But given the extremely literal nature of the translation, any Greek-Latin or Latin-Greek correspondence can be easily identified by reference to Usener's page and line numbers that I have introduced into the Latin text. Finally, in order to facilitate the understanding of the Latin text for our present purposes, but without any pretense to providing a critical apparatus, in a very light annotation I have merely registered some indispensable notes and corrections, some of which were made by Kley and Most and others by me. Matteo Di Giovanni had the kindness, amid a very busy personal schedule, to read through the Latin translation in Kley and offer some further suggestions, which I gratefully incorporate in the annotation (with the abbreviation MDG).

{62ʳ} Incipit

LIBER ARISTOTELIS DE PRINCIPIIS

translatus de greco in latinum a magistro bartholomeo de messana in curia illustrissimi maynfredi serenissimi regis Sicilie scientie amatoris de mandato suo

(1) [2]Quomodo determinare oportet et quibus speculationem que est de 4a
[3]primis que enim utique est natura multiplex est [4]et ut quidam utique aiunt ingenita [5]transmutationes habens omnimodas que autem est primorum [6]determinata et semper secundum eadem propter quod utique et in intelligibilibus [7]non sensibilibus ipsam posuerunt sicut immobilibus [8]et intransmutabilibus et universaliter autem venerabiliorem et [9]maiorem cogitant ipsam

(2) Utrum autem principio contactus [10]quis et ut communicatio ad se invicem [11]intelligibilibus et hiis que sunt nature aut nullus sed quemadmodum [12]utraque separata cooperantia autem quodam in [13]omnem substantiam rationabilius autem igitur est esse quendam [14]contactum et non confusum universum sed ut [15]hec quidem priora hec vero posteriora et principia hec autem [16]sub principiis sicut et sempiterna corruptibilibus

(3) [17]Si autem igitur ita est que est natura ipsorum et in [18]quibus si quidem enim in mathematicis solum [19]intelligibilia quemadmodum quidam aiunt neque valde bene designatus [20]et contactus sensibilibus neque omnino inutilia [21]videntur ab universo ut enim excogitate [22]videntur per nos esse figure et forme et [23]rationes circumponentium ipsa autem per se
ipsa nullam [2]habent naturam si autem non non sicut copulare [3]eis que 4b
sunt nature ut fac sicut vita [4]et motus ipsa neque enim ipse numerus [5]quem utique primum et principalissimum quidam posuerunt

---

4a 3 natura *cod.* (*Kley*) : nature *legendum* (φύσεως; *cf. Kley p. 16 ad loc.*) ‖ 20 et *cod.* : est *legendum* (*cf. Kley p. 16 ad loc.*) **4b** 3 fac *cod.*: facere *prop. Kley, MDG*

(4) [6]si autem altera quedam substantia prima et melior est [7]hanc temptandum dicere utrum una quedam secundum [8]numerum aut secundum speciem aut secundum genus rationabilius [9]autem dicetur principii naturam habentes in paucis [10]esse et imparibus si non quia primis et [11]primo

(5) quod autem igitur hoc et que sed plura [12]temptandum manifestare verum quodam modo [13]sive secundum aliam similitudinem necesse autem fortassis [14]potentia quadam et excellentia aliorum accipere [15]quemadmodum utique quid divinum divinum enim omnium principium [16]per quod omnia et sunt et permanent fortassis quidem [17]igitur facile ita assignare difficile autem manifestius [18]aut credibilius

(5.1) tali autem existente [19]principio quum autem copulat se sensibilibus [20]natura autem ut simpliciter dicere in motu et hoc est [21]ipsius proprium manifestum ut causam ponendum ipsum [22]motus quum autem immobile secundum se ipsum manifestum [23]quod non utique erit in movendo eis
5a que sunt nature [1]causa sed alii cuidam potentie meliori [2]et priori talis autem aut appetibilis natura [3]aqua circularis continua et [4]irrequieta quare secundum illud solveretur utique non esse [5]motus principio aut si motum movebit

(6) usque ad [6]hec utique ut par sermo principio [7]faciens unum omnium et actum et [8]substantiam assignans amplius autem neque divisibile neque quantum [9]quid dicens sed simpliciter auferens in meliorem quandam [10]particulam et diviniorem sic enim magis assignandum [11]quam divisibile et partibile auferendum [12]simul enim in altiori et veriori ratione [13]dicentibus negatio quod autem post hec [14]utique ratione indiget multa de desiderio [15]quale et quorum quum autem et plura circumlaria et [16]motus quodam modo subcontrarii et inutile [17]et cuius gratia inmanifestum sive enim unum movens, inconveniens [18]non omnia secundum idem sive secundum unumquodque alterum [19]principia enim plura quare consonum ipsorum in [20]appetitum euntium optimum minime manifestum (7) que [21]autem secundum multitidinem sperarum causa maiorem [22]querit rationem neque enim que est astrologorum

---

4b11 sed *cod.* (*Kley*) : si *prop. Kley* ‖ 12 *post* modo ⟨sive secundum analogiam⟩ *legendum* (εἴτε κατ᾽ ἀναλογίαν; *cf. infra 9a7*); *cf. Kley p. 17 ad loc.* **5a** 3 a qua *legendum; cf. infra 5b4* 4 solveretur *cod.* : solvetur *prop. MDG* ‖ 15 circumlaria *Kley* (*cod.?*) : circularia *legendum* (*cf. infra 5b11*) ‖ 21 multitidinem *sic cod. pro* multitudinem (*MDG*) | causa *cod.* (*Kley*) : cause *prop. Kley*

(8) [23]dubium autem et quomodo [24]naturalem appetitum quandoque habentia non quietem persequuntur [25]sed motum quid igitur simul immitationi [26]aiunt illud similiter quicumque unum et quicumque numerum [27]dicunt et enim ipsi numeros [28]aiunt unum

(8.1) si utique desiderium aliter et [1]optimi cum anima nisi aliquis dicat 5b
secundum similitudinem [2]et differentiam animata utique erunt que moventur [3]anima autem simul videtur et secundum motum inesse vita enim [4]habentibus a qua et appetitus ad unumquodque [5]quemadmodum et animalibus quia et sensus [6]quamvis in patiendo {62^{v}} existens per alia tamen amati [7]fiunt si igitur circularis causa est [8]primum non utique optime erit melior enim que [9]anime et prima utique et maxime que intellectus [10]a quo appetitus

(9) fortassis autem et hoc utique [11]quis inquiret propter quid circularia solum desiderativa [12]eorum autem que sunt circa medium nullum quamvis mobilibus existentibus [13]utro sicut impossibilia aut sicut non accedentia [14]ad primum sed hoc est inconveniens si per inbeccillitatem [15]fortius enim utique quis dignificabit homeri [16]jove sicut ait

[17]ipsa quidem terra librabit ipsa in mari

[18]sed igitur sicut inreceptibile quid et incompositum esse

(10) [19]fortassis autem primo inquiret utique aliquis quomodo se habet utrum [20]partes hec aut non partes celi et si [21]partes quomodo partes nunc enim remota a [22]dignissimis non solum secundum regiones sed [23]secundum actionem si quidem circularis huius contingit [24]secundum accidens a circulari [25]circulatione et in loca et in advicem [26]transmutationes

(10.1) si autem et optimum ab [27]optimo melius utique aliquid de primo
indigeat [28]circumallatione non igitur prohiberetur non posse [1]recipere 6a
primum enim utique et divinissimum omnia [2]optima volens forte autem hoc quidem ut [3]transcendens quid et investigabile dignificat enim qui hoc [4]dicit omnia similia et in perfectis esse [5]parvam quandam aut neque unam habentia differentiam (11) hoc autem [6]dubitabit utique aliquis fortassis apud ipsum primum [7]celum referens utrum circulatio substantie

---

5b 6 a⟨ni⟩mati *legendum; cf. supra 5b2* animata (ἔμψυχ’) ‖ 14 inbecillitatem *MDG* **6a** 3 ⟨in⟩investigabile *legendum* (ἀζήτητον) ‖ 5 hoc *cod.* : hic *in marg.* (*Kley*)

[8]est ipsius et simul in quiescendo corumpetur [9]aut si desiderio quodam et appetitu secundum accidens [10]si non igitur conatum ipsi appetere [11]et nichil prohibet talia quedam entium existere **(12)** [12]forte autem utique erit et auferentem appetitum [13]de ipso motu dubitare si ablata [14]corumpet utique celum

(13) et hoc quidem sicut [15]ab aliis rationibus assignare de hac aut ab hiis [16]principiis dignificabit utique aliquis fortassis autem et ab [17]aliis utrum utique aliquis ponit que consequuntur confestim assignare [18]et non usque hoc adveniens pausare [19]hoc enim perfecti et sapientis quod architas [20]aliquando ait amplum disponentem quosdam numeros [21]dicere enim sicut hic quidem hominis numerus [22]hic autem equi hic vero alius cuiusdam existit [23]nunc autem multi usque ad aliquid venientes quiescunt [24]quemadmodum et qui unum et indefinitam [25]dualitatem facientes numeros enim generantes [26]et superficiem et corpora fere alia [27]praeter-
6b mittunt nisi quantum tangentes et tantum [28]solum manifestantes quum hec quidem ab indefinita [1]dualitate ut locus et ricuum et infinitum [2]hoc autem a numeris et uno ut anima [3]et alia quedam tempus autem simul et celum et [4]alia quedam plura de celo autem et reliquis [5]neque unam utique faciunt mentionem similiter autem neque [6]circa peusippum neque aliorum nullus nisi [7]xenocrates iste enim omnimode circumponit [8]circa mundum similiter sensibilia et intelligibilia et [9]mathematica et adhuc utique divina temptat autem et [10]est quod usque ad aliquid non sicut dictum est de [11]primis solum plato quidem igitur in reducendo [12]ad principia [14]deinde secundum [15]generationem usque ad dicta hii autem [16]principiorum solum quidam autem et veritatem in [17]hiis entia enim solum circa principia accidit [18]autem e contrario quam in aliis methodis [19]in illis enim que sunt post principia fortiora [20]sciens forte autem et [21]rationabiliter ubi quidem enim principiorum in [22]reliquis autem a principiis questio

(14) [23]quomodo autem quandoque congruit et qualia principia supponi [24]fortassis utique dubitabit aliquis utrum informia [25]et ut potentiales quemadmodum quicumque ignem et [26]terram aut formata ut maxime convenienter hec [27]terminari sicut in timeo ait [28]honoratissumis namque

---

8 corrumpetur (*MDG*) ‖ 10 connatum (*MDG*) ‖ 27 tantum *cod.* (*Most*) : tant (*Kley*) **6b** 6 peusippum *cod.* (*Kley*) : Speusippum *legendum* (*cf. infra 11a23*) | numerus *post* aliorum *expunctum in cod.* (*Kley*) ‖ 12–14 *post* principia *lac.* (*e homoeoteleuton*) *ind. Kley* ‖ 28 honoratissumis *cod.* (*Most*) : honoratissimis *corr. Kley* (*cf. 11a12*)

valde propria ordinatio et terminari [1]videtur autem et in reliquis fere 7a
habere [2]ita quemadmodum gramatica et musica et [3]mathematicis consequitur autem et que post [4]principia amplius autem et secundum artes similiter [5]que quidem naturam imitantur et instrumenta et [6]alia secundum principia hii quidem omnia formata [7]hii vero solum materialia hii autem utraque [8]formata et que materie sicut in utrisque [9]perfectum ut enim ex oppositis [10]universam substantiam

(14.1) irrationale illis videbitur utique [11]si quidem totum celum et singule partium [12]omnes {63[r]} in ordinatione et ratione et formis et potentiis [13]et periodis in principiis autem nichil [14]tale sed quemadmodum caro si confusorum [15]pulcherimus ait heraclitus mundus et [16]secundum minimum autem ut dicere accipiunt similiter [17]in animamatis et animatis determinate singulorum [18]nature ut dicere quamvis a casu factorum [19]principia autem indefinita esse

(14.2) difficile autem [20]iterum hoc rationes singulis circumponi [21]ad propter aliquid congregantes in omnibus et in [22]animalibus et plantis et in ipsa ampulla nisi [23]secundum accidens aliorum ordinatione et trans-
mutatione formas [1]omnimodas et varietate fieri eorum que sunt circa 7b
[2]aerem et terram quorum utique maximum quidam exemplum [3]faciunt que circa tempora causas [4]in quibus et in animalium et plantarum et fructuum [5]generationes ut generante sole

(15) et hec [6]quidem hic ibi inquirunt considerationem determinationem [7]expetentia usque quo ordinatum et propter [8]quid plus impossibile si ad peius transitio **(16)** [9]in principiis autem unde utique et prima ratio [10]convenienter utique quis et quod est de quiete dubitabit [11]si quidem enim ut melius reducet utique [12]principiis si autem ut otium et privatio motus [13]non reducet sed si quidem actionem transmutandi [14]sicut priorem et honorabiliorem motum autem [15]in sensibilibus quum propter hoc [16]quiescere sicut impossibile semper movens esse [17]non enim utique erit primum periculum non [18]in speciem rationis et aliter non fide dignum sed maiorem [19]causam querit

---

7a 16 secundum *cod.* (*Most*) : secundam (*Kley*) ‖ 17 animamatis *cod.* (*Most*) : aniamatis (*Kley*) : inanimatis *legendum* (ἀψύχοις; *cf. 10b22*) **7b** 1 *fort.* varietate⟨s⟩ *legendum* (ποικιλίας) ‖ 8 tus (tus *Most* : ctus *Kley*) *post* peius *expunctum in cod.* (*Kley*)

(**16.1**) videtur autem et sensus quodammodo [20]consonare sicut contingens non oportet movens [21]alterum esse et quod movet propter agere [22]et pati amplius autem si quis agit ad ipsum [23]intellectum et deum

8a (**16.2**) inconveniens autem et alterum dictum [1]aut non mictantur adpetentia quiescentem [2]si enim ipsis entibus consequetur aliorum [3]verum fortassis non similiter sicut impartibile [4]agentes sed quomodo quum maxime consonum ipsi [5]et dependens sicut multum ut animal aut aliquid [6]aliud partibilium aut et totum celum quod utique [7]aiunt esse perfectissimum

(**17**) [8]querunt autem quedam et huius rationem quomodo [9]quandoque eorum que sunt partitio in materiam et formam [10]utrum sicut ens potentia [11]autem unum et ductum in actionem aut ens quidem [12]indefinitum autem quemadmodum in artibus generatio autem [13]substantia autem ipsorum in formando secundum [14]rationes sed ita autem in melius quidem [15]forte utique transitio erit esse autem nichil [16]minus verum existit secundum se ipsum non enim utique [17]neque fieret non existente sed neque hoc [18]neque quantum sicut indefinitum speciebus [19]potentiam autem quandam habens universaliter autem secundum rationem [20]sumendum ad artes et si qua alia similitudo

(**18**) [21]videbitur autem et hoc habere dubitationem nisi [22]quia otiositas inquirere quia utique natura [23]et tota substantia universi in contrariis est [24]et fere eque participat peius meliori magis [25]autem et multo magis est quod videtur et [26]euripedes universaliter dicere quod

non utique fieret [27]seorsum bona

8b talis autem sermo prope [1]inquirere est quod non omnia bona neque omnia similia [2]et quod de omnibus esse dicimus nichil [3]simile ad invicem quemadmodum alba et [4]nigra in se ipsis

(**18.1**) amplius autem quod videbitur inopinalius [5]sicut non possibile ens absque contrariis

7b20 20 oportet *cod.* (*Most*) : omne (*Kley*) **8a** 1 aut *cod.* (*Kley*) : ut *legendum* (ὡς) | mictantur *cod.* (*Kley*) : imitantur *legendum* (μιμοῦνται) ‖ 5 ut *Kley* (*cod.?*) : aut *legendum* ‖ 10 τὸ δὲ μὴ ὄν *om. Lat. e homoeotel.* **8b** 4 quod] d *expunctum in cod.* (Most)

(18.2) [6]qui autem pluri inopinabili utentes et [7]non ens non autem factum neque futurum connumerant [8]in universi naturam sed hec quidem ut [9]suprascendens aliqua sapientia ens autem quum multipliciter [10]manifestum sensus enim et differentias [11]considerat et causas querit forte autem verius [12]dicere sicut suprascendit intellectui hec quidem [13]simpliciter querens hec autem dubitationem operans [14]per quam quamvis non possit procedere tamen apparet [15]quedam lux in non luce querentibus [16]in plus scire quum non absque differentia [17]aliqua sive enim alia ad invicem differentia [18]aliqua in hiis que sunt pluribus entibus eis que sunt sub [19]universali differre necesse et hec sive [20]genera universalia sive species

(18.3) fere autem et omnis scientia [21]propriorum substantia enim et quod [22]quid erat esse unumquodque proprium que videntur [23]secundum sit si quid de [24]aliquo

(18.4) universaliter autem quod in pluribus idem simul videre [25]scientie
aut comuni et secundum quod dicitur [26]aut propria unumquodque quo-
dam modo singulis ut numeris lineis [27]animalibus plantis finis autem ex
utrisque sunt autem [1]quedam eorum quidem que sunt universalia finis 9a
in hoc enim [2]causa quod autem est in parte secundum quecumque divi-
sio [3]in athoma quemadmodum in practicis et factis [4]sic enim ipsorum
actio idem autem scimus [5]et substantia et numero et specie et genere
[6]et proportione et si quum circa hec {63[v]} divisione [7]plurimum autem
quod secundum anologiam sicut distantia [8]plurimum hec quidem per
nos ipsos hec autem [9]per subiectum hec vero per utraque

(19) [10]multipliciter autem existente scire quomodo singula [11]persequendum principium autem et maximum proprius [12]modus sicut prima et intelligibilia et mobilia [13]et secundum naturam ipsorum horum que in principio [14]et consequentia usque ad animalia et plantas et ultima [15]inanimamata est enim aliquid secundum unumquodque genus [16]proprium quemadmodum in mathematicis habent [17]autem et ipse discipline differentiam unius [18]generis quodam modo entes divisum est autem suf-

---

7 connumerant *cod.* (*Most*) : conumerant (*Kley*) ‖ 9 multipliciter *cod.* (*Most*) : muti- (*Kley*) ‖ 23 *post* secundum *lac. ind. Kley* ‖ 25 communi (*MDG*) **9a** 7 anologiam *cod.* (Most) : analogiam *corr. Kley* ‖ 15 inanimamata *cod.* (Most) : inaniamata (*Kley*) : inanimata *legendum* (*v. supra ad 7a17*)

ficienter si autem et quedam [19]nota in existendo ignota quemadmodum quidam aiunt [20]proprius utique modus erit divisione autem quadam indigent [21]fortassis autem in quibus contingit secundum anologiam proprius [22]dicere aut ipso ignoto sicut [23]si quis invisibili visibile

(20b) [26]difficilius autem utique videbitur [27a]non enim possibile univer-
9b sale in [1a]multipliciter dictis [27b]et comune quid accipere **(20c1)** [1b]aut et hoc
[2]dubium aut non facile dicere usque quo et [3]quorum querendum causas similiter in sensibilibus [4]et intelligibilibus via enim in infinitum [5]in utrisque aliena et interimens sapere [6]principium autem quodam modo utrumque fortassis autem hec quidem nobis [7]hec autem simpliciter aut hic quidem finis hec vero nostrum quoddam [8]principio usque ad aliquid quidem igitur possumus per causas [9]considerare principia a sensibus accipientes [10]quando autem ad ipsa extrema et prima transcendimus [11]non amplius possumus sive propter id quod non habemus causas [12]aut propter nostram imbecillitatem quemadmodum [13]ad lucidissima videre fortassis autem illud [14]verius sicut ipso intellectu [15]consideratio habenti et ut tangenti propter quod non [16]est fallatia circa ipsa **(20c2)** difficilis autem et in hoc [17]ipsum et intellectus et fides quum aut et aliter magnum [18]et ad secundum singula negotia necessarium [19]et maxime maxima in quodam faciendum [20]diffinitionem ut de natura et circa adhuc [21]priora qui enim omnium querentes rationem interimunt [22]rationem simul autem et scire magis autem [23]verius dicere quum querunt quorum non est [24]neque aptum natum est quicumque celum perpetuum arbitrantur [25]amplius autem que secundum motus et [26]magnitudines et figuras
10a et distantias et [27]quecumque alia astrologia demonstrant hec reliquerunt
[1]prima autem moventia et cuius causa dicere [2]et que est natura uniuscuiusque et que [5]ad animalia et planta

(21) astrologia quidem igitur [6]cooperatur quidem non in primis nature [7]altera principalissima utique [8]et modus ut opinantur quidam non fisicus aut [9]non omnis et etiam moveri et universaliter [10]nature proprium et maxime celi propter quod et [11]actio uniuscuiusque [12]quando agit et movetur quemadmodum in [13]animalibus et plantis si autem non equi-

19 nota in *cod.* (Most) : notam (Kley) ‖ 21 anologiam *cod.* (*Most*) : analogiam *corr. Kley* ‖ 23 invi *post* quis *expunctum in cod.* (*Most*) ‖ 23–26 πόσοι … ἐπίστασθαι *om. Lat.* **9b** 16 fallatia *cod.* (*Most*) : fallacia (*Kley*) ‖ 27 demonstrat (*MDG*) **10a** 2–5 *post* et que (πρὸς ἄλληλα … μερῶν) *lac.* (*e homoeoteleuton*) *ind. Kley* ‖ 7–8 *post* utique (εἴη … δὴ) *lac.* (*e homoeoteleuton*) *indicavi* ‖ 11 τῆς οὐσίας *om. Lat.* | καὶ τὸ καθ' ἕκαστον *om. Lat.*

voca manifestum quum [14]quamvis celum in circulatione secundum substantiam [15]erit separatum autem et quiescens equivocum ut [16]enim anima quedam circulatio universi utrum sive [17]nichil animalibus vitam utique querendum [18]neque in celo et celestibus motum [19]aut secundum aliquem modum diffinitum copulat autem quodam modo que est [20a]nunc dubitatio dubitationem et ad [21]motum [20b]ab immobili

(**22**) [22]de omnibus autem propter aliquid et nichil frustra [23]sed ut determinatio non facilis quemadmodum [24]multociens dicitur Unde autem incipere congruit et in [25]qualia finire et iam quedam in eo quod non videntur habere [26]ita sed hec quidem contingenter hec vero neccessitate [27]quadam sicut in celestibus et in hiis que sunt [28]circa terram pluribus

(**22.1**) cuius autem causa egressus [1]sursum discutiones maris aut cuius 10b
inundationes [2]aut desiccationes et humiditates [3]et universaliter ad aliud transmutationes et [4]corruptiones generationes aut quidem in ipsa terra alterationes [5]et transmutationes fiunt ad aliud [6]transmutatis et alia non pauca similia [7]hiis

(**22.2**) amplius autem in ipsis animalibus hec quidem ut [8]frustra sicut maribus mamme et [9]feminis emissio si quidem non conferunt [10]et generativus quibusdam aut omnino pilorum ortus in [11]aliquibus locis amplius autem cornuum magnitudines sicut [12]cervus [15]et per unum diem vivere et alia non pauca [16]accipiet quis utique talia et maximum utique et maxime [17]videtur circa alimenta et generationes [18]animalium nullius enim hec causa sed sinthomata [19]et per alias neccessitates oportebat enim si horum gratia [20]semper secundum hec et similiter

(**22.3**) amplius autem in [21]plantis et maxime inanimatis determinatam quandam [22]habentes naturam sicut videntur in formis et [23]speciebus et potentiis cuius causa {64^{r}} hec queret [24]utique (**23**) ipsum enim hoc indubitabile non habere [25]rationem et hec in aliis non facientibus [26]et honorabilioribus quam videtur ratio habere [27]aliquid credibile ut quia acasu hec et [28]circulatione totius accipit aliquas ydeas aut ad invicem 11a
[1]differentias

10b 2 humiditates *cod.* (Most) : humoritates (Kley) ‖ 12–15 τοῖσδε … ὀχεύει *non vert. Lat.; cf. Kley p. 26 ad loc.*

(24) si autem non hoc causa huius et [2]in optimum sumendum quorundam terminos et non in [3]omnibus simpliciter ponendi quum et huius habent [4]aliquam dibietatem et universaliter dicta singulariter [5]universaliter quidem quia natura in omnibus [6]appetit optimum et in quibus contingit [7]tradere id quod semper et ordinatum ut [8]hoc autem et in animalibus similiter ubi enim possibile est [9]medius hic nequaquam deficit ut [10]anterius guttur ysofago honorabilius [11]autem et in medio ventre cordis [12]complexionem optimam quum medium honoratissimum [13]similiter autem et quecumque ornatus gratia si enim [14]appatitus ita sed illud autem manifestat propter hoc quia multum [15]quod non obedit neque recipiens bene [16]autem multo magis paucum autem quid animatum [17]infinitum autem inanimatum et ipsorum animatorum [18]modicum et melius esse universaliter autem rarum [19]aliquod et in paucis bonum multa autem multitudo [20]est malum non autem infinitas solum et sicut [21]materie specie sicut nature indisciplinate [22]si enim et de universa substantia dicentes [23]sicut speusippus rarum quid honoratum [24]facit quod circa medii regionem extrema autem [25]et utrinque que quidem igitur entia bene existunt [26]entia

11b (24.1) [27]plato vero et pithagorii longinquam [1]distantiam inmutari autem volunt omnia [2]et quemadmodum compositionem quandam faciunt indefinite [3]dualitatis et unius in quo et infinitum [4]et inordinatum et omnis ut dicere informitas secundum [5]se ipsam universaliter autem non est possibile absque hac totius [6]naturam sed ut eque participare aut et super excellere [7]alteram aut et principia contraria propter quod et neque [8]deum quicumque deo causam attribuunt posse [9]omnes in optimum ducere sed in [10]quantum contingit forte autem neque utique eliget si quidem [11]interimi contingit universam substantiam ex contrariis [12]autem et in contrariis existentem

(24.2) videtur autem [13]et in primis visa multa et ut [14]contingit ut que circa terram dicta secundum transmutationes [15]neque enim optimum neque cuius gratia [16]sed si necessitatem quandam consequi multa autem [17]et in aere huius et in aliis maxime autem [18]videbitur habere ordinationem sensibilium quidem [19]celestia aliorum autem nisi et priora [20]mathematicis si enim et non omne sed [21]in hiis plus ordinatum nisi si quis huius

---

11a 4 dubietatem (*MDG*) ‖ 14 appatitus (*Kley*) : appetitus *legendum* (*cf. supra 5b9*) ‖ 21 indisciplinate *cod.* (Most) : indissi- (Kley) **11b** 1 inmutari *cod.* (*Kley*) : imitari *prop. Kley*

[22]accipiat formas quales democritus supponit [23]atomorum sed de hiis
[24]perscruptandum temptandum quod in principium dictum quendam
[25]accipere terminum et in natura et in [26]universisubstantia et huius causa
et in [27]melius motus (**25**) hoc enim principio [1]universi considerationis in 12a
quibus entia et quomodo se [2]habent ad invicem

Explicit

---

24 perscrutandum (*MDG*) ‖ 27 principio] o *exstinctum in cod.* (Kley).

PART III

COMMENTARY

Introduction

The commentary is structured by the Aporiae. Each Aporia is introduced by its extent, given in the page, column, and line numbers of Usener, followed in parentheses by the Greek word or words which identify the question asked in the Aporia, separating it from the rest (see Part I, Chapter 1.4 and notes 62–64). Then follows a paraphrase of the Aporia and the succeeding Diaporiae (if there are any) in italics, with my additional explanatory remarks in parentheses. Whenever not immediately apparent from the paraphrase, the structure and argument of each Aporia and the succeeding Diaporiae are then analyzed in Roman type, followed by pertinent bibliographical references. Comments on the individual words, phrases, and sentences in the body of the Aporia and the Diaporiae are then introduced by the line number in which they occur.

The philosophical context in which *On First Principles* was written and to which it refers is crucial to its understanding. To that end, but also to avoid prolixity and repetition here, the Loci Paralleli have been provided as a study aid in the upper apparatus of the Greek text. Although typographically distinct, they nevertheless constitute an integral part of the Commentary and should be consulted in all cases.

There are several general presentations of the Essay, mostly of an expository nature with different degrees of bibliographical documentation: Brandis 1860, 325–343; Usener 1861; Zeller 1879, II,2, 821–829 (English translation pp. 364–372); Regenbogen 1940, 1389–1395; Wehrli / Wöhrle / Zhmud 2004, 518–519, 541–544. Others offer and defend a particular perspective on the entire Essay, ranging from one of adherence to or criticism of views in the Old Academy to adherence to or criticism of Aristotelian positions. These should be consulted throughout and they can be listed more profitably here than referred to repeatedly under specific passages in the commentary below: Festugière 1937, Theiler 1958, Skemp 1969, D. Frede 1971, Krämer 1973, van Raalte 1988, Battegazzore 1989, Botter 1999, Rudolph 2000, Berti 2002, Dillon 2002.

Title. See Part I, Chapter 1.2.

Aporia 1

4a2–9 (πῶς καὶ ποίοις): *How and with what sort of objects are the boundaries of the study of first things to be marked? (i.e., marked off from the study of nature)?*

The opening paragraph, containing an aporia as a direct question and followed by a brief diaporia, is crucial for an understanding not only of the starting point of Theophrastus's argument and the course he is about to follow, but also of his aim and approach in the entire Essay. The force of his argument, made apparent through his use of the particles that bind it together (see the commentary below on γὰρ δή at 4a3 and on διὸ δὴ καί at 4a6), can be paraphrased as follows.

Diaporia 1. *The subject of the Essay is to mark the boundaries of the study of the first things, i.e., to identify the objects involved in such a study. If someone objects and says, Is it possible to do so, because, in the case of natural science, the objects of study are so many as to be practically innumerable, the answer is, Yes; although the study of nature is clearly more diverse given its incessant variability, the study of the first things is nevertheless bounded and always the same, and thus it should be possible to enumerate with precision its objects. Having said this, however, the fact is that some philosophers have gone to the other extreme and said that the study of first things is concerned* only *with intelligibles (because they are immutable), disregarding the objects of sense.*

In this manner the opening paragraph directly addresses the question of the identification and classification of the sciences, and in particular the science that was later to be called metaphysics. The statement of the aporia here should be seen in dialectical relationship to the numerous efforts by Aristotle to tackle the same problem in the various books of what was to become his *Metaphysics*. Of the major discussions on this subject attempted by Aristotle in that work, i.e., in books A 1–2, Γ 1–3, E 1, K 7, and Λ 8, the statement by Theophrastus in this opening paragraph is closer to the tentative remarks of Aristotle in A 1–2 and Λ 8 than to the more developed theories in E 1 and K 7 (pace Zeller 1877, 146–147); besides, in the latter two sections, Aristotle talks about theology or first philosophy as treating being qua being, while in A 1–2 and Λ 8, just as in the entire Essay by Theophrastus, there is no mention of this subject. What Aristotle says in book A 1–2, that what is called "wisdom" (σοφία) is to be identified as the science which investigates the first principles and causes (see the Loci Paralleli), actually either echoes or gives occasion to the title of Theophrastus's Essay. In Λ 8, 1073b1–8, Aristotle talks in tentative terms of two of the three theoretical sciences, with metaphysics, which as yet has no specific name but is simply called φιλοσοφία, being superior to mathematics, whose astronomical part, nevertheless, is "most akin" (οἰκειοτάτη) to "philosophy."[1] Theophrastus directly reacts to these formulations both in Aporiae 7 and 21 of this Essay, where he disputes the value of astronomy for the study of first principles (see the commentary on these Aporiae below), and also in this opening paragraph, where he silently disavows the appellation of metaphysics as "philosophy" and calls it descriptively "the study of the first things." In the rest of the Essay he tries so to identify the objects of this science and the ways to study it as to include in them an account of the connection existing between the first things and the sensible world. And this is the major theme which, as noted by Theiler and Laks & Most, runs through the entire Essay.[2]

This analysis has implications for the dating both of Theophrastus's Essay and of the books of Aristotle's *Metaphysics*. The direct verbal and contextual congruence between Λ 8 and this Essay make it certain beyond a reasonable doubt that the former antedates the latter; and since it is now equally clear that Theophrastus's Essay is early and can be dated with certainty in the period between the residence of the philosophers in Assos and the very beginning of Aristotle's return to Athens, i.e., in 347–335 (above, Part I, Chapter 1.1), the perennial question of whether Λ 8 was composed after the rest of Lambda should be settled definitively in the negative. As for Theophrastus, it appears that his Essay is situated in the initial stages of Aristotle's metaphysical speculations and was composed precisely in order to raise aporiae on the subject of first principles as was discussed in the Academy and in Aristotle's early metaphysical work, including *Metaphysics* Lambda. Theophrastus never revisited the subject of metaphysics in his writings, as far as we know; in the collection of his fragments in FHS&G, no titles other than this Essay are listed as belonging to obviously metaphysical works (fr. 246), and no fragments are cited from any reliable source as belonging to a metaphysical

---

[1] Cf. the discussion on this passage in Reale 1980, 297 and 371–372, and Devereux 1988, 173.

[2] "1. Leitmotiv," Theiler 1958, 102/292; "Le postulat fondamental de la « continuité » qui traverse le traité comme un fil rouge;" Laks & Most p. xxv.

treatise (frs. 247–250). But even so, if his aporiae in this remarkable Essay were instrumental in the elaboration of Aristotle's mature metaphysical theories, then his contribution to the discipline at its very inception was momentous.

2 ποίοις] Theophrastus here asks about the method (πῶς) to be followed in marking the boundaries of the study of the first things, and the sort of things (ποίοις) with which this study can be delimited or identified, i.e., of which things it will consist. The following sentence is intended by Theophrastus to explain the question in the first (see the second comment after next). By asking about the method of metaphysical study, Theophrastus wishes to indicate that it is different from that followed in the study of nature and how it is different, and by asking about the sorts of things involved in this investigation, he wishes to identify the objects of study marking its boundaries. Both of these questions are fully discussed in the body of the treatise (principally at 9a10 ff., and 4a17 ff., respectively). Ποίοις, therefore, rather than having the more general sense of "characteristics" (Ross, Tricot, Reale, van Raalte), is a specific reference to the objects of metaphysical study (cf. Laks & Most and Henrich, though strangely Henrich 80 understands ποίοις to depend not on the obvious ἀφορίσαι, but on a presumed or understood θεῖναι or εἶναι).

4a2 ὑπέρ] The use of ὑπέρ instead of περί here would appear to be determined by stylistic considerations (Einarson and Link 1976, pp. xliii–xlvi); otherwise they are synonymous. See further van Raalte 71.

4a3 θεωρία] For the various senses of this word in Theophrastus's time see van Raalte 71–73; here it means study in the basic sense of application of the mind to a subject. In this treatise, Theophrastus never names these two kinds of study under discussion here, i.e., metaphysics and physics, other than to call them "the study of the first things" (ἡ τῶν πρώτων θεωρία 4a3, ἡ τῶν ἀρχῶν ζήτησις 6b21–22) and "the study of nature" (ἡ τῆς φύσεως θεωρία 4a3) respectively; at most he refers to the way of studying the latter as φυσικὸς τρόπος (10a8). As Reale 1964, 30, suggests, this would indicate on the one hand that Aristotle at the time of the composition of Theophrastus's Essay had a fluctuating terminology ("terminologia fluttuante") to designate metaphysics, and on the other that the early Peripatos had not yet developed a fixed expression ("espressione fissa") for this study. See further the comment on Aporia 1 above and Chapter 1.1 on the date of this treatise.

4a3 γὰρ δή] This particle combination, coming as it does after a question, implies the following. Upon hearing Theophrastus's initial question, and especially the question about identifying precisely the sort of things (ποίοις) which would be included in the study of the first things and thus delimit it, one may reasonably object whether it is at all possible to do it, given that it is difficult to do the same in the study of nature because of its diversity. Theophrastus forestalls this objection by providing the answer, which is introduced by γὰρ δή: "Yes (assentient γάρ: Denniston 244), surely (δή) the study of nature is more diverse—some even say it is more disorderly because of its variability—but the study of the first things is bounded and hence, the implication is, it should be possible to mark its boundaries accurately, or at least discuss the problems relating to this project, which is what this treatise will discuss." The presence of ὡρισμένη at 4a6 makes this reading recommended. Theophrastus starts his whole argument from the fact that the study of the first things is bounded, and then asks how these boundaries are to be marked, though rhetorically the question comes first; the contrast with the study of nature both highlights the feasibility of Theophrastus's project and helps introduce into the discussion the sensibles and their incorporation in such a study for the further development of the argument.

4a4 τινές φασιν ἀτακτοτέρα] The reference is certainly to Platonists, but also in all likelihood to Aristotle. The question has been raised as to whether Aristotle would have thought of the study of nature as "lacking in order" (ἄτακτος). Commentators (except van Raalte) think not, some of whom have cited passages from the treatises in which Aristotle says that nature means order, not the lack of it, as in the following: ἡ γὰρ φύσις αἰτία πᾶσιν τάξεως (*Physics* 252a11–12, cited by Henrich 21), to which one could also add, ἔτι τὸ ἀτάκτως οὐθέν ἐστιν ἕτερον ἢ τὸ παρὰ φύσιν· ἡ γὰρ τάξις ἡ οἰκεία τῶν αἰσθητῶν φύσις ἐστίν (*De caelo* 301a4–6). However, two things are overlooked when this claim is made. First, in these passages Aristotle is talking about sensible objects and not the study of them, which is what Theophrastus is talking about, and second, Theophrastus does not say that the study of nature is lacking in order absolutely but that it is *more* lacking in order than the study of the first things; he uses the comparative degree (cf. van Raalte 77). Now if we look at Aristotle we find that he makes a similar distinction in the amount of order inherent in things: at the beginning of *Meteorology* he says that the object of this study (μέθοδος) is "those things that happen according to nature, certainly, but [according to a nature that is] more lacking in order than that of the first element of bodies (i.e., the ether)" (ταῦτα δ' ἐστὶν ὅσα συμβαίνει κατὰ φύσιν μέν, ἀτακτοτέραν μέντοι τῆς τοῦ πρώτου στοιχείου τῶν σωμάτων, 338b20–21).[3] Thus it is clear that although Aristotle does indeed maintain that nature is the principle of order in sensible things, he nevertheless admits different levels or degrees of order exhibited by various parts of nature; in this case, sublunar elements exhibit less order than ether. If then, on the principle that a study is as ordered as its objects, we are allowed to extrapolate from this, it stands to reason that the study of the most ordered things—the first things—would be invariable and immobile, while that of the less ordered things—the things of nature, composed of the four elements more lacking in order—would have "all sorts of changes," and that this is the clear implication of Aristotle's words in the beginning of the *Meteorology*. It thus seems more than likely that Theophrastus is referring to this very passage in his opening sentence, or at least to an earlier formulation of it, something which also has implications for the date of this Essay (see Chapter 1.1). Besides, in all extant Greek literature up to and including Theophrastus, the comparative ἀτακτότερος is used only 11 times, five of which are in Thucydides and hence irrelevant for our purposes, four in Aristotle and two in Theophrastus. Of the uses in Aristotle, only the one just quoted from the *Meteorology* is contextually relevant to what Theophrastus is talking about. Naturally it is possible that Theophrastus may have had in mind either works that have not survived or even oral statements by Aristotle to this effect. But the very close relation his opening paragraph bears to the introduction of Aristotle's *Meteorology* can hardly be accidental.

4a5 μεταβολὰς ἔχουσα παντοίας] This clause of the circumstantial participle, by its position, explains either both comparatives (πολυχουστέρα, ἀτακτοτέρα) or the one it immediately follows; no reason is given by those who maintain that it explains only πολυχουστέρα (Laks & Most 25, Henrich 81). I believe it rather explains ἀτακτοτέρα because of the parallelism in the structure of this sentence: Theophrastus first presents his own views about the study of nature and of first things, and then the views of the other philosophers, followed by the reasons for which they say what they do. In tabular form:

[3] Vallance 1988, 27 and note 8, already suggested that this passage in Aristotle may be referred to by the word ἀτακτοτέρα here, though he understood the adjective in the Essay to apply to "the works of nature" and not to the *study* of nature, as Theophrastus says.

subject	*Theophrastus*	*others*	*reasons given by the others*
ἡ θεωρία τῆς φύσεως	πολυχουστέρα	ἀτακτοτέρα	μεταβολὰς ἔχουσα παντοίας
ἡ θεωρία τῶν πρώτων	ὡρισμένη καὶ ἀεὶ κατὰ ταὐτά	same as Th.	ἐν ἀκινήτοις καὶ ἀμεταβλήτοις

4a6 ἀεὶ κατὰ ταὐτά, *sc.*, ἔχει or ἐστί, which is the usual turn of phrase (see the examples from Plato and Aristotle in van Raalte 79–80 and Laks & Most 26). The bare use of this expression, without any other qualification or specification, "[being] always the same" refers to the study of first things (as does the preceding and exactly parallel epithet, ὡρισμένη), not to its objects, as Reale (1980) 392 translates ("identical in its subject matter") and as van Raalte 81 and Laks & Most 26 are also willing to entertain; it is especially not the case that "there is possibly some confusion between natural science and its subject-matter" (Ross 41). That the objects are also unchangeable, which is not Theophrastus's concern here, is implied not by the syntax of the passage but conceptually. In this opening paragraph it is assumed rather than argued for that the study of the first things is well defined and circumscribed, never varying in what it does, while the study of nature is constantly changing and open ended. That this is due to their respective objects (the invariable first things versus the infinite variability of nature) is beyond any doubt but—and this is important because frequently misunderstood—it is left unsaid, because uncontested: it was a philosophical commonplace in all schools of the time, and Theophrastus is not interested either in mentioning it or discussing it. As Laks & Most 25–26n5 note, both Plato and Aristotle, and hence their followers, held that theoretical propositions on eternal things were themselves eternal and unchanging, just as the opposite was true for variable and corruptible things. A statement such as the following by Aristotle, *De anima* 430a4–5, ἡ γὰρ ἐπιστήμη ἡ θεωρητικὴ καὶ τὸ οὕτως ἐπιστητὸν τὸ αὐτό ἐστιν is echoed by Theophrastus himself, ἡ ἐπιστήμη ἡ θεωρητικὴ ταὐτὸ τοῖς πράγμασιν (fr. 319.7 FHS&G).

4a6 διὸ δὴ καί] The particles here appear to express some disapproval or disagreement on the part of Theophrastus. The two clauses, "they place ... and consider" (τιθέασιν ... νομίζουσιν) introduced by διὸ δὴ καί add Theophrastus's report about what the philosophers he is referring to infer from the invariable nature of the study of first things and do not constitute his own inference and argumentation. The emphasis of this clause seems to be that these philosophers put the study of the first things to be exclusively in the realm of (ἐν, see the next comment) the intelligibles to the exclusion of the sensibles, because otherwise the argumentation would have been inverse, a good case of hysteron proteron (as Henrich 195 mistakenly claims for Theophrastus: "Theophrast argumentiert umgekehrt"). In other words: if the διὸ δή clause is read as the conclusion by these other philosophers from the premise that the study of the first things is invariable, then it would have been an inverse argument because the study of the first things is not regarded as being about intelligibles *because* it, the study itself, is always the same and unchanging, but the other way round: the study is well-defined or bounded because it is about unchanging intelligibles. So since clearly no one made this inverse argument, Theophrastus could not be reporting about it in this sentence, and hence his emphasis is as I stated above. This is further indicated by his explicit mention of the sensibles in this sentence, where he says, διό δὴ καὶ ἐν νοητοῖς, *οὐκ αἰσθητοῖς*, αὐτὴν (sc. τὴν θεωρίαν) τιθέασιν (4a7). Had the point of the sentence been the inverse argument I mentioned above, namely, that because the study of the first things is invariable it is about intelligibles, Theophrastus should have just said, διὸ δὴ καὶ ἐν νοητοῖς αὐτὴν τιθέασιν. The emphatic mention of the sensibles in the sentence implies that the placement of the study of the first things among the intelligibles only and not also among the sensibles is somehow surprising and contrary to what Theophrastus would have wished or expected. The particle δή here, in the causal clause, adds a tone of surprise or disapproval (Denniston 231). Finally, what demonstrates that this is indeed the course of Theophrastus's argument, that he disapproves of those philosophers who merely look at intelligibles because he feels that the study of the first things should also consider the sensibles, is that the intelligibles and the sensibles together, and their connection, constitute the beginning of the first sentence of the following Aporia 2: "The starting point is, ..."

4a6 ἐν, "among"] The preposition ἐν describes the boundaries within which, or in reference to which, the study of the first things operates, according to the philosophers whose views Theophrastus is reporting. This is one of the basic meanings of the preposition ἐν with the dative; see the discussion and examples in Humbert 306 ("dans les limites de") and also below the commentary on 4a17–18. Cf. similar uses of the preposition with τίθημι in Plato, *Sophist* 246c8: τῶν ἐν εἴδεσιν αὐτὴν (sc. τὴν οὐσίαν) τιθεμένων, or especially Simplicius *In phys.* 453.26 Diels (*CAG*): τὴν δὲ ἀόριστον δυάδα καὶ ἐν τοῖς νοητοῖς τιθείς. The sentence ἐν νοητοῖς αὐτὴν τιθέασιν thus indicates, quite unambiguously, that this study, or "view" (in order not to forget the resonance of the word θεωρία to a Greek speaker), is operative among the intelligibles and hence it reflects upon and regards, or is in reference to, the intelligibles and not, as Theophrastus emphasizes (as discussed in the preceding comment), the sensibles. This then would appear to be the reason why Theophrastus uses this preposition rather than περί or ὑπέρ, as he did in the very first sentence, to describe the object of the study of first things; he is not interested in the objects as such *of* which it is a study (περί or ὑπέρ), but rather in indicating the level of applicability *within* which this study operates (ἐν), according to these philosophers, and this is the realm of the intelligibles and not that of sensibles.

4a4, 7, 9 τινές φασιν ... τιθέασιν ... νομίζουσιν] The first verb in third person plural has the indefinite subject τινές, while the last two have no explicit subject; all three verbs occur in the same sentence, and all three introduce views which are reported by Theophrastus as not being his. In this grammatical and semantic context it would be unnatural to assume, as all translators do, that the last two verbs refer to a different subject; if Theophrastus was interested in this passage in assigning views to specific philosophers and intended to say so he would have somehow made it explicit. It cannot be precluded that he is not referring to a different subject, but it seems that his purpose here is to refer generically to the overall mistaken approach by his contemporaries (perhaps all, or perhaps all who count) of disparaging the study of nature as disorderly and concentrating on the study of the first things with reference only to the intelligibles. This is the import of this passage; it is doubtful that we can, or need, be more specific than this.

Aporia 2

4a9–17 (πότερα ... ἤ): *Whether or not there is some connection between intelligibles and natural objects.*

Diaporia 2. *(Since the diaporia of the opening paragraph revealed that some philosophers think that the study of the first things can be conducted only within the realm of the intelligibles, disregarding the objects of sense,) the discussion can start by first determining whether there is in fact some connection between them. But if such a connection is doubted, it would* *mean that there is no contact between intelligibles and natural objects, and hence that the universe is episodic and disjointed. But it is more reasonable, (patently in the opinion of the many or the wise,) not to think so, but rather that there is some kind of ontological or causal relationship of priority and posteriority between them.*

Theophrastus begins the discussion, after the initial question that set the subject matter to be treated, with the aporia concerning the connection between intelligibles and sensibles because he has just hinted in his opening remarks at the inadequacy of the study of the first things that neglects to study also the sensibles. This aporia is resolved in proper dialectical fashion by an appeal to an *endoxon* ("it is more reasonable," εὐλογώτερον), the connectedness between intelligibles and objects of nature, which becomes a first principle on the basis of which future aporiae are resolved.

The critical reference to Speusippus in this passage has been widely commented upon; see Theiler 1958, 293n58; Tarán 1981, 321n122; and others. On Speusippus' episodic ontology and the sets of problems it raises see Happ 1971, 212–227; Tarán 1981, 49–52.

4a12 συνεργοῦντα ... εἰς] Van Raalte 92 rightly raises the question whether there is any difference between the verb συνεργοῦντα with the preposition εἰς, as here, and πρός, used by Theophrastus and others elsewhere. The distinction she draws is accurate: the former indicates the actual effect the contribution brings about, as here (both contribute to bringing about all of existence), while the latter emphasizes the proceeding towards the goal. For this causal usage of εἰς in Theophrastus see in particular Müller 1878, 8–9. The verb with the preposition, συνεργέω εἰς, here can only mean "to contribute to", not "to cooperate [in order] to;" cooperate implies a deliberate working together, something which would make no sense in this context where the two entities supposed to be cooperating, the intelligibles and natural objects, are separated, κεχωρισμένα.

4a12 δέ, "though," is adversative (and not merely additive; pace van Raalte 91), balancing the preceding opposing idea of κεχωρισμένα, though without μὲν to follow it; cf. Denniston 165.

4a13 οὐσία is used in this work 15 times, in four different Aristotelian senses. (1) In a general way, and always in the phrase ἡ (ἅ)πᾶσα οὐσία or ἡ ὅλη οὐσία, to mean "existence" in the sense of "all that exists": 4a13 (this passage), 7a10, 11a22, 11b11 (cf. this use of the word in Aristotle listed in Bonitz *Index* s.v. οὐσία 2); (2) in the main Aristotelian sense of "substance" as the first category, a subject of which the other nine categories are predicated: 4b6 (and see below on that passage), 8a13 (Bonitz *Index* s.v. οὐσία 3b); (3) in the Aristotelian sense of "the what it is to be," τὸ τί ἦν εἶναι, formal substance or essence: 5a8, 6a7–8, 8b21 (where it occurs literally as a synonym for τὸ τί ἦν εἶναι), 9a5, 10a11, 10a14 (Bonitz *Index* s.v. οὐσία 3f); (4) in the looser sense of οὐσία as form, i.e., as something's nature or formal constitution or configuration, as described by Bonitz *Index* s.v. οὐσία 3g: 8a23, 10a3, 11b26. It is significant that in the last three passages οὐσία is always used by Theophrastus in conjunction with φύσις, apparently as a discriminating marker. This, and the turn of phrase ἡ ὅλη οὐσία mentioned above under (1), indicate that Theophrastus chose his words carefully.

4a13 δ' οὖν, "at any rate"] After an enumeration of the preceding alternatives and questions and their import, the particle combination indicates that whatever the case might be ("at any rate"), the speaker wishes to concentrate on the point that he is interested in making; see Denniston 463. For this basic use of the particle combination see also Humbert 429, §750: "C'est un peu comme si le sujet parlant disait: « j'en viens donc à ce point, logiquement fondé sur ce qui précède, qui présente beaucoup plus d'intérêt à mes yeux »." Theophrastus uses this particle combination relatively frequently in this Essay.

4a15 τὰ μέν ... τὰ δέ, as a construction, could refer either to "the former ... the latter," i.e., to the intelligibles and the things of nature in line 11, or to generic "some things ... other things" (Ross, Tricot, Laks & Most). In context, the former alternative seems beyond doubt: Theophrastus just said that it is more reasonable that there does exist a connection, i.e., a connection (συναφή) between intelligibles and sensibles, as in lines 10–11, and he is giving here an example (οἷον) of what that connection might consist in, that of priority and posteriority (cf. van Raalte 98).

4a15 καὶ ἀρχάς, without τὰ μέν, meaning, "and [the former,] first principles, too ...". Τὰ μέν is clearly implied here and it was both added in the text by the scribe of J[II] and so interpreted by Isḥāq (though it cannot be precluded that Ψ also carried it). The omission, however, is not an error; see the references in Laks & Most 27n3 and van Raalte 98–99.

4a16 τῶν φθαρτῶν, *sc.* πρότερά ἐστι, "are [prior] to the perishable," is the only plausible reading in context (as also understood by Isḥāq), similar to Aristotle, *Met.* Θ 8, 1050b6–7 (cf. van Raalte 99, Laks & Most 27n4); there is no particular difficulty here (pace Laks & Most 27n4) given the structure of Theophrastus's sentence. Usener's original (1861, 264) conjecture, later abandoned by him (Usener 1890 *ad loc.*) but endorsed by Reale (1964, 167n7), to emend the text to read, καὶ ὥσπερ αἴτια τὰ ἀΐδια τῶν φθαρτῶν, is too speculative and not supported either by the manuscript tradition or the context; it is also unnecessary.

Aporia 3

4a17–4b5 (τίς καὶ ἐν ποίοις): *What is the nature of the intelligible first things and among what sort of things are they found?*

Diaporia 3 brings up the question of mathematicals, one of the major issues under discussion in Academic circles, and one which Aristotle himself had to deal with extensively. Theophrastus quickly disposes of it: *If the intelligible first things are mathematicals, they cannot account for the connection between intelligibles and objects of nature; accordingly this alternative is to be rejected on the basis of the principle established from the* endoxon *in the preceding Aporia 2.*

4a17 εἰ δ' οὖν, "If (really) so," to give the particle combination its full force, introduces the question to which the "more reasonable" theory that there *is* a connection between the intelligibles and the sensibles leads (cf. van Raalte 100).

4a17–18 ἐν ... ἐν] In the Essay, Theophrastus uses the preposition ἐν, with the verb εἶναι either expressed or understood, eleven times to indicate that something belongs to, or is found among, a particular set of items and hence that it consists of them. In this sense, the preposition is very close in meaning to its use with the verb τίθημι at 4a6, as stated in the commentary above. However, even within this sense, it is evident that two different aspects of it are expressed, one of which emphasizes the set among which something finds itself in order to differentiate that set from others, and the other emphasizes the fact that this set indicates the constitution of something, what it consists of.[4] In the former case it is translated as "among" (at 4a17, 4a18, 4b9, 4b10, 6a4, 12a1), and in the latter as "consists of" (at 6b16, 7a8, 8a23, 11b12, and "consist in" at 5b6). This point is implicitly raised in Dillon's (2002, 176n6) adaptation of a translation by Ross, though I do not agree with him on the rendering of the particular passage (4a18).

In the sentence ἐν τοῖς μαθηματικοῖς μόνον τὰ νοητά, "[it is] among the mathematicals only that the intelligibles are," Theophrastus emphasizes mathematicals by inverting the word order and putting the predicate first.

4a18 εἰ μέν, "if, on the one hand," is answered by εἰ δ', "if, on the other hand," at 4b6.

4a20–21 ἀξιόχρεα ... τοῦ (τοῦ J Ψ Λ : om. P) παντός] ἀξιόχρεως *c. gen. rei* means more than just ἄξιος *c. gen. rei*; the latter means just "worthy" or "adequate" to do something, whereas the former, taking into account its two components, ἄξιος and χρέο/ως, means, "worthy or adequate for, i.e., to perform, what is needed or called for by the specific occasion," something like "rise to the occasion," with the genitive specifying the respect in which the adequacy is to be understood. Cf. the Demosthenian passages cited by Ross 42 and van Raalte 105n6, and also Isocrates, *Philippus* 138,3, μᾶλλον γὰρ ἂν ἀξιόχρεως οὗτος ἔδοξεν εἶναι τῆς ὑποθέσεως. If that is so, then παντός, without the article, can only mean "everything" (the suggestion by Jaeger 1932, 293, to read πάντως instead of παντός, "in all ways," also means the same); with the article, however, παντός would mean "the universe." The former cannot be the sense because it is palpably wrong to maintain that mathematicals "are not at all equal to the task with regard to everything", which is the interpretation of both Laks & Most ("à la hauteur de toute chose") and Henrich ("allem gewachsen zu sein")—clearly mathematicals are useful with regard to *some* things (Ross's [not] "equal to their whole task" is not a viable interpretation of παντός). What they are not adequate to perform at all, in context, is to be the principles which will provide a

[4] These two aspects of the use of ἐν in this sense by Theophrastus were already identified by Müller 1878, 6: "So wird auch durch ἐν mit ... εἶναι, τιθέναι ausgedrückt, zu welcher Gattung diese oder jene Art gehört, gerechnet wird;" and "An andern Stellen bezeichnet εἶναι mit ἐν, worin etwas besteht, worin es sein Wesen hat."

connection between intelligibles and sensibles so that the universe will not be episodic (4a14) and thus contribute to the constitution of all being (4a13).

The reading τοῦ παντός is also attested in Ψ: the Arabic has *al-kull*, a standard translation of the word to mean the universe. Margoliouth 1892, 195, unaware of this usage in Arabic, wrongly suggested that the Arabic supports the reading πάντως: the phrase *fī l-kull* does not mean "on the whole," as he translated it, but "with regard to the universe." Finally, Bartholomew's Latin translation also points to a reading τοῦ παντός in Λ: *inutilia videntur ab universo*. Although Kley 16 may be right in saying that it is not absolutely clear what lies behind *ab universo*, the preposition *ab* can be most reasonably explained by assuming that Bartholomew took the genitive of the article in τοῦ παντός to indicate agency ("by") after the passive *videntur*; otherwise, given his slavish word by word translation, if the reading were only παντός, he would have written just *universi*. Furthermore, *universum* most plausibly can be taken to mean "the universe" rather than "all together;" if Bartholomew had been translating πᾶν without the article in his exemplar (Λ), he would have most probably used *omnis*, as elsewhere. By the same token, the suggestion by Jaeger 1932, 293, to read πάντως also is off the mark.

With three of the four independent witnesses (PJ Ψ Λ) for the text supporting the reading τοῦ παντός, the omission of the article in P can be seen as a peculair error; and if in later tradition the article is also omitted in A, this can have no significance on its own, given the stemmatic relation of the manuscripts (see Chapter 2.1 and 2.6).

An example of this use of ἀξιόχρεως, as a first principle that can effect what is needed for a specific purpose, is offered by Euripides, *Orestes* 597, ἢ οὐκ ἀξιόχρεως ὁ θεὸς ἀναφέροντί μοι / μίασμα λῦσαι. Τοῦ παντός in line 21, therefore, harks back to τὸ πᾶν in line 14 because they are both part of the same argument in which Theophrastus spells out the precise areas of his concern with regard to the quest for the first things: he is not interested in discussing possible candidates for first things with regard to their usefulness in *everything* but only in explaining, or constituting, a mutually connected universe. (Henrich's 84 reference to πάντων and ἅπαντα at 4b15–16 has nothing to do with this particular argument in which τὸ πᾶν is to be understood as the universe.)

4b2 ἔχει, "they … have"] Theophrastus uses the indicative instead of an infinitive to express his conviction that mathematicals have in fact no nature of their own. The infinitive would have placed the sentence as reported speech in subordination to the preceding φαίνεται or δοκεῖ, "they seem," and thus diminish the value of the expression as a statement of fact. All manuscripts and independent witnesses concur in the reading; only a second hand in a late MS (B) "corrected" it to the infinitive. After a verb in the infinitive as part of reported speech, Theophrastus on occasion deliberately reverts to finite verbs in order to state something as factual by contrast (cf. Laks & Most 10n7 and 29n9). These passages are not to be "corrected" to the infinitive, as in some late manuscripts and modern editions. In this case in particular ἔχει does not represent one of the primitive errors of the archetype, as listed by Fobes, p. xxvii.

4b2 εἰ δὲ μή, "or, if not," referring, as Ross notes, to οἷον γάρ in 4a21. Clearly the negative alternative refers to the totality of the preceding sentence: "or, if mathematicals are not devised by us but have a proper nature …".

4b2 οἷά τε] The Arabic translation suggests a reading in Ψ of either οὐχ οἷά τε or οὐχ οἷόν τε (see the corresponding note to the Arabic translation). Given the structure of the Greek sentence, εἰ δὲ μή … τιθέασιν (4b2–5), what is required is the former construction, which makes τὰ μαθηματικά the subject of ἐμποιῆσαι, as opposed to the latter, impersonal construction, which would leave the verb without a subject. The presence of the next subject, ὁ ἀριθμός in b4, which is parallel to τὰ μαθηματικά, also requires the personalized construction οὐχ οἷά τε: it needs to fit the same structure as the subject of the preceding sentence in order for the elliptical expression to make sense, i.e., οὐδὲ γὰρ αὐτὸς ὁ ἀριθμὸς, *sc.* οἷός τε συνάπτειν τοῖς τῆς φύσεως ὥστ' ἐμποιῆσαι ζωήν. The indefinite expression οὐχ οἷόν τε would derail the parallelism.

The reading οὐχ οἷά τε is also preferable to the other actual or suggested readings because the alternatives have grave problems. The extant Greek manuscripts have οὐχ ὥστε, and apparently so does Λ,[5] but the

[5] Bartholomew's Latin has *non sicut*, which stands for οὐχ ὥστε. It is not true, as Kley 16 states, that Bartholomew translates ὥστε with *quare*; in the five instances in which ὥστε occurs in this Essay, it is translated by *quare* (5a4, 5a20), *sicut* (here, 4b2), *ut* (4b3), and *quod* (8a25). On the other hand, *sicut* translates mainly three words, ὡς (4a7, 5b13, 6a21, etc.), ὥσπερ (4a16, 5b18, 6b10, etc.), and καθάπερ (4b3, 6b27, 10a27, etc.). Ὥσπερ, which also begins with ὡς, is thus translated by *sicut* here as well.

recurrence of ὥστε four words further down in the same sentence makes it "very awkward" (Ross 42), if not impossible, to retain (despite van Raalte's valiant efforts, 112–113, and Henrich's approval). Besides, if, in order to retain the reading of ὥστε, φύσις needs to be taken as the subject of συνάπτειν and ἐμποιῆσαι (as van Raalte 37, 112, suggests), then it would not be parallel, as subject, to ὁ ἀριθμός (as indicated in the preceding comment), and thus the syntax of the οὐδὲ γὰρ clause would not conform to that of the main sentence, ruining the parallelism and the meaning. Usener's 1890 emendation to οὕτως γε,[6] adopted by Ross and Laks & Most, has the problem, as noted by van Raalte (112), that it presupposes the conjecture ἔχειν for ἔχει in 4b2 in order to justify the infinitive in συνάπτειν and put everything in reported speech dependent on δοκεῖ at 4a22. Ross is consistent in this regard for he prints ἔχειν φύσιν and translates συνάπτειν, "they *seem* not to connect with the things of nature", but not Laks & Most. However, the reading of ἔχειν for ἔχει in 4b2 has been ruled out (see the preceding comment). There remains the reading in Ψ, which makes good sense and has the authority of one of the oldest independent witnesses. Van Raalte's (113) objection, that the intransitive συνάπτειν is "somewhat awkward" with the following active ὥστ' ἐμποιῆσαι is without any basis, especially since the two verbs are in two different clauses. Palaeographically, the corruption of οιατε to ωστε would appear to have taken place, possibly because of assimilation to the following ὥστε, in a minuscule rather than an uncial environment (OIATE < ΩCTE?), through a misreading of οι as ω and of ατ as the στ ligature.

4b4 οὐδὲ γάρ, "no, not even," assentient γάρ, with οὐδέ echoing οὐχ in line 4b2 (see Denniston 86–88, especially 88 § 2). This does not preclude the particle combination introducing an *a fortiori* argument (cf. Laks & Most 29n12, van Raalte 115).

4b5 ὅνπερ δή, "the very one which," emphatic περ further strengthened by δή (Denniston 490).

[6] Which is not, as Kley 16 claims, supported by Bartholomew's Latin; see the preceding note.

Aporia 4

4b6–11 (πότερον ... ἤ): *Whether a substance that is prior and more powerful (than mathematicals) is one in number or in species or in genus.*

Diaporia 4. The diaporia that follows makes use of another *endoxon* to settle this question, something that is considered "more reasonable" by the many or the wise, namely that *such intelligible first substances, insofar as they are principles, would be few or possibly just one.*

4b6 οὐσία, "substance"] Theophrastus asks this question in the same spirit as that in which Aristotle discusses the number of "substances" different philosophers postulated (*Met.* Z 2). For the different uses of οὐσία in this work see above, at 4a13.

4b9 δ' οὖν, "at any rate," see 4a13 above.

4b9 ἐχούσας] The plural feminine ἐχούσας here can only refer to a presumed plural οὐσίαι of the only feminine noun actually mentioned in the paragraph, οὐσία in 4b6 (and this is why Usener 1861 and 1890 tried to "correct" the text, unnecessarily, by preferring the late reading ἔχουσαν and adding δ' οὖν ⟨οὐσίαν⟩). Most of the modern translations, following the Greek, use the plural pronoun, "they", "ils", "sie," generating the impression that the antecedent is the mathematical objects. The plural form in the Greek, which is certainly correct—the Arabic and Latin translations, and thus Ψ and Λ also have it—implies the following: "It is more reasonable that, having the nature of a first principle, substances like the one that was just assumed—a substance prior and more powerful than the mathematicals—are among few and extraordinary things."

4b9–11 ἐν ὀλίγοις ... τῷ πρώτῳ] There are two interrelated difficulties in this passage. The first concerns the precise meaning of εἰ μὴ ἄρα, and the second the progression of the thought. Εἰ μὴ ἄρα, which is a favorite expression of Theophrastus both in this work and elsewhere (he uses it five times in this Essay, at 4b10, 5b28, 6a10, 8a21–22, and 11b19; cf. van Raalte 122), means, "if not, perhaps," "unless, indeed" ("indeed" suggesting the uncommon nature of the thing introduced by the hypothesis), or, affirmatively stated, "possibly even," with ἄρα denoting a just realized and novel alternative (cf. Denniston 37; van

Raalte 122). The question here is whether ἄρα is also ironic and, as is frequently the case with εἰ μὴ ἄρα, expresses that the alternative introduced is improbable or undesirable (Smyth § 2796; Humbert 382: "hypothèse … à peine croyable"). But this does not seem to be the case in the actual usage of the expression by Theophrastus (cf. the evidence and the discussion in van Raalte 122–123). What it does indicate is that the alternative introduced is actually preferable even if some people, Theophrastus appears to be implying, might not have actually thought of it or even might find the suggestion somewhat novel or perhaps surprising. Thus "if not, indeed," in the sense described above, would appear to fit Theophrastus's meaning.

If then the alternative introduced by εἰ μὴ ἄρα is not improbable but something which Theophrastus wishes actively to suggest, the next question is, how much of the εἰ μὴ ἄρα clause (i.e., how many of the words following it) is an alternative to what has preceded. There are two possibilities, and both have been taken by different scholars. The first is to take only καὶ πρώτοις as belonging to the εἰ μὴ ἄρα clause and view the final καὶ ἐν τῷ πρώτῳ as a further addition to the progression that began with ὀλίγοις and continued with περιττοῖς, so that πρώτῳ would be the third item in it (with the εἰ μὴ ἄρα clause qualifying the preceding one or two items), punctuating after πρώτοις to indicate the division (Laks & Most, Talanga 1995, 19). The second is to view the entire clause, καὶ πρώτοις καὶ ἐν τῷ πρώτῳ as part of the alternative introduced by εἰ μὴ ἄρα, in which the original suggestion, that these substances which are superior to mathematicals can be found among few and extraordinary things (ὀλίγοις and περιττοῖς), is subsituted by the alternative that they can be found rather among the first things and indeed in the very first itself. Thus what is contrasted here is the first thing(s) and non-first things. I tend to favor the second alternative, for two reasons. First, if καὶ ἐν τῷ πρώτῳ is taken as a third item in the progression—ὀλίγοις, περιττοῖς, πρώτῳ—but in a progression in which the second element at least, περιττοῖς (if not the first also, ὀλίγοις), is "corrected" by the εἰ μὴ ἄρα clause which substitutes for it the item πρώτοις, then the element of "first things" will have been already introduced into the discussion, and the further addition of πρώτῳ, as a third element, would be redundant. Secondly, and perhaps more importantly, in this entire sentence in which the εἰ μὴ ἄρα clause appears, Theophrastus makes what may be called a dialectical argument on the basis of what is more "reasonable" to suppose, one with which he could expect most of his audience readily to agree: most Greeks of his time would have found it reasonable to claim that intelligible substances which are prior and more powerful than mathematicals and which have the nature of first principles are few and extraordinary; but it is very doubtful that they would have found it equally reasonable to say that these substances are actually the very "first thing," which is what the sentence would imply if we read it with a comma after πρώτοις in πρώτοις, καὶ and if we take ἐν τῷ πρώτῳ as the third item in the progression ὀλίγοις, περιττοῖς, πρώτῳ (according to the first alternative mentioned above). It is thus semantically more correct to take καὶ πρώτοις καὶ ἐν τῷ πρώτῳ as part of the alternative clause introduced by εἰ μὴ ἄρα (for philosophical arguments see van Raalte 123 and Henrich 85–86); Theophrastus expects most people to agree that these entities are few and rare, and he adds his personal qualification that these entities could even be among the "first things" or the very "first thing" itself. The preposition ἐν in ἐν τῷ πρώτῳ is apparently to be understood in the sense (see above the comment on 4a17–18) that the set of things among which these entities are to be found includes only the "first thing," and thus these entities consist of just the first "thing" (cf. Laks & Most 31n16).

4b10 εἰ μὴ ἄρα, "if not, indeed"] See the first paragraph of the preceding comment.

Aporia 5

4b11–5a5 (τίς καὶ τίνες): *What this first intelligible substance is, or what they are, if more than one, can be revealed through (a diaporia by) analogy or some other comparison.*

It has been suggested that this aporia reflects an "epistemological pessimism" which implies that this substance (or substances) that has the nature of a first principle is not directly accessible to human knowledge (Laks & Most 31n17). Cf. below at 9a18–23 and the Appendix.

Diaporia 5 (4b13–18). The discussion is divided into two separate diaporiae. The first argues by analogy, as just suggested, and makes use of yet another *endoxon*: *(According to the opinion of the many or the wise,) the first principle of all is divine. By analogy, the first principles being sought should be assumed to have power and superiority over others, just like god is superior to all other beings.*

For Theophrastus's conception of the divine and its relation to the philosophical and general ideas of his time see the study by Pötscher 1970, 75–112.

Diaporia 5.1 (4b18–5a5). *Since the first principle is superior to others, as just mentioned, and is connected with the sensibles (according to the* endoxon *established as principle in Aporia 2), and since, moreover, the objects of nature have the unique property of being in motion, the first principle must be posited as the cause of motion. Since the first principle is motionless in itself (reference to the axiom of the impossibility of infinite regress), it causes the incessant circular motion of the heavenly spheres by being their object of desire.* In this manner Theophrastus introduces into the discussion Aristotle's major innovation concerning motion, his theory of desire.

In the final sentence in this Diaporia (5a4–5) Theophrastus refers to what may be seen as an earlier aporia (and which could perhaps be numbered as **Aporia 5a**): *If motion is initiated only by something that is itself in motion, does this not lead to an infinite regress? The theory of the unmoved mover resolves the question of the origin of movement.*

4b11 δ' οὖν, "at any rate," see 4a13 above.

4b11 αὕτη could refer either to οὐσία in the preceding paragraph or to ἀρχή, and the answer given to this question at the beginning of the following paragraph makes it clear that it is ἀρχή (Henrich 86 also points out that the explanatory θεία γὰρ ἡ πάντων ἀρχή indicates the same). However, strictly speaking, and given the immediately preceding sentence, the reference should be, for τίς, to ἀρχῆς φύσιν ἔχουσα οὐσία, and for τίνες, ἀρχῆς φύσιν ἔχουσαι οὐσίαι.

4b13 ὁμοίωσις, "[procedure through] similarity," or likening, is an act of showing that some things are similar to each other. As such it is different from ὁμοιότης, just plain similarity (in 5b1–2 and 8a20), which is the quality, or the methodological principle, on the basis of which the act of likening one thing to another is effected. Laks & Most 31 rightly point to the fact that analogy in this passage, as also in 8a20, is a species of the genus of proceeding through similarity or likening.

4b15 τὸν θεόν] The accusative makes it clear that the noun is the object of a verb, which is clearly λαμβάνειν in this context. The juxtaposition of θεόν with the immediately following θεία, the repetition of a word from the same root at the end of a clause and the beginning of the next (cf. J.D. Denniston, *Greek Prose Style*, Oxford: Clarendon Press, 1960, 92–96), together with the inverted word order in the following γάρ clause, give the latter its stately and proverbial feel and its appeal to deeply held beliefs; see the following comment.

4b16–17 τάχα μὲν οὖν, "and yes, maybe"] Τάχα, which occurs very frequently in this small treatise, sometimes presents a corrective reaction to a preceding statement in the form of internal dialogue, as in the present case (cf. van Raalte 135). Theophrastus has just noted that the first principle can perhaps be apprehended, analogously to a divine being, by taking into consideration its power and superiority over all else, which is the quality that makes it comparable to a divine being. To provide an explanation (γάρ 4b15) for why the first principle should at all have this divine quality, he gives as reason the statement, "divine is the first principle of all, through which all [things] both are and abide." Having said this, he imagines someone (or himself) saying that this is an easy explanation to give—presumably because it is a traditional explanation, an ἔνδοξον, that one could expect easily to gain assent; Laks & Most 31n18 even suggest that it may be a proverb—to which Theophrastus responds by assenting to the objection (assentient οὖν) but qualifying it in two ways. First, he casts the assent in doubtful terms ("maybe"), and second, he makes an important distinction in the manner in which an explanation is given for the statement, "divine is the first principle of all, through which all [things] both are and abide:" if it is in general and vague terms, as here (cf. van Raalte 135), then such explanation is easy; but if one wants a more explicit and (philosophically) convincing explanation, then it is very difficult. The particle combination μὲν οὖν here underscores this distinction by emphasizing the prospective μέν ("yes, maybe on the one hand thus to explain *is* easy") which is answered by Theophrastus's objection to the objection by δέ ("though on the other hand it is indeed difficult"); see Denniston 473–474.

4b17 οὕτως, "in this manner"] Given the corrective reaction that this sentence presents to the preceding one, as just discussed, the adverb οὕτως can only refer to the explanation contained in the γάρ clause, "divine is the first principle of all, through which all [things] both are and abide." (Cf. the exactly parallel use of the expression οὕτως ἀποδιδόναι and its referent, a few lines further down, at 5a10–11, where the explanation referred to is the clause ἁπλῶς ... θειοτέραν). Thus what is contrasted in the μέν ... δέ sentence here is not this easy explanation versus another, more convincing but difficult, explanation (as Laks & Most 31n19 argue), but the manner in which this same explanation is given: either in lapidary or "proverbial" form or terms, as here, which is easy, or in terms philosophically more explicit and convincing, which would be difficult.

4b18 πιστικωτέρως] All manuscripts agree on this spelling, except for D, which has πειστικωτέρως, allegedly the older spelling of the word (LSJ), and hence, the reasoning goes, the form most likely to have been used by Theophrastus. However, it is not at all clear how far back the form πιστικός goes, and whether it may not have been already in use in Theophrastus's time. We do find it in Plato (*Gorgias* 455a3), and the manuscripts there also waver between the two spellings, but Burnet prints πιστικός; I do not think that the issue has been resolved. There is also the question whether πειστικός and πιστικός mean exactly the same thing, given their respective etymologies (πείθω and πιστεύω). So in order not to eliminate good evidence from the text and prejudge the issue, I prefer to follow the reading of all the independent and oldest witnesses, including Ψ and Λ. The Arabic has an etymological translation for πιστικωτέρως, *aqrab ilā t-taṣdīq*, "more credible" (literally, "closer to being believed, or poducing belief"), where *taṣdīq* is used elsewhere (9b17) to render πίστις (in the sense of "belief"), thus verifying for us the πιστικωτέρως spelling that must have existed in Ψ. Similarly, the Latin has *credibilius*, which also stands for πιστικωτέρως. The spelling in manuscript D is clearly a Renaissance scribal emendation, for there is no evidence that D had access to an independent ancient source other than the manuscripts we already possess.

4b18–19 τοιαύτης ... ἐπείπερ] In context, "such" can only refer to the immediately preceding declarative statement (before the modificatory τάχα sentence) which specifically describes the first principle as "divine": θεία γὰρ ἡ πάντων ἀρχή ... τοιαύτης δ' οὔσης τῆς ἀρχῆς. The rhetorical connection and physical proximity of these two statements are such that they cannot be disputed. Clearly in the background there looms the entire preceding discussion that led to the declaration of the first principle as divine, but the immediate referent of τοιαύτης is θεία (not, as Laks & Most 32 suggest, "l'ensemble des acquis intermédiaires," or "vague," van Raalte 137). Besides, in all nine out of the ten uses of the word τοιοῦτος in this Essay (see the Glossary), the referent of the word is always what has immediately preceded; in the one instance where it is not (11b21–22), it points forward to the following clause. If this is the case, then the absolute genitive of the τοιαύτης clause is declarative, stating a premise for a conclusion that is to follow (4b21), and it cannot even be considered that it is concessive (Laks & Most 31–32). And this perhaps explains the emphatic περ in ἐπείπερ: the conclusion that this first principle must be posited as the cause of movement (4b21–22) has two sorts of premises; the first is the general one of the divine nature of the first principle, "through which all [things]"—and hence also motion—"both are and abide," as summarized in the absolute genitive clause beginning with τοιαύτης, and the second is the specific quality of being in motion that characterizes the natural world, which requires a mover. Ἐπείπερ introduces the second set of premises, and the particle emphasizes this point.

4b20 ἐν κινήσει, "in motion," for nature is, strictly speaking, inappropriate; nature itself is the principle of motion. Φύσις here must stand, or be an abbreviated expression, ὡς ἁπλῶς εἰπεῖν, for what Theophrastus properly calls four lines later in the passage, τὰ τοῖς φύσεως, "the [things] of nature." Theophrastus used exactly the same phrase, πάντα γὰρ ἐν κινήσει τὰ τῆς φύσεως, in his *Physics*, a fragment from which is preserved by Simplicius, *In Phys.* 20.17 ff. Diels (*CAG*) = fr. 143 FHS&G. For an analysis of this fragment and its relation to this Essay see Laks 1998 and Sharples 1998, 36–40.

4b21 ταύτην, referring to ἀρχή, of course, and not φύσις.

4b22 ἐπεὶ δ' introduces yet a third premise, after the genitive absolute and ἐπείπερ, to arrive in the end to the desired conclusion of the object of desire.

5a1 ἀλλὰ λοιπόν] See below the comment at 5b18.

5a3 ἀφ' ἧς] The feminine pronoun can only refer to φύσις in grammatical terms, and not to ἀρχή (*pace* Henrich 88), though what is meant by this prepositional phrase is clearly, ἀπὸ τῆς τοῦ ὀρεκτοῦ φύσιν ἐχούσης ἀρχῆς.

5a4 ⌜καὶ⌝ κατ' ἐκεῖνο] The phrase has generated difficulties for scholars. To begin with, the referent of ἐκεῖνο can be ambiguous, insofar as Theophrastus uses the pronoun in this Essay in two ways: either to refer back to something that immediately preceded (5a26, 6b19), or forward to an immediately following item (7a10, 9b13, 11a14). In this case, it was thought by Camotius and Usener to point forward and so they emended the transmitted reading κατ' ἐκεῖνο to κἀκεῖνο and καὶ ἐκεῖνο respectively, to mean, "and so this also would be resolved: that motion cannot begin …". However the transmitted reading κατ' ἐκεῖνο can be retained, for the phrase is a perfectly acceptable relational locution, parallel to κατὰ τοῦτο, "in accordance with this, in this respect, on the basis of this" (LSJ s.v. κατά; cf. van Raalte 144), with ἐκεῖνο pointing to the immediately preceding thought (as ἐκεῖνο normally does, cf. LSJ s.v.), namely, the desirable nature of the first principle from which the incessant and continuous circular motion derives (Reale, Laks & Most; Ross's and Tricot's understanding of the referent to be specifically τὸ ὀρεκτόν does strain κατὰ, as van Raalte 114 remarks, "to an intolerable degree"). The Arabic translation, finally, adds the word "also" in the sentence, which indicates that the translator read ὥστε καὶ κατ' ἐκεῖνο in the Greek (*fa-yajibu min ḏālika … ayḍan*). In the Greek transmission, καί before κατ' could have easily been omitted by haplography. Ὥστε καί adds the further consequence of establishing the desirable as the first principle: it helps resolve the difficulty involved in the Platonic position of a self-moved mover (for ὥστε καί see Denniston 299). For this last position see the references in Ross 42–43 and the other commentators.

5a4–5 τὸ μὴ εἶναι … κινήσει] Comparative ἤ following a negative here means "except," "unless" (Smyth § 2863a), not "or" (the literal translation by Ross 42 of this compressed clause is somewhat misleading). Ἀρχή here means literally "beginning," "starting point" (Ross, Henrich), not "principle" (Tricot, Laks & Most, van Raalte), since the problem addressed is precisely the origin of movement.

Aporia 6

5a5–20 (δεῖται λόγου, ποία καὶ τίνων, 5a14–15): *What kind the impulsion of the rotating heavenly spheres is and towards which things it is.*

In the first half of this paragraph (5a5–13) Theophrastus reviews the attributes of the first principle discussed in Aporiae 2–5 and exalts it to a divine rank adding that it is also indivisible and unquantifiable. This summary leads to the next Aporia with its accompanying

Diaporia 6 (5a13–20): *Manifestly the rotating heavenly spheres are many and their motions are opposed. Their opposed and interminable motions, as well as the final cause of their motions, cannot be explained by assuming either one or multiple first movers as the goal towards which they are impelled, i.e., as the object(s) of desire. For if the mover is one, it is absurd to suppose that the resulting movements would not be the same, and if it is not one, then it is equally absurd to suppose that they would be in concord.*

After a summary statement of the Aristotelian position on the unmoved mover(s), in the immediately following Aporiae (6–12) and in Aporia 16 Theophrastus turns to raising problems about that theory. The question whether Theophrastus in the end abandoned the unmoved mover has been variously answered, though the majority opinion would appear to be that he had, with qualifications. See the statement of the problem by Sharples 1998, 87–88 and his references. For wider discussions of the issue of motion that the problem involves see Skemp 1969, D. Frede 1971, and Berti 2002.

5a6 μὲν δή] The long μέν clause (5a5–13) sums up what has been said; it is answered by δέ in line 13. The two clauses are part of the same sentence and should not be broken up into two separate paragraphs as in previous editions. The particle δή is transitional and connective, summing up as accepted what preceded ("now"), but not inferential or consequential ("then"), without, presumably, losing its primary function of strengthening μέν (cf. Denniston 257–259).

5a6 ἄρτιος means the parts of a whole being functionally well in place (cf. the telling passage about the vertebrae cited in LSJ, s.v.: οἱ σπόνδυλοι … ἄρτιοί εἰσιν ἀλλήλοισι, Hippocrates, *De articulis* 45). What is normally given as words explaining it is εὐκρασία (well mixed together, in right measure and proportion: *SVF* III,278.28, p. 68), πληρότης (fullness or completeness, in the sense that no part is missing or out of place: *Etymologicum Magnum* 150.27), among other references given by van Raalte, 147–148. Henrich's discussion, 189–191, who translates the word as "richtig," is quite off the mark. Whatever λογώδης might mean in 7b18, its antonym (Gegenteil) is not ἄρτιος. Clearly the word implies soundness and health, insofar as proper arrangement and disposition of the parts are prerequisites for the functioning of the whole, but this is not its primary significance.

5a7 ἐνέργειαν, "actualized state"] ἐνέργεια is normally translated in philosophical terms either as "activity" or "actuality," depending on the context, in the specific senses given to the term by both Aristotle and Theophrastus. Theophrastus says that ἐνέργεια in the sense that he is using it here is "prior and more valuable" than movement (below, 7b14), and defines it as "the essence and peculiar form of each thing" (fr. 152 FHS&G; see the Loci Paralleli). In this context, a rendering of the term as "actualized state" better reflects what Theophrastus intends than "actuality." For a discussion of the term see Blair 1967, Rudolph 1988, 233–237; van Raalte 148–150; Sharples 1998, 66–70.

5a8–9 μή … λέγων] The negative goes with the participle, to which the following ἀλλά responds (cf. van Raalte 151–153). For the structure of the sentence and its implication see the comment below on 5a13.

5a9, 5a13 λέγων, τοῖς λέγουσιν, "says", "those who make the … statement." The dative plural in line 13 refers to the participle in line 9.

5a9 ἁπλῶς, "in an absolute sense"] The English adverbs "simply" and "absolutely" cannot easily convey the sense here: the argument Theophrastus is advocating exalts the first principle to a class by itself in the absolute sense, without qualifications.

5a10 μερίδα] For the meaning of μερίς as "class, division" ("rank," as in the Arabic translation, which I adopt) see LSJ s.v. II and III, and especially the reference to μέρος IV.3; cf. van Raalte 153–154.

5a11 ἀφαιρετέον] Happ 1971, 616 and note 288, makes the point that although ἀφαίρεσις had acquired the status of an epistemological technical term in the older Academy, Theophrastus uses it in the conventional sense in this passage as he does later at 6a12–13.

5a13 It is important to note that ἀπόφασις, negation, here does not refer to the actual structure of the sentence in Theophrastus's words in the text above (i.e., to the actual wording in lines 5a8–9, ἔτι δὲ μή … λέγων: Laks & Most 34n32, Henrich 90), but to the proposition to which Theophrastus's words here *point*. So when Theophrastus actually says that the argument he is discussing "says that it [the first principle] is not something divisible" (μὴ διαιρετόν … τι λέγων, lines 8–9), he is pointing to the proposition, "the first principle is not divisible" (in Greek, οὐκ ἔστι διαιρετὸς ἡ ἀρχή; cf. Aristotle, *De Interpretatione* 19b27), and this is the ἀπόφασις that he is talking about in line 13. This negative proposition is then used *in* (ἐν, line 5a12) an argument (and is not itself the argument), based on the divinity of the first principle, which overall is loftier and closer to truth than others. Aristotle frequently so describes the unmoved mover (see the Loci Paralleli), but a question may be raised (as, apparently, van Raalte 151–153, did) whether the statements that he is making on this subject are negative or affirmative; for when Aristotle makes statements like, τὸ πρῶτον κινοῦν ἀδιαίρετόν ἐστι, "the first [unmoved] mover is indivisible", etc., these statements are formally affirmative and not negative, so the question is whether Theophrastus is objecting even to Aristotle's way of putting the argument. But it appears very doubtful that Theophrastus is at all interested in this context in the logical semantics of Aristotle as set forth in *De Interpretatione*.

5a13 δέ, responding to μέν in line 5a6; see above.

5a14 ἐφέσεως] With reference to the desire for the unmoved mover, Theophrastus uses here and at 5a28 and 5b11 a different word, ἔφεσις, than the one he uses elsewhere, ὄρεξις, at 5a2 (in ὀρεκτόν), 5a20, etc. However, at 6a9 he uses both words together in asking whether the rotation of the bodies is "through some impulsion and desire," ἐφέσει τινὶ καὶ ὀρέξει, which would indicate that the two words are synonymous. The same appears to be the case with Aristotle's use of the two words in a related context in *EE* 1218a24–33, where ἐφίενται, ὀρέγεται, and ὄρεξις seem to be used interchangeably. Simplicius, *In Phys.* 250.22–23 Diels (*CAG*), explains the difference by saying that ὄρεξις is what animate beings have, ἔφεσις inanimate natural bodies. This would appear to be indicated by the passage below in the Essay (at 5a28), where Theophrastus implies that if impulsion entails soul then it is desire—but given the nine centuries of Greek usage separating Simplicius from Theophrastus, it is not clear whether Simplicius may not just be rationalizing (cf. further the references in van Raalte 165). On the other hand, on the basis of the passage in the *Eudemian Ethics* just referred to, Berti 2002, 344–345, saw in ἔφεσις a reference to Academic doctrine, suggesting that Theophrastus here is criticizing Platonists rather than Aristotle.

5a15 The genitive interrogative pronoun τίνων could theoretically refer either to the object towards which the impulsion is directed or the subject being impelled, as the commentators note, but there can be little doubt, in context, that the genitive is objective. The argument that immediately follows, in response to ποία καὶ τίνων, raises precisely the problem of how the object towards which the impulsion is directed is to be understood.

5a16 φοραί] The reference is to the motions of the celestial bodies as they are "carried along" across the heavens. Theophrastus's reference here is directly to Aristotle's *Metaphysics* Λ 8, where the word φορά is repeatedly used, and where Aristotle describes the six different motions of these bodies, conveniently summarized by Ross 43. It is accordingly inaccurate (and anachronistic) to render this word as "orbit" or "orbiting" (Umlaufbahn, Henrich).

5a16–17 καὶ τὸ ἀνήνυτον … ἀφανές] This phrase, which seems to have caused unnecessary problems, can be most naturally understood to refer to the motions of the spheres (φοραί), the interminable nature and goal of which do not seem to be apparent; i.e., one is to understand, καὶ τὸ ἀνήνυτον αὐτῶν [sc. τῶν φορῶν] καὶ οὗ χάριν ἀφανές. This can be best brought out by eliminating the comma traditionally placed after ὑπεναντίαι. Van Raalte 169–171, who has a different interpretation and suggests a different punctuation, nevertheless cites two passages (Plato, *Phaedo* 84a5–6 and Ps.-Plato *Axiochus* 371e8) which best bring out the meaning of ἀνήνυτον: the futile interminableness of Sisyphus's rolling of the stone (Σισύφου πέτρος ἀνήνυτος) and Penelope's weaving of her web (ἀνήνυτον ἔργον πράττειν Πηνελόπης). The οὗ χάριν phrase lacks the article τό immediately before it, but it is not necessary (cf. van Raalte 169n1); the article before ἀνήνυτον serves for both. It can be misleading, though, and it apparently misled Isḥāq; see the corresponding note to the Arabic translation.

5a17 ἄτοπον, "it makes no sense"] The word refers to something that is out of place, that does not fit, and hence, in Theophrastus's philosophical usage, something that is logically inconsistent and incongruous. See his usage of the term in *Ign.* § 4,3, ἄτοπον φαίνεται πρῶτον αὐτὸ (*sc.* τὸ πῦρ) λέγειν καὶ οἷον ἀρχήν, εἰ μὴ οἷόν τ' εἶναι χωρὶς ὕλης (p. 5, line 14 Coutant), i.e., to say both that fire needs "matter" or fuel in order to exist *and* that it is a primary and first principle does not make sense because contradictory. The word thus means more than "strange" in its accepted meanings of "alien, unfamiliar, and unaccountable" (Ross, Tricot, Laks & Most, Henrich; "puzzling," van Raalte; though more accurately, "assurdo,"

Reale 1964), for it points to the logical incongruity of two (sets of) facts. Cf. further Baltussen 2000, 203–204, and his references to Le Blond.

The word occurs three times in the Essay; here and at 5b14 and 7b23. Isḥāq translates the first two instances with *šaniʿ* (repugnant, horrid) and the last with *qabīḥ* (bad, ugly), which are, essentially, ethical terms referring to negative moral qualities, not intellectual incongruity. Isḥāq's choice of words is difficult to gauge. Either these terms, in 9th century Baghdad Arabic, also had an intellectual reference to them, which, however, is not recorded in the dictionaries, or, what seems more likely, Isḥāq's understanding of the term was colored by its Christian use, meaning "wicked;" cf. Lampe s.v.

5a18 τὸ μὴ πάντα τὴν αὐτήν] In the elliptical sentence of Theophrastus, the infinitive that complements the substantival use of the article τό can be either active or middle, κινεῖν or κινεῖσθαι, i.e., either τὸ μὴ πάντα τὴν αὐτὴν κινεῖν κίνησιν, or τὸ μὴ πάντα τὴν αὐτὴν κινεῖσθαι κίνησιν, in which case the noun πάντα will function either as the object or the subject of the verb, respectively ("why it [the mover] does not move all with the same motion," or "why all do not move with the same motion"). Ross prefers the former alternative, and everybody else, including Isḥāq, the second. Berti 2002, 345, takes the pronoun αὐτήν to refer to ἔφεσις and translates, "è assurdo che tutti non abbiano lo stesso desiderio," which seems quite improbable in context, as the above analysis of the clause indicates.

5a19 ὥστε, which seemingly introduces the apodosis of a conditional sentence, has long baffled scholars and does not appear to be fully understood. Hermann Bonitz wrote a substantial article on its use in Aristotle in the 1860s,[7] in which he also cited earlier references in the works of his German predecessors. He made two basic points. The first is that such use of ὥστε, beyond being a mere indication of anacolouthon in Aristotle's works, is rather a grammatically inaccurate ("sprachlich ungenauen") stylistic peculiarity of his (p. 75). The second is that, once this is understood, it should affect the punctuation of Aristotle's works

[7] Originally published in the *Sitzungsberichte der philosophisch-historischen Classe der kais. Akad. der Wissenschaften* in Vienna, 1862, 72–90, it was reprinted in his *Aristotelische Studien*, Hildesheim: Olms, 1969, 202–220. Bonitz also listed the Aristotelian passages which exhibit this use of ὥστε allegedly "in apodosi" in his *Index* 873a31–44.

where it appears in a way that will reflect it (p. 80). Minute analyses of numerous passages in Aristotle where this occurs accompanied Bonitz's observations. In the summary of his research in the *Index* (873a31–44), Bonitz mentioned that in most cases the anacolouthon is due to the longish protasis of the conditional sentence which contains many subordinate phrases (*per plura membra continuata vel parenthesibus intercepta*), though he admitted that in some instances it is also found after brief and simple (*brevem ac simplicem*) protases. Ross apparently followed this concise statement of the case in the *Index* rather than Bonitz's full study, for he repeated it both in his commentary on this text of Theophrastus (pp. 43–44) and in his commentaries on Aristotle's works (e.g., Aristotle's *Physics*, Ross 1936, p. 643 ad 233b7–11). As a matter of fact, it appears that Ross was rather uncomfortable with the appearance of this feature in short sentences, and in one instance at least he accordingly followed an inferior manuscript reading which eliminates the problem by dropping the particle δέ (*Physics* 232a12 and note on pp. 640–641; this incidentally, is the very text which Ross had given in the commentary on Theophrastus as example of the occurrence of this feature in short protases!). Subsequent commentators on Theophrastus mostly referred to Ross.

However, valuable as Bonitz's study is, and despite the acceptance by modern commentators of his analysis, it cannot be thought that ὥστε can introduce a conditional apodosis. Van Raalte, exceptionally, writes in a brief note (171n1) about the passage in Theophrastus that the ὥστε clause "takes the place of an apodosis rather than constituting an exceptional instance of ὥστε in apodosi." The question is, how. This is not the place to go into a detailed study of the issue (clearly a desideratum), but a few remarks are in order.[8] First, since this passage occurs in a work by Theophrastus, it cannot be maintained that this was a stylistic feature peculiar to Aristotle alone. I could not check thoroughly in the time at my disposal all the extant works by Theophrastus or other related Greek literature, but if the style of Theophrastus's Essay, because of its aporetic nature, is close to that of Aristotle, the possibility ought to be investigated whether this feature may not be more at home in the style of oral disputation because of the semantic jump it requires from the protasis of the conditional clause to the result clause of an assumed apodosis (as discussed below). Secondly, Bonitz's (and following him, Ross's) attempted

[8] The comprehensive Greek grammars by K.-G. and Schwyzer do not mention a feature of ὥστε "*in apodosi*" simply because it does not exist.

explanation of the feature as deriving from anacolouthon in sentences with long protases cannot hold because of its obvious appearance in shorter ones as well (see the referenes in Bonitz's article and *Index*).

The following example would appear to give a clue about the grammar and function of this use of ὥστε: *De anima* 432b21–26: εἰ οὖν ἡ φύσις μήτε ποιεῖ μάτην μηθὲν μήτε ἀπολείπει τι τῶν ἀναγκαίων, πλὴν ἐν τοῖς πηρώμασι καὶ ἐν τοῖς ἀτελέσιν, τὰ δὲ τοιαῦτα τῶν ζῴων τέλεια καὶ οὐ πηρώματά ἐστιν (σημεῖον δ' ὅτι ἐστὶ γεννητικὰ καὶ ἀκμὴν ἔχει καὶ φθίσιν)—ὥστ' εἶχεν ἂν καὶ τὰ ὀργανικὰ μέρη τῆς πορείας.[9] This is a good example of the precise function of ὥστε in the apodosis because the passage is unambiguous, in the sense that though the protasis is not particularly short, no part of it can be misconstrued as the apodosis. The function of the ὥστε clause here, then, is not to be the entire apodosis but a part of it, the part that expresses the *result* or *consequence* of an assumed grammatical apodosis. This is clear from the unambiguous sense of the text and it appears in almost all translations of the passage, which *add* a clause or a phrase to express the apodosis in the Greek which is implied but not actually stated: "then it follows too that" (D.W. Hamlyn, Oxford 1968), "il en résulte que" (Bodéüs, Paris 1993), and, most significantly, "dans ces conditions donc" (Barbotin, Paris 1966), etc. It is thus clear that the use of ὥστε in these cases is consecutive. As such, it has a number of uses (Schwyzer II,677–681), two of which would appear to be relevant here: introducing a result clause after demonstrative adjectives or adverbs (οὕτως etc.) in the principal clause, and (perhaps as an extension of this most common usage?) introducing independent sentences in the sense of "consequently" (Schwyzer II,680 §7), where apparently a principal clause, to which ὥστε answers, can frequently be semantically assumed. It thus appears that ὥστε in these conditional sentences does not so much introduce the apodosis as constitute the consequence of an assumed and unexpressed grammatical apodosis, such as, "If x and y and z obtain, ⟨then, these stated conditions are such—or, the situation so develops⟩ that the consequences are as follows." It may be too much to assume that some such phrase as, εἰ …, ⟨οὕτως ἔχει⟩ ὥστε …, is to be understood in every instance of this use of ὥστε, but clearly its function has become one which expresses the consequence of the condition in the protasis with greater emphasis than a regular apodosis without ὥστε could have done.

---

9 I follow the text and punctuation in the edition by Ross 1961, of whose dash before ὥστε I fully approve.

5a19–20 τὸ σύμφωνον … τὴν ἀρίστην] The clause is quite clear both in its syntax and meaning; the complications raised by Laks & Most 35n39 (followed and subscribed to by Henrich 91–92) appear to be unnecessary. Laks & Most translate, "leur accord en matière de désir, quand ils suivent la meilleure [des translations], n'est absolument pas manifeste." But first, the context cannot support this interpretation; the concord must refer to the concord of movements, not desires, as they claim, because the objection to the preceding alternative was also based on the concord of movements: if the mover is one, Theophrastus's argument goes, it is absurd to suppose that the resulting movements would *not* be the same; and if it is not one, then it is equally absurd to suppose that they *would* be the same, i.e., be in concord. And second, for Laks & Most's interpretation to stand, the wording in the Greek ought to have been different and differently punctuated, as follows: ὥστε τὸ σύμφωνον εἰς ὄρεξιν, ἰόντων αὐτῶν τὴν ἀρίστην, οὐθαμῶς φανερόν. Since the text is not thus worded, and the words εἰς ὄρεξιν ἰόντων τὴν ἀρίστην clearly belong together, then ὄρεξιν ἀρίστην must mean that the desire is "best" in the sense that it is desire *for* the best, and hence the object of the desire would not be desire itself (thus the difficulty identified by Laks & Most does not exist), but the Best itself (so in a sense Tricot in his translation should have capitalized *Meilleur* rather than *Désir*).[10] The correct evaluation of the preposition εἰς in the clause is important; it does not express place ("in the direction of," Jaeger 1948, 349; Ross), but purpose and end (cf. LSJ s.v. V), "in the fulfillment of;" for this causal use of εἰς, where "εἰς zunächst den Zweck angiebt, welcher bei etwas verfolgt wird," see Müller 1878, 8–9.

For the cosmological and ontological implications of Aristotle's ordering of the spheres, skeptically countenanced here by Theophrastus, see Happ 1971, 363–367. For the one system in which Aristotle argues that all the spheres for all the planets must work together, see Beere 2003, 5 ff.

Aporia 7

5a20–22 (ζητεῖ λόγον): *The great number of celestial sheres (and their separate movers) needs an explanation more pertinent than the one provided by the astronomers.*

[10] Skemp 1969, 219, interprets, "as they move towards the most excellent form of desire," which does not avoid the difficulty raised by Laks & Most.

This is a reference to the account by the astronomers Eudoxus and Calippus which Aristotle provisionally invokes in *Metaphysics* Λ 8 in explanation of the number of spheres. Aristotle introduces that section by calling astronomy "most pertinent" or "most akin" to philosophy, but ends, after having presented the astronomers' theories and his adaptation of them, by leaving the improvement of the discussion to more competent hands. Theophrastus takes Aristotle at his word and echoes the sentiment here. On the questions raised here by Theophrastus on the relevance of astronomy to metaphysics and on Aristotle's competence in astronomy, see Lloyd 2000.

5a21 δέ introduces here the related but incidental (though not necessarily parenthetical, pace van Raalte 176) aporia about the multitude of spheres and their numerous movers that the immediately preceding sentence brought to Theophrastus's mind. The main subject under discussion in the paragraph of Aporia 6, the desire for the unmoved mover(s), is interrupted for a moment for Theophrastus to register his dissatisfaction with, apparently, Aristotle's astronomical theories in *Metaphysics* Λ 8 (see the next comment and the Loci Paralleli), and is then continued with the following Aporia 8. The use of the subordinating copulative δέ here is too common to require comment.

5a22 The missing word at this point in all the extant Greek manuscripts and the Latin translation (Λ), noted by most editors, is supplied with the help of the Arabic, which has the verb *anisa* (*lam ānas*), here most likely rendering οἰκεῖος (see the corresponding commentary on the Arabic translation); there seems to be little doubt that this is the missing word. Besides, Theophrastus here is echoing Aristotle's words in *Metaphysics* Λ 8, 1073b4, where astronomy is called the science "most relevant" or "most pertinent" (οἰκειοτάτη) to philosophy with regard to establishing the number of celestial motions and hence of the spheres that cause them (see the Loci Paralleli). Theophrastus begs to differ, and is calling for a philosophical discussion of the reason for the number, and also, one would think (and as Laks & Most 35n40 suggest), for the necessity of a multiplicity of movers. In a way, Theophrastus takes up, and demands more of, the conclusion to that section by Aristotle (1074a13–17): "Let then the number of the spheres be that many, whence it is reasonable to suppose that there are as many unmoved substances and first principles. ⟨I say "reasonable" and not "necessary"⟩ because (γάϱ) necessity ought to be left to more powerful [thinkers] to state." Theophrastus seems not to find this supposition reasonable, and wants a detailed discussion of the reason for it, or the necessity for it, challenging precisely Aristotle's disclaimer that this discussion ought to be left to better thinkers.[11] Aristotle appears to have taken Theophrastus's admonition to heart, for, as Owen 1961, 90, astutely remarked, he later changed his mind about the ability of (astronomical) observation to provide knowledge about the "divine" beings, i.e., the stars and the celestial spheres; in their regard, he says, "there are few things that are evident to the senses" (ὀλίγα τὰ φανερὰ κατὰ τὴν αἴσθησιν, *PA* 644b24–28).

The expression οἰκεῖος λόγος in the sense of "relevant, pertinent argument" is common in the vocabulary of both Aristotle and Theophrastus. A passage from Aristotle's *Physics* (264a7–9) gives us a good idea about what the issue raised by Theophrastus here is. With regard to the question of the circular φορά of the celestial bodies, Aristotle provides an account of its continuous nature by having recourse to two kinds of arguments: one based on the nature of rectilinear and circular motion, which would be a physical argument, and another based on logical considerations concerning opposites, which he calls a "logical" (λογικῶς) argument (see the analysis of the passage in Ross's commentary in his edition, corr. ed. Oxford 1966, p. 715). The former, physical argument, Aristotle characterizes as "pertinent" to the subject (οἰκείοις λόγοις), insofar as the question is a physical one and so the argument most pertinent to it is also physical. The point that Theophrastus is thus making here is what has just been stated in the preceding paragraph, that the argument of the astronomers is a mathematical argument that does not satisfy the requirements of an explanation for a metaphysical subject.

For a similar use of the expression οἰκεῖος λόγος in Aristotle see *Politics* 1323b38–39; Theophrastus, as a matter of fact, even wrote an essay on the subject with the very title, Περὶ οἰκείων λόγων α′ (FHS&G fr. 1,280). It is not clear whether he may have been responding in this essay to the peculiar use made of the concept by Antisthenes, as discussed by A. Brancacci, *Oikeios logos. La filosofia del linguaggio di Antistene*, Napoli 1990.

For οἰκεῖος in this context see also the fragment by Eudemus quoted by Simplicius *In Phys.* 48,8–26 Diels (*CAG*) = fr. 34 Wehrli.

---

[11] "The question of necessity is left in abeyance," says G.E.R. Lloyd 2000, 273, of this passage; the problematic nature of Aristotle's words here is discussed by Lloyd at 262–263.

Aporia 8

5a23–5b10 (ἄπορον πῶς): *Why the rotating celestial spheres, desiring (an) immobile mover(s), pursue not rest but motion.*

This aporia is discussed in three stages, in one diaporia immediately following (Diaporia 8), in a second following that (Diaporia 8.1), and in a later discussion at 7b23–8a7 (Diaporia 16.2).

Diaporia 8 (5a25–28). *Concerning desire, the aporia is how it can be that the celestial spheres, though possessed of a natural desire for the unmoved mover (as Aristotle claims), pursue, (contrary to all logic,) not rest but motion. (But leaving Aristotle aside,) why is it that this (i.e., the pursuit of motion) can be maintained, (in an even more manifestly illogical way,)* at the same time with imitation *this time, also by (Platonists and Pythagoreans)? For they, too, maintain that the numbers are the one (as being derived from it and unmoved like it, and hence the spheres should be imitating not motion but rest).*

This diaporia, stated in one sentence only as a rhetorical question, has presented difficulies of interpretation. An initial problem is how to understand the semantic transition from Aristotle's theories (desire for the unmoved mover) to those of the Platonists and Pythagoreans (imitation of the one), and the precise rhetorical meaning of τί οὖν which opens the sentence. Is it an indirect criticism of Aristotle for having failed to base his theory of desire on a theory of imitation like the Platonists, as Laks & Most 36n42 suggest, or is it a rhetorical expression of indignation that not only Aristotle, with his theory of desire, failed to see the contradiction between the desire for the unmoved mover and the pursuit of motion rather than rest, but especially the Platonists, and in a manifestly more illogical manner, with their theory of imitation? The style in which this sentence is written, with the emphasis clearly laid on imitation, ἅμα τῇ μιμήσει, suggests the latter.

The main difficulty, however, is presented by the elliptical nature of the final καὶ γάρ clause in the sentence. To understand it, it is imperative to follow Theophrastus's argument closely and especially the point he wishes to make. Having first stated the self-contradictory nature of Aristotle's theory of desire because of the discrepancy between the desire of the celestial bodies for the unmoved mover and their pursuit of motion rather than rest, with the next sentence Theophrastus now points out a similar discrepancy in the views of those who uphold the one and the numbers as ultimate principles through whose imitation the heavenly bodies and, by extension, sensible things are in motion or come to be. As Ross 44 explains, the similarity "is that, whether we say that the sensible world 'desires' or that it 'imitates' the first principle, we should expect to find it in that case having the same characteristics as the first principle—not movement but rest." The discrepancy in the case of Aristotle's theory is obvious, in that the ultimate principle which is desired by the heavenly bodies is expressly identified as the "*unmoved* mover", and hence whatever desires it should pursue not motion but rest, as Theophrastus says. In the case of those who uphold the one and the numbers as ultimate principles whose imitation brings about motion, the situation is not as clear. The discrepancy, in the case of those who uphold the one, is real only when the one is taken to be motionless, in which case those who claim that things both imitate the one *and* are in motion can justifiably be said to fall into contradiction. Now the one is unmoved (cf. the passage from Xenocrates cited in the Loci Paralleli: *immutabile*). The problem is with the position of those who uphold the numbers as ultimate principles: they can be said to fall into contradiction only if the numbers are, as first principles, unmoved. Theophrastus's rhetorical question τί οὖν ... λέγουσιν claims that this discrepancy exists equally (ὁμοίως) in the position of those who uphold the numbers as it does in that of those who uphold the one, and the emphasis Theophrastus puts on the word ὁμοίως implies that the position that numbers as first principles are unmoved was not something that was known as commonly, or that people were willing to accept as readily, as that which claimed immobility for the one as principle. So the phrase with the word ὁμοίως points this out to the audience ("you know," Theophrastus is saying, "it is not only those who uphold the one who say that it is immobile and hence fall into this contradiction, but equally those who uphold the numbers"), and the following καὶ γάρ clause provides the explanation; καὶ γάρ explains ὁμοίως. In other words, the raison d'être of the καὶ γάρ clause is to state or explain the immobility of the numbers, so that the discrepancy in the position of those who both say that things move or come to be in imitation of the numbers *and* at the same time claim that numbers are immobile can be real; in the context, the καὶ γάρ clause can have no other purpose. Thus Henrich (95) is right in pointing out that the καὶ γάρ clause refers not to the theory of imitation but to that of numbers ("ergänzt nicht die Theorie der μίμησις, sondern ausschliesslich die Zahlenlehre").

If this is so, then the καὶ γάϱ clause can be taken at its face value to mean, "for these people too say that the numbers are the one," in the sense either that they are ultimately the one, being derived from it, and hence also unmoved, or that they are like the one, unmoved, a position ascribed to Xenocrates (fr. 16 Heinze; see the Loci Paralleli). The reference to Xenocrates would appear to be also behind the problematic passage in Aristotle's *Eudemian Ethics*, 1218a24–28, as Brunschwig 1971, 212–216, argues, where Aristotle says, οἱ ἀϱιθμοὶ ἐφίενται, the numbers are impelled, presumably towards the one, though the transmitted text does not say so, despite the numerous attempts by scholars at emending it to do precisely that (Fritzsche, Richards, Ross; see Walzer and Mingay's critical apparatus *ad loc.*). But regardless how scholarship resolves the object that is the goal of the numbers' impulsion in this passage of the *Eudemian Ethics*, what is relevant for our (and Theophrastus's) argument here is that if numbers are impelled and have desire, they must undergo some kind of κίνησις, change or movement, for they would have to have life—to say that they are lifeless is an "audacious" (παϱάβολος) and absurd statement, as Aristotle notes in criticizing this theory. Thus the implication that one would derive from such a theory, even if its adherents do not say (as Aristotle remarks) precisely how it is that numbers desire, is that numbers are moved. Theophrastus then would seem to be reacting to this implication of the theory about numbers, that they may be moved (in which case, the movement of sensible things in imitation of numbers would not be paradoxical, as Theophrastus wants to argue in the passage under discussion), and he accordingly stresses that this is not so, that even those (like Xenocrates?) who uphold the numbers say that they are the one, unmoved like it.

If the point and force of Theophrastus's argument here is as just described—to show that the numbers, *when taken as principles*, are just as unmoved as the one itself, so that the assumption of the generation of the moving sensible world through imitation of the immobile numbers would be contradictory, as Theophrastus claims—then the καὶ γάϱ clause cannot be assumed to have missing here an infinitive like μιμεῖσθαι or διώκειν ("for the latter themselves speak of the numbers as imitating the one," Ross, followed by Tricot; Theiler 1958, 103/293; Reale 1980, 394; Laks & Most; for διώκειν see Skemp 1969, 218). Because if the numbers imitate or pursue the one, they are either unmoved like it or moved. But if they are moved—as one would expect them to be since the sensibles, which imitate the one, are also moved—then they themselves would be in motion, and thus when numbers act as principles and sensible things imitate *them*, the resulting motion of the sensible things would not be contradictory, and hence the very point that Theophrastus wishes to make about imitation (imitation is untenable because imitation of unmoved principles cannot lead to movement) cannot be made. So if the numbers imitate or pursue the one, they must be unmoved. But this time the objection would be, if imitation leads to immobility when the numbers imitate the one, why does it lead to motion when sensible things imitate it or them? Thus in this case also Theophrastus cannot make the point he is making in the text because if numbers are unmoved this means that imitation *does* work, at least in the case of the numbers imitating or pursuing the one, and he would then have to discuss and explain the special circumstances concerning sensible things, in whose case imitation does not work. But neither does Theophrastus enter into such a discussion nor is there any indication that he wishes to take the argument there. Thus the point of the καὶ γάρ clause cannot be imitation (or pursuit) because it does not fit the argument that Theophrastus is making here, and the clause cannot be read by assuming a missing infinitive μιμεῖσθαι or διώκειν.

Van Raalte (and, following her, Henrich and Dillon 2002, 178 and note 11) does not think that μιμεῖσθαι or διώκειν is the missing word here either, but she offers an emendation of the text whose upshot is that it coalesces the two positions, that of those who uphold the one and that of those who uphold the numbers, which, though in the right direction, misses the point about the motion of the numbers. She records a possible emendation of the text on the suggestion of van Ophuijsen, καὶ γὰρ αὐτοὶ ⟨οἱ⟩ τοὺς ἀριθμοὺς (*sc.* λέγοντες) φασιν (*sc.* εἶναι) τὸ ἕν, which she translates as, "for the adherents of the numbers themselves too postulate the One" ("For those who favour numbers also postulate the One," Dillon 2002, 177). The emendation is quite ingenious, because palaeographically plausible, but it cannot be entertained not only because it does not fit the analysis of the argument as stated above, but also on stylistic grounds. First, the repetition of οἱ τοὺς ἀριθμοὺς (*sc.* λέγοντες), whether with or without λέγοντες, right after ὅσοι τοὺς ἀριθμοὺς λέγουσιν, which is already repeated in αὐτοί, would be more than unbearably pleonastic, it would be untenable. Second, if Theophrastus wanted to say what van Raalte wants him to say in her reconstructed sentence, he would simply have said, καὶ γὰρ αὐτοί φασιν εἶναι τὸ ἕν, or even just καὶ γὰρ αὐτοί φασιν τὸ ἕν. The presence of τοὺς ἀριθμούς in the clause, just four words after they have already been used in the sentence, makes it clear that Theophrastus wants to say something different about them, not use them in the same phrase as before, and according to the analysis I offered above, it is precisely the fact of their immobility that he wants to stress.

Diaporia 8.1 (5a28–5b10). *If the heavenly bodies have impulsion or desire, then they must have soul; and if they have soul, then they must have movement in the form of thought, but also of desire, which springs from thought. Thus the movement of the soul in the form of thought and desire is primary, whereas the rotating movement of the spheres, if it is caused by desire for the prime mover, is secondary. Hence the prime mover cannot be the cause of the best movement (because it would be contrary to the implied* endoxon *in this Aporia that the first must be the best).*

Theophrastus's argument at 5b7–10 would appear to be addressed at Aristotle's *Metaphysics* Λ 8, 1072a26, where the ὀρεκτόν causes *directly* the circular movement of the spheres, without explaining how this actually works.[12] So Theophrastus's objection claims that the ὀρεκτόν does not cause directly the circular movement, but it moves the soul, or even better, the intellect; and it is the soul or intellect, which are the best of things as principles (as Aristotle was later to state in *De anima* 410b12–15), that cause the circular movement through the ὄρεξις they develop for the first. Aristotle responds to this criticism by developing in the later in date *De anima* the mechanism of the causation of movement. In Γ 10, 433b13–21, he says there are three things:[13] (1) that which causes movement, which is subdivided into (1a) that which is unmoved (i.e., the good to be achieved by action) and (1b) that which causes movement and is itself moved (i.e., the faculty of desire, for actual desiring is a movement); (2) that with which it causes it (i.e., the corporeal organ by which desire causes movement); and (3) that which is moved (i.e., the animal). Thus Aristotle qualifies his earlier position that there can be no self-movement by saying that "it is by virtue of having desire that an animal moves itself" (433b27–28; Ross 1961, 315). In this fashion what the unmoved mover sets in motion is not the circular movement of the spheres but the desiring movement in their souls, and it is this desiring movement which in turn sets them in circular motion. This means that Theophrastus could not have written his diaporia in this passage the way

[12] Only Berti 2002, 349, thinks that Theophrastus is here using a doctrine by Plato against Plato's followers.

[13] Borrowing freely Ross's rendition of the argument in his *De Anima* 1961, 315.

he has if the *De anima* had already been written, for it seems that the passage in the *De anima* is an actual response to this difficulty raised by Theophrastus.

Grumach 1966, 51–54 and 62–64, first associated this diaporia by Theophrastus with the *De anima* passages from Aristotle and drew out its implications for the position of the Stoa (Grumach's arguments were summarized by Reale 1980, 384–385); Reale 1964, 37–55 (and especially 46–50), then discussed it at length. The issue of the movement of the celestial souls due to desire, which became subsequently standard Peripatetic doctrine, was thus first raised by Theophrastus, as pointed out by I.M. Bodnár in a written communication to G. Endress, who reports it in "Alexander Arabus on the First Cause," in C. D'Ancona and G. Serra, eds, *Aristotele e Alessandro di Afrodisia nella tradizione araba*, Padova: Il Poligrafo, 2002, 41.

5a26 The referent of the pronoun ἐκεῖνο here has been much discussed, unnecessarily, it seems; for the various theories see van Raalte 184–185 and the summary by Henrich 92–93. The most natural way to read the sentence, in the rhetorical sweep of the argument, is to take the neuter pronoun to point to what Theophrastus has just said (ἐκεῖνο referring, as it normally does, "to what has gone immediately before," LSJ s.v.), viz., the *whole* statement (and not just one word) that sensibles "pursue not rest but motion" (οὐ τὴν ἠρεμίαν διώκουσιν ἀλλὰ τὴν κίνησιν). Without any hint of having had difficulty, Isḥāq also understood it in this way, "this statement" (*hāḏā l-qawl*). There is danger in disregarding the regular meaning of words and coming up with ad hoc "rules," as Ross 45 does when he says that Theophrastus "tends to revert to the neuter when he is referring to anything inanimate;" see below the commentary at 6b16–17.

5b3 ψυχῇ ... ὑπάρχειν] This brief sentence has exercised all students of Theophrastus's work, including Isḥāq. The problem has been both the case in which the opening word, ψυχή, is to be read, and the proper understanding of the word ἅμα and the correct appreciation of the emphasis indicated by its position in the word order. The Greek manuscripts and the Latin translation have ψυχή in the nominative, except for C, which has both ψυχήν and κίνησιν in the accusative, an obvious (and negligible) scribal emendation intended to read δοκεῖ as impersonal. If, then, ψυχή is read in the nominative (as done by Wimmer and van Raalte following the Greek manuscripts), it has to be taken together with κίνησις, in which case the sentence could yield two possible understandings of ἅμα: (1) ψυχὴ δ' ἅμα καὶ κίνησις δοκοῦσιν ὑπάρχειν[14] where adverbial ἅμα nuances the conjunction καί,[15] and (2) ψυχὴ δὲ καὶ κίνησις δοκοῦσιν ἅμα ὑπάρχειν, where adverbial ἅμα modifies ὑπάρχειν. Version (1) would mean, "Soul together with movement seem to exist," which may be an inelegant way of saying what version (2) says, "Soul and movement seem to exist together," or, as understood by van Raalte: "Soul seems to be coexistent with movement." Next, if ψυχῇ is read in the dative, as originally corrected by Usener (1861) and accepted by all modern editors, then we have essentially one way to understand the sentence, (3) ἅμα δὲ δοκεῖ καὶ κίνησις ὑπάρχειν ψυχῇ, where adverbial ἅμα modifies δοκεῖ ὑπάρχειν, with the dative ψυχῇ complementing ὑπάρχειν but placed first in the sentence because of emphasis. The meaning would be, "At the same time movement also seems to pertain to soul" (as in the translation of Laks & Most). Laks & Most 38n46 mention another possibility of reading the sentence, namely, (4) δοκεῖ δ' ἅμα ⟨τῇ⟩ ψυχῇ καὶ κίνησις ὑπάρχειν, where prepositional ἅμα is directly connected with ψυχῇ in the dative, and meaning, "It seems that movement also exists together with soul." It would be difficult to maintain this because of the position of ψυχῇ preceding ἅμα in the original sentence[16] and because one would have expected an article before ψυχῇ, though if this were to be the reading, ψυχῇ δ' ἅμα would echo μετὰ ψυχῆς in 5b1 and yield a parallel meaning. In any case, Isḥāq did understand the sentence as in version (4), translating, "It seems with the existence of the soul [there is] motion" (for a discussion of this version see the corresponding commentary in the Arabic translation). It is clear that Isḥāq read in his Greek exemplar, Ψ, ψυχῇ in the dative, which corroborates Usener's conjecture.

The course of the argument, which may indicate which alternative reading of those offered above is most likely to be correct, is the following: Theophrastus starts with the position of Aristotle, that the heavenly bodies desire the unmoved mover. From this he derives the following consequences. If the heavenly bodies have desire, then they must have soul

[14] In this reconstruction of the sentence it is necessary to use the plural form, δοκοῦσιν; in the actual text, as van Raalte 193 suggests, the singular δοκεῖ can be explained by the fact that it precedes the second subject, κίνησις. In Theophrastus, in fact, δοκεῖ does precede a plural subject when it consists of a series of singular nouns, e.g., δοκεῖ δ' ἡ ἀνδράχλη καὶ ὁ κόμαρος τὰ μὲν κάτω φυλλοβολεῖν, *HP* I.9.3, line 9; cf. *HP* I.9.7, line 2; II.1.3, line 6, etc.

[15] Cf. van Raalte's apposite citation, 193, of examples for this usage, including the one from *HP* V.4.2, ἰσχυρὸν ἅμα καὶ εὔεργον τὸ ξύλον.

[16] A search in the *TLG* data base revealed no instances in Theophrastus where prepositional ἅμα follows the noun to which it is attached in the dative.

(5a28–5b2). But if they have soul, then they must also have movement (5b3). There follows a brief parenthetical section (ζωὴ γάρ ... γίνονται, 5b3–7) explaining the statement just made, i.e., the connection between movement and soul: soul implies movement just as desire implied soul precisely because desire is movement of the soul; as a matter of fact, Theophrastus argues, desires for all objects, as well as sensations and, as he is going to say a few lines later, thoughts, are all movements of the soul. So, the argument then resumes, if the unmoved mover were really the cause of circular movement, it would not be the cause of the best movement because these other movements of the soul, and especially thought, would be better and prior, because thought gave rise to the desire for the unmoved mover to begin with. Thus, the conclusion is that "what is put forward as the cause of movement (i.e., the impulse [or desire]) presupposes the existence of movement," that of the soul in the form of thought (Ross 46). Hence Aristotle's theory of the unmoved mover as the original source of movement cannot stand.

As for the significance of ἅμα and καί in this understanding of the Greek in line 5b3, it appears that Theophrastus is saying that movement *also* seems *at the same time* as desire to pertain to soul, because, in fact, as he explains later, desire *is* a movement of the soul. Thus the force and purpose of the sentence in 5b3 is not to say that soul and movement co-exist (versions 1 and 2),[17] or that movement exists together with soul (version 4, assuming it is a viable reading), but that just as desire pertains to soul, so does at the same time and a fortiori movement (version 3), because desire is, in fact, a movement of the soul.

5b4 ἀφ' ἧς] In the parenthetical section (ζωὴ γάρ ... γίνονται, 5b3–7) the tone and the references are set by the opening clause, ζωὴ γὰρ τοῖς ἔχουσιν, whose subject is understood to be ψυχή, as universally acknowledged, reading ζωὴ γὰρ ἡ ψυχὴ τοῖς ἔχουσιν αὐτήν (or, as Skemp 1969, 218, has it, ζωὴ γὰρ τοῖς ἔχουσιν ἡ ψυχή ἐστιν). This being the case, the antecedent of the feminine pronoun in ἀφ' ἧς must necessarily be ψυχή because it is closer to the understood ψυχή in the immediately preceding clause than to κίνησις in the clause before that (pace Ross 47; cf. van Raalte 199: "Like ζωή in the preceding parenthesis,

[17] This is also indicated by Theophrastus's choice of particles. He has just said at 5b2 that things in motion have soul, so if he meant to repeat or explain this in the next line at 5b3 by saying that soul and motion co-exist, he would (or should) have used an explanatory particle like γάρ rather than the oppositional δέ in ψυχῇ δ'.

ἀφ' ἧς refers to ψυχή"). As for the force of the preposition ἀπό in ἀφ' ἧς, it is similar to what Aristotle says when he talks about the affections of the soul as movements reaching *to* it and starting *from* it (ἀπ' ἐκείνης), *De anima* 408b13–18 (see the Loci Paralleli).

5b6 ὡς ἐμψύχοις. The Greek exemplar (Ψ) used by Isḥāq had, ὅμως ὡς ἐμψύχοις γίνονται (*illā annahā ʿalā ḥālin tunsabu ilā anna lahā anfusan*), with the ὡς disappearing through haplography in the extant Greek manuscripts. Thus the correct text is as Usener (1861) had originally suggested, ὅμως ὡς ἐμψύχοις γίνονται. The presence of ὡς in Ψ makes Ross's emendation, ἐν ψυχῇ, untenable. Besides, it is difficult to imagine that the textual corruption would go from the *lectio facilior*, ἐν ψυχῇ, to the *lectio difficilior*, ἔμψυχοι, in all the manuscripts. The dative in ἐμψύχοις is indicated by the Arabic *tunsabu ilā*, the phrase literally meaning, "in a state (*ʿalā ḥālin* = ὡς) that pertains (*tunsabu* = -οις) to the fact that they have souls (ἐμψύχ-)."

If it is certain that Ψ read ὡς ἐμψύχοις, it is also clear that it is the correct reading for it makes good sense. Theophrastus's point is that soul is the active agent, which through desire initiates motion. He introduces sense perception to make the further point that even when a body is supposed to be passive when it receives influences from others, as in sensation, yet nevertheless this being affected happens to it only insofar as it is an ensouled body. So the primacy for initiating both action and being acted upon belongs to the soul, and a prime mover can accordingly not be the primary mover.

5b7 εἰ δ' οὖν indicates that the parenthetical remarks (ζωὴ γάρ … γίνονται, 5b3–7; see above, comment on 5b3) have come to an end and Theophrastus is returning to his main argument, where he left it off at 5b3, κίνησις ὑπάρχειν. This also explains why Theophrastus can take for granted that κίνησις would be immediately understood to be referred to in τῆς κυκλικῆς without the need to repeat the word. The force of the particles is, as Laks & Most 38n50 indicate with reference to Denniston 465, a disapproving statement of a position that is not acceptable. For this use of εἰ δ' οὖν see above the comment at 4a17.

5b8 κρεῖττον] The neuter here is the *lectio difficilior* and present in three of the four independent witnesses (in PJ and Ψ); it is certainly correct. Naturally one would have expected the feminine form, κρείττων (and Burnikel 121 recommends it as the preferable reading), since in the text ἡ ⟨κίνησις⟩ τῆς ψυχῆς is feminine, and κρεῖττον is taken to refer to κίνησις (for the different interpretation of Isḥāq see the corresponding note), but Theophrastus is using here an impersonal construction (and the translations should accordingly reflect this). But to the scribes of the later manuscripts (including Λ, Bartholomew's exemplar) the impersonal construction did not sound natural and the word was accordingly "corrected" to the feminine form.

5b9 πρώτη δὴ καὶ μάλιστα] The expression, relatively common in classical texts, is usually fully adverbial, πρῶτον καὶ μάλιστα, as in Plato (*Philebus* 15e4, *Charmides* 157a1, *Republic* 377d8, 406b1, 415b3, etc.), and means something very much like the English "first and foremost" (suggested but not adopted by van Raalte 218), where "foremost," just like μάλιστα, emphasizes importance rather than numerical order ("most importantly," *Webster's Third New International Dictionary*). The inflectionality of the first word in Greek, however, as opposed to English, lends the expression flexibility and adaptability to context. Thus Aristotle, for example, can use the regular adverbial suffix rather than the neuter form in the *Categories* 2a11 (οὐσία δέ ἐστιν ἡ κυριώτατά τε καὶ πρώτως καὶ μάλιστα λεγομένη), while Theophrastus uses it here (πρώτη) as an adjective modifying κίνησις. Exactly parallel is the use in his *HP* VIII.1,2.4: ὧραι δὲ τοῦ σπόρου τῶν πλείστων δύο: πρώτη μὲν καὶ μάλιστα ἡ περὶ Πλειάδος δύσιν, where Hort translates (p. 143), "There are two seasons for sowing most of them; the first and most important is about the setting of the Pleiad."

Aporia 9

5b10–18 (ἄν τις ἐπιζητήσειεν διὰ τί, πότερον … ἤ): *Why are the heavenly bodies alone actuated by an impulsion or desire (for the unmoved mover and hence, by implication, move in a circle), while the sublunar elements are not?*

The assumption behind this Aporia is that everything that is actuated by a desire for the first would move with a circular motion (Laks & Most 39n53); since the sublunar elements manifestly do not, despite their capacity for motion, they must accordingly not be so actuated. Ross 47, followed by Tricot 10n2, suggests that this objection of Theophrastus is invalid.

Diaporia 9. *(In answer to the question, Theophrastus argues that) this can be either because the sublunar elements are unreceptive of and unconnected with the first principle (with the implication that this would go against the principle of connectedness established through the* endoxon *in Aporia 2), or because the first principle is too weak to infuence them, which is impossible according to the* endoxon *established in Aporia 5: the first principle, which is divine, is stronger than Zeus.*

5b11 ἐφετικός, formed from the verbal adjective ἐφετός of ἐφίεμαι, is attested only here in all of extant classical and Hellenistic Greek; after Theophrastus it is first encountered in Clement (*Stromateis* V.5.28) and Hippolytus (*Refutatio omnium haeresium* V.20.2–3). Subsequent uses are either legal (court appeals) or grammatical (expressing desire). As properly defined by LSJ, it means here "actuated by impulsion/desire," with reference to motion, which is at the center of discussion in this passage. The point Theophrastus is making (cf. Ross 47) is that if we admit that both celestial and terrestrial bodies are impelled towards (ἐφετικά) the prime mover, then we cannot explain why the former move with a circular and the latter with a linear motion. So in order to avoid having the same impulsion lead inexplicably to two different kinds of motion, ἐφετικά must apply to only one of the two kinds of bodies, celestial and terrestrial, as an explanation of their motion. But since terrestrial bodies are manifestly actuated by a host of causes other than a desire for the prime mover (if they are moved by this desire at all), then the inevitable conclusion is that only the celestial bodies are actuated by this impulsion (τὰ κυκλικὰ μόνον ἐφετικά).

5b14 τοῦτό γ' ἄτοπον] For ἄτοπον see the comment at 5a17. Τοῦτο refers to the immediately preceding alternative, i.e., to the latter alternative, that the first does not get through to the sublunar world, but restated with the added explanation why not. Thus Theophrastus restates the latter alternative in the form of a conditional sentence, as follows: "if the first did not get through to the sublunar world because of its own weakness, then *this* (τοῦτό γ'), i.e. that it doesn't get through, would make no sense," because the first cannot be weak, as the following γάρ clause explains; the Greek intended would be, εἰ δι' ἀσθένειαν οὐ διικνεῖται τὸ πρῶτον, ἄτοπον. The particle γ' emphasizes the pronoun it follows (as it preponderantly does in Greek literature; cf. Denniston 121–123), and in this way Theophrastus eliminates the second of the two alternatives he mentions in the πότερον clause so that he can turn his attention in ἀλλὰ λοιπόν (5b18) to the former alternative. The alternative that the first principle, because of weakness, cannot "get through to," or influence, the sublunar world is not attributed by Theophrastus to anyone; Happ 1971, 766n430 does not think that Theophrastus had any particular philosopher in mind but rather used the argument by way of example.

5b17 Jaeger 1948, 357 and note 2, associates Theophrastus's quotation of this Homeric line with that by Aristotle in *MA* 699b37–700a2, but the context is not similar, as he and also Ross 47 and van Raalte 1988, 199, claim (cf. Laks & Most 39n54); see the commentary by Nussbaum 1985, 320–321.

5b18 ἀλλά here, as in 5a1, is progressive (Denniston 21–22; cf. van Raalte 228); it continues the argument by directing attention to the first alternative which has not been discussed yet (ἀδύνατα in 5b13): "So, since the second alternative is impossible, there remains only the first." The combination ἀλλὰ λοιπόν has a curious history in Greek. It is extraordinary that in all classical and Hellenistic literature it is attested in our extant sources only in these two passages in Theophrastus; this would tend to indicate that ἀλλά and λοιπόν, having maintained their individual meanings and not coalesced into a single expression, just did not happen to have been used together in the extant Greek writings. After Theophrastus the expression occurs first in Herodianus (Περὶ ῥημάτων, in A. Lentz, *Grammatici Graeci*, Leipzig: Teubner 1870, III,2.804), and then, with greater frequency in later literature, especially in the Christian Greek of the Church Fathers. By then the word λοιπόν had acquired its later (and present) meaning as particle, "so, then," and the combination ἀλλὰ λοιπόν would appear to have meant, "So then, what is left next to discuss."

5b18 ἀσύνδετον] Margoliouth 1892, 196, first noted that the Arabic translation indicates that the reading was ἀσύνδετον, as correctly proposed by Usener 1890 in his apparatus, instead of the reading ἀσύνθετον transmitted in the extant Greek manuscripts and the Greek exemplar (Λ) of the Latin translation (which, however, was defended by Henrich 98, "nicht Zusammengesetztes"). Usener also pointed out in his apparatus that ἀσύνδετον would refer to τὸ μέσον as the subject. The implied connection with συναφή mentioned at the outset (Aporia 2) is obvious.

Aporia 10

5b19–6a5 (ζητήσειεν ἄν τις πῶς, πότερον ... ἤ): *Is the sublunary world part of the universe? If it is (which it must be according to the endoxon in Aporia 2), how is it part?*

Diaporia 10 (5b21–26). *The available theories do not provide the answer: they do not explain how the rotations of the heavenly spheres bring about changes in the sublunary world, for such changes seem to come about accidentally.*

This aporia with its diaporia, together with those at 6a5–14, 10a10–16, and 11b17 raise the question of the composition, in terms of their elemental structure, of the supralunar and the sublunar worlds, and in particular the issue whether Theophrastus accepted Aristotle's position on the fifth element, ether. The lengthy discussions on the whole issue are summarized by Sharples 1998, 88–94. A particularly subtle and illuminating recent analysis is that by Bodnár 2002.

Diaporia 10.1 (5b26–6a5). *Some claim that the first, or the best, produces only what is best. However, the sublunary elements not only lack rotation (as discussed in Aporia 9), which is considered an effect from the first (and the best) in the case of the heavenly spheres, but even if they had had it it would not have been the best possible outcome of what the first produced. Besides, if only the best came out of the best, there would have been no differentiation among the things that were produced by the first and best.*

The precise thrust of this diaporia and its position in the argument have been difficult to determine. All scholars until van Raalte took it to follow directly upon 5b7–10 (the last part of Diaporia 8.1), before the interruption of the flow of the argument by the two Aporiae 9 and 10 on the sublunary world (5b10–26). Van Raalte, and following her, Henrich, on the other hand, see it as continuing the discussion about the sublunary world (i.e., in Aporia 10). This makes a difference, because the ambiguity depends on the unexpressed subject of ἐκωλύετο in 5b28: the former group of scholars take it, judging by their translations, to be (presumably) τὰ κυκλικά (i.e., the heavenly spheres), while the latter take it (explicitly) to be τὰ περὶ τὸ μέσον in 5b12 (van Raalte 237, Henrich 99). Although both sides seem to have good arguments, the latter are almost certainly right.

Apart from the breakdown of the text in explicit aporiae by Theophrastus himself, which make Diaporia 10.1 part of Aporia 10, as I present the text, there are primarily philological considerations. The two intervening Aporiae 9 and 10 on the sublunary world (5b10–26) are too long, even for Theophrastus's elliptical style, to allow him to refer, without any explicit word or other hint, to a preceding subject (τὰ κυκλικά, 5a16, repeated in 5b11) in another aporia and bypass the one (τὰ περὶ τὸ μέσον, 5b12) about which the discussion had been progressing for some time. Furthermore, Theophrastus introduces this Diaporia 10.1 (5b26–6a5) with εἰ δέ (5b26), which normally indicates a continuation of the immediately preceding argument with the addition of a new consideration, but not a change of subject; see the use of εἰ δέ in 5a28 and 5b7. For a change of subject, or a new line of thought, Theophrastus uses explicit language, as at the beginning of Aporia 9, 5b10–11 (τοῦτ' ἄν τις ἐπιζητήσειεν), etc. Indeed, when Theophrastus is finished with Diaporia 10.1 about the sublunary elements at 6a5, he marks the beginning of a new Aporia 11 with a similar expression, τόδε δ' ἄν τις ἴσως ἀπορήσειεν (6a5–6). Finally, in order to allow no room for misunderstanding, he refers to his new subject—or his reversion to the old one in Diaporia 8.1 (5b7–10)—in explicit terms: αὐτὸν τὸν πρῶτον οὐρανόν.

Another point, though not necessarily binding, is of historical significance. In the Arabic translation, what must have been manifestly a gloss, marginal or otherwise, has entered into the text, which identifies the subject of the verb in question (ἐκωλύετο): "He means the bodies about the center." Since this gloss is incorporated into the text copied by the scribe at-Tikrītī and not a marginal note by some subsequent (i.e., post 11th century) reader of the Tehran manuscript, it means that the gloss was either added by some member of the 10th–11th century Baghdad Aristotelians, from whom at-Tikrītī received his exemplar of the text he copied (Part I, Chapter 3.1), or by the translator himself, Isḥāq. In either case there is a very good possibility that it goes back to a Greek marginal gloss in the Greek manuscript tradition or even in manuscript Ψ itself. And since Theophrastus's text went unnoticed in Greek philosophical history, this gloss (and a couple of others in the Arabic translation) constitutes the only commentary we have on the text from the ancient tradition. If the gloss, then, goes back to a Greek source, it demands our absolute attention; if it is due to Isḥāq or a Baghdad Aristotelian, it demands no less attention: they were as close to the late antique philosophical tradition as we can get, and they were astute.

In addition, arguments from content also indicate that Diaporia 10.1 (5b26–6a5) still refers to the sublunary world and not to the heavenly spheres. In the first place, the whole passage on the sublunary world, and its rectilinear as opposed to circular movement, cannot but be related to Aristotle's *De generatione et corruptione* B 10, and especially 336b25–337a7. This whole chapter in Aristotle is about the generation and corruption of the things "about the center" (ἐν τῷ περὶ τὸ μέσον τόπῳ, introduced in the preceding chapter, 335a25), in which Aristotle argues that "in all things nature desires the better" (336b27–28, see the Loci Paralleli), a statement reflecting Theophrastus's τὰ ἄριστα βουλόμενον (6a2). Now for Aristotle nature is the same as god; a few lines further down in the same passage he refers to the same subject that always desires the better, φύσις, as god, θεός (336b32), and in *De Caelo* 271a33 he says as much: ὁ θεὸς καὶ ἡ φύσις οὐδὲν μάτην ποιοῦσιν. In the passage from *De generatione et corruptione* Aristotle then tries to explain that some things, obviously those in the sublunar world, cannot enjoy the kind of existence enjoyed by the rotating heavenly bodies because they are "too far removed from the first principle" (διὰ τὸ πόρρω τῆς ἀρχῆς ἀφίστασθαι, 336b30–31), echoing Theophrastus's οὐ διικνουμένου τοῦ πρώτου (5b13–14). Because of this they cannot move in a circle and hence are not eternal, since the only motion that is eternal is the circular one. However, Aristotle continues, god "strung together" (συνείροιτο, 336b33, echoing Theophrastus's main concern about συναφή in this Essay), or provided continuity between the heavenly and sublunar realms by making perpetual (ἐνδελεχῆ, 336b32) not individual sublunar beings but their generation and corruption instead, and thus bringing them most close to the immortality of the supernal beings by granting them eternal generation. Now the agent of generation and corruption is the circular motion, and it is this which sublunar beings imitate by coming-to-be and passing-away, and in this fashion, Aristotle concludes, "it is by imitating circular motion that rectilinear motion [of the sublunar bodies] too is continuous" (*GC* 337a7, *CWA* 552).

It is noteworthy that in this passage Aristotle satisfies at least three of Theophrastus's concerns, or objections, regarding the cosmic significance of circular motion. First, he establishes that not only the rotating bodies are actuated by desire and hence move in a circle (διὰ τί τὰ κυκλικὰ μόνον ἐφετικά, 5b11) but also sublunar bodies, which desire to imitate the circular motion; the difference though, is that their rectilinear motion ends in circular generation and regeneration of their species, not in circular motion for the individual. Second, it is not ἄτοπον that the first principle appears to be unable to get through and influence sublunar life; the reason that this appears so is the great astronomical distance separating the first principle from the sublunar world, which dilutes the effect. However, god's desire for the best sees to it that sublunar things too enjoy immortality in species by perpetual generation and corruption. Third, sublunar bodies have not been "pushed away" from the things held in highest honor (ἀπεωσμένα τῶν ἐντιμοτάτων, as Theophrastus says, 5b21–22) like circular motion, and circular motion is not accidentally causing their changes; to the contrary, god made generation of sublunar bodies perpetual (336b32) by making circular motion the agent of generation and corruption. Aristotle makes the point explicitly: "The cause of this [perpetual generation] as we have often said, is circular motion; for that is the only motion which is continuous" (337a1, *CWA* 552). The final and major point that this whole discussion in Aristotle makes is that there is coherence (συνειρμός, 336b33) between the supralunar and sublunar worlds, "because that coming-to-be should itself come-to-be perpetually is the closest approximation to eternal being" (336b33–34, *CWA* 552), which should satisfy Theophrastus's concerns about lack of συναφή between the two worlds.

The trend of this passage in *De generatione et corruptione* is such that it makes it difficult to assume that Theophrastus could have written what he did in this passage had he known this particular Aristotelian text, because it seems clear that Aristotle is responding to Theophrastus, not that Theophrastus is objecting to Aristotle's theories. This understanding of the passages involved has implications for the relative dates of composition of Aristotle's *De generatione et corruptione* and Theophrastus's Essay; see above, Part I, Chapter 1.1.

To resume the discussion about Diaporia 10.1 in Theophrastus (5b26–6a5) and that it refers to the sublunary world and not to the heavenly spheres, a final point in support of this position needs to be considered. Theophrastus says that the argument of the philosopher who claims that the first, or prime mover, wishes, and hence effectuates, only what is best would require that everything, i.e., both heavenly spheres and the sublunary world, be identical or little differentiated, and among the best (6a3–5). The unstated conclusion of this argument is that evidently all things are neither identical nor the best, and thus the claim of that philosopher is invalid. Now if this passage were referring to the heavenly spheres, this objection would not hold: the spheres, if not identical, are nevertheless little differentiated from each other, and they certainly are among the best (ἐν ἀρίστοις)—the belief in the divinity of the spheres was commonplace. Hence the ἅπανθ' in 6a4 cannot refer to the spheres and neither does ἐκωλύετο, and so the passage is most naturally to be taken to be continuing the discussion about the sublunary world.

The two Aporiae 9 and 10 with Diaporia 10.1 (5b10–6a5) therefore neatly summarize the status of, and hence the problem about accounting for, the sublunary world, in three stages: (a) Aristotle's theory of the heavenly circular movement by means of desire for the unmoved mover does not hold because the sublunary world does not have this movement, and since it does not, it means either that the first does not penetrate in its influence to the sublunary world or that the sublunary world is unreceptive and unconnected. Since the first is absurd, the sublunary world is unconnected, and hence Aristotle's theory cannot explain the entire universe. (b) This presupposes a previous and related aspect of the same problem, whether the sublunary world is part of the universe or not, and if so, how it is connected. The Aristotelian theory that says that it is connected insofar as the circular movements of the heavenly spheres (5b24–25) cause the changes in the elements is at best dubious because no direct connection can be established between the circular movements and those changes: it appears that the connection is at best accidental (κατὰ συμβεβηκός, 5b24); and thus this theory cannot explain the entire universe either. (c) The theory (patently of Plato in the *Timaeus*, given the similar wording; see the Loci Paralleli) that explains the connection between the first and the sublunary world by saying that the best does only what is best is patently and evidently an invalid exaggeration that has not been properly thought out (ὑπερβατὸν καὶ ἀζήτητον). For all these reasons, there is no theory that satisfactorily explains the connection between the first and the sublunary world.

5b23 συμβαίνει, the reading universally attested in all witnesses, was corrected into λαμβάνει by Usener 1861, a plausible conjecture as the mistake would have happened "in anticipation of" the following συμβεβηκός (Usener 1861 and note 1, Laks & Most 6n58). Συμβαίνει, however, sometimes with the omission of the infinitive εἶναι or γίγνεσθαι, is regular Theophrastean style and is to be retained (see the parallel passages cited by van Raalte 233–234 and her reference to Hindenlang); it is not one of the primitive errors of the Neoplatonic archetype, as listed by Fobes, p. xxvii.

5b25 εἰς τοὺς τόπους appears slightly ambiguous, again because of Theophrastus's elliptical style. But it is clear that Theophrastus is speaking of the sublunary elements and their movements into the places where they would naturally tend (up or down) when not forced into the opposite direction. The article has a distributive function, "towards the place where each of them goes" when not forced (van Raalte 234–235). Similar is the use in Plato, *Phaedo* 112c6, καὶ εἰς τοὺς τόπους ἕκαστα ἀφικνούμενα εἰς οὓς ἑκάστοις ὡδοποίηται, different streams of water "find their way to their several places" (Jowett); of course, in Plato's full style εἰς τοὺς τόπους is further modified by the following εἰς οὓς ἑκάστοις ὡδοποίηται, but one could supply in the passage of Theophrastus the phrase, εἰς οὓς τείνουσιν. Isḥāq had the right idea: "from place to place."

6a1–2 πάντα ... βουλόμενον] As it is, this participial clause can only mean "willing everything that is best;" there is no justification in the text or the meaning to take βουλόμενον circumstantially as a participium coniunctum and then be forced to add a supposedly understood main verb like "does" or "operates" (πράττει, van Raalte 239); in any case, not much is gained by this reading: "willing everything that is best" means roughly the same as van Raalte's preferred reading, "operates wishing all things to be the best." Even more inaccurate is the predicative interpretation of τὰ ἄριστα, "vuole che tutte le cose siano ottime" (Reale 1964, 173; Tricot); if that were the meaning, the Greek should have read, τὰ πάντα ἄριστα.

Jaeger 1948, 451n4, sees in this statement, which he takes to represent the views of Theophrastus, as reflecting Aristotle's theory of a self-thinking mind in *Met.* Λ 7.

6a3 ἀζήτητον is passive, equivalent to οὐ ζητηθέν, "not having been [properly] looked into," "unexamined" (cf. ἀμύητος, "uninitiated," ἄκλαυτος "not wept for" [Sophocles, *Antigone* 847]), but not in the sense of οὐ ζητητέον, "not to be looked for," as in all the translators' versions; and it certainly does not mean "transcendental," as in the interpretation of Jaeger 1948, 349. What is meant here is that whoever made such a hyperbolic statement did not properly investigate its logical coherence before making it, and thus there ensues the absurd position stated by Theophrastus in the following γάρ phrase.

6a2–5 τοῦτο μέν ... τόδε δ'] The μέν ... δέ structure of this sentence is significant and should not be sundered apart as in all previous editions. As elsewhere in this Essay (see above, Part I, Chapter 1.4), Theophrastus wraps up the previous discussion in the μέν part of the sentence and introduces a new subject—in this case a new aporia—in the δέ part. The contrast intended in the sentence is between the extravagant and unexamined claim of some philosophers that only the best can come from the best first principle, the absurdity of which Theophrastus registers parenthetically in the γάρ phrase, as noted, and the question that properly deserves to be investigated, whether rotation is essential to the first heaven.

Aporia 11

6a5–12 (ἄν τις ἀπορήσειεν, πότερον ... ἤ): *Whether rotation is essential to the first heaven and with its cessation it would perish, or, if the rotation is through desire, it is accidental, unless desiring is innate to the first heaven and nothing prevents it from desiring.*

This aporia simply states the problem. It is to be noted that Theophrastus is entertaining here three alternatives, not two; (1) one is expressed in the first part of the 'whether ... or' construction (if rotating is essential to the first heaven it will perish when it stops), while the second part itself includes two alternatives: (2) if rotating is through desiring, and if desiring is not innate to the first heaven, then it is accidental, and (3) if rotating is through desiring, and if desiring is innate to the first heaven and nothing prevents it from innately desiring, then it is not accidental. See the extensive discussion in Henrich 99–103, who brings out these distinctions.

On the question of the relevance of this aporia to Theophrastus's views on ether see the comment at the end of the discussion on Aporia/Diaporia 10.

6a11–12 καὶ οὐθέν ... ὑπάρχειν, "and nothing ... from being such:" this is the interpretation of Isḥāq and of Ross, Tricot, and Reale, as opposed to that of the other translators (Laks & Most, van Raalte, Henrich), "nothing prevents some such beings from existing." The statement καὶ οὐθέν ... adds yet a further condition to that of the preceding clause (εἰ μὴ ἄρα), as indicated by the use of the conjunction καί (Tricot has the right translation and punctuation); most interpreters consider this as a justification of the preceding statement (punctuating it either with a dash or a semi-colon), but this would have required οὐθὲν γὰρ κωλύει, not καὶ οὐθὲν κωλύει. This being the case, the verb ὑπάρχειν is to be understood with τοιαῦτα, "being such," i.e., having innate desire, and not as implying existence, something which would have no meaning for the present argument. The qualification that Theophrastus has in mind is that nothing prevents some things from *acting upon* the dictates of the innate desire, not from existing. The question of existence with regard to any of these beings is not at all part of the discussion, whereas having innate desire and being able to act upon it is very much so; with reference to the celestial beings, having innate desire means being ensouled, an issue Theophrastus argued for in the opening lines of this argument (ἔμψυχ' ἂν εἴη τὰ κινούμενα, 5b2). The import of the εἰ μὴ ἄρα clause then, would be, "unless, of course, desiring is innate to the first heaven and it is granted that it is ensouled."

Aporia 12

6a12–14 (ἀπορεῖν εἰ): *Whether the heavens, desire apart, would be destroyed if they are considered to have no movement.*

This is a reformulation of the first alternative in the preceding Aporia (see above). If the heavens were to cease to exist if they were to be motionless, this would mean that motion is of their very essence.

Aporia 13

6a14–6b22 (ἀξιώσειεν ἄν τις, 6a16): *The task at hand is, beginning from a first principle or first principles like those mentioned in Aporia 6, to proceed to account for the rest of reality and not stop at a certain point.*

The diaporiae that follow take the form of brief references and discussion of positions taken on the subject by a number of philosophers (*endoxa*).

Diaporia 13.1 (6a19–22). *Eurytus, as reported by Archytas.*

Eurytus, no. 45 [33] 2 DK; no. 19, fr. 2 Timpanaro Cardini 1962, with Italian translation and commentary; Henrich 316–317. Archytas, no. 47 [35] A 13 DK; Timpanaro Cardini 1962, 295 (commentary).

Diaporia 13.2 (6a23–6b5). *Plato and the Pythagoreans.*

This is one of two testimonia passages in this work which informs about Plato's unwritten doctrines: Testimonium Platonicum 30 (Gaiser 1968, 493–494, with notes); Testimonium Platonicum 8 (Krämer 1982, with Italian translation = Krämer 1990, with English translation); Testimonium Platonicum B4 (Isnardi Parente 1998, with Italian translation and commentary); and cf. Isnardi Parente 1997, p. 394. See also Isnardi Parente 1971; Laks 1988; Henrich 320–326, 333–334; and the commentary below on 6a24–25.

Diaporia 13.3 (6b5–6). *Speusippus.*

Speusippus fr. 51 Lang; fr. 59 Tarán 1981, with commentary (379–382); fr. 87 Isnardi Parente 1980, with Italian translation (168) and commentary (322–325); also included in the longer extract constituting Testimonium Platonicum 30 (Gaiser 1968, and notes thereto), see the preceding entry on Plato. Cf. Tarrant 1974, Henrich 326–330.

Diaporia 13.4 (6b7–9). *Xenocrates.*

Xenocrates fr. 26 Heinze; fr. 100 Isnardi Parente 1982, with Italian translation (199–200) and commentary (333–335); also included in the longer extract constituting Testimonium Platonicum 30 (Gaiser 1968, and notes thereto), see the second preceding entry on Plato. Happ 1971, 241–247 discusses this passage in detail, and especially the levels of being that are indicated for Xenocrates' system here (intelligibles, sensibles, etc.) and their derivation from the first principles. See further Henrich 330–333.

Diaporia 13.5 (6b9–11). *Hestiaeus.*

Fr. 2 Lasserre 1987, with French translation (314) and commentary (533–534); see also Laks 1988; Henrich 326.

Diaporia 13.6 (6b11–16). *Plato, as distinct from the Pythagoreans and all his other disciples.*

This passage, in which Theophrastus says that Plato held the numbers to be hierarchically superior to the ideas, was the focus of a good part of the controversy last century regarding Plato's unwritten doctrines. Robin's 1906 book gave credence to this statement by Theophrastus against the evidence presented by Aristotle, who repeatedly claimed that for Plato the ideas were numbers. Ross 58–59 tried to reconcile the two views, but was famously criticized by Cherniss 1945, 26–27.

Gaiser 1968 dealt comprehensively with the issue, and Henrich 321–325 summarized the controversy with some bibliography. An accessible account of what may be taken to be, in general terms, a mainstream view is provided by Dillon 2003, 16–29. A very recent contribution with a conspectus of the issues and the latest bibliography is that by Ferber 2007.

Diaporia 13.7 (6b16–17). *Some unspecified Academics.*
The reference here is unclear. Reale 1964, 180n20 suggests Aristotle, but is disputed by van Raalte 276–277. Laks & Most 47n87 suggest a general Platonic orientation, which would appear likely, given the context of the reference. Cf. also Henrich 33–334.

Incidental **Diaporia 13** (6b17–22) on the characteristics of knowledge arrived at in the different sciences: *In studies of things other than the first principles, knowledge of what comes after the first principles is firmer than the knowledge of the first principles; this is reasonably so, because in those studies the search is from the principles whereas in studies of the first principles themselves like the present Essay, the search is of the first principles themselves.*

For the two methods of analysis referred to in this diaporia—from and to the principles—which were regular practice in the Academy, see Gaiser 1968, 81–88; Happ 1971, 158ff. and n421; Krämer 1990, 81–82.

6a14–15 καὶ τοῦτο μέν … ἀπὸ δ' οὖν] The μέν … δέ construction here also (see above at 6a2–5) is not easily to be ruptured, as all editors and translators do rather cavalierly. The meaning is, "Now (καί) X may be so, but it is Y that we are talking about (δ' οὖν), and this is as follows." Cf. the same construction below at 7b5–9. Καί is copulative (but cf. van Raalte 249), adding a further piece of information about the immediately preceding subject (referred to by τοῦτο), which then the following μέν clause defers to another discussion. For δ' οὖν, which brings the discussion back to where Theophrastus wants it ("but for the present"), see the comment on 4a13. The genitive in ἑτέρων λόγων is of belonging: the discussion of this subject belongs "more appropriately" elsewhere, hence my rendering. Furthermore, it is also clear from this μέν … δέ sentence that Theophrastus is referring to his own (prospective? existing?) discussion of the subject and not to one by somebody else: since the second half of the sentence obviously refers to his argument (which follows imediately), so must the first. But it is not clear to what Theophrastus is precisely referring. The subject is eternal or destructible bodies in motion. Later on in this Essay (10a9–19) he touches on the related question whether the motion of the heavens is essential to them; though there he says that the heavens, when divested of motion, would be the heavens only in name, not that they would be destroyed. Theophrastus's qualified way of expressing himself here would tend to indicate that he is talking in theoretical terms rather than referring to a specific treatise of his, but given the loss of most of his works, there can be no certainty. On the subject cf. his fragments 137.2, 137.8, and 184 FHS&G; and van Raalte 248.

6a17 ἄρ'] The reading transmitted in the two independent Greek manuscripts, PJ, ἄρ' , ἄν τις τίθηται, has been unnecesarily doubted. It is true that we cannot know what the third witness, Ψ, had, for the Arabic suggests that Isḥāq understood (rather than read?) ἅμα for ἄρα, but this difficult sentence taxed his capacities also and is mistranslated (see the note to the Arabic translation), and we cannot be certain about what precisely Ψ read. In the Latin translation, Bartholomew read, or perhaps understood, ἆρα (*utrum*) for ἄρα. As for the Greek, first, the conditional phrase itself, ἄν τις τίθηται, is perfectly fine and rather common; the problem has been to account for the particle ἄρα and its position, but that, too, is relatively standard. Ἄρα here is used in a context of reported speech ("one could demand that …"), and its function is, as Denniston 38 puts it, either to convey "actual scepticism" or to disclaim "responsibility for the accuracy of the statement." The latter is closer to Theophrastus's meaning, for in the parenthetical statement he is introducing an alternative about whose accuracy he is not certain, and this is the reason for his doubly circumspect expression, "perhaps" and "were one to assume". The particle adds a further note of uncertainty ("I suppose"). Theophrastus uses ἄρα in reported speech also later on (10b27), this time with ὥς, a common construction. In such uses of ἄρα the particle may be easily placed quite late in the sentence. A good example of both the use and position of this ἄρα is provided in Plato, *Gorgias* 524d3–4: ταὐτὸν δή μοι δοκεῖ τοῦτ' ἄρα καὶ περὶ τὴν ψυχὴν εἶναι, "And I should imagine that this is equally true of the soul," in Jowett's translation, where δοκεῖ ἄρα is represented by the phrase, "I should imagine," with the English subjunctive rendering very aptly the force of the particle.

6a19 τελέου καὶ φρονοῦντος] If, as Aristotle says in *Metaphysics* Δ 16, 1021b15–17 (cited by van Raalte 254), a perfect physician or musician is he who lacks nothing in his own kind of virtue, then Theophrastus's τέλεος here would be he who lacks nothing in a particular virtue, identified by the following participle, φρονοῦντος, i.e., having a sound mind (φρένες), being "sensible." It is to be noted that the virtue in question is not specifically related to education, so "adult" is to be taken in its basic meaning indicating completion (τελέου) of one's development. This is very close to the other possible meaning of τέλεος, one who is "complete" of age, i.e., adult (see the references in van Raalte 253–254). The combined expression "sensible adult" may appear to contrast with the depiction of Eurytus, for whom these laudatory epithets are intended, as somebody playing at philosophy with pebbles, but it may be Theophrastus's way of disapproving of the other philosophers' procedures which stop after the first principles: despite the seeming naiveté of Eurytus's ideas, he was consistent enough to provide an account for the entire universe. So Theophrastus clearly wants to refer favorably to the theories of Eurytus with the pebbles as those of a thinker who thought things through in order to arrive at an explanation of the entire universe and who did not stop after the first principles; it does not appear that his description of him as "sensible adult" is ironic. For if Theophrastus is being ironic here, then he must be heaping even greater ridicule on some of his contemporaries whom he goes on to accuse of not providing accounts of the entire universe even as minimally consistent and thorough as that of Eurytus. But if Theophrastus's irony extends this far, it would be inconsistent with the rather somber and decidedly non-playful tone of the entire Essay. Cf. further Laks & Most 43n75.

6a21 λέγειν, "according to Archytas"] The indirect speech reported by Archytas is indicated by the infinitive in λέγειν.

6a23 νῦν δ', "at present, however"] The temporal reference of νῦν is assured by the presence of ποτ' in the preceding sentence (6b20). Theophrastus's main subject from the beginning of the Essay is to investigate the connection (συναφή) between the first principles and the sensible world. He begins this Aporia by restating the question (6a15–18): one should not stop without providing a complete account of reality. That is what sensible philosophers of old did, like Eurytus, as Archytas *once* said. *At present*, however, many philosophers stop short of giving a complete account.

6a23 καταπαύονται, "stop completely"; the preposition κατά in compound verbs emphasizes the base meaning of the simple word. Cf. LSJ s.v., E.V.

6a24 καθάπερ καί, "as do too"] Happ 1971, 244n833, rightly notes that καί in this passage is used in the sense of "for example, among others," and refers to the same philosophers as does οἱ ἄλλοι at 6b6.

6a24–25 οἱ τὸ ἓν καὶ τὴν ἀόριστον δυάδα ποιοῦντες] This passage (6a24–6b17) has been much discussed, for it presents crucial evidence on the theories of the Old Academy concerning the first principles and cosmogony as well as the controversial issue of Plato's unwritten doctrines. A good part of the discussion has been centered on identifying "those who posit the one and the indefinite dyad," and on how they relate to the rest of the philosophers named later in the passage. Given the relatively charged atmosphere of this controversy, the passage has been given opposing interpretations which tend to overlook its context, the sweep of the argument, and the grammar. As mentioned in the third preceding comment (at 6a23), Theophrastus's main subject is the investigation of the connection between the first principles and sensible reality, and at the beginning of this Aporia he complains that many philosophers of his time posit the first principles but do not proceed therefrom to the derivation of all reality, stopping short at some point. As example, or as the group of philosophers that do this, he cites "those who posit the one and the indefinite dyad." Now to begin with, it is incontestable that he means by this the Pythagoreans and Plato because he himself ascribes to them the very doctrine later in the Essay, at 11b2–12. But he also uses the expression more broadly as a blanket description of all Platonists and members of the Academy; this is clear from the rhetoric of the passage in which he later names the *exceptions* (πλὴν, 6b6) to this blanket statement, all from the Academy. Thus in this passage Theophrastus is not interested in listing in a doxographic fashion three groups of philosophers as examples of those who hold this view (i.e., Plato and the Pythagoreans [6a24–25], Speusippus, and "the others" [6b6], as Happ 1971, 244, maintains), but describes what all of them do wrong: they posit the one and the indefinite dyad and generate the first level of beings, but then make absolutely no mention of the specifics in the constitution of the heavens and inferior reality, as exemplified by such Platonists as Speusippus and "the others." Thus the generic blanket description is indeed meant to cover all Platonists. However, having mentioned one prominent Platonist by name,

Theophrastus then proceeds to respond to the expectations and possible objections generated in the reader about his evaluation of other Platonists. And at this point he introduces his first and major exception to the blanket statement, Xenocrates, as the only philosopher to have both posited the one and the indefinite dyad and to have then proceeded to discuss the generation of all reality.[18] This is followed by a further qualification, the case of another philosopher who may be thought to be an exception, Hestiaeus, who, however, is not to be entirely absolved of this neglect because apparently he did not complete the derivation of all reality from the first principles but went up to a certain point (μέχρι τινός, 6b10). And this brings Theophrastus to a second case of a seeming exception, Plato. In anticipation of an objection by the reader, Theophrastus says, "And yes, Plato may be thought to be another exception, insofar as he *would seem* (δόξειεν ἂν) to be treating of the sensibles and providing an account of all reality through his method of proceeding from the principles and to the principles (as Aristotle also says that Plato did, *EN* 1095a30–b1 = Gaiser 1968, Test. Plat. 10 = Krämer 1990, 204 no. 6; see the Loci Paralleli)—but in fact his derivation, unlike that of Xenocrates, also is incomplete, like that of Hestiaeus." This is the meaning of the reservation implied in the optative δόξειεν with ἄν. See the discussion by Gaiser 1968, 529, 490, 493–494, 366n101, 380n146; and Happ 1971, 111n166, 161n442, 244n833, referring to Gaiser.

6a27 ἐφαπτόμενοι, "apprehending," has proven difficult for the translators to pinpoint (as the relatively divergent and imprecise translations show), especially in this passage where it is used without an objective complement, which it normally takes in the genitive; ὅσον in this sentence is adverbial.[19] The verb in the middle voice had a very wide array

[18] Pace Happ 1971, 244, who thinks that we cannot infer from this passage anything about Xenocrates' doctrine of first principles. But this is clearly implied in the reading I propose here, while the doctrine of the one and the indefinite dyad as principles is otherwise well attested for Plato, Speusippus, and Xenocrates. Even if as a technical term, "indefinite dyad" was introduced by Xenocrates (as Tarán 1981, 225, suggests, though Happ 1971, 140n327, argues for the opposite view), the fact remains that Plato's "great-and small", Speusippus' "multiplicity", and Xenocrates' "unlimited" or "everlasting" stand for the same principle of indeterminacy. See the useful summary of the positions of these thinkers in Dillon 2003.

[19] Henrich's 51 translation, "ausser den Bereich, den sie behandeln" renders ὅσου ἐφαπτόμενοι, not ὅσον, as does Tricot's 15, and van Raalte's 45: "so much as they do lay hold of." But there is no manuscript evidence for ὅσου unless one take seriously the reading ὅσων in J which, however, makes no sense in context and shows itself to be a

of uses in Attic Greek; its occurrence in Plato clearly shows this, but it also helps delineate the precise meaning when the word refers to mental action, as it does in this passage of Theophrastus. In the *Phaedo*, Plato twice uses τοιούτων ἐφαπτομένη with reference to the soul to indicate the two kinds of things which it grasps or apprehends, the changeable things of this world and the eternal and unchanging things; its apprehension of the latter constitutes φρόνησις (79c8, d6). In another passage, in the *Theaetetus* (190c6), the soul lays hold of and apprehends two contrary objects about which it could make a judgment (λέγειν, δοξάζειν). In more general terms, Plato uses the expression ἐφάπτεσθαι τῶν ὄντων to indicate someone's "grasp of reality" (*Sophist* 234d5, 259d6): young people διὰ παθημάτων ἀναγκαζομένους ἐναργῶς ἐφάπτεσθαι τῶν ὄντων, "forced by experience to apprehend things clearly as they are" (Cornford 1957, 194). Thus the word means "to apprehend" and, despite the temptation of its etymology, ἐφάπτομαί τινος with reference to mental activity does not mean "to touch upon" something (Ross; Laks 1988, 239), or "effleurer" le sujet (Laks & Most), or "fare un accenno" (Isnardi Parente 1998, 18). In another passage in Plato, *Cratylus* 404d2, this verb is used together with another one (ἐπαφάω) that *does* mean "to touch" and thus the difference in meaning between the two is highlighted: ἅτε γὰρ φερομένων τῶν πραγμάτων τὸ ἐφαπτόμενον καὶ ἐπαφῶν καὶ δυνάμενον ἐπακολουθεῖν σοφία ἂν εἴη, "for seeing that things are in motion, that which apprehends and touches and is able to follow [them] is wisdom."[20] If that is so, a number of interpretations of this passage that are based on the understanding of ἐφαπτόμενοι as "touch upon" cannot stand (mainly those of Laks & Most 44–45, Isnardi Parente 1998, 18).

6b1 τόπος καὶ κενὸν καὶ ἄπειρον] Ross 54–55 suggests that place, void, and the infinite refer to "Plato's doctrine of χώρα" in the *Timaeus*. Happ 1971, 110–113, 162n445, in general agrees with Ross despite the presence of some terminological difficulties in this position which he discusses.

---

scribal emendation. The Arabic reads *bi-qadri mā yudrikūna*, "to the extent that they grasp," and the Latin *quantum*, both obviously reflecting ὅσον.

[20] A parenthetical note: It may be just the requirements of the etymological context of this passage in *Cratylus* that make Plato express himself thus, but he appears to be contradicting himself: it was the apprehension of immobile and eternal things that he called φρόνησις in the *Phaedo* passage cited previously, whereas here he calls wisdom the apprehension of things in motion.

6b3–4 χρόνος ... πλείω] The transmitted text of this phrase, with the two masculine nouns in the accusative, cannot stand by itself, and this was felt as early as the 14th century, when the corrector of manuscript J (J^{II}) deleted it, and later, the scribe of manuscript L (mid-15th cent.), omitted it. H. Ritter in 1826, Usener on both occasions he dealt with the text (1861, 1890), and Reale secluded the phrase.[21] But there are no grounds for doing so; all four independent witnesses (PJ Ψ Λ) have it, which indicates that it was also present in the Neoplatonic archetype of the Essay (Part I, Chapter 2.5). It may be that the phrase represents some kind of gloss that entered the text before that stage,[22] or that something significant dropped out of the text, but apart from the fact that we cannot know that, we cannot argue for it either.

Most recent scholarship has tended to be more conservative and retained the phrase, but tried to explain it by assuming syntactical acrobatics on the part of Theophrastus's prose, most prominently by assuming that a verb γεννῶσι, reflecting γεννήσαντες in line 6a25, is to be understood as governing the accusatives of the phrase (Ross and others following him, Tarán 1981, 380n192; Laks 1988, 240–242; van Raalte 261–262; Henrich 105).[23] Ross 46 points to similar ellipses at 5a27 and elsewhere. However, just as in the case of 5a27 (see the comment on Diaporia 8, 5a25–28, above), here also the ellipsis cannot be assumed.[24] The intervening πλήν sentence (6a27–b3) changed the flow of the argument and its grammatical structure: the governing construction now is δηλοῦντες ὅτι with the implied verb in the reported speech being either an intransitive γέγονεν or a passive ἐγεννήθη. As a result, an active verb γεννῶσι would not naturally fit the syntactic imagination and expectation of a reader of

[21] Reale 1964, 178n14, and see the references in Laks 1988, 252n51.

[22] Cf. van Raalte 261, and Dillon 2002, 180n19, who gives a graphic account of how "an indignant reader" could have added the comment in the margin by citing the *Timaeus* passage at 38b6, χρόνος δ' οὖν μετ' οὐρανοῦ γέγονεν, and then adding what amounts to "etc.", καὶ ἕτερα δὴ πλείω. "This was then witlessly incorporated into the text by a scribe, being adapted to give grammatical coherence."

[23] A variant of this position is the solution preferred by Isnardi Parente 1971, 54n12, who views the accusatives as directly dependent on the preceding γεννήσαντες without the ellipsis of a presumed γεννῶσι. The resulting anacolouthon, as Laks 1988, 241, rightly remarks, is "intolerably rough."

[24] Ross is rather cavalier in assuming ellipses in the style of Theophrastus. Of the ellipses he mentions on p. 46, only those at 6b16, 6b25, and 10a25 exhibit the requisite obvious and grammatical implication that puts them within the acceptable limits of prose style. The rest, at 5a27, 6b3, and 8a2, are not ellipses at all but require a different parsing of the syntax and meaning of the text; see the commentary on these passages. For an analysis of the ellipses that may or may not be assumed see the discussion at 6b16–17.

the sentence χρόνος ... πλείω. Even less plausible is Laks & Most's suggestion (44n80) to understand a γεννῶσι as the implied verb of the participle ἐφαπτόμενοι. Even if γεννῶσι had been actually present in the text it would have been difficult to connect it, after the intervening πλὴν sentence, with ἐφαπτόμενοι, let alone that it is not even expressed. Besides, if the participle ἐφαπτόμενοι needs a finite verb, the one that is to be supplied mentally is, of course, οὐ παραλείπουσιν, implied by παραλείπουσιν at 6a27 and πλὴν, which supplies the negative (i.e., to paraphrase, "they leave out almost everything else except the things which, ἐφαπτόμενοι, ⟨they do not leave out⟩"). Furthermore, the meaning of ἐφαπτόμενοι is not, as discussed in the preceding comment, "effleurer," as they claim, and hence the negative meaning that ἐφαπτόμενοι must have in order for their interpretation to be valid ("but they only touch upon;" i.e., they do not do it thoroughly) is simply not there.

There remains the possibility that the Arabic translation was based on the correct text. It reads, "They say that ... some [other things] come from the numbers and the One, like soul and other things—time together with heaven and many other things. But as for investigating the question of heaven, ..." The Arabic translation implies a small variant from our transmitted text, the reading not of δ' in 6b3 but of ϑ', as Usener's 1861, 270n1, proposed emendation has it. In this rendering, then, the phrase beginning with χρόνον/χρόνος identifies the preceding ἄλλ' ἄττα and does not belong to the same sentence as the next phrase, τοῦ δ' οὐρανοῦ πέρι, because the translator felt that they say two different things. If this rendering is accurate, the Greek text should be read and punctuated as in the Arabic: time and heaven are further examples, like the soul, of things generated by the numbers and the one, and they are in the nominative. It is true that this alternative does not explain the *lectio difficilior* of the accusative nouns as transmitted in the Greek manuscripts, but this reading eliminates the need for a verb to justify the accusatives in the received text and makes it unnecessary to consider this phrase parenthetical. Also, if the need to supply a verb is eliminated so is the dilemma whether to have the supplied verb have a positive or negative connotation so that it would fit the meaning of what is said just before and just after (cf. the analysis by Laks & Most 44n80). Theophrastus simply enumerates the things that are only derived from the one and the indefinite dyad in the theories of the philosophers he mentions, and in the next sentence, which can be paraphrased as follows, he lodges his complaint and brings out the contrast with what he has just enumerated: "but as far as the *details* about heaven are concerned, they did not do anything more beyond generating it" (cf. the comment by Ross 56); this emphasis is the meaning of the inverted order of the preposition (τοῦ δ' οὐρανοῦ πέρι instead of περὶ δὲ τοῦ οὐρανοῦ) and the particular force of ἔτι. Thus, there is no discontinuity in meaning either: if we take the phrase χρόνος ϑ' to be a listing amplifying ἄλλ' ἄττα, then it talks about the *derivation* of heaven, while the following sentence, τοῦ δ' οὐρανοῦ πέρι, talks about heaven itself and the derivation of its particulars: its motion, that of the other celestial spheres, etc. And the ἔτι, which appears to have been largely disregarded in the previous discussions of this passage, removes any contradiction with what preceded: "yes, they did explain the derivation of the heavens, but once they did this they made *no more* mention of it." I.e., they made no more mention of it regardless whether temporally or logically, as Laks 1988, 241–242, who does discuss ἔτι, wishes to discriminate. Theophrastus here is not interested in discussing whether or not these philosophers developed independent disciplines of cosmology, biology, etc., as Laks objects, but in the fact that when they talked about first principles they did not discuss the details of heaven and the rest either substantively (or logically) when they were actually deriving them from the soul (as in Plato's *Timaeus*), or subsequently (temporally) in their further discussions and treatments of the same subject of first principles. In other words, they did not, *simpliciter*, effect the connection between the first principles and the rest of the universe that Theophrastus has been complaining about all along in this Essay. On the other hand, Laks 1988, 241, does disregard ἔτι when he criticizes Ross's explanation of it as the details of celestial organization (as I do here). Laks says, "not making any mention of the heaven is not the same thing as not going into the details of its organization." No, but "not making any *more* mention of the heaven" is.

Finally, one alternative (though less likely, in my opinion) which would enable us to retain the accusatives in the received text is to consider them as dependent on an understood verb that is commonly omitted, one meaning "I mean," such as λέγω (χρόνον ϑ' ἅμα καὶ οὐρανὸν ⟨λέγω⟩), viewing the entire phrase as a remark by Theophrastus himself intended to explain ἄλλ' ἄττα. But this understanding also would require changing into ϑ' the transmitted reading δ'.

This is how far a philological analysis can take us. As for the issue whether deriving the heavens from the numbers and the one, as this reading of the text implies, is "philosophical nonsense" (Tarán 1981, 380n192), it is open to question. Two considerations are of relevance. First, what cannot be gainsaid is the obvious references in Theophrastus's wording to the cosmogony in the *Timaeus*: Aristotle himself in *De anima* 404b18–27 explicitly identifies the *Timaeus* as containing an account of cosmogony in much the same terms as Theophrastus (see Ross 1951, 210 and 214, and Ross 1961, 178; cf. Laks & Most 44n80, and see the Loci Paralleli). In the *Timaeus* the soul is clearly derived from the numbers in the sense that it has a numerical structure (the geometrical progressions of 2 and 3, the "double and triple intervals," κατὰ τὴν τοῦ διπλασίου καὶ τριπλασίου διάστασιν, 36d3: Cornford [n.d.] 74, etc.), and οὐρανός and χρόνος are next "fitted" (προσήρμοττεν, 36e1) to this numerically derived soul; thus heaven and time do indeed explain and identify ἄλλ' ἄττα in Theophrastus's wording in this passage (cf. Laks 1988, 240). Second, as Dillon 2002, 181–182 pointed out, Plutarch offers an explanation of the generation of the soul in the *Timaeus* which purports to represent Xenocrates' views (fr. 68 Heinze; see the Loci Paralleli), from which the generation of the soul ultimately from the one and more immediately from the numbers can be plausibly inferred; and if soul is thus generated, so is also heaven. Now whether Theophrastus meant by this to impugne Plato (whom he appears to exonerate a few lines later), or Xenocrates and other Platonists, or even the trend of discussions in the Academy, is debatable; but the passage in question does mean that the philosophers Theophrastus is talking about derived soul, the heavens, and time from the numbers and the one.

6b5 ὡσαύτως δ' οὐδ' οἱ περὶ Σπεύσιππον] This is the correct reading, with the Paris manuscript (P) being the only one of the four independent witnesses (PJ Ψ Λ) to omit οὐδ'. The reference to Speusippus is incontestably negative: what Theophrastus means is precisely that those about Speusippus τοῦ οὐρανοῦ πέρι καὶ τῶν λοιπῶν οὐδεμίαν ποιοῦνται μνείαν, i.e., they do not explain how "the lower entities can be derived from the principles assumed" (van Raalte 264). This is the theme of this entire Aporia, that some philosophers posit the principles and then stop without explaining the derivation of everything else from them. Theophrastus's statements about Speusippus and all the others concern just this aspect of their works.

6b7 περιτίθησιν] The preposition περί in περὶ τὸν κόσμον need not indicate place ("in, dans, nell', autour au sens de distribuer, im," in the translations) but the object about which one is concerned, and the prepositional phrase then would naturally go with ἅπαντα (ἅπαντα περὶ τὸν κόσμον); cf. Plato *Symposium* 193a8, πάντ' ἄνδρα χρὴ ἅπαντα παρακελεύεσθαι εὐσεβεῖν περὶ θεούς, literally, "every man ought to be exhorted to observe [religiously] everything about the gods;"[25] in which case, the verb περιτίθησιν can have its regular meaning ("bestow, provide") as in the other two instances Theophrastus uses it in this Essay (4a23, 7a20). So the meaning here would be, "provide everything that has to do with the universe: sensibles, intelligibles, etc." This fits the context better, in which Theophrastus is concerned with showing not so much that Xenocrates assigns everything to its place but that he does not stop with the first principles but provides his universe—populates it, as it were—with all the proper ingredients and presumably also with how they are interrelated. In any case, there seems to be no need to emend to διατίθησιν, as proposed by Usener 1890.

On the other hand, the Arabic translation does not help: it translates the verb by a simple *yajʿalu*, literally "he places," which renders just τίθησιν, without specifying which preposition Isḥāq read. The whole sentence reads, *yajʿalu* (the verb) *ʿalā wajhin mina l-wujūhi* (πως) *jamīʿa l-ašyāʾi* (ἅπαντα) *fī l-ʿālami* (περὶ τὸν κόσμον) *ʿalā miṯālin wāḥidin* (ὁμοίως): literally, "he places in some manner all things in the universe in the same way." In the other two passages in this work where περιτίθημι occurs (4a23, 7a20), Isḥāq uses different words according to sense.

6b8–9 αἰσθητὰ καὶ νοητὰ καὶ μαθηματικὰ καὶ ἔτι δὴ τὰ θεῖα] The repeated conjunction καί clearly intends to distinguish among the four classes of entities. Ross 56–57, on doctrinal grounds derived from other witnesses of Xenocrates' views, wants to reduce the number to three by conflating νοητὰ and μαθηματικὰ, and accordingly translates, "objects of reason *or* mathematical objects" (emphasis added), something for which Isnardi Parente 1982, 334–335, rightly takes him to task.

6b11 μὲν οὖν, "And yes;" assentient οὖν with prospective μέν, answered by δέ in 6b15 (for this μὲν οὖν see 4b16–17 above). The implication is that Theophrastus meets the expectation (assentient οὖν) of the reader

[25] Judging from the variety of prepositions used with the essentially intransitive verb εὐσεβεῖν, it is perhaps unlikely that it would take a direct object in the accusative, as the case seems to be here, though LSJ do register a usage εὐσεβεῖν θεούς. I would guess the accusative is one of respect.

to hear about Plato's position and responds to his objection that Plato should not be included among those who stop short from deriving all reality from the principles. See the comment at 6a24–25.

It may also be mentioned, assuming that Theophrastus here has the *Timaeus* in mind (as in 6b27, and see the next comment below), that an additional reason for his reservation may be the narrative (εἰκὼς μῦθος, 29d2), and not analytical, nature of Plato's account in the *Timaeus*.

6b11–15 Theophrastus's statement here implies that Plato made a distinction between ideas and numbers, a statement which contradicts Aristotle's view that Plato held that all ideas were numbers. On the accuracy of Theophrastus's report see Cherniss 1945, 26–27 and n. 112; Ross 1951, 216; Tarán 1981, 379; Henrich 321–326, with review of the more recent literature.

6b14–15 εἶτα κατὰ τὴν γένεσιν μέχρι τῶν εἰρημένων] "The [things] mentioned," cannot refer, of course, to "such things as τόπος, κενόν, etc." (Ross 59) because these are not the things that *Plato* derives from the indefinite dyad but those which Theophrastus is criticizing; on the other hand, the expression τὰ εἰρημένα is too specific to refer merely to τῶν ἄλλων (6b12–13) as objects of sense (as suggested by Tarán 1981, 381n194, and Laks & Most 47n85). This Aporia begins at 6a14, where Theophrastus demands of philosophers to proceed to the derivation of τὰ ἐφεξῆς (6a17) and cites as examples the explanation given by Eurytus of ἄνθρωπος and ἵππος (6a22). Τὰ εἰρημένα therefore must refer to τὰ ἐφεξῆς as exemplified by such objects of sense as men and horses. And in the case of Plato, who is the subject under discussion in this sentence, the reference must again be to the *Timaeus*, which goes into the very details of human anatomy. Theophrastus's expression κατὰ τὴν γένεσιν is significant in this regard: the *Timaeus* indeed proceeds by describing the very composition of the universe and its contents "in order of generation." Finally, εἶτα indicates a change of the upward progression to its opposite, as implied in the concept of "generation" (and which justifies the addition of "[down]" in the translation): the "order of generation" is from the principles on down, not the other way.

6b16 τῶν ἀρχῶν] As repeatedly noted, the genitive makes it certain that the verb to be understood here is ἅπτομαι from 6b12; the question, however, is whether what to be understood precisely is ἅπτονται (they treat), or δόξειεν ἂν ἅπτεσθαι (they would seem to be treating), since both are possible. The answer depends on how one interprets the reservation implied by the optative (see the comment at 6b11 above). If the reservation is directed only to Plato, as I think it is, then clearly only ἅπτονται is to be understood.

6b16–17 τὴν ἀλήθειαν ἐν τούτοις. The difficult term ἀλήθεια here refers to its ontological and not epistemological dimension. For the use of the word in Aristotle in these two senses see Bonitz *Index* 31a39–42: "*nominis usus modo ad* τὸ ὂν *et* τὴν οὐσίαν, *modo ad cognitionem et scientiam vergit.*" The Aristotelian passages he cites equate ἀλήθεια with τὸ πρᾶγμα, φύσις, τὰ ὄντα, i.e., the things as they are, objective reality. This is the sense in which Theophrastus is using the word here, as in any case the definite pronoun preceding it, τήν, indicates: the universe, *the* one reality, or "reality itself," as I render it. (See also the following comment at 6b17.)

The accusative of τὴν ἀλήθειαν makes it certain that a verb like φασί or λέγουσι is to be understood; see Ross 46 note to 5a27. However, Ross exaggerates when he places all elliptical expressions on the same level as this one. Three categories should be distinguished: (a) Obvious implication. Even without any context, in a sentence like the present one, ἔνιοι δὲ καὶ τὴν ἀλήθειαν ἐν τούτοις, the implied φασί or λέγουσι can be automatically understood; there can be no other meaning. (b) Contextual (grammatical) implication. Some other elliptical expressions can be understood only in context, i.e., the syntax and context of a paragraph generate a certain structure in the reader's mind who is then able to provide the omitted word(s); e.g., 6b15–16, οἱ δὲ τῶν ἀρχῶν μόνον, where the genitive can only be understood in relation to the genitive complement (τῶν ἄλλων) of the verb ἅπτεσθαι in 6b12. (c) No implication. In some cases, there is no implication, either obvious or contextual insofar as no writer would expect his reader to make such semantic jumps without deliberately causing obfuscation. And in this case there is no indication that Theophrastus sought to cause that, which means that these so-called elliptical expressions have to be interpreted differently, i.e., by not assuming the presence of an ellipsis.

In this particular sentence, the pronoun is neuter, τούτοις (rather than masculine), and refers not so much specifically to the feminine plural noun τῶν ἀρχῶν in the preceding line—for that Theophrastus should (and would) have used a feminine pronoun—but to the *contents* of the noun ἀρχαί, things like the one and the indefinite dyad, the unmoved mover, etc., which *are* principles. Τούτοις thus here means "these things" with reference to the various items that have been taken in these philosophies to be first principles. It is dangerous to enunciate ad hoc grammatical rules, as Ross 45 does, "that Theophrastus tends to revert to the neuter when he is referring to anything inanimate;" they tend to distract one from understanding what the text really says. Of the three examples of this so-called "tendency" of Theophrastus that Ross gives, ἐκεῖνο in 5a26 does not refer to κίνησις (see my comment above), τούτοις in the present passage just discussed does not refer to ἀρχαί, as just discussed, and ἐκείνοις in 6b19 is a manifest scribal error for ἐκείναις, as discussed just below.

6b17 περὶ τὰς ἀρχάς] There appears to be almost unanimous agreement among scholars that the preposition here is to be interpreted as "in" (as in the case of 6b8); van Raalte even cites Müller's 1878 study where he states that in the botanical works Theophrastus uses περί for ἐν. Be that as it may, and without having to do a complete study of the use of this preposition in Theophrastus, it seems strange that he should have said περί where he meant to say ἐν, especially in a context where abstract ideas are discussed, as opposed to the concrete meanings of the preposition in the botanical works. Clearly there must be semantic nuances that pertain to the use of περί in Theophrastus's Greek and in that of his contemporaries that are not expressed with ἐν. This is why someone like Ross, who does translate with the preposition "in", nevertheless gives a paraphrastic and not a literal translation of the entire sentence: "for they concentrate reality entirely in the ruling principles"—to say nothing of the even more paraphrastic version of Reale (1964): "Le cose, infatti, si fondano non su altro che sui principi;" for a literal rendering with the preposition "in" would make little sense: "For beings are only in the principles." And if περί makes little sense as ἐν in the context, it is doubtful that it can be stretched to mean "in the realm of" (van Raalte), "dans le domaine des" (Laks & Most). Tricot, who also gives a paraphrastic version, nevertheless was headed in the right direction: "car la réalité tourne exclusivement autour des Principes." For the preposition περί with the accusative does mean "concerning, about, having to do with, pertaining to," and this meaning seems to fit the context better and more naturally: all things, i.e., all things that exist, τὰ ὄντα, are not "in" the first principles or are not themselves first principles (for what else would the statement, "they are in the realm of first principles," mean?), but they have to do with and pertain to, insofar as they exist and have being, the first principles. As Aristotle puts it in the passage from his *Metaphysics* α 1, 993b31, an understanding of which Theophrastus here echoes (cf. Reale 1980, 411n20, pace van Raalte 276–277), ἕκαστον ὡς ἔχει τοῦ εἶναι οὕτω καὶ τῆς ἀληθείας, "as each thing is in respect of existence, so is it in respect of reality." This whole Aristotelian passage (for which see the Loci Paralleli) is about ἀλήθεια in the ontological sense (as is clear also from the classification of relevant passages in Bonitz *Index* 31a39 ff.; see the preceding comment), and I accordingly change the word in Ross's translation of this passage just cited (*CWA*, p. 1570) from "truth" to "reality."

6b18 μεθόδοις means disciplines here. For what Theophrastus is contrasting is not the differences in procedure in the various fields but the knowledgeability of their subject matters. For this use of the word in Aristotle see Bonitz *Index* 449b60–450a30. This usage continued in later centuries; cf. Nicomachus of Gerasa, *Introductio arithmeticae* 5.19–6.2, where he gives examples of two disciplines: δύο μέθοδοι … ἀριθμητική … μουσική.

6b19 ἐν ἐκείναις] It is very difficult to insist, as all translators do, that the reading ἐκείνοις in all Greek manuscripts (for what I correct to ἐκείναις here), taken as neuter, could refer to the immediately preceding feminine noun μεθόδοις. There is simply no explanation. The reason Ross 45 gives, "that T. tends to revert to the neuter when he is referring to anything inanimate," does not apply in the two of the three examples he gives (the other two being 5a26 and 6b17; see my comments on these), and the third concerns the present case. If Theophrastus really did use the neuter to refer to inanimate things, then at least he would have been consistent and continued referring to μεθόδοις in the neuter when he next refers to them in the same sentence two lines down, ταῖς λοιπαῖς, but he does not; he uses the proper feminine pronoun, so he clearly did not "revert to the neuter." Besides, to say ἐν ταῖς ἄλλαις μεθόδοις· ἐν ἐκείνοις is also impossible Greek—to mention, that is, a noun and then, with the immediately following word that refers to it, change the gender. Nor is there any contextual justification. If μεθόδοις means here study, discipline, etc., as all agree (see the preceding note), then all the other presumably synonymous words that Theophrastus could have had in mind are also feminine (I pick the words from the parallels in Bonitz's *Index*): πραγματεία, θεωρία, ἐπιστήμη, τέχνη, ζήτησις. And I cannot think of, nor anyone has suggested, anything else that Theophrastus could have had in mind. The Arabic and Latin translations, finally, are correct, but all this means is that both translators understood the disputed word to refer to μεθόδοις, as we do, regardless whether they read ἐκείνοις or ἐκείναις. But the transmitted ἐκείνοις in the extant Greek manuscripts is wrong and cannot be justified. Though there can be no certainty, the mistake likely occurred in the minuscule stage of the transmission of the manuscripts: A and O in ἐκείνο/αις are not readily confused in uncials; on the other hand, it is just as likely that the scribal error may have come about due to the influence of ἐν τούτοις two lines up (6b17) which conditioned, through (a misunderstood) parallelism, the neuter dative in ἐν ἐκείνοις. In any case, Camotius corrected the gender to the obvious ἐκείναις and was followed by Usener 1890, both of whom I am happy to follow.

6b20 τῶν ἐπιστημῶν has created problems of interpretation and a number of readings have been proposed. The genitive phrase could function in one of the following ways: as partitive genitive depending on (a) ἐκείναις (as I emended, and as suggested by Laks & Most 47n90: "in those of the sciences"), (b) τὰ μετὰ τὰς ἀρχάς (see below), (c) ἰσχυρότερα καὶ τελεώτερα (van Raalte: "the stronger and more complete part of the sciences concerned"); (d) as objective genitive after ἰσχυρότερα καὶ τελεώτερα (Dalechampius, as cited by Laks & Most 47n90: "*ad parandam scientiam exactiora*"); and (e) as genitive of comparison after ἰσχυρότερα καὶ τελεώτερα ("more complete than the sciences"). (e) is manifestly absurd; (a) is silly and redundant: if ἐπιστημῶν means roughly the same as μεθόδοις, then ἐν ἐκείναις by itself has already said what ἐν ἐκείναις τῶν ἐπιστημῶν is presumably intended to say; (d) seems very unlikely; objective genitives are in essence passive in meaning insofar as they express a frame of mind or emotion, or else are substitutes for prepositions in expressing the relationship to the word they modify (cf. K.-G. II.1,335–336): it is very doubtful that τῶν ἐπιστημῶν τελεώτερα could stand for τελειοῖ τὰς ἐπιστήμας; and (c) for van Raalte's reading to be possible the predicative ἰσχυρότερα καὶ τελεώτερα would have to be introduced by the article, τά, so that the partitive meaning of the genitive can be elicited. This leaves (b) as the only viable alternative. The question, then, is the precise meaning of ἐπιστημῶν. Henrich 108 makes the valid observation that Theophrastus here is talking about epistemology; the parts after the first principles are ἰσχυρότερα and τελεώτερα not in a metaphysical or ontological sense but epistemologically: they are known better and more completely. If this is the case, then ἐπιστημῶν cannot and should not be translated as sciences but "knowledges," or, given the partitive construction, "parts of knowledge." This, incidentally—the little tolerance that English shows for the word "knowledge" in plural—is a frequent source of confusion and inexact renderings of the Greek word, unless one constantly keep the Latin etymon of the word `science' in mind (which in regular modern English parlance one does not). For example, in a passage where "knowledges" is manifestly the intended meaning, translators still render the plural word as "sciences:" Aristotle, *Metaphysics* A 9, 990b12–13, εἴδη ἔσται πάντων ὅσων ἐπιστῆμαί εἰσι, "there will be forms of all things of which there are knowledges ("sciences" Ross, Tredennick, etc.);" Aristotle goes on to give examples of such knowledges, forms of negation and perishable things, and it hardly makes sense to say that we have a science of negation or a science of perishable things. The same problem, by the way, exists also in English translations of philosophical Arabic, for the word for knowledge, *ʿilm*, pl. *ʿulūm*, is similar to ἐπιστήμη in its polysemy.[26]

Aporia 14

6b23–7b5 (πῶς καὶ ποίας, ἂν ἀπορήσειέν τις, πότερον … ἤ): *How and of what sort should one suppose the first principles to be?*

The argumentation of this aporia is convoluted. Theophrastus discusses three positions, and thus there are three diaporiae, numbered here in the commentary as 14.1, 14.2, and 14.3, but their various parts are actually interwoven in the text. They are disentangled here and presented consecutively. In order to avoid clutter in the presentation of the Greek text and the English translation, not all these numbers of the various parts of the diaporiae are actually given there. After the initial statement of Aporia 14 (6b23–24), Theophrastus continues:

[26] Franz Rosenthal has a very useful little chapter on the problem in his *Knowledge Triumphant*, Leiden: Brill 1970, repr. 2006, Chapter 3, "The Plural of Knowledge."

Diaporia 14.1a (6b24–26). *The first principles may be shapeless and potent, like fire and earth.* **Diaporia 14.1b** (7a7). *Some suppose that there are only material principles.* **Diaporia 14.1c** (7a10–19). *(Objection to this position:) It would seem unreasonable even to these people (were they to think seriously about it) if the entire universe were orderly and formally principled in all aspects but the first principles themselves were not. For example, Heraclitus should have realized the absurdity of his own statement when he said that the human body, made up of elements "poured out at random" (i.e., by random and indeterminate first principles), is nevertheless the most beautiful arrangement of such elements. And yet these philosophers do maintain that the nature of everything among both animate and inanimate things, down to the smallest thing, is determinate, but not the first principles.*

For references to this much discussed fragment of Heraclitus see the comment on 7a15 below.

Diaporia 14.2a (6b26–7a6). *The first principles may be already shaped, since it is necessary most of all for these to be determined, as Plato says in the* Timaeus, *for it is appropriate for the most valuable of beings to have order and be determined. (Parenthetically Theophrastus adds that) except for a few disciplines like grammar and music, the rest have principles that are determined, and so do the crafts which, in fact, imitate nature.* **Diaporia 14.2b** (7a6–7). *Some suppose that there are only enshaped first principles.* **Diaporia 14.2c** (7a19–7b5). *(Objection to this position: In the case of these people) as well it is difficult to assign to each set of things its own formal principles by a collective referral to a final cause, unless it happens that, due to the orderly arrangement and change in other beings (viz. the celestial bodies and configurations), changes come about on earth and in the air, e.g., the seasonal generation of plants and animals under the influence of the sun.*

Diaporia 14.3 (7a7–10). *Some suppose that there are both material and enshaped first principles, on the ground that what is complete is composed of both, given that all of existence derives from opposites.*

The last position is favored by Theophrastus. He returns to it in Aporia 18 below, to which this passage refers. For an analysis of this entire Aporia with its diaporiae as the introduction, thesis, and antithesis of the question whether the principles are determinate or not see Ellis 1988, 221–222.

6b25 οἷον δυναμικάς, ὥσπερ ὅσοι πῦρ καὶ γῆν] The word δυναμικός first appears in the writings of the Italian Pythagorean Philolaus as quoted by Stobaeus (*Eclogae* 1.20.2, I.172.9 Wachsmuth = fr. 21, line 5 Huffman, Timpanaro Cardini). These writings, however, are considered spurious and hence more recent than Theophrastus, and thus the first unequivocal occurrence of the word is in the historian Theopompus (fourth century BC), who uses it to describe the efficacity of a poison (δυναμικὸν ἐναργῶς ὄν), fr. 181b Jacoby. It thus means having potency rather than potentiality (pace Schnayder 1973, 55n25), and Laks & Most 48n2 are doubtless correct when they associate it with the common expression further down, 8a19, δύναμιν δέ τιν' ἔχον (cf. ὑλικός 7a7, "having matter"); for Aristotle, see, i.a., the opening sentence of the *Poetics*, ἥν τινα δύναμιν ἕκαστον ἔχει, *sc.* τῶν τῆς ποιητικῆς εἰδῶν. It should be noted that if δυναμικός is roughly equivalent to δύναμιν ἔχων, it does not mean the same thing as δυνάμει εἶναι, "potential"; LSJ list only Damascius (sixth Christian century) as evidence for the use of the word with the meaning "potential." If the reference by Theophrastus here is indeed to Parmenides, about whom he explicitly says that he posited earth and fire as principles (see the Loci Paralleli), then δυναμικός would be a very apt synonym of the participle ποιοῦν used in that passage to describe the potency of fire. The use of οἷον just before δυναμικός in the text would appear to mitigate the contrast between the shapelessness of a first principle and the fact that it is nevertheless dynamic or efficacious.

The occurrence of the word among the Pythagoreans, and especially Philolaus, even though assumed to be spurious, may not be insignificant. If the passage quoted by Stobaeus has some basis in pre-Socratic Pythagorean writings, to which Theophrastus would have had access, the dualist theory mentioned here by Theophrastus (earth and fire as principles) may well be referring to some Pythagorean cosmogony, possibly even to Philolaus and his theory, in which central fire would indeed be the δυναμικόν first principle, with earth and counter-earth as secondary (cf. Huffman 207–215, 246–248).

Alternately, commentators have also pointed out that "fire and earth" may mean "fire or earth," and thus entertained the possibility that Theophrastus is talking about here monists rather than dualists, in which case the reference would be to Heraclitus, of course, and to Hippasus. As Ross 60 points out, though, Aristotle said (*Met.* A 8, 989a5–6) that no philosopher ever treated earth as a first principle, so reading the phrase above as "fire *or* earth" cannot stand. Finally, though it is difficult to be certain, the normal reading of καί in πῦρ καὶ γῆν (as opposed to, say, πῦρ ἢ γῆν, or even better, ὅσοι πῦρ καὶ ὅσοι γῆν, which Theophrastus does not say) would be to have it join two items that belong together in the thinking of a dualist.

6b27 For a discussion of the comments by Theophrastus on the *Timaeus* see Baltussen 2003.

7a1 ἐν ταῖς λοιπαῖς refers, naturally, as in 6b21–22, to μεθόδοις, not to ἐπιστῆμαι; see above, commentary on 6b18 and 6b20.

7a1 σχεδόν] It is difficult to gauge the precise force of this adverb. (a) Most translators take it to modify what follows, οὕτω ἔχειν, so that the meaning is, "and in the rest of the sciences this seems pretty much to be so" (Ross, and similarly Tricot, Reale, Laks & Most, Henrich); whereas (b) Isḥāq and van Raalte see it as modifying ἐν ταῖς λοιπαῖς. The point is not moot. In alternative (a), if the case is "almost" so in the rest of the disciplines, i.e., if the principles are "almost" shaped and determined in the rest of the disciplines, this means that they are *not* fully determined in *any* discipline other than metaphysics, the discipline in which Theophrastus is currently engaged. In case (b), the principles are shaped and determined in "almost" all the rest of the disciplines, which means that they are fully determined in most of the disciplines other than metaphysics, except for a few in which they are not. Now if (a) is what Theophrastus means, it would imply that, in the examples he provides next, mathematics would be a discipline without fully determined principles, something which would be difficult to maintain given Aristotle's statement (see the Loci Paralleli) that most of all it is mathematics that displays determinacy. Furthermore, if (a) is meant, the examples that follow would be pointless: if all the rest of the disciplines have no fully determined principles, why single out three of them as examples? It thus appears that σχεδόν should be read as modifying ἐν ταῖς λοιπαῖς, in which case the examples immediately following can be seen as providing explanation for σχεδόν by discriminating those disciplines which do not have fully determined principles from those who do. See the following comment.

7a2 The transmitted Greek text of this line is problematic (καὶ ἐν ταῖς λοιπαῖς σχεδὸν ἔχειν οὕτω καθάπερ ἡ γραμματικὴ καὶ μουσική), as is evident from the many attempts by scholars to emend it. The Latin translation reads, *et in reliquis fere habere ita quemadmodum gramatica* *et musica*, which shows that Λ had the same text as the extant Greek manuscripts. The Arabic translation, by contrast, points the way to the solution, indicating that Ψ had the correct reading. The error can thus be located in the common parent of the Messinan (Λ) and Constantinopolitan (**α**) recensions of the text but not in the archetype.

The Arabic translation of this passage reads, "Now we find this to be so in the rest of the sciences except for a few, like writing and music, and the situation is the same with the mathematical [sciences]." This is different from the Greek text we have in two important aspects. First, Isḥāq clearly understood writing and music as two examples of the few sciences that form the exception to the rule, exemplified by mathematics, the science with the most ordered and determined principles. Since this understanding cannot be achieved from the Greek text either as we have it or as emended by the scribe of J^{II} and other modern scholars, either Isḥāq failed to understand the (relatively very simple) text, or he read before καθάπερ some word(s) that fell out in the extant Greek manuscripts, i.e., there is a lacuna before καθάπερ. Second, the Arabic does list the three disciplines one after the other, but separates the first two (writing and music) from the last (mathematics) by the expression, "the situation is the same with" (*wa-ka-ḏālika yajrī l-amru fī*). It seems quite improbable that this entire phrase would be a mere translation of καί in καὶ ταῖς μαθηματικαῖς, the only word in the Greek text separating μουσική and μαθηματικαῖς, unless something preceded in the lacuna that would impart such a sense to καί. Expressions of this sort throughout this text in Arabic translate various Greek adverbs like οὕτως and ὁμοίως (see the Glossary), but this particular one, *ka-ḏālika yajrī l-amru*, in another passage (11a8) translates ὡσαύτως. It is thus very probable that Ψ may have read, καὶ ⟨ὡσαύτως ἐν⟩ ταῖς μαθηματικαῖς, where ὡσαύτως would indicate that Theophrastus was reverting to his discussion about the order and determinacy of principles after the brief parenthetical note differentiating grammar and music from mathematics. These two aspects of the Arabic version taken together suggest that a lacuna has to be assumed at least before καθάπερ, if not also before ταῖς μαθηματικαῖς.

Apart from the evidence of the Arabic translation, a lacuna before καθάπερ has to be asssumed mainly for two reasons: first, it is difficult to account for the nominatives of ἡ γραμματικὴ καὶ μουσική in all the independent witnesses, including Ψ and Λ: they could hardly have arisen from a corruption of the text as originally reconstructed by the scribe of J^{II} and accepted by almost all modern editors (i.e., the addition of ἐν before the two nouns and of a iota subscript and circumflex of the final η of both for the dative), and they do not appear to have been a marginal gloss that was inserted into the text, as suggested by van Raalte (290n2); if they had, and they are athetized, then the phrase after οὕτω must read either καθάπερ καὶ ταῖς μαθηματικαῖς, or, if one assumes that καθάπερ also was part of the marginal gloss, just καὶ ταῖς μαθηματικαῖς. But of these the first seems unlikely and the second is "rather pointless," as van Raalte 290 rightly points out: to say καὶ ταῖς μαθηματικαῖς after having just said καὶ ἐν ταῖς λοιπαῖς without any intervening text to require the explicit declaration and affirmation of καὶ ταῖς μαθηματικαῖς makes little sense; "one would at least have expected *καὶ *δὴ* ταῖς μαθηματικαῖς." Thus the nominative in the following two words after καθάπερ must be seen not itself as a corruption that needs to be corrected but as a fossil of the correct text which indicates an adjacent corruption, namely this lacuna.

Second, if σχεδόν in 7a1 is taken as modifying ἐν ταῖς λοιπαῖς (see the preceding comment), the examples that follow must provide some explanation for Theophrastus's statement by discriminating among the various disciplines, and the two disciplines of grammar and music contrasted with mathematics would indeed provide such a discrimination. Furthermore, if it is assumed that Theophrastus intended no such discrimination, it seems rather unlikely that he would have put grammar and music at the very same level as mathematics with regard to the order and determinacy of their principles, or, for that matter, cited grammar and music *before* mathematics; for as it is, i.e., in the passage as reconstructed by the scribe of J^{II}, mathematics appears almost as an afterthought. But it is difficult not to see in this passage of Theophrastus an echo of the Aristotelian text in *Metaphysics* M 3, 1078a36–b2, τοῦ δὲ καλοῦ μέγιστα εἴδη τάξις καὶ συμμετρία καὶ τὸ ὡρισμένον, ἃ μάλιστα δεικνύουσιν αἱ μαθηματικαὶ ἐπιστῆμαι. And if numbers are the principles of mathematics, it is difficult to see that they can compare, with regard to order and determinacy, with the principles of grammar and music, which are, respectively, φωναί, articulate sounds (*Met.* Γ 2, 1003b21), and φθόγγοι, notes (*De mundo* 396b16, despite the spurious attribution of this work to Aristotle), both of which are produced by men and are accordingly quite variable. Similarly, in Plato's *Philebus* (18a6–d2), grammar and music are presented as having an infinity of elements that have to be reduced to order (18a6–d2) and as sciences based on conjecture, having little that is certain and exact, as opposed to arithmetic (56a3–d1).

It is possible to go even further. Depending on what Theophrastus had in mind with ἀρχαί in this passage, it may be possible to point to principles of music which are even further removed from order and determinacy than notes. In a passage preserved in Plutarch's *Table Talk* (I,5,2 623A), we read that Theophrastus had said that the principles of music are three, "pain, pleasure, and inspiration," λέγει δὲ μουσικῆς ἀρχὰς τρεῖς εἶναι, λύπην ἡδονὴν ἐνθουσιασμόν (fr. 719A FHS&G). Affections such as these are neither orderly nor determinate. The same applies to "grammar," in that it could be said to have principles that are themselves further removed from order and determinacy than articulate sounds. In the *Topics* Aristotle defines γραμματική in such a way as to make of it, as a discipline, a qualitatively very different thing than mathematics. It is, he says (142b31–33, p. 241 *CWA*), "the knowledge how to write from dictation and how to read" (τὴν γραμματικὴν ἐπιστήμην τοῦ γράψαι τὸ ὑπαγορευθέν … καὶ τοῦ ἀναγνῶναι). The principles of literacy, if that is what Theophrastus had in mind here with γραμματική, cannot have the same determinacy as those of mathematics. This evidence sufficiently indicates that in this passage Theophrastus is somehow making a distinction between grammar and music on the one hand and mathematics on the other with regard to the order and determinacy of the principles of these disciplines, and that the clause with the two nouns in the nominative expressed this distinction.

The Arabic translation suggests that the structure of this entire sentence in Theophrastus was as follows: Theophrastus states a general state of affairs which he qualifies by using the word σχεδόν, opens up a parenthetical aside in which he registers an exception to this general state, gives two examples of this exception (grammar and music), and finally reverts to the general state by giving an example of it, mathematics. As it turns out, Theophrastus uses such a syntactic structure, with slight variations, relatively frequently. Most immediately parallel is the following passage from *HP* VII,6,1, lines 4 ff.: ἅπαντα γάρ ἐστι τὰ γένη ταῦτα καὶ ἄγρια, καὶ *σχεδὸν* τά γε πολλὰ παραπλησίαν ἔχοντα τὴν ὄψιν τοῖς ἡμέροις, *πλὴν* τοῖς γε φύλλοις ἐλάττω ταῦτα καὶ τραχύτερα … *καθάπερ* ἥ τε θύμβρα καὶ ἡ ὀρίγανος. The following two passages have a similar structure: *HP* III,9,1, lines 1 ff., καὶ *σχεδὸν* τά γε πλεῖστα διαιροῦσι ἄρρενι καὶ θήλει … *πλὴν* ὀλίγων *ὧν* ἐστι καὶ ἡ πεύκη, and *HP* I,6,6, lines 1 ff., *σχεδὸν* δὲ καὶ τῶν λαχανωδῶν τὰ πλεῖστα μονόρριζα … *πλὴν* ἔνια καὶ ἀποφυάδας ἔχει μεγάλας, *οἷον* τὸ σέλινον.

Since the Arabic indicates that what dropped out meant to say "except for a few" (*mā ḫalā š-šāḏḏ minhā*), the evidence above suggests that the lacuna must have included the word πλήν plus another word. Πλήν is in fact translated by *mā ḫalā* in this Essay (6b6), and the evidence of the translation literature indicates that *šāḏḏ* is rendered by παῦροι and ἔνιοι (see the commentary on the corresponding passage in the Arabic translation). Since Theophrastus uses παῦροι only once in his extant writings (*HP* VIII,7.4 l. 8), ἔνιοι would be a good candidate for the lacuna (it is used in the third example just cited), but so would ὀλίγοι, which is both used by Theophrastus (as in the second passage cited) and would fit the sense better in this context. It thus appears almost certain that the text that dropped out before καθάπερ here read, καὶ ἐν ταῖς λοιπαῖς σχεδὸν ἔχειν οὕτω ⌜πλὴν ὀλίγαις,⌝ καθάπερ ἡ γραμματικὴ καὶ μουσική, καὶ ταῖς μαθηματικαῖς. If this is the Greek text that was translated by Isḥāq, then it may be possible to derive the amplified meaning of "the situation is the same with" from καί in καὶ ταῖς μαθηματικαῖς, in which case one would not have to emend the following clause as well and read καὶ ⟨ὡσαύτως ἐν⟩ ταῖς μαθηματικαῖς.

7a4 ἔτι δέ … ὁμοίως, i.e., ὁμοίως ἔχει, the structure of the sentence paralleling the earlier one in 7a1, with ἔτι δέ adding yet another item after δέ in that line (cf. van Raalte 292, Laks & Most 50n9).

7a4, 6 κατά, "in accordance with," i.e., crafts, just like most of the disciplines, bear out, as analogues, the observation made in 6b26–28 that order and determinacy are most appropriate to the first principles. For an analysis of this sentence see Henrich 110.

7a6–7 The accusatives in ἐμμόρφους and ὑλικάς are parallel to those in ἀμόρφους and δυναμικάς (6b25) and thus dependent, after the long parenthetical argument in 7a1–6, on the verb ὑποθέσθαι (6b23), to assume.

7a7 πάσας here means "nothing but, just, only" (LSJ s.v. I,4), not "all."

7a7–8 τάς τ' ἐμμόρφους καὶ τὰς τῆς ὕλης] The extant Greek manuscripts and the Latin translation add here this phrase, "both those possessed of shape and those of matter," which is absent from the Arabic translation and hence from its Greek exemplar Ψ. This is clearly a marginal gloss that entered the main text in the manuscript transmission deriving from one transliteration from uncials (see the stemma codicum). In the highly succinct style of this Essay, Theophrastus would have hardly wasted words explaining something obvious while letting stand other, more ambiguous expressions.

7a10 ἄλογον δέ, introducing the objections to the "materialists", is answered by χαλεπὸν δέ in 7a19, introducing the objections to the "formalists." It is impossible in the English translation to place these two adjectives first in their respective sentences.

7a10 κἀκείνοις, "these [people]," must refer to the "materialists," i.e., those who assume only indeterminate material first principles, one of the three groups of philosophers Theophrastus mentioned in Aporia 14. There has been much discussion on this subject (for which see the commentaries), with Laks & Most claiming that "them" refers to the "dualists," and everybody else the "materialists." The arguments in favor of the "materialists" are the following. First, the subject "they" indicated in λαμβάνουσιν in the following sentence (7a16) cannot but be the same, in context, as "them" referred to by κἀκείνοις. Laks & Most may be right in saying that it is not required that this be so ("il n'est pas requis," 52n17, which I take it to mean that there is no grammatical necessity that this be so), but then Theophrastus was writing with the purpose of being understood and, despite the elliptic nature of this Essay, he could not have violated all rules of contextual intelligibility: a verb without a subject in a sentence must necessarily refer to the subject expressed in a preceding sentence, unless there are other pointers to the contrary, and in this case there are none. Second, if it is assumed that "them" refers to anyone else other than the materialists against whom Theophrastus is arguing in this diaporia (14.1c), it would make no sense because it would be tautological: to those who held any one of the three positions mentioned by Theophrastus, the other two must have naturally seemed "unreasonable;" so why should Theophrastus say that it *would* seem unreasonable, using even the conditional and not the indicative, as if the formalists and the dualists might even consider it reasonable? And why, in addition, "*even* or *also* (καὶ in κἀκείνοις) to these [people]"?—wouldn't it be normal, and not exceptional, for the views of the materialists to seem unreasonable to the formalists and dualists to begin with? Finally, the pronoun ἐκείνοις, since Theophrastus is going to argue against the materialists in what follows, points forward to them rather than backward (as elsewhere in this Essay, at 9b13 and 11a14), and thus there is no point in arguing to which of the preceding three groups the pronoun is referring (as Most 1988b,

244–245, does). Thus κἀκείνοις refers to the materialists, and Theophrastus is saying, "it is unreasonable for the formalists and dualists—but *also* for the materialists themselves, were they to think seriously about the matter—to say that the world is ordered but not its principles, as Heraclitus does." The objection by Most 1988b, 244, in this instance that, if this were so, it would mean "that Theophrastus would be saying that Heraclitus would find one of Heraclitus' own aphorisms absurd," is precisely the case: Theophrastus *is* saying that were Heraclitus to think seriously about his paradoxical statement he might find it unreasonable.[27] As a matter of fact, in *Metaphysics* K 5 Aristotle (and/or perhaps also Theophrastus?)[28] is saying exactly the same thing about Heraclitus: "If we had questioned Heraclitus himself in this way we might have forced him to confess that opposite statements can never be true of the same subjects. But, as it is, he adopted his opinion without understanding what his statement involved" (*Met.* K 5, 1062a31–35, *CWA* 1678; referred to by Viano 1992, 472n53). The "opposite statements" in this instance, in the Heraclitus quotation cited by Theophrastus in what follows, are "things poured out at random" (εἰκῇ κεχυμένα) on the one hand and "the most beautiful arrangement" (ὁ κάλλιστος κόσμος) on the other, which Heraclitus claims both to be true of the same subject, "flesh" or human body (σάρξ); see the comment at 7a15 below.

7a12 (ἐν ...) λόγῳ, "formally principled"] This would appear to be the meaning of this polysemic word here and in the next paragraph (7a20), since what Theophrastus is talking about is the determinacy of the first principles in accordance with some "formula" or "plan" (Ross); these words, however, are hardly usable in this sense in contemporary English. "Proportion" (Isḥāq, Tricot, Reale, van Raalte) is equally applicable, but if understood in these terms. By contrast, it seems implausible that the term would mean either "raison" (Laks & Most) or "Verhältnis" and "Erklärung" (Henrich). Given that Theophrastus quotes Heraclitus in this context, it may be also that he has this philosopher's concept of λόγος in mind.

---

[27] Cf. McDiarmid's 1941, 493–494, similar analysis of Theophrastus's motive for quoting Heraclitus: "to wrest from his [Heraclitus's] own words an admission of an antithesis between the orderliness of the world of perception and the disorder of the principles from which the world is formed."

[28] On the question of the authorship of this book and its relation to Theophrastus see Aubenque 1983, and especially p. 343 where its closeness to this Essay by Theophrastus is noted.

7a15 This Heraclitean fragment (DK 22 B 124; fr. 107 Marcovich 1978, 2001; T 209 Mouraviev 1999) and its text have been much discussed; see Most 1988b, Viano 1992, van Raalte 301–306, Henrich 111–112, 298–315, Mouraviev 1999, 163–166 and their references to earlier literature. There are two contested readings in the Greek text, σάϱξ and the article ὁ before κόσμος. Σάϱξ is universally attested: all the Greek manuscripts and the Arabic (Ψ) and Latin (Λ) translations have it, so that if it is indeed erroneous it would be one of the primitive errors of the Neoplatonic archetype manuscript. With few exceptions, all scholars have thought it untenable and emended it, mostly with a word that means "a heap or a pile [of sweepings]" (σάϱμα Diels, σάϱον Bernays, σωϱός Usener, etc; see the apparatus, and in particular the complete table of proposed readings in Mouraviev 1999, 165), so that the resulting text meant, "the most fair universe is like a rubbish-heap of things thrown anyhow" (Ross), and the like. However, what is untenable is this emendation, because it presents the wrong comparison and ruins the point that Theophrastus is trying to make. In this paragraph he is objecting to those philosophers who posit only indeterminate material principles but hold that everything that derives from these indeterminate principles is nevertheless determinate and ordered, and gives the quotation of Heraclitus as example for such a belief. Thus what we need to have in the quotation is an indeterminate principle and an ordered universe. Specifically, this means the following. It is to be noted that the Heraclitean quotation is parallel in a chiasmus to the structure of the preceding statement of the problem by Theophrastus: ὁ μὲν ὅλος οὐϱανός … πεϱιόδοις is repeated in ὁ κάλλιστος κόσμος, while ἐν δὲ ταῖς ἀϱχαῖς μηθὲν τοιοῦτον is paralleled by εἰκῆ κεχυμένων (cf. Ross's 61 comment on the contrast indicated). In other words, the indeterminate principle in the quotation is represented merely by the adverb εἰκῆ and the implied agents (χέοντες) of the passive participle κεχυμένων,[29] while everything else that derives from them is represented by ὁ κάλλιστος κόσμος. So what is needed in the quotation, in order for the point Theophrastus is making to be made, is to have the word(s) representing the random principles to stand by themselves in sharp contrast, and not be subordinated syntactically, to the orderliness of the universe. In the text as emended by most scholars, however, we get instead a disordered universe: This most fair universe (i.e., what derives from the principles) is like a rubbish-heap of things thrown about at random.

[29] I.e., the indeterminate principle is not, as McDiarmid 1941, 494, thought, represented by κεχυμένα but by their agent(s) who did the outpouring.

Arguing along lines similar to those who would emend σάρξ, but "taking εἰκῇ κεχυμένων as a partitive genitive attached to ὁ κάλλιστος, and ὁ κόσμος as a predicate defining that preceding phrase," Most 1988b, 246, suggested reading σωρῶν for σάρξ as the plural word modified by κεχυμένων. He accordingly translated, "Just like the most beautiful of the heaps piled at random [is] the world-order." This is better, in that it makes what is derived from the principles to be the most beautiful of the heaps, but it is equally marred by calling it "heaps" of things, implying a pell-mell and not orderly arrangement. The problem with all these emendations is that by integrating the word that is substituted for σάρξ into the syntax of the words that follow it, there inevitably results that this syntactic unit ("a heap of random things") becomes the phrase that in the end describes "the universe" (ὁ κόσμος). But according to the sense of the comparison that Theophrastus is trying to make, the universe is what derives from the principles, and for his comparison to work, the phrase that describes the universe must say that it is absolutely ordered and determinate. But these emendations say the opposite.

The objections I raised so far against these emendations are based on the syntax that results from these emendations and on the concomitant sense, which is the opposite of the one required. A more compelling objection, however, is presented by the transmission of the text and the manuscript affiliations, or stemmatics. The corruption of an allegedly correct σάρον or σάρμα or σωρῶν, etc., into the transmitted σάρξ, given the very nature of the corruption, could only have happened in the transmission of the text in minuscule copies (as Most 1988b, 247; Marcovich 2001, 548, etc., explain), i.e., after the transliteration of an uncial exemplar into minuscule copies. But this is impossible, for the reading σάρξ is already to be found in the uncial Neoplatonic archetype: both the Arabic translation, which represents one transliteration from uncials, and the Greek manuscripts together with the Latin translation, which represent the second transliteration, read σάρξ. Accordingly, unless one assumes that the same corruption of σάρον, etc., to σάρξ occurred in both traditions *independently* of each other, the alleged corruption must have happened in uncials, something which is difficult to justify palaeographically.

All these considerations make it likely, therefore, that first, σάρξ may be the right reading after all—it certainly is supported by all the manuscripts while its derivation from a corruption is decidedly not—and second, that it must be detached syntactically from what follows in order to avoid ending up, like the proposed emendations, as just described, with a sense that is the opposite of the one desired. H. Gomperz did precisely that in 1922 (p. xxvi); he read the text of the quotation with a comma or a colon after σάρξ, he secluded both articles, thus reading, σάρξ: εἰκῆ κεχυμένων [ὁ] κάλλιστος [ὁ] κόσμος, and he translated, "der Menschenleib: zufälliger Ergiessung (d.h. des Samens) vollkommene Wohlgestalt." Diels, who printed this reading and translation in his 1922 Nachträge, dismissed them out of hand, without discussion. More responsibly, Most 1988b, 245, objected to this interpretation by finding (a) the seclusion of both articles, with the implication that there had been a double interpolation, "implausible," (b) the "separation between σάρξ and κεχυμένων scarcely tolerable," (c) the meaning of κεχυμένων as *Ergiessung* "quite strained," and (d) the meaning of κόσμος in Heraclitus as *Wohlgestalt* unlikely, suggesting that it "should refer to the universe." But none of these objections has any support. (a) It may be implausible to assume two masculine singular articles to have been interpolated in the passage, but not one, which is in fact what happened, as I will explain below. (b) Second, the separation between σάρξ and κεχυμένων is quite regular if the quotation is seen as a "definition," as Viano 1992, 471 suggested; other instances of such separation in the fragments of Heraclitus can be seen, e.g., at fr. B 33 and B 67: νόμος: καὶ βουλῆι πείθεσθαι ἑνός, and, θεός: ἡμέρη εὐφρόνη, κτλ. (c) As for Gomperz's translation of κεχυμένων, a plural passive participle, with a singular gerund, *Ergiessung*, literally an "outpouring" but specified by Gomperz as "discharge of semen," may not have been what Heraclitus had primarily in mind (though it can never be ruled out with this philosopher, so polysemic in his expression), but there can be no doubt that the word means "things poured out" in the sense of "things thrown about," which is a most apposite signification in context. But whatever the primary meaning intended by Heraclitus, this does not affect Gomperz's understanding of the syntax of the Greek, which reads σάρξ as syntactically separate from what follows. (d) Finally, not only does the word κόσμος in this fragment *not* refer to the universe, as the context, which I discuss next, makes clear, but, on the basis of all available evidence (presented in detail by Kirk 1970, 311–314), it cannot mean "universe" in Heraclitus but arrangement and order, perhaps ornament; the meaning of "world" or "universe" was a later development.[30]

After Gomperz, the word σάρξ and both masculine articles in the passage were retained by scholars representing two different approaches, those who kept σάρξ as part of the Heraclitean fragment but removed

---

[30] Most 1988b, 254n84, cites Kerschensteiner's *Kosmos* (Munich 1962) in support of his statement but not Kirk's discussion of the evidence against it.

from it the word κόσμος, and those who did the opposite. The first was introduced by McDiarmid 1941, who claimed the fragment consisted of only the following words, σὰρξ εἰκῇ κεχυμένων ὁ κάλλιστος, which he translated as, "the fairest man is flesh composed of parts scattered at random." This interpretation is problematic primarily because McDiarmid did not parse the fragment satisfactorily in its surrounding syntax[31] (though his analysis of the context in which it is found and its intended effect is accurate), but it found the approval of Kirk 1970 who accordingly did not include the Theophrastean citation in his study of Heraclitus's cosmic fragments. McDiarmid was followed by P. Friedländer 1942 who, perceiving the difficulty of forcing ὁ κάλλιστος to mean "the fairest *man*" without any other corroborating markers, suggested correcting the text to read, σὰρξ εἰκῇ κεχυμέν⟨η ἀνθρώπ⟩ων ὁ κάλλιστος, by assuming the missing letters to have dropped out through a misreading of an abbreviation in a manuscript. But the evidence of the Arabic translation, to be discussed next, indicates that the omission which Friedländer supposed must have existed in the Neoplatonic archetype of Theophrastus's Essay, which was in uncials; and uncial manuscripts of non-Christian Greek texts did not use such abbreviations by contraction like that posited by Friedländer.[32] To this group would also belong the implausible reading suggested by Mouraviev 1999, who read the fragment as, ὥσπερ σὰρξ εἰκῆι κεκυ(η)μένων ὁ κάλλιστος, and translated, "tel de la viande ⟨de fausse couche = môle⟩ en vrac ⟨est⟩ le plus beau des enfantés."[33]

The second approach to the text by those scholars who retained, like Gomperz, the word σάρξ is represented by the studies of Bollack & Wismann 1972, fr. 124, and by Viano 1992, 471. They saw both articles as

---

[31] See the objections by Most 1988b, 245–246.

[32] E.M. Thompson, *Greek and Latin Palaeography*, Oxford: Clarendon Press 1912, 76–78.

[33] On the basis of this translation one is to understand that Mouraviev took σὰρξ εἰκῆι as the predicate of the sentence, but "flesh randomly," or "miscarried embryo randomly," as he interpreted the phrase, can hardly stand alone (the noun cannot be modified by the adverb); in other words, the syntax of the fragment can hardly be, ὁ κάλλιστος τῶν κεκυ(η)μένων ἐστὶ ὥσπερ σὰρξ εἰκῆι. Besides, the sentence as a whole, if it means, "The most beautiful of babies (?, children? embryos?) is like a miscarried embryo," makes little sense both in itself and especially in the context in which Theophrastus is quoting the adage. In addition, Mouraviev introduced yet another emendation (κεκυ(η)μένων) to the transmitted text without any basis; his reference to Diog. Laert. III,72, τοῦ καλλίστου τῶν γεννητῶν as a description of κόσμος, with reference to Plato's *Timaeus*, is hardly relevant, especially since he left κόσμος out of the fragmant and otherwise did not integrate it into the overall sentence of Theophrastus.

part of the text and considered the word σάρξ, after which they punctuated the text, not as part of the Heraclitean fragment but as a word introduced by Theophrastus for the sake of comparison, while they admitted the word κόσμος into the fragment. They translated, respectively, "Des choses jetées là au hasard, le plus bel arrangement, ce monde-ci," and " « la più bella organizzazione di cose sparse a caso », dice Eraclito, « [sarebbe] l'Universo » ". In this interpretation, to arrive at the meaning they desired, both Bollack & Wismann and Viano, read κόσμος *twice* in the text, the first time as if the words ὁ κάλλιστος by themselves implied κόσμος, as follows: ὥσπερ σάρξ, "εἰκῆ κεχυμένων ὁ κάλλιστος ⟨κόσμος⟩," φησὶν Ἡράκλειτος, "ὁ κόσμος." But this again is forced and unnecessary.

The main problem in all of these interpretations except Gomperz's (both those which would emend σάρξ and those which would keep it) is that because of the context of the fragment, where Theophrastus speaks of ὁ ὅλος οὐρανός just before quoting it (7a11), it has been assumed that the word κόσμος in it has to mean the universe. But the real point of the Theophrastean context is not to speak about the universe but about *order*, τάξις and λόγος (7a12), which, according to the materialists, is found in what derives from the principles but not in the principles themselves; thus for the Heraclitean quotation to serve Theophrastus's purpose in the comparison, the word κόσμος must mean order and orderly arrangement, not universe.[34]

At this point it is useful to look at the Arabic translation; the Latin does not add anything new insofar as it has the same text as the Greek manuscripts without providing any clues about the two masculine articles in the quotation (*caro si*[35] *confusorum pulcherimus ait Heraclitus mundus*). The Arabic, on the other hand, suggests the correct reading. For the words ἀλλ' … κόσμος it reads, "but the most sublime thing is like flesh scattered to no purpose, as Heraclitus said" (*lākin ajallu l-umūri bi-manzilati laḥmin manṯūrin bāṭilan, 'alā mā qāla Irāqlīṭus*). In Greek, following the Arabic syntax, this stands for, ἀλλ' ὁ κάλλιστος κόσμος

[34] This further corroborates the argument by Kirk 1970, 311–314, about the meaning of κόσμος in Heraclitus and at the same time obviates the need (felt by Kirk 1970, 313, following McDiarmid 1941 and Friedländer 1942) to consider the word in this fragment as not belonging to Heraclitus but to Theophrastus on account of its alleged meaning "universe."

[35] *Si* translates only the εἰ part of εἰκῆ, with the κῆ part most likely omitted by haplography with the following first syllable κε of κεχυμένων, as Kley 21 suggests. Mouraviev 1999, 166, without mentioning Kley's explanation, suggests instead a misreading of εἴη for εἰκῆι.

ὥσπερ σὰρξ κεχυμένη εἰκῇ, ὥς φησιν Ἡράκλειτος. Re-arranging the same words in the order of the actual Greek text, we get, ἀλλ' ὥσπερ σὰρξ εἰκῇ κεχυμένη ὁ κάλλιστος, ὥς φησιν Ἡράκλειτος, κόσμος. Now it is doubtful that the Greek exemplar (Ψ) of the Arabic translation actually had κεχυμένη; in all likelihood it had the transmitted genitive plural, but because Isḥāq apparently could not understand κεχυμένων after the feminine σάρξ (reading, like his modern counterparts, σάρξ together with what follows rather than separating it) he translated it as if the participle were singular feminine. For the same reason it would appear that he rendered κόσμος in a general way as "things," *umūr*, rather than literally. However, the Arabic version clearly has ὥς (*'alā mā*) before φησίν (thus corroborating Hommel's and Marcovich's conjectural addition) and reads ὁ κάλλιστος κόσμος (*ajallu l-umūri*) without the article ὁ before κόσμος. The presence of ὡς in Ψ helps explain how the second article ὁ was inserted before κόσμος. To begin with, ὥς must have dropped through haplography after κάλλιστος in the other branch of the transmission represented by the Greek manuscripts and the exemplar of the Latin translation. Once ὡς disappeared from the text, the resulting reading ὁ κάλλιστος φησὶν Ἡράκλειτος prompted some copyist, "who took ὁ κάλλιστος with Ἡράκλειτος," to add the ὁ in ὁ κόσμος, as Ross 61 explains. The reading in Ψ, as it can be recovered from the Arabic translation, thus directs us to add ὥς before φησιν and eliminate the article ὁ before κόσμος.

The correct way to read the Heraclitean "definition" which Theophrastus is using in his argument thus becomes, σάρξ, εἰκῇ κεχυμένων ὁ κάλλιστος, ⌜ὥς⌝ φησιν Ἡράκλειτος, [ὁ] κόσμος, meaning, "Flesh [as the contour of the human body]: of things poured out at random, the most beautiful, as Heraclitus says, arrangement." Gomperz was right, except that he secluded the first masculine article unnecessarily and rendered his reading less likely. Heraclitus is not talking about the universe but merely about the human body, by means of whose definition he can illustrate his theory, according to Theophrastus, that the disordered and indeterminate principles, responsible for the pouring out of the elements at random, bring about in actual fact perfectly arranged and orderly wholes. And this is precisely what Theophrastus is castigating him for, pointing out the utter lack of logic in this statement, as does Aristotle in the passage from *Met.* K 5, 1062a31–35, cited in the commentary on 7a10 above.

Heraclitus's definition of the human body is in perfect accord with all we know about ancient Greek conceptions, for it was widely held that the outward part of the body, or the contours of the flesh, "adorn" (κόσμος) the aggregate that forms the human body. In a similar context Galen expresses the same view, perhaps even with the saying or definition of Heraclitus, his Ionian countryman, in mind: καὶ τί γὰρ ἄλλ' ἢ πρὸ πάντων τῶν κυρίων μερῶν εἰς ἅπασαν ἔκκειται βλάβην τὸ σαρκῶδες γένος; οὕτως ἐξ ἁπάντων ἡ φύσις ὠφελεῖ τε ἅμα καὶ κοσμεῖ καὶ φρουρεῖ τὸ ζῷον (*De usu partium* IV.10,3 Kühn).

There remains the question whether ὥσπερ belongs to the Heraclitean fragment or is Theophrastus's word. Given that Heraclitus wrote aphorisms and "definitions" rather than similes or homoeomata, which, by their very nature contain words like ὥσπερ (cf. A. Elter, *Gnomica homoeomata*, Bonn 1900–1904), the second alternative is preferable (cf. also Marcovich 2001, 549).

7a15–16 καί ... δ', "and ... even"] The conjunction καί here is used in a contrasting sense in an ascending climax (Denniston 293): not only does the self-contradictory nature of their view just mentioned in the preceding sentence (i.e., the world is ordered but its principles are not) not seem unreasonable to them, but on top of that (καί) they take this to be the case even in the *smallest* detail, for animate and inanimate beings alike.

7a16 λαμβάνουσιν, i.e., in context, ἅπαντ' ἐν τάξει καὶ λόγῳ ἐν δὲ ταῖς ἀρχαῖς μηθὲν τοιοῦτον, that is, they take things to be as described in the previous sentence.

7a16 ὁμοίως] Given the word order, the adverb ὁμοίως belongs with the following phrase, ἐν ἀψύχοις καὶ ἐμψύχοις (cf. van Raalte 307). If ὁμοίως were to be read with λαμβάνουσιν, as Laks & Most 52n18 suggest, and the phrase ἐν ἀψύχοις καὶ ἐμψύχοις were an addition for specification, then Theophrastus would have said ὁμοίως λαμβάνουσιν ἐν ἀψύχοις τε καὶ ἐμψύχοις.

7a19 χαλεπὸν δέ responds to ἄλογον δέ in the preceding paragraph, 7a10.

7a20 πάλιν αὖ] The Arabic supports Zeller's emendation of αὐτό of the Greek manuscripts to αὖ τό; πάλιν is rendered by *ayḍan*, "also, again," while there is no demonstrative pronoun that would correspond to αὐτό. The function of πάλιν here is to introduce a new set of objections to another doctrine, that of the "formalists."

7a20 Note the article in τοὺς λόγους: not *some* formal principles but its own internal principles; τούς here contrasts with ἑτέρων in line 7a23.

7a21 συνάγοντας, "collective referral"; see the relevant passages from Aristotle cited by van Raalte 312.

7b2 παράδειγμα] Rendered as "example" by all translators, the word nevertheless makes sense here if understood in its Platonic sense of "paradigmatic" cause, as also used by what has been argued is the early Aristotle, in *Metaphysics* Δ 2 and *Physics* B 3 (see the Loci Paralleli), where he equates it with the formal cause. This meaning is justified by the word λόγους (7a20) which Theophrastus is talking about in this Diaporia (14.2) and which, given the structure of his exceptive syntax, is then identified with the "shapes and varieties of atmospheric and terrestrial" phenomena. He says, in effect, that it is difficult to ascribe formal principles (λόγους) to everything in the realm of generation and corruption in all cases *unless* these formal principles can be assumed to be the atmospheric and terrestrial phenomena; that they can, in fact, be so assumed is implied in his use of πλὴν εἰ with the indicative (van Raalte 314). And he continues by saying that some philosophers (apparently his Peripatetic colleagues) do precisely that, claiming that whatever is entailed by the variation of the four seasons (i.e., the atmospheric and terrestrial phenomena) constitutes the greatest such paradigmatic cause in the realm of which is to be found (ἐν αἷς, the preposition being used roughly as at 4a6; see above and cf. Laks & Most 53n24) the very process of generation. The sun, he concludes, acts as if it were (οἷον) the begetter, echoing (and apparently referring to) Aristotle's very passage (*Phys.* B 2–3, 194b13–29) where there is mentioned both the sun's ultimate generative power and the definition of παράδειγμα. Furthermore, that παράδειγμα refers to a cause (and not to an example) is also evident from Aristotle's words in a related passage in the *Physics*, Θ 5, 257b10, ὅλως γεννᾷ τὸ ἔχον τὸ εἶδος, "in general what possesses the form begets." Theophrastus's reference to the former Aristotelian passage (in *Phys.* B 3) cannot be accidental, for Aristotle's point is the issue which concerns Theophrastus here:[36] if the student of physics knows the formal and final cause up to

[36] For Theophrastus's apparent response to another passage in Aristotle's *Physics* see Bodnár 2002, 79n10.

a certain point (μέχρι του, *Phys.* 194b11, the reading of manuscripts E and J) and it is the job of the metaphysician to know the essence of separable being, as Aristotle argues, then Theophrastus raises the question, first, of the extent to which this in fact can be accomplished beyond the admission of the causality of atmospheric phenomena, and second, with his one-word qualification of the sun's generative power (οἷον), how that is to be understood. In his own *Physics* (fr. 176 FHS&G), Theophrastus says that things are generated by something that is similar, or opposite, or in actuality; the sun generates as a cause in actuality. See the comments on the fragment by Sharples 1998, 125–127, and especially the discussion by Bodnár 2002, 79–81.

If the mention of παράδειγμα here is indeed in its Academic sense (see Bonitz *Index* s.v. for the references), as I argue, then this has implications for the date of Theophrastus's Essay (as discussed in Part I, Chapter 1.1). Ross 1936, 512, assigns this usage of the word to Aristotle's "Platonic period," during his first residence in Athens, and says that "it never occurs in his [Aristotle's] later references to εἶδος." It is justifiable to think that Theophrastus stands temporally close to this passage in Aristotle's *Physics*. For the importance of the word in later developments in Platonic and Aristotelian philosophy see Merlan's discussion in *The Cambridge History of Later Greek and Early Medieval Philosophy*, A.H. Armstrong, ed., Cambridge: Cambridge University press, 1970, 54–55.

7b3 τὰς ὥρας τὰς ἐτησίους] Usener's 1890 conjecture of ἐτησίους for the corrupt words in the extant Greek manuscripts is corroborated by the reading of Ψ as reflected in the Arabic translation. As for ὧραι in this context of generation caused by the sun and meteoric phenomena, there appears to be little doubt that it refers to seasons; cf. *CP* III.2.6 (cited by van Raalte 318), τοῦτο δ' ἐν δυοῖν ὥραιν γίνεται ... ἔαρι καὶ μετοπόρῳ· ... τότε γάρ ... ὁ ἥλιος θερμαίνων ἄγει καὶ ὁ ἀὴρ μαλακός ἐστιν καὶ ἐρσώδης ... κτλ.

Aporia 15

7b5–8 (ἀφορισμὸν ἀπαιτοῦντα μέχρι πόσου καὶ διὰ τί). *This aporia is in two parts:*

Aporia 15a, deriving from the immediately preceding diaporiae: *How far what is endowed with order extends*;

Aporia 15b, mentioned for future discussion (in Diaporia 24.1 at 11b7–12): *Why what is endowed with order cannot extend beyond a certain point for in that case the change would be for the worse.*

7b6–9 The μέν … δέ construction is clear here: in the μέν part Theophrastus wraps up the previous discussion (6b23–7b5) on the nature of the principles—whether they are determined or not—and in the δέ part (7b9) launches the next question, that of their rest or immobility. If it is not justifiable to print the second part of the sentence as a separate paragraph even for editorial convenience, then the unity of the sentence must certainly not be broken by a full stop between the two parts.

7b7 ἀπαιτοῦντα … καὶ διὰ τί] The object of ἀπαιτοῦντα for the first question, μέχρι πόσου, is clearly ἀφορισμόν, but for the second question, διὰ τί, it cannot be the same because of the sense: a "why" question cannot be answered by a delimitation or definition (pace Laks & Most: "que l'on définissse … pourquoi") but by an answer "because"; thus a word like ⟨ἀπόκρισιν⟩ ἀπαιτοῦντα is to be understood here (cf. Ross: "demanding … an account of the reason why").

7b8 τὸ πλέον, "more [of it]," i.e., of what is endowed with order; the reference to τεταγμένον is effected through the definite article in τὸ πλέον.

7b8 ἤ] There seems to be little room for the apparent disagreement among the commentators either for the correction by the scribe of J^{II} of the original εἰ (also in Ψ and Λ) into ἤ, adopted by all modern editors, or for its meaning: the phrase ἢ εἰς τὸ χεῖρον ἡ μετάβασις explains the preceding question, "Why is more of order impossible?"; because, the answer is, otherwise (ἤ = or, ⟨if more order were possible,⟩) the change would be for the worse. Van Raalte 326 points to the common use of ἤ in the sense of εἰ δὲ μή (Bonitz *Index* 312b36), while Theophrastus's view of why more order is impossible is discussed later in the Essay, at 11b7–12. There are thus here only two subjects mentioned for future discussion: the extent of reality that is endowed with order, and the impossibility of reality being completely endowed with order on the ground that more order would lead to corruption.

Aporia 16

7b9–8a7 (περὶ τῆς ἠρεμίας ἀπορήσειεν ἄν τις): *Aporia about the rest at which the first principles are (how it is to be understood).*

Diaporia 16 (7b11–19). *If the rest is conceived as something better, then it would be worthy of the first principles, but not if it is conceived as privation of motion. But if rest is ascribed to them in order to avoid an infinite regress of prime movers who initiate motion by themselves being in motion, then they should be said to be in an actualized state (ἐνέργεια) rather than motion, for motion is ascribed to the sensible world.*

Diaporia 16.1 (7b19–23). *Sense perception seems somehow to corroborate the possibility of self-movement—i.e., the identity of mover and moved—on the grounds that the mover both acts and is acted upon, something which applies (with greater cogency) to intellect and god.*

Diaporia 16.2 (7b23–8a7), re-statement and discussion of Aporia 8. *To say that the (heavenly bodies) that desire (the first principle,) which is at rest, do not imitate it (because they are not at rest but in motion) is problematic: for why is their (desire) not accompanied by (the same outcome of imitation as) that of others? This case, however, should be thought of differently. For had the heavenly bodies done so and everything else followed them, then the universe, which is taken to be most perfect, would not be a well regulated whole like a city or animal with parts but something without parts (i.e., an undifferentiated mass at rest).*

This aporia and the following analysis continue the discussion about the questions raised by the theory of the unmoved mover. See the references given in Aporia 6 above.

7b11 ὡς βέλτιον] The implied structure of this sentence is, ἀπορεῖν περὶ τῆς ἠρεμίας εἴτε ὡς βέλτιόν τι εἴτε ὡς ἀργία καὶ στέρησίς τις κινήσεως. The question raised about rest thus entails that one investigate whether it is to be taken as something better in itself or as some cessation of movement, and hence a negative attribute in itself. I take ἀργία καὶ στέρησις to be both complemented by the following genitive, κινήσεως (cessation *and* privation of movement). Cf. the various readings of this sentence in van Raalte 334 and Henrich 117.

7b13 ἀλλ' εἴπερ … ἀντιμεταλλακτέον] With this sentence Theophrastus reacts to what he perceives is a false dichotomy in the way the problem has been expressed: with regard to what qualification to ascribe to the first principles, the choice is not between rest and motion—if rest, that is, is a cessation and privation of motion—but rather between rest and ἐνέργεια, because ἐνέργεια, as an actualized state, a state of consummate being, is better than motion because it is complete, while motion is "incomplete consummation" (ἐνέργεια ἀτελής, in fr. 153A, line 13, FHS&G, and cf. the commentary by Sharples 1998, 66ff.; Rudolph 1988, 234). Objecting sharply to the false dichotomy (ἀλλ'), he says, if ⟨one is to ascribe (ἀνάπτειν) any qualification to the principles⟩ at all (εἴπερ), an actualized state of consummate being should be exchanged (-μεταλλακτέον) in the place of (ἀντι-) rest as their chief attribute. The *hapax legomenon* ἀντιμεταλλακτέον in the fifteenth century manuscript D would appear to be an apposite scribal emendation from τι μεταλλακτέον in A (from which D derives directly). Cf. Laks & Most 55n30 and van Raalte 336–337.

7b15 τὴν δὲ κίνησιν [ἐν] τοῖς αἰσθητοῖς, *sc.* ἀναπτέον] As mentioned in the preceding comment, Theophrastus says that it is an actualized state of consummate being that should be (-τέον in ἀντιμεταλλακτέον) ascribed to the principles, whereas motion, which was mentioned in the preceding clause (στέρησίς τις κινήσεως), should be ascribed, it is understood, to the sensibles. Thus Usener's suggestion that the missing verb here that would require the accusative in τὴν κίνησιν is ἀναπτέον is correct and necessary (and not "something like θετέον εἶναι," Ross 63). This verb (ἀνάπτω) takes its indirect object in the dative and this requires that ἐν in ἐν τοῖς αἰσθητοῖς be secluded; in all probability it was added by a scribe who did not see the immediate connection between ἀνάψειεν and ἀνάψει in 7b11 and 13 and the dative in this passage. Ross's reason (63 top) for keeping the manuscript reading on the grounds that Theophrastus's style is "loose" is hardly justified: Theophrastus's style is fast and elliptical but not sloppy, and he adhered to the minimum requirements of intelligibility.

7b18 λογῶδες] This is another rare word in extant classical Greek. The suffix -ώδης, like -ειδής, indicates that the basic meaning is "having the nature or form of" (Schwyzer 418). In this case, having the nature of words without substance, mere verbiage. The actual spelling in J provides a clue to its transformation from λογῶδες to λογοειδὲς in the manuscript tradition. The scribe had originally written on the line λογωϊδες, without accent, which he then changed by adding an *epsilon* over the *iota* of the word, thus resulting in λογωειδες. This must have later given rise to λογοειδες through a change from the *omega* to *omikron*. It is not clear why in the original spelling of J there should have been an *iota* after the *omega*, unless one suppose that some earlier scribe had taken the *omega* to be that of dative and added an *iota* adscript.

7b20 δεῖν is the reading corrected by Laks & Most for the transmitted δεῖ in the Greek manuscripts and apparently also in Ψ and Λ (thus constituting one of the primitive errors in the Neoplatonic archetype). See the corresponding note to the Arabic translation; and see Most 1988c, 176, for Kley's suggestion of πᾶν for δεῖ, based on a faulty transcription of the Latin manuscript reading.

7b21–22 διὰ τὸ ποιεῖν καὶ πάσχειν provides the reason for something that has just been said, but because the expression is apparently elliptical, the question is for what. It has been taken by some to mean, διὰ τὸ ποιεῖν καὶ πάσχειν ⟨ἕτερα εἶναι⟩, "en vertu de la distinction entre agir et pâtir" (Tricot), or "because the one acts and the other is acted on" (Ross, English translation in Reale 1980), understanding the phrase to explain the preceding ἕτερον. Some others have opted for a neutral rendering, as if the phrase read, διὰ τὸ ποιεῖν καὶ πάσχειν ⟨εἶναι⟩, "parce qu'il y a agir et pâtir" (Laks & Most, van Raalte, Henrich, Isḥāq). This, however, eschews the responsibility of understanding what the phrase is used to explain: certainly there is acting and being-acted-upon, but is the acting and being-acted-upon being done by the same entity or by two different ones? The whole point is that Theophrastus wishes to support the first alternative—he claims, as in his fr. 271 FHS&G, that body and soul are self-movers—and that is why he uses the phrase; the neutral translation does not make this point. There is, finally, Usener's 1861 and 1890 conjecture to read τὸ ποιοῦν instead of τὸ ποιεῖν (with the added refinement by Fobes to read τὸ ⟨τὸ⟩ ποιοῦν), adopted by Reale 1964, "perchè ciò che muove subisce anche movimento" ("because that which causes movement is also moved"), which everybody seems to like—since it obviously makes the point that Theophrastus is trying to make—but shies away from. But there seems to be no need even to emend the text to get this desired meaning. The presumably elliptical phrase is to be read with the emphasis on the καί in the sense of "also," διὰ τὸ ποιεῖν *καὶ* πάσχειν, "because of *both* acting and being acted upon," that is, on the part of that which causes movement, τὸ κινοῦν, the subject of the subordinate clause. As the subject, the explanatory phrase would naturally be taken as referring to it, and thus there would be no need to add in that phrase, διὰ τὸ ποιεῖν καὶ πάσχειν ⟨αὐτό⟩. In English the subject pronoun has to be added, "on the ground that [it] both acts and is acted upon," but the elliptical phrase turns out to be not so elliptical.

8a2 τί γάρ ... τῶν ἄλλων;] The sentence is corrupt in all the Greek manuscripts, including Ψ and Λ; the version given here and by Isḥāq depends on emendation and interpretation. Ross's correction of the transmitted οὖσιν ἀκολουθεῖ into οὐ συνακολουθεῖ can hardly be doubted, if the passage is to make any sense without substantial additions or alterations. Usener's 1890 correction of the initial εἰ to τί may be more open to doubt, and has led van Raalte to assume a lacuna after this sentence, since reading "if" for "why" would make it into a conditional protasis without an apodosis. If the sentence is emended as Ross suggests, its interpretation then hinges on the identification of the referents of the pronouns. "They" (αὐτοῖς) could hardly refer to anything other than τὰ ὀρεγόμενα insofar as that is the only plural word that immediately preceded, and the particle γάρ makes it abundantly clear that this sentence is to be understood in close relationship to the preceding one. The problem is the feminine article "that" (ἡ) and, to a lesser extent, "the others" (τῶν ἄλλων). The singular feminine article (ἡ), given the three verbal forms in the preceding sentence (μιμοῦνται, ὀρεγόμενα, ἠρεμοῦντος), has been interpreted as referring to μίμησις (Laks & Most, Henrich), ὄρεξις (van Raalte), and ἠρεμία (Ross, Tricot, Reale), while the Arabic interprets it as οὐσία, with reference to the immediately preceding οὖσιν in the manuscript reading of the sentence (see the commentary on the Arabic translation). The logic of the passage (cf. Henrich 120) would tend to support the choice of μίμησις, imitation, though immobility (ἠρεμία) is always implied, insofar as the imitation in question here would result in immobility, and it is the consequences of immobility that Theophrastus is using to find a way out of the difficulty of his own aporia. The argument seems to run as follows: "What makes no sense is that the things that desire the immobile do not imitate it. Why does this make no sense? Because (γάρ), desire implies imitation, but in the case of the rotating celestial bodies ("the things that desire"), as we can observe, imitation (and hence immobility) does not accompany their desire." This seems to be the force of the question, "For why aren't they accompanied by that [i.e., imitation] of the others?" (where the "others," according to Laks & Most 56n36, refers to everything else other than the things that desire), that is, "why is their imitation ineffective," if ἡ ⟨μίμησις⟩ τῶν ἄλλων means imitation as practiced by everything other than the celestial bodies; but this remains conjectural (and van Raalte's suggestion of a lacuna after τῶν ἄλλων remains very much a possibility). However, Theophrastus continues, if we assume successful imitation to be following desire universally and without exception, this would result in our reducing the universe to something that is undifferentiated and has no parts, because, successful imitation, i.e., followed by immobility, would make everything immobile and hence an undifferentiated mass which, though theoretically in possession of separate parts (viz., the unmoved mover, the unmoved celestial bodies, and the unmoved sublunar elements), would be practically indistinguishable.

Aporia 17

8a8–20 (ἐπιποθεῖ λόγον, πῶς, πότερον … ἤ): *How does the division of beings into matter and form take place (or is to be understood)?*

Diaporia 17. *Either: Form is being, and matter is not-being that is potentially being and driven towards actuality. Or: Form is being and matter is also being, but indeterminate, like (the raw materials) in the crafts, and generated by being shaped in accordance with formal principles. This alternative is better.*

In this aporia on matter and form, which is related to Aristotle's discussion in *Met.* Λ 2–3, Theophrastus points to some difficulties in Aristotle's concept of matter, to which he also adheres; cf. Happ 1971, 811.

8a12 ἡ δὲ γένεσις] The particle δέ is present in all the manuscripts, including Ψ and Λ. Fobes's suggestion to suppress it, followed by Laks & Most, is unjustified. The omission of δέ would require the passage καθάπερ—λόγους to be read as one unbroken sentence, in which case the ellipsis of ἔστι, as Ross 64 observes, becomes "rather difficult." But the sense also requires a comma after τέχναις, for the καθάπερ clause is intended to provide an example of the indeterminacy of matter prior to its adoption of a particular form, which is what καθάπερ ἐν ταῖς τέχναις does (i.e., ἐν ταῖς τέχναις understood as καθάπερ ἡ ὕλη ἐν ταῖς τέχναις). But if καθάπερ—λόγους is read as one sentence, then this does not talk about the indeterminacy of matter, as it should, but about its acquiring a form in accordance with its formal principle (cf. van Raalte 367 bottom). Finally, the reading preferred here (καθάπερ ἐν ταῖς τέχναις, ἡ δὲ γένεσις ἢ οὐσία γ' αὐτῶν), which was suggested by Ross himself in the commentary and endorsed by Fobes in the apparatus and which was also adopted by van Raalte, is actually found in the Arabic translation (*bi-manzilati mā fī ṣ-ṣināʿāti lākin ḥudūṯuhā aw wujūduhā*) and reflects the reading of Ψ.

8a13 The pronoun "their" (αὐτῶν) must refer to the "beings" (ὄντων) mentioned in the initial question a few lines above in 8a9 (van Raalte 366), though a case has been made for the referent to be the products of the crafts ("things generated," Ross) mentioned in the immediately preceding clause (also by Laks & Most 58n40). However, a few lines down (8a17), the subject of γίνοιτο would again have to be the beings (ὄντων) of line 8a9, and not any assumed products of the crafts, and Theophrastus cannot be jumping back and forth with the referents of his pronouns without confusing his readers.

8a14 The ἀλλ(ά) here is assentient ("but of course"), preceded as it is by a question; see Denniston 16, as noted by Laks & Most 58.

8a16–17 ἀληθὲς ὑπάρχοι ... γίνοιτο] Ὑπάρχειν, *sc.* αὐτῷ, could be taken in its logical sense here, as Ross did, whom I follow ("to be predicated of something"), or in its existential sense, "it exists." Although both ultimately mean the same thing (being which is predicated of things, or being which exists [for/in things]), the former is preferable because it predisposes the reader mentally to add τοῖς οὖσι after ὑπάρχοι, an object which reappears in the immediately following clause as the pronoun implied by the third person singular verb, γίνοιτο, and referring to a neutral plural subject, τὰ ὄντα of line 8a9, beings or things. (For the misunderstanding of the Greek syntax in the Arabic translation see the note to the English translation thereof.)

There is a further issue with the function of ἀληθές, whether it is to be taken adverbially (Ross, Tricot, Reale, Isḥāq) or predicatively (Laks & Most, van Raalte, Henrich). While both readings are theoretically possible, it would seem that the word order supports the adverbial reading: if Theophrastus intended ἀληθὲς predicatively, he most probably would have said οὐθὲν ἂν ἧττον ὑπάρχοι ἀληθές.

8a17 ἀλλὰ τὸ μήτε, etc. refers back to τὸ εἶναι in line 8a15 and modifies it as something that has being but is otherwise indeterminate (i.e., has no specific substance, quality, or quantity) and potential.

8a19–20 The method κατ᾿ ἀναλογίαν for knowing matter is discussed by Happ 1971, 667–670, with references to further literature (especially in 667n537).

Aporia 18

8a21–9a9 (ἔχειν ἀπορίαν, τί): *(It seems paradoxical) why nature consists of contraries, with the worse being equal to or greater than the better* (cf. Aporia 14).

Diaporia 18 (8a27–b4). *Putting the question in such terms implies that all things should be good or alike* (a patently indefensible position).

Diaporia 18.1 (8b4–5). *What is seemingly even more paradoxical is that being cannot exist without contraries.*

Diaporia 18.2 (8b6–20). *Some maintain that the nature of the universe includes past, present, and future non-being. Now this is too paradoxical and beyond the pale, though clearly being exists in many ways (and contraries, i.e., the fact that reality consists of differences and similarities, serve to know them). Sense perception observes differences and seeks the causes, and accordingly knowing does not occur without the presence of difference, both among individuals and universal categories such as genera and species.*

Diaporia 18.3 (8b20–24). *Almost all knowledge is of unique properties, whether this be the essence or essential attributes of something.*

Diaporia 18.4 (8b24–9a9). *The task of knowledge is to perceive simultaneously the identical in many, whether it is said of them universally or particularly, though complete knowledge is of both. Nevertheless, there are some knowledges whose end is solely either the universal or the particular. We know the identical with respect to essence, number, species, genus, and, for objects of knowledge the farthest removed from our experience, by analogy, or any other division.*

This epistemological aporia and the terms of its discussion reflect procedures in the old Academy and early Aristotle. See the elements enumerated by Krämer 1973, 211–213, and his references to earlier literature; see also Krämer 1968.

8a21–22 εἰ μὴ ... ζητεῖν] The dashes in the translation are intended to convey the force of the particle ἄρα: the realization on the spot of something else, a second thought (cf. Denniston 36–38). It may be too strong a translation to render the clause, "unless, coming to think of it, it is pedantry even to inquire."

The noun περιεργία goes together with ζητεῖν and is not to be separated from it, as suggested by some scholars; cf. the indictment against Socrates, which accused him of "meddlesome inquisitiveness" (Σωκράτης ἀδικεῖ καὶ περιεργάζεται ζητῶν τά τε ὑπὸ γῆς καὶ οὐράνια, Plato, *Apology* 19b4–5). The real question in this construction is whether to keep the transmitted reading in the Greek manuscipts, περιεργίαν τοῦ ζητεῖν, with the accusative followed by the genitive, or change it to the only possible alternative, the subject and predicate nominatives, περιεργία τὸ ζητεῖν (*sc.* ἐστίν). There are two objections to the transmitted text in the Greek manuscripts. First, if the accusative in περιεργίαν is to be retained, it would have to be construed with ἔχειν in the preceding line, but the expression τοῦτ' ἔχειν περιεργίαν is awkward and unusual, if not unidiomatic; in all instances in which περίεργον as adjective or περιεργία is used in such a context and with this meaning, the verb it is used with is εἶναι, not ἔχειν (see all the examples cited in Bonitz *Index* 580b56, Jaeger 1932, 293, and van Raalte 379–380). The reason is that the περιεργία does not lie in the subject matter itself that is to be discussed, as does the ἀπορία, but in the person who is doing the investigating. It is therefore more natural to say "there is pedantry in asking this" than "this thing has pedantry." And in fact this is precisely what Ps.-Plato, *Sisyphus* 387d7 says: ἀλλὰ μὴ ἐμὴ περιεργία ᾖ καὶ τὸ ἐρωτῆσαί σε περὶ τούτου; Dirlmeier 1938, 135, who first cited this passage, considers it decisive. This evidence indicates that the reading περιεργίαν τοῦ ζητεῖν, if at all possible, would be extremely awkward.

The second and more important objection comes from the two translations, the Arabic and the Latin. To start with the latter, it reads *otiositas inquirere*, which points to a reading of περιεργία τὸ ζητεῖν in Λ, as noted and convincingly argued by Dirlmeier 1938, 134–135. Most's 1988c, 176, objection that this construction results "in an awkwardly complicated sentence structure" is without foundation. The main sentence is very straightforward, καὶ τοῦτ' ἔχειν ἀπορίαν, τί δή ποτε ..., while εἰ μὴ ἄρα περιεργία τὸ ζητεῖν is parenthetical (as in any case indicated by the particle ἄρα, see above) and does not affect the main sentence. The Arabic translation also suggests a reading like that in the Latin translation: *in lam yakuni l-baḥṯu ʿan miṯli hāḏā huwa mina l-fuḍūli*, "if investigating the likes of this were not superfluous," where the translator adds "the likes of this" to amplify the specific demonstrative force of the article τό (without this addition, Arabic *al-baḥṯu* [= τὸ ζητεῖν] would have been taken to refer to research in general, and not to the specific investigation at hand), but the rest of the sentence translates exactly εἰ μὴ ἄρα τὸ ζητεῖν περιεργία ἐστίν.

Thus both Λ and Ψ read περιεργία τὸ ζητεῖν, which is the correct reading of the Neoplatonic archetype, while the Constantinopolitan recension represented in the extant Greek manuscipts corrupted the text to περιεργίαν τοῦ ζητεῖν.[37] The error is easily explained: ἀπορίαν in the preceding line led the scribe to write περιεργίαν in the next also in the accusative, which itself may have led to the change into the genitive of the following article or, alternately, the genitive may be due to a misreading of the ου ligature as ο.

Finally, with regard to the meaning of περιεργία in the context in which Theophrastus uses it, the sense of "overdoing it" implied in the preposition περί of the noun does not denote meddlesomeness (as in the case of Socrates in the *Apology* passage cited above) or officiousness, but excessive zeal in asking insignificant questions, hence "pedantry" in my translation.

8a23 δ' is found in all the Greek manuscripts, but the literal Latin translation by Bartholomew omits it, which led Ross 1936 to consider its absence as pointing to an original γ', a particle which Bartholomew "habitually omits to translate" (the Arabic translation cannot make the distinction between a simple καί and a καί ... δέ, as here). However, καί ... δέ is a regular construction in Attic prose at the time of Theophrastus and used elsewhere by him (see the Glossary), and it also makes sense in this context: after the mention of nature (φύσις), δ' introduces another, broader term (see Denniston 202–203).

---

[37] It is interesting to note that although Ross prints in the text περιεργίαν τοῦ ζητεῖν he nevertheless translates *both readings* simultaneously, as if the text read, περιεργία τοῦ ζητεῖν ἢ τὸ ζητεῖν, "unless indeed it be a superfluity of inquisitiveness to ask the question."

8a24 καὶ σχεδὸν] The clause introduced by καί here is semantically subordinate to the preceding one and does not introduce a second question, as normally translated, i.e., "Why is it that nature consists of contraries *and* why is it that the worse balances the better?" Rather, the sense requires that the worse and the better be one set, albeit the predominant set, of contraries of which the universe consists.

8a27 τοιοῦτος here refers to the original question asked by Theophrastus and not to the quotation of Euripides in which, in fact, contraries and the mixture of good and bad (σύγκρασις) are posited as something good (ἔχειν καλῶς). See the extensive discussion and the text of Euripides, a fragment from the lost *Aeolus* (fr. 21 Nauck) in Stobaeus, in van Raalte 383–385.

8b3 The elliptical sentence is to be understood as, καθάπερ τὰ λευκὰ καὶ μέλανα *sc.* ὅμοιόν τι ἔχουσι (van Raalte 387).

8b4 μέλανα] Burnikel 121 may be right in suggesting that the reading in manuscript A τὰ μέλανα (with the article) is the correct reading, for otherwise the phrase τὰ λευκὰ καὶ μέλανα would be understood as a hendiadys—i.e., as one group of things having two qualities rather as two groups of things—but it seems that there would be little danger of such a misunderstanding in this context, given the meaning of the words: no one would take this phrase to mean "the white-and-black things." Isḥāq also translated as if he read τὰ μέλανα here, as in the correction in manuscript A, but there can be no certainty, for the same reason, that he actually read the article τά in Ψ.

8b4–5 ἔτι δέ … ἐναντίων] For us who cannot hear the inflection of the voice speaking this sentence, its syntax would appear ambiguous (cf. van Raalte 388). Τὸ δοκοῦν is the subject, but παραδοξότερον could be either predicative or attributive with respect to it; the clause introduced by ὡς merely lists the contents of δοκοῦν. If it is predicative, the initial ἔτι would appear to complement it, in which case the sentence would mean, "And that which appears [to us, namely], that being cannot [be] without contraries, [is] even more paradoxical." If παραδοξότερον is attributive to δοκοῦν, then ἔτι δέ would have its usual sense of introducing a further point, in which case the predicate of the sentence could be supplied from the beginning of the paragraph 18, τὸ δοκοῦν παραδοξότερον ⟨ἔχει ἀπορίαν⟩, or some such phrase (Laks

& Most 61n6 even suggest—but reject—putting a comma after αὐτοῖς in 8b4 and reading our phrase as a complement of λέγομεν in 8b2), and the sentence then would mean, "And further, that which appears more paradoxical [also involves an aporia, namely,] that being cannot [be] without contraries," or simply "And further, [there is] that which appears more paradoxical ..." The former interpretation is preferred by Ross, Tricot, Reale, and van Raalte, the latter by Laks & Most and Henrich, as well as by Isḥāq. As in other instances of apparent ambiguity, in defense of Theophrastus, the word order will have to provide the clue. If Theophrastus intended παραδοξότερον as predicate, he would most probably have said, ἔτι δὲ παραδοξότερον τὸ δοκοῦν ὡς ...; as we have it, it can be taken most plausibly attributively (cf. also Laks & Most 61n6).

Henrich 124 objects to the use of the word "paradox" in modern languages to translate παράδοξον on the basis that it is "aus der Sicht gegenwärtiger Philosophie ungeschickt; Paradoxien sind Sätze, deren Wahrheitswert nicht festlegbar ist." This may be so, but paradox in common English usage (and in German, if I am not mistaken) means "a seemingly contradictory statement that may nonetheless be true," which would appear to be what Theophrastus is talking about: a thesis which is the opposite of ἔνδοξον, but because maintained by a serious thinker, to be entertained. For an understanding of how such arguments would be perceived in Academic and Peripatetic circles in Theophrastus's time, see Aristotle's discussion and classification of dialectical and other, including paradoxical, theses and problems in *Topics* I,10–11 (and cf. Baltussen 2000, 39–41).

8b8–9 ἀλλά ... μέν ... δέ] As Theophrastus wraps up the preceding discussion and moves on to the next subject (ἀλλά, progressive), he makes a last comment about an item in the preceding sentence (μέν after ἀλλά, cf. Denniston 378) which at the same time points forward to the subject of the following section (δέ). The mention of τὸ μὴ ὄν in 8b7 leads into a discussion of τὸ δὲ ὄν in 8b9. Van Raalte 393n1 aptly paraphrases the transition ("to count among the totality of being even τὸ μὴ ὄν etc. is going too far; but that τὸ ὄν applies to quite heterogeneous things is evident"). As frequently in this work, Theophrastus finishes a subject in the same sentence in which he begins a new one, and this cohesiveness of his argumentation should not be artificially sundered by breaking up the sentence in two independent paragraphs.

8b10–11 τάς … τάς. Theophrastus uses the definite article twice with obvious reference to the possessive pronouns, as is usually the case. Isḥāq translates with the appropriate pronouns instead, taking "causes" to refer to "differences": "sense-perception perceives its [the existent's] differences and investigates *their* causes."

8b12 Intransitive ὑποβάλλει here most likely is to be taken in the theatrical sense of "prompting" (an ὑποβολεύς is a prompter) or the paedagogical one of "dictating."

8b13–14 ἀπορίαν … δι' ἧς, "an aporia through whose consideration"] The feminine pronoun refers to the closest feminine antecedent, ἀπορία. Isḥāq took it to refer to διάνοια, most likely because he understood the subject of δύνηται to be αἴσθησις and not διάνοια. The preposition διά together with ἀπορία expressed in the pronoun have the meaning of the verb διαπορέω, "to consider or work through an aporia" (see the discussion of διαπορέω in the commentary on the Scholium at 12b4); so light appears in the darkness not through the aporia itself but through the process of working through or considering it.

8b21–24 ἥ τε γὰρ οὐσία … τὶ κατὰ τινός] Laks & Most 64n20 are in all probability correct in pointing out that this sentence posits that all knowledge is either knowledge of essence or of essential attributes. The dual objects of knowledge are ascertained by the construction, "both, on the one hand … and, on the other" (τε … τε, 8b21–22). Essential attribution appears from Theophrastus's description of the things that are "observed essentially (καθ' ἑαυτά) and not accidentally," a maddeningly elliptical phrase. But assuming that nothing has been left out but the verb to be, the simplest way to read that sentence would be, τὰ θεωρούμενα καθ' ἑαυτὰ ⟨εἶναι⟩ καὶ οὐ κατὰ συμβεβηκός, i.e., "what are observed [to be] essential and not accidental [attributes]." The addition of "attributes" here is justified from the preceding ἴδιον, unique characteristic, which is the subject Theophrastus is discussing. The same (i.e., the addition of the verb to be) also applies to the formula τὶ κατὰ τινός which, when coupled with a verb meaning "to say", is shorthand for predication (cf. Bonitz *Index* 368a34–35); here, though, there is no such verb, and if, as the simplest alternative, it is taken that the expression is, τὶ κατὰ τινὸς ⟨ὄν⟩, the phrase would mean, "a certain thing [belonging to, or being] of some other thing." For this, ontological, dimension of the expression τὶ κατὰ τινός see the fundamental but little noticed study by Tugendhat 2003^5, 5–23, 161.[38]

Finally, the iterative use of ἄν with the imperfect in ἦν ἄν has been remarked upon a number of times, but it is important to note that the imperfect in itself has this function (past continuous); what distinguishes it from the form with ἄν is that the latter emphasizes, instead of the continuity of the action, the individual instances in which the act is being repeated (K.-G. II,1 p. 211); hence the rendering above, "would be in each case." The least interpretive reading of this clause would thus be, "and, on the other hand, what are observed [to be] essential and not accidental [attributes] would be in each case a certain thing belonging to some other [particular] thing." For a different interpretation see Talanga 1995, 20, and for a discussion of all the alternative readings see Henrich 128–130.

8b25 ἐπιστήμη] It is quite clear in these Aporiae (18–21), which form a sort of appendix on epistemology (see Chapter 1.4 above), that Theophrastus is talking about knowing and knowledge, and not about "science" in the sense of disciplines of learning. Various forms of the verb from this root are strewn about in the passage (ἐπιστάμεθα 9a4, ἐπίστασθαι 8b16, 9a10, 9a26), as are related words (εἰδέναι 9a24, 9b22; γνωστά 9a19; τὸ φρονεῖν 9b5), so the noun ἐπιστήμη has to be seen in this context and not be translated as science as in some versions. In particular this passage (8b25) about the identical has given rise to this misunderstanding, but it appears from the continuation of the discussion in 9a4 after the parenthetical interlude (8b27–9a4) that Theophrastus is talking about knowing the identical (9a4–5 ταὐτὸ δ' ἐπιστάμεθα) and not a science of the identical or about science in general whose task it is to know the identical. Of course ἐπιστήμη here is to be understood in the Aristotelian sense of scientific knowledge, through causality (see ἐν τούτῳ γὰρ τὸ αἴτιον at 9a1–2, and cf. Aristotle, *Posterior Analytics* 71b16–19, etc.), and conceptually it comes close to the meaning of "understanding," which is, indeed, the word used by Jonathan Barnes to translate this term in the *Posterior Analytics* (cf. his translation, Barnes 1994, 82).

[38] For the meaning of κατά in the phrase Tugendhat 23 says characteristically, "Das λέγεσθαι κατά (κατηγορεῖσθαι) bedeutet nicht eine urteilsimmanente Beziehung und meint auch nicht primär … die Beziehung des Seienden zum Aussagen, … sondern es steht für eine bestimmte *Seinsstruktur*." Although paraphrastic, Ross's translation ("particular attributes belonging to particular things") thus expresses better the meaning than Laks & Most's logical rendering ("ce qui est prédiqué de quelque chose").

8b27 τέλεος is the reading in Ψ and P; Λ and J read τέλος (scil. τῆς ἐπιστήμης) for τέλεος. It would seem that this reading could be equally viable, insofar as Theophrastus does discuss the end of knowledge (i.e., the specific object to which it is directed and the purpose behind it) in the next sentence. If that were the reading, what Theophrastus would be saying is that though the end of knowledge is to comprise both universals and particulars, in some cases it is just universals while in others particulars. Thus τέλος in 8b27 would be prefiguring the same word in 9a1. And in general there would be no discussion here of which knowledge is complete (τέλεος) but only the purpose or end (τέλος) for which a particular piece of knowledge is sought (cf. van Raalte 415: seeking a universal or qualified same "is relative to … a given stage of the inquiry."). The one argument against this reading is that of the *lectio difficilior*. Having τέλος as the center of discussion in 9a1–4 could easily cause the corruption of τέλεος to τέλος in 8b27. But if τέλος were the original reading there would be little justification in the corruption into τέλεος. Besides, as the passage from *De causis plantarum* reminds us (cited by van Raalte 416), Theophrastus does believe in general that complete knowledge consists of theory and particulars: τὸ δὲ τέλειον ἐξ ἀμφοῖν (*CP* III,2.3).

8b27–9a1 εἰσὶ δ' ἔνιαι μὲν ὧν] The impossible reading ἔνια τῶν μέν, as all agree, is found in all manuscripts, including Ψ and Λ; J omits μέν, though the original scribe corrects himself and adds the particle above the line in the space between τῶν and καθόλου. A number of emendations have been offered, but the most obvious one has been overlooked. The most common correlative constructions with ἔνια (in all three genders) are normally three, ἔνια answered by another ἔνια, or by τά, or by τινά, and in each case ἔνια is followed by μέν and the answering pronoun by δέ. In the present passage the expression is of the second type, ἔνια μέν … τὰ δέ (with the appropriate inflection and gender in accordance with sense, to be discussed next). Most pertinent examples, because they also begin with ἔστι, as in this passage, are Isocrates, *Antidosis* § 10,2: ἔστιν γὰρ τῶν γεγραμμένων ἔνια μὲν ἐν δικαστηρίῳ … τὰ δὲ πρός …, and one from Aristotle (and indeed very similar to this passage), *Posterior Analytics* 96a8: ἔστι δ' ἔνια μὲν γινόμενα καθόλου … τὰ δὲ ἀεὶ μὲν οὔ … .

With regard to inflection, in the Theophrastus passage the second half of the sentence is not parallel to the first in that the article (at 9a2, τῶν), used as a pronoun in these cases, is in the genitive and not in the nominative, as in the first part (ἔνια). But this "dissymmetry" ought not to bother editors (Laks & Most 66n23) because in this μέν … δέ construction the two legs of the sentence are very flexible syntactically and each conforms to its own structure (e.g., Aristotle, *Historia animalium* 536a28: ᾄδουσι δ' ἔνια μὲν ὁμοίως τὰ ἄρρενα τοῖς θήλεσιν ... ἐνίων δὲ τὰ ἄρρενα μᾶλλον—or even Strabo, *Geographia* III,2,4.24: ἔνιαι μέν ... τινὰς δ' ...; etc.).

The problem in the text as we have it is with the gender of the expression ἔνια ... μέν ... τῶν δέ. In the text the neuter is unambiguously transmitted, ἔνια, and it has been universally accepted. There is, however, a difficulty with the sense, in that if the neuter is retained the sentence would mean that there are certain *things* whose end is the universal and not *knowledges* which aim at the universal, as the sense requires (and Theophrastus manifestly intended). Translators normally finesse this difficulty by inserting into their translations knowledge as the ultimate subject, though against the expressed words of Theophrastus: "in the case of some things there is a universal end *for knowledge*" (Ross, and similarly Tricot, "la fin du savoir)", "in alcune cose, il fine *della conoscenza* è un universale" (Reale 1964), "il *en* existe certains dont la fin est le général" (Laks & Most, where *en* refers to a preceding *savoir*). Laks & Most are aware of the problem but they dismiss it by claiming that the neuter in ἔνια refers to the feminine ἐπιστῆμαι anyway, and point to a similar occurrence at 6b9 with ἐν ἐκείνοις. But this, I argued above in my comment on that passage, cannot be maintained there and it cannot be maintained here. Only van Raalte tries to remain true to Theophrastus's text and translates what he wrote, "there are some objects of study of which the end is universal." In her commentary (p. 418) she suggests that these things which have the universal as end, or objects of study, are the intelligibles (τὰ νοητά), and then explains as follows the difficult concept of things having universals as an end: "Of some things, then, the objects of thought such as analytical concepts and explanations, the end is universal," which I take it to mean, if the English sentence is so to be construed, that the end of the objects of thought of some things is universal, or, to put it differently, the end of some things as objects of thought is universal. But this again makes the object of thought have a universal as its end (and not the thing itself, as Theophrastus says), and an object of thought is a different way of saying knowledge. It thus appears that the sense would be less forced and the passage would conform more evenly to what Theophrastus is trying to say if one read ἔνια as feminine, ἔνιαι, to refer to the obvious antecedent, ἐπιστῆμαι. This would also require to change the number of the initial verb, ἔστιν to εἰσί. The passage then will be emended to read, εἰσὶ δ' ἔνιαι μὲν ὧν ... τῶν δέ.

Palaeographically, the correction of ἔνια to the feminine gender, ἔνιαι, is the most plausible means to explain the transmitted text. If the original text was ἔνιαι μὲν ὧν, as I suggest, the initial mistake occurred through the omission (as in J) or transposition of μέν (as in the other manuscripts), thus leaving ἔνιαι ὧν. Next, ἔνιαι ὧν was read as ἔνια τῶν for a number of reasons: first, the *iota* could easily have been misread for *tau*; second, the *iota* could have been misread as *tau* especially under the influence of τῶν in line 9a2 and in an effort to make the two legs of the expression symmetrical; and third, ἔνια τῶν could have come about because of the impossibility of the hiatus generated by ἔνιαι ὧν, which even an average scribe would have recognized.[39] The need to explain the misreading in ἔνια τῶν, which most plausibly can be accounted for by assuming it to derive from an already corrupt ἔνιαι ὧν, is the primary reason for preferring the feminine gender of ἔνιαι in the emended text I propose. This, however, also required reading εἰσί for ἔστιν, which can be accounted for as a scribal "correction" of the former to the latter once ἔνιαι had been changed to ἔνια, a neuter plural subject. Finally, after ἔνιαι ὧν had been changed to ἔνια τῶν, μέν was added after τῶν either in the wrong place if it had been omitted, or, most likely, in order to balance τῶν δέ in 9a2.

The Arabic translation of the very beginning of the passage suffered its own peculiar distortion, but it is nevertheless clear that Ψ had ἔνια τῶν, like the extant Greek manuscripts (see the corresponding note). Since, however, Ψ on the one hand and PJ and Λ on the other derive from different transcriptions from uncials, the corruption of ἔνιαι μὲν ὧν to ἔνια τῶν μέν must have occurred already at the uncial stage of the transmission of the text and is one of the primitive errors of the Neoplatonic archetype (Chapter 2.5). The omission of μέν in J, with its subsequent interlinear addition by the same scribe, appears to be accidental and not causally related to this process. That it happened again, however, indicates precisely the plausibility of the original omission which led to the generation of the error.

[39] In all of extant Greek literature until the 14th century there is not a single instance of ἔνιαι ὧν, only one of ἔνιοι ὧν (Apollonius Dyscolus, *De pronominibus* II,1,1, p. 51.9), and only two of ἔνια ὧν (Aristotle, *De Memoria et reminiscentia* 451a29 and Photius, *Bibliotheca* 128b29 Bekker). Accordingly, such proposed emendations of the text in this passage as ἔνια ὧν (Laks & Most, van Raalte, Henrich) cannot be entertained, especially for an author like Theophrastus who avoided hiatus almost obsessively: see the valuable evidence presented by Einarson 1976 in the introduction to the Loeb edition of *De causis plantarum*.

This correction restores also the sense in context. Theophrastus is talking in this Diaporia (18.4) about knowledge of the identical in a plurality of objects. Perceiving the identical is the task of knowledge, he says, regardless whether the identical is understood as a universal or a shared quality in genera and species; complete knowledge, however, must consist of the perception of both. Nevertheless, he goes on, there are some kinds of knowledge which are complete without necessarily having as end a knowledge of both these kinds of the identical, but merely the universal, and that happens when one is seeking the ultimate cause (αἴτιον) of something; and there are other kinds of knowledge, equally complete, whose end is the particular something (τὸ ἐν μέρει, 9a2), and that is when one is seeking knowledge of individual things made or done (9a3–4). It appears that the entire sentence εἰσὶ δ' … ἡ ἐνέργεια, 8b27–9a4, is a parenthetical qualifying statement following the generality stated in τέλεος δ' ἡ ἐξ ἀμφοῖν. The main subject of this paragraph, that knowledge is knowing the identical, resumes then with the following sentence, ταὐτὸ δ', 9a4.

9a4 δ', "Well,"] After the introductory remarks about the identical (8b24–27), and the parenthetical comment (8b27–9a4) about knowledge whose end is only the universal or particular, δέ marks the transition to the main subject about the identical (cf. Denniston 170–171).

9a4–6 ταὐτό … διαιρέσει] Henrich 132 duly notes that these datives are not instrumental but of respect: we know the identical not *by means* of formal substance or essence, genus, etc., but with respect to these divisions, i.e., that it belongs to the division of formal substance, genus, etc.; of relevance is Aristotle's wording in the *Topics* 120b36, referred to by both Laks & Most and van Raalte. Theophrastus could just as easily have used κατά instead of the dative—as he does, as a matter of fact, in the next sentence, κατ' ἀναλογίαν at 9a7—and as Aristotle did in *Metaphysics* Δ 6, 1016b31–35 in a passage clearly echoed here by Theophrastus; see the Loci Paralleli and the discussion by Devereux 183–184 and van Raalte 421. Aristotle lists some of the ways in which things are said to be "the same" essentially at *Metaphysics* Δ 9, 1018a6–7 (things whose matter is formally or numerically one, and things whose οὐσία is one) only after he has stated that "the same" is said in as many ways as "the one" (1018a5), thus referring the reader back to the preceding discussion in that book. At 1016b31–32 he says that things are one with respect to number, species, genus, and analogy, and at 1018a7 he adds οὐσία (which here is to be understood as form, i.e., substance as form, or essence), thus completing the list of alternatives that Theophrastus gives in this passage. Stenzel 1959, 159–160, showed that the series number, species, genus, and analogy derives from the mathematical methodology in the early Academy.

9a6 διαιρέσει] With the datives in this line understood as datives of respect, there is no problem in keeping the dative διαιρέσει reading in all independent witnesses. The elliptical sentence, as it stands, can be read most obviously, and without the addition of words not easily justifiable, in only two ways: (a) καί, εἴ ἄρα παρὰ ταῦτα (*sc.* ἐστὶ διαίρεσις, or ἥ διαίρεσίς ἐστι), διαιρέσει, "and, if indeed there is a division besides these," or, "if indeed division is besides these, then with respect to division;" or (b) καί, εἴ ἄρα ⟨τις ἔστι⟩, παρὰ ταῦτα διαιρέσει, "and, if at all there is one, with respect to a division besides these." The first is the way chosen by Isḥāq, but it clearly makes no sense; "division" here means "category" in the common (English) sense of the term, and is the generic name applied to all the items that have just been listed (substance, number, etc.); "category" is not itself one of those items with respect to which we can know the identical, but a generic term describing them all. The meaning thus requires that Theophrastus say, "with respect to a category *other than* those just mentioned." This meaning can only be elicited from reading (b): the sense requires that there be a word in Theophrastus's formulation, if he is to be at all intelligible, that would express the concept of "other than" and this is provided by παρὰ ταῦτα. Παρὰ ταῦτα, therefore, has to be read with διαιρέσει, the word in the dative, "with respect to a category besides these," and εἰ ἄρα by itself can support the burden of implying "if at all ⟨there is one⟩." Εἰ ἄρα here is the affirmative of εἰ μὴ ἄρα, an otherwise favorite expression of Theophrastus in this Essay and elsewhere (cf. van Raalte 122). In any case, Theophrastus frequently uses incomplete conditional sentences as steps, too obvious to be mentioned explicitly, in building his arguments; cf. his use of ἀλλ' εἴπερ in 11b9, 11b16, and of εἴ τις in 8a20, etc. The only other acceptable alternative would be to add τις after εἰ and read, καί, εἴ ⟨τις⟩ ἄρα παρὰ ταῦτα, διαιρέσει (cf. the parallel expressions with τις in van Raalte 423). But without τις, it is impossible to read the sentence in other than the two ways suggested above, short of adding words not intended by Theophrastus.

9a7–9 διὰ πλείστου ... τἄμφω] This part of the sentence has been variously understood and interpreted; for a discussion of the different views see Henrich 183–188. Given that Theophrastus uses long periods and that accordingly one ought not to be misled by modern punctuation (the upper point after διαιρέσει in 9a6 should be changed to a comma), it is most natural to read 9a7–9 as continuing the previous sentence. I thus read, διὰ πλείστου δὲ ⟨ἐπιστάμεθα ταὐτὸ⟩ τὸ κατ' ἀναλογίαν, which it is necessary to do if ἀπέχοντες (9a7–8), the correct reading in all Greek manuscripts, is to be integrated in the syntax. Of the translators, only Isḥāq read the sentence in this way; Bartholomew apparently read (or understood?) ἀπέχοντα. Laks & Most on the one hand rightly suggest (67n29) that ἀπέχοντες is in apposition to ἐπιστάμεθα, but on the other read διὰ πλείστου δὲ τὸ κατ' ἀναλογίαν as a nominal sentence (and so do Ross, Tricot, van Raalte, and Henrich) which creates the rough syntax they complain about. If τὸ κατ' ἀναλογίαν is seen as the object of ἐπιστάμεθα, as I suggest, then the three adverbial phrases at the end (τὰ μέν … τὰ δέ … τὰ δέ) naturally complement and explain διὰ πλείστου and ἀπέχοντες: as Laks & Most note (*ibid.*), the limitation of our faculties, the obscurity of the object to be known, or both these factors together create the distance referred to between us and the object. The different interpretation by van Raalte 427 assumes that the three adverbial phrases enumerate the three ways in which analogy helps us *bridge* the distance between us and the object of knowledge, but that does not seem to be what the Greek text says. It is rather that these three factors explain how that distance was *created* in the first place.

Aporia 19

9a10–23 (πῶς): *Since knowing occurs in many ways, how is each class of things to be inquired into?*

Diaporia 19. *The starting point is to find the appropriate manner of investigating each class, from the intelligibles to inanimate things, because each genus of things has a unique way of being investigated. If there is a genus of unknown things that can be known by being unknown, they would require a unique manner of investigation, though it would entail some sort of division; however, for most of such cases the manner of knowing is by analogy.*

9a10 πλεοναχῶς] It has to be assumed, though dictionaries do not seem to be making the distinction, that πλεοναχῶς, composed as it is of the comparative form, has (or at least originally had) some implication of excessiveness (cf. πλεονάζω, πλεονεξία) as opposed to πολλαχῶς, used just before (8b10). Theophrastus was not particularly free with its use, as opposed to Aristotle; it occurs only five times in his extant writings (two of which are in this Essay), while in Aristotle it occurs 69 times. Aristotle apparently used it synonymously with πολλαχῶς: in the sentence, τὸ ἓν ὅτι μὲν λέγεται πολλαχῶς … πλεοναχῶς δὲ λεγομένου (*Metaphysics* I 1, 1052a15–16), the change from the one word to the other would appear to be for stylistic reasons. The much more restricted use by Theophrastus may imply that he was more careful with its use, especially if it carried that sense of excessiveness. Finally, of the very many things which Aristotle says λέγεται πολλαχῶς, interestingly ἐπιστήμη is not one.

9a10 ἕκαστα] Since a number of scholars translate ἕκαστα in the singular ("object" of knowledge, van Raalte; "chacun des objets particuliers," Laks & Most; "den einzelnen," Henrich, etc.), it is worth noting that the word, in the plural, refers to a class or a group of things, as Ross translates it; if Theophrastus meant to say "each particular object" he would have said ἕκαστον (the actual reading in manuscript A, apparently an attempt, by this scribe—or textual tradition—which takes excessive liberties with the text, to express precisely this). That a "class of things" is intended, i.e., that ἕκαστα here means ἕκαστον γένος, is further manifest from the classes which Theophrastus does mention (τὰ πρῶτα, τὰ νοητά, τὰ κινητά, κτλ.) and from Theophrastus's very words describing these plural terms in the list as ἕκαστον γένος (9a15–16).

9a12 τρόπος] As usual with the long periods of Theophrastus's prose in this Essay, he lets one sentence be heard in the next. The Greek to be understood here, if this were a fully explicit sentence, would be, ἀρχὴ καὶ μέγιστον ὁ οἰκεῖος τρόπος ⟨τοῦ μεταδιώκειν ἕκαστα⟩, οἷον τὰ πρῶτα καὶ νοητά, καὶ τὰ κινητά … κτλ., as translated above, a sentence which does not generate any of the syntactical problems mentioned by Henrich 132. Thus οἷον in this construction provides concrete examples for ἕκαστα.

9a14 ⌜τά⌝.] The article τά, which according to the Arabic translation was present in Ψ, is necessary here, for the reason suggested by van Raalte 431n8, to separate the two classes of things, those that lead and those that follow; without it, ἑπόμενα would be referring not to a different category from τὰ ἐν ἀρχῇ but to those very things: the things that both are at the head *and* follow, which is absurd. The absence of the article in the immediately preceding two phrases has precisely this function: τὰ πρῶτα καὶ νοητά means "the first *and* intelligible things," i.e., both first and intelligible, both belonging to the same category.

9a15–16 τι … ἴδιον] I.e., each class of things has its proper manner or method of being investigated. Theophrastus expresses himself here in general terms by saying τι … ἴδιον instead of ⟨τρόπος⟩ τις ἴδιος, as he does later in line 20 below, ἴδιος τρόπος.

9a17 An additional point, introduced by δὲ καί (on which cf. van Raalte 408 on 8b20), noted by Ross 67: these differentiations exist not only in mathematical objects but also in mathematical studies.

9a18 διῄρηται δ' ἱκανῶς, i.e., the matter has been sufficiently discussed and therefore needs no further comment; for the explicative δέ, noted by Laks & Most 68n35, see Denniston 169–170.

9a22 λέγειν could be taken in three ways here. (1) The first is to take the phrase λέγειν κατ' ἀναλογίαν absolutely and as complete in itself, i.e., without the addition of understood word(s) needed to complete the sense, in which case it would mean "to argue by analogy." (2) The second is to see the phrase as elliptical and complete it by taking the implied word τρόπον as the object of λέγειν, thus reading, λέγειν ⟨τὸν τρόπον⟩ κατ' ἀναλογίαν, "to call this manner [of knowing knowing] by analogy." (3) The third way is also to take it as elliptical and understand its object to be αὐτά (referring back to ἔνια in line 18), thus reading, λέγειν ⟨αὐτὰ⟩ κατ' ἀναλογίαν; this has been the most popular way in which the word has been interpreted: Ross uses "describe" to translate λέγειν here, Merlan "express" (see the Appendix), Laks and Most "expliquer," and Henrich "erklären." (3a) Van Raalte has a variation on the third way, further adding to the ellipsis γνωστά as the object of the verb and reading, λέγειν ⟨αὐτὰ⟩ κατ' ἀναλογίαν ⟨γνωστὰ εἶναι⟩. I prefer the second alternative (2) that makes τρόπος the implied word in the elliptical phrase and translate λέγειν by "call" because I think it is best justified by the context. The main subject of this Diaporia (19) is the οἰκεῖος τρόπος (9a11–12) and Theophrastus's main concern is to identify it; then he says that some things which some people say are known by being unknown may have their own ἴδιος τρόπος, one which would have to be added to the divisions-list; and immediately after that he adds the "perhaps" clause. The thrust of the "perhaps" clause I take it to be, "but perhaps one need not do that, i.e., add this ἴδιος τρόπος to the divisions-list, because in some cases it is more appropriate to call it τρόπος κατ' ἀναλογίαν rather than by 'being unknown', in which case the κατ' ἀναλογίαν entry already exists in the divisions-list." In any case, in the final analysis, whichever of the three alternatives is chosen, the fact remains that Theophrastus is actually comparing the two manners (i.e., by analogy and by being unknown) and finds them close enough as to suggest that one approach or appellation would be, in some cases, more appropriate than the other. Thus any one of the three ways of reading the passage would fit the interpretation I am giving here. For an analysis of this manner of something being known "by being unknown" see the Appendix.

Aporia 20

9a23–10a5. This Aporia has three parts, or succesive formulations (20a–c), the third part itself being in two parts (20c1–2). For an analysis of the structure of the argument in the entire Aporia see the comment at 9b1.

Aporia 20a, 9a23–24 (πόσος, ποσαχῶς): *How many manners of investigation are there, and in how many ways does knowing occur?*

Aporia 20b, 9a24–9b1 (ἀφορίσαι, τί): *But first, how to mark the boundaries of what knowing is? This seems to be more difficult than (20a) because it is impossible to apprehend the universal and common characteristic of things that are said in many ways (i.e., of knowledge, which has many senses).*

Aporia 20c1, 9b1–16 (ἄπορον, μέχρι πόσου καὶ τίνων): *Or rather this too is a matter of aporia, identifying precisely, in order to avoid infinite regress which destroys understanding, the sensible and intelligible things for which causes are to be sought.*

Diaporia 20c1 (9b6–16). *Sense perception provides the starting point up to a point; beyond that, it is the intellect that contemplates "the first and highest" things.*

The epistemological principle that knowledge starts from sense perception and from apprehending the phenomena (λαμβάνειν τὰ φαινόμενα—see the discussion above in Chapter 1.3) was stated by Theophrastus also in his *Physics*: see fr. 143 FHS&G and the discussion and references by Sharples 1998, 37–40.

Aporia 20c2, 9b16–10a5 (ἐν τίνι): Re-statement of Aporia 20c1. *Not only in physics, but also in mathematics and metaphysics, the question is to know where to set the boundaries of the extent of the investigation before reaching an axiomatic first principle, in order to avoid infinite regress.*

Diaporia 20c2 (9b21–10a5): *Seeking to explain everything destroys explanation itself and even knowledge—or rather, seeking to explain everything is pointless because some objects of inquiry by their very nature are axiomatic and admit of no proof. ⟨Though identifying such objects is difficult, one should nevertheless beware of the other extreme, viz., stopping too short in the quest for causes, as is done⟩ by those who posit the eternity of the heavens, taking as axiomatic the data provided by the astronomers. One should go beyond these, state the first movers and final causes, and show how everything relates to everything else all the way down to animals and plants.*

The epistemological principle that philosophical investigation should identify and apprehend the categories into which beings break themselves and take these boundaries as guideposts and thus delimit enquiry is fundamental in Theophrastus's thought (Aporia 1 begins with this very question; see the discussion of boundaries in Chapter 1.4 and note 58). In addition to the Aporiae 20c1 and 20c2 here, it occurs elsewhere in his works. See Sharples 1998, 96–97 for references and discussion.

For an analysis of Aporia 20c2 and Aporia 21 as the introduction, thesis, and antithesis of the argument that the search for explanation should be limited to those cases where it is possible, see Reale 1980, 419–420n41, and Ellis 1988, 218–220.

9a23 τρόποι] Theophrastus has just spent an entire paragraph talking about finding the proper method of investigating (the proper manner of "pursuing") each class of objects; the mention of the same word τρόποι at the beginning of the present paragraph where he summarizes the preceding and goes on to the next issue is obviously to be taken in the same sense. It is counterintuitive to argue otherwise or assume ambiguity in its use, as most commentators do.

9a26 χαλεπώτερον] This is a true comparative degree and not one used merely to "soften" the expression: τὸ ἀφορίσαι is more difficult than διελεῖν.

9b1 ἢ καί] All manuscripts have ἢ καί here, which Ross "corrects" to ᾗ, "wherefore," or "on which account," instituting a causal connection and making the following statement a consequence of the preceding one. The "correction," however, is not only not necessary (pace Laks & Most, van Raalte 444–445, and Henrich, who accept it), but it also appears to be wrong because of the sense. The argument here develops through a number of restatements or refinements of the precise nature of the aporia. Theophrastus is saying the following: (1 = [Aporia 20a]) We should try and distinguish in how many ways knowing occurs (9a24). But before we do that, (2 = [20b]) we should start by marking the boundaries, i.e., identifying precisely the objects, of what knowing is (9a26). But this would appear to be more difficult (χαλεπώτερον) than distinguishing the different ways of knowing because it is not possible to apprehend the common element of things said in many ways—i.e., to give a common and universal definition of knowledge, which has different senses in accordance with the objects known: whence the need to mark its boundaries, or identify its objects, in each case (9a27–9b1). (3a = [20c1]) Or rather (ἤ), (since the first task is to mark the boundaries of knowledge, we can specify the quest and say that) actually *this* (καὶ τοῦτο; emphatic καί, Denniston 320) is a matter of aporia—or at least it is not easy to say—how far and to which things the search for causes should extend in both sensibles and intelligibles (9b1–4). After a parenthetical discussion of sensibles and intelligibles as starting points (9b6–16, see the commentary on that passage), there is a reprise and repetition of (3a): (3b = [20c2]) So, reaching understanding and conviction is important, finally, with this very point, where to draw the line (how to "set the boundaries") in the search for causes or reasons (λόγον) in physics, mathematics, and metaphysics (9b16ff.). In this sequence of the argument, stages (1) and (2) are connected by the comparative χαλεπώτερον, which all commentators seem to ignore; stages (2) and (3a) are connected by οὐχ οἷόν τε and καὶ τοῦτ' ἄπορον, where the word ἄπορον, being a repetition of οὐχ οἷόν τε, explains the καί ("actually") in ἢ καί; and stage (3b) connects with stage (3a) through the repetition of the object of search (ἐν τίνι ποιητέον τὸν ὅρον is a reprise of μέχρι πόσου ζητητέον αἰτίας, and thus explains the precision expressed in the demonstrative αὐτὸ τοῦτο in 9b16–17, "this very [issue] here"), but it also connects with stage (2) through the use of the word χαλεπὴ in 9b16. According to this analysis, the connection between stage (2) and stage (3a) is not that the last clause in (2), "it is impossible to have a universal definition of knowledge because knowledge is used in more than one sense," gives the reason (ᾗ, "wherefore," Ross; "c'est pourquoi" Laks & Most), for stage (3a), "how far the search for causes should extend;" rather, having stated in (2) that the aporia is how to mark the boundaries of knowledge, Theophrastus rephrases the question in (3a). He rephrases the question in order to take into account the common, but unexpressed, notion that knowledge is searching for and understanding of causes (Aristotle, *Met.* B 2, 996a19; Γ 2, 1003b16–19; E 1, 1025b6–7, etc.). He thus specifies in (3a) that in this case "marking the boundaries" means establishing *how far* the search for causes should extend in each of the three areas of investigation, physics, mathematics, and metaphysics. The need to mark clearly the boundaries of the extent of the search for causes is twofold: one is to avoid infinite regress, which in the end destroys understanding (9b4–5), and the other is to stop the chain of causality because some objects of knowledge either have no cause or we have no direct causal access to them except through intellectual intuition (9b10–12). Hence Ross's emendation of ἤ to ᾗ is not acceptable here because the connection between stages (2) and (3a) is not causal but one expressing alternatives (ἤ, the transmitted reading), as analyzed above.

9b2 εἰπεῖν, "say," that is, to put it in logically and philosophically coherent language, the difficulty stemming from the difficulty of the subject. For the use of the aorist infinitive, εἰπεῖν, in this meaning here see van Raalte 446 and note 2.

9b2–3 μέχρι ... τίνων] Μέχρι governs naturally both genitives after it, πόσου and τίνων (Berti, preprint, note 15); the first asks about the extent or level of inquiry, and the second about the specific things, among both sensibles and intelligibles, which should be included in the search. If τίνων were meant to be taken with αἰτίας, Theophrastus would probably have said, μέχρι πόσου ζητητέον αἰτίας καὶ τίνων. In any case, Theophrastus is not asking here the relatively pointless question of what things in general one should investigate the causes—the answer would be clearly of everything, both sensibles and intelligibles—but the more specific question, up to what particular things in the investigation of both sensibles and intelligibles the search for causes should extend.

9b6–16 The rest of this paragraph is parenthetical, taking off on a tangent from the mention of sensibles and intelligibles and seizing the opportunity to discuss in which ways they can be starting points for knowledge and how far causality can extend. When Theophrastus returns to the main subject with χαλεπὴ δέ in 9b16, the digression makes necessary the emphatic demonstrative αὐτὸ τοῦτο.

9b10 αὐτὰ τὰ ἄκρα καὶ πρῶτα, "the first and highest",[40] is something that Plato may have used in the Academy, almost as a technical expression, to refer to the very first principles. He certainly used the pronoun αὐτό before a neuter substantive (αὐτὸ τὸ καλόν, αὐτὸ τὸ ἀγαθόν; see the Loci Parallei) to express the ideas (Berti, preprint p. 4). The only other attestation of the phrase τὰ ἄκρα καὶ πρῶτα in all extant Greek literature before the Christian era is in Plato's *Seventh Letter*, 344d5, and one is tempted to think that Theophrastus may be echoing its use by Plato (and the Old Academy?); hence my quotation marks around the phrase. Because of its extremely limited attestation, even in the meager remains of classical literature, it cannot be assumed to have been a common phrase. In imperial and later times, it becomes more current (perhaps because of its Academic use), both in pagan and Christian Greek, and both in its technical sense (Alexander of Aphrodisias, *In Met.* 240.24 Hayduck (*CAG*): αἱ ἀκρόταταί τε καὶ πρῶται ἀρχαί; Plotinus, *Enneads* V,1,1.24; Proclus, *Platonic Theology* I,118.12: τὸ μὲν θεῖον ἀκρότατον εἶναι καὶ πρώτιστον) and a general one, "the very best" (Theodoretus, *Hist. relig.*, Vita 13, 1.14; Hephaestion, *Apotelesmatica* 200,25–26).

9b13 The force of ἐκεῖνο is, as Laks & Most 70n46 observe, to point forward (cf. van Raalte 456) to a third alternative known to Theophrastus's audience, the theory that holds as possible the direct apprehension of ultimate principles by the intellect without the mediation of the search for causes. This theory at the same time appears to deny the second alternative in the preceding sentence, the weakness of our faculties.

9b16 δέ, "So"] Resumptive δέ (Denniston 182–183) with χαλεπή harking back to χαλεπώτερον in 9a26, and implied repetition of ἄπορον in 9b2. See the analysis of the structure of this passage in the commentary on 9b1.

---

[40] Literally, the topmost and very first, but I borrow the translation from G.R. Morrow (*Plato's Epistles*, New York 1962, p. 241), who puts "first" first, because in English it sounds more natural.

9b16–17 εἰς αὐτὸ τοῦθ' ἡ σύνεσις καὶ ἡ πίστις. Εἰς indicates relation, i.e., reaching understanding concerning, with regard to, this issue (K.-G. II,1.471c, cited by van Raalte 460).

Αὐτὸ τοῦθ' refers back to τοῦτ' (and all that that entails, 9b2–4) in 9b1, and forward to ἐν τίνι ποιητέον τὸν ὅρον in 9b19–20; see the discussion of the structure of the argument in the commentary on 9b1.

Σύνεσις must be understood in the way Aristotle defines and describes it in the *Nicomachean Ethics* VI,10, i.e., as learning and reaching a critical understanding περὶ ὧν ἀπορήσειεν ἄν τις καὶ βουλεύσαιτο (1143a6), of issues that are subjects of aporiae and deliberation, precisely what Theophrastus is doing here. The Arabic translates σύνεσις with the word that normally translates ζήτησις, *baḥṯ*. It seems likely that Ψ may have had ζήτησις instead of σύνεσις in this passage, and ζήτησις would make just as good sense, though it cannot be excluded that some marginal annotation to σύνεσις influenced Isḥāq's judgment, or that he himself simply understood σύνεσις as ζήτησις, complaining about the difficulty of which is otherwise a common enough motif in this Essay. For the range of the epistemological sense of σύνεσις in Aristotle see Bonitz *Index* 727b6. Πίστις is "*persuasionis firmitas*," Bonitz *Index* 595b8.

9b20 οἷον explains ὅρον, not πραγματείας, of which it was taken to provide examples. Cf. van Raalte 462n4 with reference to Bonitz *Index* 502a7–8.

9b20 ⌜τάς⌝] The reading of the Greek manuscripts, περί τε τῆς φύσεως καὶ περὶ τὰς ἔτι προτέρας, where περί is used in a pair of balanced phrases with two different cases, genitive and accusative, is rather improbable (cf. van Raalte 462). The corrections suggested by various commentators have all concentrated on replacing τε with another word, such as τάς, τήν, τά. However, it seems difficult to justify the excision through substitution of τε, both on palaeographical grounds (the presumed corruption of τάς or τήν or τά into τε cannot be easily accounted for) and on stylistic grounds, especially in this work by Theophrastus where the particle is liberally used (see the Glossary). The combination τε … καί is very frequent, and in one other instance (10a27) it is used with a preposition: ἔν τε τοῖς οὐρανίοις καὶ ἐν τοῖς … πλείοσιν; thus the combination transmitted in the manuscripts, περί τε … καὶ περί is perfectly fine and in need of no correction. Next, the pronoun τάς in the second half of the phrase (καὶ περὶ τὰς ἔτι προτέρας), which is unimpugnable, as well as the context of the entire sentence, which speaks of studies (πραγματείας), clearly refer to these very studies, and thus the obvious balance between the first and the second half of the phrase requires the presence of τάς also in the first half. The Arabic translation also supports the reading of τάς in the first half of the phrase: the word πραγματείας in 9b18 is translated by *al-ʿulūm*, and this word is repeated in the οἷον phrase, where the first half is rendered by, *ʿilm umūr aṭ-ṭabīʿa*, where *ʿilm* clearly renders Greek τάς properly understood as τὰς πραγματείας. If then τε should not be excised and τάς is needed because of both the sense and the evidence of the Arabic translation, τάς is to be added after τε, the omission of which in the MS tradition can be easily attributed to haplography. For an identical prepositional phrase see below at 11b14, οἷον τὰ περὶ τὰς τῆς γῆς λεχθέντα μεταβολάς.

9b24 The reason for assuming a lacuna here is the following. The argument in Aporia 20c2 (9b16–10a5), a nodal point of which is the difficult passage in 9b24, runs thus: In physics, mathematics, and metaphysics, setting a boundary with regard to how far inquiry is to proceed is important for these disciplines, but also difficult. It is difficult because (γάρ 9b21) if no boundary is set, one would go on seeking proof for everything, thus triggering an infinite regress, which was rejected above (9b4–5). Theophrastus, however, corrects himself at this point (ἀληθέστερον εἰπεῖν 9b23) and restates the reason in a way which he considers more accurate and which does not involve an argument from the impossibility of infinite regress, but rather one from the very nature of some of the objects of inquiry: some of them do not admit of proof and are simply to be taken axiomatically. The question then becomes, How can one identify these axiomatic principles which are, by their very nature (πέφυκεν 9b24), the boundaries of inquiry? It is easy to be mistaken in this regard, for some, trusting in astronomy as an unerring guide, stop too short in their search and take as the axiomatic and unprovable starting point the eternity of the heavens and all the other facts about their motion and shape (9b24–27). This, however, Theophrastus concludes, is not the unprovable boundary sought after because these people have yet to demonstrate other things which astronomy cannot prove, such as the first movers and the final cause (10a1–5).

The problem at the nodal point πέφυκεν ὅσοι (9b24) is that in the preceding sentence (9b23–24), Theophrastus just finished saying that those who seek causes for everything, including for those things which by their nature cannot have a cause, do away with proof. The next sentence, after ὅσοι in the transmitted text, complains about exactly the opposite position, that some people who do in fact posit an entity that is primary and cannot be proven, viz. those who take the eternal heavens as such a boundary and do not seek beyond them, stop too short of the boundary. The transition from one sentence to the next is thus very abrupt and breaks the continuity of the argument, generating almost a non-sequitur. What is needed as a transition is some statement that will say something like my reconstruction above, viz., that "though finding such a boundary is difficult, one should on the other hand beware of stopping too short in the quest of causes, as is done by those who posit the eternity of the heavens." Adding δέ after ὅσοι with Zeller (and those who followed him), despite its economy, does not solve the problem, because the particle δέ by itself cannot, in this context, carry the meaning of the sentence in quotation marks in my preceding reconstruction. As Laks & Most (72n50) suggest, δέ could have provided satisfactory text if κατάλοιπον in 9b27 meant "leave aside, not mention," instead of its opposite, "there remains to mention." As it is, however, something more is needed, and hence the supposition of a lacuna, first proposed by Usener 1861. His hypothesis, according to which about a sentence must have dropped out from the text, would best seem to account for the discrepancy and rough transition discussed above.

Furthermore, palaeographically there is no good reason why the particle δέ should have fallen out of the text at such a crucial point. Without it the text truly runs the risk of being read as Isḥāq read it, with ὅσοι being taken as the subject of ζητοῦσιν in 9b23, which would give the nonsensical sentence we find in Arabic, "those who assume the heavens to be eternal seek proof of things of which there neither is nor naturally can be any." If there were no lacuna in the text, a particle after ὅσοι would be indispensable, so by the same token the text cannot stand without it, as printed by van Raalte and Henrich: book typography with paragraph breaks (both van Raalte and Henrich start a new paragraph with ὅσοι) may provide to the modern reader the illusion of the break needed after πέφυκεν, but that is not how Greek was written or read in Theophrastus's time. Absence of particles in instances of "left dislocation" that van Raalte speaks of occurs in very explicit texts and is singularly inappropriate in this context: apart from the reasons of semantic discontinuity just given, the theme that supposedly should precede this asyndeton is exactly the opposite of what presumably the sentence beginning with ὅσοι provides: the theme of the last sentence is condemnation of the position which tries to provide causes for something which by its nature cannot have a cause, while the following sentence beginning with ὅσοι gives an instance of the position in which something *is* in fact accepted as not having a cause.

In addition, if a continuous text is supposed in 9b24 and is doctored by the mere addition of δέ, a further inconsistency occurs: without any qualifying context (such as that which would have dropped out in the lacuna), ὅσοι in the text as we have it gives the wrong impression that it refers to astronomers.[41] The reason is that in the truncated sentence (due to the lacuna) as we have it, ὅσοι and τούτοις (9b27) have to refer to the same subject because the ἔτι δέ clause needs a verb and this is supplied by ὑπολαμβάνουσιν of the ὅσοι clause (i.e., if the truncated sentence were considered complete, its structure would be, ὅσοι τὸν οὐρανὸν ἀΐδιον καὶ ὅσα ἄλλα ἀστρολογία δείκνυσιν ὑπολαμβάνουσιν). And since those who assume whatever astronomy proves cannot but be astronomers, ὅσοι by extension would also have to refer to astronomers. But this cannot be so because first, astronomers do not say anything about the eternity of the world, and second, they would be charged with the absurd task of still having to investigate everything from final causes to plants; as Laks & Most correctly note (72n50), "L'argument reste un peu surprenant, en raison du caractère hyperbolique de sa formulation: on voit mal un astronome être convaincu de la nécessité de s'intéresser aux moteurs premiers ou aux plantes en tant qu'astronome." And if this were so, i.e., if astronomers in this passage were charged with doing all that, then Theophrastus would be contradicting himself in the very next sentence when he says that though astronomy contributes to our understanding of causes it nevertheless cannot do so for those things which are prior (πρότερα) to its objects. So that in 10a1 Theophrastus would be demanding of astronomers an account of the final cause (τὸ τίνος ἕνεκα λέγειν), and in 10a6 he would be denying them the capacity to contribute to a knowledge of "the first things" (οὐκ ἐν τοῖς πρώτοις). To remove this discrepancy, ὅσοι must be somehow qualified to indicate that it refers not to astronomers, but to those who, taking over the data and the assumptions of the astronomers, stop too short of the boundary. The text in the lacuna would have provided this qualification.

---

[41] A victim of which is Steinmetz 1964, 159, who prints the text in question as, τούτοις (sc. τοῖς ἀστρολόγοις) ὑπόλοιπον, and who derives, as a result, a skewed interpretation of the passage. Theophrastus was not speaking against astronomers but against improper use of the knowledge they provide.

A lacuna is thus the only alternative which can explain all the evidence. In all likelihood a line has dropped out due to haplography or some other palaeographical mishap which, however, would appear to be difficult to conjecture.

10a3 The dative in ὑποβαίνοντι makes it clear that the structure of this new clause beginning with καί in this line is to be parallel to that of the clause beginning with τούτοις (9b27), and thus the elliptical ὑποβαίνοντι clause is to be supplemented by the words, καὶ ὑποβαίνοντι δὴ πρὸς τὰ ἄλλα ⟨κατάλοιπον ὁμοίως λέγειν⟩.

10a4 δή, "then," in a progressive sense, adding a new element in the rhetorical progression of the argument (cf. Humbert 405, "une sorte de tremplin," Denniston 239; cf. also Denniston 254 for καί ... δή). The jump to the new element justifies the switch from the plural of τούτοις to the singular in ὑποβαίνοντι and is not as "rude" as Laks & Most note (17n55).

10a4 ἢ μερῶν appears to be corrupt. See the discussion in Chapter 2.1, section on "Sub-family JCL."

Aporia 21

10a5–21 (ζητητέον 10a17, ἡ νῦν ἀπορία 10a20): *By what method is the movement of the heavens to be investigated?*

Diaporia 21. *Astronomy does not provide information about the first things; the method of investigating them is accordingly not that of physics. In the case of animals and plants, but also in the case of the heavens, motion is of their essence; without motion they would not all be what they are except in name only. For it seems that the rotation of the universe is a sort of life. Thus, just as in the case of living things life is to be investigated as being of their essence, so also in the case of the heavens their motion is to be explained as being of their essence through an investigation that is marked off (as being metaphysical). This aporia is related to the theory of the unmoved mover. (Implied conclusion: Such an investigation would obviate that theory because it would study the motion of the heavens through their essence and not through its origin in an unmoved mover.)*

This aporia identifies itself at the end rather than at the beginning, and the thrust of its argument, which hangs on a correct understanding of καίτοι at 10a9, has been difficult to ascertain; see the commentary on that word below. For the relevance of this diaporia to the question of Theophrastus's views concerning ether, see above the commentary on Aporia/Diaporia 10.

10a6–7 τῆς φύσεως must be read with ἕτερα, as Laks & Most punctuate, and it is placed first in the phrase because it is emphasized, in anticipation of what follows: τῆς φύσεως ἕτερα is echoed in, and gives meaning to, οὐ φυσικός in 10a8: the most important things are other than nature (perhaps τῆς φύσεως is used here elliptically for ⟨τῶν⟩ τῆς φύσεως, "other than ⟨those of⟩ nature"), and consequently the method to study them is other than that employed in physics.

10a7–8 καὶ γὰρ δή, "and certainly;" cf. Humbert 391–392, Denniston 243.

10a9 καίτοι, "in fact"] For progressive καίτοι, expressing an idea added as an inference or conclusion, see Humbert 415, Denniston 563–564 ("logical"). The sentence beginning with καίτοι here does not have the adversative sense in which it is normally translated ("yet" or "and yet," "pourtant," "obwohl;" only Reale 1964 has a progressive rendering, "infatti"): if it is thought, along with Henrich 141, that καίτοι is to be read as a concessive clause at the end of the preceding sentence, then the Diaporia 21 loses its meaning. Theophrastus introduces the problem of motion right after he has said that the method of studying the most important things is wholly or partly other than that of natural philosophy, meaning that it is wholly, or partly, metaphysical. He then goes on to say about motion that it may be thought that it is essential to the heavens, as it is essential to living beings, and thus, as the statement of the Aporia 21 in the final sentence of the paragraph hints (10a19–21), the metaphysical question of positing an unmoved mover as the cause of celestial motion becomes obviated. The study of motion, then, when conducted by other than a physical method, i.e. when conducted in a metaphysical way (the metaphysical approach is evident since Theophrastus is arguing from the essence of things and especially of the heavens), can answer metaphysical questions. If this is so, then the purpose of introducing here the problem of celestial motion, right after saying that the method of investigating the most important things is wholly or partly metaphysical, is to provide a case in which the method, though it might be thought to be physical, is in actuality also metaphysical. Thus καίτοι in 10a9 is not concessive ("obwohl," Henrich) because if it were, then the section about motion would have had to say that the method of investigating motion is only physical. Since, however, this section makes the claim that the method of investigating motion is metaphysical, or primarily metaphysical, a concessive καίτοι would make no sense. The use of καίτοι is accordingly progressive, expressing an idea added unto the argument as an inference from the preceding.

10a11 Reading καὶ ⟨εἰ⟩ ἡ, combining the two conjectures by Usener and Wimmer to produce what I believe is the proper text. The article, the reading of all Greek manuscripts (the Arabic translation has an omission at this point, while the Latin is inconclusive), is needed because it has possessive force: "each thing, *its* actualized state belongs to its essence." Cf. 9a4, οὕτως αὐτῶν ἡ ἐνέργεια, and 5a7, τὴν ἐνέργειαν [*sc.* τῆς ἀρχῆς] … ἀποδιδούς, where the function of the article is clearly possessive, as opposed to 8a11, ἀγόμενον εἰς ἐνέργειαν, where the noun is used indefinitely. In addition, without the article the word ἐνέργεια runs the risk of being read attributively or as a predicate. Thus εἰ (which is clearly needed for the sentence to make sense, cf. van Raalte 479 top) should be added to the text, not substituted for ἡ.

10a10–11 διὸ καί … οὐσίας ἑκάστου] Οὐσίας is emphasized, apparently, through καί after διό in a causal clause (Denniston 296–297).

10a12 κινεῖται] Three of the four independent witnesses (JP and Ψ) read κινῆται; the Latin translation is inconclusive. With the subjunctive, however, the sentence is incomplete, and this led to the scribal correction into κινεῖται in later manuscripts. Unless, in an effort to preserve the readings of PJ and Ψ, one assumes a loss of that part of the sentence that would have completed it if κινῆται is to be read, the corruption of κινεῖται into κινῆται most likely occurred in an uncial manuscript and is accordingly one of the primitive errors in the Neoplatonic archetype.

10a17–19 μηδ' … ἤ, οὐδ' … ἤ] Ἤ means "except" here, having the same use as that after a comparative (K.-G. II,304, Anmerk. 4, cited by van Raalte 482). Disjunctive ἤ would make no sense in this context: Theophrastus just finished saying in the previous sentence that it is obvious (δῆλον) that in the case of both animals and the heavens movement belongs to their essence. Hence the life of both should be investigated in accordance with this fact *only*. Disjunctive ἤ would destroy this exclusivity that Theophrastus wants to present and make one of the alternatives possible, viz. not investigating the life of both at all (as in the translations of Ross, Tricot, Laks & Most, Henrich, and Sharples 1998, 97), which would be contradictory to the previous sentence.

Aporia 22

10a22–10b24 (ἀφορισμός, τίνος ἕνεκα 10a22, 28, 10b18, 23; μηδὲν μάτην 10a22, 10b8): *How is the final cause and that nothing is in vain to be understood? In general, it is difficult to mark the boundaries within which these considerations apply: where should one start and end? In particular, some objects seem to happen by coincidence and others by some necessity, and hence are not subject to these stipulations.*

Aporiae 22–24, on the subject of teleology, have been rightly much discussed in the literature, for they provide valuable insight into Theophrastus's theory of scientific method; the question, though, has been to gauge accurately how to interpret the examples of "dysteleology" that he gives in the succeeding diaporiae and whether he accepts, partially or wholly rejects, or modifies the Aristotelian concept. See in particular Lennox 1985; Vallance 1988, 27–39; Repici 1990; Botter 1999; Lennox 2001, 226–227; and the comprehensive study of Aristotelian teleology by Johnson 2005, 35–39.

Diaporia 22.1 (10a28–10b7). *Terrestrial and geological changes and generation take place for the sake of no obvious end.*

This Diaporia, which appears wordy and repetitive, has exercised the commentators, perhaps because the precise reference of each technical term used in it is not grasped. The text, however, as transmitted in the four independent witnesses (JP Ψ and Λ), with the addition of καὶ ἀναχωρήσεις from Ψ, seems unimpeachable, and one would have to think of, and account for, a catastrophic alteration or interpolation at some much earlier stage of the transmission to justify the proposed emendations. As it is, the sense of the paragraph is plain enough. For a discussion of the wording used in this paragraph see Vallance 1988, 28–30. The presumed references to the work of Aristotle have been problematic; see Lennox 1985, 156; Repici 1990, 202–204.

Diaporia 22.2 (10b7–20). *In animals, the growth of certain body parts, or some biological functions, are for the sake of no obvious end, and neither is the variety of their nourishment or generation: had there been one specific end for all, they would not have exhibited wide divergences among them in these respects.*

For a discussion of the examples of "dysteleology" given here by Theophrastus and their relation to the work of Aristotle see Lennox 1985, 147–149, 156–158; Vallance 1988, 30–31; Most 1988a, 226–229; Repici 1990, 205–212.

Diaporia 22.3 (10b20–24). *Changes and generation in plants and inanimate things take place for the sake of no obvious end.*

10a23 Usener's 1861, 1890, conjectural addition of τε in ἄλλως ⟨θ'⟩ is convincing because it builds the parallel construction ἄλλως τε ... καὶ δή (10a25), giving to the passage the sense of "in any case ... in particular;" cf. the examples in Denniston 249–250 of τε ... καὶ δή. For the particle combination itself see Plato, *Sophist* 259e1: ἄλλως τε οὐκ ἐμμελὲς καὶ δὴ καὶ παντάπασιν ἀμούσου τινός καὶ ἀφιλοσόφου, literally, "[it] is in any case not graceful and in particular [the work] of an uncultured non-philosopher;" translated more elegantly and imaginatively, but using a "not only ... but" expression for the combination, by Cornford 1957, 300, "not only strikes a discordant note but amounts to a crude defiance of the philosophic Muse." Closer to Theophrastus's use of the combination is Aristotle's text in *Physics* 193b28–30.

Palaeographically, the omission of θ before ὁ can be easily ascribed to haplography in the uncial stage of transmission of the text (two successive round letters written as one; Ψ does not have it either). Without it, ἄλλως sits awkwardly in the sentence, and necessarily leads to reading ἄλλως with μάτην, as in the Arabic translation. This in turn has its own problems, and Zeller, who adopted it, felt the need to athetize μάτην, causing an even greater disruption to the transmitted text. The adoption of Usener's addition of θ' appears to be the least problematic alternative to restoring the text.

10b1–2 Usener's 1890 conjectural addition of καὶ ἀναχωρήσεις after προχωρήσεις here is actually found in Ψ. See the corresponding note to the Arabic translation.

10b4 ᾗ] Bignone's correction of the transmitted ἥ to ᾗ is necessary for both the syntax and the sense. The reference here is to the entire set of problems in Aristotle's *De generatione et corruptione* viewed as problematic when considered from the point of view of their final end. The specific reference to these problems is also clear from the existence of the article αἱ in αἱ ... ἀλλοιώσεις ... γίνονται, which points to *the* alterations talked about in the Peripatos. Had Theophrastus been speaking in general terms here he would not have used the article. All this indicates that the whole clause ᾗ αἱ μέν ... μεθισταμένων was intended by Theophrastus as qualification of φθοραὶ καὶ γενέσεις and is part of his text and not a marginal gloss to be athetized. Furthermore, the particle μέν in the clause, without a corresponding δέ, would be pointless if this were only a gloss and the entire gloss (as Ross's seclusion of the clause, 32, and Henrich's express suggestion, 145, maintain). Laks & Most 77n10 make the additional point that Theophrastus is talking here about subterranean changes (if indeed that is what ἐν αὐτῇ τῇ γῇ indicates), a subject not mentioned in what preceded.

10b6 μεθισταμένων, "as [things] shift" places, is apparently to be taken in its literal sense, as frequently in Aristotle (cf. Bonitz *Index* 449b13 ff.). The absent subject of the absolute genitive is apparently to be supplied according to sense; cf. similar constructions at 5a24 and 8b15–16.

10b6 καὶ ἕτερα δ', "and ... besides"] Preparatory μέν in line 4 is answered by non-adversative καί (Denniston 374) in a καί ... δέ combination which introduces the last item in a series in "the form of an etcetera" (Denniston 202). MS A of the Σ group and the Latin translation omit the δ', which Burnikel 129 seems to prefer by comparing it to 10b15; but the particle combination of the transmitted reading here (10b6) can hardly be doubted.

10b12 τοῖσδε] Usener's 1861, 1890, "correction" of this word is actually very close to the transmitted manuscript readings: τοισδε P, without any accents, and τοῖσδὲ, J written as one word but with a grave on the δὲ (the Latin translation omits three lines here). Only Ψ must have had τοῖς δέ, or at least Isḥāq so read it, because he wrote, "to the point that some of them (i.e., deer) actually suffer harm" (*ḥattā anna baʿḍahā qad yataʾaḏḏā*). Usener's reading is the only possible reading, given the text, and is not as unsatisfactory as Ross 71 thinks. Τοῖσδε is part of the καθάπερ clause, and if read continuously in an expanded form (i.e., reading τοῖς κέρασι for τοῖσδε), it presents no difficulties: καθάπερ τῶν ἐλάφων τοῖς κέρασι καὶ λελωβημένων κινήσει τε καὶ παραιωρήσει καὶ ἐπιπροσθήσει τῶν ὀμμάτων.

10b12 κινήσει τε καὶ παραιωρήσει] Usener's 1861, 1890, emendation of the transmitted κινήσει to κνήσει, brilliant though it is, does not yield better sense. Usener was led to his conjecture by the Aristotelian passage, *Historia Animalium* 611b16, ὅταν δὲ μηκέτι πονῶσι (*sc*. οἱ ἔλαφοι) πρὸς τὰ δένδρα κνώμενοι αὐτὰ (*sc*. τὰ κέρατα), τότ' ἐκλείπουσι τοὺς τόπους τούτους διὰ τὸ θαρρεῖν ὡς ἔχοντες ᾧ ἀμυνοῦνται, where the verb κνάω is brought into direct relationship with κέρατα. But the meaning in the Aristotelian passage is directly the opposite of that in Theophrastus: in Aristotle deer scratch their horns against trees to test them and thus ensure that their contact with something hard will not be painful to them; so the scratching is done for a beneficial purpose, whereas the word in question in Theophrastus, if it is indeed κνήσει, implies that harm is being done to the animal. Thus the two contexts are entirely different and the Aristotelian passage cannot be used to emend the text in Theophrastus. The word itself, κνῆσις, is not attested either in Aristotle or Theophrastus; the former uses κνησμός instead, and apparently the latter, too, in the derivative κνησμώδης (fr. 9 Wimmer). The meaning of κνῆσις, moreover, cannot be anything other than either scratching (rather than "rubbing," Ross), or, apparently, its counterpart, itching (cf. LSJ; "abrasion" in van Raalte, and "Abschürfung" in Henrich, indicate the *result* of scratching, not scratching itself). Laks & Most prefer "itching" (démangent), but that can hardly be true for itching in itself is not harmful to the animal because the animal can easily cure it by scratching the affected part, if it can reach it, or by rubbing it gainst something, if it cannot. There remains the meaning of scratching and rubbing, two verbs, however, which need an object—scratch or rub against what? Ross and Tricot provide the missing object ("obstacles"), but that is not in Theophrastus, as opposed to the case of ἐπιπροσθήσει, which does require an object, and which Theophrastus provides with the objective genitive τῶν ὀμμάτων. So if Theophrastus had meant to say "horns rub against obstacles/trees" he ought to have provided the object in such an inexplicit context. Besides, judging from the next two words, παραιωρήσει and ἐπιπροσθήσει, which have a parallel function in the sentence, it is clear that all three words describe qualities that horns have in themselves *because of their size*, regardless of their environment (i.e., regardless whether there are trees around for the horns to rub against). Thus "scratching" or "rubbing" does not yield a satisfactory sense either. Laks & Most's comment (78n17) is to the point when they remark that the passage, as reconstructed with Usener's emendation, "reste étrange." For all these reasons, then, κνήσει cannot be sustained. The transmitted word, κινήσει, on the other hand, in addition to having the authority of all the Greek manuscripts and the Arabic translation (the Latin translation omits the passage), is perfectly compatible with the sense of the sentence as just described: because of their large size, horns of deer move (sway) in an ungainly way as the head moves, their extremes necessarily dangle (παραιωρήσει: the horns dangle, it is not that the deer are "hung up by their horns," Ross 72, or "suspended," van Raalte 61), and obstruct their vision in the direction where the horns dangle (the proper meaning of ἐπιπροσθέω, ἐπιπρόσθησις, cf. Aristotle, *Topics* 148b27) presumably by restricting the free movement of the head.

10b14 Connective δή, "then again"; cf. Denniston 254, 240.

10b20–22 ⟨αἱ⟩ ἐν ... τοῖς ἀψύχοις ... ἔχουσαι φύσιν] There is a significant problem here, with three interrelated parts, one grammatical, one codicological, and the third having to do with the Arabic translation. In the first place, the phrase τοῖς ἀψύχοις ὡρισμένην τιν' ἔχουσι φύσιν, in which the transmitted ἔχουσαι is "corrected" to ἔχουσι as accepted in all editions, cannot stand; the word order of the attributive participle ἔχουσι with the article τοῖς is wrong. There are five different ways in which this phrase can be said,[42] but the one we have in the text is not one of them. The easiest way to emend this would be to adopt one of them, τοῖς ἀψύχοις ⟨τοῖς⟩ ὡρισμένην, and very plausibly blame haplography for the omission, but then we are confronted with the second part of the problem, the reading ἔχουσαι for ἔχουσι. Ἔχουσαι is the reading

[42] I.e., as follows: (1) τοῖς ὡρισμένην τιν' ἔχουσι φύσιν ἀψύχοις, (2) τοῖς ἀψύχοις τοῖς ὡρισμένην τιν' ἔχουσι φύσιν, (3) τοῖς ἔχουσιν ὡρισμένην τινὰ φύσιν ἀψύχοις, (4) τοῖς ἔχουσιν ἀψύχοις ὡρισμένην τινὰ φύσιν, (5) τοῖς ὡρισμένην τινὰ φύσιν ἀψύχοις ἔχουσι. See K.-G. I,623I; Smyth § 1166 lists only four ways, omitting (5).

of all four independent witnesses, certainly of PJ and Λ, and apparently also of Ψ as reflected in the Arabic translation (see further below). Impugning this reading in the best witnesses is not easy, especially if it is difficult to account for the error—if it is an error, as in this case: how would ἔχουσαι have arisen? In addition, the form accepted in the editions, ἔχουσι, is found only in CL and A, our least reliable manuscripts (see Part I, Chapter 2.1), and can hardly be more than a conjecture on the part of scribes or revisers; for according to the stemma codicum, CL and A could have gotten the reading ἔχουσι, assuming it is the correct one, only from their common source with J, and if so, then J would have committed an error by writing ἔχουσαι. This might be acceptable if it were an isolated error, but P, a manuscript completely independent from the J tradition, also committed on its own the same error.[43] This is straining credibility; but even if it is accepted, then we have the same error occurring independently for yet a third time in Λ and a fourth in Ψ, a manuscript which belongs not only to a different tradition from P J and Λ but also to a different transcription from uncials. So ἔχουσι is difficult, if not impossible, to accept both because CL and A could not have gotten the reading from any independent source (other than conjecture), and because all four independent witnesses could not have made the same error and written ἔχουσαι for a presumed correct original ἔχουσι.

Thus ἔχουσι cannot be a true reading, and is to be rejected, while ἔχουσαι may or may not be the true reading; in other words, either the paradosis has ἔχουσαι which is a primitive error of the Neoplatonic archetype, or ἔχουσαι is the true reading. At this point the Arabic translation interjects yet a third part of the problem; it reads, "One should also investigate with regard to plants—or rather, with regard to souls, the reason on account of which they have come to have a determinate nature" (*wa-li-l-insāni ayḍan an yabḥaṯa mina amri n-nabāti, bal min amri l-anfusi ʿani s-sababi llaḏī lahū ṣāra lahā ṭabīʿatun maḥdūdatun*). The translator understood the structure of the sentence quite correctly, but there are some other difficulties. The first has to do with the word ἀψύχοις; Isḥāq either read or interpreted what he read as ψυχαῖς, souls, and not inanimates. It is possible that the original version of the translation did read

[43] Burnikel 119 thinks that there are only two common errors between P and J: one of them is this one (which in reality is not an error), and the other is the spelling of ἐνμόρφους at 7a6 (which, as a spelling peculiarity, could have arisen independently)—there are thus no common errors between P and J.

"inanimate" and the word was later corrupted within the Arabic tradition, but that seems unlikely. Alon in his edition silently corrected the reading of the manuscript, *al-anfus*, souls, to *al-lā-nafs*, the inanimate, but this is unacceptable; first "the inanimate" does not mean "inanimate things," what Theophrastus is talking about here, and second the translator does not use this neologism with *lā* to render ἄψυχος: in two other places where the word occurs in the Essay it is translated by *mā lā nafsa lahū* (11a17) and *allatī lā nafsa lahū* (9a15). If one were to emend the manuscript reading of *al-anfus*, therefore, it would be more plausible to suggest reading ⟨*m*⟩*ā lā nafsa* ⟨*lahū*⟩. In Arabic, ⟨*m*⟩*ā lā nafsa* is written in a practically identical way with *al-anfus*, while the following ⟨*lahū*⟩ could have been omitted as meaningless at a later stage, once the mistaken transition from *mā lā nafsa* to *al-anfus* was effected. However, there are two difficulties with this emendation. First, there seems to be no obvious reason why the mistake should have occurred, and second, the pronoun that is used right after this emended passage to refer back to it is feminine (*-hā* in *ṣāra lahā ṭabīʿatun*), i.e., plural, while *mā lā nafsa lahū* would have taken the masculine pronoun. And *lahā* does not refer back to *an-nabāt* either because of the intervening *bal*, which changes the subject to *al-anfus* (or *mā lā nafsa lahū*, as the case might be). In any case, it is clear from this plural pronoun that it refers to *al-anfus* and points to a reading of ἔχουσαι in Ψ; for the question is, what could have (mis)led the translator to assume that ψυχαί are somehow meant in the Greek, and the only thing I can think of is that he also read ἔχουσαι in his manuscript and the only plural feminine subject he could find was to assume somehow ψυχαί from the ἀψύχοις (or whatever else might have stood for it) in his source.

The Arabic evidence thus supports the reading ἔχουσαι but does not prove it, so we are back to the question of whether to accept or reject ἔχουσαι, and if the first, how so. Rejecting it would entail assuming some major corruption in the text which we would have no means of correcting. But the text in general seems to make sense along the general lines we have it, so it is worth considering how to explain ἔχουσαι. Facing the same problem as Isḥāq, the question we need to answer is what the plural feminine subject of the participle could be. The problem posed in this Aporia 22 (beginning at 10a22) is discussed in three diaporiae: In the first one (22.1, 10a28–10b7) Theophrastus asks the question about the τέλος of terrestrial and geological changes; in the second, introduced by ἔτι δέ (22.2, 10b7–20), he asks the same about animals, and in the third, also introduced by ἔτι δέ (22.3, 10b20–11a1), about plants and inanimate things. The first Diaporia (22.1) ends by asking about the purpose of the μεταβολαὶ καὶ φθοραὶ καὶ γενέσεις on and in the earth, and the second (22.2) by asking about the purpose of the variety of τροφὰς καὶ γενέσεις of animals—nouns which are all feminine plural. It is thus not far-fetched to assume that a feminine plural participle, especially when introduced by a sentence beginning with ἔτι δέ which would bring the other questions to mind, is referring to the same general feminine gender subjects, and perhaps specifically to μεταβολαί or γενέσεις (for elliptical ἔτι δέ sentences in a series in this Essay see 8b4); μεταβολαί, in particular, hovers in the air in the last part of the Essay and it recurs, in the same context and with reference to this passage, at 11b14–15, τὰ περὶ τὰς τῆς γῆς λεχθέντα μεταβολάς. Thus if it is assumed that the reader can see the word μεταβολαί or γενέσεις reflected in ἔχουσαι, the sentence in question can be most easily emended to read correctly by the addition of the nominative feminine plural article, ἔτι δ' ⟨αἱ⟩ ἐν τοῖς φυτοῖς καὶ μᾶλλον τοῖς ἀψύχοις ὡρισμένην τιν' ἔχουσαι φύσιν (*sc.* μεταβολαί or γενέσεις). The article would have fallen out through the similarity of sound, ε, in three consecutive vowels: in δ(έ), in the Middle Greek pronunciation of the article αἱ as unaspirated ε, and in ἐν—in a sense, all three ε sounds would be contracted into one in the resulting corrupt δ' ἐν. It is also almost certain that Theophrastus would have written δ' αἱ instead of δὲ αἱ to avoid at least one hiatus, though in his extant writings he tends to write δὲ αἱ three times as frequently as δ' αἱ. The hiatus at αἱ ἐν was unavoidable but excusable; in one passage Theophrastus actually writes, ἅπασαι δ' αἱ εὐώδεις (*HP* VII,9,4.10).

Beyond saving the reading of our oldest manuscripts, one further advantage of this emendation is that it includes φυτῶν γενέσεις in the ταῦτα of line 10b23. Because without this emendation, with the phrase ὡρισμένην τιν' ἔχουσι φύσιν taken to refer only to ἀψύχοις (Laks & Most 80n23), plants are left without any specific question having been asked about them. With the emendation proposed here, the purpose of the determinate nature of the generation of both plants and inanimates is questioned in the sentence. Furthermore, this emendation explains the source of the confusion of Isḥāq and the resulting mistranslation through the introduction of souls in the passage, as discussed above.

10b21 τιν'] The indefinite τιν' here following a participle with an adjectival function, has, in context, a strengthening effect. Cf. Smyth § 1268; Humbert § 29.

Aporia 23

10b24–11a1 (ἄπορον): *On spontaneous causation. These things must have a cause in something prior and nobler, whence the mechanistic view that appears credible, viz., that they come about spontaneously and through the rotation of the universe.*

For Theophrastus's hesitant attitude towards spontaneous generation, especially in plants, see Balme 1962.

10b24 αὐτὸ γὰρ τοῦτο ἄπορον] The expression αὐτὸ γὰρ τοῦτο provides a strong connection between the preceding and following sentence and points forward; the comma should come after ἄπορον. This is a further aporia in connection with teleology, though brief, but it is not parenthetical, as Ross translates. Cf. the parallel expression in Plato, *Symposium* 204a4, αὐτὸ γὰρ τοῦτό ἐστι χαλεπὸν ἀμαθία, τό ... δοκεῖν ... (cf. LSJ s.v. οὗτος VIII.1).

10b25 λόγον] In this reading of the text λόγος seems to mean a cause in the Aristotelian sense, especially formal and final; cf. Aristotle, *GA* 715a5–9, *PA* 639b14–16, *GC* 335b6–7.

10b25 δὴ ποιοῦσιν] The transmitted reading in the Greek manuscripts and Λ, μὴ ποιοῦσιν, is problematic, as Laks & Most 80n26 note. Ross's intepretation is difficult to maintain. First, as Laks & Most observe, reading ποιοῦσιν as masculine plural dative, presumably referring to some people, and sandwiching it between three neuter plural datives governed by ἐν, is more than "intolérable", it is quite impossible Greek. One would have at least expected an article to indicate the different nature of that dative (τοῖς ποιοῦσιν), otherwise normal when referring to groups of people (cf. Aristotle, *GC* 330b13–14, 17–18, οἱ ποιοῦντες, etc.). Even more to the point is that the sense of the passage requires ποιοῦσιν to be read as "agents" together with the other datives. If the sentence that follows begins with ᾗ, as emended, which means "for this reason," "on which account," then there must be something in this sentence to which ᾗ refers. With ποιοῦσιν read as "agents," the revolution of the universe mentioned in the following sentence finds its referent. Without it, there is no real reason why the assumption that plants and inanimates have no explanation should lead one to assume that everything is caused by the rotation of the heavens. Laks & Most's reading of the sentence is thus basically correct. The Arabic translation helps refine the reading. The phrase μὴ ποιοῦσιν is indeed problematic (and was accordingly considered corrupt by Usener 1861). The Arabic translation, however, does not have the negative particle but a word meaning "then" (*ṯumma*). Clearly Isḥāq read something other than μή in Ψ, and indeed something that made him break the sentence before ἐν ἑτέροις; in other words, a particle. The particle that fits best this context would be δή, which was taken by the translator in its temporal and connective rather than emphatic function (see, for example, the use of connective δή above at 10b27). Reading δή instead of μή makes for a smoother sentence and removes the need to assume the "indirect" influence which Laks and Most talk about but not explain.

10b27 ἄρα, "allegedly"] Theophrastus wants to distance himself from this view; cf. Denniston 38–39. Not, "after all" (Ross).

Aporia 24

11a1–11b27 (ληπτέον τινὰς ὅρους, διστασμός): *So if this does not come about for the sake of an end, we should identify and apprehend (in nature and the universe) the boundaries (within which teleology is applicable) and not apply it indiscriminately.*

Based on the epistemological principle enunciated earlier (Aporiae 19–20) that each class of objects has its proper method of being investigated, this crucial Aporia asks the main question of how to recognize and identify the boundaries existing in reality among the various classes of objects. The realization and apprehension of these boundaries (λαμβάνειν ὅρους, a key concept in Aristotelian and Theophrastean aporetic method—see the discussion in Part I, Chapter 1.3, and the comment below at 11a1), in connection with the teleological principle that states everything is for the best, will lead to investigating each thing by its proper method and avoid applying a principle such as teleology indiscriminately. The discussion of this aporia is wide-ranging and breaks down into three diaporiae. The first one, Diaporia 24, is marred by textual corruption toward the end, while the second, Diaporia 24.1, is particularly complex in its argumentation.

Diaporia 24 (11a1–26). *Indiscriminate application of teleology is inappropriate because the following statements are dubious both when said without qualification and with reference to each genus of things. Without qualification, when it is said that nature (a) always desires the best, and (b) gives a share in eternity and order to those things that can accept it. With reference to each genus, as in the case of animals, when it is said that (a) the better is never lacking wherever it is possible (e.g., the windpipe is in front of the oesophagus because it is nobler), and that (b) there is orderly arrangement (no examples given). The reason why the statements above are dubious, making indiscriminate application of teleology inappropriate, is that even if the desire of nature is for the best, it is nevertheless obvious that what neither obeys nor receives the good in nature is by far much more than what does. The animate part of nature is little, the inanimate infinite. Hence, and in general, the good is something little, the evil much.* (Corrupt text in the following three lines makes the flow of the argument unclear.) *Speusippus claimed that the noble, which is only about the center of the universe, is something rare. Though (?) the things that are happen to be good.*

For a discussion of the biological examples given here by Theophrastus (11a8–13) and their relation to the work of Aristotle see Lennox 1985, 149–155; Most 1988a, 229–231; Repici 1990, 197–200.

Diaporia 24.1 (11a27–b12). *(In contrast with Speusippus,) Plato and the Pythagoreans make the distance between the principles and the sensible world great, and posit that everything wishes to imitate fully (the first principles). And yet, (from this premise, and from the one that the principles are the best, one should not conclude that nature imitates the best, because, in fact,) Plato and the Pythagoreans posit two contrary principles, the one and the indefinite dyad, in the first of which reside order and determinacy and in the other lack of order and shapelessness, and accordingly the entire universe cannot dispense with this principle of indeterminacy which equals, if not even exceed, the other; hence the principles are contrary to each other. (The unstated conclusion is therefore that everything imitates or derives from the two principles together, both order and disorder, and accordingly Plato and the Pythagoreans avoid the philosophically indefensible position that "everything is for the best.") Because of this opposition in the first principles according to these philosophers, not even god is able to, or even would want to if he could, lead everything towards the best (and thus remove the principle of the indefinite dyad) because it would destroy the universe, whose very being consists in contraries.*

This is the second of the two testimonia in this work which inform us about Plato's unwritten doctrines: Testimonium Platonicum B3 in Isnardi Parente 1998 (with Italian translation and commentary), and cf. Isnardi Parente 1997, p. 394. Theophrastus provides here evidence for the dualist nature of Plato's system, "despite the monistic tendencies" (Happ 1971, 169 and n478). But the passage is also significant for the discussion about teleology, as mentioned above in the comment on Aporia 22. Vallance 1988, 31, argues for an understanding of Theophrastus "as a dyed-in-the-wool Aristotelian," while Botter 1999, 61–62, brings out Theophrastus's closeness, on the matter of teleology, to the Platonic and Academic position.

Though the overall trend of the argument in this diaporia is clear, as just summarized, its precise logic has been difficult to determine, primarily because there are many variables, and as each one shifts so does the overall meaning. There is first a problem with the context: because of the corruption in the immediately preceding paragraph, it has not been possible to say precisely in what light Theophrastus cast the ideas of Speusippus, and hence we do not know with what kind of rhetorical momentum he is now introducing the ideas of Plato and the Pythagoreans on teleology. Secondly there is a textual problem—indeed three; the result, obviously, of the indeterminacy of meaning I just described which may have occasioned scribal manipulation of the text. The first two have to do with the transmitted words ἐπιμιμεῖσθαι γ' at 11b1, and the third with δ' at 11b5.

Ἐπιμιμεῖσθαι, found in all Greek manuscripts, is a *hapax legomenon*, apparently, in the extant Greek writings up to the 14th century (according to the *TLG*), and thus either suspect or, if accepted, of indeterminate meaning. The Arabic and Latin translations, which both render it as "imitate", could point as the reading in Ψ and Λ to either ἐπιμιμεῖσθαι or μιμεῖσθαι, since they cannot (or do not) give the precise sense of the preposition in the compound verb. Some scholars tried to resolve the difficulty by assuming a hiatus between ἐπι and μιμεῖσθαι, but their suggestions (for which see the Supplementary Apparatus) appear arbitrary and beyond discussion. Laks & Most, following a suggestion by Allan, emended the compound verb to read ἐπεὶ μιμεῖσθαι, an emendation subsequently approved by both van Raalte and Henrich. My argument against it would be that the sense it yields is wrong. As van Raalte translates it, "Plato and the Pythagoreans ⟨hold⟩ the distance to be a great one, seeing that all things wish to imitate ⟨the good⟩." I would add in this translation, since van Raalte retains the particle γ' that follows the verb, "seeing that all things wish to imitate, at any rate, ⟨the good⟩." But this means, as Theophrastus allegedly presents it,[44] that Plato and the Pythagoreans believed the distance between the good and the sensible world to be great *because* all things wish to imitate the good; but this can hardly be imputed to Theophrastus—if anything, what is, or should be, meant is the converse: all things wish to imitate the good *because* they are separated by such a great distance from it. There is also the additional problem of the connection that is implied, through this emendation, between imitation and distance: if the emphasis in the first clause of this problematic sentence is on μακράν, it is not clear why imitation should imply great distance rather than any other kind of difference. The emendation, therefore, though palaeographically sound and plausible in itself, cannot stand.

The original reading ἐπιμιμεῖσθαι, even though a *hapax*, need not cause problems and can be retained. As for its meaning, it will have to be divined from the context, for the preposition ἐπί is very versatile in compound verbs. LSJ offer "imitate further," which I take it to mean "imitate additionally or besides," insofar as the concept of accumulation or addition is one of the commonest meanings of the preposition in compounds, as in ἐπιμανθάνω. But this would raise the question, in context, 'additionally to what?', and accordingly van Raalte (564n2) rightly disagrees; she suggests instead, "go as far as actual μίμησις," which is the meaning the preposition contributes in such compounds verbs as ἐπιτελεῖν. However, the general meaning of "up to a point" of the preposition in ἐπιτελεῖν does not mean "go as far as" but "go to the end of and actually finish" something.[45] This latter, then, is in this instance the meaning of ἐπί, for it functions to emphasize and intensify the root meaning of the verb; and hence ἐπιμιμεῖσθαι means "to imitate fully."

The problem of the particle that follows the verb, γ', attested in all the Greek manuscripts, is closely related to it. If the original ἐπιμιμεῖσθαι is retained, and since there is no other particle connecting the verb with the preceding clause, γ' can be taken in either of two senses, which are essentially one, epexegetic (Denniston 138) or quasi-connective and

---

[44] Acording to Laks & Most 86n54, the willingness by all things to imitate (the one) is presented by Theophrastus as an indication of the great distance between the one and the many, without which, γε implies, imitation would not be meaningful (see also van Raalte 566 and n. 3).

[45] Apparently basing themselves on this mistaken interpretation of the meaning of "up to a point" of ἐπί in compound verbs, Reale 1964, p. 205, and Isnardi Parente 1998, p. 15, mistranslate as "tendono ad imitare" and "tendenza all'imitazione," respectively.

explanatory, like γάρ (Denniston 144–145). To his credit, Isḥāq so took it, seeing a causal connection between the two clauses and translating, "because they thought that all things imitate it" (*bi-mā ra'awhu mina l-ašyā'i kullihā yataqayyaluhū*). It is clear that the translator saw the particle γ' in his exemplar (Ψ) and not ἐπεί because in the five other instances where ἐπεί occurs in this work it is translated differently: by *wa-ḏālika anna* (7b15, 9b17, 11a3), *min qibali anna* (4b22), and *fa-inna* (5b5). The lighter causal connection indicated by *bi-mā* (as opposed to the stronger expressions used for ἐπεί in the other passages) is thus due to his taking the particle γ' correctly in its epexegetic and quasi-connective sense. But if this is the meaning of the Greek sentence with γ', as also correctly understood by Isḥāq, then we have the same problem with regard to sense as we did with the proposed correction ἐπεί: the fact that people wish to imitate the good does not explain the great distance between them but rather, if anything, the opposite.

Ross tried to resolve the difficulty by emending the particle to read δ' (translating it as "but") and was pleased to note, in his review (Ross 1938) of the subsequent publication by Kley of Bartholomew's Latin translation, what he took as confirmation in the Latin text (*autem*) of his emendation. The problem, however, is that though *autem* does indeed occasionally translate δέ in Bartholomew's version, it also translates γε. The particle γε occurs fifteen times in Theophrastus's Essay, and in five of these it is translated as *autem* by Bartholomew.[46] There is thus little doubt that Bartholomew's exemplar (Λ) also had the same reading as that in the extant Greek manuscripts, ἐπιμιμεῖσθαι γ'. Nevertheless, Ross's thinking seems to be in the right direction, for a particle like δ' removes the causal connection between the two parts of the sentence which yields the objectionable *proteron-hysteron* meaning discussed above, and replaces it with a parataxis. But if δ' is difficult to defend on grounds both of transmission and palaeography, τ' could be most plausibly suggested as the original reading whose corruption to γ', common enough in Greek manuscripts, should be counted among the primitive errors in the Neoplatonic archetype. τ' also has the additional advantage that it removes any kind of connection between the great distance and imitation (even the slight adversative one implied by δ'), and simply states in sheer parataxis the two legs of the Platonic and Pythagorean position. In this context, the "great distance" (if, as suggested above, the emphasis in that

[46] At 8a13 and 14, 11a14, 11b1, and 11b12. In nine other passages it is not translated at all, and in the tenth, at 4b12, ἁμῶς γέ πως is rendered by *verum quodam modo*.

first clause is on μακρὰν) would be seen as forming a contrast with what preceded: if Speusippus located the noble, rare as it is, about the center of the universe, i.e., among us humans, Plato and the Pythagoreans by contrast put it at a great distance from us. The sentence then will read, μακρὰν τὴν ἀπόστασιν, ἐπιμιμεῖσθαι τ' ἐθέλειν ἅπαντα, and will depend, as Ross 74 suggests, on ποιοῦσιν, understood from ποιεῖ referring to Speusippus at 11a24.

This initial declaratory sentence, actually a categorical premise, and what follows it are best understood as a syllogistic argument. The clue to this is the word καίτοι (11b2), the adversative nature of which has been difficult to asses with precision. In syllogistic arguments of this sort, καίτοι usually introduces the major premise and the conclusion is usually left unexpressed (Denniston 561–563). In this case, the syllogism can be reconstructed when one keeps in mind the main subject of the entire Aporia 24, a discussion of the difficulties involved with the assumption of a teleological impetus for the best in nature (εἰς τὸ ἄριστον 11a2, εἰς τὸ βέλτιον ὁρμή 11b27). In this context, once Theophrastus utters his opening sentence about Plato and the Pythagoreans, which can be taken as the minor premise of a syllogistic argument (in a categorical syllogism), the rest would be formed as follows in the mind of his audience:

Minor: everything (ἅπαντα) imitates the principles (11a27–b1);
Major: the principles are the best (universally accepted premise);
Conclusion: therefore everything imitates the best.

This conclusion, however, is precisely what Theophrastus wishes to contest, or has been contesting, by pointing out in the preceding paragraphs the numerous aspects of nature, "everything" or reality, where this conclusion is not valid. What Theophrastus is arguing for is a conclusion that would state that nature imitates both the best and its contrary, because that is what can be observed empirically and because reality (οὐσία at 11b11) consists of contraries. In order to arrive at this conclusion, therefore, and given the minor premise which he has just expressed, he has to construct a different major premise, and this is precisely what the sentence beginning with καίτοι offers. The syllogistic argument that Theophrastus actually puts together, instead of the one most people would normally think of, as just stated, is the following:

Minor: everything (ἅπαντα) imitates the principles (11a27–b1);
Major: the principles are two contrary ones, one for order and one for disorder (11b2–7);
Conclusion: therefore everything imitates and includes both order and disorder (unexpressed but implied).

A final problem concerns the syntax of the passage containing the major premise and the conclusion, 11b2–7, centered around the presence or absence of particle δ' at 11b5. Ross 75 points out that καθάπερ at 11b2 can be taken either adverbially with ἀντίθεσίν τινα, in which case the clause beginning with ὅλως would be coordinated with it and require the particle δ' ("they create as it were some opposition ..., *and* it is altogether impossible ..."), or as introducing a subordinate clause which is answered by the main clause beginning with ὅλως, in which case the particle δ' has to be omitted ("as they make some opposition ..., *then* it is altogether impossible ..."). The manuscript transmission is clearly in favor of retaining δ'. The particle is omitted only in the Paris manuscript (P), while all three other independent winesses, JΨΛ, have it. Stemmatically this can only mean that P is mistaken and the other three correct, for it is difficult to assume that all three erroneously added the particle independently of each other, though Ross 75, strangely, claims precisely this.[47] The alternative, if one thinks that the absence of δ' is the correct and original reading, would be to assume that its inclusion was one of the primitive errors in the Neoplatonic archetype, that it was naturally copied in the subsequent exemplars JΨΛ, and that the editors of the text as it was redacted in the Paris manuscript excised it, recognizing its spuriousness. But it would be too much to assume that these editors, capable as they were, could actually perform the kind of analysis of the meaning of the text undertaken here. Besides, the whole passage beginning with καίτοι (11b2–7) which aims to introduce a new major premise, as discussed above, concludes with τὰς ἀρχὰς ἐναντίας, which *is* the major premise, and the clause introduced by δ' naturally fits into the progression of the argument leading to it.

Diaporia 24.2 (11b12–27). *Even among the first things one can observe many things (like the geological changes mentioned above) that are at random and thus happen not for the best or for the sake of some end, but comply with some sort of necessity. Among sensibles, the heavenly bodies possess order; among other things, the mathematicals, for in these the ordered is the greater part (unless one follows Democritus's understanding of the shapes of atoms).*

[47] Ross mentions as reason of the alleged confusion the "failure to notice the idiomatic use of the participle ποιοῦσιν" at 11b2, but I cannot see what he is aiming at; ποιοῦσιν is certainly not used as a participle in that sentence (cf. the commentary above at 10b25), but as the main verb on which depend all clauses, with εἶναι naturally understood after φύσιν at 11b6.

Concluding summary and re-statement of Aporia 24. *We should try and identify some boundary, both in nature and in the substance of the universe, both for the final cause and for the impulse for the best.*

11a1 εἰ δὲ μὴ τοῦθ'] This is the reading in all Greek manuscripts and the two translations. Usener 1890 punctuated after μή, changing the meaning of the sentence and the flow of the argument, and he was followed by all subsequent editors. The original reading was restored by Repici 1990. Repici's article is important for drawing attention to the meaning of λαμβάνειν ὅρους and ἀφορισμός in this Essay, namely, apprehending and identifying in nature and the universe the boundaries among things that exist objectively, and then basing our studies and analyses on these data rather than applying wholesale preconceived theories upon nature. The word ἀφορισμός is crucial in this Essay; Theophrastus wishes basically to mark the boundaries of the various disciplines, that is, identify the objects of study that are proper for each on the basis of discriminations that are provided by these objects themselves, and then find the appropriate method for their study.

11a3 ἁπλῶς] Laks & Most 81n30 and Henrich 149 make the distinction that the word ἁπλῶς, ("without qualification," "absolutely"), because of its position, may modify either the prepositional phrase ("for everything without qualification") or the verb ("posited without qualification") and ask themselves whether Theophrastus is emphasizing the quantity of teleological explanation (the former case) or its modality (the latter); they prefer the former. But given that, in essence, the one affects the other, I am not sure I see the distinction: qualifying the positing (θετέον) can only have meaning with reference to the objects for which these rules are posited, and hence it also qualifies the "everything" (πάντων). Thus in a way ἁπλῶς modifies both the prepositional phrase and the verb; the implication is, "We posit these two teleological principles not absolutely for absolutely everything, but absolutely for some things and in a qualified way for other things."

11a3 For ἐπεὶ καί, "for in fact," see Denniston 297.

11a5 ὅτι] It appears that ὅτι is causal or explanatory, meaning "because/when," i.e., something is the case. This meaning is required by, and explains, τοιάδε ἔχει τινὰ διστασμόν in 11a3–4, in which case the "irregularity" in the syntax seen by the translators (cf. van Raalte 544) disappears as the infinitives in the sentence reflect reported speech dependent on λέγεται which, in context, is clearly to be understood *after* ὅτι: ἁπλῶς μὲν ὅτι τὴν φύσιν ὀρέγεσθαι ⟨λέγεται⟩ καὶ μεταδιδόναι (i.e., one is *not* to read, ἁπλῶς μὲν ⟨λέγεται⟩ ὅτι τὴν φύσιν ὀρέγεσθαι, which ceates the problems with the following infinitives). To paraphrase what Theophrastus is saying, "there is some ambiguity in the following, both when they speak generally and with reference to particulars: generally, because/when they say that nature always desires the best ..., and with reference to particulars, because/when they say ...".

11a7–8 ὡς δ' αὐτό is the reading of Λ, the exemplar of the Latin translation (*ut hoc autem*), which seems preferable to αὐτά if only for reasons of stemmatic affiliation. J^II^, the only independent witness to have αὐτά, is nevertheless the later and restored text of the missing final bifolium of J, P has αύτος, which may be a corruption of an original αὐτό, while the Arabic translation cannot give conclusive evidence. It reads, *wa-ka-ḏālika yajrī l-amr*, "thus" (literally, "like this runs the case with ..."), which could translate either ὡς δ' αὐτό or ὡς δ' αὐτά; in addition, Isḥāq does not translate ὁμοίως at the end of the phrase, doubtless because he felt that *wa-ka-ḏālika yajrī l-amr* covered both adverbs: this is contrary to his practice because in all other instances of ὁμοίως in the Essay he renders it with *ʿalā miṯāl wāḥid* (see the Glossary). Thus *wa ka-ḏālika yajrī l-amr* must stand for both ὡς δ' αὐτά/-ό and ὁμοίως, and accordingly it is not possible to say what Isḥāq read in Ψ. Both αὐτό and αὐτά fit the context well by referring to the preceding teleological principles (either in the singular referring to the preceding ὅτι clause or in the plural referring to the two principles separately) which are next going to be applied to particular instances from the animal kingdom, as van Raalte 546 explains. The reading then, is, either ὡς δ' αὐτό ... ὁμοίως or ὡς δ' αὐτά ... ὁμοίως, a sentence which, when normally expressed, would read, ὁμοίως δ' ὡς αὐτὸ καὶ ἐπὶ τῶν ζῴων (the expression ὁμοίως ὡς is too common to need special documentation; see above the text at 8a3 and also cf. Theophrastus, *CP* IV,9,1.5). I prefer the former for stemmatic reasons.

As for the other transmitted reading, αὕτως, there is no good manuscript evidence for it; it is carried only by A, a manuscript representing a revised edition of the work (see Part I, Chapter 2.1). In addition, and regarding the style of the Greek text, the redundancy in having both ὡσαύτως and ὁμοίως in the same phrase would be almost intolerable, and the allegedly "loose" style of this Essay is no excuse (especially for someone who was nicknamed θεόφραστος). Besides, in the two other passages in this work where Theophrastus uses the adverb αὕτως together with the particle δ', he says ὡσαύτως δέ (6b5, 11a3) and does not split it as ὡς δ' αὕτως.

11a8 καὶ ἐπὶ τῶν ζῴων ὁμοίως ⟨λέγεται⟩ is understood here (see the second preceding comment). Having stated what the ἁπλῶς λεγόμενα are in 11a5–7, Theophrastus now proceeds to say what the καθ' ἕκαστα λεγόμενα are. Having mentioned in the former category the two absolute claims by those who make them, namely that nature [a] desires the best, and [b] bequeaths eternity and order, he engages in the second category to talk about individual cases for each one of the claims. He starts with [a] τὸ βέλτιον in lines 8–12 and then continues in line 13 with [b] κόσμος, which stands for τὸ ἀεὶ καὶ τὸ τεταγμένον in line 7, without, however, providing any examples for [b]. He may have considered the case as self-evident, though Wimmer was moved to suggest a lacuna after χάριν. Κόσμος is a more comprehensive and traditional term for τὸ τεταγμένον, while his complaint about the ἀκαριαῖον in line 18 indicates that he is including both τὸ ἀεὶ καὶ τὸ τεταγμένον in his discussion of κόσμος.

11a8 γάρ introduces the list of examples of the best arrangement of biological matter in nature; ὡσαύτως at the end of the parenthesis refers to the orderly arrangement of the same.

11a9 παραλείπειν] There is patent need to read the infinitive παραλείπειν here: the view presented is reported speech, which depends on the presumed λέγεται of the preceding sentence (and not, as Ross suggests, the ὅτι of the preceding sentence). For an author like Theophrastus, writing reported speech in infinitives if he is not sharing that view—and here he is clearly not—would be automatic and independent of how "polished" or "rough" his style in any work is.

11a13 κόσμου] Given τὸ τεταγμένον in line 7, it is clear that κόσμος here must be referring neither to ornaments nor to the universe ("the cosmos"), but to order as a teleological principle, eternally valid (cf. ἡ τοῦ κόσμου τάξις ἀΐδιός ἐστιν, Aristotle, *De Caelo* 296a33). A fragment attributed to Aristotle (Rose fr. 17) makes κόσμος an axiomatic principle permeating the world: the argument that there is only one ἀρχή hinges on the axiomatic truth that there must be κόσμος in the cosmos;

otherwise οὐκ ἔστι κόσμος ὁ κόσμος ἀλλ' ἀκοσμία. Bonitz *Index* 406a33 compares the similar notion in Plato, *Gorgias* 508A.

11a13 εἰ γὰρ καί … ἀλλ', "for if it is true that …, nevertheless," is a common style of argumentation, especially with Aristotle (e.g., *APo* 79a8, 87b28, 92b20; *Phys.* 225a27, 254a24; *DC* 307a4; *GC* 316b12; *Mete.* 358a32; *GA* 716a27; *Met.* K 11, 1067b32; *EE* 1227a1, etc.); Theophrastus himself uses it once more further below, at 11b20. The conditional protasis repeats or states a position that was being discussed, and the apodosis, beginning with ἀλλά, introduces an objection or exception to it. The particle γάρ is essentially epexegetic, explaining something that has been said; in this case it explains the word διστασμόν at 11a4: after the examples which corroborate the view that biological organisms do, in fact, exhibit excellent and orderly arrangement, γάρ introduces the reason why ambiguity exists about the universal applicability of this principle. The particle καί is asseverative (not "also" or "even"); it states what in fact the case may be, as described in the preceding discussion. The structure of this paragraph therefore is such that the main statement about the ambiguity concerning the universal applicability of the teleological principle (11a3–5) is followed by the reason for it in lines 11a13–18. The intervening lines provide the details and illustration of the original statement. This structure has not been properly understood and has accordingly led to a misunderstanding of the function of γάρ here; Tricot went even so far as to suggest emending it to δέ.

11a14 For ἀλλά … γε in apodosis see Denniston 12–13.

11a14 διότι here used as ὅτι; see Laks & Most 20n41 and van Raalte 552.

11a18 κἂν] Laks & Most are doubtless right in adopting the marginal correction by an anonymous "homo italicus" in the margin of the Florentine Riccardiana copy of the Gemusaeus (Oporinus) edition of this Essay. One of the arguments used by those who advance the doctrine of βέλτιον is that the animate is better than the inanimate (Aristotle, *GA* 731b29: τὸ δ' ἔμψυχον τοῦ ἀψύχου βέλτιον). Theophrastus is throwing this back at Aristotle, saying, this may be so (κἂν βέλτιον), but what good is it given the momentary nature (ἀκαριαῖον) of our existence? This is related to Theophrastus's complaint about the brevity of life in the saying attributed to him both by Cicero and the *Ṣiwān al-ḥikma* (Gutas 1985, 92–93).

11a18 δ'] We are here entering a passage that appears to be corrupt beyond redemption, and I indicate the corrupt places with an obelisk. With manuscript J missing the original page (even if it was replaced at the turn of the 14th century by its copy) and the evidence from the Arabic and Latin translations inconclusive, our oldest witness for the text is the Paris manuscript P, whose readings I give in the text. The precise meaning of δ' at this point depends on how one interprets the passage. For the different—valiant but, I believe, unsuccessful—attempts at restoration and interpretation of the text see the apparatus, the references below, the commentators, and Tarán 1981, fr. 83 and pp. 444–449. Since it is uncertain how the following phrases and clauses are to be connected to each other, I do not translate this and the following particles.

11a19 πλήθει] The error πλῆθος at the very beginning of this corrupt passage can be corrected with certainty. All the main Greek manuscripts (PJ^{II}CLA) read πλῆθος η, with varying accents and breathing signs on the ēta. The Arabic translation also reflects the word πλῆθος in the nominative but disregards the following *ēta* (*wa-r-radī'u kaṯīru l-ʿadadi*, "the evil is much in number" = πολὺ δὲ πλῆθος τὸ κακόν). The nominative πλῆθος also appears in the Latin translation, *multitudo est*, where the second word, *est*, must reflect how Bartholomew understood the *ēta* after πλῆθος. This error is accordingly one of the primitive errors of the Neoplatonic archetype (Part I, Chapter 2.5). The correction is simple and it was proposed by Laks & Most, who read πλήθει for πλῆθος η. The dative of respect in πλήθει is common after words indicating amount, and the very expression πλήθει πολύ (i.e., "much/many as to number") is found elsewhere in Theophrastus (*HP* IV,2,1.13 and IV,2,5.16) and also in Aristotle (*HA* 581a5: γίνονται δὲ πλήθει πολλοί). It is even more common in Plato (e.g., ὄντα πολλὰ πλήθει *Phaedo* 111a2), one of whose favorite phrases is, ἄπειρον πλήθει, as in ἄπειρον δὲ πλήθει τὸ μὴ ὄν (*Sophist* 256e6). Would this latter Platonic maxim resonate in Theophrastus's sentence here?

As for the error itself, I would think it was occasioned by the neuter form πολύ at the beginning of the sentence, following which some scribe changed the dative πλήθει to the nominative πλῆθος to agree with it. The following *ēta* in the manuscripts is difficult to account for. Usener 1861, pp. 279–280, suggested that it is an abbreviation for εἶναι, but that, as Ross 74 explains, can be the case only if one reads ει instead of η, and ει is present only in the later manuscripts, i.e., RBHD in Ross. But RBHD derive ultimately from J, which has the *ēta*, and thus the corruption went from *ēta* to *epsilon iota* and not the other way around as Ross suggests. The abbreviation theory explaining *ēta*, then, can hardly be correct. It may be that the *ēta* in the oldest Greek manuscripts represents the original ending of πλήθει, after it was corrupted to πλῆθος, miswritten in a marginal note as η instead of ει and eventually incorporated into the main text. But there can be no certainty.

11a20 οὐκ] The Arabic omits or does not translate οὐκ, but rather has something which would seem to indicate that he read or understood the relative οὗ in its stead, reading, πλῆθος τὸ κακὸν οὗ ἡ ἀοριστία μόνον: *wa-r-radīʾ kaṯīr al-ʿadad wa-ḫurūj hāḏā* (*sc.*, *ar-radīʾ*) *ʿan al-ḥadd faqaṭ*, "evil is great of number and the departure of this (*sc.* of evil) from limit only," where, as is frequently the case, *ḫurūj ʿan*, "departure from," translates the *alpha privativum* in ἀοριστία.

11a22–23 καὶ γάρ … Σπεύσιππος] καὶ γάρ is well attested in the oldest Greek manuscripts, while εἰ γὰρ καί and καί in C and L respectively would appear to be scribal emendations for the impossible εἰ καὶ γάρ in P and J. Sylburg's emendation of ει και to εἰκῆ fails to convince both because of the sense and because of the syntax. As Laks & Most note (84n48), Theophrastus cannot be accusing Speusippus of "arbitrary" speech if he thinks that the theory about the center position of the noble is plain wrong (if this theory is interpreted cosmologically, i.e., as referring to the central position of the world-fire), or even less so, if he thinks that the theory about the center position of the noble is right (if this theory is interpreted ethically and is similar to that of Aristotle: see Tarán 1981, 444–449, and the parallel passages). To say nothing of the fact that it is inconceivable that Theophrastus could have used an expression like "a most ignorant person" (ἀμαθέστατος) to describe, however indirectly, Speusippus. Syntactically, the sentence as reconstructed with εἰκῆ and accepted by Ross (and then by Tarán 1981), is incomplete. It does not mean, as Ross, translates, "For quite random is the talk of those who speak of the whole of reality as Speusippus does when he makes the valuable element to be something scanty, namely, what is found in the region of the centre of the universe;" if that were the meaning of the sentence it should have read not as transmitted but instead as, εἰκῆ γὰρ οἱ περὶ τῆς ὅλης οὐσίας λέγουσιν ὥσπερ Σπεύσιππος, σπάνιόν τι τὸ τίμιον ποιῶν τὸ περὶ τὴν τοῦ μέσου χώραν. The corruption stands: see the following comment. For the Speusippus fragment itself see also the texts and commentaries in fr. III 41 Lang, fr. 83 Tarán 1981, fr. 71 Isnardi Parente 1980.

11a22–25 καὶ γάρ ... ἑκατέρωθεν] The sentence has no finite verb in the Greek manusctipts and in Λ. In Arabic, Isḥāq understood the verb referring to Speusippus, ποιεῖ, as the main verb and apparently interpreted it as ποιοῦσι. It is not clear whether this was also the reading in Ψ. Given our lack of certainty about what precisely the issues in question here are because of the corrupt text, it would be rash to supply a verb according to sense (οὕτως ὑπολαμβάνουσιν or ποιοῦσιν Laks & Most 84n48, λέγουσιν van Raalte 559).

11a25 μὲν οὖν] Since we do not know the precise sense of this corrupt passage, the connecting particle combination, μὲν οὖν, is ambiguous, for it could be either adversative (corrective to previous statements) or assentient (cf. Denniston 479–480), and it has accordingly been interpreted in both ways (Ross 74 vs. van Raalte 563, depending on the interpretation given to the passage). Again, I do not translate. It is certain, however, that μὲν οὖν rounds out the discussion of the preceding paragraph and points forward to the δέ in the next sentence introducing the views of Plato and the Pythagoreans.

11a25 ἔτυχεν] If this brief sentence is indeed an expression of Theophrastus's own views, then the fortuitous element implicit in ἔτυχεν needs to be made explicit in view of ὡς ἔτυχεν further down (11b14). Cf. Laks & Most "se trouve être" vs. Ross "is and always has been."

11b1 ἐπιμιμεῖσθαι τ'] τ' is my correction from the transmitted γ'. See the discussion following Diaporia 24.1 above.

11b1 ἐθέλειν, "wish," indicating natural tendency and disposition rather than actual desire; see the passages assembled by van Raalte 567–568.

11b2 Logical καίτοι ("and yet") here introduces the major premise of the syllogistic argument. See the discussion following Diaporia 24.1 above.

11b2 ἀντίθεσιν] It is is interesting to note that the Latin translation has *compositionem* for this word, suggesting a Greek original σύνθεσιν. This may well have been the reading of Λ, if it was not a marginal comment incorporated into the text, because both ἀντίθεσιν and σύνθεσιν would actually mean, in context, the same thing. As analyzed above in the discussion of Diaporia 24.1, the argument Theophrastus is making is that the first principle for Plato and the Pythagoreans is actually two, one for order and one for disorder, and as such they are antithetical, and hence the original reading of the text (ἀντίθεσιν); but they also work together as a team to "produce" all reality, with its ordered and disordered aspects, and thus present a synthesis at the highest level of principles, and hence the "correction" or marginal note of σύνθεσιν in Λ.

11b5 δ'] Only P omits the particle δ' here. See the discussion following Diaporia 24.1 above.

11b12 The word ἐν, added by scribes to manuscripts L and B, was present in Ψ.

11b16 κατακολουθεῖν with the dative, "to comply with or obey" (cf. LSJ), harks back to ὑπακοῦον at 11a15. The infinitive indicates that it continues to be indirect speech dependent on "appear", φαίνεται, in 11b12.

11b17–19 Μάλιστα ... οὐράνια] This passage was used by Steinmetz 1964, 158, to dispute Theophrastus's adherence to the theory of ether, and was criticized by Gottschalk 1967, 23; see also Happ 1971, 764n418, and the comment on Aporia/Diaporia 10 above. For an analysis of the passage as it relates to Democritus see Henrich 317–320.

11b20 εἰ γὰρ καί ... ἀλλά] See above at 11a13.

11b23–24 ἀλλὰ δή ... μέν ... ὃ δ' ἐξ ἀρχῆς] The ἀλλὰ δή sentence completes the previous thought; it does not start a new paragraph as originally printed by Usener 1890 and then, following him, by all the editors. The particle combination is resumptive, brushing aside the brief (and irrelevant?) digression of the mention of Democritus (cf. Denniston 241). As Theiler 1958, 102 / 292, remarks, and van Raalte 584–585 amply documents, ἀλλὰ δή is a typically Theophrastean way of wrapping up a previous argument before moving on to the next point, here marked by the particle, δ', which summarizes the main and original (ἐξ ἀρχῆς; cf. LSJ, s.v. ἀρχή I.1.b) question of Aporia 24 at 11a1–3. Τούτων in this line thus refers back to the question of the amount of order possessed, respectively, by the heavenly bodies and mathematicals, which are prior with regard to order. They all are, Theophrastus says, subsidiary subjects for further research.

Aporia 25

11b27–12a2 (ἐν τίσιν, πῶς): *The initial aporia in the study of the universe is this: (to determine) among what (different sets of) things all beings belong and how they relate to each other.*

The final aporia restates the initial one in a comprehensive manner, as a result of the investigation throughout the Essay. The question is to determine the different categories—intelligibles, mathematicals, sensibles, and the different sub-categories of each—into which all beings belong and the ways in which they are connected and associated with each other, in order to understand how all reality works. The initial aporiae were asking about the boundaries of the categories or sets of things in which the first principles belong, but given the connectedness of all reality, which is the leitmotif of the Essay (see Part I, Chapter 1.4), the final restatement focuses on the study of the universe and hence on the assignment of all beings to their proper categories. For the use of the preposition ἐν in this context (ἐν τίσιν τὰ ὄντα;) see the comment on 4a17–18.

Scholium

12b4 οἷον προδιαπορίαι] The term προδιαπορία bears some investigation, for it is not a common term. As a matter of fact, it is a *hapax legomenon*: this is the only recorded instance of the word. LSJ list it in the latest (1996) *Supplement* only (defining it as "preliminary problems") and refer to its use in this scholium alone, while the *TLG* shows no record of it at all up to the 12th century (apparently this scholium was not copied in their data-base). It is not so much its meaning that is problematic as its usage, which requires some analysis.

It is a doubly compound word, with the προ- prefix clearly intending to signify "preliminary," as everybody agrees. Removing this prefix for the moment, we are left with the word διαπορία, which is the base upon which the προ- was added. Now διαπορία itself is not a common word. Again, for the period up to the 12th century the *TLG* lists only 14 occurrences. It derives from the verb διαπορέω, which is much more common, and which means, with the preposition διά adding the sense of intensity and completion, "to raise and run through problems/aporiae thoroughly," or, in common usage, a more intensive form of ἀπορέω (cf. LSJ; Bonitz *Index* 187b11 defines Aristotle's use of the word as, διέρχεσθαι τὰς ἀπορίας). The verbal noun, raising such a question, was διαπόρησις, while διαπόρημα and not διαπορία was the noun derivative from this verb (as in the title of Theophrastus's lost work, Περὶ τῶν ἁπλῶν διαπορημάτων, Diog. Laert. V,46 = fr. 1,178 FHS&G, or even Aristotle's own reference to the aporiae in *Met.* B as διαπορήματα, *Met.* M 2, 1076a39–b1, etc.). Διαπορία in the sense of διαπόρημα or even διαπόρησις (a vexed or difficult questioning), was not used or used very rarely, and hence its very low incidence in ancient literature. Exceptionally, Epicurus used the word διαπορίαι as the title of one of his books, and this accounts for eight of the fourteen occurrences of the word mentioned above; it was a good choice by Epicurus for it was distinctive in that it was a term not in use. Of all extant ancient literature the only place where διαπορία occurs outside of Epicurus is in Aristoxenus's *Harmonics* (62,13), where it appears to be used like ἀπορία. Of the remaining five recorded uses, one occurs in Galen and four in late antiquity. It is again surprising that the voluble Galen used it only once in all his extant writings, together with πλάναι to refer to the difficult problems faced by physicians (*De plac. Hipp. et Plat.* IX.1.4,2); clearly it was a rare term not in use either in medical or philosophical parlance in his time.

On the other hand, the uses of the word in late antiquity are instructive,[48] for they are philosophical: they occur in the *Metaphysics* commentary of Syrianus (*In Met.* 29.17 Kroll [*CAG*]) and the *De anima* commentary of (Ps.-) Simplicius (*In De an.* 24,1 and 24,6 Hayduck [*CAG*]).[49]

This philosophical use and the reference to Aristotle are crucial for our purposes. Διαπορέω, of course, is a key term in Aristotelian dialectic method, and Book B, the aporetic book par excellence of his *Metaphysics*, starts off with a first chapter built around the term (995a28, 35, and 996a17). The subject itself is well known, but what is important is that Syrianus and (Ps.-)Simplicius use the noun διαπορία, in the pas-

---

[48] With the exception of the one Christian occurrence in John Climacus, *Scala Paradisi*, ch. 7, col. 809, line 41, where it is apparently used in its Middle Greek sense of "doubt," like διαπόρησις.

[49] Blumenthal summarizes the literature that discusses the spuriousness of the attribution to Simplicius, but this does not affect my argument here; whoever the author was, he was one of the "Neoplatonists who worked in Athens at the end of the fifth century and the beginning of the sixth." See H.J. Blumenthal, "Some Notes on the Text of Pseudo-Simplicius' Commentary on Aristotle's *De Anima*, III.1–5," in M. Joyal, ed., *Studies in Plato and the Platonic Tradition* [Esays Presented to John Whittaker], Ashgate: Aldershot, 1997, 213–214. See also H.J. Blumenthal, *'Simplicius.' On Aristotle, On the Soul 3.1–5*, London: Duckworth, 2000, 1–7.

sages just indicated, precisely in the same way as Aristotle uses the verb διαπορέω in Met. B—Syrianus, as a matter of fact, expressly calls Book B διαπορητικόν (διαπορητικὸν γάρ ἐστιν ὅλον τὸ B, 1,19–20 Kroll). In other words, Simplicius and the Neoplatonists of late antiquity used διαπορία as the noun for that verb, and this apparently for the first time. What is astonishing is that there is no record of this usage of the noun any time during the nine centuries separating Aristotle and these late antique philosophers, despite the extensive philosophical—and indeed, Aristotelian philosophical—Greek that has survived. In this instance the argument from silence is valid, it seems. I draw the conclusion that διαπορία rather than διαπόρημα or διαπόρησις became current in late antiquity among the Neoplatonic commentators as the noun for διαπορέω precisely because it began to be used as a technical term in the Aristotelian sense.

If that is the case, it has implications for the Scholium at the end of Theophrastus's Essay. In the first place, the word προδιαπορία which we see in the Scholium would appear to be a neologism either on the part of the author of the Scholium or his circle. If διαπορία in the restricted technical Aristotelian sense had little currency in late antiquity, then προδιαπορία must have hardly had any, and there is justification in seeing it as a neologism.[50] As a matter of fact, just as διαπορία was used as the noun for διαπορέω in the Aristotelian sense by the Neoplatonic commentators, so also was προδιαπορία derived from the verb προδιαπορέω as its noun. The verb προδιαπορέω itself was very rarely used: we have only three recorded occurrences. The first is in Apollodorus Dyscolus (see LSJ), and the other two, again significantly for our purposes, are in the works of the Neoplatonic philosophers, both in the Aristotelian sense of a preliminary run-through of problems. Philoponus writes (*In An. pr.* 42.35 Wallies [*CAG*]), τούτων ἡμῖν ... προδιηπορημένων, ἄξιόν ἐστι καὶ τάς ... ἀπορίας ἐπιλύσασθαι; and Damascius (*In Parm.* 169,6 Ruelle), Περὶ τῆς τρίτης τῶν νοερῶν διακοσμήσεως τάδε προδιαπορητέον, ἓν μέν ... .

In addition, προδιαπορία would appear to be a slightly redundant term, and this redundance would also speak for its neologism status in

[50] That (προ)διαπορία in this sense was not used before the Neoplatonists in late antiquity is also indicated, however circumstantially, by the variant προδιαπορήσεις in manuscript A of the Essay for the original προδιαπορίαι (P) in this Scholium (see the apparatus). Manifestly the scribe of A did not know the neologism προδιαπορία and wrote the usual προδιαπορήσεις instead.

late antiquity (as languages develop, redundant use of prepositions and adverbs increases). It is redundant because the Aristotelian διαπορία by itself implies a *preliminary* consideration of a problem. At the very beginning of *Met.* B, where Aristotle establishes the importance of διαπορέω, he writes (995a27–30), ἔστι δὲ τοῖς εὐπορῆσαι βουλομένοις *προὔργου* τὸ διαπορῆσαι καλῶς· ἡ γὰρ ὕστερον εὐπορία λύσις τῶν *πρότερον* ἀπορουμένων ἐστί. Προὔργου, which refers to διαπορῆσαι, means doing something in advance for the furtherance of a project, and the πρότερον ἀπορούμενα are the objects of διαπορῆσαι. Nine centuries later, (Ps.-) Simplicius does exactly the same, using διαπορία in a way which indicates that it is a preliminary undertaking. Commenting on Aristotle's use of διαποροῦντας in *DA* 403b20 (a passage, incidentally, parallel to the one from *Met.* B cited above), (Ps.-)Simplicius writes, Διὰ τὸ μὴ αὐτόθεν ἡμῖν τὴν τῶν πραγμάτων προσπίπτειν ἀλήθειαν, ... προηγεῖται ἡ ζήτησις καὶ ἡ πρὸς τὰ ἀντικείμενα ἡμῶν φορὰ καὶ τούτων διαπορία.[51] Finally, there is the evidence in favor of the neologism status of the word provided by the use of the word οἷον before it; the scholiast says, οἷον προδιαπορίαι. Οἷον here cannot cast doubt upon or qualify the προδιαπορία nature of the work of Theophrastus—in good Aristotelian fashion the Essay is a work raising problems about issues of first principles in a thorough manner in order to further their eventual resolution; it is not a work that "sort of raises," or that "can be considered to raise" problems.[52] Laks & Most, p. xvi, suggest, with reference to Stephanus's *Thesaurus*, that οἷον here might be an annotator's mark. But the word here is not used in a gloss and does not refer to a specific passage in the Essay, which is the proper usage of a glossator's οἷον. Thus οἷον in this context would appear to point to a self-conscious use of the term προδιαπορία by the scholiast, aware of its novelty.

And this brings us to the date in which the last sentence of the Scholium was written. If προδιαπορία, which may be a neologism as it occurs in the Scholium, is based on the use of διαπορία and προδιαπορία as an Aristotelian technical term only in late antiquity, then this sentence was composed in late antiquity.[53] And if this term was current among

---

[51] J.O. Urmson translates: "Since the truth about the facts does not fall spontaneously into our laps, ... first must come a search and our movement towards the opposed opinions, and the raising of the problems about them;" in *Simplicius. On Aristotle's On the Soul 1.1–2.4*, Ithaca, N.Y.: Cornell University Press, 1995, 40.

[52] As interpreted by Laks & Most, p. xvi, "en quelque sort," and by Hecquet-Devienne 2004, p. 174, "what may be considered to be."

[53] On the strength of an argument based on the order occupied by the Essay among

the philosophers and commentators of the time, then it must have been composed by somebody in their circle. This conclusion is corroborated by the accuracy of the description of Theophrastus's Essay as a διαπορία, or προδιαπορία. The person who made this evaluation knew his Aristotle and he could associate the Aristotelian methodological procedure of διαπορεῖν, as set forth in *Met.* B and mentioned elsewhere (see the frequent use of the verb in Bonitz *Index*), with the actual performance of Theophrastus. Modern scholarhip is gradually coming around to appreciate this evaluation of Theophrastus's Essay. See the discussion in Part I, Chapter 1.1–3, on the date and nature of the work and the Scholium.

Aristotle's works in the Paris manuscript (P), and the athetization of Book Alpha of Aristotle's *Metaphysics* from some manuscripts in the medieval Arabic and Latin translations (on the grounds that the Scholium at the end of the Essay restored Book Alpha and not the Essay itself to Theophrastus), Jaeger 1932, 290–292, came to the conclusion that the author of the Scholium was the editor of the Roman edition of the works of Aristotle. Valuable as this argument is, it cannot be maintained in view of our current knowledge of the history of the texts preserved in the Paris manuscript as analyzed by Hecquet-Devienne 2004, 184–189. For his part, Theiler 1958, 102 / 292, simply guessed, without argument, that the whole Scholium was probably composed by Nicolaus of Damascus.

APPENDIX

"KNOWN BY BEING UNKNOWN" (9a18–23)

There is considerable uncertainty about what and whom Theophrastus is referring to in this passage. The general brevity of his style in this work, the presence of the paradoxical but philosophically cute phrase γνωστὰ τῷ ἄγνωστα εἶναι, and the existence of a variant in a crucial part of the argument (ὁρατόν/ἀόρατον, 9a23), have indeed made the passage "notoriously" difficult to understand and translate (van Raalte 435).

The crux of the matter is to understand precisely what the people who used the phrase γνωστὰ τῷ ἄγνωστα εἶναι meant (and what Theophrastus understood by it). Since Theophrastus does not specify who said it (καθάπερ τινές φασιν) and how they meant it, we can only proceed by trying to see what Theophrastus is actually saying in this passage and eliminating the impossible interpretations.

First it is necessary to eliminate the impossible interpretation given by Ross, which appears unfortunately to have confused the issue much more than helped it. Ross (followed by Laks & Most) read this passage by Theophrastus in the light of the sophistry mentioned by Aristotle in the *Rhetoric* (1402a4–7): ἐπιστητὸν τὸ ἄγνωστον, ἔστιν γὰρ ἐπιστητὸν τὸ ἄγνωστον ὅτι ἄγνωστον ("the unknown is known, for the unknown is known to be unknown"). Ross 68 thus interprets the whole passage in Theophrastus as a flippant sophistry and "a mere play on words" ("une position extrême, ou « éristique »", Laks & Most 68n36).

Looked at closely, however, it is seen that the sophistry in the *Rhetoric* passage is not what Theophrastus is talking about here. First, the sophistry itself is not about the *manner* (τρόπος) of knowing the different classes of being—Theophrastus's express purpose here—but rather is intended to prove and maintain, and indeed in a paradoxical way, that nothing is unknown, that the unknown does not exist: if we know that something is unknown, our mere knowledge that it is unknown makes it known and hence there is no unknown: the unknown does not exist epistemologically and, conversely, this would seem to imply (though it is not stated either by Aristotle or Theophrastus), that if we do not know that something is unknown, it does not exist anyway because our mere lack of knowledge that it is unknown makes it epistemologically non-existent.[1]

Second, the sophistry, a play on words as it is, is not about the manner or respect in which, or the means by which, we may come to know the unknown—again, Theophrastus's express purpose here—but rather about our knowledge *that* the unknown is unknown. But Theophrastus calls knowing τῷ ἄγνωστα εἶναι an ἴδιος τρόπος (9a20) of knowledge, while it is clear that knowledge *that* the unknown is unknown is not a τρόπος of knowledge but itself a piece of knowledge (arrived at, presumably, after a certain τρόπος has been employed).

Third, a comparison between the text of Theophrastus and that of Aristotle's sophistry corroborates the previous two points: Theophrastus says that some people claim that some things are known τῷ ἄγνωστα εἶναι. The dative here is almost certainly instrumental, or possibly of respect; it is in any case clear that it is identical with αὐτῷ τῷ ἀγνώστῳ at 9a22, which is parallel in meaning to the *κατά* in κατ' ἀναλογίαν, which in turn is identical to the datives in the previous passage, 9a5–6. There is no doubt that what Theophrastus means is that some things are known through or by means of or with respect to (τῷ) their epistemogical status or quality as unknown (τῷ ἄγνωστα *εἶναι*; cf. Henrich 134); the sophistry says that they are known *that* (ὅτι) they are unknown. It thus seems unavoidable to suppose that had Theophrastus had in mind the sophistry mentioned by Aristotle, he would have said at 9a19, γνωστὰ *ὅτι* ἄγνωστα εἶναι.

Fourth, in order for the parallelism between the known and seen things to hold up in Ross's 68 reconstruction of the argument, Ross has to interpret ἔνια at 9a18 as if it meant τὰ ἄγνωστα. But reading this word in the context of this entire paragraph, there can be little doubt that ἔνια refers to the objects of knowledge whose proper manner of investigation is being sought; i.e., the Greek would presumably be, ἔνια ⟨ὧν ζητεῖται ὁ οἰκεῖος τρόπος τοῦ ἐπίστασθαι⟩, viz., the list of things enumerated in lines 9a12–15, from the first to the inanimate things. These are simply beings as objects of knowledge, τὰ γνωστά in the descriptive sense (or, in logical terms, *simpliciter*), without reference to their inherent or actual epistemic status (i.e., to their modality as either possible or necessary objects of knowledge): things that we would like

[1] In a similar fashion, Merlan 1968, 188 note *, criticizes Ross's interpretation by pointing out that "Theophrastus is speaking of a whole class of things ... and not at all of sophisms as Aristotle does."

to know about and for which reason we are seeking the proper method of doing so (just as, e.g., τὰ αἰσθητά in the title of Aristotle's Περὶ αἰσθήσεως καὶ αἰσθητῶν is to be taken: study of things that are objects of sense perception, without reference to their inherent or actual capacity of being sensed). Thus it seems very inappropriate to call these things τὰ ἄγνωστα since Theophrastus does not intend to portray them as such. The same applies to the (un)seen thing at 9a23: with one exception, the manuscripts have all τὸ ὁρατόν; Ross's preferred reading τὸ ἀόρατον in manuscript A only is clearly a scribal correction, to be disregarded, apparently introduced for the same reason that prompted modern editors to effect the same emendation (for this manuscript see Part I, Chapter 2.1, section on "Sub-family Σ"). Accordingly, both words necessary for Ross's interpretation to work, a presumed τὰ ἄγνωστα at 9a18 and an actual τὸ ἀόρατον at 9a23, are neither attested nor implied in Theophrastus's text.

Fifth, and perhaps most importantly, in order to make rhetorical sense, the phrase that Ross wants to read at 9a23, τῷ ἀοράτῳ ⟨ὁρατὸν⟩ τὸ ἀόρατον (instead of τῷ ἀοράτῳ ⟨ὁρατὸν⟩ τὸ ὁρατόν, the transmitted reading), must provide, by analogy, the absurd consequence of the position of something being γνωστὸν τῷ ἀγνώστῳ. That is, the rhetorical argument would go as follows: if someone maintains that the unknown is known by being unknown (τῷ ἄγνωστον εἶναι γνωστὸν ⟨τὸ ἄγνωστον⟩, as Ross wants to read it), then he must also maintain that the unseen can be seen by being unseen (τῷ ἀόρατον εἶναι ⟨ὁρατὸν⟩ τὸ ἀόρατον, as Ross wants to read it), and since this latter position is manifestly absurd, so must the former. But this rhetorical *reductio ad absurdum* cannot be accomplished by adopting the reading τὸ ἀόρατον in line 9a23 simply because τῷ ἀόρατον εἶναι ⟨ὁρατὸν⟩ τὸ ἀόρατον makes as good (perverse and sophistical) sense as τῷ ἄγνωστον εἶναι γνωστὸν ⟨τὸ ἄγνωστον⟩ (as Ross would have it): to follow Ross, who rephrased this interpretation accurately (p. 68), to say that the unknown "can be known because it can be known to be unknown ... would be like saying that the unseen can be seen because it can be seen to be unseen." Now to someone who accepts as a valid manner of knowledge of the unknown the proposition that the unknown can be known because it can be known to be unknown, the proposition that follows, that the unseen can be seen because it can be seen to be unseen, must appear equally valid; in other words, the latter proposition is not inherently or even in context absurd, and thus it canot have the intended effect, to show by analogy the untenability of the former.

Because of all these reasons, Ross's interpretation cannot stand. Another major interpretation that has been offered is also difficult to defend. Merlan's 1968, 187–189, thesis that Theophrastus is here referring to what was later to become the Neoplatonic theory of *docta ignorantia* has two main problems, the text of Theophrastus itself, which can hardly be translated as Merlan does (187–188), and the fact that Theophrastus talks about knowledge "by being unknown" as if it were of the same order as knowledge by analogy and not, as Merlan would have it, as the *via negationis*, the negation of all positive forms of knowledge (see further below on this aspect and the references to the work of Krämer).

With the sophistical and the "Neoplatonic" interpretations eliminated, we come back to the question of the precise meaning of the phrase γνωστὰ τῷ ἄγνωστα εἶναι. First, and to eliminate another misconception, the existence of the word εἶναι in this formulation makes it clear that both in this phrase (at 9a19) and in the phrase αὐτῷ τῷ ἀγνώστῳ further down (at 9a22), the term ἄγνωστον denotes an attribute, or a quality, and not an object (as already noted by Henrich 134, pace van Raalte 439–440). The phrase thus means, "some things are known by way of/through their very attribute of being unknown/unknowable."[2] In order to know something about these things, then, one has to employ this attribute of theirs, their unknownness. The only positive signification that I can find for this statement (apart from being a mere verbal paradox, which, as discussed, is to be excluded) is that it means that some things cannot be known directly, and hence some knowledge of them can be gained by indirect means and in an indirect manner, perhaps by some kind of similarity or relationship that exists between the unknown object and something we know: it would seem this is what Theophrastus himself may be referring to when he says at 4b12–13, εἴτε κατ' ἀναλογίαν εἴτε κατ' ἄλλην ὁμοίωσιν, bringing together again the method by analogy in close proximity to some other method, as in this passage. Τῷ ἀγνώστῳ would thus seem to be some other kind of ὁμοίωσις, or at least Theophrastus would seem to be considering it as such, an indirect means of gaining access to the unknown object.

[2] The distinction between unknown and unknowable may well be, as van Raalte 436 observes, a problem for English, which makes it, and not for Greek, which does not, with its single term ἄγνωστος for both meanings. In any case, it is inconsequential in this discussion. The reader should concentrate on thinking about γνωστόν and ἄγνωστον in Greek.

We do not know what the people who said this meant precisely by this indirect manner. But Theophrastus, who thought in terms of the discussions conducted in Aristotle's circle, had a very clear idea about what the manners (τρόποι) of knowing were. He mentions them, with regard to knowledge of identity, in the list of διαιρέσεις he provides at 9a5–6, a list which echoes that of Aristotle in *Metaphysics* Δ 6, 1016b31–1017a3. Now Theophrastus says that this manner of knowing, viz., through the object's attribute of being unknown, would be another separate way of knowing and it would need to be placed in some scheme of such διαιρέσεις (9a20–21). But, he adds, it would be more *appropriate* to call (οἰκειότερον λέγειν) this manner of knowing knowledge "by analogy" (κατ' ἀναλογίαν) rather than "through the very attribute of being unknown." This means, first, that knowledge through unknownness is of the same genus as knowledge by analogy, and second, that knowledge by analogy somehow covers the same area as, and is parallel to, knowledge by unknownness. Thus Theophrastus would seem to be saying that, although knowledge by unknownness may be acceptable in some cases,[3] in others knowledge by analogy would be a more appropriate term to cover the same manner of knowing. Thus we may guess that the people who said that something is known by its being unknown indicated thereby an indirect manner (or indirect manners) of knowledge of some objects without apparently either specifying this manner (these manners?) more precisely or using a more intelligible (and less paradoxical) term. Thus Theophrastus's objection is not so much to the manner of knowledge itself—the fact that he is willing to accord to this manner its proper διαίρεσις and the reservations expressed at 9a21 clearly prove this—as to its appellation. He seems to be saying that the manner by means of unknownness, τῷ ἀγνώστῳ, may indeed be a separate manner of knowing that would require its own διαίρεσις—this would have to be investigated—but, he goes on, in some cases at least, it would be more proper to call this manner of knowing knowing by analogy because the paradoxical expression ("known by being unknown") is as counterintuitive and absurd as saying that something that is seen (thus keeping the attested reading τὸ ὁρατόν) is seen through its very attribute of being unseen. And just as, upon first hearing this, someone will find

[3] The reserve shown by Theophrastus himself with the words τάχα δ' ἐφ' ὧν ἐνδέχεται (cf. van Raalte 438–439) would indicate that he, too, under certain conditions, might accept it.

this nonsensical, so also someone hearing the manner of knowing by analogy called knowing by unknownness will find it equally nonsensical.

The question is, who these philosophers—or philosopher—who held this view were. It would seem beyond serious doubt that they have to be sought in the Academy, given the closeness of Theophrastus's Essay to a number of their positions; Berti even aired the thought that it might be Plato himself.[4] But a more likely suggestion is that it was Speusippus,[5] and his theory that "the essential nature of each thing is identical with the complex of all its relations to all other things," in the words of Cherniss 1945, 42, or, as Tarán 1981, 58 put it, "the very essence of anything is simply to be the focus of all the relations that make it different from everything else and that knowledge of anything requires knowledge of the whole system of relations." This can be likened to an algebraic equation in which we stipulate the unknown, x, and, starting from the fact that it is unknown, we come to know it once we have all the determinate or known terms in the equation which express their relation to it. That something like this was the theory of Speusippus is derived from Aristotle's passage on definition in the *Posterior Analytics* II,13, 97a6–22 (fr. 63a Tarán 1981), who, however, does not mention Speusippus, and from the later commentators on this passage who do (frs. 63b–e Tarán 1981).

There have been divergent views about the precise purpose of Speusippus in making this argument and about the function of division as method in the process, but there seems to be agreement that at the very minimum Speusippus held that "to define a thing is to know the relations that this thing has with all surrounding things."[6] This is certainly an indirect way of coming to know something, and we know for a fact that Speusippus did maintain that some things are known indirectly. In a reference preserved by Proclus, Speusippus is reported to have said that "in the hunt for knowledge," some things our mind "is unable to grasp immediately and therefore advances on them step by step and endeavors

---

[4] Berti, preprint, pp. 2–3, refers to Plato's view that the ideas can never be known adequately (ἱκανῶς, *Resp.* 505a5, e2). Although he admits that Plato never said that they can be known by being unknown, he entertains the possibility that such a thing could have been said in Academic circles.

[5] Made to me privately by Paul Kalligas, for which I am most grateful.

[6] See the detailed discussion by Falcon 2000; the quotation above is on p. 413. Cf. also the analysis of the Aristotelian passage by Barnes 1994, 245–247.

to capture them by their consequences"[7] (κατὰ μετάβασιν ἐπ' ἐκεῖνα [*sc.* τὰ οὐκ εὐθέως αἱρεῖν ἀδυνατοῦσα ἡ διάνοια] διαβαίνουσα κατὰ τὸ ἀκόλουθον αὐτῶν ἐπιχειρεῖ ποιεῖσθαι τὴν θήραν, fr. 73 Tarán 1981). It is not known whether Speusippus meant to call this knowledge that comes οὐκ εὐθέως but κατὰ μετάβασιν and κατὰ τὸ ἀκόλουθον as the knowledge that makes things γνωστὰ τῷ ἄγνωστα εἶναι, or what precisely Theophrastus meant when, for his part, he said that this manner of knowledge "by being unknown" would be more appropriately called knowledge by analogy, κατ' ἀναλογίαν, and how this is to be understood in this context. In a number of studies, Krämer also identified Speusippus as the philosopher to whom Theophrastus is here referring by this manner of "known by being unknown," but he has likened the process to the one κατ' ἀφαίρεσιν, as developed in Middle and Neo-Platonism. Krämer did not explain, beyond these general statements, how objects known by a method κατ' ἀφαίρεσιν could be γνωστὰ τῷ ἄγνωστα εἶναι, though it is true that he expressed himself with caution.[8] The problem with Krämer's analysis, though, is that Theophrastus himself never mentions ἀφαίρεσις in this Essay,[9] and indeed neither does Speusippus in the few fragments we have, but he says, instead, as just cited, κατὰ μετάβασιν κατὰ τὸ ἀκόλουθον. The subject deserves more detailed scrutiny than can be afforded to it here; in general, though, it would seem to be a fruitful line of approach to investigate how Speusippus's idea of reaching the unknown through its relations and especially its consequences, κατὰ τὸ ἀκόλουθον, relates to mathematical procedure and possibly the Aristotelian discovery of the middle term described in the *Posterior Analytics*.[10]

---

[7] Translation by G.R. Morrow, *Proclus. A Commentary on the First Book of Euclid's* Eements, Princeton: Princeton University Press, 1970, 141.

[8] I.e., "Die Erkenntnis der πρῶτα durch Negation, die Theophrast referiert ..., dürfte in diesem Zusammenhang der mathematisierenden Methode κατ' ἀφαίρεσιν entsprechen, die im späteren Platonismus terminologisch fixiert ist," Krämer 1973, 212; as opposed to the bolder unsubstantiated claims by Merlan mentioned earlier. See also similar general statements in Krämer 1967, 105–106, 350–351; Krämer 1968, 327n125; Krämer 1971, 177–178. Theiler 1958, 105/296–297 also saw points of contact between later Platonism and this passage in Theophrastus, but without claiming this to be an expression of *docta ignorantia*, despite his reference to Merlan.

[9] At 5a11 (for which see the commentary) the word ἀφαιρετέον has its literal meaning "to remove," without any epistemological implications, and similarly at 6a12–13.

[10] The issue is also related to the knowledge, and hence derivation, of sensible objects from and through the principles, something which Theophrastus accuses Plato to have done not completely, and Speusippus not at all, at 6a24–6b15; see the commentary on this passage and cf. Gaiser 1968, 366n101.

As to the question what these objects of knowledge are that can be known indirectly (though this question is not immediately relevant to this discussion), the answer depends on how ultimately the process described by Theophrastus is understood. If the reference is indeed to Speusippus, then in all likelihood the object of this indirect knowledge will be the sensibles, since the upper three substances in Speusippus' ontology, numbers, magnitudes, and soul, are known directly (cf. Tarán 1981, 53–60). Alternately, in Aristotelian terms, direct knowledge cannot be had of objects like the ultimate principles, matter, etc. A statement like Aristotle's ἡ δὲ ὑποκειμένη φύσις ἐπιστητὴ κατ' ἀναλογίαν (*Physics* 191a7–8) seems to be relevant in this regard (see the evidence collected by van Raalte 436–437).

I conclude that knowing by unknownness is neither a sophism, as Ross would have it, nor what a loaded interpretation like that of Merlan suggests (a prefiguring of the Neoplatonic *docta ignorantia*), but merely an indirect manner of knowing for those objects of which there cannot be a direct knowledge. There is a very strong possibility that Theophrastus may be referring here to an aspect of Speusippus's epistemology, but we have relatively little direct evidence, and it may appear strange, even given our scant knowledge of this thinker's works, that there has survived no other testimony to it. Whether by Speusippus or not, in all likelihood the theory was part of internal discussions in the Old Academy before Aristotle and Theophrastus returned to Athens in 335, which the participants would recognize even when briefly referred to through the catch phrase γνωστὰ τῷ ἄγνωστα εἶναι, but which, through its very paradoxical nature and lack of explicitness, was soon abandoned, leaving just this trace in this Essay.

WORD INDICES AND GLOSSARIES

1. *Greek Word Index and Greek-Arabic Glossary*

The Greek word index and glossary follows the alphabetical order and manner of citation of words in LSJ (i.e., words printed in bold). It includes all the words that occur in the text of Theophrastus except for the article, the various uses of which are listed only in representative samples; a complete index of its occurrence can be found in van Raalte 645–647. The words in the Scholium are listed in a separate index at the end.

In addition, because the word index is at the same time also a glossary, it includes all those words which, though they do not occur independently in the text of Theophrastus, are components of compound words, translated individually by Isḥāq ibn-Ḥunayn in accordance with his etymological analysis of the compound word. For example, the word ἀστρολογία at 9b27 and 10a5 is translated as *ṣināʿatu n-nuǧūmi*, literally, "the science of the stars," with the two Arabic words standing for ἄστρον and λόγος respectively. The word ἄστρον is accordingly listed independently in the word index, although it does not occur as such in the text of Theophrastus, while an additional reference to the translation of λόγος as "science" is added in its own entry.

In the compilation of the glossaries I followed the general rules adopted by Gerhard Endress and myself in our *A Greek and Arabic Glossary* (*GALex*), references to the entries of which are added in the Arabic-Greek glossary. Additional instances of a Greek-Arabic correspondence, with citations of passages from the translation literature, can be found in these references, listed under the Arabic word. Some of the technical terms used in the entries below, whose abbreviations are given in the list that follows, conform to the rules in *GALex*, but are for the most part self-explanatory. For more detailed information the reader is referred to the introduction in *GALex*. In addition, several signs have been used that are particular to this publication, the key to which is given at the end of the abbreviations.

Abbreviations

abs.	absolute use; a word without any syntactic governance
acc.	according
accus.	accusative
act.	active voice
add.	adds, added (by)
adj.	adjective(s)
adv.	adverb(s), adverbial
affirm.	affirmative
amplif.	amplification
Ar.	Arabic
Ar. synt.	required by the Arabic syntax
circumst.	circumstantial
comp.	comparative
concentr.	concentration
conj.	conjunction
corr.	corrected (by), -ion in
dat.	dative
def.	definite
demonstr.	demonstrative
encl.	enclitic
etym.	etymology
expr.	expression(s)
foll.	following, followed (by)
fut.	future tense
gen.	genitive
Gr.	Greek
hend.	hendiadys
impers.	impersonal
impf.	imperfect
indef.	indefinite
indic.	indicative
inf.	infinitive(s)
inflect.	inflection
interpr.	interpretation, -tive translation; as -ted by
interr.	interrogative, -ion
intrans.	intransitive
juss.	jussive
lac.	lacuna
masc.	masculine
med.	middle voice
morph.	morphology
neg.	negative
n.t.	not translated (analysis of the omission is usually offered in the corresponding note to the Arabic translation)
obj.	object

om.	omits, omitted by / in
opt.	optative
paraphr.	paraphrase, -phrastic
part.	participle
pass.	passive voice
perf.	perfect
pers.	person(al)
pl.	plural
prep.	preposition, -nal
pres.	present tense
pron.	pronoun(s), -nominal
ref.	reference
sc.	scilicet
sem.	semantic
sem. amplif.	semantic amplification
sing.	singular
s.th.	something
subj.	subjunctive
subst.	substantive(s)
superl.	superlative
synt.	syntax
transl.	translated, -tes, -tion
w.	with, used with
w.o.	without

Signs

1,2,3	a raised, exponential number next to a page-column-line reference indicates the first, second, or third occurrence in the same line of the word indexed.
*	an asterisk following a page-column-line number indicates that the word so glossed is the result of editorial emendation and is not to be found in the manuscripts; for supporting arguments see the corresponding entry in the commentary (Part III) or the note to the Arabic translation.
{1a1}	a page-column-line reference so bracketed indicates a different, inaccurate, or misapprehended interpretation by the Arabic translator; for explanation see the corresponding note to the Arabic translation.
1a1 (1a2)	page-column-line references in parentheses following immediately after another such reference point to the occurrence of the word in the Arabic text in a different line than that in the Greek, and vice-versa for the Arabic-Greek glossary.
†	a raised obelisk following a page reference indicates that the word in question is corrupt in the MSS.
|	a vertical line separates different definitions within the same lemma.
▬	a bold rectangle separates different lemmata within the same entry.
(a)	a bold lower case letter in the longer entries separates different categories of meaning or usage for the word concerned.
-/-	(e.g, τε/καί) a slash in Greek and Arabic entrics indicates a correlative use of the words concerned. In such instances, when one side of the slash has only a hyphen and not a word, it indicates that one of the correlatives is not expressed in the translation.

ἀγαθός 8b1 ḫayrun | *as the positive degree of* κρείττων 4b6 faḍlun – τὸ ἀγαθόν 11a19 al-ǧayyidu – *comp.* → βελτίων, κρείττων – *superl.* → ἄριστος
ἄγαν 4a19 *n.t.*
ἄγνωστος 9a19, 9a22 ġayru maʿlūmin
ἄγω 7b22, 8a4 (8a3) radda | 11b9 qāda – ἄγομαι *pass.* 8a11 uḫriǧa
ἄδεκτος 5b18 ġayru qābilin
ἀδύνατος 7b8 ʿāǧizun | 7b16 ʿaǧzun ʿan | 5b13 *in hend.* ḍuʿfun wa-ʿaǧzun
ἀεί 7b16, 10b20 dāʾiman | 4a6 *om. Ar.* (*in lac.*) – τὸ ἀεί 11a7 ad-dawāmu
ἀζήτητος 6a3 lā yaqaʿu fīhi baḥṯun
ἀήρ 7b2, 11b17 hawāʾun
ἀΐδιος 9b24 azaliyyun – τὰ ἀΐδια 4a16 al-ašyāʾu l-azaliyyatu
αἴσθησις (*sense-perception*) 7b19, 8b10 ḥissun – αἱ αἰσθήσεις (*the senses*) 5b5, 9b9 al-ḥawāssu (*sing.* ḥāssatun)
αἰσθητός 6b8 maḥsūsun | 4a7 *om. Ar.* (*in lac.*) – τὰ αἰσθητά 4a20, 4b19, 7b15, 9b3, 11b18 al-ašyāʾu l-maḥsūsatu
αἰτία 4b21, 5a1, 5a21, 7b19, 8b11, 9b11 sababun | 11b8 ʿillatun | 9b3 mabdaʾun
αἴτιος – αἴτιον 5b7, 9a2 (9a1), 9b8 sababun
ἀκαριαῖος 11a18 asraʿu
ἀκίνητος 4b22, 10a20 ġayru mutaḥarrikin | 4a7 *om. Ar.* (*in lac.*)
ἀκολουθέω *in* συνακολουθέω 7a3 tabiʿa – ἀκολουθεῖ (*thus in the MSS; corr. by Ross to* οὐ συνακολουθεῖ) 8a2* tabiʿa
ἄκρον – τὰ ἄκρα 9b10 al-aṭrāfu | 11a24 an-nihāyātu
ἀλήθεια 6b16 ḥaqqun
ἀληθής 8a16 mina ṣ-ṣiḥḥati – ἀληθέστερος *comp.* 8b11, 9b14, 9b23 aṣaḥḥu
ἀληθινός – ἀληθινώτερος 5a12 aṣdaqu
ἀλλά 4a14, 5a1, 7a14, 7b13, 7b18, 8a4, 8b8, 10a26, 11b6, 11b9, 11b16 lākin | 5b14, 8a14, 8a17, 11b23 illā anna | 5a9, 10b18 bal | 5a25 innamā | 5b18 fa-qad | 5b22 *n.t.* | 4a11 *om. Ar.* (*in lac.*) – εἰ γὰρ καί/ἀλλά 11a14 iḏā/illā anna | 11b20 (11b21) fa-inna ... wa-in/fa-
ἀλλήλων 5b25, 8b3, 8b17, 10a2, 12a2 baʿḍun/baʿḍun | 10b28 ({11a1a}) aṣnāfun | 4a10 *om. Ar.* (*in lac.*)
ἀλλοίωσις 10b4 (10b5) istiḥālatun
ἄλλος 6a17, 6b18, 9b27 sāʾiru *w. gen.* | 4b13, 5a1, 8a5 āḫaru | 6b3, 8a20 ġayru *w. gen.* | 6a22 āḫaru ġayruhū – ἄλλο 10b3, 10b5 šayʾun – οἱ ἄλλοι 6b6 ġayruhū – ἄλλα 11b17 ašyāʾu uḫaru ġayruhū – τὰ ἄλλα 4b14, 6b12, 8a2, 10a4, 11b19 sāʾiru l-ašyāʾi | 6a26 sāʾiru mā siwā ḏālika | 7a6 sāʾiru mā fīhā
ἄλλοτε – ἄλλοτ᾽ ἄλλο 10b3 šayʾun baʿda šayʾin | 10b5 šayʾun ilā šayʾin
ἀλλότριος 9b5 *in hend.* muǧtanabun ġayru maʾlūfin
ἄλλως 7b18 ayḍan | 10a23 lā maʿnā lahū – ἄλλως τε καί 5a28 wa- ... maʿa ḏālika – καὶ ἄλλως/καί 9b17–18 -/wa- ... maʿa ḏālika
ἄλογος 7a10 ġayru munqāsin (*see Part I, Chapter 3.3*)
ἅμα 5a25, {5b3}, 6a8, 9b22 maʿa – ἅμα ... τε καί 5a12 wa- – ἅμα καί 6b3 maʿa
ἀμαθής – ἀμαθέστατος /-ον 11a21 ġāyatu l-ǧahli
ἀμερής 8a3 lā ǧuzʾa lahū
ἀμετάβλητος 4a8 *om. Ar.* (*in lac.*)

ἅπας 7a10 kullu *w. gen.* – ἅπαντα 7a12 (7a11) ǧamīʿu *w. gen.* | 4b16, 6a4, 6b7, 7a21 ǧamīʿu al-ašyāʾi | 11a5 kullu šayʾin | 9b21 al-ʿulūmu kulluhā | 11b1 al-ašyāʾu kulluhā
ἀπάτη 9b16 zalalun
ἄπαυστος 5a4 allaḏī lā yatafattaru
ἄπειρος 11a17 lā yuḥṣā kaṯratan – (τὸ) ἄπειρον 6b1 mā lā tanāhā | 9b4 mā lā nihāyata lahū | 11b3 al-ḫurūǧu ʿani t-tanāhī
ἀπέχω 9a7 baʿuda
ἁπλῶς 4b20, 5a9, 8b13, 9b7, 10a9, 11a4, 11a5 ʿalā l-iṭlāqi | 11a3 muṭlaqan
ἀπό *w. gen.* 5b26, 6a15, 6a16, 6a28, 6b2, 9b9 min | 5a3, 5b4, 5b10 ʿan | 6b22 *sem. amplif.* yaʾḫuḏu min
ἀποδίδωμι 4b17 wafāʾun bi- | 5a8 (5a7) waṣafa | 5a10 waṣfun | {6a17} iʿtaqada
ἀπορέω 6a6 mawḍiʿu tašakkukin | 6b24 tašakkaka fī | 7b10 taḥayyara fī | 6a13 ǧaʿala baḥṯahū fī | *in* ἄπορον 9b2 irtabaka fī
ἀπορία 10a20 (10a19) šakkun | 8a21 mawḍiʿu tašakkukin | 8b13 *in hend.* šakkun wa-ḥayratun
ἄπορος – ἄπορον 5a23 mā yutaḥayyaru fīhi | 9b2 mā yurtabaku fīhi | 10b24 mawḍiʿu ḥayratin
ἀπόστασις 9b26, 11b1 buʿdun
ἀπόφασις 5a13 salbun
ἅπτω – ἅπτομαι *med.* 9b15 māssa | *w. gen.* 6b12 šaraʿa fī
ἀπωθέω 5b21 *in hend.* qaḏafa bi- ʿan ... wa-aqṣā
ἄρα 8b16 iḏan | 10b27 ḫalīqun an | {6a17} maʿa (*i.e., Ar. (mis-?) read as* ἅμα) | 8a22, 9a6 *n.t.* – εἰ μὴ ἄρα 4b10, 6a10 allāhumma illā an | 5b28, 11b19 illā an
ἆρα 10a16 yā layta šiʿrī
ἀργία 7b12 taʿṭīlun
ἀριθμός 4b4, 4b8, 5a26, 5a27, 6a21, 6a25, 6b2, 6b14, 8b26, 9a5 ʿadadun
ἄριστος 5a20 afḍalu | {5b8} afḍalu l-umūri | 11a12 *om. Ar.* (*in lac.*) – τὸ ἄριστον 11a6 al-afḍalu | 5b1 afḍalu l-umūri | 5b26, 5b27 mā huwa fī ġāyati l-faḍīlati | 11a2, 11b9 al-amru l-afḍalu – τὰ ἄριστα 6a2 afḍalu l-umūri | 6a4 afāḍilu l-umūri
ἄρρην 10b8 ḏakarun
ἄρτιος 5a6 kāmilun
ἀρχή 4a15, 4a16, 4b9, 4b15, 4b19, 5a5, 5a6, 5a19, 6a16, 6b12, 6b14, 6b16, 6b17, 6b19, 6b21, 6b22, 6b23, 7a4, 7a6, 7a13, 7a19, 7b9, 7b12, 9a11, 9a13, 9a25, 9b6, 9b8 (9b7), 11b7, 11b27 mabdaʾun | 9b9 awwalu | 11b24 awwalu l-amri – *title**, 4a9 *om. Ar.* (*in lac.*)
Ἀρχύτας 6a19 Arḫūṭas
ἄρχω – ἄρχομαι *med.* 10a24 badaʾa
ἀσθένεια 9b12 ʿaǧzun | 5b14 *in hend.* ḍuʿfun wa-kalālun
ἀστήρ → ἄστρον
ἀστρολογία 9b27, 10a5 ṣināʿatu n-nuǧūmi
ἀστρολόγος 5a22 munaǧǧimun
ἄστρον *in* ἀστρολογία 9b27, 10a5 naǧmun
ἀσύνδετος 5b18 lā muḥtamilun li-l-irtibāṭi
ἄτακτος – τὸ ἄτακτον 11b4 al-ḫurūǧu ʿani n-niẓāmi – ἀτακτότερος *comp.* 4a4 *om. Ar.* (*in lac.*)
ἄτομος – ἄτομον 9a3 šaḫṣun – τὰ ἄτομα 11b23 al-aǧzāʾu llatī lā tataǧazzaʾu
ἄτοπος 5a17, 5b14 šaniʿun | 7b23 qabīḥun
ἄττα 6a11 baʿḍu *w. gen.* | 6b3 *n.t.*
αὖ – πάλιν αὖ 7a20* ayḍan
αὐτόματος – τῷ αὐτομάτῳ 10b27 min ḏātihā – αὐτομάτως 7a18 min ḏātihī

αὐτός (**a**) (*self*) 6a13, 7b22, 9a8, 9a17, 9b10, 9b14, 9b16[2], 10b24 nafsu *w. attached pron.* | 4b4[2] *sem. amplif.* nafsuhū faḍlan ʿan ġayrihī | 5b17 kullu *w. attached pron.* | 6a6 amru *w. gen.* | 7a22 mā huwa ayḍan – αὐτός *in* αὐτομάτως 7a18, 10b27 ḏātun – {9a22} *transl. as if it were a pers. pron. w. ref. to* λέγειν – 10b7 *n.t. as such, but its emphasis is rendered by the assertive* qad yakūnu *add. for the implied copula* – 10b4, 11a17 *n.t.* (**b**) (*pers. pron.*) 4a17, 4b4[1], 4b21, 5a19, 6a8, 6a10, 8a2, 8a13, 8b4, 9a4, 9b16[1] *transl. by the attached pron.* | 5a27, 8a16 *transl. by the subst. to which it ref.* | 11a8 ḏālika *in* ka-ḏālika | 9a13, 9a25 *n.t.* | 4a7, 4a9 *om. Ar.* (*in lac.*) (**c**) (*same*) αὐτά 4a23 hiya – ὁ αὐτός 5a18 wāḥidun bi-ʿaynihī – τὸ αὐτό 8b24 aš-šayʾu bi-ʿaynihī | 9a4 aš-šayʾu wāḥidun bi-ʿaynihī – ταὐτά 10b20 ḥālun wāḥidatun – κατὰ ταὐτά 10b20 ʿalā ḥālin wāḥidatin | 4a6 *om. Ar.* (*in lac.*)

αὑτοῦ 4a23, 4b22 nafsu *w. attached pron.* | 11b5 *n.t.* – → ἑαυτοῦ

ἀφαιρέω 6a12 ḥaḏafa | 5a11 rafaʿa ʿan – ἀφαιροῦμαι *pass.* 6a13 *sem. metathesis; pass. / act. transformation* zāla

ἀφανής 5a17 *sem. metathesis; neg./affirm. transformation* mā yaḫfā

ἀφορίζω 9a25 laḫḫaṣa | 4a2 *om. Ar.* (*in lac.*) – ἀφωρισμένος 10a19 maḥdūdun

ἀφορισμός 7b6 (7b7) ḥadda | 10a23 talḫīṣun

ἄχρι 10a5 ilā

ἄψυχος 7a17 al-ʿadīmu li-n-nafsi | 9a15, 11a17 lā nafsa lahū | {10b21} nafsun

βελτίων – βέλτιον 11a18 aǧwadu – τὸ βέλτιον 8a24 al-afḍalu | 7b11, 8a14, 11a9, 11b15, 11b27 al-amru l-afḍalu

βία 10b14 *om. Ar.* (*in lac.*)

βλέπω – βλέπειν 9b13 an-naẓaru

βούλομαι 6a2 šāʾa

γάρ 4a18, 5a10, 5a17, 5a22, 5a27, 5b24, 6a1, 6a3, 6a19, 6a21, 6a25, 6b7, 6b17, 6b27, 7a17, 7b11, 7b17, 8a2, 9a1, 9a4, 9b4, 9b21, 10a28, 10b18, 10b24, 11a22, 11b15, 11b27 fa-inna | 4a21, 4b4, 4b15, 5a12, 5b3, 5b8, 5b15, 5b21, 6b19, 7a9, 8a16, 8b10, 8b17, 8b21, 9a15, 9a27, 10a16, 10b19, 11a8, 11a16 wa-ḏālika anna | 6b21 min qibali anna | 11a11 li-anna | 4a3 *om. Ar.* (*in lac.*) – καὶ γὰρ δή 10a7 fa-inna – εἰ γὰρ καί/ἀλλά 11a13–14 iḏā/illā anna | 11b20 fa-inna ... wa-in/fa-

γε 5b14 *the repetition of the whole clause to which* τοῦτο *refers may express the emphasis of the particle* | 5a22 *n.t., though its force may be reflected in the first person verb* (ānas) *selected to transl.* οἰκεῖος | 6a23, 7b15, 8a13, 8a14, 9b2, 10a9, 11a14, 11b12, 11b18 *n.t.* | 4a4 *om. Ar.* (*in lac.*) – ἁμῶς γέ πως 4b12 ʿalā waǧhin min al-wuǧūhi – {10a17} *Ar. read* εἴτε *for* εἴ γε

γένεσις 8a12 ḥudūṯun | 6b15, 10b17 tawalludun | 7b5 (7b4) tawallada | 10b4 kawnun

γεννάω 6a25 walada | 7b5 wallada

γένος 4b8, 8b20, 9a5, 9a15 ǧinsun – γένος *in* ὁμογενής 9a18 ǧinsun

γῆ 5b17, 7b2, 10b4, 11b14 arḍun | 10a28 arḍun *in* arḍiyyun | 6b26 *om. Ar.* (*in lac.*)

γίνομαι 7a18, 8a17 ḥadaṯa | 7b1 ḥudūṯun | 10b5 (10b4) ʿaraḍa | 8a26 wuǧida | 5b7 *transl. by the implied copula of an Ar. nominal sentence* annahā (hiya) ʿalā ḥālin – γεγονός 8b7 kāna mawǧūdan

γνωστός 9a19 yuʿlamu *pass.* | γνωστός *in* ἄγνωστος 9a19, 9a22 maʿlūmun

γραμματικός – ἡ γραμματική 7a2 kitābatun

γραμμή 8b26 ḫaṭṭun

δέ *w.o. preceding* μέν (**a**) *abs.* 4a15[2], 4b2, 4b13, 4b20, 5a2, 5a23, 5b3, 5b10, 5b19, 5b26, 6a12, 6b5, 6b9, 6b13, 6b14, 6b15, 6b16, 6b18, 6b20, 6b23 (6b24), 7a1, 7a3, 7a10, 7a19[2], 7b14, 7b19, 7b22, 7b23, 8a8, 8a19[2], 8a21, 8a27, 8b6, 8b11, 8b20, 8b24, 8b27[1], 9a4, 9a18[1,2], 9a20, 9a21, 9a25, 9a26, 9b6[1], 9b13, 9b16, 9b22[1], 9b25, 10b7, 10b11, 10b20, 11a13, 11a17, 11a18, 11a19, 11a20, 11b5, 11b12, 11b16 wa- | 4b18, 5a28, 6a2, 9a10, 10a13, 10a24, 11a1 fa- | 4a23, 5a21, 5b12, 6b4, 7a19[1], 10a22 (10a23b), 11a24 wa-(fa-)ammā ... fa- | 4a12, 6a23, 8a11 (8a10), 8a19[1], 9a7, 9b6[2], 10a19, 11b17 illā anna | 4b22, 8a12 lākin | 10a15 ḥattā | 9a7 fa-inna (?) | 11a20 *n.t.* | 4a5, 4a9, 8b27[2], 9a17 *om. Ar.* (*in lac.*) (**b**) *in compounds* δέ *in* οὐδέ 5b12, 6b5, 6b6, 9b24, 11a15, 11b7 (11b8) wa- *in* wa-lā – δέ *in* μηδέ 5a8, 8b7[1,2] wa- *in* wa-lā (**c**) *in combinations* δ' οὖν 4a13, 4b9 wa- | 4a17, 4b11, 5b7 fa- | 9a23 (9a24) fa-qad *w. perf.* – ἔτι δέ 5a8, 7a4, 8b4 wa- – μᾶλλον δέ 8a25, 9b22[2], 11a16 (11a15) bal – τάχα δὲ 6a16 *paraphr.* aw | 11b10 *n.t.* (**c**) *see also* καί/δέ → καί – μέν/δέ → μέν

δεῖ 7b20, 10b19 (10b20) waǧaba | 4a2 *om. Ar.* (*in lac.*) – δέον 6b26 *in hend.* ḥaqīqun wa-awlā bi- *in* aḥaqqu wa-awlā bi-

δείκνυμι 9b27 bayyana

δέχομαι 11a15 qabila | 6a1 qabūlun – δέχομαι *in* ἄδεκτος 5b18 qabila

δέω – δέομαι *deponent* 5a14, 5b27, 9a20 iḥtāǧa ilā – → δεῖ

δή (**a**) *abs.* 5a6 fa- | 7b2 qad *w. impf.* | 10b25* ṯumma | 4b5, 5b9, 6a1, 6b4, 6b9, 8a22, 10a4, 10b16, 11b23 *n.t.* | 4a3, 4a4, 4a6, 10b14 *om. Ar.* (*in lac.*) (**b**) δή *transl. by a ḥāl clause*: ὅθεν δή 7b9 wa-hiya llatī minhā | ὃν δή 8a6 wa-hiya llatī (**c**) *in combinations* καὶ δή 10a25 fa-inna qad naǧidu – καὶ γὰρ δή 10a8 fa-inna

δῆλος – δῆλον 4b21, 10a13 min al-bayyini

δηλόω 6a28 dalla ʿalā

Δημόκριτος 11b22 dymwqryṭs

διά (**a**) *w. gen.* 4b16, 5b6, 8b14 bi- | 4a23 fī | {9b8} *n.t.* – *introducing the subject of a pass. verb* 4a22 *sem. metathesis*; *pass. Gr. verb transl. by an act. Ar. verb* – διά *in* διὰ πλείστου 9a7 *transl. by the accus. of the adv.* akṯara (**b**) *w. accus.* 7b21, 9a8, 9a9[1,2], 9b11, 9b12, 10b19 min qibali *w. gen.* | 5b14 li- | 7b15 *n.t.* – *in* διὰ τί 5b11, 7b7 li- *in* li-mā – *in* διό 9b15 li- *in* li-ḏālika

διαίρεσις 9a2, 9a6, 9a20 qismatun

διαιρετός 5a8 mutaǧazziʾun – τὸ διαιρετόν 5a11 at-taqsīmu

διαιρέω 9a24 mayyaza – διαιροῦμαι *med. & pass.* 9a18 luḫḫiṣa *pass.*

διαμένω 4b16 baqāʾun

διάνοια 5b9 fahmun | 8b12 fikrun

διατίθημι 6a20 ṣāra lahū

διαφέρω 8b19 iḫtalafa

διαφορά 6a5, 8b16, 8b17, 9a17 iḫtilāfun | 11a1 muḫtalifun | 8b10 faṣlun – 5b2 διαφορά *in the MSS corr. to* μεταφορά *in the editions*

διϊκνέομαι 5b13 balaġa ilā

διό – διὸ καί 9b15 wa-li-ḏālika | 11b7 wa-min qibali ḏālika | 4a6, 10a10 *om. Ar.* (*in lac.*)

διότι 11a14 anna
διστασμός 11a4 ǧihatāni *dual*
διώκω 5a24 ṭalaba
δοκέω 10b22 ra'ā – δοκεῖ *impers.* 4a22 qad yurā fīhi | 5b3 qad yurā | 7b19 qad yuẓannu bi- – δόξειεν ἄν 6b12, 8a21 qad yuẓannu | 9a26 qad yuẓannu bi- | 11b18 an yuẓanna bi- | 7a10 an yaqūlū – δοκεῖν 8a25 qad yuẓannu | 10a25 qad yuẓannu bi- – τὸ δοκοῦν 8b4 mā yuẓannu bihī | 10b17 *interpr.* mā yadḫulu š-šakku fīhi
δυάς 6a25, 6b1, 11b3 uṯnūwatun
δύναμαι 11b8 qadara | 9b11 qadara ʿalā | 9b8 amkana *w. pers. pron. and* an | 8b14 tahayya'a lahū an – μὴ δύνασθαι 5b28 *sem. metathesis, neg. / affirm. transformation* ʿaǧzun ʿan
δυναμικός 6b25 ašbahu bi-l-quwā
δύναμις 7a12, 8a19, 10b23 quwwatun | *in* δυναμικός 6b25 quwwatun – δυνάμει 4b14, 5a1 bi-quwwatin | 8a10 bi-l-quwwati

ἐάν 7b22 lahū an – *in* κἄν (καὶ ἐάν) 8b14 in – ἐάν/ἐάν 8b19–20 kāna/kāna
ἑαυτοῦ 8b23 ḏātun – σύμφωνος ἑαυτῷ 8a4 *morph.; transl. by the reflexive sense of form VIII of the Ar. verb* ittafaqa – → αὑτοῦ
ἐγγύς *w. gen.* 8a27 qarībun min
ἐγώ – ἡμεῖς 4a22 naḥnu | 9a8, 9b6 *transl. by the attached pron.*
ἐθέλω 11b1 *n.t.*
εἰ (**a**) *abs.* 4a17, 4a18, 4b2, 4b6, 4b11, 5a5, 5a28, 5b7, 5b14, 5b20, 5b26, 7b11, 7b12, 8a20, 8a21, 8b17, 9a6, 9a18, 10a13, 11a1 in | 9a23 law | 10a5 iḏā | {10a16*} *Ar. read* εἴτε, *not* εἴ γε | 11a20† *Ar. misread it as* ἤ | 11a22† *n.t.* | 10a11* *om. Ar.* (*in lac.*) – εἰ *in indirect questions* (*whether*) 6a13 hal | *in indirect discourse* (*that*) 7a11 an *w. subj.* – 8a2 εἰ *in the MSS corr. to* τί *in the editions* (**b**) *in combinations* εἰ μή 5b1 illā an – εἰ μὴ ἄρα 4b10, 6a10 allāhumma illā an | 5b28, 11b19 illā an | 8a21–22 in lam – εἰ γὰρ καί/ἀλλά 11a13–14 iḏā/illā anna | 11b20 fa-inna ... wa-in/fa- – πλὴν εἰ 7a22–23, 11b21 illā an – ὥσπερ ἂν εἰ {4b15} ʿalā mā huwa ʿalayhi
εἶδος 4b8, 8b20, 10a4, 10b23 nawʿun | 8a18, 9a5 ṣūratun | 11a21 *n.t.*
εἴδω (*perf.* οἶδα) – τὸ εἰδέναι 9b22 al-maʿrifatu | 9a24 *in hend.* al-maʿrifatu ... innahū yuʿlamu
εἰκῇ 7a14 bāṭilan
εἰκότως 7b10 bi-l-wāǧibi
εἰμί (**a**) *copula* 4b18, 5b2, 5b6, 7b16, 7b21, 8a15[1], 8b18, 9a10, 10a15 (10a14) kāna | 8a23 ṣāra | 4a22, 6a8, 8b23, 10a7 *transl. by the pron. of separation* (*ḍamīr al-faṣl*) hiya | 5b12, 5b18, 7a19, 8a7, 8a25, 9a18, 9a20, 11b12 *transl. by the copula expressed by the Ar. nominal sentence* – ᾖ (*emended from* ἤ *in the MSS*) 8a6* aw – *in* κίνδυνος εἶναι {7b17} *sem. concentr.* ḫāfa (**b**) *neg. copula* εἰμί *w. neg.* 4b23, 5a4, 5b8 laysa (**c**) *existential uses* 4a13 kāna | 4b10 kāna wuǧūduhū | 4b16 wuǧūdun | 6a4 yūǧadu | 4b6, 9a19 (9a18) *in hend.* kāna hāhunā | 9b16 waqaʿa | 9b23 fīhi | 9a15 *synt.; expressed by the indef. nominal sentence with the prep. phrase preceding the indef. subject* anna fī ... ǧinsan – ἂν εἴη *w. foll. inf.* 6a12 lahū an *w. foll. subj.* – 8b27 *om. Ar.* (*in lac.*) (**d**) *part.* ὄν 8a10[1,2], 8a11[1,2], 8b7 mawǧūdun – τὸ ὄν 8b5, 8b9 al-mawǧūdu – τὰ ὄντα 6b17, 12a1 al-mawǧūdātu | 6a11, 8a9 al-ašyā'u l-mawǧūdatu | 11a26 hiya | 11a25 *n.t.* (**e**) *inf.* τὸ εἶναι 11a18 *in hend.* takawwunun

wa-wuǧūdun | 8b2 innahū mawǧūdun | 8a15[2] al-qawlu bi-annahū mawǧūdun – τὸ τί ἦν εἶναι 8b22 mā huwa š-šay'u

εἶμι 5a20 ṣāra

εἴπερ 5b23 in | 11b9, 11b10 iḏ | 10b19 law | 7b13, 11b16 *n.t.* | 10b9 *om. Ar.* (*in lac.*) – εἴπερ ὀρέξει 6a9 *sem. metathesis; conditional / affirm. transformation* hiya bi-šahwatin

εἶπον – εἰπεῖν 4b20, 8b12, 9b23 al-qawlu | 9b2 an yuqāla – ὡς εἰπεῖν 7a16, 7a18 maṯalan | 11b4 bi-l-ǧumlati

εἰς *w. accus.* (**a**) *abs.* 5a9, 5a19, 6b12, 6b13[1,2], 6b14, 7b8, 8a3, 8a9, 8a11, 8a14, 9a3, 10a24, 11b9, 11b26 (11b27) ilā | 5b25[1,2] min ... ilā | 9b16 ʿan (*after* baḥṯun) *and* bi- (*after* taṣdīqun) | 4a12 ʿalā (*after* taʿāwana) (**b**) *sem. amplif.* 9b4 sulūkun | 11a2 quṣida bihī | 8b8 mā yadḫulu fī

εἷς, μία, ἕν 4b7, 5a7, 5a17 wāḥidun – τὸ ἕν 5a26, 5a28, 6a24, 6b2, 11b3 al-wāḥidu

εἶτα 6b14 fa-

εἴτε/εἴτε 4b12–13 immā/aw | 9b11–12 immā/wa-immā | 5a17–18 in/wa-in

ἐκ *w.gen.* 6b14, 11b11 min | 7a9 ʿan | 11b24 munḏu | 8b27 *om. Ar.*

ἕκαστος 5a18, 5b4, 7a11, 7a17, 8b22, 9a10 (9a11), 9a15, 9b18, 10a2 kullu wāḥidin min | 8b26 kullu wāḥidin | 11a4 wāḥidun wāḥidun | 7a20* *transl. by the attached pron.* | 10a4 *n.t.* | 10a11[1,2] *om. Ar.* (*in lac.*)

ἑκάτερος – ἑκάτερα 4a12 kullu wāḥidin minhumā/al-āḫaru | *in* ἑκατέρωθεν 11a25 ǧanbatāni *dual*

ἑκατέρωθεν 11a25 ʿan ǧanbatayni *dual*

ἐκεῖνος 5a4, 7a10 ḏālika | 5a26 hāḏā | 6b19 *sem. amplif.* sāʾiruhā mā ḫalā hāḏihī | 9b13 *sem. amplif.* hāḏā l-qawlu l-āḫaru | 11a14 *transl. by the emphasis expressed by the foll.* qad yaẓharu

ἔκφυσις 10b10 nabātun

ἔλαφος 10b12 ayyilun

ἐλάχιστος *in* τοὐλάχιστον 7a16 aṣġaru *in* aṣġaru l-umūri

ἔμμορφος 7a6 mušakkalun | *in gloss* 7a8 *om. Ar.*

ἐμποιέω 4b3 aḥdaṯa fī

ἔμπροσθεν 11a10 min muqaddami *w. gen.*

ἐμφαίνω 4b12 awḍaḥa | 11a14 ẓahara – ἐμφαίνομαι *med.* 8b14 ẓahara li-

ἔμψυχος 5b2, 7a17, 11a16 ḏū nafsin | 5b6, 11a17 lahū nafsun

ἐν *w. dat.* (**a**) 4a17, 4b20, 5a12, 6a4, 6b16, 6b18, 6b19*, 6b21, 6b27, 7a1, 7a8, 7a13, 7a17, 7a21[1], 7a22, 7b4, 7b15*, 8a12, 8b4, 8b15, 8b24, 9a3, 9a13, 9a16, 9a27, 9b3, 9b5, 9b19, 10a6, 10a12, 10a27[1,2], 10b4, 10b7, 10b10, 10b25, 11a5, 11a19, 11b3, 11b12*, 11b13, 11b17[1,2], 11b25[1,2], 12a1 fī | 4a18, 4b9, 4b10, 5b6, 8a23, 9a1 wuǧūduhū fī | 7b9 (7b10), 10b20 (10b21[1,2]) min | 6b11 ʿinda | 10a14 ʿalā ḥāli *w. gen.* | 7a12 ǧarā ʿalā | 7a21[2], 8b18, 11b21 *n.t.* | 4a6, 11a11 *om. Ar.* (*in lac.*) – *in* ἐν μέρει 9a2 *morph.; transl. by the nisba ending* -iyyun *in* ǧuzʾiyyun – 10a17 *Ar. read* μηδέν *for* μηδ' ἐν | 10a18 *Ar. read* οὐδέν *for* οὐδ' ἐν (**b**) *in compound adj., expressing the possession of a quality* (*LSJ E.I.2*) 5b2, 7a17 ḏū | 5b6 lahū

ἕν → εἷς

ἐναντίος 11b7 mutaḍāddun – τοὐναντίον 6b18* mutaḍāddun – ἐναντία 11b11, 11b12 ašyāʾu mutaḍāddatun – (τὰ) ἐναντία 8a23, 8b5 al-mutaḍāddātu

ἐνδέχομαι – ἐνδέχεται *impers.* 9a21 yumkinu an | 11a6 iḥtamala | 11b10 kāna bihī an – ἐνδεχόμενος 7b20 mumkinun
ἕνεκα 10a1, 10a28, 10b23 li- *in* la-hū | 10b18, 11a1 min qibali *w. gen.* | 10a22, 11b26 min aǧli *w. gen.* – {7a21} *Ar. read* ἓν ἕκαστον *for* ἕνεκά του
ἐνεργάζομαι 8b13 aḥdaṯa li-
ἐνέργεια 5a7, 5b23, 7b13, 8a11, 9a4 fiʿlun | 10a11 *om. Ar.* (*in lac.*)
ἐνεργέω 10a12 faʿala
ἔνθα 6b21 *interpr.* fī hāḏihi s-sabīli
ἔνιοι 6b16 baʿḍun | 10b10 baʿḍu *w. gen.* – ἔνιαι {9a1*} min – ἔνια 9a18, 10a25 ašyāʾu | 10b14 *om. Ar.* (*in lac.*)
ἐνταῦθα 7b6 fī hāḏā l-mawḍiʿi | 11a9 *n.t.*
ἔντιμος – ἐντιμότατος 5b22 fī ġāyati š-šarafi
ἐξαίρω 5a9 rafaʿa
ἔοικα 10b26 aḫlaqu bi-
ἐπεί 4b22 min qibali anna | 5b5 fa-inna | 7b15, 9b17, 11a3 wa-ḏālika anna
ἐπειδή 5a15 min qibali anna
ἐπείπερ 4b19 min qibali anna
ἐπεισοδιώδης 4a14 madḫūlun
ἐπί (**a**) *w. gen.* 9a21, 11a8 fī | 11a2 (11a3) ʿalā – ἐφ' ὧν 11a6 fī-mā (**b**) *w. accus.* 7b22, 9b10 ilā | 8a20 fī – ἐφ' ὅσον 11b9 ayḍan – ἐπὶ πλέον 8b16 amʿana
ἐπιζητέω 5b11 *paraphr.* fīhi mawḍiʿu ṭalabin wa-baḥṯin
ἐπιθεωρέω – ἐπιθεωροῦμαι *pass.* 11b13 *n.t.*
ἐπιμιμέομαι 11b1 taqayyala
ἐπίπεδος – ἐπίπεδον 6a26 saṭḥun
ἐπιποθέω 8a8 iqtaḍā
ἐπιπρόσθησις 10b13 satrun
ἐπίσταμαι 9a4 waqafa ʿalā – τὸ ἐπίστασθαι 8b16, 9a10 al-maʿrifatu | 9a26 ʿulima
ἐπιστήμη 6b20 ʿilmun | 8b20, 8b25 maʿrifatun
ἕπω – ἑπόμενα 9a14 lawāḥiqu
ἐρύω {5b17} ǧabara
ἔρχομαι 6a23 balaġa
ἐρῶ – εἴρηται 6b10 (6b11) waṣafa – τὰ εἰρημένα 6b15 *transl. by the subst. to which it refers* – τῶν εἰρημένων (?) {10a4*} allatī qulnā
ἐρῳδιός 10b14 *om. Ar.* (*in lac.*)
ἐσθλός – ἐσθλά 8a27 al-ḫayrātu
Ἑστιαῖος {6b10} annahū yatadāwalu
ἔσχατος 9a14 bi-aḫaratin
ἕτερος 4b6, 7b23, 10b19, 11b7 (11b6) āḫaru | 5a18, 7b21 ġayru *w. gen.* | 6a15 *sem. metathesis; affirm. / neg. transformation* laysa hāḏā – ἕτερα 7a23 ašyāʾu | 6b4, 10b6 ašyāʾu uḫaru| 5b6, 8b17, 10a7, 10b25 ġayru *w. gen.* | 10b15 *om. Ar.* (*in lac.*)
ἐτήσιος 7b3 as-sanati, *foll. in the gen. after a subst.*
ἔτι 7b22, 9b25, 10b7, 10b20 (10b24a) ayḍan | 6b5 *in context,* faḍlan ʿan an yašraʿū fīhi | 10b11 *sem. amplif. acc. to sense*: mimmā yaǧrī ayḍan hāḏā l-maǧrā | 5a8, 7a4, 8b4 *n.t., but included in* wa- *transl.* ἔτι δέ | 8b6 *n.t., but included in the foll. elative* abdaʿu *transl.* πλέον παράδοξον | 9b20 *om. Ar.* (*in lac.*) – ἔτι δή 6b9 maʿa ḏālika – ἔτι *in* οὐκέτι 9b11 ḥīnaʾiḏin
εὖ – τὸ εὖ 11a15 al-amru l-afḍalu – *in* Εὔρυτος {6a20} salisun
εὐθύς 6a17 dufʿatan
εὔλογος – εὐλόγως 6b21 wāǧiban – εὐλογώτερος *comp.* 4b8 al-awlā | 4a13 *sem.; etym.* al-awlā fī l-qiyās
Εὐριπίδης 8a26 ʾwrybydys
Εὔρυτος {6a20} *sem.; etym.* salisu l-ǧaryi
εὔσημος 4a19 bayyinun
ἐφάπτω – ἐφάπτομαι *med.* 6a27 adraka

ἐφεξῆς – τὰ ἐφεξῆς 6a17 sāʾiru l-ašyāʾi llatī tattaṣilu bi-hā

ἔφεσις 5a14, 5a28, 6a9 tašawwuqun

ἐφετικός 5b11 ḏū tašawwuqin

ἔφοδος 10a28 maḏhabun

ἔχω (**a**) (*to have*) 4b2, 5b4, 8a19, 9a16, 9b11 li- *w. attached pron. or subst.* | 10b22 ṣāra li- *w. gen.* | 5a24 kāna fī *w. attached pron.* | 6a5 kāna bayna *w. attached pron.* | 11a3 māla ilā | 8a21, 10b26, 11b18 fī *w. gen.* | 4b9 *transl. by the pron. attached to the subst. being possessed* ṭabīʿatuhā | 4a5 *om. Ar.* (*in lac.*) – ἔχω λόγον 10b24 *sem. concentr.* munqāsun (**b**) (*to be in a state*) 5b19 al-ḥālu fīhi | 12a2 ḥālu *w. gen.* – ἔχειν οὕτως 10a25 ǧarā hāḏā l-maǧrā | 7a1 *sem. concentr.* ka-ḏālika

Ζεύς 5b16 Zʾws

ζητέω (**a**) *transl. by* baḥaṯa: 5b19, 8b11, 8b13, 9b3, 10a17, 10b23 (10b24a) baḥaṯa ʿan | 8b1 baḥaṯa | 8b15 *in hend.* al-baḥṯu wa-t-taftīšu – τὸ ζητεῖν 8a22 al-baḥṯu ʿan – *in* ἀζήτητος 6a3 baḥṯun | *in* ἐπιζητέω 5b11 *in hend.* ṭalaba wa-baḥaṯa (**b**) *transl. by other verbs* 9b21 ṭalaba | 5a22, 7b19 iqtaḍā | 7b6 iḥtāǧa ilā | 9b23 iltamasa

ζήτησις 6b22 (6b21) baḥṯun

ζῶ 10b15 *om. Ar.* (*in lac.*)

ζωή 4b3, 5b3, 10a16, 10a17 ḥayātun

ζῷον 5b5, 7a22, 7b4, 8a5, 8b27, 9a14, 10a5, 10a13, 10a17, 10b7, 10b18 (10b17), 11a8 ḥayawānun

ἤ (**a**) *disjunctive* 4b8[1,2], 4b18, 5a5, 6a5, 6a15, 8a5[1,2], 8a13, 9b2, 9b7, 10a8, 10a17, 10a19, 11b6 aw | 10b1, 10b2, 10b10, 10b28 (11a1a) wa- | 9b1 wa-laʿalla | {7b8} in (*transl. the variant* εἰ *in the MSS*) | {10a4*} *n.t.* | 6b26, 10b14 *om. Ar.* (*in lac.*) – ἤτοι/ἤ 8b25–26 immā/wa-immā – πότερον/ἤ → πότερος (**b**) *comparative* 5a11, 9a22 min – τοὐναντίον ἤ 6b18 mutaḍaddāni (*transl. by the Ar. dual*)

ᾗ 10b26* fa- | 10b4* wa-ka-ḏālika (*emendation for* ἤ *in all sources*) | 11b7* aw (*emendation for* ἤ *in all sources*)

ἤδη 5a14 *n.t.*

ἥλιος 7b5 šamsun

ἡμεῖς → ἐγώ

ἡμερόβιος – τὸ ἡμερόβιον 10b15 *om. Ar.* (*in lac.*)

ἡμέτερος 9b7 la-nā | 9b12 *transl. by the attached pron. w. postpositive pers. pron. and* nafsun: ...nā naḥnu anfusunā

Ἡράκλειτος 7a15 ʾrʾqlyṭs

ἠρεμέω 8a1, 10a15 sakana – τὸ ἠρεμεῖν 7b16 as-sukūnu

ἠρεμία 5a24, 7b10 sukūnun

ἤτοι (ἤ τοι) → ἤ

ἥττων *in* ἧττον *adv.* 8a16 ʿalā dūni *w. gen.*

θάλασσα 5b17 baḥrun – θάλαττα 10b1 māʾu l-baḥri

θεῖος 4b15 ilāhiyyun – τὰ θεῖα 6b9 (al-ašyāʾu) l-ilāhiyyatu – θειότερος *comp.* 5a10 ašbahu bi-llāhi – θειότατος *superl.* 6a1 aḥaqqu l-ašyaʾi bi-annahū llāhu

θεός 4b15, 7b23, 11b8[1,2] allāhu

θέσις 10a3 (10a2) waḍʿun

θεωρέω 8b11 waqafa ʿalā | 9b9 (9b8) adraka – τὰ θεωρούμενα 8b22 al-ašyāʾu llatī tuʿlamu

θεωρία 9b15, 12a1 naẓarun fī | 4a3 *om. Ar.* (*in lac.*)

θῆλυς 10b9 *om. Ar.* (*in lac.*)

θιγγάνω 9b15 misāsun

θρίξ 10b10 šaʿrun

ἰδέα 6b13, 10b28 ṣūratun

ἴδιος 9a20 ḫāṣṣiyyun ▬ ἴδιον 8b22, 9a16 ḫāṣṣun ▬ τὸ ἴδιον 4b21 al-amru lladī yaḫuṣṣu ▬ τὰ ἴδια 8b21 al-ašyāʾu l-ḫāṣṣiyyatu ▬ ἰδίᾳ 8b26 ḫāṣṣiyyan

ἱκανός ▬ ἱκανῶς 9a18 bāliġan *modifying a mafʿūl muṭlaq*

ἵππος 6a22 farasun

ἰσομοιρέω 8a24 kāna muʿādilan | 11b6 muḍāhin

ἰσόμοιρος *in* ἰσομοιρέω 8a24 muʿādilun

ἰσχυρός ▬ ἰσχυρότερος *comp.* 5b15, 6b19 aqwā

ἴσως 4b13 aḫlaqu bi- | 8a3 ḫalīqun an | 6a12 fī-mā aḥsibu | 6a6 *n.t.*

καθά ▬ καθάπερ 6a24, 8a12, 8b3, 9a3, 10a12, 10b8, 10b11, 11a21 bi-manzilati (mā) | 4a19, 9a19, 10a23 ʿalā mā | 6b27, 9a22, 10a27 ka-mā| 7a2 miṯla | 4b3 maṯalan | 11b2 *n.t.*

καθόλου 9a1, 9a27 kulliyyun | 8b25 kulliyyan | {8a26} ṣawābun ▬ τὰ καθόλου 8b20 al-kulliyyātu | 8b18 al-ašyāʾu l-kulliyyatu | 8b19 *transl. by a pron.*

καὶ **(a)** (*and*) 4a14, 4a15, 4a17, 4b4, 4b5, 4b6, 4b14, 4b20, 5a2, 5a10, 5a11, 5a15[1,2], 5a17, 5b2, 5b9[1,2], 5b18, 5b20, 5b22, 5b25[2], 6a3, 6a8, 6a9, 6a11, 6a14, 6a18, 6a24[2], 6a26[1,2], 6a27, 6b1[1,2], 6b2, 6b3[1,3], 6b4, 6b20[1], 6b23, 6b25[1], 6b28, 7a2[1], 7a11, 7a12[1,2,3], 7a13, 7a17, 7a23, 7b2, 7b7, 7b12, 7b14, 7b18, 7b22, 7b23[1], 8a5, 8a9, 8a20, 8a24, 8b2, 8b3 (8b4), 9a3, 9a11, 9a12[2], 9a14[1,2,3], 9a24, 9a25, 9b2 (9b3), 9b5, 9b15[1], 9b19, 9b25 (9b26[1]), 9b26[1,2,3], 10a2[1,2], 10a3[1,2], 10a5, 10a7[1], 10a10[1], 10a12, 10a13, 10a15, 10a18, 10a22, 10a24, 10b1, 10b2[1*,2], 10b3[1,2] (10b3–4[1]), 10b4, 10b5, 10b16[1], 10b16[2] (10b17), 10b17, 10b20, 10b26[1], 11a2, 11a6, 11a7, 11a17 (11a18a), 11a19, 11a25, 11a27, 11b3[1], 11b12, 12a1 wa- | *in* κἄν (καὶ ἐάν) 8b14 wa- | καὶ (*adding a limiting or defining expr.*: *LSJ A I 2*) 8a11 wa-qad *w. impf.* (*ḥāl*) | 7b5 fa- | 4b11 aw | 5a17[1] wa- ... ayḍan | 9b17[1] wa-kaḏālika | 4a16, 4b10[1,2,3], 5a3, 6a19, 6b9[2], 7b21, 8b25, 9a12[1], 9a13, 9a27, 9b10, 10b19, 10b27, 11a1, 11a3, 11a8, 11a13[2], 11a20, 11a22, 11b13[2] *n.t.* | 4a2, 4a4, 4a6[1], 4a8[1], 4a8[3], 4a10, 6b25, 9b20, 10a10[2], 10a11, 10b8, 10b13[2], 10b15[1,2], 11a11 *om. Ar.* (*in lac.*) **(b)** καί (*also*) 5a4*, 5a23, {5a27}, 5b10[2], 6a1, 6a4, 6b16, 7a4, 7b23[2], 8a8, 8a21, 8b19, 9a16, 9b16, 11b7[1] ayḍan | 7a2[2] *sem. amplif.* wa-ka-ḏālika yaǧrī l-amru | 9a6[2] *sem. amplif.* wa-maʿa ḏālika ayḍan | 5b3, 5b4, 5b5, 5b10[1], 5b25[1], 6a16, 6a24[1], 6b9[2], 7a1, 7a3, 7b10, 8a6, 8b6, 8b20, 9a18, 9b15[2], 9b22, 10a8, 10a14 (*in* κἄν), 10a20, 10b25, 10b26[2], 11a13[1] *n.t.* | 10a10[2] *om. Ar. in lac.* **(c)** καί (*even*) 6a12, 11b13[1] ayḍan | 10b12[1] ḥattā anna | 7b9 *transl. by the emphasis indicated in the inverted Ar. word order* minhā btadaʾnā bi-l-kalāmi | 5b5, 5b26, 6b20[2], 7a10, 7b19, 8a25[1,2], 9a17, 9b1, 11b6, 11b7[2], 11b19 *n.t.* | 4a6[2] *om. Ar.* (*in lac.*) **(d)** *in combinations* καὶ/καὶ 4b16, 7a5, 8b10–11, 10a9–10a10[1], 11a4, 11b17, 11b25 -/wa- | 5a7, 11b26 wa-/wa- ▬ καὶ ἄλλως/καί 9b17–18 -/wa- ... maʿa ḏālika ▬ καὶ/καὶ/καὶ 6b8[1,2]–6b9[1], 7a21–22, 7b4, 9a5–6[1], 10b22–23 (10b23a), 11b3[2]–4[1,2] -/wa-/wa- ▬ καὶ ... δέ 8a23, 10b6, 10b10 wa- | 7a15–16 wa- ... ayḍan | 4a8[2] *om. Ar.* (*in lac.*) ▬ καὶ γὰρ δή 10a7 fa-inna ▬

κυκλοφορία 5b28 al-ḥarakatu d-dawriyyatu
κύριος *in* κυριώτατος 4b5 ḫaṭarun | 10a7 qadrun ‒ κυριώτατος *superl.* 4b5 aʿẓamu ḫaṭaran ‒ τὰ κυριώτατα 10a7 al-umūru llatī hiya aǧallu qadran
κωλύω 6a11 manaʿa ‒ κωλύομαι *med.* 5b28 imtanaʿa min

λαμβάνω 8a3, 9a27, 9b9 aḫaḏa | 10b28 qabila | 8a20 fahima | 11a2 waqafa ʿalā | 4b14 idrākun | 11b22 iʿtaqada | 7a16 istaʿmala n-naẓara | 11b25 *n.t.* | 10b16 *om. Ar.* (*in lac.*)
λέγω 4b7, 5b1, 6a21, 8a26, 8b2, 10a24, 11b24 qāla | 5a27 (5a26b), 9a22 qāla bi- | 5a9 (5a8), 10a1 (9b27), 11b14 ḏakara ‒ λέγων *act. part.* 5a13 man qāla bi- | 6a4 al-qāʾilu bi- | 11a22 allaḏīna takallamū ‒ λεγόμενος *pass. part.* 8b25 (8b24b), 9b1 allaḏī yuqālu | 11a4 iḏā qīla ‒ τὸ λεχθέν 7b23 al-qawlu
λευκός ‒ τὰ λευκά 8b3 al-ašyāʾu l-bīḍu
λόγος 4a23, 7a12, 8a14 nisbatun | 5a6, 5a14, 8a27, 10b26 qawlun | 5a12 martabatun | 5a22, 6a15, 7b9, 8a8 kalāmun | 9b21, 9b22 ḥuǧǧatun | 7a20 ḥaddun ‒ λόγος *in* λογώδης 7b18 nuṭqun | *in* ἀστρολογία 9b27, 10a5 ṣināʿatun ‒ ἔχω λόγον 10b25 *sem. concentr.* munqāsun
λογώδης 7b18 ḏū nuṭqin
λοιπός ‒ λοιπόν 5a1 allaḏī baqiya | 5b18 baqiya ‒ αἱ λοιπαὶ (*sc.* μέθοδοι) 6b22 sāʾiru s-subuli | (*sc.* ἐπιστῆμαι) 7a1 sāʾiru l-ʿulūmi ‒ τὰ λοιπά 6b4 sāʾiru l-ašyāʾi
λύω ‒ λύομαι *med.* 5a4 infasaḫa
λωβάομαι ‒ λελωβημένος *pass. part.* 10b12 taʾaḏḏā

μάθημα ‒ τὰ μαθήματα 9a17 at-taʿālīmu
μαθηματικός ‒ αἱ μαθηματικαί (*sc.* ἐπιστῆμαι) 7a3 at-taʿālīmu ‒ τὰ μαθηματικά 4a18, 9a16, 11b20 at-taʿālīmu | 6b9 (al-ašyāʾu) t-taʿālīmiyyatu
μακρός 11a27 bāʿada kaṯīran
μάλα (**a**) *comp.* μᾶλλον 5a10 awlā ‒ μᾶλλον δέ 8a24, 9b22, 11a15 bal ‒ καὶ μᾶλλον 10b21 bal (**b**) *superl.* μάλιστα 9b19, 10a10 ḫāṣṣatan | 10b16 (10b17) aḫaṣṣu bi- | 5b9, 11b17 awlā bi- | 6b26 *morph.; transl. the elative form in the hend.* aḥaqqu wa-awlā bi- ‒ μάλιστα *in* ὅ τι μάλιστα 8a4 fī ġāyat *in* fī ġāyati mā yumkinu an yakūna ʿalayhi
μαστός 10b8 ṯadyun
μάταιος 10b8 bāṭilun
μάτην 10a22 bāṭilun
μέγας 9b17 ʿaẓīmu l-ʿġanāʾi ‒ *comp.* μείζων 5a21 aǧallu | 7b18 (7b19) aʿẓamu | 4a9 *om. Ar.* (*in lac.*) ‒ *superl.* μέγιστος 7b2, 10b16 aʿẓamu *w. gen.* | 9b19 aǧallu *w. gen.* ‒ (τὸ) μέγιστον 9a11 malākun
μέγεθος 9b26 miqdārun | 10b11 ʿaẓīmun
μεθίστημι ‒ μεθίσταμαι *pass.* 10b6 (10b5) tanaqqulun *w.* min
μέθοδος 6b18 sabīlun
μείζων → μέγας
μέλας ‒ μέλανα 8b4 al-ašyāʾu s-sūdu
μέλλω *in* μέλλον 8b7 *morph.; transl. by the future sense of the impf.*, yakūnu mawǧūdan
μέν/δέ (**a**) 4a15, 4a18–4b6, 6a28–6b2, 6b21, 7a11–13, 7b11–12, 8a10, 8b2–3, 8b12–13, 9a1–2, 9b6–7, 9b7, 10a26, 11a5–7 -/wa- (**b**) 5a6–13, 6a2–5, 7b6–9 fa-ammā ... fa-/wa-ammā ... fa- (**c**) 8b8–9, 11b23–24 -/fa-ammā ...

ὁ, ἡ, τό *the following entries do not include all the occurrences of the article but are representative of its various uses, as translated by the Ar.* (**a**) *in its pronominal uses, the Gr. article is transl. by a corresponding Ar. pron. or subst.* ‒ οἱ *masc. pl.* 5a13[1] man | 7a6b, 7a7[1,2] baʿḍun | 6b15 baʿḍu n-nāsi | 6a23 mina n-nāsi | 6a24, 8b6 qawmun | 9b21, 11a22 allaḏīna | 6b6 (οἱ περί), 11a27 šīʿat *w. gen.* ‒ τὰς 4a16 tilka | ὁ 10a8 hāḏā ‒ τό 8b24[1] allaḏī | τά 9a15, {10a4[2]} allatī ‒ *with* ὁ μέν/ὁ δέ 8a10 aḥaduhumā/al-āḫaru | 9b6–7, 9b7 ḏālika/hāḏā ‒ *with* τὰ μὲν/τὰ δὲ/(τὰ δέ) 4a15, 10a26 baʿḍuhā/wa-baʿḍuhā | 6a28–6b2 baʿḍu l-ašyāʾi/wa-baʿḍuhā | 8b12–13 ašyāʾu/wa-ašyāʾu | 9a8–9 baʿḍu l-umūri/wa-baʿḍuhā/ wa-baʿḍuhā ‒ *substituted in Ar. with the noun to which it refers*: ἡ (*sc.* κίνησις) 5a3 al-ḥaraka | ὅ (*sc.* λόγος) 5a22 kalāmun | τάς (*sc.* ἀρχάς) 7a7 al-mabādiʾu | τάς (*sc.* πραγματείας) 9b20[1*,2] ʿilmun | 7a7, 7a8 *om. Ar.* ‒ *in attributive position preceding an adj., transl. by a relative clause in Ar.*: ὄρεξις ἡ ἀρίστη 5a20 hāḏihi š-šahwatu llatī hiya afḍalu š-šahawāti ‒ *interpr.; demonstr. as possessive, transl. by attached pron.*: τὰς ἀρχάς 7a19 mabādiʾuhā | τῇ περιφορᾷ 10a14 ḥarakatuhā (**b**) *the Gr. article in its function as subst. maker is transl. either* (b1) *by the Ar. article, or* (b2) *by a generic Ar. subst. or pron.* (mā, šayʾun, amrun), *or* (b3) *by an Ar. nominal clause introduced by* an *or* anna, *or* (b4) *by an Ar. subst. add. acc. to sense in context* (**b1**) *transl. by the Ar. article*: τὸ *in* τὸ ἄριστον 11a6 al-afḍalu | τὸ ἀεί 11a7 ad-dawāmu | τὸ τεταγμένον 11a7 an-niẓāmu | τὸ ἀγαθόν 11a19 al-ǧayyidu | τὸ κακόν 11a20 ar-radīʾu | τὸ τίμιον 11a23 aš-šarīfu | τὸ ἕν 11b3 al-wāḥidu | τὸ ἄπειρον 11b3 al-ḫurūǧu ʿani t-tanāhī | τὸ ἄτακτον 11b4 al-ḫurūǧu ʿani n-niẓāmi | τὸ ἀποδοῦναι 4b17 al-wafāʾu ‒ τά *in* τὰ ἐναντία 8b5 al-mutaḍāddātu | τὰ πρῶτα 6b11, 9a12, 10a1, 10a6, 11b13 al-awāʾilu | τὰ μαθηματικά 11b20 at-taʿālīmu (**b2**) *transl. by an Ar. generic subst. or pron.* ‒ *transl. by* mā: τό/τά 5a13[2], 5b4, τό 5b26[1,2], 6b19, 7a3, 7b1, 9a13, 9a14*, 10b16, 11a17, 11a21, 11b14 mā; *examples*: τὸ χεῖρον 7b8 mā huwa aḫassu | τὸ ἀμερές 8a3 mā lā ǧuzʾa lahū | τὸ μὴ ὄν 8b6 mā laysa bi-mawǧūdin | τὸ ἄψυχον 11a17 mā lā nafsa lahū | τὸ μὴ ὑπακοῦον 11a15 mā lā yuʾātī | τὸ ἕνεκά του 11b26 mā huwa min aǧli šayʾin | τὸ τί ἦν εἶναι 8b22 mā huwa š-šayʾu ‒ *transl. by* šayʾun: τά 4a16, 4a16–17, 4a19, 4a20, 4b3, 4b14, 4b19, 4b23, 5a15, 6a17, 6a28, 8a6, 8b22, 9a12, 9b1, 10a4, 10b7, 11b18 al-ašyāʾu | τὰ τοιάδε 8a8, 11a3 hāḏihi l-ašyāʾu | τὸ ὑποκείμενον 9a9 aš-šayʾu l-mawḍūʿu ‒ *transl. by* amrun: τὸ ἄριστον 11a2, 11b9 al-amru l-afḍalu | τὸ βέλτιον 11a9, 11b27 al-amru l-afḍalu | τὸ εὖ 11a15 al-amru l-afḍalu | τοὐλάχιστον 7a16 aṣġaru l-umūri | τὸ ἐν μέρει 9a2 al-umūru l-ǧuzʾiyyatu | τὸ περὶ τῆς ἠρεμίας 7b10 amru s-sukūni | τὰ οὐράνια 10a27[1] al-umūru s-samāwiyyatu | τὰ ἄριστα 6a4 afāḍilu l-umūri | τὰ τιμιώτατα 6b27 (6b28) ašrafu l-umūri | τὰ τοιαῦτα 9b14 ašbāhu hāḏihī mina l-umūri | τὰ περί τὰς ὥρας 7b3 amru l-awqāti | τὰ περὶ τὴν γῆν 10a27[2] al-umūru l-arḍiyyatu | τὰ κατὰ τὰς φορὰς 9b25 amru ḥarakātihā (**b3**) *transl. by a nominal clause introduced by* an *or* anna: τὸ περιθεῖναι 7a20 an naǧmaʿa | τὸ (*sc.* κινεῖσθαι) 5a18 an takūna tataḥarraku ‒ τὸ ἀνήνυτον 5a16 annahā lā tafturu | 10a22 τὸ πάντα (*sc.* εἶναι) καὶ (τὸ) μηδὲν (*sc.* εἶναι) 10a22 annahā takūnu wa-annahū laysa | τὸ μὴ ἔχειν 10b24 annahū laysa | τὸ (*sc.* εἶναι) 11a10 annahā ǧuʿilat ‒ τὸ περὶ τὴν τοῦ μέσου χώραν 11a24 *n.t.* | τὰ τῆς φύσεως 4a11 *om. Ar.* (*in lac.*) (**b4**) *transl. by a subst. add. acc. to sense in context*: τά 5b11, 5b12, 5b21 al-ağsāmu | τό 8b15 mawḍiʿun | τό 5a4 al-qawlu bi-annahū

ὅδε *demonstr. pron.* 6a22[1,2] hāḏā | 8b8 hāḏā l-amru | 6a21 hāḏā l-mušāru ilayhi | 8a17 hāḏā š-šayʾu l-mušāru ilayhi ‒ 10b12 baʿḍu *w. gen.* ‒ 6a5 *paraphr.* mā anā qāʾiluhū

ὁδός 9b4 ṭarīqun

ὅθεν 7b9 hiya llatī minhā

οἰκεῖος 9a11 mulāʾimun | 10a10 *in hend.* mulāʾimun wa-ḫāṣṣun | 5a22* anisa ilā ‒ οἰκειότερος *comp.* 9a21 alyaqu ‒ οἰκειότατος *superl.* 6b28 awlā wa-aḥaqqu bi- ‒

οἴομαι 10a8 ẓanna

οἷος (**a**) *as relative to a demonstr.* (*LSJ II.1*) 11b22 mā (**b**) *able to do* (*LSJ III.2*) οἷός τε *w. inf.* 4b2* amkana ‒ οἷόν τε 8b5, 9a27, 11b5 amkana an | 11a8 amkana (**c**) *adv.* (*LSJ V*) οἷον 4a14, 5a6, 5b21, 5b24, 6a2, 6b20, 6b25, 7a9, 7b5, 8b8, 9b15, 11b6 ka-anna | 4a21, 8b26, 10a15 (10a16) bi-manzilati *w. gen. or* mā | 6b1, 6b2, 11b14 miṯla | 9b20 miṯāluhū | 9a12, 11a9 miṯālu ḏālika | 11a20 *n.t.* | 4a10 *om. Ar.* (*in lac.*)

οἰσοφάγος 11a10 marīʾun

ὀλίγος 11a16 qalīlun | 10b6, 11a19 yasīrun | 7a2* šāḏḏun | {4b9} kaṯīrun | 10b15 *om. Ar.* (*in lac.*)

ὅλος 7a11, 8a6, 8a23, 11a22, 11b11 bi-asrihī ‒ τὸ ὅλον *subst.* 10b28, 11b5 al-kullu ‒ τὸ ὅλον *adv.* 11a18 bi-l-ǧumlati | 4a8 *om. Ar.* (*in lac.*) ‒ ὅλως 4a20, 8a19, 8b24, 10b3, 10b10, 11b5 bi-l-ǧumlati

Ὅμηρος 5b15 Umīrūs

ὄμμα 10b13 ʿaynun

ὁμογενής 9a17 min ǧinsin wāḥidin

ὅμοιος 8b1, 8b3 mutašābihun | *in* ὁμοίως 7a4 miṯālun | {6a4} maʿan wa-hiya llatī (*Ar. misread* ὅμοια *as* ἅμα ἅ) ‒ ὁμοίως 5a26, 6b8, 8a3, 9b3 (9b4) ʿalā miṯālin wāḥidin | 7a4, 7a16 ʿalā hāḏā l-miṯāli | 11a8 *n.t.*

ὁμοιότης 5b1 šabahun | 8a20 mušākalatun

ὁμοίωσις 4b13 tašbīhun

ὁμός *in* ὁμογενής 9a17 wāḥidun *in* min ǧīnsin wāḥidin

ὁμώνυμος 10a13, 10a15 samiyyun

ὅμως 5b6, 8b14 illā anna

ὄν → εἰμί

ὅπου 11a8 ḥayṯu

ὅπως 8a4 ʿalā anna

ὁρατός 9a23 mubṣarun

ὄργανον 7a5 ālatun

ὀρέγω ‒ ὀρέγομαι *med.* 11a6 tašawwaqa ilā | 6a10 tašawwuqun ‒ ὀρέγομαι, *as implied in* ἕκαστον (*sc.* τῶν ὀρεκτῶν) 5b4 ištahā ‒ τὰ ὀρεγόμενα 8a1 ⟨al-ašyāʾu⟩ l-mutašawwiqatu

ὀρεκτός 5a2 mutaššawaqun ilayhi

ὄρεξις 5a20, 5a24, 5b4, 5b10, 6a9, 11a14 šahwatun | 6a12 šawqun

ὁρίζω ‒ ὁρίζομαι *pass.* 6b27, 6b28 taḥdīdun ‒ ὡρισμένος 7a17, 10b21 (10b22) maḥdūdun | 4a6 *om. Ar.* (*in lac.*)

ὁριστός *in* ἀόριστον 8a18 ḥaddun *in* ḫurūǧun ʿani l-ḥaddi

ὁρμή 11b27 ḥarakatun
ὅρος 9b20, 11a2, 11b25 ḥaddun | *in* ἀοριστία 11a20 ḥaddun *in* ḫurūǧun ʿani l-ḥaddi
ὅς, ἥ, ὅ (a) *demonstr. pron.* 7b2 ḏālika | *in* διό 9b15 ḏālika *in* li-ḏālika (b) *relative pron.* 5a17, 5b10, 5b16, 8a6 allaḏī | 7b21 aš-šayʾu llaḏī | ὅ *in* ὅθεν 7b9 allaḏī ▬ 9a21, 9b23, 11a6, 11b24 mā | ἅ in καθάπερ 4a19 mā ▬ 4b16, 5a3, 5b4, 7b4, 11b3 *pron. attached to a prep.* ▬ δι' ἧς 8b14 bi-l-fikri (*transl. by the noun to which it refers*) ▬ 9a1* *n.t.*
ὅσος 9a2 qadrun | 9b27 mā ▬ ὅσον *adv.* 6a27 bi-qadri mā ▬ ἐφ' ὅσον 11b10 ayḍan ▬ ὅσα 11a13 kullu mā ▬ ὅσοι 9b24, 11b8 allaḏīna | ὅσοι λέγουσιν 5a26[1,2] *morph.; transl. by the act. part.* al-qāʾilūna ▬ 6b25 *om. Ar.* (*in lac.*)
ὅσπερ 4b5 huwa llaḏī | 6a19 wa-huwa mā | {7a5} fa-inna
ὅστις → ὅ τι
ὅταν 9b10, 10a12 iḏā
ὅ τι 8b1, 8b2 li-mā ▬ ὅ τι μάλιστα 8a4 fī ġāyati mā yumkinu an yakūna ʿalayhi
ὅτι 8b9, 10a13, 11a5 anna | 6a28 inna *after* qāla | 9b23 qawlun | 11a12 *om. Ar.* (*in lac.*)
οὐ (οὐκ, οὐχ) 5a24, 5b13, 6b10, 7b18, 8b1, 8b23, 9b15, 9b23, 10a6, 11a2, 11a15 lā | 4b2, 5b20, 7b17, 8a1, 8a3, 8a26, 8b5, 8b16, 9a27, 9b2, 10a8, 10a9, 10a23, 10b6, 11b5 laysa | 5a22, 7b13 lam | 8a2* wuǧūdun (*transl. the MS reading* οὖσιν) | 11a20† *understood as* οὗ, hāḏā, *in Ar.* | 5b22 *n.t.* | 4a7, 10b15 *om. Ar.* (*in lac.*) ▬ οὐ *w.* εἰμί 4b23, 5b8 laysa ▬ *in* οὐδέ 6b5, 6b6, 9b24, 11a15, 11b7 (11b8) lā *in* wa-lā ▬ *in* οὐκέτι 9b11 lam ▬ *in double neg.*, οὐ/οὐδέ 8a16–17 lam
οὐδαμοῦ 11a9 fī mawḍiʿin mina l-mawāḍiʿi *w. neg.*
οὐδέ 6b5, 6b6, 8b1, 9b24, 11a15, 11b7 (11b8) wa-lā | 4b4 laysa | 11b10 lā ... aṣlan | 10a18 *Ar. read* οὐδέν *for* οὐδ' ἐν ▬ οὐδέ *in* οὐθαμῶς 5a21 laysa ▬ *in double neg.* οὐ/οὐδέ 8a16–17 lam
οὐδείς/οὐθείς 6b6 aḥadun *w. neg.* | 10b18 laysa šayʾun | 4a23 laysa qāʾimun (*see note to the Ar. transl.*) | 6a11 laysa māniʿun | 5b12 *sem., etym.* laysa ... wa-lā wāḥidun | 6b5 lam ... aṣlan | 4a11 *om. Ar.* (*in lac.*) ▬ οὐδέν 8a15, 8b2 laysa
οὐθαμῶς 5a20 laysa ... bi-waǧhin mina l-wuǧūhi
οὐθείς → οὐδείς
οὐκέτι 9b11 lam ... ḥīnaʾiḏin
οὖν 5a25, 7a6, 10a5, 10a16 fa- | 6a15, 11a25 *n.t.* ▬ *in* δ' οὖν → δέ ▬ *in* μὲν οὖν → μέν
οὐράνιος ▬ τὰ οὐράνια 10a18, 11b19 al-aǧrāmu s-samāwiyyatu | 10a27 al-umūru s-samāwiyyatu
οὐρανός 5b20, 6a7, 6a14, 6b3, 6b4, 7a11, 8a6, 9b24, 10a14, 10a18 samāʾun | 10a10 *om. Ar.* (*in lac.*)
οὐσία 4a13, 4b6, 5a8, 6a7, 7a10, 8a13, 8a23, 8b21, 9a5, 10a3, 10a14, 11a22, 11b11, 11b26 ǧawharun | 10a11 *om. Ar.* (*in lac.*)
οὔτε/οὔτε 4a19–20 laysa/wa-lā | 11b15 lam/wa-lā
οὗτος *demonstr. pron.* 4b21, 5b20, 6a15[1,2], 6a19, 6b7, 6b17, 8a21, 8b19, 9a1, 9a6, 9a13, 9b1, 9b17 (9b16), 10b7, 10b18, 10b24, 10b27, 11a1, 11b23, 11b27 hāḏā | *in* οὕτως 4b17 hāḏā | *in* τοιοῦτος 4b18 hāḏā | 4b20 *sem. amplif.* hāḏā l-amru | 6a2, 6a14, 7b5 *sem. amplif.* hāḏā l-maʿnā | 4b11 *sem. amplif.* hāḏā l-ǧawharu | 5a6 *sem. amplif.* hāḏā l-mawḍiʿu ▬ 5a13, 5b14, 6a3, 9a25, 10b25, 11b5,

11b20 ḏālika | *in* οὕτως 4a17 ḏālika ▬ 4b7 fīhi, 9b27 ʿalayhim, 11b21 akṯaruhā: *transl. by the attached pron.* ▬ 6b13, 6b14, 6b26 *transl. by the subst. to which it refers* ▬ 5b10 *sem.amplif.* mā anā qāʾiluhū ... aʿnī ▬ 7b15, 10b23 *n.t.*

οὕτω, -ς 7a2, 8a14 ka-ḏālika | 4a17 kāna l-amru ka-ḏālika | 4b17 ʿalā hāḏā l-waǧhi | 5a10 ʿalā hāḏā n-naḥwi | 9a4, 11a14 ǧarā hāḏā l-maǧrā | 10a26 hāḏā *in* ǧarā hāḏā l-maǧrā

ὀχεύω 10b15 *om. Ar.* (*in lac.*)

πάλιν ▬ πάλιν αὖ 7a20 ayḍan

παντοῖος 7b1 *in hend.* āḫaru ġayruhū | 4a5 *om. Ar.* (*in lac.*)

παρά *w. gen.* 5b27 min ▬ *w. accus.* 9a6 ḫāriǧun ʿan | 10b14 *om. Ar.* (*in lac.*)

παράδειγμα 7b2 dalīlun

παράδοξος ▬ τὸ παράδοξον 8b6 *in hend.* badīʿu š-šanāʿati ▬ παραδοξότερος *comp.* 8b4 abdaʿu

παραιώρησις 10b13 istiqlālun

παραλείπω 6a27 amsaka ʿan | 11a9 qaṣara

παρόμοιος 10b6 naẓīrun

πᾶς 7a7, 8b21, 11b20 kullu *w. gen.* | 10a9 bi-asrihī | 4a13, 11b4 *n.t.* ▬ τὸ πᾶν 4a14, 4a21, 8a23, 8b8, 10a16 al-kullu | πᾶν *in* τὸ σύμπαν 10a3 al-kullu ▬ πάντα 4b15, 5a7, 11a3 ǧamīʿu l-ašyāʾi | 8b1[1], 8b2, 10a22, 11b9 al-ašyāʾu kulluhā | 5a18, 8b1[2] kulluhā | 6a1 al-umūru kulluhā

πάσχω ▬ τὸ πάσχειν 5b6, 7b22 al-infiʿālu

παύω ▬ παύομαι *med.* 6a8 sukūnun | 6a18 *in hend.* inqaṭaʿa wa-nḥalla | *in* ἄπαυστος 5a4 tafattara

πείθω ▬ πείθομαι, πέποιθα *in* πιστός 10b27 waṯiqa bi-

πειράω ▬ πειρῶμαι *med.* 4b7, 6b9 rāma (*or* rāma an yubayyina? *see note*) | 4b12, 9a24, 11b24 iltamasa

περ → εἴπερ, ἐπείπερ, καίπερ, ὅσπερ

πέρας *in* ἄπειρον 9b4 nihāyatun | 11b3 tanāhin

περί (**a**) *w. gen.* 5a14, 6b4, 11a22 fī | 6b10 ʿinda | 11b23 ʿan (*following* baḥaṯa) | τὸ περί 7b10 amru *w. gen.* | *title** *om. Ar.* (*in lac.*) (**b**) *w. accus.* 6b8, 6b17, 7b1, 9b16, 11a24 fī | 11b14 min | 10b17 amru *w. gen.* | τὰ περί 7b3 amru *w. gen.* | 5b12 waliya | 9b20[1,2] *n.t.* ▬ περι- *in* περιτίθημι 4a23 waṣf ▬ οἱ περί 6b6 šīʿat *w. gen.* ▬ περὶ τὴν γῆν 10a28a *transl. by the nisba ending* -iyyun *in* arḍiyyun

περιεργία 8a22 fuḍūlun

περίοδος 7a13 dawrun

περιτίθημι 4a23 waḍaʿa waṣfan | 6b7 ǧaʿala | 7a20 ǧamaʿa

περιττός 4b10 zāʾidun

περιφορά 5b25, 6a7, 10a14, 10a16, 10b28 ḥarakatun

πέφυκα → φύω

πιστικός ▬ πιστικοτέρως 4b18 aqrabu ilā t-taṣdīqi

πίστις 9b17 taṣdīqun bi-

πιστός 10b27 mā yaǧibu an yūṯaqa bihī

Πλάτων 6b11, 11a27 Aflāṭun

πλεῖστος ▬ πλεῖστον *adv.* 9a8 kaṯīran ▬ διὰ πλείστου 9a7 akṯara mā

πλείων 4b11, 6b4, 8b18, 10a28 (10a27), 11a16 kaṯīrun | 5a15, 5a19 akṯaru min wāḥidin| 5a14 ablaġu ▬ πλέον 8a25, 11b21 akṯaru | 8b6 *morph.; transl. by the comp. degree in the foll. elative* abdaʿu ▬ τὸ πλέον 7b8 al-akṯaru ▬ πλείονα 8b24 ašyāʾu kaṯīratun ▬ ἐπὶ πλέον 8b16 amʿana

πλεονάκις 10a24 fī mawāḍiʿa kaṯīratin

πλεοναχῶς 9a10 ʿalā wuǧūhin kaṯīratin | 9b1 min ǧihātin šattā πλῆθος 5a21 kaṯratun | 11a19 ʿadadun

πλήν *conj.* 6b6, 7a2* mā ḫalā | 6a27 illā anna | {8a3} fa-inna – πλὴν εἰ 7a22, 11b21 illā an

πόθεν 10a24 min ayyi l-umūri layta šiʿri

ποιέω 5a7, 9b19, 10b25, 11a24 (11a23) ǧaʿala | 11b2 waḍaʿa | 6a25 qāla bi- | *in* ποιητός 9a3 ʿamila | {6a20} *sem. amplif.* fiʿluhū an yaǧʿala mā yaǧʿaluhū – τὸ ποιεῖν 7b21 al-fiʿlu – ποιοῦμαι *med.* 7b3 ǧaʿala – ποιοῦμαι μνείαν 6b5 *sem. concentr.* ḏakara

ποιητός 9a3 (al-ašyāʾu llatī) tuʿmalu

ποικιλία {7b1} *Ar. transl.* ποικίλος *instead*

ποικίλος {7b1*} *in hend.* kaṯīrun muḫtalifun

ποῖος *interr.* 4a18, 10a25 ayyu *w. foll. gen.* | 5a15 ayyu šayʾin | 6b23 ayyu l-ašyāʾi | 4a2 *om. Ar.* (*in lac.*)

ποιός 8a18 kayfa

πόλις 8a5 madīnatun

πολλαχῶς 8b9 ʿalā anḥāʾin šattā

πολύς 11a14 (11a15), 11a19 kaṯīrun – πολλῷ *dat. of manner, w. comp.* 8a25, 11a16 kaṯīran – πολλά 11b13 ašyāʾu kaṯīratun | *in* πολλαχῶς 8b9 šattā | 11b16 *n.t.* – οἱ πολλοί 6a23 al-kaṯīru mina n-nāsi – *comp.* → πλείων, πλέον – *superl.* → πλεῖστος

πολύχους – πολυχούστερος *comp.* 4a3 *om. Ar.* (*in lac.*)

πομφόλυξ {7a22} bayna l-ḥayawāni wa-n-nabāti

ποσαχῶς 9a24 ʿalā kam

πόσος 7b7 ayna | 9a23 *n.t.* – πόσον 9b2 ayyu mawḍiʿin

ποσός 8a18 kam | 5a8 ḏū miqdārin

ποτε *indef. encl.* 5a24 fī waqtin mina l-awqāti | 6a20 marratan | 6b23, 8a9, 8a22 *n.t.*

πότερος – πότερον/ἤ *adv.* 4b7–8, 5b13, 5b19–20, 6a7–9, 6b24 hal/aw | 8a10–11 a/aw | 4a9–11 *om. Ar.* (*in lac.*)

που *encl.* 7b6 *n.t.*

πραγματεία 9b18 ʿilmun

πρακτός – τὰ πρακτά 9a3 al-ašyāʾu llatī tufʿalu

πρό *in* πρότερος 4b6, 7b14 taqaddumun | 10a7 buʿdun – *comp.* → πρότερος – *superl.* πρῶτος → πρότερος

προαιρέω – προαιροῦμαι *med.* 11b10 šāʾa

προβαίνω 8b14 naǧaḥa

προέρχομαι 6a18 balaġa

πρόεσις 10b9 *om. Ar.* (*in lac.*)

πρός *w. accus.* 7a21, 9b13, 10a4, 10b3, 10b5 ilā | 6a6, 9a25, 10a20 fī | 10a2 maʿa | 12a2 ʿinda | 5b4 *sem. amplif.* dāʿin ilā | 9b18, 10b28 *n.t.* | 4a10 *om. Ar.* (*in lac.*) – πρός *in* προσκαταριθμέω 8b7 adḫala

προσκαταριθμέω 8b7 *sem., etym.* adḫala fī ʿidādi *w. gen.*

πρότερος **(a)** *comp.* 4a15, 11b19 mutaqaddimun | 4b6, 7b14 ašaddu taqadduman | 5a2 aqdamu | 10b25 mā huwa aqdamu | 9b21 qabla | 10a7 ašaddu buʿdan – πρότερον *adv.* 5b19 qabla ḏālika **(b)** πρῶτος *superl.* 4b5, 4b10, 9a25, 9b10 awwalu | 5b9 aqdamu | 7b9 ibtadaʾa bi- | 6a6 *n.t.* – πρῶτον 7b17 al-awwalu – τὸ πρῶτον 4b11, 5b8, 5b14, 5b27, 6a1 al-awwalu – τὰ πρῶτα 6b11, 9a12, 10a1, 10a6, 11b13 al-awāʾilu | 4a3, 4a5 *om. Ar.* (*in lac.*)

προχώρησις 10b1 (10b2) maddun ilā

πρῶτος → πρότερος

Πυθαγόρειος 11a27 Fūṯāġūras *in the gen., as the second element of a gen. construction (iḍāfa)*

πῦρ 6b25 *om. Ar.* (*in lac.*)

πώγων 10b10 liḥyatun

πῶς *interr.* 5a23 as-sababu llaḏī lahū | 5b19, 5b21, 6b23, 8a8, 12a1 kayfa | 4a2 *om. Ar.* (*in lac.*) ▬ 9a10 *sem. metathesis; interr. / affirm. transformation* aṭ-ṭarīqu llaḏī bihī

πως *indef. encl.* 4a12, 6b7 ʿalā waǧhin mina l-wuǧūhi | 9a18, 10a19 ka-anna *w. pron.* | 8b26 *n.t.* ▬ ἁμῶς γέ πως 4b12 ʿalā waǧhin min al-wuǧūhi

ῥᾴδιος 4b17, 9b2, 10a23 sahlun

ῥυτός *in* Εὔρυτος {6a20} ǧaryun

σάρξ 7a14 laḥmun

σαφής ▬ σαφεστέρως 4b17 awḍaḥu

σεμνός ▬ σεμνότερος *comp.* 4a8 *om. Ar.* (*in lac.*)

σκέπτομαι 11b24 baḥaṯa ʿan

σκέψις 7b6 baḥṯun

σοφία 8b9 ḥikmatun

σπάνιος 11a18 yasīrun | 11a23 (11a24) *in hend.* qalīlun ʿazīzun

Σπεύσιππος 6b6, 11a23 sbwsbs

στέρησις 7b12 ʿadamun

συμβαίνω ▬ συμβαίνει *impers.* 6b17 ʿaraḍa | 5b23 naǧidu (waǧada) | 7a23 lazima ▬ συμβήσεται *fut.* 11b11 ʿaraḍa ▬ κατὰ συμβεβηκός 5b24 ʿaraḍun | 6a9 bi-ṭarīqi l-ʿaraḍi | 8b23 ʿalā ṭarīqi l-ʿaraḍi

συμβάλλω ▬ συμβάλλομαι *med.* 10b9 *om. Ar.* (*in lac.*)

σύμπας ▬ τὸ σύμπαν 11b26, 12a1 al-kullu | 10a3 *sem., etym.* al-kullu bi-asrihī

σύμπτωμα 10b18 *sem., etym.* ʿaraḍun lazima | *in* συμπτωματικῶς 10a26 *in hend.* al-ittifāqu wa-l-ʿaraḍu

συμπτωματικῶς 10a26 ʿalā ṭarīqi l-ittifāqi wa-l-ʿaraḍi

σύμφυτος 6a10 ġarīziyyun

σύμφωνος ἑαυτῷ 8a4 ittifāqun ▬ τὸ σύμφωνον 5a19 ittifāqun

συν- *in* συνακολουθέω 7a3 lazima | συν- *in* τὸ σύμπαν 10a3 bi-asrihī

συνάγω 7a21 (7a20) radda

συνακολουθέω 7a3 *in hend.* tabiʿa wa-lazima | *as emended from the MS reading* οὖσιν ἀκολουθεῖ 8a2* yatbaʿu wuǧūdahā

συνάπτω *intrans. w. dat.* 4b2, 4b19 ittaṣala bi- | *w.* πρός 10a19 qurina bi- ... fī

συναυδάω 7b20 šahida bi-

συναφή 4a14, 4a20 ittiṣālun | 4a9 *om. Ar.* (*in lac.*)

συνδέω ▬ συνδέομαι *med. in* ἀσύνδετος 5b18 irtabaṭa

συνεργέω 10a6 aʿāna | *w.* εἰς 4a12 taʿāwana ʿalā

σύνεσις 9b17 baḥṯun (*for* ζήτησις?)

συνεχής 5a3 muttaṣilun

συνοράω ▬ συνιδεῖν 8b24 (8b25a) al-wuqūfu ʿalā

σφαῖρα 5a21 kuratun

σχεδόν 6a26, 8a24 kāda an | 8b20 aḫlaqu bi- | 7a1 *n.t. ut vid.*

σχῆμα 4a22, 9b26 šaklun

σῶμα 6a26 ǧismun

τάξις 7a12, 7a23, 11b18 niẓāmun | *in* ἄτακτον 11b4 niẓāmun | 6b28 tartībun |

τάττω ▬ τὸ τεταγμένον 7b7 al-manẓūmu | 11a7 an-niẓāmu | 11b21 ʿalā niẓāmin

τάχα 4b16, 5b19, 6a2, 6b20, 6b24, 8a15, 8b11, 9a21, 9b6, 9b13 aḫlaqu bi- | 5b10 *n.t.* ▬ τάχα δὲ 6a16 *paraphr.* aw | 11b10 *n.t.*

τε *encl.* 5b17 maʿa | 6b3*, 9a13 wa- | 11b1* bi-mā (*transl. the transmitted* γ') ▬ τε/τε 8b21–22 wa-/wa- | 8b17–18 -/wa- | 8b19–20 -/aw ▬ εἴτε/τε 5a19 wa-(in)/wa- ▬ τε/καί 5a26, 8b21, 9b3–4, 9b20, 10a27 -/wa- | 7b1, 8b23 *n.t.* | *in gloss* 7a8 *om. Ar.* | 4a10–11 *om. Ar.* (*in lac.*) ▬ τε καί/καί 4a22, $10b12^{2}$–13^{1} wa-/wa- ▬ τε/καί/καί/(καί) 5a6–7, 10a1–3 -/wa-/wa-/(wa-) ▬ οἷός, τε (*continued*) οἷόν τε → οἷός ▬ ἅμα ... τε καί → ἅμα ▬ ἄλλως τε καί → ἄλλως

τέλεος 6a19, 8b27 kāmilun ▬ τὸ τέλεον 7a9 al-kamālu ▬ τελεώτερος *comp.* 6b20 akmalu ▬ τελεώτατος *superl.* 8a7 fī ġāyati l-kamāli

τελευτάω 10a25 intahā

τέλος 9a1 ġāyatun | 9b7 *in hend.* ġāyatun yuqṣadu lahā

τέχνη 7a4, 8a12, 8a20 ṣināʿatun

τίθημι 4b21 ǧaʿala *w. two accus.* | 11a3 waḍaʿa | 4b5 iʿtaqada fīhī anna | {6a17} kāna | 4a7 *om. Ar.* (*in lac.*) ▬ *in* περιτίθημι 4a23 waḍaʿa

Τίμαιος (*title*) 6b27 al-kitābu l-mansūbu ilā Ṭymʾws

τιμή *in* ἐντιμότατα 5b22 šarafun | *in* τιμιώτερος 7b14 faḍlun

τίμιος ▬ τὸ τίμιον 11a23 aš-šarīfu ▬ τιμιώτερος *comp.* 7b14 ašaddu faḍlan | 10b26, 11a10 (11a11) ašrafu ▬ τιμιώτατος *superl.* 6b28 ašrafu | 11a12 *om. Ar.* (*in lac.*)

τις, τι (**a**) *indef. pron., encl.* (*see also* ἄττα*)* 4b6, 4b14, 5a1, 6a18, 6a20, 6b10, 8a19, 8b17, 9a20, 10a16, 10a19, 11a2, 11b24 (11b25) mā | 5a9, 5b18, 5b27, 6a22, 8a6, 8b15, 8b23, 8b24, 9a27, 10a22, 10b19, 10b27, 11a1, 11b15, 11b26 šayʾun | 6a16, 6b24, 7b10, 7b22, 10b24 insānun ▬ τινές 4a19, 4b5, 7b2, 9a19, 10a8 baʿḍu n-nāsi ▬ *transl. in context*: 11b16 imāmun | 6a3 mawḍiʿun ▬ *morph.; transl. by the indef. nunation of the noun*: 4a13 ittiṣālun (4a14) | 6a9 bi-šahwatin wa-tašawwuqin | 7b19 sababan | 8a20 mušākalatun | 8b9 ḥikmatun | {9a15} ǧinsan (*mistaken parsing of the syntax*) | 9b7 mabādiʾu | 10a27 bi-ḍarūratin | 10b11 mawāḍiʿu | 11a23 (11a24) qalīlan ʿazīzan ▬ *synt.*; *transl. by the act. part. of the verb whose subject it is*: 5b1 qāʾilun | 5b19 bāḥiṯun | 6a6 nāẓirun | 9a23 qāʾilun | 11b21 muʿtaqidun ▬ *transl. by partitive* min: 6a5 min *w. foll. gen. of the noun that introduces the encl.* | {5a9} *n.t., but apparently present in the sem. amplif.* (afḍal) min ḏālika *in the Ar. transl. (see the note)* | *in the indef. expr.* 6a23, 9b8 mawḍiʿun mina l-mawāḍiʿi | *in the expr.* τρόπον τινὰ 5a16, 7b20, 9b6 ʿalā waǧhin mina l-wuǧūhi ▬ 11a4 (11a3) *sem. amplif.; indefiniteness expressed by* ka-anna ▬ *in the expr.* τὸ ἕνεκά του {7a21} *Ar. read* τὸ ἓν ἕκαστον *instead* ▬ 4b7, 5b11, 5b15, 6a17, {7b12}, 8a8, 8b18, 10b21, 10b28, 11a16, 11a19, 11b2 *n.t.* | 4a4, 4a10, 10b16 *om. Ar.* (*in lac.*) (**b**) *interr. pron.* τίς, τί (**b1**) *abs.* 4a17, 9a26, 10a2 mā | 5a25, 8a22 li-mā | *in* διὰ τί 5b11, 7b8 mā *in* li-mā | 4b11[1,2] ayyu *w. gen.* | 9b19 ayyu šayʾin | 5a15, 9b3, 12a1 ayyu l-ašyāʾi | 8a2* in (εἰ *in the MSS, emended to* τί *in the editions*) | 10b1 *n.t.* (**b2**) *in expr.* τίνος ἕνεκα 10a1, 10a28, 10b23 as-sababu llaḏī lahū (ṣāra ḏālika ka-ḏālika) ▬ τὸ τί ἦν εἶναι 8b22 mā huwa š-šayʾu

τοῖος *in* τοιοῦτος 9b14 šibhu *w. gen.* | 7a14 min

τοιόσδε 8a8 hāḏā llaḏī anā ḏākiruhū | 11a3 hāḏā

τοιοῦτος 5a2, 8a27 hāḏā | 4b18 ǧarā hāḏā l-maǧrā | 5b23, 6a11 ka-ḏālika | 11b17 miṯla ḏālika | 7a14 min ḏālika | 9b14 ašbāhu hāḏihī mina l-umūri | 11b21 *n.t.* | 10b16 *om. Ar.* (*in lac.*)

τόπος 5b25, 10b11 mawḍiʿun | 6b1 makānun

τοσοῦτος 6a27 bi-qadri mā ... wa- ... ḏālika
τοὐλάχιστον → ἐλάχιστος
τρόπος 9a20, 9a23 (9a24) ǧihatun | 9a12 waǧhun | 10a8 fannun ▬ τρόπον τινά 5a16, 7b19–20, 9b6 ʿalā waǧhin mina l-wuǧūhi | 10a19 ʿalā ǧihatin mā
τροφή 10b17 ġiḏāʾun
τυγχάνω 11b14 ittifāqun | 6a22 min šaʾnihī an yakūna ▬ καλῶς ἔτυχεν 11a25 ʿalā mā yanbaġī
τῷ *abs.* 9a19, 9a22, 9a23 min ṭarīqi anna | 5b28 min qibali | 8a13 bi- | {10a25} *n.t.*

ὑγρότης 10b2 ballun
ὕλη 8a9 māddatun | *in* ὑλικός 7a7 māddatun ▬ *in gloss* 7a8 *om. Ar.* | 11a21 *n.t.*
ὑλικός 7a7 mušārikun li-l-māddati
ὑπακούω 11a15 ātā
ὑπάρχω 6a11, 8a16 kāna | 5b3 wuǧūdun | 8a17 kāna mawǧūdan
ὑπεναντίος 5a16 mutaḍāddun
ὑπέρ *w. gen.* 6a13 fī | 10a22 ḥattā yuʿlama | 4a2 *om. Ar.* (*in lac.*)
ὑπερβατός 6a3 taḫaṭṭā | 8b9 *sem. amplif.* taǧāwaza kulla ḥaddin
ὑπερέχω 11b6 faḍala ʿalā
ὑπεροχή 4b14 faḍlun ʿalā
ὑπό *w. gen.* 10a20 ʿan | 5b24 lazimahū ʿan ▬ *w. accus.* 4a16, 8b18 taḥta | 9a13 *sem. amplif.* dāḫilatun taḥta
ὑποβαίνω 10a3 inḥaṭṭa
ὑποβάλλω 8b12 awqaʿa
ὑπόκειμαι ▬ ὑποκείμενος 9a9 mawḍūʿun
ὑπολαμβάνω 9b24 iʿtaqada fī
ὑποτίθημι ▬ ὑποτίθεμαι *med.* 6b23 waḍaʿa | 11b22 iʿtaqada
ὕστερος 4a15 mutaʾaḫḫirun
ὑψηλός ▬ ὑψηλότερος 5a12 aʿlā

φαίνω ▬ φαίνεται *pass. impers.* 4a21 huwa min(mā ...) | 7a1, 11b12 qad naǧidu
φανερός ▬ φανερόν 4b22, 5a20, 8b10 (8b9) bayyinun
φάρυγξ 11a10 ḥanǧaratun
φημί 4a19, 5a26, 5a28, 5b16, 6a20, 6b27, 7a15, 8a7, 9a19 qāla | 4a4 *om. Ar.* (*in lac.*)
φθαρτός ▬ τὰ φθαρτά 4a16 al-ašyāʾu l-qābilatu li-l-fasādi
φθείρω {6a14} kāna buṭlānun ▬ φθείρομαι *med.* 6a8 kāna buṭlānun ▬ *in* φθαρτός 4a16 fasādun
φθορά 10b4 fasādun
φορά 5a16, 9b25, 10a18 ḥarakatun | *in* κυκλοφορία 5b28 ḥarakatun
φρονέω ▬ φρονῶν 6a19 al-ʿāqilu ▬ τὸ φρονεῖν 9b5 al-maʿqūlu
φυσικός 5a24, 10a8 ṭabīʿiyyun
φύσις 4a17, 4b2, 4b9, 4b20, 4b23, 5a2, 7a18, 8a22, 8b8, 9a13, 9b20, 10a2, 10a6, 10a10, 10b22, 11a5, 11a21, 11b6 (11b5), 11b25 ṭabīʿatun | 7a5 ṭabʿun | 4a3, 4a11, 10b14 *om. Ar.* (*in lac.*) ▬ τῆς φύσεως 4b3 aṭ-ṭabīʿiyyu
φυτόν 7a22, 7b4, 8b27, 9a14, 10a5, 10a13, 10b21 nabātun
φύω ▬ πέφυκε *abs.* 9b24 min šaʾnihī an
φῶς 8b15[1,2] ḍawʾun
φωτεινός ▬ τὰ φωτεινότατα 9b13 al-ašyāʾu llatī fī ġāyati ḍ-ḍiyāʾi

χαλεπός 4b17, 9b16 ṣaʿbun | 7a19 ṣaʿuba ▬ χαλεπώτερον *comp.* 9a26 aṣʿabu
χάρις ▬ χάριν *adv. accus. w. gen.* 5a17 li- | 10b19, 11b15 min aǧli *w. gen.* | 11a13 tahayyaʾa bi-
χείρων ▬ τὸ χεῖρον 8a24 al-aḫassu | 7b8 mā huwa aḫassu
χέω ▬ κεχυμένος 7a14 manṯūrun
χράω ▬ χρῶμαι *med.* 8b6 istaʿmala

χρεία (*or* χρέως) *in* ἀξιόχρεως 4a20 *in hend.* iḥtiyāğun ilayhi wa-ntifāʿun bihī

χρέως → χρεία

χρή *impers.* 6b23, 10a24 yanbaġī an

χρόνος 6b3 zamānun

χώρα 5b22 makānun | 11a24 mawḍiʿun

χωρίζω ▬ χωρίζομαι *pass.* 10a15 *sem. metathesis; pass./act. transformation* fāraqa ▬ κεχωρισμένος 4a12 munfaṣilun ʿan

χωρίς 8a27 ʿalā l-infirādi

ψῆφος 6a20 ḥiṣṣatun

ψυχή 5b1, 5b3, 5b9, 6b2 nafsun ▬ ψυχή *in* ἔμψυχος 5b2, 5b6, 7a17 nafsun ▬ ψυχή *in* ἄψυχος 7a17 nafsun

ᾠδί {10a17} *Ar. read* τόδε *for* ᾠδί

ὥρα 7b3 waqtun

ὡς (**a**) *adv.* (*LSJ A.II*) 5b6 ʿalā ḥālin | 7a15*, 10a8 ʿalā mā | 8a10 ʿalā anna | 7b11, 11b13 ʿalā ṭarīqi *w. gen.* | 7b12 ṭarīqi *w. gen.* | 8a18 ka-anna | 11a7 (11a8) ka- *in* ka-ḏālika | 4a4, 10b14 *om. Ar.* (*in lac.*) (**b**) *conj.; w. subst. clauses, "that"* (*LSJ B.I.1*) 4b21, 4b23, 7b20, 8b5, 8b12, 9b14, 10b27 anna ▬ 6a21, 8a26 inna (*after* qāla) ▬ *w. inf.* (*LSJ B.II.3*) ὡς εἰπεῖν 7a16, 7a18 maṯalan | 11b4 bi-l-ğumlati | 4b20 mina l-qawli ▬ 8a1 *sem. amplif.* al-qawlu llaḏī qīla fīhi inna (**c**) *w. part., expressing reason or motive* (*LSJ C.I.1*) 5b13[1,2], 6b26, 7b16 min qibali, min qibali anna | 7a8, 7b14, 9a7 iḏ | 8a3 ḥattā | 4a7 *om. Ar.* (*in lac.*)

ὡς ἄν 8a5 bi-manzilat *w. gen.* | 9a7 *where* ἄν *is not transl. and* ὡς *is merged with the foll. circumst. part. as* iḏ

ὡσαύτως 11a13 ka-ḏālika | 10b20 ʿalā miṯālin wāḥidin | 6b5 *in context* lam yaḏkur ḏālika

ὥσπερ 4a16, 5b5 ka- | 9a16 ka-mā | 10b7 ka-anna | 11a23 miṯla | 6b10, 10b22 ʿalā mā | 7a14, 9b12 bi-manzilat *w. gen.* | 5b18 min ṭarīqi anna | 6a14 aḫlaqu bi- | 4a11, 6b25, 10b14 *om. Ar.* (*in lac.*) ▬ ὥσπερ ἂν εἰ {4b15} ʿalā mā huwa ʿalayhi

ὥστε 4b3, 8a25 ḥattā | 5a4 fa-(yağibu) | 5a19 fa-(yakūnu)

Translation of Greek Morphology, Syntax, and Semantics

α- (*alpha privative*) *in* ἀκίνητος 4b22, *in* ἄδεκτος 5b18, *in* ἀόριστος 6a24, 11b2 (11b3), *in* ἄμορφος 6b24, *in* ἄγνωστος 9a19, 9a22 ġayru *w. gen.* | *in* ἄψυχος 7a17 ʿadīmun li-| *in* ἄπαυστος 5a4, *in* ἀνήνυτος 5a16, *in* ἀσύνδετος 5b18, *in* ἀζήτητος 6a3, *in* ἀμερές 8a3 lā *w. verb or part.* | *in* ἀοριστία 11a20, *in* ἄπειρον 11b3, *in* ἄτακτον 11b4, *in* ἀμορφία 11b4 ḫurūğun ʿan ▬ *sem. metathesis; neg./affirm. transformation* ἀφανής 5a17 mā yaḫfā

-ειος *indicating descent or affiliation*: Πυθαγόρειος 11a27 *transl. by the gen. case in* Fūṯāġūras *as the second element of a gen. construction* (*iḍāfa*)

-εω *suffix of denominative verbs indicating a condition or activity*: ἰσομοιρέω 8a24 kāna *in* kāna muʿādilan

-θεν: ὅθεν 7b9, πόθεν 10a24, ἔμπροσθεν 11a10 min | ἑκατέρωθεν 11a25 ʿan

-ικός *suffix indicating relation or ability in* ἐφετικός 5b11 ḏū *w. gen.* | δυναμικός 6b25 ašbahu bi- | ὑλικός 7a7 mušārikun li-

-ιος *suffix indicating descent in* θεῖος (*in* θειότερος) 5a10 šabīhun bi-

-τέος *suffix of verbal adj.* 4b7, 4b12, 7b13, 8a20, 10a17, 11a2–3 qad yanbaġī an | 4b21, 9a11, 9b3, 9b19, 11b24 yanbaġī an | 9a24 baqiya an | 5a11 *transl. by the subj. in* an yurfaʿa ʿan | 5a10 *n.t.*

-τος *suffix of verbal adj. in* ἀσύνδετος 5b18 muḥtamilun li- | φθαρτός 4a16 qābilun li- | ἀζήτητος 6a3 waqaʿa fī | πιστός 10b27 yaǧibu an ▪ *morph.; transl. by the reflexive and pass. meaning of the verbal Form II pass.* (fuʿʿila) *and verbal Form V act. and pass.* (tafaʿʿala, tufuʿʿila) διαιρετός 5a11 taqsīmun (*pass. sense of the maṣdar*)| ὀρεκτός 5a2 mutašawwaqun ilā | ἄπαυστος 5a4 lā yatafattaru | διαιρετός 5a8 mutaǧazziʾun | μεριστός 5a11 taǧazzuʾun

-ώδης *adj. suffix* 7b18 ḏū

-ως *adv. suffix in* ὁμοίως 5a26, 6b8, 7a4, ὡσαύτως 10b20, οὕτως 5a10, πολλαχῶς 8b9 ʿalā

accusative, adverbial, in τρόπον 10a19 ʿalā

accusative, of respect, in τὰ μέν/τὰ δέ/τὰ δέ 9a8–9 fī *in* fī/wa-fī/wa-fī

active participle; morphology of, in λέγων 5a13 man

comparatives, morphology of, 4b6, 4b18, 5a12, *etc., transl. by the* afʿalu *pattern*

dative, transl. by bi-: δυνάμει 4b14 bi-quwwatin | τῷ νῷ 9b14 bi-l-ʿaqli | ἀνάγκῃ 10a26 bi-ḍarūratin | μορφαῖς καὶ εἴδεσιν καὶ δυνάμεσιν 10b22–23 (10b23a) bi-ṣ-ṣuwari wa-l-anwāʿi wa-l-quwā ▪ *transl. by* fī: τοῖς ἄρρεσιν 10b8 fī l-ḏukūrati | ἐνίοις 10b10 fī baʿḍihā | ζῴοις {5b5} fī l-ḥayawāni ▪ *transl. by* li-: τοῖς εἴδεσιν 8a18 li-ṣ-ṣuwari | ἀλλήλοις 8b3 baʿḍuhā li-baʿḍin | τῇ διανοίᾳ 8b12 li-l-fikri | ἡμῖν 9b6 lanā | τοῖς ζῴοις 10a17 li-l-ḥayawāni | τούτοις 10b7 li-hāḏihī ▪ *transl. by* ʿalā: τούτοις 9b27 ʿalayhim ▪ *transl. by* min: τῷ αὐτομάτῳ 10b27[1] (10b27a) min ḏātihā | τῇ περιφορᾷ 10b27[2] (10b28a) min ḥarakati *w. gen.* ▪ *transl. by* ḥawla: γαίῃ {5b17} ḥawla l-arḍi ▪ *transl. by* nasaba ilā: ἐμψύχοις 5b6 tunsabu ilā anna lahā anfusan

future tense, in κινήσει 5a5 yakūnu ⟨muḥarrikan⟩

genitive absolute 4b18, 8b18 iḏ | 5a24 lammā | 8a17 law

genitive after a comparative adj. 5b15, 5b27 min

genitive of belonging, transl. by fī: ὧν 9b23 fī-mā | τῆς γῆς 11b14 allatī taʿriḍu fī l-arḍi ▪ *transl. by* li-: τοῦ ἕνεκά του 11b26 li-mā huwa min aǧli šayʾin | τῆς ... ὁρμῆς 11b26 (11b27) li-l-ḥarakati

genitive of comparison and ruling, transl. by li-: τὰ ἀΐδια τῶν φθαρτῶν (*sc.* πρότερα) 4a16[1] taqaddumu l-ašyāʾi al-azaliyyati li-l-ašyāʾi l-qābilati li-l-fasādi

genitive, partitive, transl. by min: τῶν μεριστῶν 8a6 mina l-ašyāʾi l-ǧuzʾiyyati | τῶν μὲν αἰσθητῶν ... τῶν δ᾽ ἄλλων 11b18–19 mina l-ašyāʾi l-maḥsūsati ... min sāʾiri l-ašyāʾi

genitive of possession used as a predicate (*with* εἰμί *implied*) *to denote duty or nature, transl. by* ḥaqqu *w. gen.*: ἐπιστήμης (*sc.* ἐστί) 8b25 ḥaqqu l-maʿrifati

participle, aorist, indicating antecedent action, transl. by ṯumma *preceding the main verb*: προελθόντα παύεσθαι 6a18 tabluġu ilā ... ṯumma tanqaṭiʿu
participle, circumstantial, transl. by iḏ: ποιῶν 5a7 iḏ ǧaʿala | ὥς ... ἀπέχοντες 9a7 iḏ kunnā nabʿudu ‒ *transl. by* iḏā: ζητούντων 8b15 iḏā amʿannā fī l-baḥṯi | ὑποβαίνοντι 10a3 iḏā nḥaṭṭū | λεγόμενα 11a4 iḏā qīlat ‒ *transl. by* illā an: ἔχοντα 6a5 illā an yakūna ‒ *transl by* bi-: λαμβάνοντες 9b9 bi-an naʾḫuḏa ‒ *transl. by* ḥattā: ἰόντων 5a20 ḥattā ṣārat | συνάγοντας 7a21 (7a20) ḥattā narudda ‒ *transl. by* min qibali : οὖσαν 11b12 (11b11) min qibali annahū
participle, gender and number, transl. by hāḏā: γεννήσαντες 6a25 hāʾulāʾi lammā waladū
participles; subordination of a participial clause to the main clause, indicated by fa- *introducing the participial clause*: χρώμενοι ... προσκαταριθμοῦσιν 8b6 qadi staʿmala qawmun ... fa-adḫalū
passive voice, transl. by qabila: μορφοῦμαι 8a13 qabūlu ṣ-ṣūrati
superlatives, morphology of, 4b5 *transl. by the* afʿalu *pattern w. foll. gen. and tamyīz acc.*

Index of Words in the Scholium

2. *Arabic Word Index and Arabic-Greek Glossary*

The Arabic word index and glossary is arranged according to the Arabic roots, except for certain compound but common words, such as *allaḏī* and *lammā*, which are listed alphabetically for the sake of simplicity and easy location, as in *GALex*. Within each root, the discrete entries follow the order of the verbal stems, identified through the corresponding Roman numeral in parentheses, each of which is followed immediately by its *maṣdar* and participles. At the end of the verbal stems follow derivative nominal forms in order of their length and complexity, as in *WKAS* and again as in *GALex*. Substantives enclosed within parentheses indicate that the word in question occurs in the text of Theophrastus in the plural (given right after the parentheses) but not in the singular.

The index and glossary includes all the words and particles that occur in the Arabic translation of the text of Theophrastus except for the article, which is listed only selectively to illustrate its various uses in the translation, and the attached pronouns, which are not listed at all.

The principles that guided the compilation of this glossary are those employed in *GALex*, the introduction to which is again recommended to readers for their orientation. The abbreviations and signs in this glosary are the same as those used there (though the layout is necessarily divergent) and in the preceding Greek-Arabic glossary, to which the reader is referred.

The compilation of *GALex* being a long-term project, the completion of which still lies in the inscrutable future, it is hoped that the Arabic-Greek glossary of Theophrastus presented here, containing as it does, despite its brevity, a representative sample of terms from the entire alphabet and especially the particles and other service words, will provide a bueprint for the complete *GALex* and a preview of its contents and potential use.

ʾa
a/aw 8a10*–11 πότερον/ἤ (*GALex I,2 §1.1*)
ʾty
ātā (III) 11a15 ὑπακούω (*GALex I,29*)
ʾǧl
aǧlun – min aǧli šayʾin 10a22, 11b26 ἕνεκά του (*GALex I,51 §1.2*) | 10b19 του χάριν | 11b15 τινὸς χάριν (*GALex I,52 §1.3*)
ʾḥd
aḥadun 6b6 εἷς *in* οὐθείς (*cf. GALex I,59 §1.1*) – aḥaduhumā/ al-āḫaru 8a10 ὁ μέν/ὁ δέ (*GALex I,65 §3.7*)
ʾḫḏ
aḫaḏa (I) 8a3, 9a27, 9b9 λαμβάνω (*GALex I,77 §1.1*) – aḫaḏa *w.* fī: *sem. amplif.; add. acc. to sense in* lammā aḫaḏa fī l-kalāmi fī t-tawalludi 6b14 κατὰ τὴν γένεσιν (*cf. GALex I,80*) – aḫaḏa *w.* min 6b22 *sem. amplif. for* ἀπό
maʾḫaḏun 6b18[1,2] *sem. amplif.; add. acc. to sense* (*GALex I,90*)
ʾḫr
mutaʾaḫḫirun (V) *act. part.* 4a15 ὕστερος (*GALex I,93 §1.1*)
āḫaru (**a**) *abs.* 4b6, 6b4, 7b23, 10b6, 10b19, 11b6 (11b7) ἕτερος (*GALex I,100 §1.3.1*)| 4b13, 5a1, 8a5 ἄλλος (*GALex I,97 §1.1*) (**b**) *sem. amplif.; modifying a subst. add. acc. to sense*: ašyāʾu uḫaru 6b4, 10b6 ἕτερα – al-qawlu l-āḫaru 9b13 ἐκεῖνος (**c**) *in hend.* āḫaru ġayruhū 6a22, 11b17 ἄλλος | 7b1 παντοῖος – ašyāʾu uḫaru ġayruhū 11b17 ἄλλα (**d**) *in correlative constructions*: aḥaduhumā/al-āḫaru 8a10 ὁ μέν/ὁ δέ (*GALex I,65 §3.7*) – kullu wāḥidin minhumā/al-āḫaru 4a12 ἑκάτερος (*GALex I,64 §3.4*) – kullu wāḥidin minhā/al-āḫaru 5a18 ἕκαστος (**e**) *morph.; transl. the sense of the comp. in hend. with an elative subst.*: sulūku sabīlin uḫrā hiya awḍaḥu aw aqrabu ilā t-taṣdīqi 4b17–18 σαφεστέρως ἢ πιστικωτέρως
aḫaratun – bi-aḫaratin 9a14 ἔσχατος (*GALex I,96 §3*)
ʾḏ
iḏ 11b9, 11b10 εἴπερ (*GALex I,149 §3.2*) | 7a8, 7b14, 9a7 ὡς (*GALex I,150 §4.5*) – *synt.* 5a6 (5a7) *transl. the circumst. sense of the part.* ποιῶν (*GALex I,150 §5.1*) | 9a7 *transl. simultaneously the circumst. sense of the part. and* ὡς *in* ὡς ἀπέχοντες – *synt.; transl. the Gr. gen. absolute* 4b18 οὔσης | 8b18 ὄντων (*GALex I,152 §5.2*)
ʾḏʾ[1]
iḏā 9b10, 10a12 ὅταν | 10a5, 11a13 εἰ – *synt.; transl. the gen. absolute* 8b15 ζητούντων (*GALex I,165 §3.1*) – *synt.; transl. the circumst. sense of the part.* 4b9 ἐχούσας | 6a6 (6a7) ἀναφέρων | 6a13 ἀφαιρεθεῖσα | 10a3 ὑποβαίνοντι | 10a15 χωριζόμενος | 11a4[1,2] λεγόμενα (*GALex I,166 §3.2*)
ʾḏʾ[2]
iḏan 8b16 ἄρα (*GALex I,181 §3.1*)
ʾḏy
taʾaḏḏā (V) 10b12 λωβάομαι (*GALex I,189*)
ʾrḫwṭs 6a19 Ἀρχύτας
ʾrḍ
arḍun 5b17, 7b2, 10b4, 11b14 γῆ (*GALex I,196 §1*)
arḍiyyun 10a28 περὶ τὴν γῆν (*GALex I,202*)
ʾrʿqlyṭs 7a15b Ἡράκλειτος

ʾzl

azaliyyun 4a16, 9b24b ἀΐδιος (*GALex I,208 §1.1*)

ʾsr

asrun ‒ bi-asrihī 7a11, 8a6, 8a23, 11a22, 11b11 ὅλος | 10a9 πᾶς | 10a3 *sem., etym.* σύν *in* τὸ σύμπαν (*GALex I,216–218*)

ʾṣl

aṣlun ‒ *w. neg.* lā ... aṣlan 11b10 δέ *in* οὐδέ | 6a5 δὲ εἷς *in* μηδείς ‒ *w. neg.* lam ...aṣlan 6b5 δὲ μίαν *in* οὐδεμίαν (*GALex I,231–233*)

Aflāṭun 6b11, 11a27 Πλάτων

ʾkr ‒ ukratun → kry (*cf. Dozy I,30b*)

ʾl

al- (*article; selective references*) ‒ *transl.* τό *w. inf.*: al-wafāʾu 4b17 τὸ ἀποδοῦναι ‒ *transl.* τό *w. adj.*: al-afḍalu 11a6 τὸ ἄριστον | al-ǧayyidu 11a19 τὸ ἀγαθόν | aš-šarīfu 11a23 τὸ τίμιον ‒ *transl.* τό *w. part.*: an-niẓāmu 11a7 τὸ τεταγμένον ‒ *transl.* τό *w. adv.*: ad-dawāmu 11a7 τὸ ἀεί

ʾlʾ

illā (in lā), illā an 5b1 εἰ μή | 5b28, 11b19 εἰ μὴ ἄρα (*GALex I,250 §1*) | 7a22–23, 11b21 πλὴν εἰ (*GALex I,253 §3*) | 8a17* ἀλλά (*GALex I,255 §4*) ‒ *morph.; transl. the concessive sense of the circumst. part.* 6a5 ἔχοντα (*GALex I,258 §9*) ‒ *in combinations* lā/illā → lā, allāhumma illā an → allāhumma

illā anna 6a27 πλήν (*GALex I,264 §1*) | 5b14, 8a14a, 11a14, 11b23 ἀλλά (*GALex I,264 §2*) | 4a12, 6a23, 8a10 (8a11), 8a19, 9a7, 9b6, 10a19, 11b17 δέ *w.o. preceding* μέν (*GALex I,266 §3*) | 5b6, 8b14 ὅμως (*cf. GALex I,267 §3.1.1*) ‒ -/illā anna 8a12 (8a11–12), 8a15b, 10a6 μέν/δέ

ʾlḏy

allaḏī (**a**) *transl. Gr. relative pron. and adv.* (*GALex I,277–279 §A*): 5a17, 5b10, 5b16, {6a4*}, 7b21, 8a6 ὅς ‒ huwa llaḏī 4b5 ὅσπερ ‒ allaḏīna 9b24b, 11b8 ὅσοι | 9b25 *sem. amplif. add. w. ref. to* ὅσοι *at 9b24b* ‒ allatī minhā 7b9 ὅ *in* ὅθεν ‒ hāḏihi llatī anā ḏākiruhā 8a8 *sem. amplif. for* τοιάδε ‒ allaḏī qīla fīhi inna 8a1 *sem. amplif.* ὡς ‒ aṭ-ṭarīqu llaḏī bihī 9a10 *paraphr.* πῶς ‒ *in expr.* as-sabab allaḏī lahū 5a23 πῶς | 10a1, 10a28, 10b23b τίνος ἕνεκα ‒ al-ašyāʾu llatī yanbaġī an nabḥaṯa ʿanhā 9b2 *paraphr.* τίνων (**b**) *introduces a relative clause that transl. adj. and other attributes in attributive position* (**b1**) *transl. adj.* (*GALex I,281 §5*): allatī hiya afḍalu 5a20 ἀρίστη ‒ allaḏī lā yatafattaru 5a3 ἄπαυστος (**b2**) *transl. part.* (*GALex I,281 §6*): allaḏī baqiya 5a1 λοιπόν (**b3**) *transl. prep. phrasses* (*GALex I,281 §7*): allatī talī al-wasaṭa 5b12 τὰ περὶ τὸ μέσον (**b4**) *transl. subst. in attributive gen.* (*GALex I,281 §9*): allatī taʿriḍu (fī l-arḍi) 11b14 τῆς (γῆς) (**c**) *introduces a relative clause that transl. the article in its subst. making function* (*GALex I,281 §10*): allaḏī 8b15, 8b24b[1] τό ‒ allatī 9a15, {10a4} τά ‒ allaḏīna 6a24, 9b21, 11a22 οἱ (**d**) *sem. amplif.; introduces a relative clause that modifies the generic subst. add. in Ar. to express the subst. implied by the Gr. article* (*GALex I,282 §11*): al-amru llaḏī yaḫuṣṣuhū 4b21 τὸ ἴδιον

ʾlḏy: allaḏī (*continued*)
- al-aǧsāmu llatī fī ġāyati š-šarafi 5b22 τὰ ἐντιμότατα - sāʾiru l-ašyāʾi llatī tattaṣilu bihā 6a17 τὰ ἐφεξῆς - al-ašyāʾu llatī tuʿlamu 8b22 τὰ θεωρούμενα - al-ašyāʾu llatī tufʿalu 9a3 τὰ πρακτά - (al-ašyāʾu llatī) tuʿmalu 9a3 τὰ ποιητά - al-ašyāʾu llatī tuqālu 9b1 τὰ λεγόμενα - al-ašyāʾu llatī fī ġāyati ḍ-ḍiyāʾi 9b13 τὰ φωτεινότατα - al-umūru llatī hiya aǧallu qadran 10a7 τὰ κυριώτατα - al-ǧuzʾu llaḏī lā yataǧazzaʾu 11b23 τὸ ἄτομον (**e**) *sem. amplif.; introduces a relative clause add. acc. to sense* (*GALex I,283 §12*): 10b3, 10b11, 10b26

ʾlf
maʾlūfun (I) *pass. part.* - ġayru maʾlūfin *in hend. w.* muǧtanabun 9b5 ἀλλότριος (*GALex I,284*)

ʾlh
ilāhiyyun 4b15b θεῖος (*GALex I,309 §1.1.1*) - al-ašyāʾu l-ilāhiyyatu 6b9 τὰ θεῖα (*GALex I,311 §1.3.2*)
allāhu 4b15a, 7b23, 11b8 θεός (*GALex I,313 §1*) - *sem., etym.* ašbahu bi-llāhi 5a10 θειότερος - *sem., etym.* aḥaqqu l-ašyaʾi bi-annahū llāhu 6a1 θειότατος
allāhumma illā an 4b10, 6a10 εἰ μὴ ἄρα (*GALex I,251 §1.1b; I,319 §1.1*)

ʾly
ilā (**a**) *abs.* (*GALex I,319 §§1–4*): 5a9, 5a20 (5a19), 6b14, 7b8, 8a3, 8a9, 8a11, 8a14b, 9a3, 10a24, 11b9, 11b27 εἰς | 5a4b (5a5), 6a18, 6a23, 6b10, 7b7, 9a14[1], 9b8 μέχρι | 7a21, 9b13, 10a4, 10b3, 10b5 πρός | 7b22–23, 9b10 ἐπί | 10a5[1] ἄχρι (**b**) *sem. amplif.*: dāʿin ilā 5b4b πρός - min ... ilā b25b[1,2] εἰς - ilā ... an yantahiya 9b2 μέχρι (**c**) *with verbs and verbal nouns*: → anisa, → balaġa, → iḥtāǧa, → daʿā, → radda, → tašawwaqa, → asāra, → muḍṭarrun, → aḍāfa, → aqrabu, → qaṣada, → maddun, → māla, → nasaba, → intahā

ʾmm
imāmun 11b16 τις (*cf. GALex I,339 §1*)

ʾmʾ
ammā - wa- (fa-)ammā ... fa- 4a23, 5a21a, 5b12, 6b4, 7a19, 10a23b–23a, 11a24, {11a27} δέ *w.o. preceding* μέν (*GALex I,344–5 §2, 3.1*) - -/wa- (fa-) ammā ... fa- 8b8–9, 11b23–24 μέν/δέ - ammā ... fa-/wa- (fa-)ammā ... fa- 6a25, 7b6–9 μέν/δέ (*GALex I,341 §1.1.1*) - fa-ammā ... fa-/wa-ammā ... fa- 5a4b (5a6)–13 μὲν δή/δέ (*GALex I,342 §1.1.2*) - (fa-) ammā ... fa-/fa-ammā ... fa- 6b11–15, 9b8–11* μὲν οὖν/δέ
immā - immā/aw 4b12b–13 εἴτε/εἴτε (*GALex I,356 §3*) - immā/wa-immā 8b25b–26 ἤτοι/ἤ (*GALex I,352 §2*) | 9b11–12 εἴτε/εἴτε (*GALex I,353 §3*) | 11b18–19 μέν/δέ (*GALex I,354 §5.2*)

ʾmr
amrun, *pl.* umūrun (**a**) *transl. pron. and pron. adj.* (*GALex I,373 §25*): 6a6 αὐτός (*cf. 6a13 where* αὐτός *is doubly determined by* amr *and* nafs) - al-umūru kulluhā 6a2 (6a1) πάντα - min ayyi l-umūri 10a24 πόθεν (**b**) *transl. Gr. prep.* (*GALex I,375 §27*): 10b17 περί *w. accus.* (**c**) *sem. amplif.; stands for the subst.*

implied by a pron. (*GALex I,376 §32.1*): hāḏā l-amru 4b20, 11b23 οὗτος | 8b8 ὅδε **(d)** *stands for a noun implied by predicate adj.* (*GALex I,378 §33*): οἰκεῖον 10a10 amrun mulāʾimun ḫāṣṣun **(e)** *sem. amplif.; stands for the subst. implied by the article in its subst. making function* (*GALex I,378 §34*): al-amru llaḏī yaḫuṣṣuhū 4b21 τὸ ἴδιον – afḍalu l-umūri 5b1, {5b8} τὸ ἄριστον – afāḍilu l-umūri 6a4 τὰ ἄριστα – ašrafu l-umūri 6b28 τὰ τιμιώτατα – aṣġaru l-umūri 7a16 τοὐλάχιστον – amru *w. gen.* 7b3, 7b10[2] τὸ/τὰ περί | 9b25 τὰ κατά – al-amru l-afḍalu 8a14b, 11a9, 11b15, 11b27 τὸ βέλτιον | 11a2, 11b9 τὸ ἄριστον | 11a15 τὸ εὖ – al-aḫassu mina l-umūri 8a24 τὸ χεῖρον – al-umūru l-kulliyyatu 9a1 τὰ καθόλου – al-umūru l-ǧuzʾiyyatu 9a2 τὸ ἐν μέρει – baʿḍu l-umūri/wa-baʿḍuhā/wa-baʿḍuhā 9a8–9 τὰ *in* τὰ μέν/τὰ δέ/τὰ δέ – ašbāhu hāḏihī mina l-umūri 9b14 τῶν τοιούτων – al-umūru llatī hiya aǧallu qadran 10a7 τὰ κυριώτατα – al-umūru s-samāwiyyatu wa-l-umūru l-arḍiyyatu 10a27 τὰ οὐράνια καὶ τὰ περὶ τὴν γῆν **(f)** *sem. amplif.; add. as the implied object of a transitive verb* (*GALex I,380 §35*): bi-misāsi l-amri 9b15 θιγόντι **(g)** *sem. amplif.; added to help in the transl. of adv.* (*GALex I,388 §43.1*): kāna l-amru ka-ḏālika 4a17 οὕτως **(h)** *partitive use* (*GALex I,390 §45a*): amru s-samāʾi 6b4 οὐρανός – amru l-mabādiʾi 6b23, 7b10 (7b9) ἀρχαί – amruhā (*sc.* al-mabādiʾi) 7b10[1] *w. ref. to* ἀρχαί *at 7b9* – umūru ṭ-ṭabīʿati 9b20 τῆς φύσεως – amru n-nabāti ... amru l-anfusi {10b21[1,2]} φυτοῖς ... ἀψύχοις **(i)** *individuating use of* amr (*GALex I,392 §46*): al-amru l-afḍalu 7b11 βέλτιον – mabdaʾu l-amri 9a11 ἀρχή – awwalu l-amri 11b24 ἀρχή **(j)** *sem. amplif.;* 7b18, 8a14a, 8a19, 9a26, 9b17, 10a12, 10a23b, 10a28 al-amru *add. to refer to the general subject under discussion* – *sem. amplif.; add. acc. to sense* 5a17, 7a4, 11a8 **(k)** *in paraphr. and interpr. uses* (*GALex I,393 §I*): wa-ka-ḏālika yaǧrī l-amru 7a2 καί – al-umūru 7a15a *interpr.* κόσμος

ʾ**myrws** 5b16 Ὅμηρος

ʾ**n**

an **(a)** *introduces a nominal clause which transl. Gr. inf.* (*GALex I,408 §A*): an yakūna 4a13, 4b9–10, 5b18, 7b16, 7b20 (7b21) εἶναι | 6a11 ὑπάρχειν | 4a14, 4b17, 7a11, 8a17, 9a21, 9b6 *sem. amplif.; add. for implied* εἶναι – an nūḍiḥa 4b12a ἐμφαίνειν – allā takūna tataḥarraku 5a18 τὸ μὴ (*scil.* κινεῖσθαι) – an naǧmaʿa 7a20 τὸ περιθεῖναι – an nakūna nabḥaṯu 8a27 (8b1) ζητεῖν – an yanǧaḥa 8b14 προβαίνειν – an nulaḫḫiṣa 9a25 ἀφορίσαι – an yuqāla 9b2 εἰπεῖν – an nudrika 9b8 (9b9) θεωρεῖν – an yaḏkurū 9b27 (10a1) λέγειν – an yartafiʿa 11b11 ἀναιρεῖσθαι **(b)** *paraphr.* an yakūna 8a15a ἂν εἴη – an nakūna fī ḏālika muḍṭarrīna 4b13 ἀνάγκη *sc.* ἡμῖν ἐστι **(c)** *add. as required by Ar. synt.*

ʾ**n**: an (*continued*)
5a1, 5a11, 5b1, 5b9, 5b19, 6a14, 6a16b, 6a20^{1,2}, 6a21, 6b5, 6b10, 6b20, 6b24, 7a10b, 7b7, 7b17, 7b18, 8b11, 8b21, 9a14, 9b9, 9b13, 10a5, 10b25, 11b17 (**d**) *in various phrases*: illā an → illā, allāhumma illā an → ʾlh, ẖalīqun an → ẖlq, min šaʾnihī an → šʾn, lahū an → li- ▬ *for its use foll. verbs see the verbs themselves*

anna (**a**) *transl. Gr. conj.* (*GALex I,416 §A*): 4b21, 4b23, 7b20, 8b5, 8b12, 9b14, 10b27 ὡς | 8b9, 10a13, 11a5 ὅτι | 11a6 *add. w. ref. to* ὅτι *at 11a5* | 11a14 διότι (**b**) *introduces nominal clause transl. subst.* (*GALex I,420 §7.1*): 4b5, 5a16b, 5b6 (**c**) *introduces nominal clause transl. inf.* (*GALex I,421 §8*): 5a4a, 5b3a, 8a15b^{2}, 8a21, 8a25, 10a25, 10b24b, 11b18 ▬ *sem. amplif.; introduces nominal clause transl. the implied* εἶναι 5a8, 6a1, 8b4, 10a22, 11a10 (**d**) *add. as required by Ar. synt.* 6a2, 6a16b*, {6b10}, 6b12, 6b13, 6b18, 7b19, 7b20, 8a26, 9a4, 9a26, 9b24b (**e**) *in various phrases*: illā anna → illā, ḥattā anna → ḥattā, wa-ḏālika anna → ḏālika, min ṭarīqi anna → ṭarīqun, min qibali anna → qibalun, (hāḏā) ʿalā anna → ʿalā, ka-anna → ka, li-anna → li-

in (**a**) *abs.* (*GALex I,438 §1*): 4a17, 4a18, 4b2, 4b6, 4b11^{2}, 5a5, 5a28b, 5b7, 5b14, 5b20, 5b26b, {7b8}, 7b11, 7b12, 8a20, 8a21, 8b17, 9a6, 9a18, 10a13, 11a1b, 11b20 εἰ | 5b23 εἴπερ | 8b14 ἐάν *in* κἄν ▬ *sem. amplif.* 4b11^{1} εἰ (*implied from what foll.*) ▬ in/wa-in 5a17–18 εἴτε/εἴτε (*GALex I,447 §4.1*) ▬ *sem. amplif.; add. acc. to sense* 8a14a (**b**) wa-in 5b6, 7a18 καίπερ (*GALex I,462 §1.3*)| 8b14 κἄν (*GALex I,461 §1.1.3*) | {8a2*} εἰ *the MS reading, emended to* τί *in the edition* (**c**) *w. neg.* εἰ μή → illā

in lā → illā

inna (**a**) *transl. conj.* (*GALex I,466 §A*): 6a21, 8a26 ὡς ▬ (al-qawlu) llaḏī qīla fīhi inna 8a1 *sem. amplif.* ὡς ▬ *after* qāla 6a28 ὅτι (**b**) *add. as required by Ar. synt., after* qāla 5b16, 6a14, 6b16, 7a6b, 7a7^{1,2}, 7a10b, 7b11, 7b12*, 8a7, 8b2, 9a23, 9a24, 9a26, 9b6, 11b8 ▬ *add. as required by Ar. synt.* 4b17, 5a22, 5a28a, 5b1, 6b11, 8b25a, 10a18, 11a18b, 11a27, 11b5

fa-inna 4a18, 5a10, 5a17, 5a22b, 5a27a, 5b23 (5b24), 6a1, 6a3, 6a19, 6a21, 6a25, 6b7, 6b17, 6b27, 7a17, 7b11, 7b17, 8a2, 9a1, 9a4, 9b4, 9b21, 10a28, 10b18, 10b24b, 11a22, 11b20, 11b15, 11b27 γάρ (*GALex I,484 §1.1*) | 10a7 καὶ γὰρ δή | 5b5 ἐπεί | 7a5b -περ | {8a3} πλήν | 9a16* δέ | 7b4, 9b25 *sem. amplif.; add. acc. to sense* ▬ fa-inna qad naǧidu 10a25 καὶ δή

innamā (**a**) *rendering the emphasis expressed by inverted Greek word order* (*GALex I,494 §8.3*): 4a21b, 6b21, 7a8, 9a1 (9a1–2), 10b27a (**b**) *highlights the emphasized word in the Greek sentence* (*GALex I,501 §11*): 8b21 ἰδίων | 8b23 κατά (**c**) innamā ... faqaṭ 4a18, 6b15–16 (6b16), 6b17, 7a7 μόνον (*adv.*) (*GALex I,503 §12.1b*) – innamā ... wa-lā 5a25a οὐ ... ἀλλά (**d**) *sem. amplif.; add. acc. to a perceived emphasis or restriction in the Gr.* 5a18, 5b6, 5b7, 5b14, 5b26b, 5b28, 6a1, 6a18, 6a23, 6b16, 8a13, 8a23, 10a22, 10b18, 10a12

ʾnʾ

anā *pers. pron.* – *periphr.*; mā anā qāʾiluhū ... aʿnī 5b10 οὗτος | 6a5 ὅδε – *sem. amplif.* hāḏihi llatī anā ḏākiruhā 8a8 τοιάδε (*cf. GALex I,513 §6*)

ʾns

anisa (I) *w.* ilā 5a22b* οἰκεῖος (*cf. GALex I,523–524*)

nāsun – al-kaṯīru mina n-nāsi 6a23 οἱ πολλοί (*GALex I,536 §14.4*) – baʿḍu n-nāsi 4a19, 4b5, 7b2, 9a19, 10a8 τινές (*GALex I,535 §13.1a*) | 6b15 οἱ

insānun 6a16b, 6b24, 7b10, 7b22, 10b24a τις (*GALex I,546 §5*)

ʾw

aw 4b18, 6a5, 6a15b, 8a5[1,2], 8a6* (ἤ *in the MSS, emended to* ᾖ *in the edition*), 8a13, 9b2, 9b7, 10a8, 10a19, 11b6, 11b7 (ἤ *in the MSS, emended to* ᾖ *in the edition*) ἤ *disjunctive* (*GALex I,591 §1*)| 4b11b καί (*GALex I,594 §3*) | 6a16a *paraphr.* τάχα δέ – {5a5} ἤ *comparative* – —/aw 8b19–20 τε/τε (*GALex I,593 §2*) – a/aw → a – immā/aw → immā – hal/aw → hal

ʾwrybydys 8a26 Εὐριπίδης

ʾwl

(ālatun) *pl.* ālātun 7a5b ὄργανον (*GALex I,614 §1.1*)

awwalu *pl.* awāʾilu, uwalu 4b5, 4b10, 9a25, 9b10 πρῶτος (*GALex I,630 §2*) | 9b9, 11b24 ἀρχή (*GALex I,624 §1.1*) – al-awwalu 4b11a, 5b7 (5b8), 5b14, 5b27, 6a1, 6b11, {7b17} τὸ πρῶτον – al-awāʾilu 9a12, 10a1, 10a6, 11b13 τὰ πρῶτα

(ayyilun) *pl.* ayāʾilu 10b12 ἔλαφος (*GALex I,655 §1.1*)

ʾyy

ayyu *w. gen.* 4a18, 5a15[1], 6b23, 10a25 ποῖος (*GALex I,688 §3.1*) | 4b11b[1,2], 5a15[2], 9b3, 9b19, 12a1 τίς, τί (*interr.*) (*GALex I,681 §1.1*) – ayyu mawḍiʿin 9b2 πόσος (*cf. GALex I,692 §4*) – min ayyi l-umūri 10a24 πόθεν (*GALex I,695 §6.2.1*)

iyyā *w. attached pron.* 10b2 *sem. amplif.; transl. an accus. object implied in Greek* (*GALex I,701 §1*)

ʾyḍ

ayḍan (**a**) *transl.* καί: 5a4b*, 5a23, 5a27a, 5b10, 6a1, 6a4, 6a12, 6b16, 7a4, 7b23, 8a8, 8a21, 8b19, 9a16*, 9b16, 11b7, 11b13 καί (*GALex I,704 §1*) – wa-maʿa ḏālika ayḍan 9a6[2] *sem.amplif.* καί – *sem. amplif.; add. acc. to sense* 4b17, 10a17, 12a1 (**b**) *transl.* ἔτι: 7b22, 9b25, 10b7, 10b24a (10b20) ἔτι (*GALex I,715 §3*) – mimmā yaǧrī ayḍan hāḏā l-maǧrā 10b11 *sem. amplif.* ἔτι (**c**) *in other uses*: 7a20 πάλιν αὖ (*GALex I,720 §4.4*) | 7b18 ἄλλως | 11b10 ἐφ' ὅσον | 7a22 mā huwa ayḍan 7a22 αὐτός (*self*) – *in combinations*: wa-/ayḍan → wa-, wa-/wa-ayḍan → wa-

ʾyn

ayna 7b7 πόσος

b

bi- (**a**) *transl. Gr. prep. and particles* (*GALex II,2 §A*): 4b16, 5b6, 8b14 διά | 5b1, 8b23, 9a2, 9a7, 9a21[2,3] κατά *w. accus.* ▬ bi-ṭarīqi(n) 4b12b, 4b13 κατά *w. accus.* ▬ bi-manzilati (mā) 6a24, 8a12, 8b3, 9a3, 10a12, 10b8, 10b11, 11a21 καθάπερ ▬ bi-mā {11b1} γε *epexegetic* (*emended to* τε *in the edition*) (**b**) *morph.; transl. the morph. of Gr. pron. adj.* (*GALex II,21.1 §19.4a*): bi-ʿaynihī 5a18, 8b24b, 9a4 ὁ αὐτός (**c**) *transl. the dat.* (*GALex II,21 §21*): bi- 8a13 τῷ ▬ bi-quwwatin 4b14a, 5a1, 8a10 δυνάμει ▬ bi-šahwatin wa-tašawwuqin 6a9 ἐφέσει καὶ ὀρέξει ▬ bi-l-ǧawhari wa-bi-l-ʿadadi wa-bi-ṣ-ṣūrati wa-bi-l-ǧinsi wa-l-muqāyasati wa- ... bi-l-qismati 9a5–6 οὐσίᾳ καὶ ἀριθμῷ καὶ εἴδει καὶ γένει καὶ ἀναλογίᾳ καὶ ... διαιρέσει ▬ bihī 9a22 αὐτῷ ▬ bi-l-ʿaqli 9b14* τῷ νῷ ▬ bi-ḍarūratin 10a26 ἀνάγκῃ ▬ bi-ṣ-ṣuwari wa-l-anwāʿi wa-l-quwā 10b23a (10b22–23) μορφαῖς καὶ εἴδεσιν καὶ δυνάμεσιν (**d**) *transl. the adv. use of the accus.* (*GALex II,25 §22*): bi-manzilati mā 4a21b οἷον ▬ bi-qadri mā 6a27 ὅσον ▬ bi-l-ǧumlati 11a18b τὸ ὅλον (**e**) *morph.; transl. the adv. suffix* -ως (*GALex II,27 §24*): bi-(l-ǧumlati) 4a20, 8a19, 8b24a, 10b3, 10b10, 11b5 (ὅλ)ως ▬ bi-(waǧhin mina l-wuǧūhi) 5a21 (οὐθαμ)ῶς ▬ bi-l-wāǧibi 7b10 εἰκότως (**f**) *synt.; transl. the circumstantiality implied by a circumst. part.* (*GALex II,28 §25*): bi-taḥarrukihī 5a5* κινούμενον ▬ bi-annahū radda 6b13 ἀνάπτων ▬ bi-an naʾḫuḏa 9b9 λαμβάνοντες ▬ iḏā zālat ... bi-zawālihā 6a13 ἀφαιρεθεῖσα ▬ bi-misāsi l-amri 9b15 θιγόντι (**g**) *helps transl. primitive adv.* (*GALex II,30 §27*): bi-ġayri *w. gen.* 8b16 ἄνευ (**h**) *helps transl.* ὥς *and derivatives* (*GALex II,31 §28*): bi-l-ǧumlati 11b4 ὡς εἰπεῖν ▬ aṭ-ṭarīqu llaḏi bihī 9a10 *sem. amplif.* πῶς (**i**) *synt.; in act./pass. transformation, it introduces the subject of the pass. verb*: yubayyanu bi-ṣināʿati n-nuǧūmi 9b27 (ἡ) ἀστρολογία δείκνυσιν (**j**) *sem. amplif.; add. acc. to sense* 9a7[1,2], 9a24, 11a5, 11b2 (**k**) *in expr.* bi-aḫaratin → ʾḫr, bi-asrihī → ʾsr, aḥaqqu bi- → ḥqq, ḫalīqun bi- → ḫlq, ašbahu bi- → šbh, awlā bi- → wly (**l**) *w. verbs: when introducing the object of* laysa → lys ▬ *see also the verbs* ibtadaʾa, ḫaṣṣa, šahida, ṣaddaqa, ẓanna, iqtadā, qaḏafa, qarana, qaṣada, qāla, kāna, tahayyaʾa, waṯiqa, ittaṣala

bḥṯ

baḥaṯa (I) (*GALex II,62 §§1–2*) ▬ *abs.* 8b1 ζητέω ▬ *w.* ʿan 5b19, 8b11, 8b13, 10b24a (10b23) ζητέω | 9b3, 10a17 ζητέω *in* ζητητέον | 11b24 σκέπτομαι | 9a11 μεταδιώκω | 6a7 *sem. amplif.; added to express the implied verb of the indirect question introduced by* πότερον

baḥṯun *maṣdar* (*GALex II,66 §§1–8*) ▬ *abs.* 7b6 σκέψις | 6a3 *sem., etym.; transl.* ζητέω *in* ἀζήτητος | *in hend.* al-baḥṯu wa-t-taftīšu 8b15 ζητέω ▬ *w.* ʿan 6b21[1,2] (6b22) ζήτησις | 8a22 τὸ ζητεῖν | {9b16} (9b17) σύνεσις (*or* ζήτησις?) | 9a12, 9a20 *sem. amplif.; add. w. reference to* μεταδιώκω *at 9a11* – *paraphr.; in expr.* fīhi mawḍiʿu ṭalabin wa-baḥṯin 5b11 ἐπιζητέω (*where the hend.* ṭalaba wa-baḥaṯa *would appear to transl.* ζητέω) | ǧaʿala baḥṯahū fī 6a13 ἀπορέω

bāḥiṯun 5b19 τις – 6a12 *sem. amplif.; add. to express the indef. subject of the foll. part.* ἀφελόντα

bḥr

baḥrun 5b17 θάλασσα – māʾu l-baḥri 10b1 θάλαττα (*GALex II,70 §1*)

bdʾ

badaʾa (I) 10a24 ἄρχομαι (*GALex II,96 §1*)

ibtadaʾa (VIII) *w.* bi- 7b9 πρῶτος (*GALex II,106 §4.1*)

mabdaʾun, *pl.* mabādiʾu 4a15, 4a16, 4b9, 4b15b, 4b19, 5a5, 5a6, 5a19, 6a15b [6a16], 6a16a, 6a17, 6b12, 6b14, 6b16, 6b17, 6b19, 6b21, 6b22, 6b23, 7a4, $7a6b^1$, 7a13, 7a19, 7b9, 7b12, 9a11, 9a13, 9a25, $9b6^{1,2}$, 9b7 (9b8), 11b7, 11b27 ἀρχή | 9b7 ἡ *w. ref. to* ἀρχή | 7a7 τάς *w. ref. to* ἀρχαί | 6b26 αὗται *w. ref. to* ἀρχαί | $7a6b^2$ *sem. amplif.; add. to complement* πάσας *w. ref. to* ἀρχαί (*GALex II,114 §1*) – 9b3 αἰτία

bdʿ

abdaʿu 8b4 παραδοξότερον | *in hend.* min aš-šanāʿati mā huwa abdaʿu 8b6 ἔτι πλέον τὸ παράδοξον (*cf.* šaniʿ 5a18* ἄτοπος) (*GALex II,120 §1*)

bdn

badanun 10b11 *sem. amplif.; add. acc. to sense*

bṣr

mubṣarun (IV) *pass. part.* $9a23^1$ ὁρατός | $9a23^2$ ὁρατός *in* ἀόρατος

bṭl

buṭlānun (I) *maṣdar* – kāna buṭlānun 6a8, 6a14 φθείρω, φθείρομαι

bāṭilun *act. part.* 10a22 μάτην | 10b8 μάταιος – bāṭilan 7a14b εἰκῇ

abṭala (IV) 9b21 ἀναιρέω | 9b22 *sem. amplif.; add. w. ref. to* ἀναιρέω *at 9b21*

bʿd

baʿuda (I) 9a7 ἀπέχω

buʿdun, *pl.* abʿādun *maṣdar* 9b26, 11b1 ἀπόστασις | 9a7 *cognate accus. for* baʿuda *transl.* ἀπέχω | 10a7 πρό *in* πρότερος

bāʿada (III) – bāʿada kaṯīran 11b27 μακρός

baʿda 5a13b, 6b19, 7a3 μετά – *in expr.* šayʾun baʿda šayʾin 10b3 ἄλλοτ' ἄλλο – *in* baʿda an yaṣīra lahū 6a20 *morph.; transl. the circumstantiality of part.* διατιθέντα 6a20

bʿḍ

baʿḍun (**a**) *abs.* 7a6b, $7a7^{1,2}$ οἱ | 6b16, 10b10 ἔνιοι | 6a11 ἄττα | 10b12 οἵδε | 10a6, 10b11 *sem. amplif.; add. acc. to sense* (**b**) *in expr.* baʿḍu n-nāsi 4a19, 4b5, 7b2, 9a19, 10a8 τινές | 6b15 οἱ – baʿḍun/baʿḍun 5b25b, 8b3, 8b17, 10a2, 12a2 ἀλλήλων – baʿḍu *w. gen.*/wa-baʿḍu *w. gen.*/(wa-baʿḍu *w. gen.*) 4a15, 6a28–6b2, 9a8–9, 10a26 τὰ μέν/τὰ δέ/(τὰ δέ)

bġy

inbaġā (VII) – yanbaġī an 4b7, 4b12a, 4b21, 7b13, 8a3, 8a19 (8a20), 9a11, 9b2–3 (9b3), 9b19, 10a17, 11a2, $11b24^{1,2}$ *morph.* -τέον | 6b23, 10a24

bġy: inbaġā (*continued*)
χρή | 10a25 *sem. amplif.; add. w. ref. to* χρή *at 10a24* – ʿalā mā yanbaġī 11a25 καλῶς ἔτυχεν
bqy
baqiya (I) 5b18 λοιπόν | 9b27 κατάλοιπον – baqiya an 9a24 -τέον *in* πειρατέον
baqāʾun *maṣdar* 4b16 διαμένω
bl¹
bal 5a9, 10b18 ἀλλά | 8a24, 9b22, 11a15 μᾶλλον δέ | 10b21 καὶ μᾶλλον – laysa bi-wāḥidin bal akṯaru min wāḥidin 5a16 (5a15) *sem. amplif. & metathesis; affirm. / neg. transformation* πλείων
bll²
ballun (I) *maṣdar* 10b2 ὑγρότης
blġ
balaġa (I) *w.* ilā 6a18 προέρχομαι | 5b14^1,2^ (5b13) διϊκνέομαι | 6b15, 7b7, 9a14 *sem. amplif.* μέχρι | 10a5 *sem. amplif.* ἄχρι – balaġa *w.* bi- 6a23 ἔρχομαι
bāliġun *act. part.* 9a18 ἱκανῶς
ablaġu 5a14 πλείων
byḍ
abyaḍu 8b3 λευκός
byn
bayānun (I) *maṣdar, w.* ʿan 4b12b *sem. amplif.; added as mafʿūl muṭlaq to the preceding* nūḍiḥa *at 4b12a*
bayyana (II) 9b27 δείκνυμι – yarūmu an yubayyina 6b9–10* πειρῶμαι
bayna 4a13 *sem. amplif.; implied by the foll.* συναφήν (4a14) ittiṣālun – bayna l-ḥayawāni wa-n-nabāti {7a22} *mistranslation of* πομφόλυξ – *w. verbs* → kāna
bayyinun 4a19–20 εὔσημος | 4b21, 10a13 δῆλος | 4b23, 5a20, 8b9 (8b10) φανερός

tbʿ
tabiʿa (I) 8a2* ἀκολουθέω | 11b16 κατακολουθέω – *in hend.* tabiʿa wa-lazima 7a3 συνακολουθέω
tḥt
taḥta 4a16, 8b18 ὑπό – *in phrase* dāḫilun taḥta 9a13 ὑπό

ṯdy
ṯadyun 10b8 μαστός
ṯmm
ṯumma 10b25 δή – *morph.; expresses the priority in time of aorist part.*: προελθόντα παύεσθαι 6a18 tabluġu ṯumma tanqaṭiʿu | ἐλθόντες καταπαύονται 6a23 yabluġūna ṯumma yuʿaṭṭilūna
ṯmr
(ṯamarun) *pl.* ṯimārun 7b4 καρπός
ṯny
uṯnūwatun 6a25, 6b1, 11b3 δυάς

ǧbr
ǧabara (I) {5b17} ἐρύομαι
ǧrf
muǧtarifatun (VIII) *act. part., in hend. w.* tašaʿʿubun 10b1 ἀνάρροια
ǧrm
(ǧirmun) *pl.* aǧrāmun – al-aǧrāmu s-samāwiyyatu 10a18, 11b19 *sem. amplif.* τὰ οὐράνια
ǧry
ǧarā (I) (**a**) *w. prep.*: ǧarā ʿalā 7a12 ἐν – *in expr.* as-sababu llaḏī lahū ṣāra l-amru yaǧrī ʿalā mā yaǧrī ʿalayhi 10a28 τίνος ἕνεκα – ǧarā bi-ḥasabihī 7a6b κατά (**b**) *w.* maǧrā: *in* ǧarā hāḏā l-maǧrā 4b19 τοιοῦτος | 9a4, 11a14 οὕτως | 10a25–26 ἔχειν οὕτως – mimmā yaǧrī ayḍan hāḏā l-maǧrā 10b11 *sem. amplif.* ἔτι (**c**) *w.* amrun:

in wa-ka-ḏālika yağrī l-amru 7a2 καί ▬ *sem. amplif.; add. acc. to sense* 7a4 tağrī l-umūru | 11a8 yağrī l-amru (**d**) *sem. amplif.*: 10a26[1,2] *add. w. ref. to* ἔχειν *(of a state) at 10a25*

ğaryun *maṣdar* {6a20} *sem., etym.; transl.* ῥυτός *in* Εὔρυτος

mağrā *see above under* ğarā (b)

ğzʾ

tağazzaʾa (V) ▬ al-ğuzʾu llaḏī lā yatağazzaʾu 11b23 τὸ ἄτομον

tağazzuʾun *maṣdar* ▬ at-tağazzuʾu 5a11 τὸ μεριστόν

mutağazziʾun *act. part.* 5a8 διαιρετός

ğuzʾun, *pl.* ağzāʾun 5b20[1,2], 5b21[1,2], 7a11 μέρος ▬ mā lā ğuzʾa lahū 8a3 τὸ ἀμερές ▬ al-ğuzʾu llaḏī lā yatağazzaʾu 11b23 τὸ ἄτομον

ğuzʾiyyun 8a6 μεριστός | 9a2 ἐν μέρει

ğzr

ğazrun (I) *maṣdar, w.* ʿan 10b1 (10b2) ἀναχώρησις

ğsm

(ğismun) *pl.* ağsāmun 6a26 σῶμα ▬ *sem. amplif.*; *transl. the article* τά *as the implied* σώματα: al-ağsāmu 5b11 τὰ κυκλικά | 5b12 τὰ περὶ τὸ μέσον | {5b22} τὰ ἐντιμότατα ▬ al-ağsāmu 5b20 *sem. amplif.; added after the pron.* ταῦτα *referring to* σώματα

ğʿl

ğaʿala (I) (**a**) *abs.* 5a6 (5a7), 10b25, 11a23 ποιέω | 9b19 ποιέω *in* ποιητέον | 7b2 (7b3) ποιοῦμαι ▬ 4b21 τίθημι *in* θετέον *w. two accus.* | 6b7 περιτίθημι ▬ ğuʿila *pass.* 11a10 *transl. the implied copula,* τὸ ἔμπροσθεν τὴν φάρυγγα *sc.* εἶναι (**b**) *sem. amplif.*: *in* fiʿluhū an yağʿala mā yağʿaluhū 6a19–20 ποιέω ▬ 11a13 *add. w. reference to* ğuʿila *at 11a10* ▬ 11b15 *add. acc. to sense* (c) *in expr.*: ğaʿala naẓarahū fī 6a6 (6a7) ἀναφέρω *w.* πρός ▬ ğaʿala baḥṯahū fī 6a13 ἀπορέω

ğff

ğafāfun (I) *maṣdar, w.* ʿan (*see Dozy*) 10b2 ἀναξήρανσις

ğll

ağallu 5a21b μείζων (*comp. of* μέγας) | 9b19 μέγιστος | 7a15a κάλλιστος ▬ *morph.; in* ağallu qadran 10a7 *transl. the superl. suffix* -ώτατος *in* κυριώτατος

ğmʿ

ğamaʿa (I) 7a20 περιτίθημι

ğamīʿun 7a11 (7a12) ἅπας ▬ ğamīʿu l-ašyāʾi 4b16, 6a4, 6b7, 7a21 ἅπαντα | 11a3 πάντα | 5a7 πᾶς ▬ *in hend.*: *w.* kull 4b15b πᾶς | *w. preceding dual subst. or pron.* 7a7, 7a8, 9a9 ἄμφω

ğml

ğumlatun ▬ bi-l-ğumlati 4a20, 8a19, 8b24a, 10b3, 10b10, 11b5 ὅλως | 11a18b τὸ ὅλον | 11b4 ὡς εἰπεῖν

ğnb

muğtanabun (VIII) *pass. part.* ▬ *in hend. w.* ġayru maʾlūfin 9b5 ἀλλότριος

ğanbatun ▬ ğanbatāni 11a25 ἑκάτερα

ğns

ğinsun 4b8, 8b20, 9a5, 9a15 γένος ▬ min ğinsin wāḥidin 9a18 ὁμογενής

ğhl

ğahlun *maṣdar* ▬ ġāyatu l-ğahli 11a21 ἀμαθέστατος/-ον

ğwd

ğayyidun ▬ al-ğayyidu 11a19 τὸ ἀγαθόν

ağwadu 11a18b βέλτιον

ǧwz
tağāwaza (VI) – *in* tağāwaza kulla ḥaddin 8b9 ὑπερβαίνω *in* ὑπερβατός

ǧwhr
ǧawharun, *pl.* ǧawāhiru 4a13, 4b6, 5a8, 7a10a, 8a23, 8b21, 9a5, 10a3, 10a14, 11a22, 11b11, 11b26 οὐσία | 4b11b[1,2,3] *sem. amplif.; add. w. ref. to* οὐσία *at 4b6*

ḥtt
ḥattā (**a**) *transl. Gr. conj. or particles*: 4b3, 8a25 ὥστε | 10a15 δέ – ḥattā anna 10b12 καί (*even*) – *paraphr.* ḥattā yuʿlama 10a22 ὑπέρ (*"with regard to the subject"*) (**b**) *morph.; transl. the circumst. part.*: ḥattā narudda 7a20 (7a21) συνάγοντας – ḥattā ṣārat 5a19 ἰόντων – ḥattā turaddu 8a3 (8a3–4) *in hend.* ὡς ἄγοντας

ḥǧǧ
ḥuǧǧatun 9b21, 9b22 λόγος | 9b23b, 9b24a *sem. amplif.; add. w. ref. to* λόγος *at 9b22*

ḥdd
ḥadda (I) 6a25 (6a24), 6b1 (6a28) ὁρίζω *in* ἀόριστος | 7b7 (7b6) ἀφορίζω *in* ἀφορισμός
maḥdūdun *pass. part.* 7a17, 10b22 (10b21) ὡρισμένος | 10a19 ἀφωρισμένος – ġayru maḥdūdin 6a25 (6a24), 6b1 (6a28), 7a19, 8a12, 11b3 (11b2) ἀόριστος
taḥdīdun (II) *maṣdar* 6b27, 6b28 ὡρίσθαι
ḥaddun, *pl.* ḥudūdun 9b20*, 11a2, 11b25 ὅρος | 11a20 ὅρος *in* ἀοριστία | 8a18 ὅρος *in* ἀόριστον | 7a20 λόγος – tağāwaza kulla ḥaddin 8b9 *sem. amplif.* ὑπερβατός

ḥdṯ
ḥadaṯa (I) 7a18, 8a17 γίνομαι
ḥudūṯun *maṣdar* 7b1 γίνομαι | 8a12 γένεσις
aḥdaṯa (IV) 4b3 ποιέω *in* ἐμποιέω – *w.* li- 8b13 ἐνεργάζομαι

ḥḏf
ḥaḏafa (I) 6a12 ἀφαιρέω

ḥrk
ḥarraka (II) 7b21 κινέω | 5a5 *sem. amplif.; add. acc. to sense* | 5a1 *sem. amplif. and sem. metathesis, pass. / act. transformation for* κινεῖσθαι *at 4b23*
muḥarrikun *act. part.* 5a5* κινέω | 5a17b, 7b16[1]*, 7b16[2], 7b20, 10a1 κινοῦν | 5a18[1,2] *sem. amplif.; add. w. ref. to* κινοῦν *at 5a17*
taḥarraka (V) 10a12 κινοῦμαι | 5a18 *sem. amplif. for* κινεῖσθαι
taḥarrukun *maṣdar* 5a5* κινούμενος
mutaḥarrikun *act. part.* 5b2 κινούμενος | 5b12, 9a12 κινητός | 4b22, 10a20 κινητός *in* ἀκίνητος
ḥarakatun (**a**) 4b4a, 4b20, 4b22, 5a5, 5a25a, 5b3a, 6a13, 7b12, 7b14, 10a20, 10b12 κίνησις | 5a3, 5a18, 5b7, 5b23 *sem. amplif. for the implied* κίνησις – al-ḥarakatu 4b23, 10a9 τὸ κινεῖσθαι (**b**) 5b25a, 6a7, 10a14, 10a16, 10b28a περιφορά | 10a15 *sem. amplif.; add. w. ref. to* περιφορά *at 10a14* – 5a16, 9b25, 10a18 φορά | 5b28 φορά *in* κυκλοφορία (**c**) 11b27 ὁρμή

ḥss
maḥsūsun (I) *pass. part.* – al-ašyāʾu l-maḥsūsatu 4a20, 4b19, 6b8, 7b15, 9b3, 11b18 τὰ αἰσθητά
ḥissun 7b19, 8b10 αἴσθησις

(ḥāssatun) *pl.* al-ḥawāssu 5b5, 9b9 αἱ αἰσθήσεις
ḥsb
ḥasiba (I) - fī-mā aḥsibu 6a12 ἴσως
ḥasabun - ʿalā ḥasabi *w. gen.* 8a13 κατά - *sem. amplif.; in* ǧarā bi-ḥasabihī 7a6b κατά
ḥṣṣ
(ḥiṣṣatun) *pl.* ḥiṣaṣun 6a20 ψῆφος
ḥṣy
aḥṣā (IV) - lā yuḥṣā 11a17 ἄπειρος
ḥṭṭ
inḥaṭṭa (VII) 10a3 ὑποβαίνω
ḥqq
istaḥaqqa (X) 7b18 *sem., etym.; transl.* ἄξιος *in* ἀξιόπιστος
ḥaqqun 6b16 ἀλήθεια - *morph.; transl. the gen. of possession used as predicate to denote duty or task*: ḥaqqu l-maʿrifati 8b25 ἐπιστήμης (*sc.* ἐστί)
aḥaqqu bi- 6a1 *morph.; transl. the superl. suffix in* θειότατον - *in hend.* aḥaqqu wa-awlā bi- 6b26 δέον | 6b28 οἰκειότατος
ḥkm
ḥikmatun 8b9 σοφία
ḥll
inḥalla (VII) - *in hend.* inqaṭaʿa wa-nḥalla 6a18 παύομαι
ḥml
iḥtamala (VIII) 11a6 ἐνδέχομαι
muḥtamilun *act.part.* 5b18 *morph.; transl.* -τος *(denoting possibility) in* ἀσύνδετος
ḥnǧr
ḥanǧaratun 11a10 φάρυγξ
ḥwǧ
iḥtāǧa (VIII) *w.* ilā 5a14, 5b27, 9a20 δέομαι (δέω *deponent*) | 7b6 ζητέω| 4a20–21 *sem., etym.; transl.* χρέος (*or* χρεία) *in* ἀξιόχρεως - *in hend.* yuḥtāǧu ilayhi ḥāǧatan ḍarūratan 9b18 ἀναγκαῖον
ḥāǧatun 9b18 *as mafʿūl muṭlaq to* iḥtāǧa ilā
ḥwl
istiḥālatun (X) *maṣdar* 10b5 (10b4) ἀλλοίωσις
ḥālun (**a**) *in phrases w.* ʿalā: ʿalā ḥālin 10a14 ἐν | 5b6 ὡς | {8b14} *add. in Ar.* - ʿalā kulli ḥālin {5b15} *corrupt text*? (**b**) *in other expr.*: ḥālun wāḥidatun 10b20 ταὐτά - al-ḥālu fīhi 5b19 ἔχω *denoting a state* - ḥāluhū 12a2 ἔχω *denoting a state*
ḥawla {5b17} *morph.; transl. the dat. in* γαίῃ
ḥyy
ḥayātun 4b3, 5b3b, 10a16, 10a17 ζωή
ḥayawānun, *pl.* ḥayawānātun 5b5, 7a22, 7b4, 8a5, 8b27, 9a14, 10a5, 10a13, 10a17, 10b7, 10b17 (10b18), 11a8 ζῷον - *in phrase* bayna l-ḥayawāni wa-n-nabāti {7a22} *mistranslation of* πομφόλυξ
ḥyṯ
ḥayṯu 11a8 ὅπου
ḥyr
taḥayyara (V) *w.* fī 7b10 ἀπορέω | 5a23 ἀπορέω *in* ἄπορον
ḥayratun - *in* mawḍiʿu ḥayratin 10b24b ἀπορία *in* ἄπορον - *in hend.* šakkun wa-ḥayratun 8b13 ἀπορία
ḥyn
ḥīnaʾiḏin 9b11 ἔτι *in* οὐκέτι

ḫrǧ
ḫurūǧun (I) *maṣdar w.* ʿan 8a18, 11a20, 11b3, 11b4[1,2] *sem.; etym.; transl the privative alpha in* ἀόριστος, ἀοριστία, ἄπειρον, ἄτακτον, ἀμορφία
ḫāriǧun *act. part. w.* ʿan 9b5 ἀναιρέω | 9a6 παρά *w. accus.*
aḫraǧa (IV) 8a11 ἄγω

ḫrʿ
iḫtaraʿa (VIII) 4a21b μηχανάομαι
ḫss
aḫassu 7b8, 8a24 χεῖρον
ḫṣṣ
ḫaṣṣa (I) 4b21 ἴδιον
ḫāṣṣun *act. part.* 8b22, 9a16 ἴδιος
- *in hend.* mulāʾimun ḫāṣṣun 10a10 οἰκεῖος
ḫāṣṣatun – ḫāṣṣatan 9b19, 10a10 μάλιστα
ḫāṣṣiyyun 8b21, 8b26, 9a20 ἴδιος
- ḫāṣṣiyyan 8b26 ἰδίᾳ
aḫaṣṣu *w. gen. and* bi- 10b17 (10b16) μάλιστα
ḫṭṭ
(ḫaṭṭun) *pl.* ḫuṭūtun 8b26 γραμμή
ḫṭr
ḫaṭarun 4b5 κύριος *in* κυριώτατον
ḫṭw
taḫaṭṭā (V) 6a3 ὑπερβαίνω *in* ὑπερβατόν
ḫfy
ḫafiya (I) 5a17 *sem. metathesis; neg. / affirm. transformation* οὐ φαίνομαι *in* ἀφανής
ḫlf
iḫtalafa (VIII) 8b19 διαφέρω
iḫtilāfun *maṣdar* 5b2*, 6a5[1,2], 8b16, 8b17, 9a17 διαφορά
muḫtalifun *act. part.* 11a1a διαφορά – *in hend.* kaṯīrun muḫtalifun 7b1* *transl. Gr. variant* ποικίλος *instead of* ποικιλία
ḫlq
ḫalīqun an 8a3 ἴσως | 10b27 ἄρα
aḫlaqu bi- 4b16, 5b19, 6a2, 6b20, 6b24, 8a15a, 8b11, 9a21, 9b6, 9b13 τάχα | 4b13 ἴσως | 8b20 σχεδόν | 6a14 ὥσπερ | 10b26 ἔοικα
ḫlw
ḫalāʾun (I) *maṣdar* 6b1 κενόν
ḫilwun min 8b5, 11b5 ἄνευ
mā ḫalā 6b6, 7a2* πλήν – *sem. amplif.;* sāʾiru s-subuli mā ḫalā hāḏihi s-sabīli 6b19[1] ἐκεῖναι (*sc.* αἱ μέθοδοι)
ḫwf
ḫāfa (I) 7b17 κίνδυνός ἐστι
ḫyr
ḫayrun 8b1 ἀγαθός
(ḫayratun) *pl.* al-ḫayrātu 8a26 (8a27) ἐσθλά

dḫl
daḫala (I) – *in phrase* mā yadḫulu fī 8b8 εἰς – *in phrase* mā yadḫulu š-šakku fīhi 10b17 *paraphr.* τὸ δοκοῦν – 11b3 *sem. amplif.; add. acc. to sense*
dāḫilun *act. part.* – *in phrase* dāḫilun taḥta 9a13 ὑπό
madḫūlun *pass. part.* 4a14* ἐπεισοδιώδης
adḫala (IV) *in* adḫala fī ʿidādi *w. gen.* 8b7 πρός *in* προσκαταριθμέω
drk
adraka (IV) 6a27 ἐφάπτομαι | 9b8 (9b9) θεωρέω
idrākun *maṣdar* 4b14b λαμβάνω
dʿw
daʿā (I) *w.* ilā 10a26 *sem. amplif.; add. acc. to sense*
dāʿin *act. part.* – *sem. amplif.* dāʿin ilā 5b4b πρός
dfʿ
dufʿatun – dufʿatan 6a17 εὐθύς
dll
dalla (I) *w.* ʿalā 6a28 δηλόω | 7b12 *sem. amplif.; add. acc. to sense*
dalīlun ʿalā 7b2 παράδειγμα
dwr
(dawrun) *pl.* adwārun (I) *maṣdar* 7a13 περίοδος
dawriyyun 5a3, 5a16, 5b7, 5b11, 5b23, 5b25a (5b24) κυκλικός | 5b28 κύκλος *in* κυκλοφορία
dwl
tadāwala (VI) {6b10} Ἑστιαῖος

dwm
dawāmun (I) *maṣdar* – ad-dawāmu 11a7 τὸ ἀεί
dāʾimun *act. part.* – dāʾiman 7b16, 10b20 ἀεί
dwn
dūnun – *in phrase* ʿalā dūni *w. gen.* 8a16 ἧττον
dūna – *in expr.* dūna ġayrihī 5b11 μόνον *adv.*
dymwqryṭs 11b22 Δημόκριτος

ḏʾ
ḏālika (**a**) *transl. various Gr. pronouns*: 5b14, 6a3, 9a25, 10b25, 11b5, 11b20 οὗτος | 7a14a οὗτος *in* τοιοῦτος | *in* ka-ḏālika 4a17 οὗτος *in* οὕτως – *in* ka-ḏālika 11a8 αὐτός – 5a4a, 7a10b ἐκεῖνος – 7b2 ὧν *rel. pron.* | *in* li-ḏālika 9b15 ὅ *in* διό – *in* ḏālika/hāḏā 9b6–7, 9b7 ὁ/ὁ *in* ὁ μέν/ὁ δέ | 4a16 τάς (**b**) *in expr.*: wa-ḏālika anna 4a21, 4b4a, 4b15b, 5a12a, 5b3a, 5b8, 5b15, 5b21, 6b19, 7a9a, 8a16, 8b10, 8b17, 8b21, 9a15, 9a27, 10a16, 10b19, 11a8, 11a16 γάρ | 7b15, 9b17, 11a3 ἐπεί – maʿa ḏālika 5a28b ἄλλως τε | 6b9 ἔτι δή – wa- ... maʿa ḏālika 9b18 (9b17–18) καὶ ἄλλως ... καί ... – wa-maʿa ḏālika ayḍan 9a6² *sem. amplif.* καί – wa-min qibali ḏālika 11b7 διὸ καί – ka-ḏālika → ka- (**c**) *sem. amplif.*: *add. to refer to a stated antecedent* 6a27², 7a1, 7a3, 7b11, 7b18, 8a10, 9a7, 9a18, 9a26, 9b9, 9b11, 9b20, 9b22, 10a4, 10a19, 10a27, 10b17, 11b10 – *add. to refer to a prospective statement* 7b20, 11a6 – *add. in the transl. of Gr. comp. adj. after* min 5a21b, 7b19 – *add. to express the subject of the verb* {5b1}, 5b28 – *add. acc. to sense* 4b12b, 4b17, 5a9, 5a22b, 5b5, 5b13, 5b18, 5b19, 8a19 (**d**) *sem. amplif.*; *add. in the expanded transl. of various terms and expressions*: miṯālu ḏālika 9a12, 11a9 οἷον – miṯla ḏālika 11b17 τοιοῦτος – as-sababu llaḏī lahū ṣara ḏālika ka-ḏālika 5a17b οὗ χάριν | 10a1 τὸ τίνος ἕνεκα – sāʾiru mā siwā ḏālika 6a27¹ (6a26) τὰ ἄλλα – an nakūna fī ḏālika muḏṭarrīna 4b13 ἀνάγκη, *sc.* ἡμῖν – lam yaḏkur ḏālika 6b5 *in context* ὡσαύτως
ḏkr
ḏakara (I) 5a8 (5a9), 9a27 (10a1), 11b14 λέγω | 6b5 *sem. concentr.* μνείαν ποιοῦμαι – *paraphr.* lam yaḏkur ḏālika 6b5 *in context* ὡσαύτως – *sem. amplif.*; *add. acc. to sense* 6b15, 9b25, 10a4
ḏākirun *act. part.* – ḥāḏihi llatī anā ḏākiruhā 8a8 *sem. amplif.* τοιάδε
(ḏakarun) *pl.* ḏukūratun 10b8 ἄρρην
ḏhb
(maḏhabun) *pl.* maḏāhibu 10a28 ἔφοδος
ḏw
ḏū *morph.*; *in compound words, it transl. suffixes and prefixed prep.*: *in* ḏū tašawwuqin 5b11 -ικός (*suffix indicating relation or ability*) *in* ἐφετικός – *in* ḏū nuṭqin 7b18 -ώδης *in* λογῶδες – *in* ḏū miqdārin 5a8 -ος (*masc. personal suffix*) *in* ποσός – *in* ḏū nafsin 5b2, 7a17, 11a16 ἐν- *in* ἔμψυχος
ḏātun 8b23 ἑαυτός – *in* min ḏātihā 7a18 *transl.* αὐτός (*self*) *in* αὐτομάτως | 10b27b αὐτός (*self*) *in* αὐτόματον

rʾy
raʾā (I) 10b22 δοκέω – *pass.* (yurā) 4a22, 5b3a δοκέω (*impers.* δοκεῖ) – 11b1 *sem. amplif.; add. acc. to sense*
rbb
rubba-mā 4b18 *sem. amplif.; added to reflect* τάχα *in 4b16 (see note to the Ar. transl.)*
rbṭ
irtibāṭun (VIII) *maṣdar* 5b18 *sem., etym.;* συνδέω *in* ἀσύνδετος
rbk
irtabaka (VIII) *w.* fī 9b2 ἀπορέω *in* ἄπορον
rtb
tartībun (II) *maṣdar* 6b28 τάξις
martabatun 5a9 (5a10) μερίς | 5a12 λόγος (*see note to the Ar. transl.*)
rdd
radda (I) *w.* ilā 7b22 ἄγω ἐπί | 8a3 (8a4) ἄγω εἰς | 6b11 ἀνάγω εἰς | 7a20 (7a21) συνάγω πρός | 6b13[1,2] ἀνάπτω εἰς
rdʾ
radīʾun – ar-radīʾu 11a19 (11a20) τὸ κακόν
rfʿ
rafaʿa (I) 5a9 ἐξαίρω – *w.* ʿan 5a11 ἀφαιρέω *in* ἀφαιρετέος
irtafaʿa (VIII) 11b11 ἀναιροῦμαι
rqy
taraqqā (V) 9b10 μεταβαίνω | 6b14 *sem. amplif.; add. acc. to sense*
rwm
rāma (I) 6b9 πειρῶμαι | 4b7 πειράω *in* πειρατέον

zʾws 5b16 Ζεύς
zll
zalalun 9b16 ἀπάτη
zmn
zamānun 6b3 χρόνος
zwl
zāla (I) 6a13 *sem. metathesis; pass. / act. transformation* ἀφαιροῦμαι *pass.*
zawālun *maṣdar* 6a13 *sem. amplif.; added to refer to* ἀφαίρεσις *in* ἀφαιρεθεῖσα
zyd
zāʾidun (I) *act. part.* 4b10 περιττός
zyn
zīnatun 11a13 κόσμος

sʾr
sāʾirun (**a**) *abs., w. gen.* 6a17[1], 6b18, 9b27, 11b19 ἄλλος (**b**) *w. a foll. subst. add. to express the implied Gr. referent*: sāʾiru l-ašyāʾi 4b14a, 6b12, 8a2, 10a4, 11b19 τὰ ἄλλα | 6b4 τὰ λοιπά – sāʾiru s-subuli 6b22 αἱ λοιπαί – sāʾiru l-ʿulūmi 7a1 αἱ λοιπαί – sāʾiru l-ağsāmi 5b12 τά (*pl. neuter article as subst. maker*) (**c**) *sem. amplif.; interpr.*: sāʾiru mā siwā ḏālika 6a27 (6a26) τὰ ἄλλα – sāʾiru mā fīhā 7a6a τὰ ἄλλα – sāʾiru s-subuli mā ḫalā hāḏihi s-sabīli 6b19 ἐκεῖναι (*sc.* αἱ μέθοδοι) – *in hend. w.* allatī tattaṣilu bihā 6a17[2] ἐφεξῆς
sʾl
saʾala (I) *w.* ʿan 10a28, 10b3, 10b4, 10b6 *sem. metathesis; direct /indirect question transformation: add. to express the interrogation indicated by* τίνος *at 10a28*
sāʾilun *act. part.; sem. metathesis as above*
sbb
sababun (**a**) *abs.* 4b21, 4b23 (5a1), 5a22, 7b19, 8b11, 9b11 αἰτία | 5b7, 9a1 (9a2), 9b8 αἴτιον (**b**) *sem. amplif.*: 5b8[1] *add. for the implied* αἴτιον *at 5b7* | {5b8[2]}, {5b9} *add. for* αἴτιον *at 5b7,*

(mis)understood as αἰτία – 11b2 *add. acc. to sense* (c) *sem. amplif. in expr.*: as-sababu llaḏī lahū 5a23 πῶς | 10b23b τίνος ἕνεκα – as-sababu llaḏī lahū ṣāra ḏālika ka-ḏālika 5a17b οὗ χάριν | 10a1 τὸ τίνος ἕνεκα – as-sababu llaḏī lahū ṣāra l-amru yaǧrī ʿalā mā yaǧrī ʿalayhi 10a28 τίνος ἕνεκα

sbl

sabīlun, *pl.* subulun (a) *abs.* 6b18[2] μέθοδος (b) *morph*: sulūku sabīlin uḫrā 4b17 *transl. the adv. suffix* -ως *in* σαφεστέρως *and* πιστικωτέρως (c) *sem. amplif.*: *transl. the subst. referred to by pron.*: 6b19[1] ἐκείναις | 6b22 λοιπαῖς – fī ḥādihi s-sabīli 6b21 ἔνθα – 6b18[1], 6b19[2] *add. acc. to sense*

sbwsbs 6b6, 11a23 Σπεύσιππος

str

satrun (I) *maṣdar* 10b13 ἐπιπρόσθησις

srʿ

asraʿu 11a18a ἀκαριαῖος

sṭḥ

(saṭḥun) *pl.* suṭūḥun 6a26 ἐπίπεδον

skn

sakana (I) 10a15 ἠρεμέω

sukūnun *maṣdar* 5a24b, 7b10 ἠρεμία | 7b16 τὸ ἠρεμεῖν | 6a8 τὸ πεπαῦσθαι

sākinun *act. part.* 8a1 ἠρεμῶν

slb

salbun (I) *maṣdar* 5a13 ἀπόφασις

sls

salisun {6a20} *sem. etym.; transl.* εὖ *in* Εὔρυτος

slk

sulūkun (I) *maṣdar* 9b4 εἰς | 4b17 *morph.; in phrase* sulūku sabīlin uḫrā *transl. the adv. suffix* -ως *in* σαφεστέρως *and* πιστικωτέρως

smw

samāʾun 5b20, 6a7, 6a8, 6a14, 6b3, 6b4, 7a11, 8a6, 9b24b, 10a14, 10a18 οὐρανός

samāwiyyun 10a18, 10a27, 11b19 οὐράνιος

smy

samiyyun 10a13, 10a15 ὁμώνυμος

snh/w/y

sanatun – *in gen., as second element in an iḍāfa construction* as-sanati 7b3 ἐτήσιος

shl

sahlun 4b17, 9b2, 10a23a ῥᾴδιος

swd

aswadu 8b4 μέλας

swy

siwan – sāʾiru mā siwā ḏālika 6a27 (6a26) *sem. amplif.* τὰ ἄλλα

šʾn

šaʾnun – *in expr.* min šaʾnihī an 9b24a πέφυκε (*GALex I,415 §7*) – *in expr.* min šaʾnihī an yakūna 6a21 τυγχάνω

šbh

tašbīhun (II) *maṣdar* 4b13 ὁμοίωσις

mutašābihun (VI) *act. part.* 8b1, 8b3 ὅμοιος

(šibhun) *pl.* ašbāhun *w. gen.* 9b14 τοῖος *in* τοιοῦτος

šabahun, *pl.* ašbāhun 4a22 μορφή | 5b1 ὁμοιότης

šabīhun bi- 5a10 *morph.; transl. the* -ιος *suffix indicating descent in* θεῖος *in* θειότερος

ašbahu bi- 5a10 *morph.; transl. the comp. suffix* -τερος *in* θειότερος | 6b25 *transl. the suffix* -ικός *in* δυναμικός

štt

(šatītun) *pl.* šattā 8b9 *sem. etym.; transl.* πολλά *in* πολλαχῶς – min ǧihātin šattā 9b1 πλεοναχῶς

šḫṣ
(šaḫṣun) *pl.* ašḫāṣun 9a3 ἄτομον
šdd
ašaddu 4b6, 7b14, 10a7 *morph.; transl. the comp. suffix* -τερος *in* πρότερος
šḏḏ
šāḏḏun 7a2* ὀλίγος
šrʿ
šaraʿa (I) *w.* fī 6b12 ἅπτομαι *w. gen.* – faḍlan ʿan an yašraʿū fīhi 6b5 *sem. amplif.* ἔτι
šrf
šarafun 5b22 *sem., etym.*; *transl.* τιμή *in* ἐντιμότατα
ašrafu *w.* min 10b26, 11a11 τιμιώτερος | *w. foll. gen.* 6b28 τιμιώτατος
šrk
mušārikun (III) *act. part.*; *in* mušārikun li-l-māddati 7a7 *morph.; transl.* -ικός *in* ὑλικός
šʿb
tašaʿʿubun (V) *maṣdar; in hend. w.* muġtarifatun 10b1 ἀνάρροια
šʿr
šaʿrun 10b10 θρίξ
šiʿrun – *in expr.* layta šiʿrī {6a16b} ἀξιώσειεν ἄν | 10a24 *morph.; transl. the interr. sense in* πόθεν – *in expr.* yā laita šiʿri 10a16 ἆρα
škk
šakkun (I) *maṣdar* 10a19 (10a20) ἀπορία | 10a20 *sem. amplif. w. ref. to* ἀπορία *in the same line* – *in hend.* šakkun wa-ḥayratun 8b13 ἀπορία – *interpr.* mā yadḫulu š-šakku fīhi 10b17 τὸ δοκοῦν
tašakkaka (V) 6a6, 6b24 ἀπορέω
tašakkukun *maṣdar* 8a21 ἀπορία
škl
mušakkalun (II) *pass. part.* 7a6b ἔμμορφος – ġayru mušakkalin 6b24 ἄμορφος – 7a7 *sem. amplif.; add. acc. to sense to refer to* ἔμμορφος
mušākalatun (III) *maṣdar* 8a20 ὁμοιότης
(šaklun) *pl.* aškālun 4a22, 9b26 σχῆμα | 7a12 μορφή
šms
šamsun 7b5 ἥλιος
šnʿ
šaniʿun 5a17*, 5b14 ἄτοπος
šanāʿatun – *in hend.* min aš-šanāʿati mā huwa abdaʿu 8b6 τὸ παράδοξον
šhd
šahida (I) *w.* bi- 7b20 συναυδᾶν
šhw
šahwatun, *pl.* šahawātun (I) *maṣdar* 5a20[1], 5a24a, 5b4b, 5b10, 6a9, 11a14 ὄρεξις | 5a20[2] *sem. amplif. for* ὄρεξις *in the same line*
ištahā (VIII) 5b4b ὀρέγομαι *as implied in* ἕκαστον (*sc.* τῶν ὀρεκτῶν)
šwb
šāba (I) {7b11}, {7b13} ἀνάπτω
šwr
mušārun (IV) *pass. part.* – *in expr.* hāḏā (š-šayʾu) al-mušāru ilayhi 6a21, 8a17 ὅδε
šwq
šawqun (I) *maṣdar* 6a12 ὄρεξις
tašawwaqa (V) *w.* ilā 11a6 ὀρέγομαι | 5a15 *sem. amplif. for* ἐφίεμαι *in* ἔφεσις *5a14*
tašawwuqun *maṣdar* 5a14, 5a28b[1,2], 6a9 ἔφεσις | 5b11, 5b12 *transl.* ἔφεσις *in* ἐφετικός | 6a10 τὸ ὀρέγεσθαι
mutašawwiqun *act. part.* 5a15 *sem. amplif. for* ἐφίεμαι *in* ἔφεσις *at 5a14* – ⟨al-ašyāʾu⟩ l-mutašawwiqatu 8a1 τὰ ὀρεγόμενα
mutašawwaqun *pass. part., w.* ilā 5a2 ὀρεκτός

šyʾ
šāʾa (I) 6a2 βούλομαι | 11b10 προαιροῦμαι
šayʾun, *pl.* ašyāʾu (**a**) *abs.; transl. Gr. indef. pron. and pron. adj.*: 5a8 (5a9), 5b18, 5b27, 6a22, 8a5 (8a6), 8b15, 8b23, 8b24a, 9a27, 10b27a, 11b15 τι *indef. encl.* | 10a22, 10b19, 11a1b, 11b26 του *indef. encl.* | 10b3 ἄλλο ▬ ašyāʾu 7a23 ἕτερα | 9a18, 10a25 ἔνια ▬ *w. neg.*: 7a13 εἷς *in* μηδείς | 10b18 εἷς *in* οὐθείς | 10a17 (*Ar. read* μηδέν *for* μηδ᾽ ἐν), 10a22 ἕν *in* μηδέν | 10a18 (*Ar. read* οὐδέν *for* οὐδ᾽ ἐν) ἕν *in* οὐδέν ▬ *in expr.* šayʾun baʿda šayʾin 10b3 ἄλλοτ᾽ ἄλλο ▬ *in expr.* šayʾun ilā šayʾin 10b5 πρὸς ἄλλοτ᾽ ἄλλο ▬ *in expr.* min aǧli šayʾin 10a22, 11b26 ἕνεκά του | 11b15 τινὸς χάριν (**b**) *abs.; transl. the neuter article, sing. and pl., in its function as subst. maker* (**b1**) *sing.*: aš-šayʾu bi-ʿaynihī 8b24b τό *in* τὸ αὐτό ▬ aš-šayʾu wāḥidun bi-ʿaynihī 9a4 τό *in* τὸ αὐτό ▬ aš-šayʾu l-mawḍūʿu 9a9 τὸ *in* τὸ ὑποκείμενον ▬ mā huwa š-šayʾu 8b22 τὸ τί ἦν εἶναι (**b2**) *pl.*: ašyāʾu 10b7 τά *in* τὰ μέν *w.o.* δέ ▬ ašyāʾu/ašyāʾu 8b12–13 τά *in* τὰ μέν/τὰ δέ ▬ *in alphabetical order of the Ar. qualifying subst.* al-ašyāʾu l-azaliyyatu 4a16 τὰ ἀΐδια | al-ašyāʾu l-bīḍu 8b3 τὰ λευκά | al-ašyāʾu l-ǧuzʾiyyatu 8a6 τὰ μεριστά | al-ašyāʾu l-mutaḥarrikatu 5b2, 9a12 τὰ κινούμενα, τὰ κινητά | al-ašyāʾu l-maḥsūsatu 4a20, 4b19, 7b15, 9b3, 11b18 τὰ αἰσθητά | al-ašyāʾu l-ḫāṣṣiyyatu 8b21 τὰ ἴδια | al-ašyāʾu d-dawriyyatu 5a15 τὰ κυκλικά | al-ašyāʾu s-sūdu 8b4 (τὰ) μέλανα | ⟨al-ašyāʾu⟩ l-mutašawwiqatu 8a1* τὰ ὀρεγόμενα | al-ašyāʾu llatī fī ġāyati ḍ-ḍiyāʾi 9b13 τὰ φωτεινότατα | al-ašyāʾu ṭ-ṭabīʿiyyatu 4b3, 4b23 τὰ τῆς φύσεως | al-ašyāʾu l-maʿqūlatu 4a19, 9b4 τὰ νοητά | al-ašyāʾu llatī tuʿlamu 8b22 τὰ θεωρούμενα | al-ašyāʾu llatī tuʿmalu 9a3 τὰ ποιητά | al-ašyāʾu l-qābilatu li-l-fasādi 4a16–17 τὰ φθαρτά | al-ašyāʾu llatī tufʿalu 9a3 τὰ πρακτά | al-ašyāʾu llatī tuqālu 9b1 τὰ λεγόμενα | al-ašyāʾu l-kulliyyatu 8b18 τὰ καθόλου | al-ašyāʾu l-mawǧūdatu 6a11, 8a9 τὰ ὄντα ▬ baʿḍu l-ašyāʾi 6a28 τὰ μέν ▬ sāʾiru l-ašyāʾi 4b14a, 6b12, 8a2, 10a4, 11b19 τὰ ἄλλα | 6a17 τὰ ἐφεξῆς | 6b4 τὰ λοιπά ▬ hāḏihi l-ašyāʾu 8a8, 11a3 τά *in* τὰ τοιάδε (**c**) *sem. amplif.; transl. the implied subst. in Gr. pron., pron. adj., and adj.* (**c1**) *interr. pron.*: ayyu šayʾin, ayyu l-ašyāʾi 5a15², 9b3, 9b19, 12a1 τίς, τί | 4a18, 5a15¹, 6b23 ποῖος (**c2**) *relative and demonstr. pron.*: aš-šayʾu llaḏī 7b21 ὅ ▬ hāḏā š-šayʾu l-mušāru ilayhi 8a17 τόδε (**c3**) *pron. adj.*: ašyāʾu uḫaru 6b4, 10b6 ἕτερα ▬ ašyāʾu uḫaru ġayruhū 11b17¹ ἄλλα ▬ al-ašyāʾu kulluhā 8b1, 8b2, 10a22, 11b9 πάντα | 11b1 ἅπαντα ▬ ǧamīʿu l-ašyāʾi 4b16, 6a4, 6b7, 7a21 ἅπαντα | 5a7, 11a3 πάντα ▬ *in hend.* ǧamīʿu l-ašyāʾi kulluhā 4b15b πάντα ▬ kullu šayʾin 11a5 ἅπαντα ▬ kullu wāḥidin mina l-ašyāʾi 8b22, 9a11 (9a10) ἕκαστος ▬ al-ašyāʾu ... ġayru *w. gen.* 8b17 ἕτερα (**c4**) *adj.*: ašyāʾu

šyʾ: šāʾa (*continued*)
mutaḍāddatun 11b11, 11b12 ἐναντία – ašyāʾu katīratun {4b9} ὀλίγα | 11b13 πολλά | 8b24b πλείονα – ašyāʾu yasīratun 11a19 ὀλίγα (**d**) *sem. amplif.; add. acc. to sense* 6a1, 6b13, 8a20, 9a23[1,2], 9a24, 9a26, 9b2, 11b17[2] (**e**) *individuating use of* šayʾun, *helping to transl. abstract Gr. subst.* (*cf. GALex I,392*, amrun 46) ašyāʾu ḍarūriyyatun 10b19 ἀνάγκαι

šyʿ
šīʿat *w. gen.* 6b6 οἱ περί | 11b27 οἱ

ṣḥḥ
ṣiḥḥatun 8a16 ἀλήθεια *in* ἀληθές
aṣaḥḥu 8b11, 9b14, 9b23a ἀληθέστερος

ṣdq
ṣaddaqa (II) *w.* bi- 7b18 πίστις *in* ἀξιόπιστος
taṣdīqun *maṣdar, w.* bi- 9b17 πίστις – *in* aqrabu ilā t-taṣdīqi 4b18 *sem., etym.; transl.* πίστις *in* πιστικοτέρως
aṣdaqu 5a12 ἀληθινότερος

ṣʿb
ṣaʿuba (I) 7a19 χαλεπόν
ṣaʿbun 4b18 (4b17), 9b16 χαλεπός
aṣʿabu 9a26 χαλεπώτερος

ṣġr
aṣġaru 7a16 ἐλάχιστος *in* τοὐλάχιστον

ṣnʿ
ṣināʿatun, *pl.* ṣināʿātun 7a4, 8a12, 8a20[1,2] τέχνη – *in* ṣināʿatu n-nuǧūmi 9b27, 10a5 λόγος *in* ἀστρολογία

ṣnf
ṣinfun, *pl.* aṣnāfun {11a1a} (10b28) ἀλλήλων | 7a7, 7b4, 8b27 *sem. amplif.; add. acc. to sense*

ṣwb
ṣawābun {8a26} καθόλου

ṣwr
ṣūratun, *pl.* ṣuwarun 6b13[1], 10b28b ἰδέα | 8a18, 9a5 εἶδος | 7b1 (7a23), 8a9, 10b23a (10b22), 11b22 μορφή (**b**) *sem.; etym.;* 8a13 *transl.* μορφή *in* μορφοῦμαι | 11b4 μορφή *in* ἀμορφία (**c**) *interpr.*: 6b13[2] *add. as the subst. referred to by* ταύτας | 6b15 *add. as the subst. referred to by* τῶν εἰρημένων

ṣyr
ṣāra (I) (**a**) *abs.* 5a20 εἶμι |8a22 (8a23) εἰμί | 5b11, 5b21, 7b8, 8a9 *add. for the unexpressed copula* εἰμί (**b**) *in phrase* ṣāra lahū 6a20 διατίθημι | 10b22 ἔχω (**c**) *synt., as auxiliary verb*: ṣāra yaṭlubu 5a24a διώκω – ṣāra yaqūlu 5a25b φημί – ṣirnā naqūlu 8b2 λέγομεν – ṣāra lā yaqaʿu 9b15 οὐκ ἔστιν (**d**) *interpr.; sem. amplif.*: as-sababu lladī lahū ṣāra dālika ka-dālika 5a17 οὗ χάριν | 10a1 τὸ τίνος ἕνεκα – as-sababu lladī lahū ṣāra l-amru yaǧrī ʿalā mā yaǧrī ʿalayhi 10a28 τίνος ἕνεκα (**e**) 11b8 *sem. amplif. add. acc. to sense*

ḍdd
taḍāddun (VI) *maṣdar* 11b2 ἀντίθεσις
mutaḍāddun *act. part.* 11b7 ἐναντίος | 5a16 ὑπεναντίος | 6b18* τοὐναντίον – al-mutaḍāddātu 8a23, 8b5 (τὰ) ἐναντία | 7a9b ἀντικείμενα – ašyāʾu mutaḍāddatun 11b11, 11b12 ἐναντία

ḍrr
muḍṭarrun (VIII) *pass. part., w.* ilā 4b13 ἀνάγκη
ḍarūratun 10a26 ἀνάγκη – *in hend.* waǧaba ḍarūratan 8b19

ἀνάγκη – *in hend.* yuḥtāğu ilayhi ḥāğatan ḍarūratan 9b18 ἀναγκαῖον
ḍarūriyyun 11b16 ἀνάγκη – ašyāʾu ḍarūriyyatun 10b19 ἀνάγκαι

ḍʿf
ḍuʿfun – *in hend.* ḍuʿfun wa-ʿağzun 5b13 ἀδύνατος – *in hend.* ḍuʿfun wa-kalālun 5b14 ἀσθένεια

ḍhy
muḍāhin (III) *act. part.* 11b6 ἰσομοιρέω

ḍwʾ
ḍawʾun 8b15[1,2] φῶς
ḍiyāʾun 9b13 φῶς *in* φωτεινότατα

ḍyf
aḍāfa (IV) *w.* ilā 11b8 ἀνάπτω

ṭbʿ
ṭabʿun 7a5a φύσις
ṭabīʿatun, *pl.* ṭabāʾiʿu 4a17, 4b2[1,2], 4b4b, 4b9, 4b20, 5a2, 7a17 (7a18), 8a22, 8b8, 9a13, 9b20, 10a2, 10a6, 10b22, 11a5, 11a21, 11b5 (11b6), 11b25 φύσις | 9b21* *sem. amplif.; add. w. ref. to 9b20*
ṭabīʿiyyun 5a24a, 10a8 φυσικός | 4b3, 5a1 τῆς φύσεως | 10a9 *sem. amplif.; add. w. ref. to* φυσικός *at 10a8*

ṭrf
(ṭarafun) *pl.* aṭrāfun 8b10 ἄκρον

ṭrq
ṭarīqun **(a)** *abs.* 9b4 ὁδός – *w. gen.* 7b12 ὡς **(b)** *w. prep.* bi-, ʿalā, min **(b1)** bi-ṭarīqi *w. gen.*, bi-ṭarīqin 4b12b, 4b13, 6a9 κατά *w. accus.* – aṭ-ṭarīqu llaḏī bihī 9a10 *sem. metathesis; interr. / affirm. transformation* πῶς **(b2)** ʿalā ṭarīqi *w. gen.* 7b11, 11b13 ὡς | 8b23 κατά | 10a26 *morph.; transl. the adv. suffix* -ως *in* συμπτωματικῶς **(b3)** min ṭarīqi anna 5b18 ὥσπερ | 9a19, 9a22, 9a23 τῷ

ṭlb
ṭalaba (I) 5a24b διώκω | 9b21 ζητέω | 5a25a *sem. amplif. for* διώκω *at 5a24*
ṭalabun *maṣdar* 9b2 ζητέω *in* ζητητέον *implied in* μέχρι πόσου (*sc.* ζητητέον) – *in hend.* ṭalabun wa-baḥṯun (*in paraphr.* fīhi mawḍiʿu ṭalabin wa-baḥṯin) 5b11 ζητέω *in* ἐπιζητέω
maṭlūbun *pass. part.* 9b15 *sem. amplif.; add. acc. to sense*

ṭlq
iṭlāqun (IV) *maṣdar* – *in expr.* ʿalā l-iṭlāqi 4b20, 5a9, 8b13, 9b7, 10a9, 11a4, 11a5 ἁπλῶς
muṭlaqun *pass. part.*– muṭlaqan 11a3 ἁπλῶς

ṭymʾws 6b27 Τίμαιος

ẓnn
ẓanna (I) *abs.* 6b12, 8a21, 8a25 δοκέω | 10a8 οἴομαι – *w.* bi- 7b19, 8b4, 9a26, 10a25, 11b18 δοκέω

ẓhr
ẓahara (I) 11a14 ἐμφαίνω – *w.* li- 8b14 ἐμφαίνομαι

ʿğz
ʿağzun (I) *maṣdar* 9b12 ἀσθένεια – *w.* ʿan 7b16 ἀδύνατος | 5b28 *sem.metathesis; neg. / affirm. transformation* μὴ δύνασθαι – *in hend.* ḍuʿfun wa-ʿağzun 5b13 ἀδύνατος
ʿāğizun *act. part.* 7b8 ἀδύνατος

ʿdd
ʿadadun, *pl.* aʿdādun 4b4a, 4b8, 5a26b, 5a27b, 6a21, 6a22[1,2], 6a25, 6b2, 6b14, 8b26, 9a5 ἀριθμός | 11a19 πλῆθος – *sem. amplif.*: 5a27a *add. for*

ʿdd: ʿadadun (*continued*)
ἀριθμός *at 5a26* | 6b14 *add. as the referent of the pron.* τούτων
ʿidādun – *in expr.* fī ʿidādi *w. gen.* 8b7 καταριθμέω *in* προσκαταριθμέω

ʿdl
muʿādilun (III) *act. part.* 8a24 ἰσόμοιρος *in* ἰσομοιρέω

ʿdm
ʿadamun (I) *maṣdar* 7b12 στέρησις
ʿadīmun – *sem., etym.; transl. privative alpha in* ʿadīmu n-nafsi 7a17 ἄψυχος

ʿrḍ
ʿaraḍa (I) 6b17, 11b11 συμβαίνω | 10b4 (10b5) γίνομαι | 9b13, 10b3, 11b14 *sem. amplif.; add. acc. to sense*
ʿaraḍun, *pl.* aʿrāḍun 6a9, 8b23 συμβεβηκός | 5b24 κατὰ συμβεβηκός – ʿaraḍun lazima 10b18 σύμπτωμα – *in hend.* al-ittifāqu wa-l-ʿaraḍu 10a26 σύμπτωμα *in* συμπτωματικῶς

ʿrf
maʿrifatun (I) *maṣdar, w.* bi- 8b21[1,2] (8b20), 8b25 ἐπιστήμη | 8b27 *sem. amplif.; add. as the referent of the article* ἡ (ἐπιστήμη) – al-maʿrifatu 8b16, 9a10 τὸ ἐπίστασθαι | 9b22 τὸ εἰδέναι – *in hend. w.* innahū yuʿlamu 9a24 τὸ εἰδέναι

ʿzz
ʿazīzun – *in hend. w.* qalīlun 11a24 (11a23) σπάνιος

ʿṭl
ʿaṭṭala (II) 6a23 καταπαύομαι
taʿṭīlun *maṣdar* 7b12 ἀργία

ʿẓm
ʿaẓīmun 10b11 μέγεθος
aʿẓamu *w. gen.* 7b2, 10b16 μέγιστος | 7b19 (7b18) μείζω | 4b5 *morph.; transl. the superl.* -ώτατος *in* κυριώτατον

ʿqd
iʿtaqada (VIII) 11b21 λαμβάνω | 11b22 ὑποτίθεμαι | {6a16b} (6a17) ἀποδίδωμι – iʿtaqada fīhī anna (*to regard s.th. as*) 4b5 τίθημι *w. two accus.* | 9b24b ὑπολαμβάνω
muʿtaqidun *act. part.* (*following its own verb*) 11b21 τις

ʿql
ʿaqlun (I) *maṣdar* 7b23, 9b14 νοῦς
ʿāqilun *act. part.* 6a19 φρονῶν
maʿqūlun *pass. part.* 4a19, 9a12 νοητός | 9b5 φρονεῖν – al-ašyāʾu l-maʿqūlatu 6b8, 9b4 νοητά

ʿll[1]
laʿalla – wa-laʿalla 9b1 ἤ

ʿll[2]
ʿillatun 11b8 αἰτία

ʿlm
ʿalima (I) – ʿulima *pass.* 9a26 τὸ ἐπίστασθαι | 9a19 γνωστός | 9a22 *sem. amplif.; add. for* γνωστός *at 9a19* – *in hend.* al-maʿrifatu ... wa-innahū yuʿlamu 9a24 τὸ εἰδέναι – al-ašyāʾu llatī tuʿlamu 8b22 τὰ θεωρούμενα – *paraphr.* ḥattā yuʿlama 10a22 ὑπέρ (*"with regard to the subject"*)
(ʿilmun) *pl.* ʿulūmun *maṣdar* 6b19 (6b20) ἐπιστήμη | 7a1 *sem. amplif.; add. w. ref. to* ἐπιστήμη *at 6b20* | 9b18 πραγματεία | 9b20[1,2*] τάς *add. w. ref. to* πραγματείας *at 9b18* | 9b21 *sem. amplif.; add. w. ref. to* πραγματείας *at 9b18*
maʿlūmun *pass. part.* – *in* ġayru maʿlūmin 9a19, 9a22 γνωστός *in* ἄγνωστος
taʿlīmun (II) *maṣdar* – at-

ʿny
a ʿnā (I) – a ʿnī, *first person sing.*: *sem. amplif.; demonstrative use of the verb to introduce the referent of a previous pron. or term*: 5b11 *w. ref. to* mā (5b10) οὗτος | 7a16, 8a22, 8b12 *w. ref. to* hāḏā | 7a21 *w. ref. to* ǧamīʿu | 7b20 *w. ref. to* ḏālika | 8a8 *w. ref. to* hāḏihi l-ašyāʾu | 9b14 *w. ref. to* hāḏā l-qawlu l-āḫaru | 9b19 *w. ref. to* hāḏā l-amru *at 9b17* | 10b24b *w. ref. to preceding* hāḏā | 11a5 *w. ref. to the repeated term* ʿalā l-iṭlāq
maʿnan – *sem. amplif.; add. to complement demonstr. pron.* hāḏā l-maʿnā 6a2, 6a14, 7b5 τοῦτο, ταῦτα – *in expr.* lā maʿnā lahū {10a23a} ἄλλως – *sem. amplif.; added acc. to sense* 9a26

ʿwn
aʿāna (IV) 10a6 συνεργέω
taʿāwana (VI) *w.* ʿalā 4a12 συνεργέω εἰς
maʿūnatun 10a6 *sem. amplif.; add. as mafʿūl muṭlaq after* aʿāna

ʿyn
ʿaynun 10b13 ὄμμα – bi-ʿaynihī *in* wāḥidun bi-ʿaynihī 5a18, 9a4 αὐτός *in* ὁ αὐτός – *in* aš-šayʾu bi-ʿaynihī 8b24b αὐτό *in* τὸ αὐτό

ġḏw
(ġiḏāʾun) *pl.* aġḏiyatun 10b17 τροφή

ġrz
ġarīziyyun 6a10 σύμφυτος

ġny
ġanāʾun – *in* ʿaẓīmu l-ġanāʾi 9b17 *sem. amplif.* μέγας

ġyy
ġāyatun **(a)** *abs.* 9a1 τέλος – *in hend.* ġāyatun yuqṣadu lahā 9b7 τέλος **(b)** ġāyatu *w. gen.: morph.; transl. the superl.*: ġāyatu š-šarafi 5b22 ἐντιμότατα – ġāyatu l-faḍīlati 5b26b, 5b27 τὸ ἄριστον – ġāyatu l-ǧahli 11a21 ἀμαθέστατος, -ον **(c)** fī ġāyati *w. gen.: morph.; transl. the superl.*: fī ġāyati mā yumkinu an yakūna ʿalayhi 8a4* ὅ τι μάλιστα – fī ġāyati l-kamāli 8a7* τελεώτατον – al-ašyāʾu llatī fī ġāyati ḍ-ḍiyāʾi 9b13 τὰ φωτεινότατα

ġyr
(taġyīrun) *pl.* taġāyīru (II) *maṣdar* 10b3, 10b5, 11b14 μεταβολή
taġayyara (V) 7b13 ἀντιμεταλλάττω
taġayyurun *maṣdar* 7a23 μεταβολή
ġayru **(a)** *w. foll. gen.* 5a18, 5b6, 7b21, 8b17, 10a7, 10b25 ἕτερος | 6b3, 8a20 ἄλλος | 6b6 οἱ ἄλλοι | 7b17, 8a10 μή – *in* ġayru maʾlūfin 9b5 ἄλλος *in* ἀλλότριος – *in hend.* āḫaru ġayruhū 6a22, 11b17 ἄλλος | 7b1 παντοῖος **(b)** *w. prep.* bi-ġayri *w. gen.* 8b16 ἄνευ – dūna ġayrihī 5b11 μόνον *adv.* **(c)** *morph.; transl. the alpha privative*: ġayru mutaḥarrikin 4b22, 10a20 ἀκίνητος – ġayru qābilin 5b18 ἄδεκτος – ġayru maḥdūdin 6a25 (6a24), 6b1 (6a28), 7a19, 8a12, 11b3 (11b2) ἀόριστος – ġayru mušakkalin 6b24 ἄμορφος – ġayru munqāsin 7a10b ἄλογος – ġayru maʿlūmin 9a19, 9a22 ἄγνωστος – ġayru mubṣarin 9a23 ἀόρατος **(d)** *sem. amplif.*; faḍlan ʿan ġayrihī 4b4a αὐτός, *self* (*in* οὐδὲ αὐτός, *see note to the Arabic transl.*)

f

fa- (**a**) *abs.* 4b6, 4b18, 5a28b, 6a2, 10a13[1], 10a24, 11a1b δέ *w.o. preceding* μέν | δ' οὖν *w.o. preceding* μέν 4a17[1], 4b12a (4b11), 5b7, 9a10 | 5a25b, 7a6b, 10a5 οὖν | 5a4a, 5a19 ὥστε | 5a6 δή | 6b14 εἶτα | 7b5 καί | 10b26 ἤ | 11b21 (11b20) ἀλλά (**b**) *synt.*: *expresses the temporal shift from a perf. tense to a present tense in the Gr. part.*: naḫtariʿuhū fa-naḍaʿuhū 4a21b–23 μεμηχανημένα δι' ἡμῶν *foll. by* περιτιθέντων – *synt.; introduces a part. clause subordinated to the main clause*: qadi staʿmala qawmun ... fa-adḫalū 8b6 χρώμενοι ... προσκαταριθμοῦσιν (**c**) *add. as required by the Ar. synt.* 4a17[2], 4a19, 4b2, 4b7, 4b17, 4b21, 4b22, 5a5, 5a17, 5b1, 5b3b, 5b8, 5b14, 5b21, 5b27, 6a7, 6a9, 7b11, 7b13, 8a15a, 8a19, 8b14, 8b17, 8b19, 8b25a, 9a20, 9b27, 10a7[1], 10a13[2], 11a2, 11a9, 11a17a, 11a18b, 11b5, 11b19, 11b20* (**d**) *see also* fa- *in* fa-inna → inna, fa-qad → qad, fa- *before and after* ammā → fa-ammā ... fa-

ftr

fatara (I) 5a16 ἀνύω *in* ἀνήνυτος
tafattara (V) 5a4a *sem., etym.* παύω (*med.* παύομαι) *in* ἄπαυστος

ftš

taftīšun (II) *maṣdar* – *in hend.* al-baḥṯu wa-t-taftīšu 8b15 ζητέω

frd

infirādun (VII) *maṣdar* – *in expr.* ʿalā l-infirādi 8a27 χωρίς

frs

farasun 6a22 ἵππος

frq

fāraqa (III) 10a15 *sem. metathesis; pass. / act. transformation* χωρίζομαι

fsḫ

infasaḫa (VII) 5a4b λύομαι *med.*

fsd

fasādun (I) *maṣdar* – *in* al-ašyāʾu l-qābilatu li-l-fasādi 4a16–17 *sem.; etym.; transl.* φθορά *in* τὰ φθαρτά

fṣl

(faṣlun) *pl.* fuṣūlun (I) *maṣdar* 8b10 διαφορά
munfaṣilun (VII) *act. part.; w.* ʿan 4a12 κεχωρισμένος

fḍl

faḍala (I) *w.* ʿalā 11b6 ὑπερέχω
faḍlun *maṣdar* 4b6 ἀγαθός *as the positive degree of the comp.* κρείττων – faḍlun ʿalā 4b14a ὑπεροχή *w. gen.* – *in* ašaddu faḍlan 7b14 τιμή *in* τιμιώτερος – faḍlan ʿan ġayrihī 4b4a *sem. amplif.* αὐτός, *self* (*in* οὐδὲ αὐτός, *see note to the Arabic transl.*) – *in* faḍlan ʿan an yašraʿū fīhi 6b5 *sem. amplif.; paraphr.* ἔτι
fuḍūlun 8a22 περιεργία
faḍīlatun 5b26b, 5b27 τὸ καλόν *as the positive degree of the superl.* τὸ ἄριστον
afḍalu 5a20, 5b1, {5b8}, 6a2, 6a4, 11a2, 11a6, 11b9 ἄριστος | 7b11, 8a14b, 8a24, 11a9, 11b15, 11b27 βέλτιον | 5a1, 5a9, 5b9 (5b8) κρείττων | 5b27 καλλίων | 11a15 εὖ

fʿl

faʿala (I) 10a12 ἐνεργέω | 9a3 πράττω *in* πρακτά
fiʿlun *maṣdar* 5a7, 5b23, 7b13, 8a11, 9a4 ἐνέργεια | 7b21 ποιεῖν – *in* fiʿluhū an yaǧʿala mā yaǧʿaluhū 6a19–20 *sem. amplif.* ποιέω
infiʿālun (VII) *maṣdar* 5b6, 7b22 πάσχειν

fqṭ
faqaṭ 6a28, 6b11, 11a20 μόνον *adv.* – innamā ... faqaṭ 4a18, 6b15–16 (6b16), 6b17, 7a7 μόνον *adv.* (*GALex I,503 §12.1b*)
fkr
fikrun 8b12 διάνοια | 8b14 *transl. the pron. referring to* διάνοια *at 8b12*
fnn
fannun 10a8 τρόπος
fhm
fahima (I) 8a19 (8a20) λαμβάνω
fahmun *maṣdar* 5b9 διάνοια
Fūṯāġūras 11b27 Πυθαγόρας *in* Πυθαγόρειοι
fy
fī (**a**) *transl. Gr. prep.* 4a17, 4a18, 4b20, 5a12, 6a4, 6b16, 6b18[2], 6b19*, 6b21, 6b27, 7a1, 7a3 (*w. ref. to 7a1*), 7a8, 7a13, 7a17, 7a21, 7b4, 7b15*, 8a12, 8b4, 8b15, 8b24b, 9a3, 9a13, 9a16, 9a27, 9b3, 9b5, 9b19, 10a6, 10a12, 10a27, 10b4, 10b7, 10b10[2], 10b25, 11a5, 11a19, 11b3, 11b12, 11b13, 11b17[1,2], 11b25[1,2], 12a1 ἐν | 4b3 ἐν *in* ἐμποιέω | 6b21 ἐν *in* ἔνθα – *sem. amplif.* wuǧūduhū fī 4a18, 4b9, 4b10, 5b6, 8a23, 9a1 ἐν (*cf. Ross 65 ad loc.*) – fī hāḏā l-mawḍiʿi 7b6 ἐν *in* ἐνταῦθα – 4b7–8, 4b22, 5b22, 5b23, 6b14, 7a4, 7a16, 8a16, 8b2, 8b22, 8b26[1], 9a15, 9b18, 9b19 (*w. ref. to 9b18*), 10a4 κατά *w. accus.* | 8b23 κατά *w. gen.* – 5a14[2], 6b4[1,2], 6b8, 6b17, 7b1, 7b2 (*w. ref. to 7b1*), 11a22, 11a24 περί – 8a20[1], 9a21[1], 11a6, 11a8 ἐπί – 6a6, 9a25, 10a20 πρός – fī (anfusihā) 4a23 διά *in* δι' αὐτῶν – 6a13 ὑπέρ – mā yadḫulu fī 8b8 *sem. amplif.* εἰς (**b**) *transl. the verbs* ἔχω (*denoting a state*) *and* ἔστιν – *w. gen.* 8a21, 10b26, 11b18 ἔχω | *in hend.* al-ḥālu fīhi 5b19 ἔχω – *w. gen.* 9b23b[2] ἔστιν (*there is*) | *w.* yakūnu 9b24a *sem. amplif.; add. w. ref. to* ἔστιν *at 9b23* (**c**) *morph.; transl. the gen., dat., and accus., and the morph. of adj. and adv.* (**c1**) *transl. the gen.*: fī l-kulli 4a21 τοῦ παντός – fī l-ʿulūmi ⟨kullihā⟩ 9b21 ἁπάντων – fī-mā 9b23b[1] ὧν – allatī taʿriḍu fī l-arḍi 11b14 τῆς γῆς (**c2**) *transl. the dat.*: fī l-ḥayawāni {5b5} τοῖς ζῴοις – fīhā 6a10 αὐτῷ – fī ḏ-ḏukūrati 10b8 τοῖς ἄρρεσιν – fī baʿḍihā 10b10[1] ἐνίοις – fī l-ḥarakati 10b12 κινήσει (**c3**) *transl. the accus.* – *of specification (synecdoche)* fī ṭabʿihā 7a5a* τὴν φύσιν – *of respect* 9a8–9 τὰ μέν/τὰ δέ/τὰ δέ (**c4**) *transl. the morph. of adj.*: *in* fī ġāyat *with foll. gen. transl. superl.*: fī ġāyat š-šarafi 5b22 ἐντιμότατος – fī ġāyati l-faḍīlati 5b26b, 5b27 ἄριστος – fī ġāyati ḍ-ḍiyāʾi 9b13 φωτεινότατος (**c5**) *transl. the morph. of adv.*: fī waqtin mina l-awqāti 5a24b ποτε *indef. encl. correlative adv.* – fī mawaḍiʿa kaṯīratin 10a24 πλεονάκις – fī mawḍiʿin mina l-mawāḍiʿi *w. neg.* 11a9 οὐδαμοῦ (**d**) *sem. amplif.* (**d1**) *add. after Ar. verbs or nouns meaning "to say"*: *after* qawlun 4b7, 5b16, 9a23 λέγω, φημί – *after* kalāmun 5a23 λόγος – lā yaqūlūna wa-lā fīhi (i.e., Allāhi) 11b8 οὐδὲ τὸν θεόν (*sc.* λέγουσιν) – (al-qawlu) llaḏī qīla fīhi inna 8a1 ὡς (**d2**) *add. acc. to sense* 4a22, 5a13a, 5a14[1], 5a22b, {5a27b}, 5b12, 6a14, 6b18[1], 8a7, 8a8, 8a19,

8a20², 8b1, 8b14, 8b15, 8b26²,³, 8b27, 9a21², 9a24, 9a26, 9b2, 10b3, 11a3, 11a21, 11b22 (**e**) *in paraphr. expr.*: al-awlā fī l-qiyās 4a13 εὐλογώτερον – fīhi mawḍiʿu ṭalabin wa-baḥṯin 5b11 ἐπιζητέω – sāʾiru mā fīhā 7a6a τὰ ἄλλα – an nakūna fī ḏālika muḍṭarrīna 4b13 ἀνάγκη *sc.* ἡμῖν – *in phrase* kullu mā fīhā {7a20} ἕκαστος, *misreading* ἓν ἕκαστον *for* ἕνεκά του *in the Greek* (7a21) (**f**) *in phrases*: fī ġāyati *w. gen.* → ġāyatun, fī-mā aḥsibu → ḥasiba, fī ʿidādi *w. gen.* → ʿidādun (**g**) *w. verbs*: → aḫaḏa, → taḥayyara, → daḫala, → ḏakara, → irtabaka, → šaraʿa, → tašakkaka, → iʿtaqada, → amʿana, → naẓara,→ waqaʿa

fyd

afāda (IV) 11a7 μεταδίδωμι

qbl

qabila (I) 10b28b λαμβάνω | 11a15 δέχομαι

qabūlun *maṣdar* 6a1 δέχομαι – qabūlu ṣ-ṣūrati 8a13 *morph.; transl. the pass. morph. of the verb* μορφοῦμαι

qābilun *act. part.* – *in* al-ašyāʾu l-qābilatu li-l-fasādi 4a16 *morph.; transl.* -τος *in* τὰ φθαρτά – 11a16 *sem. amplif.; add. w. ref. to* qabila *at 11a15*

qabla 9b21* πρότερος – qabla ḏālika 5b19 πρότερον

qibalun – min qibali *w. gen.* 7b21, 9a8, 9a9¹,², 9b12, 10b19 διά | 10b18, 11a1b ἕνεκα | 5b13¹, 7b16 ὡς | 5b28 τῷ *w. infinitive* – min qibali anna 9b11 διά | 4b22 ἐπεί | 5a15 ἐπειδή | 4b19 ἐπείπερ | 5b13², 6b26 ὡς | 6b21 γάρ | 11b11 (11b12) *morph.: transl. the circumst. part. in* οὖσαν – wa-min qibali ḏālika 11b7 διὸ καί

qd

qad (**a**) *transl. Gr. particles*: wa-qad *w. impf.* 7b2 δή – fa-inna qad naǧidu 10a25 καὶ δή – fa-qad *w. perf.* 9a24 (9a23) δ' οὖν | 5b18 ἀλλά (**b**) *w. impf.* (*possible*) qad yuḥtāǧu 5b27 δέοι ἄν – qad yataḥayyaru 7b10 ἂν ἀπορήσειεν – qad yuẓannu 6b12, 8a21, 9a26 δόξειεν ἄν | 8a25, 10a25 δοκεῖν (**c**) *w. impf.* (*assertive, emphatic; see note 21 to the Arabic translation*); *in alphabetical order of the Ar. verbs*: qad yataʾaḏḏā 10b12 λελωβημένος (*sc.* ἐστίν) (*where the assertion in the use of* qad *comes from the preceding* καί) – qad yubṭilūna 9b21 ἀναιροῦσιν – qad yanbaġī an 4b7, 4b12a, 7b13, 8a19 (8a20), 10a17, 11a2, 11b24 -τέον – qad yabqā 9b27 κατάλοιπον (*sc.* ἐστίν) – qad yaḥtāǧu ilā 7b6 ζητεῖ – qad yurā 4a22, 5b3a δοκεῖ – qad yaṣʿubu 7a19 χαλεπόν (*sc.* ἐστίν) – qad yuẓannu 7b19 δοκεῖ – qad yaẓharu (lahū) 8b14 ἐμφαίνεται | 11a14 ἐκεῖνό γ' ἐμφαίνει (*where* qad *transl. the emphasis expressed by* ἐκεῖνό γ') – qad yaʿriḍu 11b11 συμβήσεται – qad yastaʿmilūna n-naẓara 7a15b λαμβάνουσι – kānat qad tuʿīnu 10a6 συνεργεῖ – qad yaqtaḍī 8a8 ἐπιποθέω – qad yakūnu 9a10 ὄντος *gen. abs.* | 10b7 *add. for the implied copula to render the emphasis expressed by* αὐτοῖς, *which is otherwise not translated* – qad yalzamu 7a23 συμβαίνει – qad yumkinu 9b8 δυνάμεθα

qd: qad (*continued*)
- qad yağibu 8b19 ἀνάγκη - qad yūğadu 6a4 εἶναι - qad nağidu 7a1, 11b12 φαίνεται | 11b16 *sem. amplif.; add. w. ref. to* φαίνεται *at 11b12* - qad naqifu ʿalā 9a4 ἐπιστάμεθα (**d**) *w. impf. and* wa- *of ḥāl*: wa-qad yuḫrağu 8a11 *transl. the circumstantial sense of the part. in* καὶ ἀγόμενον (**e**) *w. perf.* (**e1**) *expresses completed action*: qad šaraʿa 6b12 ἅπτεσθαι - qad ʿaraḍa 6b17 συμβαίνει - qadi staʿmala 8b6 χρώμενοι - qad qaḏafa 5b21 ἀπεωσμένα - qad luḫḫiṣa 9a18 διῄρηται - qad kāna yağibu 10b20 (10b19) ἔδει - *sem. amplif.* qad waqaʿa l-iḫtilāfu 8b17 διαφορά τις (*sc.* ἔστιν) (**e2**) *expresses completed action in the apodosis of a conditional sentence* qad šāba 7b11 ἀνάψειεν ἄν

qdr
qadara (I) *w.* an 11b8 δύναμαι | *w.* ʿalā 9b11 δύναμαι
qadrun 10a7 κύριος *in* κυριώτατος - bi-qadri *w. gen.* 6a27, 9a2 *transl. the indef. quantity indicated in* ὅσος
miqdārun, *pl.* maqādīru 9b26 μέγεθος | 5a8 *sem., etym.; transl. the root meaning* ποσ- *in* ποσός

qdm
muqaddamun (II) *pass. part.* - min muqaddami *w. gen.* 11a10 ἔμπροσθεν
taqaddumun (V) *maṣdar* 4b6, 7b14 πρό *in* πρότερος | 4a16 (4a15) *sem. amplif. for* πρότερος
mutaqaddimun *act. part.* 4a15, 11b19 πρότερος
aqdamu 5a2, 10b25 πρότερος | 5b9 πρῶτος

qdw/y
iqtadā (VIII) *w.* bi- 8a1 μιμέομαι

qḏf
qaḏafa (I) *w.* bi- *of obj. and* ʿan, *and in hend. w.* aqṣā 5b21 ἀπωθέω

qrb
qarībun *w.* min 8a27 ἐγγύς *w. gen.*
aqrabu *w.* ilā 4b18 *morph.; transl. the comp. suffix* -τερος *in* πιστικωτέρως

qrn
maqrūnun (I) *pass. part., w.* bi- 10a19 συνάπτω *intransitive*
qarnun 10b11 κέρας

qsm
taqsīmun (II) *maṣdar* - at-taqsīmu 5a11 τὸ διαιρετόν
qismatun 8a9 μερισμός | 9a2, 9a6[1], 9a20 διαίρεσις | {9a6[2]} *add. for* διαίρεσις *acc. to sense*

qṣd
qaṣada (I) - quṣida *pass., w.* bi- 11a2 εἰς | 11b15 *sem. amplif.; add. acc. to sense w.* τέλος - *in hend.* ġāyatun yuqṣadu lahā 9b7 τέλος
maqṣūdun *pass. part., w.* ilā 9a1 *sem. amplif.; add. acc. to sense*

qṣr
qaṣara (I) 11a9 παραλείπω

qṣw/y
aqṣā (IV) - *in hend. w.* qaḏafa 5b21 ἀπωθέω

qḍy
iqtaḍā (VIII) 5a22a, 7b19 ζητέω | 7b7 ἀπαιτέω | 8a8 ἐπιποθέω

qṭʿ
inqaṭaʿa (VII) - *in hend.* inqaṭaʿa wa-nḥalla 6a18 παύομαι

qll
istiqlālun (X) *maṣdar* (*to be lifted, picked up*) 10b13 παραιώρησις
qalīlun - *in hend. w.* ʿazīzun 11a24 (11a23) σπάνιος

qwd

qāda (I) 11b9 ἄγω

qwl

qāla (I) (**a**) *abs.* 4a19, 5a26b, 5a28a, 5b16, 6a19 [6a20], 6b27, 7a15b, 8a7, 9a19 φημί | 5b1, 6a21, 8a26, 8b2, 8b24b (8b25), 9b1, 10a24, 11a4[1,2], 11b24 λέγω | 7a10b δοκέω ‒ *sem. amplif.; added acc. to sense* 6a14, 6a28, 6b16, 7a6b, 7a7[1,2], 7b11, 7b12, 7b23, 8b26, 9a21, 9a23, 9a24, 9b6, 11b8 ‒ allatī qulnā {10a4*} εἰρημένων? (ἐρῶ) (**b**) qāla *w.* bi- 5a13 λέγω | 6a24 ποιέω

qawlun *maṣdar* (**a**) *abs.* 5a6, 5a14[1], 8a27, 10b26 λόγος | 7b23 τὸ λεχθέν | 4b7 λέγειν | 4b20, 8b11, 9b23a[1] εἰπεῖν | 9b23a[2] ὅτι ‒ *sem. amplif.; add. as the subst. implied by the pron.* 5a26a, 9b13 ἐκεῖνο | 9a22 αὐτό ‒ *sem. amplif.; add. to refer to a preceding statement* 7b22, 11a3[1,2], 11a5 ‒ *sem. ampl.; add. acc. to sense* 5a14[2], 8a16, 8a26[1,2], 9a26 (**b**) qawlun *w.* bi- 9a21[1,2] (9a22) λέγειν | 5a25c *sem. amplif. for* φημί (5a26) ‒ *sem. amplif.; transl. the subst. implied by the neuter article* τό: al-qawlu bi-annahū mawǧūdun 8a15b τὸ εἶναι ‒ al-qawlu bi-annahū laysa 5a4a τό μὴ εἶναι

qāʾilun *act. part.* (**a**) *abs.* 5b1, 9a23 *add. after its own verb transl. the indef. pron.* τις ‒ *synt.; add. acc. to sense after its own verb* 9a26 ‒ *periphr. transl. of Gr. pron.*: mā anā qāʾiluhū ... aʿnī 5b10 οὗτος | mā anā qāʾiluhū 6a5 ὅδε (**b**) qāʾilun *w.* bi-: al-qāʾilu bi- 6a3 (6a4) ὁ λέγων ‒ al-qāʾilūna bi- 5a26b[1,2] *sem. concentr.* ὅσοι λέγουσιν | 5a27a *sem. amplif.; add. as the subst. implied by the pron.* αὐτοί

qwm

qāʾimun (I) *act. part.* 4b2[1,2], 4b4b *sem. amplif.; add. acc. to sense (see note to the Arabic transl.)*

qawmun 6a24, 8b6 οἱ

qwy

quwwatun, *pl.* quwan 4b14a, 5a1, 7a12, 8a19, 10b23a δύναμις ‒ bi-l-quwwati 8a10 δυνάμει ‒ *in* ašbahu bi-l-quwā 6b25 *sem. etym.; transl.* δύναμις *in* δυναμικός

aqwā 5b15, 6b19 ἰσχυρότερος

qys

qiyāsun (III) *maṣdar* 8a19 ἀναλογία ‒ *in* al-awlā fī l-qiyāsi 4a13 *sem.; etym.; transl.* λόγος *in* εὐλογώτερον

muqāyasatun (III) *maṣdar* 4b12b, 9a6, 9a7, 9a21[1,2] ἀναλογία

munqāsun (VII) *act. part.* 10b25 (10b24–25) ἔχω λόγον (*see Part I, Ch. 3.3*)

qyl

taqayyala (V) 7a5a μιμέομαι | 11b1 ἐπιμιμέομαι

taqayyulun *maṣdar* 5a25c μίμησις

k

ka- 4a16 ὥσπερ ‒ ka- *in* ka-ḏālika 11a8 (11a7) ὡς *in* ὡς δ' αὐτό ‒ {9a1} *sem. amplif.; add. acc. to sense*

ka-anna 4a14, 5a6, 5b21, 5b24, 6a2, 6b20, 6b25, 7a9b, 7b5, 8b8, 9b15, 11b6 οἷον | 8a18 ὡς | 10b7 ὥσπερ | 9a18, 10a19 πως | 11a3 (11a4) τις *indef. enclitic*

ka-ḏālika (**a**) *abs.* 4a17, 8a14a* οὕτως | 7a1 ἔχειν οὕτω | 5b23, 6a11 τοιοῦτος | 11a13 ὡσαύτως | 11b21 *sem. amplif.; add. w. ref. to* τὸ τεταγμένον

k: ka-ḏālika (*continued*)
(**b**) *in expr.*: as-sababu llaḏī lahū ṣara ḏālika ka-ḏālika 5a17 οὗ χάριν | 10a1 τὸ τίνος ἕνεκα – wa-ka-ḏālika yağrī l-amru 7a2 καί – wa-ka-ḏālika 9b17 καί (**c**) *sem. amplif.; add. acc. to sense* 7a7
ka-mā 6b27, 9a22, 10a27 καθάπερ | 5b5, 9a16 ὥσπερ

ktb
kitābun – al-kitābu l-mansūbu ilā Ṭym'ws 6b27 *sem. amplif., interpr.;* Τίμαιος
kitābatun 7a2 γραμματική

kṯr
kaṯratun 5a21 πλῆθος – *in* lā yuḥṣā kaṯratan 11a17a ἄπειρον
kaṯīrun 11a15 (11a14), 11a19 πολύς | 4b11b*, 8b18, 10a27 (1028) πλείων – ašyā'u kaṯīratun 11b13 πολλά | 6b4, 8b24b πλείονα | {4b9} ὀλίγα – al-kaṯīru mina n-nāsi 6a23 οἱ πολλοί – fī mawāḍi'a kaṯīratin 10a24 πλεονάκις – 'alā wuğūhin kaṯīratin 9a10 πλεοναχῶς – *in hend.* kaṯīrun muḫtalifun 7b1* *transl. variant* ποικίλος *instead of* ποικιλία – kaṯīran *adv.* 8a25, 11a16 πολλῷ | 9a8 πλεῖστον *adv.* – *in* bā'ada kaṯīran 11b27 μακρός
akṯaru 8a25, 11a16, 11b21 πλέον – al-akṯaru 7b8 τὸ πλέον – *in expr.* akṯara mā 9a7 διὰ πλείστου – akṯaru min wāḥidin 5a19 *sem. amplif.* πλείων – laysa bi-wāḥidin bal akṯaru min wāḥidin 5a15 *sem. amplif. & metathesis; affirm. / neg. transformation* πλείων

kry
(ukratun) *pl.* ukarun 5a21a σφαῖρα | 5a24a *sem. amplif.; added w. ref. to* σφαῖρα *at 5a21a (GALex I,239 §1)*

ks'nwqr'ṭys 6b7 Ξενοκράτης

kll
kalālun (I) *maṣdar* – *in hend.* ḍu'fun wa-kalālun 5b14 ἀσθένεια
kullun (**a**) kullu *w. gen.* 5a18, 6a2 (6a1), 7a6b (7a7), 8b1[1,2], 8b2, 8b21, 10a22, 11b9, 11b20 πᾶς | 7a10a, 9b21*, 11a5, 11b1 ἅπας | 5b17 αὐτός *self* – *in hend. w.* ğamī' 4b15b πᾶς – *in phrase* kullu mā 11a13 ὅσα – tağāwaza kulla ḥaddin 8b9 *sem. amplif.* ὑπερβατός – kullu mā fīhā {7a20} ἕκαστος, *misreading* ἓν ἕκαστον *for* ἕνεκά του *at 7a21* – 'alā kulli ḥālin {5b15} *corruption* (**b**) *in phrase* kullu wāḥidin 8b26 ἕκαστος – kullu wāḥidin min 5b4b, 7a11, 7a17, 8b22, 9a11 (9a10), 9a15, 9b18, 10a2 ἕκαστος – kullu wāḥidin minh(um)ā/al-āḫaru 5a18 ἕκαστος | 4a12 ἑκάτερος (*GALex I,64 §3.4*) (**c**) al-kullu 4a14, 4a21a, 8a23, 8b8, 10a16 τὸ πᾶν | 10a3 τὸ πᾶν *in* τὸ σύμπαν | 10b28a, 11b5 τὸ ὅλον | 11b26, 12a1 τὸ σύμπαν
kulliyyun 8b18, 9a1, 9a27 καθόλου – al-kulliyyātu 8b20 τὰ καθόλου – kulliyyan 8b25b καθόλου

klm
takallama (V) 11a22 λέγω
kalāmun 5a22a, 6a14 (6a15), 7b9, 8a8 λόγος – 5a22b *sem. amplif.; transl. demonstrative* ὅ *w. ref. to* λόγος *at 5a22a* – *sem. amplif.;add. acc. to sense* lammā aḫaḏa fī l-kalāmi fī 6b14 κατά

km
kam 8a18 ποσόν – 'alā kam 9a24 ποσαχῶς

kml
kamālun (I) *maṣdar* 7a8 (7a9) τὸ τέλεον - fī ġāyati l-kamāli 8a7 τελεώτατος
kāmilun *act. part.* 5a6 ἄρτιος | 6a19, 8b27 τέλεος
akmalu 6b20 τελεώτερος
kwd
kāda (I) *w.* an 6a26, 8a24 σχεδόν
kwn
kāna (I) **(a)** *abs.* 4b9 (4b10), 4b18, 5b2, 5b6, 7b16^{2}, 7b20 (7b21), 8a14a (8a15), 8b18, 9a10^{2}, 10a14 (10a15) εἰμί | 6a11, 8a16 ὑπάρχω | 4b9 *paraphr.* ἔχω | {6a17} τίθημι - yakūnu *impf.* 8b7^{2} μέλλω *in* μέλλον **(b)** kāna/kāna *introducing two correlative clauses* 8b19–20 ἐάν/ἐάν **(c)** *sem. amplif.; added to transl. the implied copula* εἰμί 4a17, 4a18, 4b10, 4b11b, 4b17^{1,2}, 5a3, 5a17, 5a20, 5b7, 5b9, 5b10, 5b20, 5b23, 5b26b^{2}, {6a1}, 6a2, 6a9, 6a10, 6b20, 7a8, 7a11, 7a13, 7b8, 7b14, 7b16^{1}, 7b17, 8a17^{3}, 8a20, 8a21, 8b1^{1,2}, 8b5, 8b11, 8b16, 8b17, 8b21, 9a6, 9a10^{3*} (9a11), 9b6, 9b7, 9b13, 9b14, 10a12, 10a13, 10a15, 10a22, 10b7, 10b19, 10b20^{2}, 10b27a, 11a1b, 11a21, 11b5, 11b7, 11b19, 11b20 **(d)** *sem. amplif.; added to express the implied existential* εἰμί (*there is*) {5a28b^{1,2}}, 5b4b, 6a28, 6b2, 10b25 **(e)** *w. prep.*: *w.* bi- 11b10^{1} ἐνδέχομαι - *w.* bayna 6a5^{1,2} ἔχω - *w.* ʿalā 8a4 ἐστί (*implied*) - *w.* fī 5a24a ἔχω | 9b24a *sem. amplif.; add. w. ref. to* ἔστιν *at 9b23* - *w.* li- 4b2 ἔχω | *in* mā kāna li- *w. subj.* (*to be such that; see WKAS I,458b*) 8a17^{1} *transl. the neg. optative in* οὐδὲ γίνοιτο **(f)** *morph.; in* kāna muʿādilan 8a24 *transl. the* -εω *suffix of denominative verb* ἰσομοιρέω - *in* yakūnu (muḥarrikan) 5a5 *transl. the future tense in* κινήσει - *in* kāna mawǧūdan 8b7^{1} *transl. the perf. tense of the part.* γεγονός - *in* an yakūna munfasiḫan 5a4a *helps transl. the optative in* λύοιτο ἄν - *w. impf. it transl. the Greek impf.* qad kāna yaǧibu 10b20^{1} (10b19) ἔδει **(g)** *in expr.*: kāna mawǧūdan 8a17^{2} ὑπάρχω - *in hend.* kāna hāhunā 4b6, 9a18 (9a19) εἰμί - min šaʾnihī an yakūna 6a21 τυγχάνω - kāna / yakūnu *foll. by* buṭlān 6a8, 6a13–14 φθείροι(τ') ἄν **(h)** *add. as auxiliary verb required by the Ar. synt.* 4b13, 5a1, 5a5^{1}, 5a18, 5a19, 5b14, 5b26b^{1}, 5b28, 7a18, 7a23, 8a2, 8a3, 8a14a, 8a27, 9a7, 9a10^{1}, 10a5, 11a13, 11b10^{2}, 11b11, 11b22
takawwunun (V) *maṣdar* - *in hend.* takawwunun wa-wuǧūdun 11a18a–18b τὸ εἶναι
makānun, *pl.* amākinu 5b22 χώρα | 6b1 τόπος
kyf
kayfa 5b19, 5b21, 6b23, 8a8, 12a1 πῶς | 8a18 ποιός

l[1]
la- *part.* 10b20 *Ar. synt.; introducing the apodosis after* law
l[2]
li- *prep.* **(a)** *transl. Gr. prep.*: 5b14, 7b7 διά - *in* li-ḏālika 9b15 διά *in* διό - *transl. the prep.* ἐν- *in compound adj. expressing the possession of a quality* (*LSJ E.I.2*): lahū nafsun 5b6, 11a17b ἔμψυχος - *transl. the distributive use of the prep.* κατά *in the sense of "to have"*: li-kulli wāḥidin

l²: li- (*continued*) minhā muḥarrikun 5a18 τὸ καθ' ἕκαστον (*scil.* κινοῦν) (**b**) *expressing cause*: as-sabab allaḏī lahū 10a1*, 10a28, 10b23b ἕνεκα | 5a17b χάρις *in* οὗ χάριν | 5a23 πῶς ποτε (**c**) *expressing duty*: lahū an *w. subj.* 6a12 ἂν εἴη *w. inf.* | 6a16b, 10b24a ἄν τις *w. opt.* | 7b22 *paraphr.* ἐάν τις | 10a28[1] *sem. amplif.; add. acc. to sense* (**d**) *expressing possession*: *w. attached pron.* 4b2[1,2], 5b4a, 8a19, 9a17* (9a16), 9b11 ἔχω | 4b4b (4b2), 5b3b (5b4), 7b11 *sem. amplif.; add. acc. to sense to mean* ἔχω – la-nā 9b7 ἡμέτερος – *in expr.* lā maʿnā lahū {10a23a} ἄλλως – *sem. amplif.; add. acc. to sense* 10b11 (**e**) *morph.; transl. the gen. case suffix*: li-l-ḥarakati 4b22 τῆς κινήσεως – li-ǧamīʿi l-ašyāʾi 5a7 πάντων – li-s-samāʾi 5b20 τοῦ οὐρανοῦ – la-hā (*sc.* li-s-samāʾi) 5b20, 5b21[1,2] *sem. amplif. for* τοῦ οὐρανοῦ – li-ǧawharihā 6a7 τῆς οὐσίας αὐτοῦ – li-l-insāni 6a21 ἀνθρώπου – li-l-farasi 6a22 ἵππου – li-šayʾin 6a22 τινὸς – li-ṭ-ṭabīʿati 10a10 τῆς φύσεως – li-mā huwa min aǧli šayʾin 11b26 τοῦ ἕνεκά του – li-l-ḥarakati 11b27 (11b26) τῆς ... ὁρμῆς (**f**) *morph.; transl. the dative case suffix*: li-man 5a13 τοῖς – li-ulāʾika 7a10b ἐκείνοις – li-ṣ-ṣuwari 8a18 τοῖς εἴδεσιν – baʿḍuhā li-baʿḍin 8b3 ἀλλήλοις – li-l-fikri 8b12 τῇ διανοίᾳ – lanā 9b6 ἡμῖν – li-l-ḥayawāni 10a17 τοῖς ζῴοις – li-s-samāʾi wa-li-l-aǧrāmi 10a18 τῷ οὐρανῷ καὶ τοῖς οὐρανίοις – li-hāḏihī 10b7 τούτοις – *sem. amplif.; add. acc. to sense* 9b9, 9b13 (**g**) *morph.; transl. morph. of Gr. adj. by making adj. out of nouns and nominal phrases* (**g1**) *transl. the suffix* -ικος: lahū tašawwuqun 5b12 ἐφετικός (*w. reference to 5b11*) (**g2**) *transl. the suffix* -ος *in compound adj. w. alpha privative*: allaḏī/mā lā nafsa lahū 9a15, 11a17a ἄψυχος – lā nihāyata lahū 9b4 ἄπειρος – mā lā ǧuzʾa lahū 8a3 ἀμερής (**h**) *synt.; add. acc. to the requirements of Ar. synt. to introduce the object* 4a16[2], 7a7, 7a17, 8a24, 9b7, 11b3[1,2], 11b6, 11b20 (**i**) *w. verbs* → aḥdaṯa, → ṣāra, →ẓahara, → kāna, → tahayyaʾa

li-anna 11a11 γάρ – *morph.; transl. the circumst. sense of the part.*: li-annahū yašāʾu {6a2} βουλόμενον

li-ḏālika 9b15 διό

li-mā 5a25b, 8a22 τί *interr.* | 5b11 διὰ τί | 8b1[1,2], 8b2 ὅ τι

lʾ

lā (**a**) *abs.* 4a14, 5a18, 5b1, 8b15, 9b11 μή | 6a5 μή *in* μηδείς | 5a8, 8b7[1,2] μή *in* μηδέ – 5a24b, 5b14[1,2] (5b13), 6b10, 7b18, 8b1, 8b23, 9b15, 9b23b, 10a6, 11a2, 11a15[1] οὐ | 6b5, 6b6, 8b1, 9b24a, 11a15[2], 11b8[2] (11b7) οὐ *in* οὐδέ | 11b8[1] *sem. amplif.*; *add. w. ref. to* οὐδέ *at 11b7* | {4b17} οὐ (*misreading for* οὖν) (**b**) *in combinations*: wa-lā 6b5, 6b6, 11a15, 11b8 (11b7) οὐδέ – lam/wa-lā 11b15 οὔτε/οὔτε – lā (*in* allā)/wa-lā/wa-lā 8a17–18 μήτε/μήτε/μήτε – lā ... aṣlan 6a5 μηδείς | 11b10 οὐδέ – lā ...

šay'un 7a13 μηδείς - laysa ... wa-lā → laysa (c) *sem., etym.; transl. the alpha privative*: lā tatafattaru 5a4a ἄπαυστος - lā tafturu 5a16b ἀνήνυτος - lā muḥtamilun li-l-irtibāṭi 5b18 ἀσύνδετος - lā yaqa'u fīhi baḥṯun 6a3 ἀζήτητος - lā tanāhā 6b1 ἄπειρον - lā ğuz'a lahū 8a3 ἀμερής - lā nafsa lahū 9a15, 11a17a ἄψυχος - mā lā nihāyata lahū 9b4 τὸ ἄπειρον - lā yuḥṣā 11a17 ἄπειρος - al-ğuz'u llaḏī lā yataǧazza'u 11b23 ἄτομον (d) *sem. metathesis; affirm. / neg. transformation* : lā yašā'u illā 6a2 βουλόμενον - lā yakūnu illā 7b16 *sem. amplif. for the implied copula* εἰμί - lā ma'nā lahū {10a23a} ἄλλως

l'kn

lākin(na) 4a14, 5a1, 7a14a, 7b13, 7b18, 8a4, 8b8, 10a26, 11b6, 11b9, 11b16 ἀλλά | 4b22, 8a12 δέ *adversative, w.o. preceding* μέν | 6a16b (6a15) δέ *adversative w. preceding* μέν

l'm

mulā'imun (III) *act. part.* 9a11 οἰκεῖος - *in hend.* mulā'imun ḫāṣṣun 10a10 οἰκεῖος

lḥq

laḥiqa (I) 11b13 *sem. amplif.; add. acc. to sense*

(lāḥiqatun) *pl.* lawāḥiqu 9a14 ἑπόμενα

lḥm

laḥmun 7a14b σάρξ

lḥw/y

liḥyatun 10b10 πώγων

lḫṣ

laḫḫaṣa (II) 9a18 διαιρέω | 9a25 ἀφορίζω

talḫīṣun *maṣdar* 10a23b ἀφορισμός | 9a18 *maf'ūl muṭlaq to a preceding* luḫḫiṣa

lzm

lazima (I) 7a23 συμβαίνω | 7a3 συν- *in* συνακολουθέω | 10b18 συν- *in* σύμπτωμα | 11b16 κατά *in* κατακολουθέω - *in hend.* tabi'a wa-lazima 7a3 συνακολουθέω | 11b16 κατακολουθέω - 5b24 *sem. amplif. of prep.* 'an *transl.* ὑπό

l'l

la'alla → 'll

lm

lam *w. juss.* 4b2, 8a17², 8a21, 8b14, 10a13, 11a1b, 11b20 μή | 5a22b, 7b13 οὐ | 6b5 οὐ *in* οὐδεμίαν | 9b11 οὐ *in* οὐκέτι | 8a17¹ (8a16–17) *in double negative*, οὐ ... οὐδέ - lam/wa-lā 11b15 οὔτε/οὔτε - *paraphr.* lam yaḏkur ḏālika 6b5 *in context* ὡσαύτως

lm'

lammā - *synt.; transl. the gen. absolute* lammā kānat fīhā 5a24a ἐχόντων | lammā kānat 9a10 ὄντος - *morph.; transl. the past tense in the aorist part.* lammā waladū 6a25 γεννήσαντες - *sem. amplif.; add. acc. to sense* lammā aḫaḏa fī l-kalāmi 6b14

lms

iltamasa (VIII) 4b12a, 9a24, 11b24 πειράω | 9b23b ζητέω

iltimāsun *maṣdar* 9b13 *sem. amplif.; add. acc. to sense*

lw

law 9a23 εἰ | 10b19 εἴπερ | 8a17 *morph.; transl. the Gr. gen. absolute*

lyt

layta ši'rī {6a16b} ἀξιώσειεν ἄν | 10a24 *morph.; transl. the interr. sense in* πόθεν - yā laita ši'ri 10a16 ἆρα

lys

laysa (**a**) *neg. of existential* εἰμί (**a1**) *expressed* 4b23, 5b8 οὐκ ἂν εἴη | 5a4a μὴ εἶναι (**a2**) *not expressed* 5b20 οὐ (*sc.* ἐστί) ▬ laysa šay'an 10a17 μηδέν (*sc.* ἐστί) (*Ar. read* μηδέν *for* μηδ' ἐν) | 10a18 οὐδέν (*sc.* ἐστί) (*Ar. read* οὐδέν *for* οὐδ' ἐν) ▬ laysa šay'un 10a22 μηδέν (*scil.* ἐστί) ▬ laysa/wa-lā 4a19–20 οὔτε (*scil.* ἐστί)/οὔτε φαίνεται (**b**) *neg. particle* 4b2, 7b17, 8a1, 8a3, 8a26, 8b5, 8b16, 9a27, 9b2, 10a8, 10a9, 10a23a, 10b6, 11b5 οὐ | 6a18, 7b20, 10a25, 10b24b μή | 4a23, 5b12, 6a11, 8a15b, 8b2, 10b18 οὐ *in* οὐδείς | 5a20, 11a9 οὐ *in* οὐδαμοῦ, οὐθαμῶς | 4b4b οὐ *in* οὐδέ ▬ laysa bi-/wa-lā/(wa-lā) 5a8, 8b7 μὴ/μηδέ/(μηδέ) ▬ laysa hāḏā 6a15a *sem. metathesis; affirm. / neg. transformation*: ἕτερος ▬ laysa bi-wāḥidin bal akṯaru min wāḥidin 5a16 (5a15) *sem. amplif. & metathesis; affirm. / neg. transformation*: πλείων

lyq

alyaqu 9a22 (9a21) οἰκειότερον *adv.*

m'

mā *indef. encl.* 4b6, 4b14a, 5a1, 6a20², 8a19¹, 8b17, 9a20, 10a16, 10a19, 11a2, 11b25 (11b24) τις, τι ▬ muddatun mā 6a18, 6b10 *sem. amplif.* τι ▬ 8a19² *sem. amplif.; add. acc. to sense*

mā *interr.* 4a17, 7b7 (7b8), 9a26, 10a2 τίς, τί ▬ *in expr.* mā huwa š-šay'u 8b22 τὸ τί ἦν εἶναι

mā *pron.* (**a**) *transl. Gr. pron.* (**a1**) *transl. the neuter article* 5a13b, 5b4a, 5b26b^{1,2}, 6b19², 7a3, 7b1, 7b8, 8a3, 8b4, 8b7 (8b6), 8b18, 9a13, 9a14*, 9b4, 9b20*, 10b16, 11a15, 11a17a, 11a17b, 11a21, 11a25 (11a24), 11b14, 11b26 τό, τά | 6a27 (6a26), 7a6a τά *in* τὰ ἄλλα ▬ *in* mā yuštahā 5b4b *sem. amplif.; transl.* τά *in the implied* ἕκαστον (*sc.* τῶν ὀρεκτῶν) ▬ *sem. ampl.; add. acc. to sense* 8a16 (**a2**) *transl. relative pron.* 9a21, 9b23b, 11a6 ὧν | 11b24 ὅ | huwa mā 6a19 ὅπερ | 4a19 ἅ in καθάπερ ▬ *in* mā yumkinu an yakūna ʿalayhi 8a4 ὅ τι (**a3**) *transl. correlative pron.*: 9b27 ὅσος ▬ kullu mā 11a13 ὅσα ▬ *in* bi-qadri mā 6a27 *transl. the indef. subst. indicated by* ὅσος *in adv.* ὅσον, *and by* τόσος *in* τοσοῦτο ▬ 11b22 οἷος (**a4**) *transl. demonstr. pron.: periphr.; in expr.* mā anā qā'iluhū (... aʿnī) 5b10 οὗτος | 6a5 ὅδε | 5b19 *sem. amplif.; add. acc. to sense* (**a5**) *other pron.*: *in* mā huwa ayḍan {7a22} αὐτός ▬ *in* kullu mā fīhā {7a20} ἕκαστος, *misreading* ἓν ἕκαστον *for* ἕνεκά του *in the Greek* (7a21) (**a6**) *sem. amplif.; in* bi-manzilati mā 4a21b, 8b26 οἷον | 8a12, 9a3, 10a12 καθάπερ (*GALex II,25 §22.1.2*) | 9b13 (9b12) ὥσπερ (**b**) *morph.; transl. the morph. of subst. used as adj.* : mā yuḥtāǧu ilayhi wa-yuntafaʿu bihī 4a20 ἀξιόχρεως ▬ mā lā yaqaʿu fīhi baḥṯun 6a3 ἀζήτητον ▬ mā yastaḥiqqu an yuṣaddaqa bihī 7b18 ἀξιόπιστον ▬ mā yaḫfā 5a17 *sem. metathesis; affirm. / neg. transformation* ἀφανής ▬ mā lā tanāhā 6b1 *sem.; etym.* ἄπειρον ▬ akṯaru mā 9a7 πλεῖστον ▬ mimmā yurtabaku fīhi 9b1–2 ἄπορον - mā huwa aqdamu 10b25 πρότερος - mimmā yağibu an yūṯaqa bihī 10b27a πιστόν (c) *sem. amplif.; in other para-/periphr. uses*: mimmā yağrī ayḍan hāḏā l-mağrā 10b11 ἔτι - mā yadḫulu fī 8b8 εἰς - ʿalā mā yanbaġī 11a25 καλῶς ἔτυχεν - *in* mā nağidu ḏālika {5b5}, {6a20[1]} *add. acc. to sense* | 11a16 *sem. amplif.; add. w. ref. to* mā *at 11a15* (d) *Ar. synt.; add. in construction* mā ... min ... 8a4, 10b4, 11b1 - *in* min aš-šanāʿati mā huwa abdaʿu 8b6 ἔτι πλέον τὸ παράδοξον (e) *in other expr.*: bi-mā → bi-, fī-mā aḥsibu → ḥasiba, mā ḫalā → ḫalā, ʿalā mā → ʿalā, ka-mā → ka-, li-mā → li-

mṯl

mīṯlun - miṯla 6b1, 6b2, 11b14 οἷον | 7a2 καθάπερ | 11a23 ὥσπερ | 8a22, 10a4 *sem. amplif.; add. acc. to sense* - miṯla ḏālika 11b17 τοιοῦτος

maṯalun - maṯalan 4b4a (4b3) καθάπερ | 7a16, 7a18 ὡς εἰπεῖν

miṯālun - *w. gen.* miṯāluhū *and* miṯālu ḏālika 9a12, 9b20, 11a9 οἷον - *in phrase* ʿalā miṯālin wāḥidin 5a26, 6b8, 8a3 ὁμοίως | 10b20 ὡσαύτως - *in phrase* ʿalā hāḏā l-miṯāli 7a4, 7a16 ὁμοίως

mdd

maddun (I) *maṣdar, w.* ilā 10b2 (10b1) προχώρησις

muddatun - muddatun mā 6b10 τι *indef. encl.* | 6a18 *sem. amplif.; add. acc. to sense*

māddatun 8a9 ὕλη - *in* mušārikun li-l-māddati 7a7 *morph.; transl.* ὕλη *in* ὑλικός

mdn

madīnatun 8a5 πόλις

mrr

marratun - marratan 6a19 (6a20) ποτε *indef.*

mrʾ

marīʾun 11a10 οἰσοφάγος

mss

māssa (III) 9b15 ἅπτομαι

misāsun *maṣdar* 9b15 θιγγάνω

msk

amsaka (IV) *w.* ʿan 6a27 παραλείπω

mʿ

maʿa 5a25c, 5b3a, 6a8, 9b22 ἅμα | 6b3 ἅμα καὶ | 5b1 μετά | 5b17 τε | 10a2 πρός | {6a17} ἄρ' ἄ[ν] - maʿa ḏālika 6b9 ἔτι δή - wa- ... maʿa ḏālika 5a28b ἄλλως τε καί | 9b18 (9b17–18) καὶ ἄλλως/καί - wa-maʿa ḏālika ayḍan 9a6[2] *sem. amplif.* καί

maʿan 6a4* ἅμα

mʿn

amʿana (IV) *w.* fī 8b16 (8b15) ἐπὶ πλέον

mkn

amkana (IV) 11a8 οἷόν τε - amkana *w.* an 8b5, 9a27, 11b5 οἷόν τε | 4b2 οἷός τε | 9b8 δύναμαι | 9a21 ἐνδέχεται - mā yumkinu an yakūna ʿalayhi 8a4 ὅ τι

mumkinun *act. part.* 7b20 ἐνδεχόμενος

mlk

malākun 9a11 (τὸ) μέγιστον

mn[1]

man *relative pron.* 5a13 ὁ

mn[2]

min *prep.* (a) *transl. Gr. prep.*: 5b26b, 6a15b[1,2], 6a16a, 6a28, 6b2[1,2], 6b22, 9b9 ἀπό | 7b10 (7b9), 10b21[1,2] (10b20) ἐν | 6b14, 11b11 ἐκ | 5b27 παρά | 5a4a κατά | 11b14 περί

mn²: min (*continued*) (**b**) *of source or provenance, transl. Gr. pron.*: 7a14a τοῖος *in* τοιοῦτος – {9a1, 9a2} ἔνιαι (**c**) *morph.* (**c1**) *transl. the Gr. gen. abs.* 6b19* (6b20) τῶν (**c2**) *morph.; transl. Gr. partitive gen.*: mina l-ašyāʾi l-ǧuzʾiyyati 8a6 τῶν μεριστῶν – mā min hāḏihī 9a13 τούτων τά – ašbāhu hāḏihī mina l-umūri 9b14 τῶν τοιούτων – mina l-ašyāʾi l-maḥsūsati ... min sāʾiri l-ašyāʾi 11b18–19 τῶν αἰσθητῶν ... τῶν ἄλλων – 10b11, 10b17 *sem. amplif.; add. acc. to sense* (**c3**) *transl. the Gr. dat.*: min ḏātihā 10b27b τῷ αὐτομάτῳ – min ḥarakati *w. gen.* 10b28a τῇ περιφορᾷ (**c4**) *transl. the adv. accus.*: min aǧli 10b19, 11b15 χάριν (**c5**) *transl. the adv. suffix* -ως: min ḏātihā 7a18 αὐτομάτως – min ǧihātin šattā 9b1 πλεοναχῶς (**c6**) *transl. the suffix* -θεν: hiya llatī minhā 7b9 ὅθεν – min ayyi l-umūri 10a24 πόθεν – min muqaddami *w. gen.* 11a10 ἔμπροσθεν (**c7**) *transl. the adj. morph.*: mina ṣ-ṣiḥḥati 8a16 ἀληθής – min ǧinsin wāḥidin 9a18 ὁμογενής (**d**) *after comparatives* 5a11, 9a22 ἤ | 5b15 τῶν – *sem. amplif.; add. in the transl. of comp. adj.* 4b18, 5a9, 5a14, 5a16, 5a19, 5a21b, 5b9^1,2^, 7b19, 8a24, 8a25, 8b4, 8b6, 9a26, 10b26, 11a11, 11a16, 11a17b (**e**) *individuating use; introducing a subject of universal validity in a nominal sentence*: mina l-bayyini 4b21, 10a13 δῆλον | 4b22 φανερὸν ὡς | 8b9 (8b10) φανερὸν ὅτι – wa-mimmā yaḫfā ... anna 5a17 ἀφανής – mimmā yutaḥayyaru fīhi 5a23 ἄπορον – mimmā lā yaqaʿu fīhi baḥṯun 6a3 ἀζήτητον – mimmā yastaḥiqqu an yuṣaddaqa bihī 7b18 ἀξιόπιστον – mina l-qabīḥi 7b23 ἄτοπον – mina l-fuḍūli 8a22 περιεργία – mimmā yurtabaku fīhi 9b1–2 ἄπορον – mimmā yaǧibu an yūṯaqa bihī 10b27a πιστόν – *sem. amplif.;* mimmā yaǧrī ayḍan hāḏā l-maǧrā 10b11 ἔτι (**f**) *partitive use* (**f1**) *restricting universal application*: yašāʾu mina l-umūri kullihā 6a2 πάντα βουλόμενον – mina l-iḫtilāfi 6a5 διαφορά – mimmā 7b1 τά (**f2**) *restricting the application of adj.*: al-kaṯīru mina n-nāsi 6a23 οἱ πολλοί – aš-šāḏḏu minhā 7a2* ὀλίγαι – al-mušakkalatu minhā 7a7 *add. w. ref. to* ἐμμόρφους *at 7a6* – al-aḫassu mina l-umūri 8a24 τὸ χεῖρον – kaṯīrun mina l-umūri 10a27 (10a28) τὰ πλέονα – šayʾun min ġayrihī 8a20 ἄλλος (**g**) *indicating indefiniteness*: ʿalā/bi-waǧhin mina l-wuǧūhi 4a12, 6b7, 9b6 πως | 4b12a ἀμῶς γέ πως | 5a16, 7b19–20 τρόπον τινά | οὐθαμῶς 5a21 – fī waqtin mina l-awqāti 5a24b ποτε – mawḍiʿun mina l-mawāḍiʿi 6a23², 9b8 τινός – fī mawḍiʿin mina l-mawāḍiʿi *w. neg.* 11a9 οὐδαμοῦ – *paraphr.*: *serves to transl. the indef. sense of* φαίνεται: mimmā yuḥtāǧu ilayhi wa-yuntafaʿu bihī 4a20 (4a21) ἀξιόχρεα φαίνεται – *indef., preceding a def. noun (Wright II, §48f, Rem. a)*: bi-ṭarīqin mina ttašbīhi āḫara 4b13 *transl. the indef. sense in* κατ' ἄλλην ὁμοίωσιν (**h**) *in various expr.* (**h1**) min aǧli šay'in 10a22, 11b26 ἕνεκά του | 10b19 του χάριν | 11b15 τινὸς χάριν (**h2**) min ša'nihī an 9b24a πέφυκε ‒ min ša'nihī an yakūna 6a21 τυγχάνω (**h3**) kullu wāḥidin min 5b4b, 7a11, 7a17, 9a11 (9a10), 9a15, 9b18, 10a2 ἕκαστος ‒ kullu wāḥidin minhā ... al-āḫaru 5a18 ἕκαστος ‒ kullu wāḥidin minhumā .. al-āḫaru 4a12 ἑκάτερος (*GALex I,64 §3.4*) (**i**) *sem. amplif.; add. epexegetically* (*li-t-tabyīn*: *Wright II,137 §48g*): ʿalā l-iṭlāqi min al-qawli 4b20 ὡς ἁπλῶς εἰπεῖν ‒ al-maḥsūsatu minhā (*sc.* al-ašyā'i) 6b8 αἰσθητά ‒ ġayruhā mimmā huwa aqdamu 10b25 ἕτερος πρότερος (**j**) *sem. amplif.; add. acc. to the requirements of Ar. synt., in* mā ... min *construction*: 8a4, 8b6, 10b4, 11b1 (**k**) *sem. amplif.; added acc. to* sense: 5a17 min amrihā; 6a25 min hāḏayni; 8b15 šay'un min; 9a23 šay'un mina l-ašyā'i (**l**) *w. verbs or verbal nouns*: → ḫilwun, → qarībun, → imtanaʿa, → tanaqqulun (**m**) *in phrases*: min ṭarīqi anna → ṭarīqun ‒ min qibali, min qibali an/na → qibalun

mnḏ

mundu 11b24 ἐκ

mnʿ

manaʿa (I) 6a11 κωλύω

māniʿun *act. part.; as indef. subject of the same verb* 6a11 εἷς *in* οὐθέν

imtanaʿa (VIII) *w.* min 5b28 κωλύομαι

mūsīqā 7a2 μουσική

mwh

mā'un ‒ mā'u l-baḥri 10b1 θάλαττα

myz

tamyīzun (II) *maṣdar* 9a24 διελεῖν (διαιρέω)

myl

māla (I) *w.* ilā 11a3 ἔχω

nbt

nabātun (I) (**a**) *maṣdar* 10b10 ἔκφυσις (**b**) nabātun, *pl.* nabātātun 7a22, 7b4, 8b27, 9a14, 10a5, 10a13, 10b21 φυτόν ‒ *in phrase* bayna l-ḥayawāni wa-n-nabāti {7a22} *mistranslation of* πομφόλυξ

nṯr

manṯūrun (I) *pass. part.* 7a14b κεχυμένος

nǧm

munaǧǧimun (II) *act. part.* 5a22b ἀστρολόγος

(naǧmun) *pl.* nuǧūmun ‒ *in phrase* ṣināʿatu n-nuǧūmi 9b27, 10a5 ἀστρολογία

nḥn

naḥnu 4a22 ἡμεῖς ‒ *in hend.* naḥnu anfusunā 9b12 ἡμέτερος ‒ *as expressed in the personal suffixes of verbs and the attached pron.* annā, innā 5b21, 5b23 (5b24), 9b19 *sem. amplif.; personalizing the impersonal expression in Gr.* ‒ 8b15 *sem. amplif.; add. to refer to the implied subject of the circumst. clause*

nḥw

naḥwun, *pl.* anḥā'un ‒ *morph.; in hend. w.* ʿalā *transl. the adv. suffix* -ως: ʿalā hāḏā n-naḥwi 5a10 οὕτως | ʿalā anḥā'in šattā 8b9 πολλαχῶς

nzl
manzilatun - bi-manzilati *w. gen. or* mā 6a24, 8a12, 8b3, 9a3, 10a12, 10b8, 10b11, 11a21 καθάπερ (*GALex II,25 §22.1.2*) | 4a21b, 8b26, 10a16 (10a15) οἷον | 7a14b, 9b12 ὥσπερ | 8a5 ὡς ἄν | 8a6 ὡς ἄν *sem. amplif., add. acc. to sense*
nsb
nasaba (I) - nusiba *pass. part. w.* ilā 5b6* *morph.; transl the dat. case in* ἐμψύχοις
mansūbun *pass. part.* - al-kitābu l-mansūbu ilā Ṭym'ws 6b27 *sem. amplif.* Τίμαιος
(nisbatun) *pl.* nisabun 4a23, 7a12, 8a14a λόγος
nṭq
nuṭqun (I) *maṣdar* - *in* ḏū nuṭqin 7b18 λόγος *in* λογώδης
nẓr
naẓara (I) 12a1 *sem. amplif.; add. w. ref. to the preceding* θεωρία - 10a6 *sem. amplif.; add. acc. to sense*
naẓarun *maṣdar* 9b13 βλέπειν - *w.* fī 9b14 (9b15), 12a1 θεωρία - *in expr.* istaʿmala n-naẓara 7a16 λαμβάνω - *in expr.* ğaʿala naẓarahū 6a6 (6a7) ἀναφέρω - 6b4 *add. acc. to sense*
nāẓirun *act. part., used w. its maṣdar* 6a6 τις
(naẓīrun) *pl.* naẓā'iru 10b6 παρόμοιος
nẓm
manẓūmun (I) *pass. part.* 7b7 τεταγμένος
niẓāmun 7a12, 7a23, 11b18 τάξις | 11b4 τάξις *in* ἄτακτος | 8a5 ἀπηρτισμένος - an-niẓāmu 11a7 τὸ τεταγμένον - ʿalā niẓāmin 11b21 τὸ τεταγμένον
nfs
nafsun, *pl.* anfusun (**a**) *soul* 5b1, 5b3a, 5b9, 6b2 ψυχή | 5b2, 5b7, 7a17, 11a16, 11a17b ψυχή *in* ἔμψυχος | 7a17, 9a15, 11a17a, {10b21} ψυχή *in* ἄψυχος| 5b4a *sem. amplif.; add. w. ref. to* ψυχή *at 5b3a* (**b**) *self, w. attached pron.* 4a23, 4b22, 6a13, 9a8 αὐτός *reflexive* - 4b4a, 7b23 (7b22), 9a8, 9a17, 9b10, 9b14, 9b16, 10b24b αὐτός *intensive* - *in hend.* naḥnu anfusunā 9b12 ἡμέτερος (**c**) *synt.* 6b21 *expresses the emphasis generated by inverted Gr. word order*
nfʿ
intafaʿa (VIII) *c.* bi- 4a20–21 *sem., etym.; transl. the component* χρέος (*or* χρεία) *in* ἀξιόχρεως
nql
tanaqqulun (V) *maṣdar, w.* min 10b5 (10b6) μεθίσταμαι
intiqālun (VIII) *maṣdar* 5b26a μεταβολή
nuqlatun 7b8, 8a15a μετάβασις
nhw/y
tanāhā (VI) - *in* mā lā tanāhā 6b1 *sem., etym.* πέρας *in* ἄπειρον
tanāhin *maṣdar* - *in* al-ḫurūğu ʿani t-tanāhī 11b3 *sem., etym.* πέρας *in* ἄπειρον
intahā (VIII) *w.* ilā 10a25 τελευτάω | 9b2 μέχρι | 9a14 *add. acc. to sense to complement* bi-aḫaratin
nihāyatun, *pl.* nihāyātun 11a24 ἄκρον - *in* mā lā nihāyata lahū 9b4 πέρας *in* ἄπειρον
nwʿ
nawʿun, *pl.* anwāʿun 4b8, 8b20, 10a4, 10b23a εἶδος

h'
hāḏā (**a**) *transl. Gr. demonstr. and other pron.* 4b11b, 4b20, 4b21, 5a6, 5b20, 6a15b[1,2], 6a19, 6b7, 6b17, 8a21, 8b19, 9a1, 9a6,

9a13, 9b1, 9b16 (9b17), 10b18, 10b27, 10b24b, 11a1b, 11b23, 11b27 οὗτος | 5a26a, 9b13 ἐκεῖνος | 10a8 ὁ *demonstr. pron.* | 6a22[1,2], 8b8, {10a17} ὅδε| 5a2, 8a27 τοιοῦτος | 8a8, 11a3 τοιόσδε | 10a20 (10a19) νῦν – ḏālika/hāḏā 9b6–7, 9b7 ὁ/ὁ *in* ὁ μέν/ὁ δέ – hāḏā l-maʿnā 6a2, 6a14, 7b5 *sem. amplif.* τοῦτο, ταῦτα – hāḏā ... al-mušāru ilayhi 6a21 *sem. amplif.* ὅδε – hāḏā š-šayʾu l-mušāru ilayhi 8a17 *sem. amplif.* τόδε – laysa hāḏā 6a15a *sem. metathesis; affirm. / neg. transformation* ἕτερος – sāʾiru s-subuli mā ḫalā hāḏihi s-sabīli 6b19 *sem. amplif.* ἐκεῖναι (*sc.* αἱ μέθοδοι) – {11a20} *misreading in Ar. of* οὐκ *as* οὗ (**b**) *transl. Gr. relative adv.*: fī hāḏihi s-sabīli 6b21 ἔνθα – fī hāḏā l-mawḍiʿi 7b6 ἐνταῦθα (**c**) *in expr. denoting similarity*: ʿalā hāḏā l-miṯāli 7a4, 7a16 ὁμοίως – ʿalā hāḏā l-waǧhi 4b17 οὕτως – ʿalā hāḏā n-naḥwi 5a10 οὕτως – ašbāhu hāḏihi mina l-umūri 9b14 τοιοῦτος – yaǧrī hāḏā l-maǧrā 9a4, 11a14 οὕτως | 4b19 (4b18) τοιοῦτος – mimmā yaǧrī ayḍan hāḏā l-maǧrā 10b11 *sem. amplif.* ἔτι (**d**) *sem. amplif.; added in the transl. of comp. or superl. adj.*: awwalu hāḏihi 4b5 πρῶτον – awḍaḥu min hāḏihi 4b18 σαφεστέρως – ablaġu min hāḏā l-qawli 5a14 πλείων – abdaʿu min hāḏā 8b4, 8b6 παραδοξότερος, πλέον παράδοξον (**e**) *sem. amplif.; added to refer to an understood antecedent* 5a24a, 5b18, 6a23, 7a17, 7b22, 8a22, 9a15, 9a20, 9a26, 10a7, 11a3, 11b15, 11b19, 11b20 – *in phrase* hāḏā ʿalā anna 5b12 καίπερ | 10a9, 11b1 (11b2) καίτοι (**f**) *sem. amplif.; add. acc. to sense* 6a25, 6b18, 7a10b, 8b11, 9b17, 10a23b – *used to mark a subst. foll. by an article in attributive position preceding an adj.* hāḏihi š-šahwatu llatī hiya afḍalu š-šahawāti 5a20 ὄρεξις ἡ ἀρίστη

hāʾulāʾi *pl.* 6a25 *morph.; transl. the pl. morph. of the part.* γεννήσαντες

hāhunā – *in hend.* kāna hāhunā 4b6, 9a18 (9a19) εἰμί (*there is*) – {5a28b}, 8a20 *sem. amplif.*; *add. to express the implied or understood existential* εἰμί (*there is*)

hl

hal *in indirect questions* 6a13 εἰ | 6b23 (6b24) πότερον – hal/aw 4b7–8, 5b13, 5b19–20, 6a7–9 πότερον/ἤ | {10a16}–17 εἴτε/ἤ

hw

huwa (**a**) *transl. Gr. pron.* huwa llaḏī 4b5 ὅσπερ – huwā mā 6a19 ὅπερ – mā huwa ayḍan 7a22 αὐτός (**b**) *sem. amplif.; add. as the implied subject of the sentence* 4b23, 5a4a, 5a5, 5a21, 5b6, 5b7, 5b8, {6a4}, 6a5, 7a8, 8a22, 8a25, 8a26, 8b14 (**c**) *sem. amplif.; copulative pronoun (ḍamīr al-faṣl)* 4b7, 4b11b, 4b21, 4b22, 5a15, 6b16, 6b21, 6b28, 8a13, 8a20, 9a11, 9a26, 10a8, 10a9, 10a23a, 10b25, 10b27a, 11a15, 11a20, 11b26 (**d**) *sem. amplif.; transl. the implied copula*: mā huwa fī ġāyati l-faḍīlati 5b26b[1,1] τὸ ἄριστον sc. ὄν – huwa afḍalu 5b27 κάλλιον – mā huwa aḫassu 7b8 τὸ χεῖρον – huwa aʿẓamu 7b19 (7b18) μείζων

hw: huwa (*continued*)
- huwa abdaʿu 8b6 πλέον παράδοξον (**e**) *in expr.* ʿalā mā huwa ʿalayhi 4b15a ὥσπερ ἂν εἰ - mā huwa š-šayʾu 8b22 τὸ τί ἦν εἶναι

hwy
hawāʾun 7b2, 11b17 ἀήρ

hy
hiya - *transl. Gr.* εἰμί: 4a22, 6a7 (6a8) εἰμί | 10a7 ἂν εἴη | 11a25 (11a26) ὄντα - *transl. Gr. pron.*: 4a23 αὐτά - *sem. amplif.; add. as the implied subject of the sentence* 6b23^{1,2}, 8b3, 8b21, 8b23 - *sem. amplif.*; *copulative pronoun (ḍamīr al-faṣl)* 4a18, 4a20, 4b11b, 4b18, 4b20, 5a2, 5a9, 5a20, 5b22, 6a9, 6b17, 7a7, 8a9, 8b27, 9a2, 9b3, 10a7, 10a16, 10a17, 10b18 - → wa-hiya

hyʾ
tahayyaʾa (V) *w.* li- 8b14 δύναμαι - *w.* bi- 11a13 χάριν *adv.*

w
wa- (**a**) *transl.* καί (**a1**) *abs.* 4a14, 4a15, 4a17, 4b4, 4b5, 4b6^{2}, 4b14a, 4b20, 5a2, 5a10, 5a15, 5a16 (5a15^{2}), 5a17^{2}, 5a26b, 5a28b, 5b2, 5b9^{1,2}, 5b18, 5b20, 5b25b, 6a3, 6a8, 6a9, 6a11, 6a14, 6a18, 6a25 (6a24^{2}), 6a26^{1,2}, 6b1^{1,2}, 6b2^{2}, 6b3^{1}, 6b4^{1} (6b3^{3}), 6b4^{2}, 6b8, 6b9^{1} (6b8^{2}), 6b9^{2}, 6b20, 6b23, 6b25, 6b28, 7a2^{1}, 7a11, 7a12^{1,2,3}, 7a13^{1}, 7a17, 7a23, 7b2^{1}, 7b7, 7b12, 7b18, 7b23, 8a5, 8a9, 8a20, 8a24, 8b2, 8b11^{1}, 8b22 (8b21), 9a12^{2}, 9a14^{1,2,3}, 9a24, 9a25^{2}, 9b3 (9b2), 9b5, 9b15^{1}, 9b19, 9b27 (9b26^{3}), 10a3^{2}, 10a7, 10a10, 10a12, 10a13, 10a15, 10a18, 10a22, 10a24, 10b1^{1}, 10b2^{1,3}, 10b3, 10b4^{1} (10b3^{2}), 10b4^{2}, 10b5^{1}, 10b16, 10b17^{1} (10b16^{2}), 10b17^{2}, 10b20, 10b26, 11a2, 11a4, 11a6, 11a7, 11a18a (11a17), 11a19^{1}, 11a25, 11a27, 11b3, 11b12, 11b20, 12a1 καί | 8b14 καί *in* κἄν | 5b22 οὐ μόνον ... ἀλλὰ καί | 4b5, 6a19 -περ | 11a18b καί *in the MSS, corrected to* κἄν *in the edition* (**a2**) *in combinations*: - /wa 4b16, 7a6a (7a5), 8b10–11, 10a9–10a10^{1}, 11a4, 11b17, 11b25 καί/καί | 8a23, 10b6, 10b10^{1} καί/δέ - wa-/wa- 5a7–8, 11b26–27 (11b26) καί/καί - -/wa-/wa- 7a22 (7a21–22), 7b4, 9a5^{1,2,3,4}–6^{1}, 9b26, 10b23a (10b22–23), 11b4 (11b3–4) καί/καί/καί - wa-li-ḏālika 9b15 διὸ καί - wa-min qibali ḏālika 11b7 διὸ καί - wa- ... maʿa ḏālika 9b18 (9b17–18) καὶ ἄλλως ... καί ... - wa-... ayḍan 5a17^{1} (5a16) καί | 7a15b–16 καί ... δέ (**a3**) *sem. amplif.*: wa-ka-ḏālika yağrī l-amru 7a2 καί - wa-ka-ḏālika 9b17 καί - wa-maʿa ḏālika ayḍan 9a6^{2} καί (**b**) *transl.* δέ (**b1**) *abs.* 4b2, 4b6^{1}, 4b13, 4b20, 5a2, 5a23, 5b3a^{1}, 5b10, 5b19, 5b26b, 6a12, 6b5^{1}, 6b9^{3}, 6b13, 6b14, 6b15, 6b16, 6b17 (6b18), 6b20, 6b21, 6b24 (6b23), 7a1, 7a3^{1}, 7a10b, 7a19, 7b14, 7b19, 7b22, 7b23, 8a8, 8a19, 8a21, 8a27, 8b6, 8b11^{2}, 8b20, 8b24a, 8b27^{3}, 9a4, 9a18^{1,2}, 9a20, 9a21, 9a25^{1}, 9a26, 9b6, 9b13, 9b16, 9b22, 9b25, 10b7, 10b11, 10b24a (10b20), 11a13, 11a17a, 11a18b, 11a19^{2}, 11b5, 11b12, 11b16^{2}, δέ *w.o. preceding* μέν | 5b12 δέ *in* οὐθέν | 6b5, 6b6, 8b1, 9b24a, 11a15, 11b8 (11b7) δέ *in* οὐδέ

wǧd: wuǧūdun (*continued*) ᾗ – *in hend.* takawwunun wa-wuǧūdun 11a18a–18b τὸ εἶναι – *in phrase* wuǧūduhū fī 4a18, 4b9, 4b10, 5b6, 8a23, 9a1 *sem. amplif.; transl. the concept of existence implied in the Gr. prep.* ἐν (*cf.* *Ross 65 ad loc.*)

mawǧūdun *pass. part.* 8a10[1*], 8a10[2], 8a11[1,2], 8b7[1] ὄν – al-mawǧūdu 8b5, 8b9 τὸ ὄν – al-ašyāʾu l-mawǧūdatu 6a11, 8a9 τὰ ὄντα – al-mawǧūdātu 6b17, 12a1 τὰ ὄντα – kāna mawǧūdan 8a17 ὑπάρχω | 8b7[2] γεγονός – innahū mawǧūdun 8b2 τὸ εἶναι – yakūnu mawǧūdan 8b7[3] μέλλον *sc.* εἶναι – al-qawlu bi-annahū mawǧūdun 8a15b *sem. amplif.* τὸ εἶναι

wǧh

ǧihatun, *pl.* ǧihātun 9a20, 9a24 (9a23), 10a19 τρόπος – min ǧihātin šattā 9b1 πλεοναχῶς – ǧihatāni 11a4 διστασμός

waǧhun, *pl.* wuǧūhun 5a16[1,2], 7b20[1,2] (7b19), 9a11 (9a12) τρόπος – *in* waǧhun mina l-wuǧūhi 5a21 ἁμός *in* οὐθαμῶς – *morph.*; *in hend. w.* ʿalā *transl. the adv. suffix* -ως: ʿalā hāḏā l-waǧhi 4b17 οὕτως | ʿalā wuǧūhin kaṯīratin 9a10 πλεοναχῶς – *in phrase* bi-waǧhin mina l-wuǧūhi *w. neg.* οὐθαμῶς 5a20 – *in phrase* ʿalā waǧhin mina l-wuǧūhi 4a12, 6b7 πως | 4b12a ἀμῶς γέ πως | 5a16a, 7b20 (7b19–20), 9b6 τρόπον τινά

wḥd

wāḥidun (**a**) *abs.* 4b7–8, 5a7, 5a17b μία, ἕν | 5b12 ἕν *in* οὐθέν | 4b11b *sem. amplif.; add. for the implied* μία – al-wāḥidu 5a26b, 5a28a, 6a24, 6b2, 11b3 τὸ ἕν | {7a21} τὸ ἕν, *misreading* τὸ ἓν ἕκαστον *for* τὸ ἕνεκά του *in the Gr.* (**b**) *in expr. denoting identity*: min ǧinsin wāḥidin 9a18 ὁμός *in* ὁμογενής – wāḥidun bi-ʿaynihī 5a18, 9a4 ὁ αὐτός – ḥālun wāḥidatun 10b20 ταὐτά – ʿalā miṯālin wāḥidin 5a26, 6b8, 8a3 ὁμοίως | 10b20 ὡσαύτως (**c**) *in expr. denoting multiplicity*: akṯaru min wāḥidin 5a19 πλείων – laysa bi-wāḥidin bal akṯaru min wāḥidin 5a16 (5a15) πλείων (**d**) *in expr. transl. Gr.* ἕκαστος *and* ἑκάτερος *denoting individuals*: kullu wāḥidin min 5a18, 5b4b, 7a11, 7a17, 9a11 (9a10), 9a15, 9b18, 10a2 ἕκαστος – kullu wāḥidin 8b26 ἕκαστος – wāḥidun wāḥidun 11a4 ἕκαστος – kullu wāḥidin minhumā/al-āḫaru 4a12 ἑκάτερος (*GALex I,64 §3.4*)

wsṭ

wasaṭun 11a24 μέσος – al-wasaṭu 5b12 τὸ μέσον | 11a25 *sem. amplif.; add. w. ref. to* μέσος *at 11a24*

wṣf

waṣafa (I) 5a7 (5a8) ἀποδίδωμι | 6b11 (6b10) εἴρηται

waṣfun *maṣdar* 5a10 ἀποδίδωμι *in* ἀποδοτέον |4a23 *sem., etym.; transl.* περι- *in* περιτίθημι (*see note to the Arabic transl.*)

wṣl

ittaṣala (VIII) *w.* bi- 4b2, 4b19 συνάπτω | 6a17 *sem. amplif.; add. acc. to sense*

ittiṣālun *maṣdar* 4a14 συναφή – ittiṣālun *w.* bi- 4a20 συναφή

muttaṣilun *act. part.* 5a3 συνεχής

wḍḥ
awḍaḥa (IV) 4b12a ἐμφαίνειν
awḍaḥu 4b18 σαφέστερος *in* σαφεστέρως
wḍʿ
waḍaʿa (I) 11a3 τίθημι | 4a23 *sem., etym.; transl.* τίθημι *in* περιτίθημι (*see note to the Arabic transl.*) | 6b23 ὑποτίθεμαι | 11b2 ποιέω – wuḍiʿa *pass.* 9a9 ὑπόκειμαι *in* ὑποκείμενον
waḍʿun *maṣdar* 10a2 (10a3) θέσις
mawḍūʿun *pass. part.* 9a9 ὑποκείμενον
mawḍiʿun, *pl.* mawāḍiʿu (**a**) *abs.* 5b25b[1,2], 10b11 τόπος | 11a24 χώρα (**b**) *sem. amplif.* (**b1**) *transl. indef.* τι *in context*: mawḍiʿun tuḫuṭṭiya 6a3 ὑπερβατόν τι – mawḍiʿun mina l-mawāḍiʿi 6a23[1,2], 9b8 τινός (**b2**) *transl. the subst. implied by the article* τό 8b15 mawḍiʿun (**b3**) *stands for a subst. implied by the pron.* hāḏā l-mawḍiʿu 5a6 οὗτος (**c**) *paraphr.; in various expr.*: fī mawḍiʿin mina l-mawāḍiʿi *w. neg.* 11a9 οὐδαμοῦ – laysa hāḏā mawḍiʿahū 6a15a ἕτερος – fī mawāḍiʿa kaṯīratin 10a24 πλεονάκις – mawḍiʿu ḥayratin 10b24b ἄπορον – ayyu mawḍiʿin 9b2 πόσος – fī hāḏā l-mawḍiʿi 7b6 ἐνταῦθα – fīhi mawḍiʿu ṭalabin wa-baḥṯin 5b11 ἐπιζητέω – mawḍiʿu tašakkukin 6a6 ἂν ἀπορήσειεν | 8a21 ἀπορία (**d**) *sem. amplif.* 10b1, 10b2 *add. acc. to sense*
wfq
ittifāqun (VIII) *maṣdar* 11b14 τυγχάνω | 5a19 τὸ σύμφωνον | 8a4 σύμφωνος ἑαυτῷ – *in hend.* al-ittifāqu wa-l-ʿaraḍu 10a26 σύμπτωμα *in* συμπτωματικῶς
wfy
wafāʾun (I) *maṣdar, w.* bi- 4b17 ἀποδίδωμι
wqt
waqtun, *pl.* awqātun 7b3 ὥρα – *in phrase* fī waqtin mina l-awqāti 5a24b ποτε *indef. encl.*
wqʿ
waqaʿa (I) *w.* fī 9b16 ἔστιν (*there is*) | 6a3 *morph.; transl. the verbal adj. suffix* -τος *in* ἀζήτητος – qad waqaʿa 8b17 *sem. amplif.; expresses the implied emphatic statement of fact* – waqaʿa *abs.* 9a24 *sem. amplif.; add. acc. to sense*
awqaʿa (IV) 8b12 ὑποβάλλω
wqf
waqafa (I) *w.* ʿalā 8b10 (8b11) θεωρέω | 8b25 συνοράω | 9a4 ἐπίσταμαι | 11a2 λαμβάνω *in* ληπτέον | 9a7 *sem.amplif.; add. w. ref. to* ἐπίσταμαι – waqafa *abs.* 6b10 *sem. amplif.; add. acc. to sense*
wuqūfun *maṣdar, w.* ʿalā 9a10 *add. acc. to sense*
wld
walada (I) 6a25 γεννάω
wallada (II) 7b5 γεννάω
tawallada (V) 7b4 (7b5) γένεσις
tawalludun *maṣdar* 6b15, 10b17 γένεσις
wly
waliya (I) – yalī 5b12 περὶ (*sc.* εἶναι)
awlā 5a10 μᾶλλον – al-awlā 4b8 εὐλογώτερον – al-awlā fī l-qiyāsi 4a13* *morph. and etym.; transl. the prefix adv.* εὐ *and the comp. degree in* εὐλογώτερον – awlā bi- 5b9, 11b17 μάλιστα – *in hend.* aḥaqqu wa-awlā

wly: awlā (*continued*)
bi- 6b26 μάλιστα δέον - *in hend.* awlā wa-aḥaqqu bi- 6b28 οἰκειότατον

y'
yā - yā layta šiʿri 10a16 ἆρα

ysr
yasīrun 6a5 μικρός | 10b6, 11a19[2] ὀλίγος | 11a19[1] (11a18) σπάνιος

BIBLIOGRAPHY

The bibliography lists all publications of relevance to the present study. Incidental single references to unrelated books and articles are supplied with full publication details at the time of their occurrence in the text and are not repeated here.

References to incidental Greek, Latin, and Arabic texts are to the standard editions, identified by the name of the editor following the volume and page numbers. These also are not listed separately here.

All references in the body of the work are by name of author and year of publication. Names of authors not followed by date of publication, names of scholars who made private communications, names of authors of reference materials, and other abbreviations are listed under Abbreviations and Reference Works.

Alon, I. "The Arabic Version of Theophrastus' *Metaphysics*," *Jerusalem Studies in Arabic and Islam* 6 (1985) 163–217

Aubenque, P., "Sur la notion aristotélicienne d'aporie," in S. Mansion 1961, 3–19

——, ed., *Études sur la Métaphysique d'Aristote*, Paris: Vrin, 1979 (6. Symposium Aristotelicum)

——, "Sur l'inauthenticité du livre K de la *Métaphysique*," in Moraux and Wiesner 1983, 318–344

Badawī, ʿA., *Manṭiq Arisṭū*, Cairo: Maṭbaʿat Dār al-Kutub al-Miṣriyya, 1948–1952.

——, *Arisṭūṭālīs, aṭ-Ṭabīʿa*, Cairo: ad-Dār al-qawmiyya li-ṭ-ṭibāʿa wa-n-našr, 1964–1965

Balme, D.M., "Development of Biology in Aristotle and Theophrastus: Theory of Spontaneous Generation," *Phronesis* 7 (1962) 91–104

Baltussen, H., *Theophrastus against the Presocratics and Plato. Peripatetic Dialectic in the* De sensibus, Leiden: Brill, 2000 (Philosophia Antiqua 86)

——, "Theophrastean Echoes? The *De Sensibus* in the Platonic and Aristotelian Tradition," in Fortenbaugh and Wöhrle 2002, 39–58

——, "Early Reactions to Plato's *Timaeus*: Polemic and Exegesis in Theophrastus and Epicurus," in Sharples and Sheppard 2003, 49–71

Barnes, J., *Aristotle. Posterior Analytics*, Oxford: Clarendon Press, 1975[1], 1994[2]

——, "Roman Aristotle," in J. Barnes and M. Griffin, eds, *Philosophia Togata II*, Oxford: Clarendon Press, 1997, 1–69

Battegazzore, A.M., "La posizione di Teofrasto tra metafisica e fisica," *Epistemologia* 12 fasc. speciale (1989) 49–72

——, "L'originalità della posizione teofrastea nel contesto del pensiero animalistico aristotelico e della fisiognomica zoo-etica tra Peripato, Stoa e loro critici," in van Ophuijsen and van Raalte, 1998, 223–266

Bauloye, L., "Note sur la traduction d'ἀπορία dans la traduction arabe de la *Métaphysique*," in Motte and Rutten 2001, 433–436

Beere, J.B., "Counting the Unmoved Movers: Astronomy and Explanation in Aristotle's *Metaphysics* XII.8," *Archiv für Geschichte der Philosophie*, 85 (2003) 1–20

Bergk, T., "Theophrastus Metaph. p. 314,8 ed. Brandis [= fr. 12, 15, vol. III. p. 155 Wimmer]," in his *Kleine philologische Schriften*, Halle: Waisenhaus, 1886, II,302–303

Berti, E., "Note sulla tradizione dei primi due libri della *Metafisica* di Aristotele," *Elenchos* 3 (1982) 5–37

——, *Le ragioni di Aristotele*, Roma/Bari: Laterza, 1989

——, "Teofrasto e gli Accademici sul moto dei cieli," in Migliori 2002, 339–356

——, "La connaissance des principes selon Théophraste, *Métaphysique* 9a10–b24," preprint

Bertolacci, A., "On the Arabic Translations of Aristotle's *Metaphysics*," *Arabic Sciences and Philosophy* 15 (2005) 241–275

Bignone, E., review of Ross and Fobes 1929, in *Rivista di Filologia e di Istruzione Classica*, N.S. 9 (1931) 112–114

Blair, G.A., "The Meaning of 'Energeia' and 'Entelecheia' in Aristotle," *International Philosophical Quarterly* 7 (1967) 101–117

Blum, R., *Kallimachos. The Alexandrian Library and the Origins of Bibliography*, transl. by H.H. Wellisch, Madison: The University of Wisconsin Press, 1991

Bodnár, I.M., "Theophrastus' *De igne*: Orthodoxy, Reform and Readjustment in the Doctrine of Elements," in Fortenbaugh and Wöhrle 2002, 75–90

Bollack, J., and H. Wismann, *Héraclite ou la séparation*, Paris: Les Éditions de Minuit, 1972

Bonitz, H., *Index Aristotelicus* (I. Bekker, *Aristotelis Opera* vol. V), Berlin: Georg Reimer, 1870[1]; repr. ed. O. Gigon, Berlin: Walter de Gruyter, 1961[2]

Botter, B., "Teofrasto e i limiti della teleologia aristotelica," in C. Natali and S. Maso, eds, *Antiaristotelismo*, Amsterdam: A.M. Hakkert, 1999, 41–62 (Supplementi di *Lexis* VI)

Brandis, C.A., *Aristotelis et Theophrasti Metaphysica*, Berlin: Georg Reimer, 1823

——, *Uebersicht über das Aristotelische Lehrgebäude und Erörterung der Lehren seiner nächsten Nachfoger* (*Handbuch der Geschichte der griechisch-römischen Philosophie* III,1) Berlin: G. Reimer, 1860

Brunschwig, J., "EE I 8, 1218a15–32 et le περὶ τἀγαθοῦ," in Moraux and Harlfinger 1971, 197–222

Burnikel, W., *Textgeschichtliche Untersuchungen zu neun Opuscula Theophrasts*, Wiesbaden: Franz Steiner, 1974 (Palingenesia 8)

Camotius, J.B. (Camozzi, Giambattista de), *Commentariorum in primum Metaphysices Theophrasti libri tres*, Venice, *apud* F. Turrisanum, 1551

Cherniss, H., *The Riddle of the Early Academy*, Berkeley and Los Angeles: University of California Press, 1945[1]; repr. ed. L. Tarán, New York & London: Garland Publishing, Inc., 1980[2]

Cleary, J.J., "Working through Puzzles with Aristotle," *The Journal of Neoplatonic Studies* Vol. I, No. 2 (1993) 83–179

——, "*Phainomena* in Aristotle's methodology," *International Journal of Philosophical Studies* 2 (1994) 61–97

Cornford, F.M., *Plato's Theory of Knowledge*, Indianapolis and New York: Bobbs-Merrill Company, Inc., 1957 ([1]1935)

——, *Plato's Cosmology*, Indianapolis and New York: Bobbs-Merrill Company, Inc., n.d. [ca. 1959], ([1]1937)

Crubellier, M., "La version arabe de la *Métaphysique* de Théophraste et l'établissement du texte grec," *Revue d'Histoire des Textes* 22 (1992) 19–45

Crubellier, M. and A. Laks, eds, *Aristotle*: Metaphysics *Beta. Symposium Aristotelicum*, Oxford: Oxford University Press, 2009.

Daiber, H., *Aetius Arabus*, Wiesbaden: Franz Steiner, 1980

——, "The *Meteorology* of Theophrastus in Syriac and Arabic Translation," in Fortenbaugh and Gutas 1992, 166–293

D'Ancona, C. and G. Serra, eds, *Aristotele e Alessandro di Afrodisia nella tradizione araba*, Padova: Il Poligrafo, 2002 (Subsidia Mediaevalia Patavina 3)

Devereux, D.T., "The Relationship between Theophrastus' *Metaphysics* and Aristotle's *Metaphysics* Lambda," in Fortenbaugh and Sharples 1988, 167–188

Diels, H., *Die Fragmente der Vorsokratiker*, Berlin: Weidmann 1922[4]

Dillon, J., "Theophrastus' Critique of the Old Academy in the *Metaphysics*," in Fortenbaugh and Wöhrle 2002, 175–187

——, *The Heirs of Plato. A Study of the Old Academy (347–274 BC)*, Oxford: Clarendon Press, 2003

Dirlmeier, F., review of Kley 1936, in *Gnomon* 14 (1938) 129–137

Dorandi, T., "Qualche aspetto della vita di Teofrasto e il Liceo dopo Aristotele," in van Ophuijsen and van Raalte 1998, 29–28

Drossaart Lulofs, H.J., *Nicolaus Damascenus on the Philosophy of Aristotle*, Leiden: E.J. Brill, 1969 (Philosophia Antiqua 13)

Düring, I., *Aristotle in the Ancient Biographical Tradition*, Göteborg: Almqvist & Wiksell, 1957 (Studia Graeca et Latina Gothoburgensia 5)

——, *Aristotle's Protrepticus*, Stockholm: Almqvist & Wiksell, 1961

——, ed., *Naturphilosophie bei Aristoteles und Theophrast*, Heidelberg: Lothar Stiehm Verlag, 1969 (4. Symposium Aristotelicum)

Einarson, B., and G.K.K. Link, eds and translators, *Theophrastus, De causis plantarum*, 3 vols, Cambridge: Harvard University Press, 1976–1990 (The Loeb Classical Library)

Ellis, J., "The Aporematic Character of Theophrastus' *Metaphysics*," in Fortenbaugh and Sharples 1988, 216–223

Endress, G., "Alexander Arabus on the First Cause. Aristotle's First Mover in an Arabic Treatise Attributed to Alexander of Aphrodisias," in D'Ancona and Serra 2002, 19–74

Falcon, A., "Aristotle, Speusippus, and the Method of Division," *Classical Quarterly* 50 (2000) 402–414

Ferber, R., *Warum hat Platon die "ungeschriebene Lehre" nicht geschrieben?*, München: Beck, 2007[2].

Festugière, A.J., "Le sens des apories métaphysiques de Théophraste," *Revue Neo-*

Scolastique de Philosophie 33 (1931) 40–49; repr. in his *Études de philosophie grecque*, Paris: Vrin, 1971, 357–366

Fortenbaugh, W.W., and D. Gutas, eds, *Theophrastus. His Psychological, Doxographical and Scientific Writings*, New Brunswick and London: Transaction, 1992 (*RUSCH* 5)

Fortenbaugh, W.W., P.M. Huby, and A.A. Long, eds, *Theophrastus of Eresus. On His Life and Work*, New Brunswick and London: Transaction, 1985 (*RUSCH* 2)

Fortenbaugh, W.W., and R.W. Sharples, eds, *Theophrastean Studies. On Natural Science, Physics and Metaphysics, Ethics, Religion, and Rhetoric*, New Brunswick and London: Transaction, 1988 (*RUSCH* 3)

Fortenbaugh, W.W., and G. Wöhrle, eds, *On the* Opuscula *of Theophrastus*, Stuttgart: Franz Steiner, 2002 (Philosophie der Antike 14)

Franceschini, E., "Le traduzioni latine aristoteliche e pseudaristoteliche del codice Antoniano XVII, 370," *Aevum* 9 (1935) 3–26

Frede, D., "Theophrasts Kritik am unbewegten Beweger des Aristoteles," *Phronesis* 16 (1971) 65–79

Frede, M., and D. Charles, eds, *Aristotle's* Metaphysics *Lambda*, Oxford: Oxford University Press, 2000

Friedländer, P., "Heracliti frag. 124," *The American Journal of Philology* 63 (1942) 336

Gaiser, K., *Platons ungeschriebene Lehre*, Stuttgart: Ernst Klett, 1968²

——, *Theophrast in Assos. Zur Entwicklung der Naturwissenschaft zwischen Akademie und Peripatos*, Heidelberg: Carl Winter, 1985 (Abhandlungen der Heidelberger Akademie der Wissenschaften, Philosophisch-historische Klasse, 1985 / 3)

Gomperz, H., "Nachträge zum ersten Band ('brieflich')," in Diels 1922⁴

Gottschalk, H.B., review of Steinmetz 1964, *Gnomon* 39 (1967) 17–26

Graf., G., *Geschichte der christlichen arabischen Literatur*, vol. 2, Vaticano: Biblioteca Apostolica Vaticana, 1947 (Studi e Testi 133)

Grumach, E., *Physis und Agathon in der alten Stoa*, Berlin/Zürich/Dublin: Weidmann, 1966² (= *Problemata* 6, Berlin, 1932¹)

Gutas, D., "The Life, Works, and Sayings of Theophrastus in the Arabic Tradition," in Fortenbaugh, Huby, and Long (1985) 63–102; repr. in Gutas 2000, no. VII

Gutas, D., *Greek Philosophers in the Arabic Tradition*, Aldershot: Ashgate, 2000 (Variorum Collected Studies Series)

Happ, H., *Hyle. Studien zum aristotelischen Materie-Begriff*, Berlin and New York: Walter de Gruyter, 1971

Harlfinger, D. [1971a], *Die Textgeschichte der pseudo-aristotelischen Schrift ΠΕΡΙ ΑΤΟΜΩΝ ΓΡΑΜΜΩΝ*, Amsterdam: A.M. Hakkert, 1971

——[1971b], "Die Überlieferungsgeschichte der Eudemischen Ethik," in Moraux and Harlfinger 1971, 1–50

——, "Die Überlieferungsgeschichte der *Metaphysik*," in Aubenque 1979, 7–33

Hecquet-Devienne, M., "Les mains du *Parisinus Graecus* 1853," *Scrittura e Civiltà* 24 (2000) 103–171

——, "A Legacy from the Library of the Lyceum? Inquiry into the Joint Transmission of Theophrastus' and Aristotle's *Metaphysics* Based on Evidence Provided by Manuscripts E and J," *Harvard Studies in Classical Philology* 102 (2004) 171–189

Heinze, R., *Xenokrates. Darstellung der Lehre und Sammlung der Fragmente*, Leipzig: Teubner, 1892; repr. Hildesheim: Olms, 1965

Henrich, J., *Die Metaphysik Theophrasts. Edition, Kommentar, Interpretation*, München and Leipzig: K.G. Saur, 2000 (Beiträge zur Altertumskunde 139)

Hort, A., ed. and translator, *Theophrastus, Enquiry into Plants*, 2 vols, London: Heinemann, 1916 (The Loeb Classical Library)

Huby, P., "The Transmission of Aristotle's Writings and the Places Where Copies of His Works Existed," *Classica et Mediaevalia* 30 (1969) 241–257

——, review of Laks and Most 1993 and van Raalte 1993, in *Journal of Hellenic Studies* 115 (1995) 208–209

——, "When Was Theophrastus' *Metaphysics* Written?" preprint.

Huffman, C.A., *Philolaus of Croton. Pythagorean and Presocratic*, Cambridge: Cambridge University Press, 1993

Irigoin, J., *Tradition et critique des textes grecs*, Paris: Les Belles Lettres, 1997

Ibn-Abī-Uṣaybiʿa, *ʿUyūn al-anbāʾ fī ṭabaqāt al-aṭibbāʾ*, ed. A. Müller, Königsberg i. Pr., 1884

Ibn-an-Nadīm, *Kitāb al-Fihrist*, mit Anmerkungen hrsg. von Gustav Flügel, nach dessen Tode besorgt von Johannes Roediger und August Mueller, Leipzig: F.C.W. Vogel, 1871–1872

Isnardi Parente, M., "Théophraste, Metaphysica 6a23 ss." *Phronesis* 16 (1971) 49–64

——, *Speusippo. Frammenti*, Napoli: Bibliopolis, 1980

——, *Senocrate—Ermodoro. Frammenti*, Napoli: Bibliopolis, 1982

——, *Testimonia Platonica. Le testimonianze di Aristotele*, Roma, 1997 (Atti della Accademia Nazionale dei Lincei. Cl. di sc. mor. stor. e filol., Ser. IX, vol. viii, fasc. 4)

——, *Testimonia Platonica. Testimonianze di età ellenistica e di età imperiale*, Roma, 1998 (Atti della Accademia Nazionale dei Lincei. Cl. di sc. mor. stor. e filol., Ser. IX, vol. x, fasc. 1)

Jaeger, W. [$Jaeger^2$], review of Ross and Fobes 1929, in *Gnomon* 8 (1932) 289–295

——[$Jaeger^1$], *Aristotle. Fundamentals of the History of His Development*, transl. by R. Robinson, Oxford: Oxford University Press, 1948^2 (1923^1)

Johnson, M.R., *Aristotle on Teleology*, Oxford: Clarendon Press, 2005 (Oxford Aristotle Studies)

Kahn, Ch.H., *Anaximander and the Origins of Greek Cosmology*, New York: Columbia University Press, 1960

Kirk, G.S., *Heraclitus. The Cosmic Fragments*, Cambridge: Cambridge University Press, 1970

Kley, W., *Theophrasts Metaphysisches Bruchstück und die Schrift περὶ σημείων in der lateinischen Übersetzung des Bartholomaeus von Messina*, Diss. Berlin 1936, Würzburg: Konrad Triltsch, 1936. Reviewed by Dirlmeier 1938, A. Mansion 1938, Ross 1938

Krämer, H.J., *Der Ursprung der Geistmetaphysik*, Amsterdam: B.R. Grüner, 1967^2 (1964^1)

——, "Grundbegriffe akademischer Dialektik in den biologischen Schriften von Aristoteles und Theophrast," *Rheinisches Museum* 111 (1968) 293–333

——, *Platonismus und hellenistische Philosophie*, Berlin/New York: Walter de Gruyter, 1971.
——, "Zum Standort der 'Metaphysik' Theophrasts," in *Zetesis. Album amicorum door vrienden en collega's aangeboden aan Prof. Dr. E. de Strycker ... ter gelegenheid van zijn 65e verjaardag*, Antwerpen/Utrecht: De Nederlandsche Boekhandel, 1973, 206–214
——, *Platone e i fondamenti della metafisica*, traduzione di G. Reale, Milano: Università Cattolica del Sacro Cuore, 1981; English transl. *Plato and the Foundations of Metaphysics*, transl. (from the Italian) by J.R. Catan, Albany, N.Y.: State university of New York Press, 1990
Krische, A.B., *Forschungen auf dem Gebiete der alten Philosophie I (Die theologischen Lehren der griechischen Denker)*, Göttingen: Dieterich, 1840
Laks, A., "Eurytus in Theophrastus' *Metaphysics*," in "Four Notes on Theophrastus' *Metaphysics*" with G.W. Most and E. Rudolph, in Fortenbaugh and Sharples 1988, 237–243
——, "Le début d'une physique: Ordre, extension et nature des fragments 142–144 A/B de Théophraste," in van Ophuijsen and van Raalte 1998, 143–169
Laks, A., and G.W. Most, *Théophraste. Métaphysique*, Paris: Les Belles Lettres, 1993. Reviewed by Huby 1995, Talanga 1995
Lasserre, F., *De Léodamas de Thasos à Philippe d'Oponte* [*La Scuola di Platone*, II], Napoli: Bibliopolis, 1987
Lennox, J.G., "Theophrastus on the Limits of Teleology," in Fortenbaugh, Huby, and Long 1985, 143–163; repr. in Lennox 2001, 259–279
——, *Aristotle's Philosophy of Biology: Studies in the Origins of Life Science*, Cambridge: Cambridge University Press, 2001
Lloyd, G.E.R., "*Metaphysics* Λ 8," in Frede and Charles 2000, 245–273
Long, A.A., "Theophrastus and the Stoa," in van Ophuijsen and van Raalte 1998, 355–383
Lord, C., "On the Early History of the Aristotelian Corpus," *American Journal of Philology* 107 (1986) 137–161
Mansion, A., review of Ross and Fobes 1929 and Kley 1936, in *Revue Néoscolastique de Philosophie* 41 (1938) 447–451
Mansion, S., ed., *Aristote et les problèmes de méthode*, Louvain: Publications Universitaires, 1961 (1er Symposium Aristotelicum 1960)
Marcovich, M., *Eraclito. Frammenti*, Firenze: La Nuova Italia, 1978
——, *Heraclitus. Greek Text with a Short Commentary*, Second Edition, Sankt Augustin: Academia Verlag, 2001 (International Pre-Platonic Studies 2)
Margoliouth, D.S., "The Book of the Apple, ascribed to Aristotle," *Journal of the Royal Asiatic Society* (1892) 188–252 (192–201 on Theophrastus)
Martini, C., "La tradizione araba della *Metafisica* di Aristotele. Libri α—Α," in D'Ancona and Serra 2002, 75–112
McDiarmid, J.B., "Note on Heraclitus, Fragment 124," *The American Journal of Philology* 62 (1941) 492–494
Mejer, J., "A Life in Fragments: The *Vita Theophrasti*," in van Ophuijsen and van Raalte 1998, 1–28
——, *Überlieferung der Philosophie im Altertum. Eine Einführung*, Copenhagen: The Royal Danish Academy of Sciences and Letters, 2000 (Historisk-filosofiske Meddelelser 80)

Merlan, P., *From Platonism to Neoplatonism*, The Hague: Martinus Nijhoff, 1968^3 (1953)

Migliori, M., ed., *Gigantomachia. Convergenze e divergenze tra Platone e Aristotele*, Brescia: Morcelliana, 2002

Moraux, P., *Les listes anciennes des ouvrages d'Aristote*, Louvain: Éditions Universitaires, 1951

——, *Der Aristotelismus bei den Griechen. Von Andronikos bis Alexander von Aphrodisias*, vol. 1, Berlin: Walter de Gruyter, 1973 (Peripatoi 5)

——, "La critique d'authenticité chez les commentateurs grecs d'Aristote," *Mansel'e Armağan* (*Mélanges Mansel*), Ankara: Türk Tarih Kurumu, 1974, I,265–288

Moraux, P., and D. Harlfinger, eds, *Untersuchungen zur Eudemischen Ethik*, Berlin: Walter de Gruyter, 1971 (5. Symposium Aristotelicum: Peripatoi 1)

Moraux, P. and J. Wiesner, *Zweifelhaftes im Corpus Aristotelicum. Studien zu einigen Dubia*, Berlin: Walter de Gruyter, 1983 (9. Symposium Aristotelicum, Peripatoi 14)

Most, G.W. [1988a], "The Relative Date of Theophrastus' *Metaphysics*," in "Four Notes on Theophrastus' *Metaphysics*" with A. Laks and E. Rudolph, in Fortenbaugh and Sharples 1988, 224–233

——[1988b] "Heraclitus, D–K 22 B 124 in Theophrastus' *Metaphysics*," in "Four Notes on Theophrastus' *Metaphysics*" with A. Laks and E. Rudolph, in Fortenbaugh and Sharples 1988, 243–248

——[1988c], "Three Latin Translations of Theophrastus' *Metaphysics*," *Revue d'Histoire des Textes* 18 (1988) 169–200

Motte, A., and Chr. Rutten, eds, *Aporia dans la philosophie grecque des origines à Aristote*, Louvain-la-Neuve: Peeters, 2001

Mouawad, R.J., "La prière selon Yaḥyā ibn Ǧarīr (XIe siècle)," *Parole de l'Orient* 22 (1997) 393–404

Mouraviev, S.N., *Heraclitea*: II. *Traditio*, A. *Témoignages et citations*, 1. *D'Épicharme à Philon d'Alexandrie* (vol. II.A.1), Sankt Augustin: Academia Verlag, 1999

Müller, W., *Über den Sprachgebrauch des Theophrasts* (*Beobachtungen über die Präpositionen*), Arnstadt: Programm des Fürstlichen Gymansiums, 1878

Nussbaum, M.C., *Aristotle's* De Motu Animalium, Princeton: Princeton U.P., 1985^2 (1978)

Ophuijsen, J.M. van, and M. van Raalte, eds, *Theophrastus. Reappraising the Sources*, New Brunswick and London: Transaction, 1998 (*RUSCH* 8)

Oporinus, H. (H. Gemusaeus), *Theophrasti ... opera ... omnia*, Basel, *apud* J. Oporinum, 1541

Owen, G.E.L., "Τιθέναι τὰ φαινόμενα," in S. Mansion 1961, 83–103

Pötscher, W., *Strukturprobleme der aristotelischen und theophrastischen Gottesvorstellung*, Leiden: E.J. Brill, 1970 (Philosophia Antiqua 19)

Primavesi, O., "Ein Blick in den Stollen von Skepsis: Vier Kapitel zur frühen Überlieferung des *Corpus Aristotelicum*," *Philologus* 151 (2007) 51–77

Raalte, M. van, "The Idea of the Cosmos as an Organic Whole in Theophrastus' *Metaphysics*," in Fortenbaugh and Sharples 1988, 189–215

——, *Theophrastus Metaphysics. With an Introduction, Translation/Commentary*, Leiden: Brill, 1993. Reviewed by Huby 1995, Talanga 1995

Reale, G., *Teofrasto e la sua aporetica metafisica*, Brescia: La Scuola Editrice, 1964; English translation of Part I, Chapter 4, and Part II by J.R. Catan, *The Concept of First Philosophy and the Unity of the* Metaphysics *of Aristotle*, Albany, N.Y.: SUNY Press, 1980, pp. 364–423

Regenbogen, O., "Theophrastos (Nr. 3) von Eresos," *Paulys Realencyclopädie der classischen Altertumswissenschaft*, Supplementband VII, Stuttgart: Alfred Druckenmüller 1940, coll. 1354–1562

Repici, L., "Limits of Teleology in Theophrastus' *Metaphysics*?" *Archiv für Geschichte der Philosophie* 72 (1990) 182–213

Robin, L., *La théorie platonicienne des idées et des nombres d'aprés Aristote*, Paris: F. Alcan, 1908; repr. Hildesheim: Olms, 1963

Romani, S., *Teofrasto. La metafisica*, Milano 1994

Rose, V., *Aristoteles pseudepigraphus*, Leipzig: Teubner, 1863; repr. Hildesheim: Olms, 1971

Ross, W.D., *Aristotle's Physics. A Revised Text with Introduction and Commentary*, Oxford: The Clarendon Press, 1936

——, "Latin Versions of Theophrastus," *The Classical Review* 52 (1938) 16–17 (review of Kley 1936)

——, *Plato's Theory of Ideas*, Oxford: Oxford University Press, 1951

——, *Aristotle. De anima. Edited, with Introduction and Commentary*, Oxford: The Clarendon Press, 1961

Ross, W.D., and F.H. Fobes, *Theophrastus Metaphysics*, Oxford: Oxford University Press, 1929; repr. Chicago: Ares Publishers, 1978. Reviewed by Bignone 1931, Jaeger 1932, A. Mansion 1938

Rudolph, E., "*Energeia* in Aristotle and Theophrastus," in "Four Notes on Theophrastus' *Metaphysics*" with A. Laks and G.W. Most, in Fortenbaugh and Sharples 1988, 233–237

——, "Destruktion Der Metaphysik?" in M. Erler and A. Graeser, eds, *Philosophen des Altertums. Von der Frühzeit bis zur Klassik*, Darmstadt: Primus Verlag, 2000, 204–214

Schnayder, J., "Der Begriff 'Dynamis' in den Werken des Theophrastos," *Eos* 61 (1973) 49–56

Sedley, D., "Theophrastus and Epicurean Physics," in van Ophuijsen and van Raalte 1998, 331–354

Sharples, R.W., *Theophrastus of Eresus. Sources for His Life, Writings, Thought and Influence; Commentary Volume 3.1: Sources on Physics*, With Contributions on the Arabic Material by Dimitri Gutas, Leiden/Boston/Köln: Brill, 1998 (Philosophia Antiqua 79)

——, "Aristotelian Theology after Aristotle," in D. Frede and A. Laks, eds, *Traditions of Theology. Studies in Hellenistic Theology, Its Background and Aftermath*, Leiden/Boston/Köln: Brill, 2002, 1–40 (Philosophia Antiqua 89)

Sharples, R.W., and A. Sheppard, eds, *Ancient Approaches to Plato's* Timaeus, London: Institute of Classical Studies, 2003 (Bulletin of the Institute of Classical Studies Supplement 78)

Skemp, J.B., "The *Metaphysics* of Theophrastus in Relation to the Doctrine of κίνησις in Plato's Later Dialogues," in Düring 1969, 217–223

Smith, R., *Aristotle, Topics, Books I and VIII*, translated with a commentary, Oxford: Clarendon Press, 1997

Spengel, L., review of H. Bonitz, *Observationes criticae in Aristotelis libros Metaphysicos* (Berlin 1842), in *Gelehrte Anzeigen*, Bayer. Akad. d. Wiss., München 17 (1843), no. 243, coll. 913–918

Steinmetz, P., *Die Physik des Theophrastos von Eresos*, Bad Homburg vor der Höhe / Berlin / Zürich: Max Gehlen, 1964 (Palingenesia 1)

——, "Ansatzpunkte der Elementenlehre Theophrasts im Werk des Aristoteles," in Düring 1969, 224–249

Stenzel, J., *Zahl und Gestalt bei Platon und Aristoteles*, Darmstadt: Wissenschaftliche Buchgesellschaft, 1959[3]

Sylburg, F., *Aristotelis opera quae exstant*, Frankfurt, *apud* Andrea Wecheli heredes, 1584–1587

Takahashi, H., "Syriac Version by Ḥunain (?) of Nicolaus Damascenus' Compendium of Aristotelian Philosophy and Accompanying Scholia," *Journal of the Canadian Society for Syriac Studies* 5 (2005) 18–34

Talanga, J., review of Laks and Most 1993 and van Raalte 1993, in *The Classical Review*, N.S. 45 (1995) 18–21

Tarán, L., *Speusippus of Athens. A Critical Study with a Collection of the Related Texts and Commentary*, Leiden: Brill, 1981

Tarrant, H.A.S., "Speusippus' Ontological Classification," *Phronesis* 19 (1974) 130–145

Theiler, W., "Die Entstehung der Metaphysik des Aristoteles. Mit einem Anhang über Theophrasts Metaphysik," *Museum Helveticum* 15 (1958) 85–105; repr. in F.-P. Hager, ed., *Metaphysik und Theologie des Aristoteles*, Darmstadt: Wissenschaftliche Buchgesellschaft, 1969, 266–298 (Wege der Forschung 206); reference is to the pages of both publications

Timpanaro Cardini, M., *Pitagorici. Testimonianze e frammenti*, Fascicolo secondo, Firenze: La Nuova Italia, 1962, 1969

Tricot, J., *Théophraste. La Métaphysique. Traduction et Notes*, Paris: Vrin, 1948

Tugendhat, E., *TI KATA TINOΣ. Eine Untersuchung zu Struktur und Ursprung aristotelischer Grundbegriffe*, München: Verlag Karl Alber Freiburg, 2003[5] (1958)

Usener, H. [Us.[1]], "Zu Theophrasts metaphysischem Bruchstück," *Rheinisches Museum* 16 (1861) 259–281, repr. in his *Kleine Schriften* I, Leipzig and Berlin: Teubner, 1912, 91–111

——[Us.[2]], *Theophrasti de prima philosophia libellus*, in *Index Scholarum ... in Universitate Friderica Guilelmia Rhenana ... anni 1890–1891*, Bonn: Typis Caroli Georgi Univ. Typogr., 1890

Vallance, J., "Theophrastus and the Study of the Intractable: Scientific Method in *De lapidibus* and *De igne*," in Fortenbaugh and Sharples 1988, 25–40

Viano, C., "Eraclito nella *Metafisica* di Teofrasto: il fr. *124 DK* e la discussione sui principi dei cap. IV e V," *Rivista di Storia della Filosofia* 47 (1992) 455–476

Vuillemin-Diem, G., "Untersuchungen zu Wilhelm von Moerbekes Metaphysikübersetzung," in A. Zimmermann, ed., *Studien zur mittelalterlichen Geistesgeschichte und ihren Quellen*, Berlin: W. de Gruyter, 1982, 102–208 (Miscellanea Medievalia 15)

——, *Wilhelm von Moerbekes Übersetzung der Aristotelischen Metaphysik*, Leiden: E.J. Brill, 1995

Walzer, R., *Al-Farabi on the Perfect State*, Oxford: Clarendon Press, 1985

Wehrli, F., G. Wöhrle, und L. Zhmud, "Der Peripatos bis zum Beginn der römischen Kaiswerzeit," in H. Flashar, ed., *Die Philosophie der Antike, Band 3, Ältere Akademie, Aristoteles, Peripatos*, Basel: Schwabe Verlag, 2004, pp. 506–557 on Theophrastus (*Grundriss der Geschichte der Philosophie*, begründet von Friedrich Ueberweg)

White, S., "Opuscula and Opera in the Catalogue of Theophrastus' Works," in Fortenbaugh and Wöhrle 2002, 9–37

Wimmer, F. [Wim.[1]], *Theophrasti Eresii Opera quae supersunt omnia*, 3 vols, Leipzig: Teubner, 1862

——, [Wim.[2]] *Theophrasti Eresii Opera, quae supersunt, omnia*, Paris: Firmin Didot, 1866

Zeller, E., "Über die Benutzung der aristotelischen Metaphysik in den Schriften der älteren Peripatetiker," *Abhandlungen der königlichen Akademie der Wissenschaften zu Berlin*. Philosophisch-historische Klasse 1877, 145–167; repr. O. Leuze, ed., *Eduard Zellers kleine Schriften*, Berlin: Georg Reimer, 1910, vol. I,191–214

——, *Die philosophie der Griechen in ihrer geschichtlichen Entwicklung*, II 2, Leipzig: R. Reisland, 1879[3]

Zonta, M., "Il compendio aristotelico di Nicola Damasceno: nuovi dati dalla tradizione siriaca," in R.B. Finazzi and A. Valvo, eds, *Pensiero e istituzioni del mondo classico nelle culture del Vicino Oriente*, Alessandria: Edizioni dell'Orso, 2001, 315–339

INDEX NOMINUM

A. *Ancient and Medieval*

(Articles and diacritical marks are disregarded in the alphabetization.)

B. *Geographical*

C. *Modern*

(Reference is given only to the page number when the name appears in both the text and the notes of that page.)

INDEX LOCORUM